LIABILITY OF CORPORATE GROUPS AND NETWORKS

What happens when a corporate subsidiary or network company is unable to pay personal injury victims in full? This book sets out to tackle the 'insolvent entity problem', especially as it arises in cases of mass wrongdoing such as those involving asbestos exposure and defective pharmaceuticals. After discussing the nature of corporate groups and networks from the perspectives of business history, organisation studies, and social theory, the book assesses a range of rules and proposed rules for extending liability for personal injuries beyond insolvent entities. New proposals are put for an exception to the rule of limited liability and for the development of a flexible new tort based on conspiracy that encompasses not only control-based relationships but also horizontal coordination between companies. The book concludes with a general discussion of lessons learned from debates about extended liability and provides guidelines for the development of new liability rules.

CHRISTIAN A. WITTING is Professor of Private Law at Queen Mary University of London where he teaches Company Law and Torts. He qualified as a lawyer in Australia and was previously employed by the Commonwealth Attorney General's Department.

INTERNATIONAL CORPORATE LAW AND FINANCIAL MARKET REGULATION

Corporate law and financial market regulation have major implications for how the modern economy is organised and regulated and for how risk is managed and distributed – domestically, regionally, and internationally. This Series seeks to inform and lead the vibrant scholarly and policy debate in this highly dynamic area by publishing cutting-edge, timely, and critical examinations of the most pressing and important questions in the field.

Series Editors

LIABILITY OF CORPORATE GROUPS AND NETWORKS

CHRISTIAN A. WITTING
Queen Mary University of London

CAMBRIDGE
UNIVERSITY PRESS

CAMBRIDGE
UNIVERSITY PRESS

University Printing House, Cambridge CB2 8BS, United Kingdom

One Liberty Plaza, 20th Floor, New York, NY 10006, USA

477 Williamstown Road, Port Melbourne, VIC 3207, Australia

314–321, 3rd Floor, Plot 3, Splendor Forum, Jasola District Centre, New Delhi – 110025, India

79 Anson Road, #06–04/06, Singapore 079906

Cambridge University Press is part of the University of Cambridge.

It furthers the University's mission by disseminating knowledge in the pursuit of education, learning, and research at the highest international levels of excellence.

www.cambridge.org
Information on this title: www.cambridge.org/9781107039926
DOI: 10.1017/9781139626828

First published 2018

Printed in the United Kingdom by Clays, St Ives plc

A catalogue record for this publication is available from the British Library.

Library of Congress Cataloging-in-Publication Data
Names: Witting, Christian A., author.
Title: Liability of corporate groups and networks / Christian A. Witting.
Description: Cambridge [UK] ; New York : Cambridge University Press, 2018. | Series: International corporate law and financial market regulation | Includes bibliographical references and index.
Identifiers: LCCN 2017053761 | ISBN 9781107039926 (hardback)
Subjects: LCSH: Tort liability of corporations. | Corporation law. | Corporate veil. | BISAC: LAW / Corporate.
Classification: LCC K1329.5 .W58 2018 | DDC 346/.066–dc23
LC record available at https://lccn.loc.gov/2017053761

ISBN 978-1-107-03992-6 Hardback

To academic colleagues past and present

CONTENTS

Acknowledgements *page* xii
Table of Cases xiv
Table of Legislation xxiv

1 Introduction 1

1.1 General 1

1.2 Definition of Corporate Group 3

1.3 Definition of Network 5

1.4 Growth of Groups 6

1.5 Problems of Corporate Groups and Networks 6

1.6 Regulation 8

1.7 Compensation 12

1.8 Development of Liability Rules 15

1.9 Summary of Recommendations 18

1.10 Structure of Book 19

PART I **Business Context** 21

2 The Formation of Corporate Groups and Networks 23

2.1 Introduction 23

2.2 The Growth of Business 24

2.3 Business Form 34

2.4 International Dimension 51

2.5 Conclusions 62

3 Structuring of Corporate Group Relations 64

3.1 Introduction 64

3.2 Separate Legal Personality 64

3.3 Corporate Capacity 68

3.4 Limited Liability 69

3.5 Judgment-Proofing and Malpractice 79

3.6 Multinationals and Private International Law 90

3.7 Position of Tort Creditors 94

3.8 Conclusions 100

4 Insolvent Entity Case Studies 102

4.1 Introduction 102

4.2 Case Study I: Asbestos Claims 103

4.3 Case Study II: Pharmaceutical Claims 122

4.4 Case Study III: 'The Next Catastrophe' 137

4.5 Legal Responses 144

4.6 Conclusions 146

PART II **Theory** 147

5 Conceptions of Group and Network Liability 149

5.1 Introduction 149

5.2 Theorising the Group of Persons 149

5.3 Theorising the Organisation 159

5.4 Theorising the Corporate Group 167

5.5 The Network: A Brief Contrast 172

5.6 Entity or Enterprise Approach? 174

5.7 Conclusions 185

PART III **Statute** 187

6 **General Protections for Creditors** **189**

6.1 Introduction 189

6.2 Ex ante Protections for Creditors 189

6.3 Ex post Protections for Creditors 197

6.4 Conclusions 203

7 **Group-Specific Protections for Creditors** **204**

7.1 Introduction 204

7.2 Statutory Recognition of Groups 204

7.3 Protections in Administration and Insolvency 212

7.4 Conclusions 233

8 **Statutory Torts** **235**

8.1 Introduction 235

8.2 Extended Liability: Products 235

8.3 Extended Liability: Polluter-Pays Legislation 254

8.4 Conclusions 266

9 **Modified Limited Liability** **268**

9.1 Introduction 268

9.2 Existing Proposals for Reform 270

9.3 Control as the Basis for Shareholder Liability 282

9.4 Modified Limited Liability 287

9.5 Conclusions 303

PART IV **Common Law** 307

10 Veil-Piercing 309

10.1 Introduction 309

10.2 Defining Veil-Piercing 309

10.3 Power to Pierce the Veil 313

10.4 Recent History of Veil-Piercing 314

10.5 Corporate Groups 318

10.6 Elements of a Veil-Piercing Action 324

10.7 Grounds of Veil-Piercing 327

10.8 US Position 339

10.9 Deficiencies in Veil-Piercing Doctrine 342

10.10 Alternatives to Veil-Piercing 343

11 Direct Liability in Tort 346

11.1 Introduction 346

11.2 Tort of Negligence 352

11.3 Unlawful Means Conspiracy 381

11.4 Multiple Entity Recklessness 389

11.5 Conclusions 395

12 Vicarious and Joint Liability in Tort 396

12.1 Introduction 396

12.2 Vicarious Liability 396

12.3 Non-delegable Duties 405

12.4 Joint Liability 406

12.5 Conclusions 412

13 Conclusions 413

13.1 The Problem 413

13.2 Current Law 414

13.3 Assumptions Underlying the Present Law 417

13.4 Proposals 420

Bibliography 423

Index 451

ACKNOWLEDGEMENTS

The 'insolvent entity problem' (as I term it) presents a series of extraordinarily difficult challenges that span statute, company law, and private law. This book on corporate groups and networks is my contribution to resolving the problem. I have many to thank for the assistance that they have given me in writing it.

Professor Helen Anderson of Melbourne Law School (MLS) was the first believer in this project, and I thank her for supplying me with ideas, materials, and goodwill. Professors Phillip Blumberg and Kurt Strasser were excellent hosts at the University of Connecticut, when I first set out my own ideas for resolving the insolvent entity problem. I thank them for talking at length with me about this project. Professor Blumberg urged me to find a new approach to the problem of corporate groups. I hope he is not offended by how different an approach I have chosen to take!

Another very important collaborator from the early years was James Rankin, who was my research assistant at MLS. He provided an excellent array of materials on veil-piercing and other matters. I congratulate James on his stellar career since our time together as articled clerk, solicitor, municipal councillor, and graduate student at Georgetown University.

And while I am on the topic of research assistance, I sincerely thank the Australian Research Council for funding Discovery Project No 86544 on 'The Liability of Corporate Groups'. I thank also my current employer, Queen Mary University of London, for providing me with funds to attend the American Bar Association Business Law Section Conference in New Orleans, Louisiana, where a number of papers were given about the oil and gas industry, *Deepwater Horizon*, and mass-torts.

At a later stage in this project, I was fortunate to meet Dr Martin Petrin of University College London, and he generously read the entire manuscript and prompted a number of important changes. Professor Richard Garnett of MLS read over the private international law section in Chapter 3, and helped me to convey its essential messages. I thank Richard, also, for being my longest-standing friend in academia!

Thanks go also to a range of people who helped at various stages, providing explanations on various issues: Paula Darvas, Alan Dignam, Michael Faure, Russell Hinchy, Paddy Ireland, Cally Jordan, Andrew Keay, Rob Merkin, Richard Mitchell, John Murphy, Sharon Oded, Ian Ramsay, Chris Riley, Andrew Simester, Peta Spender, Willem Van Boom, and Wee Meng Seng.

Paul Ali, Pamela Hanrahan, and Cally Jordan (again), former colleagues at MLS, helped me a great deal in the early days when I was learning the ropes teaching Corporations Law.

Finally, I thank Kim Hughes of Cambridge University Press for awarding me a contract for a book that I really wanted to write, and for not abandoning me during the significant delays in producing it.

And so my part is done. I hope this book proves to be of use in thinking through the insolvent entity problem. Even if it does not, I must say that I enjoyed every single moment that I worked on it. This book is dedicated to the exceptional people who have served beside me in my employer universities, and whom I have met in the wider world of academia. My academic colleagues have helped make for a very enjoyable career thus far. I pay tribute to them for their integrity, diligence, and brilliance.

The law and literature referred to in this book are such as were available to me up to Australia Day, 26 January 2017.

TABLE OF CASES

Australia

Amaca Pty Ltd v. *Ellis* (2011) 283 ALR 461
Australian Competition and Consumer Commission v. *April International Marketing Services Australia Pty Ltd (No 6)* [2010] FCA 704
Australian Securities and Investments Commission v. *Hellicar* (2012) 247 CLR 345
Baxter v. *Obacelo Pty Ltd* (2001) 205 CLR 635
Beach Petroleum NL v. *Johnson* (1993) 43 FCR 1
Briggs v. *James Hardie & Co Pty Ltd* (1989) 5 NSWLR 549
CC Containers Pty Ltd v. *Lee* [2011] VSC 537
Re Charter Travel Co Ltd (1997) 15 ACLC 1685
Chen v. *Karandonis* [2002] NSWCA 412
Commissioner for Fair Trading v. *TLC Consulting Services Pty Ltd* [2011] QSC 233
Commissioner for Probate Duties (Vic) v. *Mitchell* (1960) 105 CLR 126
Commonwealth Bank of Australia v. *Kojic* [2016] FCAFC 186
CSR Ltd v. *Wren* (1997) 44 NSWLR 463
CSR Ltd v. *Young* [1998] Aust Torts Reports 81–468
Day v. *The Ocean Beach Shell Harbour Pty Ltd* [2013] NSWCA 250
Dean-Willcocks v. *Soluble Solution Hydroponics Pty Ltd* (1997) 24 ACSR 79
Dennis Willcox Pty Ltd v. *Federal Commissioner of Taxation* (1988) 79 ALR 267
Dresna Pty Ltd v. *Misu Nominees Pty Ltd* [2004] FCAFC 169
Re Enterprise Gold Mines NL (1991) 3 ACSR 531
Fatimi Pty Ltd v. *Bryant* (2004) 59 NSWLR 678
Federal Commissioner of Taxation v. *BHP Billiton Finance Ltd* (2010) 182 FCR 526
Federal Commissioner of Taxation v. *Casuarina Pty Ltd* (1970–1) 127 CLR 62
Geraldton Building Co Pty Ltd v. *Woodmore* (1992) 8 ASCR 585
Heytesbury Holdings Pty Ltd v. *City of Subiaco* (1998) Aust Torts Rep ¶ 81–488
Ho v. *Akai Pty Ltd (in liq)* (2006) 24 ACLC 1526
ICT Pty Ltd v. *Sea Containers Ltd* (1995) 39 NSWLR 640
Industrial Equity Ltd v. *Blackburn* (1977) 137 CLR 567
Jaensch v. *Coffey* (1984) 155 CLR 549
James Hardie & Co Pty Ltd v. *Hall* (1998) 43 NSWLR 544
James Hardie & Co Pty Ltd v. *Putt* (1998) 43 NSWLR 554
Kondis v. *State Transport Authority* (1984) 154 CLR 672
Leichhardt Municipal Council v. *Montgomery* (2007) 230 CLR 22

McKernan v. *Fraser* (1931) 46 CLR 343
Mentha v. *GE Capital Ltd* (1997) 27 ACSR 696
New South Wales v. *Lepore* (2003) 77 ALJR 558
O'Brien v. *Dawson* (1942) 66 CLR 18
Oceanic Crest Shipping Co v. *Pilbara Harbour Services Pty Ltd* (1986) 160 CLR 626
Premier Building and Consulting Pty Ltd (rec apptd) v. *Spotless Group Ltd* (2007) 64 ACSR 114
Scott v. *Davis* (2000) 175 ALR 217
Stanley v. *Layne Christensen Co* [2006] WASCA 56
State Rail Authority (NSW) v. *Wallaby Grip Ltd* (1999) 18 NSWCCR 193
Sullivan v. *Moody* (2001) 207 CLR 562
Re Switch Telecommunications Pty Ltd (in liq); Ex parte Sherman [2000] NSWSC 794
Terranora Leisure Time Management Ltd v. *Harris* [2004] 1 Qd R 93
Theosophical Foundation Pty Ltd v. *Commissioner of Land Tax* (1966) 67 SR (NSW) 70
Voth v. *Manildra Flour Mills Pty Ltd* (1990) 171 CLR 538
Walker v. *Wimborne* (1976) 137 CLR 1

Canada

671122 Ontario Ltd v. *Sagaz Industries Canada Inc* [2001] 2 SCR 983
Athey v. *Leonati* [1996] 3 SCR 458
Bazley v. *Curry* [1999] 2 SCR 534
Blackwater v. *Plint* (2005) 258 DLR (4th) 275
Canada Cement LaFarge Ltd v. *British Columbia Lightweight Aggregate Ltd* [1983] 1 SCR 452
Choc v. *Hudbay Minerals, Inc* 2013 ONSC 1414
Clements v. *Clements* [2012] 2 SCR 181
Cooper v. *Hobart* [2001] 3 SCR 537
Doe v. *Bennett* [2004] 1 SCR 436
Lange v. *Bennett* [1964] 1 OR 233
Odhavji Estate v. *Woodhouse* [2003] 3 SCR 263
R v. *Waverley Construction Co Ltd* (1972) 30 DLR (3d) 224
Resurfice Corporation v. *Hanke* [2007] 1 SCR 333
Ryan v. *Victoria (City)* [1999] 1 SCR 201

European Union

Case 21/76, *Handelskwekerij GJ Bier BV* v. *Mines de Potasse d'Alsace SA* [1976] ECR 1735; [1978] QB 708
Case C–52/00, *European Commission* v. *France* [2002] ECR I-3827
Case C-97/08 P, *Akzo Nobel NV* v. *Commission of the European Communities* [2009] ECR I-8237
Case C–127/04, *O'Byrne* v. *Sanofi Pasteur MSD Ltd* (2006) 91 BMLR 175
Case C–183/00, *Sanchez* v. *Medicina Asturiana SA* [2002] ECR I-3901

Cases C-201/09 and C216/09, *Arcelormittal Luxembourg SA* v. *European Commission* [2011] 4 CMLR 21
Case C-281/02, *Owusu* v. *Jackson* [2005] ECR I-1383
Case C–358/08, *O'Byrne* v. *Aventis Pasteur* (2009) 113 BMLR 1
Case T-77/08, *Dow Chemical Co* v. *European Commission* [2012] 4 CMLR 19
Case T-102/92, *Viho Europe BV* v. *Commission of the European Communities* [1995] ECR II-17
Case T-117/07, *Areva* v. *European Commission* [2011] 4 CMLR 26
Case C-172/12 P, *EI du Pont Nemours & Co* v. *European Commission* [2014] 4 CMLR 7

India

MC Mehta v. *Union of India* 1987 AIR 965

New Zealand

Dairy Containers Ltd v. *NZI Bank Ltd* [1995] 2 NZLR 30
Lewis v. *Poultry Processors* (1988) 4 NZCLC 64,508
Mountfort v. *Tasman Pacific Airlines of NZ Ltd* [2006] 1 NZLR 104
Nathan v. *Dollars & Sense Ltd* [2008] 2 NZLR 557
Re Pacific Syndicates (NZ) Ltd (1989) 4 NZCLC 64
Steel & Tube Holdings Ltd v. *Lewis Holdings Ltd* [2016] NZCA 366

Singapore

EFT Holdings Inc v. *Marinteknik Shipbuilders (S) Pte Ltd* [2014] 1 SLR 860

United Kingdom and Privy Council

A v. *National Blood Authority* [2001] 3 All ER 289
A Company, Re [1985] BCLC 333
Abouzaid v. *Mothercare (UK) Ltd* [2000] All ER (D) 2436
Adams v. *Cape Industries plc* [1990] Ch 433
Alcock v. *Chief Constable of South Yorkshire Police* [1992] 1 AC 310
Allen v. *Flood* [1898] AC 1
Atlas Maritime Co SA v. *Avalon Maritime Ltd (No 1)* [1991] 4 All ER 769
Antonio Gramsci Shipping Corpn v. *Recoletos Ltd* [2013] EWCA Civ 730
Antonio Gramsci Shipping Corp v. *Stepanovs* [2011] 1 Lloyd's Rep 617
Avonwick Holdings Ltd v. *Castle Investment Fund Ltd* [2015] EWHC 3832 (Ch)
Baker v. *Quantum Clothing Group Ltd* [2011] 1 WLR 1003
Baldwin v. *Berryland Books* [2010] EWCA Civ 1440
Re Bank of Credit and Commerce International SA (No 3) [1993] BCLC 1490
Bank of Tokyo Ltd v. *Karoon (note)* [1987] AC 45

Banque Financière de la Cité v. *Parc (Battersea) Ltd* [1998] 1 All ER 737
Barber v. *Somerset County Council* [2004] 1 WLR 1089
Barker v. *Corus UK Ltd* [2006] 2 AC 572
In re Barned's Banking Company (1867) 3 LR Ch 105
Barnett v. *Chelsea and Kensington Hospital Management Committee* [1969] 1 QB 428
Belmont Finance Corp v. *Williams Furniture (No 2)* [1980] 1 All ER 393
Ben Hashem v. *Ali Shayif* [2009] 1 FLR 115
Bilta (UK) Ltd (in liq) v. *Nazir* [2015] 2 WLR 1168
Bird v. *Holbrook* (1828) 4 Bing 628
British Thomson-Houston Company Ltd v. *Sterling Accessories Ltd* [1924] 2 Ch 33
Campbell v. *Peter Gordon Joiners Ltd* [2016] AC 1513
Canadian Pacific Railway Company v. *Lockhart* [1942] AC 591
Caparo Industries plc v. *Dickman* [1990] 2 AC 605
Cape plc, In the Matter of [2006] 3 All ER 1222
Capital For Enterprise Fund A LP v. *Bibby Financial Services Ltd* [2015] EWHC 2593 (Ch)
Carmarthenshire CC v. *Lewis* [1955] AC 549
CBS Songs Ltd v. *Amstrad Consumer Electronics plc* [1988] 1 AC 1013
Chandler v. *Cape plc* [2012] 1 WLR 3111
Chandler v. *Lopus* (1603) Cro Jac 4; 79 ER 3
Charterbridge Corporation Ltd v. *Lloyds Bank Ltd* [1970] Ch 62
Connelly v. *RTZ Corp plc (No 2)* [1998] AC 854
Re Continental Assurance Co of London plc [2007] 2 BCLC 287
Cooper Tire & Rubber Co Europe Ltd v. *Dow Deutschland Inc* [2010] EWCA Civ 864
Cox v. *Ministry of Justice* [2016] AC 660
Crawford Adjusters Ltd v. *Sagicor Insurance Ltd* [2014] AC 366
Creasey v. *Breachwood Motors Ltd* [1992] BCC 638
Credit Lyonnais v. *ECGD* [1998] 1 Lloyd's L Rep 19
Crofter Hand-Woven Harris Tweed Co Ltd v. *Veitch* [1942] AC 435
Darby, ex parte Brougham, Re [1910] 1 KB 95
Denham v. *Midland Employers Mutual Assurance Ltd* [1955] 2 All ER 561
DHN Food Distributors Ltd v. *Tower Hamlets LBC* [1976] 3 All ER 462
Digicel (St Lucia) Ltd v. *Cable & Wireless plc* [2010] EWHC 774 (Ch)
Dimbleby & Sons Ltd v. *National Union of Journalists* [1984] 1 WLR 427
Distillers Co (Biochemicals) Ltd v. *Thompson* [1971] AC 458
Donoghue v. *Stevenson* [1932] AC 562
Dorset Yacht Co Ltd v. *Home Office* [1970] AC 1004
Durham v. *BAI (Run Off) Ltd (in scheme of arrangement)* [2012] 1 WLR 867
E v. *English Province of Our Lady of Charity* [2013] QB 722
Ebbw Vale Urban District Council v. *South Wales Traffic Area Licensing Authority* [1951] 2 KB 366
Emerald Supplies Ltd v. *British Airways plc (No 1)* [2016] Bus LR 145
Enviroco Ltd v. *Farstad Supply A/S* [2011] 1 WLR 921
Fairchild v. *Glenhaven Funeral Services Ltd* [2003] 1 AC 32

Gardiner v. *Gray* (1815) 4 Camp 144
Gas Lighting Improvement Co Ltd v. *Inland Revenue Commissioners* [1923] AC 723
Gencor ACP Ltd v. *Dalby* [2000] 2 BCLC 734
Gilford Motor Co Ltd v. *Horne* [1933] Ch 935
Glasgow Corporation v. *Muir* [1943] AC 448
Grant v. *Ralls* [2016] All ER (D) 113
Grupo Torras SA v. *Al Sabah* [1999] CLC 1469
Haley v. *London Electricity Board* [1965] AC 778
Hawley v. *Luminar Leisure Ltd* [2006] PIQR P17
Hedley Byrne & Co Ltd v. *Heller & Partners Ltd* [1964] AC 465
Holcombe v. *Hewson* (1810) 170 ER 1194
Holtby v. *Brigham & Cowan (Hull) Ltd* [2000] 3 All ER 421
Home Office v. *Dorset Yacht Co Ltd* [1970] AC 1004
Huntly v. *Thornton* [1957] 1 WLR 321
Hydrodan (Corby) Ltd, Re [1992] BCC 161
Ide v. *ATB Sales Ltd* [2009] RTR 8
Inland Revenue Commissioners v. *Sansom* [1921] 2 KB 492
Intel Corporation v. *General Instrument Corporation* [1991] RPC 235
Jeromson v. *Shell Tankers UK Ltd* [2001] PIQR P19
JH Rayner (Mincing Lane) Ltd v. *Department of Trade and Industry* [1989] Ch 72
Jones v. *Fay* (1865) 4 F & F 525
Jones v. *Lipman* [1962] 1 All ER 442
Kensington International Ltd v. *Republic of Congo* [2005] EWHC 2684 (Comm)
Khan v. *Miah* [2001] 1 WLR 2123
Kodak Ltd v. *Clark* [1903] 1 KB 505
Kriegel, Waring and Co; Ex parte Trotman, Re (1893) 68 LT 588
Kuwait Asia Bank EC v. *National Mutual Life Nominees Ltd* [1990] 2 Lloyd's Rep. 95
Kuwait Oil Tanker v. *Al Bader* [2000] 2 All ER (Comm) 271
Lazarus Estates Ltd v. *Beasley* [1965] 1 QB 702
Limpus v. *LGO Co* (1862) 1 H & C 526
Linsen International Ltd v. *Humpuss Transportasi Kimia* [2012] Bus LR 1649
Lister v. *Hesley Hall Ltd* [2002] 1 AC 215
Lonrho plc v. *Fayed* [1992] 1 AC 448
Lonrho v. *Shell Petroleum Co Ltd* [1982] AC 173
Lubbe v. *Cape plc* [2000] 1 WLR 1545
Lungowe v. *Vedanta Resources plc* [2016] BCC 774
MacDonald Dickens & Macklin v. *Costello* [2012] QB 244
Margereson v. *JW Roberts Ltd* [1996] Env LR 304
Marini Ltd, Re [2004] BCC 172
Mattis v. *Pollock* [2003] 1 WLR 2158
Mbasago v. *Logo Ltd (No 1)* [2007] QB 846
MCA Records Inc v. *Charly Records Ltd* [2002] BCC 650
McDermid v. *Nash Dredging & Reclamation Co Ltd* [1987] 3 WLR 212
Meretz Investments NV v. *ACP Ltd* [2008] Ch 244
Michael v. *Alestree* (1675) 2 Lev 173; 83 ER 504

Michael v. *Chief Constable of South Wales Police* [2015] AC 1731
Miraflores (Owners) v. *George Livanos (Owners)* [1967] 1 AC 826
Mogul Steamship v. *McGregor Gow & Co* (1889) 23 QBD 598
Mohamud v. *Wm Morrison Supermarkets plc* [2016] AC 677
Morris v. *Breaveglen Ltd* [1993] ICR 766
Morris v. *West Hartlepool Steam Navigation Co Ltd* [1956] AC 552
Nash v. *Eli Lilly & Co* [1993] 4 All ER 383
Newton-Sealy v. *ArmorGroup Services Ltd* [2008] EWHC 233 (QB)
In re Nortel GmbH (in admin) [2014] AC 209
Oasis Merchandising Services Ltd, Ward v. *Aiken, Re* [1997] 1 BCLC 689
OBG Ltd v. *Allan* [2008] 1 AC 1
O'Byrne v. *Aventis Pasteur SA* [2010] 1 WLR 1412
Okpabi v. *Royal Dutch Shell plc* [2017] EWHC 89 (TCC)
Ord v. *Belhaven Pubs Ltd* [1998] 2 BCLC 447
Orr v. *Milton Keynes Council* [2011] EWCA Civ 62
Page v. *Smith* [1996] AC 155
Paycheck Services 3 Ltd, Re [2011] 1 BCLC 141
Performing Right Society Ltd v. *Ciryl Theatrical Enterprises Ltd* [1924] 1 KB 1
Polly Peck International (in administration), Re [1996] 2 All ER 433
Prest v. *Petrodel Resources Ltd* [2013] 2 AC 415
R v. *Boyle Transport (Northern Ireland) Ltd* [2016] 4 WLR 63
R v. *Lord Chancellor; Ex p Child Poverty Action Group* [1999] 1 WLR 347
R v. *Siricusa* (1989) 90 Cr App R 340
Rainham Chemical Works Ltd v. *Belvedere Fish Guano Co Ltd* [1921] AC 465
Revenue and Customs Commissioners v. *Total Network SL* [2008] 1 AC 1174
Rhesa Shipping Co SA v. *Edmunds ('The Popi M')* [1985] 1 WLR 948
Richardson v. *LRC Products Ltd* (2000) 59 BMLR 185
Rothwell v. *Chemical & Insulating Co Ltd* [2008] 1 AC 281
Royal Brompton Hospital NHS Trust v. *Hammond (No 3)* [2002] 1 WLR 1397
Said v. *Butt* [1920] 3 KB 497
Salomon v. *A Salomon & Co Ltd* [1897] AC 22
Sandman v. *Panasonic UK Ltd* [1998] FSR 651
Scala Ballroom (Wolverhampton) Ltd v. *Ratcliffe* [1958] 1 WLR 1057
Sea Shepherd UK v. *Fish v Fish Ltd* [2015] 2 WLR 694
Secretary of State for Trade and Industry v. *Deverell* [2001] Ch 340
Sienkiewicz v. *Greif (UK) Ltd* [2011] 2 AC 229
Sithole v. *Thor Chemical Holdings Ltd* [1999] All ER (D) 102
Sithole v. *Thor Chemicals Holdings Ltd* 2000 WL 1421183 (Court of Appeal, 28 September 2000)
Smith, Stone and Knight Ltd v. *Birmingham Corporation* [1939] 4 All ER 116
Spiliada Maritime Corporation v. *Consulex Ltd* [1987] AC 460
Standard Chartered Bank v. *Pakistan International Shipping Corp (No. 2)* [2003] 1 AC 959
Stevenson, Jordan and Harrison Ltd v. *MacDonald and Evans* [1952] 1 TLR 101
Re T & N Ltd [2006] 1 WLR 1728

In re T & N Ltd and ors (No 4) [2007] Bus LR 1411
Taylor v. *Morris* [1992] BCC 440
The Gramophone and Typewriter Ltd v. *Stanley* [1908] 2 KB 89
The Print Factory (London) 1991 v. *Millam* [2007] ICR 1331
Thompson v. *The Renwick Group plc* [2015] BCC 855
Trevor v. *Whitworth* (1887) 12 App Cas 409
Trustor AB v. *Smallbone (No 2)* [2001] 1 WLR 1177
Unilever plc v. *Gillette (UK) Ltd* [1989] RPC 583
Vacwell Engineering Co Ltd v. *BDH Chemicals* [1971] 1 QB 88
Various Claimants v. *Catholic Child Welfare Society* [2013] 2 AC 1
Viasystems (Tyneside) Ltd v. *Thermal Transfer (Northern) Ltd* [2006] 2 WLR 428
VTB Capital plc v. *Nutritek International Corpn* [2013] 2 AC 337
WH Newson Holdings Ltd v. *IMI plc* [2014] 1 All ER 1132
Wilkinson v. *Downton* (1897) 2 QBD 57
Williams v. *Natural Life Health Foods Ltd* [1998] 1 WLR 830
Wills v. *Corfe Joinery Ltd* [1997] BCC 511
Wilsher v. *Essex AHA* [1988] 1 All ER 871
Wilsons and Clyde Coal Ltd v. *English* [1938] AC 57
Woodland v. *Essex County Council* [2014] AC 537
Woolfson v. *Strathclyde Regional Council* 1978 SC (HL) 90
Worsley v. *Tambrands Ltd* [2000] PIQR P95
Wragg Ltd, In re [1897] 1 Ch 796
Wright v. *Cambridge Medical Group* [2013] QB 312
Zurich Insurance plc v. *International Energy Group Ltd* [2016] AC 509

United States

80 Nassau Associates v. *Crossland Federal Savings Bank (In re 80 Nassau Associates)* 169 BR 832 (Bankr. SDNY 1994)
1438 Meridian Place, NW, Inc, In re 15 Bankr. 89 (Bankr. DDC 1981)
Abdel-Fattah v. *Pepsico, Inc* 948 SW 2d 381 (Tex App 1997)
Abel v. *Eli Lilly & Co* 343 NW 2d 164 (Mich 1984)
Amchem Products Inc v. *Windsor* 521 US 591 (1997)
American Needle Inc v. *National Football League* 130 S Ct 2201 (2010)
Anglo Eastern Bulkships, Ltd v. *Ameron, Inc* 556 F Supp 1198 (SDNY 1982)
Apple Computer, Inc, In re 243 F Supp 2d 1012 (ND Cal 2002)
Aubin v. *Union Carbide Corporation* 177 So 3d 489 (Fla 2015)
Bayer Corp v. *MascoTech, Inc (In re Autostyle Plastics Inc)* 269 F 3d 726 (6th Cir. 2011)
Bean Dredging LLC v. *United States* 773 F Supp 2d 63, 86 (DDC 2011)
Beck v. *Prupis* 529 US 494 (2000)
Bell Petroleum Services, Inc, In re 3 F 3d 889 (5th Cir. 1993)
Benjamin v. *Diamond (In re Mobile Steel Co)* 563 F 2d 692 (5th Cir. 1977)
Beshada v. *Johns-Manville Products Corp* 447 A 2d 539 (NJ 1982)
Bhopal I 634 F Supp 842 (SDNY 1986)

Boggs v. *Blue Diamond Coal Co* 590 F 2d 655 (6th Cir. 1979)
Borel v. *Fibreboard Paper Products Corp* 493 F 2d 1076 (5th Cir. 1973)
Brown v. *Superior Court* 751 P 2d 470 (Cal 1988)
Browning-Ferris Industries v. *Ter Maat* 195 F 3d 953 (7th Cir. 1999)
Burlington Northern & Santa Fe Railway Co v. *United States* 129 S Ct 1870 (2009)
Celotex Corp v. *Copeland* 471 So 2d 533 (Fla 1985)
Chemical Bank New York Trust Co v. *Kheel* 369 F 2d 845 (2nd Cir. 1966)
Christofferson v. *Kaiser Foundation Hospitals* 15 Cal App 3d 76 (1971)
Cohen v. *Bowdoin* 288 A 2d 106 (Me 1972)
Combustion Engineering, Inc, In re 391 F 3d 190 (3d Cir. 2004)
Copperweld Corp v. *Independence Tube Corp* 467 US 752 (1984)
Crabtree, In re 39 Bankr. 718 (Bankr. ED Tenn 1984)
Craig v. *Lake Asbestos of Quebec Ltd* 843 F 2d 145 (3rd Cir. 1988)
Cyberco Holdings, Inc, In re 431 BR 404 (Bankr. WD Mich 2010)
Dalehite v. *United States* 346 US 15 (1953)
Dazo v. *Globe Airport Security Services* 295 F 3d 934 (9th Cir. 2002)
Delaney v. *Deere & Co* 999 P 2d 930 (Kan 2000)
Doney v. *TRW Inc* 39 Cal Rptr 2d 292 (Cal App 6 Dist 1995)
Drabkin v. *Midland-Ross Corp (In re Auto-Train Corp)* 810 F 2d 270 (DC Cir. 1987)
Escola v. *Coca Cola Bottling Co* 150 P 2d 436 (Cal 1944)
Esmark, Inc v. *National Labor Relations Board* 887 F 2d 739 (7th Cir. 1989)
Federal Deposit Insurance Corporation v. *Hogan* (*Re Gulfco Investment Corp)* 593 F 2d 921 (10th Cir. 1979)
Federal Deposit Insurance Corporation v. *Sea Pines Company* 692 F 2d 973 (4th Cir. 1982)
Feldman v. *Lederle Laboratories* 479 A 2d 374 (NJ 1984)
Feszczyszyn v. *General Motors Corp* 248 AD 2d 939 (NY 1998)
Flora Mir Candy Corp v. *RS Dickson & Co* 432 F 2d 1060 (2nd Cir. 1970)
Forsythe v. *Clark USA, Inc* 864 NE 2d 227 (Ill 2007)
Frazier v. *Bryan Memorial Hospital Authority* 775 P 2d 281 (Okl 1989)
Freeman v. *Complex Computing Co* 119 F 3d 1044 (2nd Cir. 1997)
Gass v. *Anna Hospital Corporation* 911 NE 2d 1084 (Ill App 5 Dist 2009)
Greater Southeast Community Hospital Corp, In re 333 BR 506 (Bankr. DDC 205)
Greenman v. *Yuba Power Products, Inc* 377 P 2d 897 (Cal 1963)
Heacock & Lockwood v. *Sherman* 14 Wend 58 (NY Sup Ct 1835)
Horst v. *Laidlaw Waste Systems Inc* 917 F Supp 739 (D Colo 1996)
Hymowitz v. *Eli Lilly Co* 539 NE 2d 1069 (NY 1989)
James Talcott, Inc v. *Wharton* (*In re Continental Vending Machines Corp)* 517 F 2d 997 (2nd Cir. 1975)
Johnson v. *Abbe Engineering Company* 749 F 2d 1131 (5th Cir. 1984)
Kansas City Journal-Post Co (Bostian v. *Shapiro), In re* 144 F 2d 791 (8th Cir. 1944)
Karjala v. *Johns-Manville Products Corp* 523 F 2d 155 (8th Cir. 1975)
Kreisler, In re 546 F 3d 863 (7th Cir. 2008)
Leannais v. *Cincinnati Inc* 565 F 2d 431 (7th Cir. 1977)
Lifschultz Fast Freight, In re 132 F 3d 339 (7th Cir. 1997)

Little v. *Delta Steel, Inc* 409 SW 3d 704 (Tex App 2013)
Lohrmann v. *Pittsburgh Corning Corp* 782 F 2d 1156 (4th Cir 1986)
MacPherson v. *Buick Motor Co* 111 NE 1050 (NY 1916)
McAndrew v. *Lockheed Martin Corp* 206 F 3d 1031 (11th Cir. 2000)
McQuade v. *Draw Tite Inc* 659 NE 2d 1016 (Ind 1995)
Morvant v. *Oil States International, Inc* 3 F Supp 3d 561 (ED La 2014)
Murray Industries, Inc, In re 119 BR 820 (Bankr. MD Fla 1990)
N & D Properties, Inc, In re (Estes v. *N & D Properties, Inc)* 799 F 2d 726 (11th Cir. 1986)
O'Brien v. *Muskin Corp* 463 A 2d 298 (NJ 1983)
Oil Spill by Oil Rig 'Deepwater Horizon' in the Gulf of Mexico, on April 20, 2010, In re 21 F Supp 3d 657 (ED La 2014)
Ortiz v. *Fibreboard Corp* 527 US 815 (1999)
Owens Corning, In re 419 F 3d 195 (3rd Cir. 2005)
Piper Aircraft Co v. *Reyno* 454 US 235 (1981)
Polygram International Publishing, Inc v. *Nevada/TIG, Inc* 855 F Supp 1314 (D Mass 1994)
Ray v. *Alad* 560 P 2d 39 (Cal 1977)
Reid-Walen v. *Hansen*, 933 F 2d 1390 (8th Cir. 1991)
Rice v. *Harken Exploration Co* 250 F 3d 264 (5th Cir. 2001)
Riddle v. *Leuschner* 335 P 2d 107 (Cal 1959)
Ritter v. *BJC Barnes Jewish Christian Health Systems* 987 SW 2d 377 (Mo App ED 1999)
Robertson v. *Sea Pines Real Estate Companies Inc* 679 F 3d 278 (4th Cir. 2012)
Rogers v. *RJ Reynolds Tobacco Co* 761 SW 2d 788 (Tex App 1988)
Royster v. *Baker* 365 SW 2d 496 (Mo 1963)
Rutherford v. *Owens-Illinois, Inc* 941 P 2d 1203 (Cal 1997)
Satin v. *Satin* 69 App Div 2d 761 (NY 1979)
Schwartz v. *Abex Corp* 106 F Supp 3d 626 (ED Penn 2015)
Sea Pines v. *United States* 346 US 15 (1953)
Seinfeld v. *Slager* (Del Ch, 29 June 2012)(unreported)
Seixas v. *Woods* 2 Cai 48 (NY Sup Ct 1804)
Silicone Gel Breast Implants Products Liability Litigation, In re 837 F Supp 1128 (11th Cir. 1993)
Sindell v. *Abbott Laboratories* 26 Cal 3d 588 (1980)
Smith v. *Eli Lilly & Co, Inc* 560 NE 2d 324 (Ill 1990)
SubMicron Systems Corp, In re 432 F 3d 448 (3rd Cir. 2006)
The Coastal Corporation v. *Torres* 133 SW 3d 776 (Tex App 2004)
Trenwick America Litigation Trust v. *Ernst & Young* 906 A 2d 168 (Del Ch. 2006)
Trilegiant Corporation, Inc, In re 11 F Supp 3d 132 (D Conn 2014)
Union Carbide Corporation Gas Plant Disaster at Bhopal, India in Dec 1984, In re 809 F 2d 195 (2nd Cir. 1987)
Union Savings Bank v. *Augie/Restivo Baking Co Ltd (In re Augie/Restivo Baking Co Ltd)* 860 F 2d 515 (2nd Cir. 1988)
United States v. *Bestfoods* 524 US 51; 118 S Ct 1876 (1998)
United States v. *Cello-Foil Products Inc* 100 F 3d 1227 (6th Cir. 1996)
United States v. *Chem-Dyne Corp* 572 F Supp 802 (SD Ohio 1983)

United States v. *Kayser-Roth Corp* 272 F 3d 89 (1st Cir. 2001)
United States v. *TIC Investment Corp* 68 F 3d 1982 (8th Cir. 1996)
Urban v. *American Legion Post* 184 NW 2d 153 (Minn App 2005)
Vandermark v. *Ford Motor Co* 391 P 2d 169 (Cal 1964)
Waste Management, Inc v. *Superior Court of San Diego* 119 Cal App 4th 105 (Cal 2004)

TABLE OF LEGISLATION

Australia

Statutes

Asbestos Safety and Eradication Agency Act 2013 (Cth)
Civil Liability Act 2002 (NSW), Pt. 4
Civil Liability Act 2002 (NSW), s. 3B
Civil Liability Act 2002 (NSW), s. 5B
Civil Liability Act 2002 (NSW), s. 5D
Competition and Consumer Act 2010 (Cth), Sched. 2
Corporations Act 2001 (Cth), Part 2 M.6
Corporations Act 2001 (Cth), Part 5.1
Corporations Act 2001 (Cth), Part 5.6
Corporations Act 2001 (Cth), s. 516
Corporations Act 2001 (Cth), s. 553
Corporations Act 2001 (Cth), s. 556
Corporations Act 2001 (Cth), s. 563 C
Corporations Act 2001 (Cth), s. 571
Corporations Act 2001 (Cth), s. 579E
Corporations Act 2001 (Cth), s. 588FE
Corporations Act 2001 (Cth), s. 588 G
Corporations Act 2001 (Cth), s. 588 V
Workplace Injury, Rehabilitation and Compensation Act 2013 (Vic)

Subordinate legislation

ASIC Class Order 98/1418

Canada

Environmental Protection Act RSO 1990, s. 91
Environmental Protection Act RSO 1990, s. 99

European Union

Clinical Trials Regulation, Council Regulation 536/2014, OJ L158/1

Commission Directive 1999/77/EC of 26 July 1999 on the marketing and use of certain dangerous substances and preparations, OJ 1999 No. L207/18

Council Directive 65/65/EEC of 26 January 1965 on the approximation of provisions laid down by Law, Regulation or Administrative Action relating to proprietary medicinal products, OJ 1965 No. P369

Council Directive 1985/374/EEC of 25 July 1985 on the approximation of the laws, regulations and administrative provisions of the Member States concerning liability for defective products, OJ L210/29

Council Directive 2004/35/EC of 21 April 2004 on environmental liability with regard to the prevention and remedying of environmental damage, OJ 2004 No. L143/56

Council Directive 2004/109/EC of 15 December 2004 on the harmonisation of transparency requirements in relation to information about issuers whose securities are admitted to trading on a regulated market, OJ 2004 No. 390/38, Art 12

Council Directive 2004/109/EC of 15 December 2004 on the harmonisation of transparency requirements in relation to information about issuers whose securities are admitted to trading on a regulated market, OJ 2004 No. 390/38, Art 13

Council Directive 2004/109/EC of 15 December 2004 on the harmonisation of transparency requirements in relation to information about issuers whose securities are admitted to trading on a regulated market, OJ 2004 No. 390/38, Art 13a

Council Directive 2006/49/EC of 14 June 2006 on capital adequacy of investment firms and credit institutions, OJ 2006 No. L177/201

Council Directive 2007/36/EC of 11 July 2007 on the exercise of certain rights of shareholders in listed companies, OJ 2007 No. L184/17

Council Directive 2013/34/EU of 26 June 2013 on the annual financial statements, consolidated financial statements and related reports of certain types of undertakings, OJ 2013 No. L182/19

Council Directive 2013/34/EU of 26 June 2013 on the annual financial statements, consolidated financial statements and related reports of certain types of undertakings, OJ 2013 No. L182/19, Art. 2

Council Directive 2013/34/EU of 26 June 2013 on the annual financial statements, consolidated financial statements and related reports of certain types of undertakings, OJ 2013 No. L182/19, Art. 22

Council Directive 2013/34/EU of 26 June 2013 on the annual financial statements, consolidated financial statements and related reports of certain types of undertakings, OJ 2013 No. L182/19, Art. 24

Council Directive 2013/34/EU of 26 June 2013 on the annual financial statements, consolidated financial statements and related reports of certain types of undertakings, OJ 2013 No. L182/19, Art. 34

Council Directive 2015/849 of 20 May 2015 on the prevention of the use of the financial system for the purposes of money laundering or terrorist financing, OJ 2015 No. L141/73

Council Directive 2015/849 of 20 May 2015 on the prevention of the use of the financial system for the purposes of money laundering or terrorist financing, OJ 2015 No. L141/73, Art. 1
Council Directive 2015/849 of 20 May 2015 on the prevention of the use of the financial system for the purposes of money laundering or terrorist financing, OJ 2015 No. L141/73, Art. 2
Council Directive 2015/849 of 20 May 2015 on the prevention of the use of the financial system for the purposes of money laundering or terrorist financing, OJ 2015 No. L141/73, Art. 3
Council Directive 2015/849 of 20 May 2015 on the prevention of the use of the financial system for the purposes of money laundering or terrorist financing, OJ 2015 No. L141/73, Art. 11
Recast Brussels Regulation, Council Regulation 1215/2012, OJ 2012 No L351/1, Art. 4
Recast Brussels Regulation, Council Regulation 1215/2012, OJ 2012 No L351/1, Art. 7
Recast Brussels Regulation, Council Regulation 1215/2012, OJ 2012 No L351/1, Art. 8
Recast Brussels Regulation, Council Regulation 1215/2012, OJ 2012 No L351/1, Art. 33
Recast Brussels Regulation, Council Regulation 1215/2012, OJ 2012 No L351/1, Art. 34
Recast Brussels Regulation, Council Regulation 1215/2012, OJ 2012 No L351/1, Art. 63
Rome Regulation II, Council Regulation 864/2007, OJ 2007 No L199/40, Art. 5

India

Bhopal Gas Leak Disaster (Processing of Claims) Act 1985 (Ind)

Ireland

Companies Act 1990 (Ire), s. 138
Companies Act 1990 (Ire), s. 141

New Zealand

Companies Act 1993 (NZ), s. 135
Companies Act 1993 (NZ), s. 136
Companies Act 1993 (NZ), s. 271
Companies Act 1993 (NZ), s. 272
Companies Act 1993 (NZ), s. 292
Companies Act 1993 (NZ), s. 297
Injury Prevention, Rehabilitation and Compensation Act 2001 (NZ)

United Kingdom

Statutes

Child Maintenance and Other Payments Act 2008, Part 4
Civil Liability (Contribution) Act 1978
Civil Liability (Contribution) Act 1978, s. 1
Civil Liability (Contribution) Act 1978, s. 2
Companies Act 1862, sch. 1, cl. 49
Companies Act 2006, Part 15
Companies Act 2006, Part 21A
Companies Act 2006, Part 26
Companies Act 2006, Sched. 7
Companies Act 2006, s. 16
Companies Act 2006, s. 399
Companies Act 2006, s. 405
Companies Act 2006, s. 479A
Companies Act 2006, s. 479B
Companies Act 2006, s. 479C
Companies Act 2006, s. 761
Companies Act 2006, s. 763
Companies Act 2006, s. 790B
Companies Act 2006, s. 790C
Companies Act 2006, s. 790M
Companies Act 2006, s. 790N
Companies Act 2006, s. 830
Companies Act 2006, s. 831I
Companies Act 2006, s. 831L
Companies Act 2006, s. 836
Companies Act 2006, s. 847
Companies Act 2006, s. 897
Companies Act 2006, s. 899
Companies Act 2006, s. 1159
Companies Act 2006, s. 1162
Companies Act 2006, s. 1173
Company Directors Disqualification Act 1986, s. 22
Compensation Act 2006, s. 3
Consumer Protection Act 1987
Consumer Protection Act 1987, s. 1
Consumer Protection Act 1987, s. 2
Consumer Protection Act 1987, s. 3
Consumer Protection Act 1987, s. 4
Consumer Protection Act 1987, s. 5
Consumer Protection Act 1987, s. 6
Consumer Rights Act 2016

Criminal Finances Act 2017, Part 3
Defective Premises Act 1972
Employer's Liability (Defective Equipment) Act 1969
Insolvency Act 1986, Part 1
Insolvency Act 1986, Sched. 4
Insolvency Act 1986, Sched. 6
Insolvency Act 1986, s. 40
Insolvency Act 1986, s. 74
Insolvency Act 1986, s. 123
Insolvency Act 1986, s. 167
Insolvency Act 1986, s 176A
Insolvency Act 1986, s. 176ZA
Insolvency Act 1986, s. 176ZB
Insolvency Act 1986, s. 213
Insolvency Act 1986, s. 214
Insolvency Act 1986, s. 215
Insolvency Act 1986, s. 238
Insolvency Act 1986, s. 239
Insolvency Act 1986, s. 240
Insolvency Act 1986, s. 241
Insolvency Act 1986, s. 246ZB
Insolvency Act 1986, s. 246ZD
Insolvency Act 1986, s. 249
Insolvency Act 1986, s. 423
Insolvency Act 1986, s. 435
Law Reform (Contributory Negligence) Act 1945
Mesothelioma Act 2014, s. 2
Mesothelioma Act 2014, s. 4
Mesothelioma Act 2014, s. 10
Mesothelioma Act 2014, s. 12
Mesothelioma Act 2014, s. 13
Pensions Act 2004, s. 38
Pensions Act 2004, s. 39
Pensions Act 2004, s. 40
Pensions Act 2004, s. 43
Pensions Act 2004, s. 44
Pensions Act 2004, s. 46
Pensions Act 2004, s. 52
Pensions Act 2004, s. 53
Pensions Act 2004, s. 54
Pensions Act 2004, s. 55
Pensions Act 2004, s. 56
Pneumoconiosis etc (Workers' Compensation) Act 1979
Small Business, Enterprise and Employment Act 2015
Third Parties (Rights against Insurers) Act 1930

Third Parties (Rights against Insurers) Act 2010
Unfair Contract Terms Act 1977, s. 2
Workmen's Compensation (Silicosis and Asbestosis) Act 1930

Subordinate Legislation

Asbestos Industry (Asbestosis) Scheme 1931
Companies (Authorised Minimum) Regulations 2009 (SI 2009/2425), reg. 2
Draft Register of People with Significant Control Regulations 2016
Financial Conduct Authority, 'Disclosure and Transparency Rules Sourcebook', Ch. 5
Financial Conduct Authority, 'Handbook', Listing Rules, LR 11.1
Financial Services and Markets: The Transparency Regulations 2015 (SI 2015/1755)
Insolvency (England and Wales) Rules 2016 (SI 2016/1024), r.14.1
Insolvency (England and Wales) Rules 2016 (SI 2016/1024), r.14.2
Insolvency (England and Wales) Rules 2016 (SI 2016/1024), r.14.12

United States

Statutes

An Act Relative to Incorporations for Manufacturing Purposes 1811 (NY)
Arizona Revised Statutes Annotated, Title 12, Courts and Civil Proceedings, § 12–684
California Labor Code, Div. 4 Workers' Compensation and Insurance, Ch. 3, § 3601
Delaware Code, Title 8, § 102 (2002)
Employee Retirement Income Security Act of 1974, § 1301 (Pub. L. 93–406, 88 Stat. 829)
Indiana Code, Title 34, Civil Law and Procedure, Art. 20, Ch 3, § 1
Louisiana Products Liability Act (La Rev Stat Ann § 9:2800.52 (2009))
Minnesota Statutes Annotated, Ch. 114 C-116i, Environmental Protection, § 115B.05
Minnesota Statutes Annotated, Ch. 114 C-116i, Environmental Protection, § 115B.14
Model Business Corporation Act § 6.22 (3d ed. Supp. 1997)
Uniform Voidable Transactions Act 1984, § 4
Uniform Voidable Transactions Act 1984, § 5
US Code, Title 11, Bankruptcy, § 101
US Code, Title 11, Bankruptcy, § 105
US Code, Title 11, Bankruptcy, § 502
US Code, Title 11, Bankruptcy, § 507
US Code, Title 11, Bankruptcy, § 524
US Code, Title 11, Bankruptcy, § 542
US Code, Title 11, Bankruptcy, § 547
US Code, Title 11, Bankruptcy, § 548
US Code, Title 11, Bankruptcy, § 1123
US Code, Title 11, Bankruptcy, § 1126
US Code, Title 18, Providing material support or resources to designated foreign terrorist organizations, § 2339B
US Code, Title 26, Hazardous Substance Superfund, § 9507

US Code, Title 26, Hazardous Substance Superfund, § 9509
US Code, Title 33, Chapter 40, Oil Pollution
US Code, Title 33, Chapter 40, Oil Pollution, § 2701
US Code, Title 33, Chapter 40, Oil Pollution, § 2702
US Code, Title 33, Chapter 40, Oil Pollution, § 2703
US Code, Title 33, Chapter 40, Oil Pollution, § 2704
US Code, Title 33, Chapter 40, Oil Pollution, § 2708
US Code, Title 33, Chapter 40, Oil Pollution, § 2712
US Code, Title 33, Chapter 40, Oil Pollution, § 2716
US Code, Title 33, Chapter 40, Oil Pollution, § 2717
US Code, Title 42, Comprehensive Environmental Response, Compensation and Liability
US Code, Title 42, Comprehensive Environmental Response, Compensation and Liability, § 9601
US Code, Title 42, Comprehensive Environmental Response, Compensation and Liability, § 9604
US Code, Title 42, Comprehensive Environmental Response, Compensation and Liability, § 9607
US Code, Title 42, Comprehensive Environmental Response, Compensation and Liability, § 9608
US Code, Title 42, Comprehensive Environmental Response, Compensation and Liability, § 9611
US Code, Title 42, Public Health and Welfare
US Code, Title 42, Public Health and Welfare, § 282

Restatements

American Law Institute, Restatement (Second) of Torts (1977)
American Law Institute, Restatement (Second) of Torts (1977), § 402A
American Law Institute, Restatement (Second) of Torts (1977), § 431
American Law Institute, Restatement (Second) of Torts (1977), § 433A
American Law Institute, Restatement (Second) of Torts (1979), § 870
American Law Institute, Restatement (Second) of Torts (1979), § 876
American Law Institute, Restatement (Third) of Agency (2006), § 7.03
American Law Institute, Restatement (Third) of Torts: Apportionment of Liability (2000), § 10
American Law Institute, Restatement (Third) of Torts: Apportionment of Liability (2000), § 15
American Law Institute, Restatement (Third) of Torts: Liability for Physical and Emotional Harm (2009), § 2
American Law Institute, Restatement (Third) of Torts: Products Liability (1998)
American Law Institute, Restatement (Third) of Torts: Products Liability (1998), § 1
American Law Institute, Restatement (Third) of Torts: Products Liability (1998), § 2
American Law Institute, Restatement (Third) of Torts: Products Liability (1998), § 4
American Law Institute, Restatement (Third) of Torts: Products Liability (1998), § 6
American Law Institute, Restatement (Third) of Torts: Products Liability (1998), § 12

American Law Institute, Restatement (Third) of Torts: Products Liability (1998), § 14
American Law Institute, Restatement (Third) of Torts: Products Liability (1998), § 15
American Law Institute, Restatement (Fourth) of the Foreign Relations Law of the United States: Jurisdiction (TD No 2, 2016)
American Law Institute, Restatement (Fourth) of the Foreign Relations Law of the United States: Jurisdiction, (TD No 2, 2016), § 304

International Treaties

Council of Europe, European Convention on Products Liability in regard to Personal Injury and Death (ETS No 91), Strasbourg, 27 January 1977
Treaty on the Functioning of the European Union OJ [2012] C 326/01, Art 107(1)

1

Introduction

1.1 General

This book is concerned with the 'insolvent entity problem'. This problem can arise in two ways. In the first case, a subsidiary company within a corporate group becomes insolvent and is unable to pay its creditors in full. In the second case, a company participating in a business network becomes insolvent and cannot pay its creditors in full. In both cases, the insolvent entity problem involves the question whether liability can be extended beyond the insolvent company to another company, whether in the group or in the network.

Much of the law in this area is concerned with corporate groups rather than networks. In this way, this book focusses predominantly on the insolvent entity problem in the group context. However, reasons will be given for which the problem of corporate groups is linked inextricably to the problem of networks. In brief, many companies cooperate with each other on projects through purely contractual relations. Any increase in the liability of corporate groups will encourage reorganisation in the network form. Such reorganisation has the potential to push the insolvent entity problem from groups to networks, which indicates the need for a principle of extended liability applicable in the latter case as well as the former.

The insolvent entity problem tends to arise (as we will see) in medium-size and smaller businesses, and less so in larger businesses. The reason for this has to do with the importance to larger businesses of their commercial reputations, as well as their greater dependence upon key suppliers, who are likely to deal only with solvent companies. However, the insolvent entity problem has arisen in certain larger corporate groups dealing in hazardous substances (such as asbestos and toxic chemicals), to which corporate reputation does not seem to matter a great deal.

This book will argue for new principles of extended liability applicable in cases of unsatisfied personal injury claims. Personal injury claims are deserving of special treatment because they involve the most important interests protected by law – interests in the human mind and body. One of the fundamental premises of this book is that the law regarding the insolvent entity problem must give priority to interests in mind and body over commercial and financial interests. The law should strive to protect the integrity of mind and body effectively and, if necessary, subordinate commercial interests to this end. While this book argues for an exception to limited liability in favour of personal injury claims, it accepts that no strong argument can be made for any exception applicable to purely financial claims arising in insolvency. In cases involving purely financial claims, the law of limited liability generally should prevail.

The argument in this book is made against a background of legislative and judicial failure in dealing with the insolvent entity problem. The legislation which addresses the insolvent entity problem does so in an unsystematic way, for example facilitating extensions of liability with respect to certain dangerous activities and certain transactions which impede companies' ability to pay their debts. This book argues for a comprehensive statutory exception to limited liability in cases of unsatisfied personal injury claims.

Failure in the common law is seen most explicitly in the doctrine of veil-piercing. Veil-piercing has failed because it does not sufficiently respect the fact that each company in a corporate group is a separate legal entity, and because courts have not properly determined the reasons for which this doctrine should be available independent of other common law actions. Indeed, there appears to be little justification for a principle of extended liability directed solely at controlling shareholders. By contrast, the 'equivalence principle' adhered to in this book states that common law doctrines applicable to individuals should be applicable to corporate entities on similar terms, unless there is a good reason for exemption. This book argues that the common law can facilitate extended liability through development of the tort of unlawful means conspiracy. A modified tort of conspiracy would facilitate extensions of liability horizontally to co-subsidiaries, or to other network participants.

Of course, there are policy choices to be made in determining an appropriate liability regime for dealing with the insolvent entity problem. A policy issue which looms large concerns the way in which the legal system in a modern economy ought to balance the interests of big business, on the one hand, and the victims of big business, on the other. In the typical case, the insolvent entity problem impacts disproportionately on the poor and the weak. The failure of legislatures and courts, when addressing this problem, to make proper provision for personal injury victims represents their *choice in favour* of businesses that injure the poor and the weak. As Guido Calabresi stated long ago: 'even leaving accident burdens where they happen to fall is an implicit decision of what an accident costs and which act or activity ought to bear the costs.'[1] The inability of personal injury victims to obtain redress from parent companies, or from other network participants, represents a gap in the law that needs to be justified[2] or eliminated – and this gap is a large one when one considers (as this book does) the strong senses in which those engaging in collective commercial endeavours have a real responsibility for injuries that they cause.

In setting the stage for the discussion which follows in this book, some preliminary observations should be made about what corporate groups and networks are, about the growth of corporate groups and the problems to which they give rise, and about regulation, compensation, and the development of appropriate liability rules.

1.2 Definition of Corporate Group

Our discussion begins with definitions of the terms 'corporate group' and 'network'. In its core conception, a 'corporate group' comprises separate legal entities related hierarchically through shareholdings. Shareholding is 'hierarchical' in the intended sense when company A is the *controlling shareholder* in companies B and C.[3] This does not necessarily entail that A Co has majority voting rights in B Co and C Co. Control can arise through indirect[4] and minority shareholdings.[5] However, the premise is that A Co has the capacity to control its subsidiaries B Co and C Co on an *ongoing basis*, whether or not control actually is exercised.[6] The conception of the corporate group can be extended to other structures where the exercise of a

[1] G. Calabresi, *The Costs of Accidents* (1970), p. 133.

[2] See J. C. P. Goldberg and B. C. Zipursky, 'The Easy Case for Products Liability Law: A Response to Professors Polinsky and Shavell' (2010) 123 *Harvard Law Review* 1919, 1938; P. Spender, 'Blue Asbestos and Golden Eggs: Evaluating Bankruptcy and Class Actions as Just Responses to Mass Tort Liability' (2003) 25 *Sydney Law Review* 223, 254.

[3] See L. Sealy and S. Worthington, *Sealy and Worthington's Cases and Materials in Company Law* (10th edn., 2013), p. 69; UNCITRAL, 'Legislative Guide on Insolvency, Part Three: Treatment of Enterprise Groups in Insolvency' (2012), pp. 2 and 7.

[4] See S. Haddy, 'A Comparative Analysis of Directors' Duties in a Range of Corporate Group Structures' (2002) 20 *Company & Securities Law Journal* 138, 140.

[5] See, e.g., Companies Act 2006, s 1159(1).

[6] *Walker* v. *Wimborne* (1976) 137 CLR 1, 6. See also A. Muscat, *The Liability of the Holding Company for the Debts of its Insolvent Subsidiaries* (1996), p. 441; M. A. Eisenberg, 'Corporate Groups', in M. Gillooly (ed.), *The Law Relating to Corporate Groups* (1993), p. 3.

different kind of common control is possible, such as where a family owns several companies which are not hierarchically structured.[7] In such a group, each company, D Co, E Co, and F Co, is related to the others as 'sibling', but no parent exercises control over those companies.[8]

There are wider conceptions of the corporate group which are not based upon hierarchical shareholdings. Thus, corporate groups might be said to exist in cases of significant but non-controlling shareholdings, combined with common management,[9] such as where there are 'cross-holdings' or 'circular holdings' of shares. An example of a cross-holding arrangement arises when three companies each have a 26 per cent shareholding in the others, and there is overlapping management. This arrangement 'enables the companies to be operated as a group so long as there is an agreement between the directors of the three companies'.[10] Under the circular shareholding arrangement, A Co holds 40 per cent of the voting shares in B Co, which holds 40 per cent of the voting shares in C Co, which in turn holds 40 per cent of the voting shares in A Co. 'The effect of this is that, although there is not de jure control of the various companies, when the directors of each company act in unison, they can control effectively the various companies in which the circular holdings are held.'[11]

The wider conceptions of the corporate group just explained should be kept in mind, but cannot always be relied upon for the purposes of determining an appropriate extended liability regime. In contentious areas of law, such as that under discussion, courts revert to narrow and legalistic criteria of liability. They prefer to limit the conception of the corporate group 'to entities linked by direct equity interests and control'. This is because 'this narrow approach gives due regard to the formal legal structure of the group' and distinguishes the corporate group 'more clearly from general agency relationships'.[12]

[7] I. Mevorach, *Insolvency within Multinational Enterprise Groups* (2009), p. 16 (example of Parmalat); D. D. Prentice, 'Some Aspects of the Law Relating to Corporate Groups in the United Kingdom' (1999) 13 *Connecticut Journal of International Law* 305, 314.

[8] See, e.g., *Charterbridge Corporation Ltd* v. *Lloyds Bank Ltd* [1970] Ch. 62, 66.

[9] *Re Enterprise Gold Mines NL* (1991) 3 ACSR 531, 540; V. Harper Ho, 'Theories of Corporate Groups: Corporate Identity Reconceived' (2012) 42 *Seton Hall Law Review* 879, 944; S. Elson, 'Legal Liability of Holding Companies for Acts of Subsidiary Companies' [1930] *Commercial Law Journal* 680, 682. Some would say that common management is more important than equity ownership in defining a corporate group: e.g., P. Nygh, 'The Liability of Multi-national Corporations for the Torts of Their Subsidiaries' (2002) 3 *European Business Organization Law Review* 51, 53.

[10] Prentice, 'Some Aspects', 313. [11] Prentice, 'Some Aspects', 314.

[12] Harper Ho, 'Theories of Corporate Groups', 932.

1.3 Definition of Network

The core conception of the corporate group can be distinguished from the 'corporate network', in which the relationship between constituent companies does not include the potential for equity-based control.[13] Network participants are related, instead, by detailed cooperation agreements, and/or repeated transactions.[14] For the most part, we focus upon the former case, cooperative agreements facilitating stable relationships between two or more companies over the medium term. For a number of reasons related, for example, to the increased importance of technology and know-how in the manufacture and distribution of products, the availability of instantaneous communications, and the need for quick adaptability to changing market conditions, corporate networks of this nature have become common in the modern, commercial world.

Whether we speak of corporate groups or networks (and the distinction between them is not always sharp),[15] the insolvent entity problem is capable of resolution only when there is a solvent company to which liability can be extended. In the corporate group context, this means extension either to the parent company or to a co-subsidiary. In the network context, it means extension of liability to another network participant. Given that businesses can choose between corporate group and network forms, and given the potential this presents for the evasion of liability rules directed at corporate groups alone, any extended liability regime must take this fact into account. The regime must, to the extent possible, be neutral as between business forms (hereafter, the 'business form neutrality principle') so as not to distort commercial operations. This gives rise to the need for rules by which liability can be extended among network participants. One of the challenges is to construct an appropriate way of doing this, based on the ability to bind together companies that coordinate with each other in ways that cause harm.[16]

[13] See fuller discussion in Chapter 2.

[14] G. Jones, *Merchants to Multinationals: British Trading Companies in the Nineteenth and Twentieth Centuries* (2000), p. 181.

[15] R. Whittington and M. Mayer, *The European Corporation: Strategy, Structure, and Social Science* (2000), p. 179.

[16] See, e.g., A. Nolan, 'The Position of Unsecured Creditors of Corporate Groups: Towards a Group Responsibility Solution which Gives Fairness and Equity a Role' (1993) 11 *Company & Securities Law Journal* 461, 468.

1.4 Growth of Groups

Corporate groups are extremely important economic, social, and political actors. Large, listed companies are characterised by control over multiple subsidiary companies. In order to understand the subject matter of this book properly, it will be necessary to examine the economic, tax, and regulatory reasons which stimulate the formation of corporate groups. Briefly, many large businesses prefer the group form for reasons that include: the convenience of organising business activity into separate units with their own products, services, and brands; the implementation of management control over and accountability for unit activities; ease of purchase and sale of assets held at the subsidiary level; the desire to adopt different financing models for different group activities; the ability of the parent company to limit its own liability for subsidiary debts; and so on. These matters are discussed at length in Chapters 2 and 3.

1.5 Problems of Corporate Groups and Networks

While corporate groups and networks contribute much to economic activity, employment, wealth creation, and political stability, they are the source of the insolvent entity problem as well. This book provides three case studies as illustrations. These involve mass asbestos-related injuries, mass pharmaceutical-related injuries, and what is described as 'the next catastrophe'. Asbestos-related injuries have given rise to significant social and legal problems in a number of jurisdictions. These arose, in part, because asbestos producers sought to divorce themselves from legal liability for the causation of personal injuries through their activities and their products. Mass pharmaceutical-related injuries began to appear in the 1950s and 1960s, notably with the Thalidomide poisoning cases. Given the ever-increasing importance of pharmaceuticals in modern medicine, outpatient treatment, and everyday life, there is the potential for many more mass-tort claims against producers in the future. 'Big pharma' has anticipated such problems, and this manifests itself in the ways in which they are, today, organising their developmental, testing, manufacturing, and distribution activities. Their methods of organisation encompass both the corporate group and the network. While we do not necessarily know what harms will be done when 'the next catastrophe' occurs, we can predict some of the circumstances that will make it possible. These include large-scale industrial processes, which are tightly coupled or interconnected, where disaster might begin anywhere in the chain.[17] The Bhopal chemical plant explosion of 1984 and the *Deepwater Horizon* oil spill of 2010 are illustrations of this type of event, which will be discussed in Chapter 4.

It is likely that the insolvent entity problem will become more critical over time. This is because we inhabit a world of 'synthetic living', dependent upon mass producers for food and drink, 'cures and complexions, apparel and gadgets'.[18] 'Synthetic living' involves the use of artificial products, the deployment of new technologies, and scientific discoveries the medium- to long-term risks of which might not become apparent until many years after testing is over and consumption has begun.[19] Moreover, the mass production, storage, and distribution of goods means that catastrophes become large-scale events which have a substantial impact upon persons, property, and the environment.[20] In the circumstances, one cannot characterise corporate insolvency 'at the hands of involuntary tort creditors as a fat-tail risk, a risk of a high-impact event that has a low probability of occurring. These kinds of risks are real and present for firms of all kinds'.[21] Indeed, both large and small companies face potential 'financial ruin as a result of having placed defective products in the stream of commerce', or having engaged in risky activities with the ability to injure on a wide scale. This is not simply because of the 'increasing sophistication of technology, marketing, and systems of distribution' which 'likely make the problem a recurring one for large corporations'.[22] The problem arises also because businesses engage in conscious decisions to structure their relationships so as to protect assets and to reduce potential exposure to liability. This is evident, for example, when the parent company operates as no more than a holding company, with no substantial operations of its own, and/or

[17] C. Perrow, *The Next Catastrophe* (2007); A. C. Hutchinson, 'Out of the Black Hole: Toward a Fresh Approach to Tort Causation' (2016) 39 *Dalhousie Law Journal* 651; J. B. Ruhl, 'Managing Systemic Risk in Legal Systems' (2014) 89 *Indiana Law Journal* 559, 563 and 588.

[18] *Dalehite* v. *United States* 346 US 15, 51–2 (1953).

[19] W. K. Viscusi and R. J. Zeckhauser, 'Deterring and Compensating Oil-Spill Catastrophes: The Need for Strict Two-Tier Liability' (2011) 64 *Vanderbilt Law Review* 1717, 1726. See also *MC Mehta* v. *Union of India* 1987 AIR 965; P. Bartrip, 'Changing Attitudes to Risk? Managing Myxomatosis in Twentieth-Century Britain', in B. Hutter (ed.), *Anticipating Risks and Organising Risk Regulation* (2010), p. 68.

[20] Viscusi and Zeckhauser, 'Deterring and Compensating', 1727.

[21] P. Conti-Brown, 'Elective Shareholder Liability' (2012) 64 *Stanford Law Review* 409, 462.

[22] M. Lyle, 'Mass Tort Claims and the Corporate Tortfeasor: Bankruptcy Reorganization and Legislative Compensation versus the Common-Law Tort System' (1983) 61 *Texas Law Review* 1297, 1299–300.

when operating companies in the group are separated from asset-holding companies. An alternative strategy involves disaggregating the corporate group, so as to reorganise as a network of companies joined through contractual agreements to cooperate in the design, production, storage, marketing, and distribution of goods.

1.6 Regulation

The aim of this book is to determine the ways in which parent companies and other companies within corporate groups and networks should be held to account through means of statute and/or tort law. It situates the development of rules aimed at resolving the insolvent entity problem, as well as their enforcement, in a framework of business regulation. In so doing, this book adopts a wide view of what passes for 'regulation'. This is in accordance with modern regulatory theory,[23] which sees the most effective regulatory strategy as a mixed one that combines traditional top-down command-and-control with more devolved approaches.[24]

Command-and-control regulation is epitomised by legislation setting out standards of conduct and penalties for non-compliance, as well as enforcement actions by regulatory bodies which undertake inspections, prosecutions, and civil suits. This type of regulation is important in creating proper standards of conduct in industries that have the potential to injure on a mass scale. However, command-and-control regulation is not effective when the subject matter of regulation changes quickly, for example in the technology and financial sectors. Part of the problem is that legislators and regulators cannot hope to understand advances in technology and finance in the way that those who work within these sectors do.[25] This makes it inevitable that regulatory rules do not cater for all potential problems, and that gaps in the rules can be exploited. Even if the rules are well-tailored to the subject matter, there might be difficulties of enforcement on account of limited budgets, limited numbers of personnel with proper training and expertise, the time and cost of

[23] R. Baldwin, M. Cave, and M. Lodge, *Understanding Regulation: Theory, Strategy, and Practice* (2nd edn., 2012), p. 2: 'think of the word regulation [as] all state actions that are designed to influence business or social behaviour.' This view is increasingly influential among tort lawyers: see, e.g., Goldberg and Zipursky, 'The Easy Case', 1930–1; T. M. Schwartz, 'The Impact of the New Products Liability Restatement on Prescription Products' (1995) 50 *Food & Drug Law Journal* 399, 410–11.

[24] Baldwin, Cave, and Lodge, *Understanding Regulation*, pp. 3, 63, 80, and 132.

[25] Baldwin, Cave, and Lodge, *Understanding Regulation*, p. 110; B. Fisse and J. Braithwaite, *Corporations, Crime and Accountability* (1993), p. 196.

enforcement actions, and so on.[26] Deficiencies such as these played their part in disasters such as the *Deepwater Horizon* oil spill and the global financial crisis.[27]

Today, experts accept that command-and-control regulation is not sufficient, in itself, to achieve all regulatory goals. Regulation is seen as a multifaceted activity which can take – and should take – a number of forms, so that the system has in-built redundancy, and so that each regulatory prong reinforces the others.[28] Mixed regulation takes advantage of the 'corporatisation' of work and other forms of business activity, which provides ready-made organisational structures for pursuing regulatory objectives.[29] The ultimate goal of regulation involves proper understanding of the risks of activity,[30] proper planning of those activities, and the formulation of general standards of conduct for business activities and interactions.[31] These standards derive from a number of sources. Courts have a role to play when deciding legal cases because they not only look back at what has happened in the past, but also set standards for future conduct. But regulation goes beyond the 'official' level of statutes, courts, and regulatory agencies, and includes various levels of delegated or self-regulation, which have advantages that include greater expertise about the issues and lower costs for the state.[32] Delegated regulation occurs, for example, when trade and industry associations establish guidelines for action, when companies adopt codes of conduct, and when they devise internal policies and procedures.[33] Companies and other organisations are typified by features which assist in the dissemination and implementation of policies and procedures that control action, including their specialisation of function, hierarchy of authority, commitment by members to organisational objectives, and reproachability amongst members when

[26] See, generally, Perrow, *The Next Catastrophe*. See also K. Greenfield, 'The Disaster at Bhopal: Lessons for Corporate Law?' (2008) 42 *New England Law Review* 755, 759.

[27] See, e.g., J. Ray, 'Offshore Safety and Environmental Regimes: A Post-Macondo Comparative Analysis of the United States and the United Kingdom' (2014) 33 *Mississippi College Law Review* 11; H. M. Osofsky, 'Multidimensional Governance and the BP *Deepwater Horizon* Oil Spill' (2011) 63 *Florida Law Review* 1077, 1102; Viscusi and Zeckhauser, 'Deterring and Compensating', 1753–4.

[28] Baldwin, Cave, and Lodge, *Understanding Regulation*, p. 80; J. Braithwaite, *Regulatory Capitalism* (2008), p. 29.

[29] Braithwaite, *Regulatory Capitalism*, p. 4. See also ibid. pp. 29 and 157.

[30] Baldwin, Cave, and Lodge, *Understanding Regulation*, p. 83.

[31] See C. Macrae, 'Regulating Resilience? Regulatory Work in High-Risk Arenas', in B. Hutter (ed.), *Anticipating Risks and Organising Risk Regulation* (2010), pp. 141–3 and 153.

[32] Baldwin, Cave, and Lodge, *Understanding Regulation*, pp. 139, 148, and 289.

[33] Baldwin, Cave, and Lodge, *Understanding Regulation*, pp. 65 and 266.

things go wrong.[34] These features create conditions conducive to the deterrence of wrongful and injurious conduct by organisations and their employees.[35] Both statute law and tort law have a role to play at the industry and corporate level in encouraging this type of proactive regulation of activity.[36]

Different levels of regulation of corporate groups exist in different jurisdictions, ranging from the more intrusive regimes of Germany and several other civil law countries[37] to the less intrusive regimes in the common law countries examined in this book. In countries like the United Kingdom and Australia, the current main objectives of the regulation of corporate groups include promoting transparency of ownership and availability of information about group operations, facilitating management of groups, preferment of employee entitlements to other debts, and protection of general creditors.[38] The latter objective is achieved largely through prohibitions on certain kinds of transaction which deplete the assets of indebted companies, and through the imposition of directors' duties which might be capable of extension to the parent company.[39]

However, some potentially helpful statutory means of extending liability exist, although they have had limited impact on the insolvent entity problem to this point. First, these jurisdictions feature protections of consumers and bystanders injured by defective products.[40] Liability is strict or 'stricter', so as to either negate or reduce the importance of fault in liability determinations. However, in their present incarnation, product liability rules are limited by a wide development risks defence and by restrictive long-stop time limits. Second, various common law jurisdictions give courts powers to consolidate group debts in cases of abuse,[41]

[34] These matters are discussed in Chapter 5. See also Fisse and Braithwaite, *Corporations, Crime and Accountability*, pp. 29, 53, 79, and 97; B. L. Garrett, 'The Corporate Criminal as Scapegoat' (2015) 101 *Virginia Law Review* 1789.

[35] This is a crucial point: see W. K. Viscusi, 'Pricing Lives for Corporate Risk Decisions' (2015) 68 *Vanderbilt Law Review* 1117, 1122.

[36] This lesson was reinforced by the *Deepwater Horizon* oil spill (discussed, e.g., in Chapter 4): see M. Greenstone, 'Liability and Financial Responsibility for Oil Spills under the Oil Pollution Act of 1990 and Related States' (Testimony before US House of Representatives Committee on Transportation and Infrastructure)(9 June 2010), available at: www.brookings.edu/research/testimony/2010/06/09-oil-spill-greenstone.

[37] K. J. Hopt, 'Groups of Companies: A Comparative Study on the Economics, Law and Regulation of Corporate Groups' (ECGI Law Working Paper 286/2015), 9.

[38] See also Hopt, 'Groups of Companies', 2–3.

[39] Such as Insolvency Act 1986, s. 214. See Chapter 6.

[40] See Chapter 8.

[41] See Chapter 7.

but this is a remedy which is used rarely because of its adverse impact on general creditor expectations. Consolidation of group debts has not been deployed in response to mass-tort cases. And no such power of consolidation is available (for reasons which are inherent) with respect to participants in corporate networks.

The multiple jurisdictions of the United States take a similar approach; however, protections for creditors are stronger in a number of areas. First, US courts have been more willing to use the corporate law doctrine of veil-piercing in order to extend liability from insolvent subsidiaries, although this occurs rarely in public companies.[42] Second, legislatures have developed specific statutory schemes allowing the extension of liability to parent companies in cases, for example, involving oil spills and environmental pollution. As will be seen,[43] these schemes have the potential to be effective in their areas of operation, but as yet do not provide a model for comprehensive protection of personal injury claimants.

What is clear from this brief survey of how corporate groups are regulated in common law countries is that the 'regulatory system' is underdeveloped, and that a more comprehensive approach needs to be taken to several issues including the protection of personal injury claimants. That is the main preoccupation of this book. In general terms, there are a number of reasons for which the common law could encourage better delegated- or self-regulation of risky activities – especially those which pose the threat of personal injury. First, the imposition of a form of extended liability upon parent companies for the wrongs of insolvent subsidiaries should result in better reporting to parent companies, better planning, and more effective control over subsidiary activities[44] – so long as the exercise of control is not itself a prerequisite for parent company liability. The parent company as shareholder in the subsidiary has the ability to implement change because it can appoint directors to the subsidiary board and transmit group policies either to the subsidiary board or directly to subsidiary managers. Second, the imposition of a form of extended liability within the corporate network has the potential to achieve some of the same goals.[45] This will not be through the

[42] See Chapter 10. [43] See Chapter 8.

[44] See T. Hadden, 'Regulating Corporate Groups: An International Perspective', in J. McCahery, S. Picciotto, and C. Scott (eds.), *Corporate Control and Accountability: Changing Structures and Dynamics of Regulation* (1993), pp. 343–4.

[45] See, e.g., M. A. Cohen, M. Gottlieb, J. Linn, and N. Richardson, 'Deepwater Drilling: Law, Policy, and Economics of Firm Organization and Safety' (2011) 64 *Vanderbilt Law Review* 1853.

exercise of formal control, but through other mechanisms, such as joint planning of projects by network participants, contractual specification of performance standards, the exercise of market power over the unwilling, and the imposition of 'penalties' for non-compliance with expectations of safety through such things as removal of recalcitrant companies from tender lists and withholding of progress payments.

1.7 Compensation

This book takes the view, then, that it is extremely important to provide adequate causes of action for personal injuries in the insolvent entity situation as part of the regulation of corporate activity, the maintenance of proper standards of conduct, and the achievement of justice in individual cases. The development of appropriate statutory and common law liability rules presents one means by which to deal with the problem. However, other mechanisms of redress exist, either alongside liability rules, or in place of them. Something must be said about some of the advantages and disadvantages of these alternatives.

Labour, social security, and other laws in many advanced nations facilitate access by injured persons to medical care, sickness benefits, and compensation for injury without the need to bring legal actions. This is the case, for example, in the United Kingdom, where the National Health Service (NHS) offers medical care which is free at the point of delivery for most persons,[46] where the Industrial Injuries Disablement Benefit (IIDB) is available to employees who become disabled through accidents at work or as a result of occupational diseases,[47] and where employers are required, under the Employers' Liability (Compulsory Insurance) Act 1969, to take out insurance to cover bodily injury and disease in their workers.[48] These schemes have softened the blow

[46] National Health Service, 'About the NHS' (2016), available at www.nhs.uk/NHSEngland/thenhs/about/Pages/overview.aspx. In the United States, it appears that a proportion of those personally injured and unable to obtain employer-sponsored health insurance have been forced to undergo expensive treatment and 'pay' for it through the bankruptcy process: M. Cole, 'Limiting Liability through Bankruptcy' (2002) 70 *University of Cincinnati Law Review* 1245, 1292. Cole says: 'Consumer bankruptcy . . . acts as social insurance, particularly in the context of "catastrophic illness". Bankruptcy and its discharge permit society to shift the cost of such illnesses from the [un]fortunate victims of the condition to healthcare providers and their "paying" patients': ibid., 1292–3.

[47] Explanatory Notes to the Mesothelioma Bill 2013, [10]; A. Boggio, *Compensating Asbestos Victims: Law and the Dark Side of Industrialization* (2013), pp. 73ff.

[48] Section 1.

delivered by certain mass-torts, such as those arising from asbestos and defective pharmaceuticals.[49] However, they have limitations of their own. First, the NHS offers what are, in many respects, basic levels of care, and the system is subject to levels of resource rationing which are likely to become more pronounced in the future as costs of care rise at the same time as the population's average age increases. Second, non-resident, non-European Economic Area nationals injured in the United Kingdom are not permitted access to the NHS free of charge, and usually need to pay for services.[50] This means that they have greater need to rely upon legal proceedings for compensation. Third, taxpayers fund the NHS (and IIDB),[51] which means that the costs of injuries caused by corporate misconduct are partly socialised.[52] Many would view this situation as unacceptable. Fourth, employment-related benefits are available to limited groups of persons and are subject to gaps which become more pronounced with long latency periods in the development of injury and disease.[53]

In addition to more comprehensive forms of assistance, the United Kingdom and other advanced nations have various ad hoc statutory schemes that permit redress for persons injured by mass- and other torts. Employment-related mesothelioma victims unable to take advantage of employer-funded insurance cover, for example, have access in the United Kingdom to assistance under the Mesothelioma Act 2014. The reason for this is that the UK government considered the 'condition to be unique, in particular because of its near universal fatality, its speed of death following diagnosis and its causation arising exclusively from exposure to asbestos'.[54] The 2014 Act creates the Diffuse Mesothelioma Payment Scheme. It makes provision for payments to eligible persons, who include sufferers of mesothelioma and certain dependants.[55] Power is given, also, to the scheme administrator to assist sufferers and dependants to bring

[49] See D. D. Prentice, 'Veil Piercing and Successor Liability in the United Kingdom' (1996) *Florida Journal of International Law* 469, 485.

[50] Department of Health, 'Summary of Changes Made to the Way the NHS Charges Overseas Visitors for NHS Hospital Care' (2016), available at: www.gov.uk/government/publications/guidance-on-overseas-visitors-hospital-charging-regulations/summary-of-changes-made-to-the-way-the-nhs-charges-overseas-visitors-for-nhs-hospital-care.

[51] See Boggio, *Compensating Asbestos Victims*, p. 75.

[52] Boggio, *Compensating Asbestos Victims*, p. 235; J. Stapleton, 'Products Liability in the United Kingdom: The Myths of Reform' (1999) 34 *Texas International Law Journal* 45, 47.

[53] Explanatory Notes to the Mesothelioma Bill 2013, [5] and [11].

[54] Explanatory Notes to the Mesothelioma Bill 2013, [17].

[55] Sections 2 and 3.

legal proceedings against negligent employers or relevant insurers.[56] The scheme is funded by a levy on active insurers,[57] and the regulations passed pursuant to the Act 'may require different active insurers to pay different amounts based on criteria relating to their relative market share in the reference period'.[58] Another example of an ad hoc statutory scheme is that applicable to injuries arising from defective vaccines. Benefits for such injuries are available in the United Kingdom by way of the Vaccine Damage Payment,[59] and in the United States under the National Vaccine Injury Compensation Program.[60] Congress legislated for the latter in light of 'unique' risks arising in the development of vaccines, which might cost many billions to develop and yet prove dangerous because of inherent limits in medical science and unforeseen biological reactions.[61]

Many would find the ad hoc nature of these schemes and the justifications for their implementation inadequate. After all, personal injury is personal injury no matter the way in which it is caused – whether by an employer, product manufacturer, or other actor. It seems arbitrary, and even unfair, to single out certain kinds of injured persons for better treatment than others, especially when schemes are financed from general taxation, and not from imposts upon injuring actors. A fairer scheme would embody a universal right to redress for personal injuries, including not only compensation for medical treatment, but full recovery of lost income and other benefits. But such schemes have become somewhat utopian in conception. Two problems with compensating personal injury by universal accident compensation relate to cost[62] and the reduced incentives for the deterrence of injurious conduct which

[56] Section 10. [57] Section 13.

[58] Section 12(5). Other ad hoc compensation schemes are available for sufferers of asbestos-related diseases: See Child Maintenance and Other Payments Act 2008, Part 4 (providing lump sum payments for those suffering from diffuse mesothelioma, where the victim was self-employed, secondarily exposed, or suffered environmental exposure); Pneumoconiosis etc. (Workers' Compensation) Act 1979 (providing lump sum payments for persons suffering from certain asbestos-related conditions unable to claim against a former employer); House of Commons Library, 'Asbestos-Related Diseases: Payments from the Department for Work and Pensions' (SN/SP/6102, 2014).

[59] UK Government, 'Vaccine Damage Payment' (2016), available at www.gov.uk/vaccine-damage-payment/overview.

[60] National Vaccine Injury Compensation Program: US Code, Title 42, Public Health and Welfare, §§ 300aa-10 to -34. See US Department of Health and Human Services, 'National Vaccine Injury Compensation Program' (2016), available at www.hrsa.gov/vaccinecompensation/.

[61] Goldberg and Zipursky, 'The Easy Case', 1932–3.

[62] K. S. Abraham, 'Individual Action and Collective Responsibility: The Dilemma of Mass Tort Reform' (1987) 73 *Virginia Law Review* 845, 894–5.

accompany such schemes.[63] In many countries, finding solutions to the problems of mass-tort and other personal injury cases that are not dependent upon government funding is becoming more important as they struggle with ageing populations and a narrowing tax base (exacerbated by the problems of corporate tax avoidance, examined in Chapter 2).

The avenues of redress promoted in this book would not increase impositions upon general taxpayers, but would help to build the costs of injury into the costs of injuring activities. Moreover, they are consistent with tort law's deterrence goals (as explained in Chapter 11).

1.8 Development of Liability Rules

As adumbrated, this book argues for the development of new principles of extended liability applicable in cases of unsatisfied personal injury claims. Before making that case, something should be said about the parameters of the ensuing discussion. First, this book focusses (as indicated) upon development of legal principles in common law countries. The United Kingdom is the main point of reference here, given its historical influence as a source of common law rules and as a major commercial jurisdiction. However, this book incorporates a great deal of comparative material, especially from the United States of America, Australia, and New Zealand. Apart from the United States' position as the world's biggest economy, US jurisdictions have developed several significant statutory schemes for extending liability beyond insolvent companies and new common law approaches to the insolvent entity problem. Australia has had decades-long experience in dealing with unfunded asbestos liabilities. And New Zealand has long been a leader in developing innovative legislative solutions to social problems.

Second, this book adopts the entity approach to the regulation of corporate activity and thus takes the company, rather than the group or network, as the basic unit of legal accountability. This is despite the fact that several influential corporate groups scholars have promoted an economics-based 'enterprise liability approach' to the insolvent entity problem, and that much literature argues that enterprise liability is the basis for modern product liability, vicarious liability, and even veil-piercing

[63] Lyle, 'Mass Tort Claims', 1345. This is a problem not only with taxpayer-funded schemes, but with industry-funded schemes as well: C. M. E. Painter, 'Tort Creditor Priority in the Secured Credit System: Asbestos Times, the Worst of Times' (1984) 36 *Stanford Law Review* 1045, 1075.

rules applicable to corporate groups.[64] As is especially apparent in the law on veil-piercing, courts struggle with the idea of the enterprise as a unit of accountability. The reason for this is that the law generally equates companies with natural persons, it being individuals who are the basic subjects of legal rights and obligations. Thus, the whole edifice of contract law is premised upon respect for the 'separate legal personality' of the company. And the same is true for tort law. Attempts to tackle the insolvent entity problem by selective application of rules regarding separate legal personality give rise to inconsistency and the potential for arbitrariness. As we shall see, there has been a move away from this kind of thinking both in the courts and in the scholarly writing on groups.

Third, this book departs from prior analyses of corporate group problems by accepting that control is not always an appropriate factor in determining liability principles. Contrary to a frequently made assumption, business history and the case studies examined in this book prove that parent companies do not always exercise day-to-day control over their subsidiaries. The reason for this is quite simple: a lack of substantial ability to control, especially when it comes to the parent company attempting to oversee the operation of foreign subsidiaries or subsidiaries which conduct businesses that differ from the parent's own. Corporate groups have the potential to comprise very large and unwieldy business operations, in which control is exercised through the setting of broad performance targets and reviews of operating results, rather than through behavioural restrictions. If control were to be the talisman of parent company liability for injuries inflicted by their subsidiaries, then the scope of liability would be modest. Moreover, the imposition of liability based upon control creates a disincentive to exercise control over subsidiary companies, and has the potential to undermine a group liability regime based upon the deterrence of future wrongdoing.

This book finds that there are other, more satisfactory reasons for extending liability beyond insolvent companies within corporate groups and networks. To summarise, corporate groups have strong attributes such as structure, hierarchical decision-making direction, coordination of activity, economic unity, group identity, and strong deterrability which provide the backdrop to the formulation of more effective liability rules and accommodate shareholder strict liability.[65] Corporate networks have fewer attributes by which to justify rules of extended liability. However, their attributes do include coordination of activity (as in the allocation of

[64] See discussion in Chapters 5, 8, and 12. [65] See discussion in Chapters 5 and 9.

functional roles and planning), commitment to common objectives, and conformity to those objectives. Although these attributes, without more, do not justify rules of extended liability, such rules are justifiable when combined with the presence of fault or fault-like conduct in the undertaking of coordinated activity.[66]

Fourth, this book does not seek to resolve the insolvent entity problem by way of extended liability rules which target directors or senior managers – although it is open to such rules. There have been various recommendations to impose new or extended forms of liability upon directors and/or senior managers. Timothy Glynn, for example, would create a new form of vicarious liability attaching to 'tort and tort-like statutory violations' by 'high-ranking' company officers (but not directors), who make important strategic decisions for their companies – on the assumption that such persons are 'best able to observe and alter firm activities, placing the burden of risk avoidance on them'.[67] However, such forms of extended liability, taken alone, would be far from adequate in providing redress for mass-torts. The reasons for this include: the fact that they restrict liability to a small group of actors; recovery made from a small group of individuals, even if insured, is likely to be inadequate in the face of mass-torts like those affecting the asbestos industry; and such proposals do no more than complement existing reasons for directors to do their jobs competently and within the limits of the law. In sum, more important avenues of redress for personal injury victims must be developed.

As adumbrated, this book sees two viable ways of extending liability from the insolvent company. The first is through a statutory exception to limited liability. This would be the simplest, most direct, and effective way of extending liability within corporate groups. However, the existence of extended forms of liability imposed upon corporate groups could encourage some businesses to reorganise their riskier activities in the network form in order to escape the prospect of heavy liabilities. In order to prevent circumvention of the rules – and to adhere to the business form neutrality principle – there is a need for the adoption of appropriate rules of extended liability in corporate networks. The second viable way of extending liability from the insolvent company is likely to be found in tort law. This book examines ways in which various torts, and tort doctrines which encompass three-party relationships, might be utilised

[66] See discussion in Chapters 5 and 11.

[67] E.g., T. P. Glynn, 'Beyond "Unlimiting" Shareholder Liability: Vicarious Tort Liability for Corporate Officers' (2004) 57 *Vanderbilt Law Review* 329.

in order to create an extended form of liability applicable in both the corporate group and network cases. Much of this book focusses upon the application or development of torts and doctrines capable of application in three-party situations – such as negligence, product liability, unlawful means conspiracy, vicarious liability, and joint liability.

1.9 Summary of Recommendations

This book makes several recommendations as to the best ways to regulate, through statute and tort law, corporate groups and networks whose activities give rise to risks of personal injury. In dealing with groups, this book recommends statutory amendments so as to create pro-rata strict liability in shareholders for unsatisfied personal injury claims. This is on the basis that shareholders represent an appropriate (although last resort) pool of persons for bearing the risks of corporate group activity that result in personal injuries. The problem of insolvent companies in corporate networks is more difficult to resolve and requires the use of a relatively flexible tort or tort doctrine. This book highlights advances in the law of vicarious liability, which potentially open the way for a greater array of claims against corporate groups. Vicarious liability is strict in nature, which entails the ability to sue without proving fault. However, the imposition of strict liability upon parent companies for the debts of their subsidiaries would contradict statutory laws on limited liability. This book also highlights advances in the application of ordinary negligence rules in the group context. Courts in various jurisdictions have recognised duties of care owed by parent companies to their subsidiaries' injured employees. However, this has proven to be a narrow basis of responsibility because of its insistence upon the exercise by parent companies of operational control over subsidiaries' injury-causing activities, in order to create the requisite proximity. This book argues that the greatest potential for extending liability horizontally in corporate groups, as between co-subsidiaries, and in corporate networks, lies in the tort of unlawful means conspiracy. Argument is made that this tort should be adapted in order to create a cognate form of liability called 'multiple entity recklessness' that operates where a company acts in a way that is objectively reckless, liability being capable of extension to other companies having substantial commercial relations with that reckless entity for their part in facilitating personal injuries. This is on the basis of their deemed agreement with that risky conduct. Each company satisfying the basic criteria for liability would become jointly liable with the risk-creating entity where personal injury ensues. This would ensure that, whether in corporate groups or in networks of companies, there is the potential for extended liability. It would then be up to the jointly liable entities to prove that they took every step to avoid the future causation of personal injury to others by doing such things as blowing the whistle on the risky conduct and ceasing coordination with the risk-creating company.

1.10 Structure of Book

This book proceeds to examine the liability of corporate groups and networks as follows: Part I sets out the context of the insolvent entity problem, explaining the reasons which drive business growth and the ways in which businesses structure their legal relationships. It includes a chapter devoted to case studies that add flesh to conceptual bones, illustrating the insolvent entity problem in cases of asbestos, defective pharmaceutical products, and the 'next catastrophe'. Part II contains a single chapter, the aim of which is to examine corporate groups and networks in more theoretical terms, and to determine whether their attributes provide a basis for extending liability to other companies involved in the group's or network's injurious activities. Part III is concerned with statute law in common law countries. It is broken down into chapters dealing successively with statutes creating general protections for creditors, statutes creating group-specific protections for creditors, and statutory torts. Given the real limitations of current statutory provisions, the final chapter in Part III sets out the proposal for an exception to limited liability operating in cases of unsatisfied personal injury claims. Part IV turns to common law causes of action of potential assistance in resolving the insolvent entity problem. The first chapter deals with veil-piercing in common law courts and explains why this has failed. The next two chapters examine torts and tort doctrines which accommodate the three-party structure of tort claimant, injuring company, and liability target. As adumbrated, we find that both the tort of negligence and the doctrine of vicarious liability are unable to provide satisfactory redress. A modified form of unlawful means conspiracy would permit the extension of liability in a satisfactory way in both corporate group and network contexts.

Various issues are touched upon in this book, but not explored in detail. Two notable topics that will require further work by relevant experts relate to the appropriate procedural rules for mass-tort actions, and rules of recognition and enforcement of judgments in multi-jurisdictional claims.

PART I

Business Context

2

The Formation of Corporate Groups and Networks

2.1 Introduction

This chapter commences our examination of corporate groups and networks, helping to set the context for discussion of the insolvent entity problem (explained in Chapter 1). This chapter begins by recounting the economic reasons for the growth of large-scale businesses. It is informed by the writings of business historians (especially Alfred Chandler and Geoffrey Jones) and economists (especially Ronald Coase and Oliver Williamson). These writers are considered 'mainstream', and their views, although subject to scholarly debate, have attracted widespread acceptance. Moreover, their views are consistent with each other with Williamson's work following directly from that of both Chandler and Coase.[1] Having outlined the main economic reasons for which businesses pursue growth strategies, this chapter turns to business forms available to those engaging in large-scale commercial activity. Reasons are given for the attractiveness of the corporate form and for the formation of corporate groups. The discussion of business form is accompanied by an initial consideration of the exercise of 'control' within corporate groups, given that this is an important element in both existing and proposed liability rules aimed at resolving the insolvent entity problem. This chapter casts doubt over the usual assumption made in the literature on extended liability, that parent companies invariably exercise operational control over their subsidiaries. There are many examples of corporate groups in which this does not occur. This chapter concludes with consideration of the multinational dimensions of corporate group growth, involving expansion beyond home country borders. It finds that parent companies are less likely to exercise operational control over their foreign subsidiaries than over their domestic subsidiaries.

[1] See O. E. Williamson, 'The Modern Corporation: Origins, Evolution, Attributes' (1981) 19 *Journal of Economic Literature* 1537.

2.2 The Growth of Business

We begin with reasons for which businesses pursue growth strategies, and the ways in which this growth is achieved. Growth is pursued in order to lower costs of operation and to increase revenues and profits. In brief, business growth can be achieved through strategies including horizontal combination, vertical integration and internalisation, diversification, and expansion into foreign markets.[2] The choice of strategy will depend upon the industry, or sector, in which the business operates.[3] Alfred Chandler undertook an important study of capital-intensive, industrial enterprises (those undertaking 'modern production processes').[4] In his book *Scale and Scope: The Dynamics of Industrial Capitalism*, Chandler observed:[5]

> Whatever the initial motivation for its investment in new operating units, the modern industrial enterprise has rarely continued to grow or maintain its competitive position *over an extended period of time* unless the addition of new units (and to a lesser extent the elimination of older ones) has actually permitted its managerial hierarchy to reduce costs, to improve functional efficiency in marketing and purchasing as well as production, to improve existing products and processes and to develop new ones, and to allocate resources to meet the challenges and opportunities of ever-changing technologies and markets. Such a process of growth has provided this bureaucratic institution with the internal dynamic that has made it powerful and enabled it to maintain its position of dominance as markets and technologies have changed ... Reductions in costs and efficient resource utilization have resulted ... from the exploitation of economies of scale in production and distribution, from exploiting economies of joint production or joint distribution, or from reduction in the costs of transactions involved.[6]

Business historians have found that many of the strategies adopted for business growth and cost reduction in the 'old', industrial economy

[2] A. D. Chandler, *Scale and Scope: The Dynamics of Industrial Capitalism* (1990), p. 146.

[3] Thus, pursuing both economies of scale and scope simultaneously has been difficult in the automotive industry: Chandler, *Scale and Scope*, p. 213. Ford Motor Company was unable successfully to move into production of tractors and airplanes: ibid., p. 223.

[4] Chandler, *Scale and Scope*, p. 14.

[5] Although there have been subsequent debates about their validity, many of Chandler's observations about 'big business' remain apposite. See, e.g., N. R. Lamoreaux, D. M. G. Raff, and P. Temin, 'Economic Theory and Business History', in G. Jones and J. Zeitlin (eds.), *The Oxford Handbook of Business History* (2007), ch. 3.

[6] Chandler, *Scale and Scope*, p. 17. Of course, corporate groups do not always form or grow on account of purely economic considerations. For example, business acquisitions are more likely to take place when the share price of the acquirer is inflated (and thus provides a strong type of consideration) and when takeover activity is high.

feature in the 'new', knowledge-based economy, in areas such as telecommunications, media, retailing, and finance.[7] Let us examine the main strategies in turn.

2.2.1 Economies of Scale

Economies of scale are those savings that 'result when the increased size of a single operating unit producing or distributing a single product reduces the unit cost of production or distribution'.[8] Such economies are realised by the use of new technologies, rather than increased labour inputs. Producing a greater number of cars on a semi-automated production line, for example, reduces fixed investment costs per vehicle and provides a competitive advantage over a more labour-intensive business.[9] Economies of scale are not confined to manufacturing, because they are not confined to the production process, but extend to purchasing, marketing, and distribution.[10]

The financial pressure to mass-produce provides business managers with incentives to expand the market for their outputs. Industrial businesses have sought to increase sales and profits by looking to new domestic and international markets. A business might expand into new markets by increasing output 'organically', that is, by selling more company-developed products. In newer industries, the first business to establish itself in a particular market often enjoys the 'first mover' advantage. Every competitor starts behind it, and must convince customers that there is reason to change from one brand to another. 'In many instances, the first company to build a plant of minimum efficient scale and to recruit the essential management team remained the leader in its industry for decades.'[11] In the alternative, a business might be anxious for more rapid sales growth than can be achieved organically. This might be pursued through the acquisition of an existing business, such as when one car manufacturer takes over another.[12] This type of growth can be

[7] Y. Cassis, 'Big Business', in G. Jones and J. Zeitlin (eds.), *The Oxford Handbook of Business History* (2007), p. 188.

[8] Chandler, *Scale and Scope*, p. 17. [9] Chandler, *Scale and Scope*, p. 23.

[10] J. Micklethwait and A. Wooldridge, *The Company: A Short History of a Revolutionary Idea* (2003), p. 69.

[11] Chandler, *Scale and Scope*, p. 26.

[12] Such as occurred when the Chinese manufacturer Geely bought the Swedish manufacturer Volvo: S. Arnott, 'China's Geely Buys Volvo for $1.5bn', *The Independent*, 3 August 2010, available at: www.independent.co.uk/news/business/news/chinas-geely-buys-volvo-for-15bn-2041772.html.

achieved, in the usual case, either by purchasing target company shares or by purchasing desired assets directly. Where one business takes over another in the same industry in order to increase its market size or capture new markets, horizontal integration occurs.

2.2.2 *Economies of Scope*

Economies of scope are those savings 'resulting from the use of processes within a single operating unit to produce or distribute more than one product'.[13] The business uses 'much the same raw and semifinished materials' and utilises the same intermediate processes to produce additional products, thereby reducing fixed investment costs per unit of output.[14] Such economies arise, for example, when an electrical equipment manufacturer starts producing new gadgets that utilise some of the same facilities, technologies, and suppliers as its existing products.[15] Chandler found that the ability of General Electric and Westinghouse successfully to exploit their investments in research and development in the generation, transmission, and application of electric power by offering related new products prevented the growth of large single-line business competitors.[16] But economies of scope are not restricted to manufacturing. Financial institutions, for example, can achieve them by extending their services from banking to insurance, personal finance planning, and so on.[17]

2.2.3 *Internalisation*

Chandler identified another type of efficiency made possible by manufacturing to scale and scope.[18] When a business produces many outputs, various operational costs increase. A point comes at which it is no longer cost-effective to rely upon external suppliers of inputs, marketing, and/or distribution of products. 'Internalisation' is the process by which businesses 'cut out the middleman' and bring within the single company or

[13] Chandler, *Scale and Scope*, p. 17. [14] Chandler, *Scale and Scope*, p. 24.

[15] Chandler, *Scale and Scope*, pp. 217–18.

[16] Chandler, *Scale and Scope*, pp. 218 and 220–1. Chandler believes that successful business growth came more from *development* of initial innovative products and systems than from research breakthroughs: ibid., p. 228. Also very important was the development of sales and servicing networks: ibid., p. 229.

[17] P. A. Gaughan, *Mergers, Acquisitions and Corporate Restructurings* (4th edn., 2007), p. 129.

[18] Chandler, *Scale and Scope*, pp. 7–8.

within the corporate group transactions that would otherwise take place in the market. Removing transactions from the marketplace reduces opportunities for profiteering by external businesses and allows the company or group to retain profits. The desire to internalise transactions leads, once again, either to the creation of new group entities or to the takeover of existing businesses.

Internalisation theory (and the 'make-or-buy' decision) was described initially by Ronald Coase[19] and developed subsequently by other economists. Coase wrote about the costs of price discovery and entry into multiple contracts ('transaction costs'), which could be reduced by bringing transactions within the 'firm'. 'Within a firm these market transactions are eliminated, and in place of the complicated market structure with exchange transactions is substituted the entrepreneur-co-ordinator, who directs production.'[20] Coase's hypothesis was that transaction costs have a very important impact upon the organisation of business, given that they amount annually to 50 per cent of gross national product.[21] The firm will grow in size as long as the relative cost of organising production within it is lower than are the costs of market transactions. Coase recognised, however, that as a firm grows larger, it becomes more difficult to coordinate internally all the functions that must be undertaken (for example, because of leakage of information as it flows up and down the decision-making hierarchy, difficulties in interpreting information, and delays in acting upon it),[22] so that mistakes will be made, losses incurred, and an endpoint to growth reached.[23]

Building upon Coase's ideas, Oliver Williamson distinguishes between transactions which can be undertaken in the anonymity of the marketplace and 'idiosyncratic' transactions requiring longer-term relationships.

[19] See R. H. Coase, *The Firm, the Market and the Law* (1988); R. H. Coase, 'The Nature of the Firm' (1937) 4 *Economica* (NS) 386; R. H. Coase, 'The Nature of the Firm: Origin' (1988) 4 *Journal of Law, Economics & Organization* 3; R. H. Coase, 'The Nature of the Firm: Meaning' (1988) 4 *Journal of Law, Economics & Organization* 19; and R. H. Coase, 'The Nature of the Firm: Influence' (1988) 4 *Journal of Law, Economics & Organization* 33.

[20] Coase, *The Firm, the Market*, pp. 35–6.

[21] Coase, 'The Nature of the Firm: Influence', 36.

[22] M. G. Colombo and M. Delmastro, 'Delegation of Authority in Business Organizations: An Empirical Test' (2004) 52 *Journal of Industrial Economics* 53, 54–5. This is a matter of theory, given that the authors' empirical study was equivocal as to the effect of these factors in decisions whether to decentralise: ibid., 76. Delays in decentralising will result in reduced adaptation to external circumstances, including changing market opportunities: P. Joskow, 'Vertical Integration', in C. Menard and M. Shirley (eds.), *Handbook of New Institutional Economics* (2005), ch. 13.

[23] Coase, *The Firm, the Market*, pp. 43–6.

Idiosyncratic transactions involve investments in special-purpose plant and equipment, and/or the development of transaction-specific skills in the course of executing contracts.[24] The need for long-term relations entails both the impossibility of providing for all eventualities in advance by way of contract, and the need for flexibility between the parties. In circumstances where contracts are not fully specified, the parties must develop governance 'structures which attenuate opportunism and otherwise infuse confidence'.[25] Williamson observes that:

> For some transactions, a shift from one structure to another may permit a simultaneous reduction in both the expense of writing a complex contract (which economizes on bounded rationality) and the expense of executing it effectively in an adaptive, sequential way (by attenuating opportunism). Indeed, this is precisely the attraction of internal procurement for transactions of a recurrent, idiosyncratic kind. Not only are market-aggregation economies negligible for such transactions – since requisite investments are transaction-specific – but market trading in these circumstances is [typified by] quasi-rent hazards.[26]

The two types of transaction-specific governance structure available are bilateral structures (such as the joint venture, discussed later in this chapter), which maintain participant autonomy, and 'unified structures, where the transaction is removed from the market and organized within the firm subject to an authority relation (vertical integration)'.[27] As between these possibilities, Williamson believes that vertical integration is preferable when 'human and physical assets become more specialized to a single use' (in which case economies of scale can be realised fully), and when it becomes necessary to organise production 'without the need to consult, complete, or revise interfirm agreements'.[28] Vertical integration has the advantage that, when disputes arise in the coordination of the factors of production, resolution is aided by better access to all relevant information and the ability to exercise administrative fiat.[29]

[24] O. E. Williamson, 'Transaction-Cost Economics: The Governance of Contractual Relations', in P. J. Buckley and J. Michie (eds.), *Firms Organizations and Contracts: A Reader in Industrial Organization* (1996), p. 174.

[25] Williamson, 'Transaction-Cost Economics', 175. Coase came to agree with this basic proposition, remarking that 'the costs of contracting increase more than the costs of vertical integration as assets become more specific and quasi rents increase': 'The Nature of the Firm: Influence', 43.

[26] Williamson, 'Transaction-Cost Economics', 178.

[27] Williamson, 'Transaction-Cost Economics', 181–2.

[28] Williamson, 'Transaction-Cost Economics', 184–5.

[29] Williamson, 'The Modern Corporation', 1549.

Internalisation theory has a number of salient aspects. First, as noted, the more external suppliers on which a business depends in manufacturing its product and getting it to market, the lower the potential ability to profit in a competitive market environment. Businesses can reduce their costs by expanding into new levels of production by 'vertical integration'. Vertical integration might occur backwards into raw materials required for production, so that the business secures its supply when the raw materials are finite in amount or costly, or in order to ensure their quality. A steel producer, for example, might buy an iron ore mine. Alternatively, vertical integration might occur forwards through acquisition of a distribution capacity, such as has been typical in the agribusiness and oil sectors, which invested in specially equipped ships.[30] Other examples of forward integration include the acquisition of storage facilities and the development of marketing competence.[31]

Second, certain 'agency' costs arise when coordinating activities with independent actors. Licensing agreements, for example, might be abused and/or difficult to enforce, especially when involving agreements with companies in foreign jurisdictions. This was a reason for which the Singer Sewing Machine Company, after an unsatisfactory experience in licensing technology, thereafter manufactured only through its own foreign subsidiaries.[32] A business will want to internalise transactions involving potential transfers of intellectual property and other 'firm-specific advantages'.[33] Again, marketing and distribution agreements often come with 'high transaction costs in the enforcement of agreements, especially when foreign operations are involved'.[34] One reason for this is the temporary nature of such agreements, which means that agents have few incentives to act in the interests of their principals. Singer found the need to invest in product distribution because of shirking by its former agents, who did not like to have too many machines in inventory or to invest time and effort in understanding their operation.[35]

30 G. Jones, *Multinationals and Global Capitalism: From the Nineteenth to the Twenty-First Century* (2005), p. 113.
31 Chandler, *Scale and Scope*, pp. 31–2.
32 Jones, *Multinationals and Global Capitalism*, p. 89.
33 P. T. Muchlinski, *Multinational Enterprises and the Law* (2nd edn., 2007), p. 28.
34 Jones, *Multinationals and Global Capitalism*, pp. 89–90.
35 J.-F. Hennart, 'Theories of the Multinational Enterprise', in A. M. Rugman (ed.), *The Oxford Handbook of International Business* (2nd edn., 2009), p. 137.

The benefits of internalisation and vertical integration have been sufficiently powerful that an estimated 40 per cent of world trade now takes place within single businesses.[36] However, internalisation is not always cost-effective. Some types of market transaction are more easily integrated within single businesses than others. Thus, the diffusion of knowledge within a business, especially when multinational in operation, can be challenging. This is because '[t]acit knowledge or "know-how" is complex, difficult to codify, and "sticky".'[37] For the most part, knowledge within a business lies with specific people, and this can be diffused only under conditions of sufficient mobility and/or effective lines of communication.[38] Occasionally, vertical integration of different stages of production is unsuccessful, so that the combination must be unwound through a process of 'vertical disintegration' by which 'a large company outsources many of its activities to separate businesses'.[39]

Although the validity of the transaction cost analysis has been repeatedly affirmed by empirical studies,[40] the make-or-buy choice necessarily encompasses considerations other than those relating to transaction costs.[41] This means that the distinction between the market and the 'firm' must not be overplayed. The difference between the two ways of transacting is one of degree.[42] While 'the market' encompasses interactions between different businesses, it has an influence on input and labour costs *within* unified businesses.[43] The corporate group is a form of business organisation located between the 'firm' and the market. This is because the vertically integrated corporate group inevitably engages in significant intra-firm trade. Some of the transaction costs that characterise markets will resurface within the group, even if there is a high degree of coordination of activity.

[36] Jones, *Multinationals and Global Capitalism*, p. 40.
[37] Jones, *Multinationals and Global Capitalism*, p. 191.
[38] Jones, *Multinationals and Global Capitalism*, p. 192.
[39] G. Teubner, *Networks as Connected Contracts* (ed. H Collins; tr. M. Everson)(2011), p. 1.
[40] Joskow, 'Vertical Integration'; O. E. Williamson, 'Transaction Cost Economics and Business Administration' (2005) 21 *Scandinavian Journal of Management* 19, 33.
[41] A point emphasised in H. Demsetz, 'The Theory of the Firm Revisited' (1988) 4 *Journal of Law, Economics & Organization* 141, 150.
[42] Thus, Richardson has written of the 'dense network of co-operation and affiliation by which firms are inter-related': G. B. Richardson, 'The Organization of Industry', in P. J. Buckley and J. Michie (eds.), *Firms, Organizations and Contracts: A Reader in Industrial Organization* (1996), p. 60.
[43] Demsetz, 'The Theory of the Firm Revisited', 145. *Semble* Coase, 'The Nature of the Firm: Meaning', 28.

2.2.4 *Diversification*

A business that has become established in a particular industry might want to ensure revenue stability by insulating itself from the economic cycle.[44] It might look, also, for additional, sustainable means of earning revenue. In the case of declining sectors, businesses might look for new, stable sources of revenue.[45] In each case, business goals might be achievable through diversification strategies. Product diversification comes from 'opportunities to use existing production, marketing and research facilities and personnel by developing products for new and more profitable markets. Such expansion [is] based on organizational capabilities that had been developed by exploiting economies of scope'.[46] Diversification also has other potential benefits, as Chandler found in the case of large chemical companies:

> One division was able to use intermediate products produced or developed in others, to exploit research and development information and techniques perfected in other divisions, to apply knowledge acquired in other divisions that used comparable production technologies and served similar markets.[47]

A business might diversify into either related or unrelated business activities, the latter strategy resulting in a 'conglomerate'.[48] The oil producer could diversify into related activities, for example, by manufacturing petrochemicals; and the car manufacturer could do so by diversifying into, say, forklift production. The advantages of diversification are available not only to manufacturers, but also to service-related businesses. Thus, dynamic trade intermediaries have diversified into shipping, insurance, real estate, and banking.[49] Keys to successful diversification are the competence of the parent company in managing diverse businesses and – what is entirely consistent with this – the 'decentralization contract' by which the parent sets financial performance targets but otherwise gives profit centre managers 'the freedom to make their own decisions'.[50]

44 Du Pont noted in its Annual Report (1924), p. 6: 'Such diversification [as had been undertaken] tends to produce a more even rate of business throughout the year and tends to avoid violent fluctuations in total sales, should one industry suffer a depression', quoted in Chandler, *Scale and Scope*, p. 176.

45 G. Jones, *Merchants to Multinationals: British Trading Companies in the Nineteenth and Twentieth Centuries* (2000), pp. 141 (e.g., of Ocean Wilsons (Holdings) Ltd) and 348–9.

46 Chandler, *Scale and Scope*, p. 39.

47 Chandler, *Scale and Scope*, p. 188.

48 Richardson, 'The Organization of Industry', 65.

49 Jones, *Merchants to Multinationals*, pp. 17, 23, 27, 43, 45, 75, 129, 146–8, and 153.

50 A. Campbell, M. Goold, and M. Alexander, 'Corporate Strategy: The Quest for Parenting Advantage' [1995] *Harvard Business Review* 120, 128.

Theory aside, it is notorious that diversification is a risky strategy, especially where businesses move well away from previous areas of operation and expertise.[51] Even superficially similar businesses will have their own quirks. Oil majors such as BP and Exxon, for example, found this to be the case in their acquired minerals subsidiaries. Although the minerals sector, like oil, involves technically complex projects of exploration, extraction, and refinement, a key to successful exploitation lies in the simple fact of access to cheap deposits – which oil companies did not understand.[52] Unsurprisingly, there has been movement away from strategies of radical business diversification and a return to 'core competencies'.[53] Businesses have become hesitant to diversify into unrelated activities in which their knowledge of products and markets is limited, preferring new opportunities in contiguous areas of activity. But there have been diversification success stories, especially where acquisitions have proceeded incrementally and made use of existing competencies.[54] General Electric Corporation is a notable example of a successful business conglomerate.[55]

2.2.5 Finance

Businesses pursue growth strategies for additional reasons. Generally speaking, larger and more profitable businesses can obtain finance at lower cost. Thus, finance is easier to obtain when revenues are higher, when a financial institution is more dependent upon a business's custom, and when there are more assets over which security can be taken. The larger the sums borrowed, the more favourable are the loan terms. Although businesses ordinarily seek finance from external providers, this is another area in which internalisation might occur. A parent company might finance the operations of subsidiaries itself, or else establish a specialist financing arm to make loans to group

[51] Gaughan, *Mergers, Acquisitions*, pp. 46–7.

[52] Campbell, Goold, and Alexander, 'Corporate Strategy', 122.

[53] Campbell, Goold, and Alexander, 'Corporate Strategy', 120; Jones, *Merchants to Multinationals*, p. 348.

[54] Jones, *Merchants to Multinationals*, p. 155 (discussing trade intermediation businesses).

[55] B. Roach, 'A Primer on Multinational Corporations', in A. D. Chandler and B. Mazlish (eds.), *Leviathans: Multinational Corporations and the New Global History* (2005), p. 29. Yet even GE is unwinding some of its diversified business, selling stakes in electrical appliances and finance: E. Crooks, 'GE Eyes Consumer Finance Unit IPO', *Financial Times*, 23 May 2013, available at: www.ft.com/content/21fd2034-c303-11e2-9bcb-00144feab7de; R. Milne, 'Electrolux to Buy General Electric's Appliance Arm for $3.3bn', *Financial Times*, 8 September 2014, available at: www.ft.com/cms/s/0/c3819660-371f-11e4-8472-00144feabdc.html.

companies.[56] On a related point, larger businesses are better able to organise, finance, and attract the talent necessary to engage in competitive research and development.[57]

2.2.6 *Specialised Management*

'The actual economies of scale or of scope, as determined by throughput, are organizational. Such economies depend on knowledge, skill, experience and teamwork – on the organized human capabilities essential to exploit the potential of technological processes.'[58] This is to say that specialised management is needed to oversee business growth. This has a number of dimensions. Managers of industrial businesses must coordinate effectively 'the fluctuating flow of a variety of materials into several production facilities, through them, and then on to wholesalers, retailers, and final consumers'.[59] In order to achieve this, management has developed along functional lines, so that different managers look after different aspects of the business.[60] A pioneer of this method of organisation was Alfred Sloan, who was president of General Motors when the business took the decision to divisionalise its car, truck, parts, and accessory functions.[61] There is a need, moreover, for proper supervision of each management division through top-level executives and company directors, who monitor and coordinate overall operations and determine 'continuing strategies for market share and growth'.[62] Again, General Motors provided the template, creating:

> a powerful general office, packed full of numbers men, to oversee this elaborate structure . . . Divisional managers looked after market share; the general executives monitored their performance, allocating more resources to the highest achievers. At the top, a ten-man executive committee, headed by Du Pont and Sloan, set a centralized corporate strategy.[63]

This is the way that corporate groups manage their businesses. Indeed, the centralisation of management in the parent company facilitates

[56] As in the case of Airbus: M. Stothard, 'Airbus to Create In-House Bank to Lend to Customers', *Financial Times*, 15–16 February 2014, available at: www.ft.com/content/48f07248-9569-11e3-8371-00144feab7de.

[57] Muchlinski, *Multinational Enterprises and the Law*, p. 33.

[58] Chandler, *Scale and Scope*, p. 24. [59] Chandler, *Scale and Scope*, p. 28.

[60] Chandler, *Scale and Scope*, p. 32.

[61] Micklethwait and Wooldridge, *The Company*, pp. 104–5.

[62] Chandler, *Scale and Scope*, p. 230.

[63] Micklethwait and Wooldridge, *The Company*, p. 104.

higher-level planning for and control over each separate company, as well as a level of efficiency in their management. The parent company might enter into 'an intercompany services agreement' with its subsidiaries, whereby it provides general group services. 'These contracts permit the entire corporate family to obtain goods or services on a more efficient or less expensive basis than any of the companies could achieve on its own. The goods or services obtained may include items such as legal services, office space, communications, accounting services, benefit plans, cash management services, and insurance.'[64]

Deficiencies in the ability to manage large and diversified businesses are major causes of failure in mergers and acquisitions. Top managers might fail fully to understand the nature of acquired businesses, their decision-making structures, culture and way of doing things, their customers, and so on. The result of managerial overload brought about by over-diversification has been either divestment or devolution of managerial autonomy to those closer to day-to-day business operations.[65]

2.3 Business Form

Having outlined the importance of growth in the business world and how it can be pursued, something must be said now about business form. While much of the focus of this book is upon corporate groups involving parent and subsidiary companies, there are a number of other forms that large businesses might take. These are of interest because they represent alternative ways of facilitating the coordination of business activities,[66] and will attract different liability principles. Many of these alternative business forms are encompassed in the term 'corporate network' (defined in Chapter 1). Let us examine some of the more important business forms.

The unitary form of business (U-Form) is one in which most decisions are taken at the highest level of management.[67] This form is appropriate for single-activity companies in which the number of decisions requiring

[64] B. B. Erens, S. J. Friedman, and K. M. Mayerfield, 'Bankrupt Subsidiaries: The Challenges to the Parent of Legal Separation' (2008) 25 *Emory Bankruptcy Developments Journal* 65, 77.

[65] Chandler, *Scale and Scope*, p. 627.

[66] Muchlinski, *Multinational Enterprises and the Law*, p. 7.

[67] D. A. Palmer, P. D. Jennings, and X. Zhou, 'Late Adoption of the Multidivisional Form by Larger US Corporations: Institutional, Political, and Economic Accounts' (1993) 38 *Administrative Science Quarterly* 100, 101.

execution is relatively small.[68] It relies upon the exercise of hierarchical control and clear decision-implementation rules.[69] The U-Form becomes ineffective when a business grows large in size. Increased operational complexity places excessive pressure on senior management and decision-making is slowed down.[70] In the typical case, a large business will have no alternative other than to restructure management along more functional lines.[71]

The multidivisional form (M-Form) is a response to the realities of modern, complex businesses, which are no longer in the hands of extended families, and persons of restricted social backgrounds.[72] The M-Form features the separation of business strategising from operations, the division of business activities along functional lines, and the semi-autonomous operation of divisions.[73] This decentralised form of management has several advantages. First, breaking down management tasks simplifies those tasks and avoids the problem of information overload and the slow response times that characterise the U-Form.[74] The M-Form provides an efficient 'means to administer several different, though related, product lines; and it also provide[s] the means to administer a single line ... sold worldwide by creating comparable integrated divisions for major geographical regions'.[75] Chandler found that management of production in industrial businesses has been organised so that:

> The general managers of the operating divisions – still middle managers – came to monitor and coordinate the activities of production, distribution, and often research for a single line of products or a major geographical area. Top managers coordinated the activities of several operating divisions, planned and allocated resources for future production and distribution in these divisions, and determined the long-term direction of continuing growth.[76]

[68] J. H. Dunning, *Multinational Enterprises and the Global Economy* (1993), p. 216.

[69] M. Eroglu, *Multinational Enterprises and Tort Liabilities* (2008), p. 46.

[70] Eroglu, *Multinational Enterprises and Tort Liabilities*, pp. 46–7.

[71] M. J. Hatch, *Organization Theory: Modern, Symbolic, and Postmodern Views* (3rd edn., 2013), pp. 272–5.

[72] Chandler, *Scale and Scope*, p. 235. Family control of industrial enterprise is more apparent in continental Europe (e.g., Italy), South America, and Asia: Jones, *Multinationals and Global Capitalism*, pp. 183 and 186.

[73] Jones, *Multinationals and Global Capitalism*, p. 30.

[74] Colombo and Delmastro, 'Delegation of Authority', 56. See also R. Whittington and M. Mayer, *The European Corporation: Strategy, Structure, and Social Science* (2000), p. 156.

[75] Chandler, *Scale and Scope*, p. 45. See also Williamson, 'The Modern Corporation', 44.

[76] Chandler, *Scale and Scope*, p. 232.

Divisionalisation permits, in other words, businesses to 'fully exploit economies arising from local capabilities and task specialization'.[77] Second, divisionalisation permits higher management to be free of day-to-day operational concerns and to concentrate on decisions of system-wide importance, including business strategy, planning and review, and the allocation of resources among divisions.[78] Third, the M-Form permits the assimilation of large numbers of managers and employees, who are brought under 'control through the use of written guidelines and formalised reporting'.[79] Finally, divisionalisation permits greater accountability of performance in the production of various lines of goods. Each line is 'assessed in comparison with its competitors',[80] which has consequences for the allocation of resources. Resources, such as loan funds, are allocated according to anticipated performance.[81]

The term 'M-Form' can be used to refer to either a single company with multiple divisions or, what is more likely, a corporate group organised along functional lines. The single M-Form company is uncommon among larger and/or diversified businesses, given that the single company does not benefit from limited liability for subsidiary company debts (explained in Chapter 3). On the other hand, the adoption of a business form featuring only a single legal entity does reduce the chances of infringing competition rules in some jurisdictions, and reduces susceptibility to civil actions (such as those discussed in this book) based on relationships between separate legal entities (although it does not necessarily eliminate this possibility, given that there still will be shareholders, directors, and so on).

2.3.1 *Corporate Groups*

As explained in Chapter 1, the corporate group comprises a parent company and subsidiaries, whether wholly or partly owned. The corporate group first became significant as a business form in the early twentieth century,[82] at which time the largest and most significant merger movement in US history occurred.[83] These mergers were mostly horizontal in nature,

[77] Colombo and Delmastro, 'Delegation of Authority', 54.
[78] Whittington and Mayer, *The European Corporation*, p. 68.
[79] Jones, *Multinationals and Global Capitalism*, p. 176. See also Whittington and Mayer, *The European Corporation*, p. 156.
[80] Hatch, *Organization Theory*, p. 275.
[81] Williamson, 'The Modern Corporation', 1556.
[82] See Chapter 3.
[83] Chandler, *Scale and Scope*, p. 75.

but much greater efforts followed at vertical integration.[84] However, the process of transforming holding companies[85] into meaningful, centralised administrations (parent companies) took longer, and was not evident until World War One.[86] Thereafter, it became more important for large businesses to adopt the divisional form in order properly to manage their diversified business activities.[87] 'Company by company, the M-form proliferated, and within companies it multiplied too.'[88] 'By the late 1960s the largest industrial corporations had evolved into nested multidivisional hierarchies. What had been divisions split into multiple divisions, organised into Groups; then Groups clustered in Sectors. By the time the industrial corporation lumbered into the 1970s, a series of intermediate layers separated the operating divisions from corporate headquarters.'[89] The M-Form group of companies had become the predominant mode of organisation among larger US businesses.[90] There has been a level of convergence in its use elsewhere in the world. Although European businesses were slow to adopt the M-Form, it is now predominant on the Continent and in other parts of the developed world. This is so, no matter whether the group offers a small range of related products and/or services or operates as a 'conglomerate', and no matter whether the group is domestic, regional, or truly multinational in nature.[91]

The corporate group permits fulfilment of the M-Form ideal, with the separate incorporation of parent companies and subsidiaries, organised along both hierarchical and functional lines. The parent company is responsible mainly for development of group strategy and for assessment of the financial performance of subsidiaries, which report to it on a continual basis. In larger, more complex groups, various committees develop group strategies dealing with investments, finance, and personnel/remuneration.[92] The parent company sets ongoing financial and

[84] Chandler, *Scale and Scope*, p. 77.

[85] The holding company, or 'H-form', is one which does little more than monitor its investments: R. W. Griffin, *Fundamentals of Management* (8th edn., 2011), p. 178.

[86] Chandler, *Scale and Scope*, p. 78.

[87] N. Nohria, D. Dyer, and F. Dalzell, *Changing Fortunes: Remaking the Industrial Corporation* (2002), p. 102.

[88] Nohria, Dyer, and Dalzell, *Changing Fortunes*, p. 102.

[89] Nohria, Dyer, and Dalzell, *Changing Fortunes*, p. 102.

[90] Williamson, 'The Modern Corporation', 1559.

[91] Williamson, 'The Modern Corporation', 1560–1.

[92] F. Chiappetta and U. Tombari, 'Perspectives on Group Corporate Governance and European Company Law' (2012) 3 *European Company and Financial Law Review* 261, 267.

operating targets for group companies, and leaves the fulfilment of these to the subsidiaries.[93] In this sense, the M-Form ideal does not involve the exercise of detailed day-to-day control. However, while the exercise of control over operational affairs is seen as a 'corruption' of the M-Form ideal,[94] variations exist in the level of control parent companies exert over their subsidiaries.[95]

Control is easier to exercise in stable operating environments than in changing environments. The 1980s brought significant change to industrial and non-industrial business sectors. This was reflected in reorganisation by management of corporate group structures, and in the movement by groups in some sectors from hierarchical decision-making structures to the network form of business.[96] In this section, something is said about the former, while the latter issue is dealt with later in this chapter.

The structuring of corporate groups has evolved because integrated manufacturing processes have declined in importance, for reasons including the globalisation of markets and increased competition. These developments have created the need for quicker adaptation of product offerings,[97] as well as greater emphasis upon innovation and design and provision of associated services. In such cases, top-down control is less effective. Such control reduces the capacity for responsive decision-making and innovation.[98] Moreover, falling trade barriers and better and cheaper means of communication[99] have reduced transaction costs (relative to the internal costs of management hierarchies), enabling groups to move towards flatter hierarchies and increased cooperation with other businesses.[100] This has included such things as streamlining decision-making processes in order to make them faster and more responsive, or pushing decision-making downstream so that it is closer

[93] Nohria, Dyer, and Dalzell, *Changing Fortunes*, p. 99.

[94] C. W. L. Hill, 'Oliver Williamson and the M-Form Firm: A Critical Review' (1985) 19 *Journal of Economic Issues* 731, 740. Hill believes that such corruptions are to be found in practice: ibid., 744.

[95] Jones, *Multinationals and Global Capitalism*, p. 182.

[96] J. Zeitlin, 'The Historical Alternatives Approach', in G. Jones and J. Zeitlin (eds.), *The Oxford Handbook of Business History* (2007), p. 126.

[97] Zeitlin, 'The Historical Alternatives Approach', 124.

[98] Hatch, *Organization Theory*, pp. 98–9.

[99] Nohria, Dyer, and Dalzell, *Changing Fortunes*, p. 125.

[100] Nohria, Dyer, and Dalzell, *Changing Fortunes*, p. ix; G. S. Geis, 'The Space between Markets and Hierarchies' (2009) 95 *Virginia Law Review* 99, 147–8. E.g., C. A. Bartlett and S. Ghoshal, 'Beyond the M-Form: Toward a Managerial Theory of the Firm' (1993) 14 *Strategic Management Journal* 23 (example of ABB).

to products and markets. It has encompassed also the outsourcing of auxiliary functions such as information technology, and 'opening systems and processes to outside partners in order to tighten coordination with suppliers, distributors, and the like'.[101] As such, many modern corporate groups operate as extended networks with multiple external linkages.[102]

All of these changes must be acknowledged. However, for the most part the M-Form has endured in the industrial setting[103] and remains relevant in determining an appropriate liability regime for the redress of mass-torts involving personal injuries. Part of the reason for its continuing relevance is that the network form does not always work as intended and is attended by coordination problems. Let us now move to an examination of the network form.

2.3.2 Corporate Networks

While corporate groups are based upon hierarchical shareholdings which permit the exercise of top-down control, networks are based upon contractual arrangements between independent businesses, and typically are more cooperative in nature. In the usual case, they encompass a combination of businesses specialising in product development, manufacture, and distribution,[104] links being maintained through the use of modern forms of communication, information technology, and transportation.[105] But networks can be structured in different ways.[106] They might subsist in the sort of flat, cooperative linkages which the contractual model implies. Alternatively, networks might have elements of hierarchy and control. Whether flatter or more hierarchical, there will be some type of governance arrangement to ensure that the contracting parties fulfil their collaborative obligations.[107]

[101] Nohria, Dyer, and Dalzell, *Changing Fortunes*, p. 121.

[102] D. E. Westney and S. Zaheer, 'The Multinational Enterprise as an Organization' in A. M. Rugman (ed.), *The Oxford Handbook of International Business* (2nd edn., 2009), pp. 360–1.

[103] Whittington and Mayer, *The European Corporation*, p. 179 (finding 'little evidence for a fundamental break in organizing principles among our large industrials').

[104] Teubner, *Networks as Connected Contracts*, pp. 96–7. See also ibid., pp. 89–100, for a description of variants.

[105] W. M. Fruin, 'Business Groups and Interfirm Networks', in G. Jones and J. Zeitlin (eds.), *The Oxford Handbook of Business History* (2007), p. 255.

[106] Teubner, *Networks as Connected Contracts*, p. 67.

[107] Teubner, *Networks as Connected Contracts*, pp. 92–3.

Networks have evolved in response to several business imperatives already alluded to. First, there are the demands of research and development. Parent company executives are not always aware of the most worthy research and development projects being undertaken in their divisions, so that resources are not allocated effectively in order to generate advances in knowledge and technological innovation.[108] The importance of knowledge and innovation shifts the emphasis in business interactions, 'from command and control to exchange', and 'from managerialism to networking'.[109] Knowledge requires investment in high-level expertise and grows in cumulative ways. Innovation requires thinking outside the box and experimentation, which means that no single business dominates the field.[110] The complexity of modern 'technology and increase[s] in the rate of change have made it difficult for a single firm to sustain state-of-the-art capacity across all the technologies necessary for successful product development'.[111] 'Rather than relying entirely on in-house R&D capacity, firms in many high-technology industries ranging from pharmaceuticals to semiconductors' have strengthened their R&D efforts through contractual alliances.[112] The network form enables the right combinations of business and people to be brought together,[113] and networks can be dismantled with relative ease.[114]

In order to maximise opportunity, pharmaceutical companies have moved from reliance upon internal research and development to the financing of smaller, research-intensive external businesses.[115] A typical modus operandi involves the identification of small companies with promising research agendas which can be expanded and commercialised through the injection of funds. As an example, a pharmaceutical company with expertise in the metabolic pathways that produce a particular condition might 'search for therapeutic compounds in concert with a

[108] W. Lazonick, 'Business History and Economic Development', in G. Jones and J. Zeitlin (eds.), *The Oxford Handbook of Business History* (2007), p. 76.

[109] Whittington and Mayer, *The European Corporation*, p. 83.

[110] M. Jennejohn, 'The Private Order of Innovation Networks' (2016) 68 *Stanford Law Review* 281, 298; R. J. Gilson, C. E. Sabel, and R. E. Scott, 'Contracting for Innovation: Vertical Disintegration and Interfirm Collaboration' (2009) 109 *Columbia Law Review* 431, 434.

[111] Gilson, Sabel, and Scott, 'Contracting for Innovation', 448.

[112] Jennejohn, 'The Private Order of Innovation Networks', 284.

[113] Hatch, *Organization Theory*, p. 99.

[114] R. E. Miles and C. C. Snow, 'Organizations: New Concepts for New Forms', in P. J. Buckley and J. Michie (eds.), *Firms, Organizations and Contracts: A Reader in Industrial Organization* (1996), p. 433.

[115] Lazonick, 'Business History and Economic Development', 76.

small start-up company that has developed tools for identifying, among billions of possibilities, the classes of molecules most likely to correct the metabolic defect without producing toxic side effects'.[116] As another example, GlaxoSmithKline plc (GSK) and Anacor Pharmaceuticals, Inc. joined forces in order to research, develop, and commercialise boron-based systemic anti-infective treatments. Their cooperative agreement gave GSK options exclusively to commercialise compounds developed. In return, Anacor secured an upfront payment, milestone payments, royalties, and an interest in jointly developed intellectual property, as well as access to regulatory and marketing expertise.[117] In Chapter 4, more will be said about the operation of such pharmaceutical businesses. That chapter discusses potential problems which the organisation of 'big pharma' poses for tort claimants injured by product defects.

A second imperative to which the corporate network responds is rapidly-changing business environments. In such environments, growth is pursued by 'economies of variety, understood as the capacity to adjust the volume and/or composition of output flexibly and to introduce new products rapidly in response to shifting demand and business strategy'.[118] The capacity quickly to alter product ranges is important especially in fast-moving industries such as clothing, computing, and electronics.[119] The typical network operates as a fluid business form that is 'more interconnected with suppliers, customers, and partners'.[120] It allows for flexible production and other work arrangements designed to respond quickly to changes in the marketplace and to new opportunities for innovation, cooperation, and cost reduction.[121] Some types of producer have adopted it with enthusiasm, shedding their interests in the physical production of goods (the infrastructure for which is costly, but yields low returns),[122] and outsourcing

116 Gilson, Sabel, and Scott, 'Contracting for Innovation', 439–40.

117 Jennejohn, 'The Private Order of Innovation Networks', 329.

118 Zeitlin, 'The Historical Alternatives Approach', 122.

119 Jones, *Multinationals and Global Capitalism*, pp. 104–5.

120 Nohria, Dyer, and Dalzell, *Changing Fortunes*, pp. xii–xiii.

121 Nohria, Dyer, and Dalzell, *Changing Fortunes*, p. 97; Fruin, 'Business Groups and Interfirm Networks', 256.

122 Gilson, Sabel, and Scott, 'Contracting for Innovation: Vertical Disintegration and Interfirm Collaboration', 441. A well-known example of this phenomenon is Apple's relationship with Foxconn, which specialises in contract manufacturing and can open up and close down manufacturing sites with rapidity as it responds (with Apple) to changes in demand for various products: S. Mishkin and S. Pearson, 'Foxconn Faces Culture Clash as its Global Reach Grows', *Financial Times*, 4 January 2013, 13. An example from the pharmaceutical industry is offered later. See also Chapter 4.

products and components.[123] Under this operational model, the producer retains a direct role only in research and development, product definition, quality control, and 'brand management' processes of design and marketing.[124] The network has become an attractive form of business for professional services organisations as well. It has provided an important mechanism by which such firms have entered new markets.[125] In new markets, firms need to be capable of offering professional services based upon 'local specialized knowledge', including knowledge of local laws, standards, and procedures.[126] They must come to grips also with local culture, preferences, and customers.[127] Collaborative, network relationships facilitate these things.

Having examined the general features of corporate networks, we now turn to more specific discussion of network structures. These structures include joint ventures, franchising agreements, business licensing, and strategic alliances.

A joint venture is a contractual agreement between independent businesses to cooperate in the exploitation of a commercial opportunity. A precondition for its formation is that the participants have complementary business activities and goals.[128] Some of the usual reasons for pursuing joint ventures are: enhancing research and development capabilities;[129] sharing the costs and wider risks arising from capital-intensive ventures; achieving economies of scale or scope in operation; gaining access to key supplies; enhancing distribution networks; and entering foreign markets in which local contacts and/or knowledge are important.[130] A non-business reason for entering a joint venture is that, although the desire to cooperate

123 Gilson, Sabel, and Scott, 'Contracting for Innovation', 436–7; G. Jones, 'Multinationals from the 1930s to the 1980s', in A.D. Chandler and B. Mazlish (eds.), *Leviathans: Multinational Corporations and the New Global History* (2005), p. 101.

124 G. Jones, 'Globalization', in G. Jones and J. Zeitlin (eds.), *The Oxford Handbook of Business History* (2007), pp. 104 and 150.

125 Jones, 'Multinationals from the 1930s', 90–1.

126 Jones, *Multinationals and Global Capitalism*, p. 126.

127 Jones, *Multinationals and Global Capitalism*, pp. 151–3. An example is the failure of AOL (centralised and controlling) to understand the unique ways of doing business at Netscape (independent and informal): H. Bennett, 'People at Core of Culture Clash', *Weekend Australian*, 13–14 December 2008, Weekend Professional Section, 1.

128 See, e.g., Jones, *Merchants to Multinationals*, p. 312.

129 Gaughan, *Mergers, Acquisitions*, pp. 521–2; J. Pfeffer and P. Nowak, 'Joint Ventures and Interorganizational Interdependence', in P. J. Buckley and J. Michie, *Firms, Organizations and Contracts: A Reader in Industrial Organization* (1996), p. 390.

130 Jones, *Multinationals and Global Capitalism*, pp. 132–3 (on growth of the sogo shosha joint ventures), and 159.

exists, cooperation is feasible on a limited basis only because of the potential for breaches of competition laws.[131]

The parties to a joint venture combine property, money, efforts, skill, and knowledge, and work jointly towards a common business objective and profits, usually over a limited duration of time[132] (although there are prominent joint ventures which have taken on a degree of permanence, such as that between automotive companies Renault and Nissan,[133] which were saved from ruin by collaboration in research and development, purchasing of resources, and factory tooling-up).[134] Agreement to share in the profits and losses of the enterprise is essential.[135] While 'equal voice and joint control' are important also, one of the joint venturers might entrust physical production processes to the other.[136] Joint ventures appear to work well when they result in deep operational integration, sharing (rather than the transfer) of technology, and opening up of new markets with foreign partners.[137]

A joint venture is not a legally recognised entity. The simple fact of two businesses joining together with a view to a profit might mean, however, that they become subject to the law of partnership.[138] Whether or not this is the case, the parties might find it convenient to carry on their cooperative venture through a subsidiary company to the board of which they appoint nominee directors. The joint venture might combine, therefore, elements of contract, partnership, and the corporate form.[139]

Franchising agreements are similar to joint ventures insofar as they involve contractual agreements between independent businesses to cooperate in the exploitation of opportunities. However, the terms of agreement are likely to be more formulaic.[140] The franchisor permits the franchisee 'to exploit a trade name, trademark, process, or other resource

[131] Pfeffer and Nowak, 'Joint Ventures', 394.

[132] Gaughan, *Mergers, Acquisitions*, p. 520.

[133] See Muchlinski, *Multinational Enterprises and the Law*, p. 67.

[134] H. Foy, 'Renault and Nissan Deepen Alliance with €4.3bn Savings Pledge', *Financial Times*, 30 January 2014, available at: www.ft.com/cms/s/0/9bb39342-89b2-11e3-abc4-00144feab7de.html.

[135] *Shell Oil Company* v. *Prestidge* 249 F 2d 413, 416 (9th Cir. 1957).

[136] *Shell Oil Company* v. *Prestidge* 249 F 2d 413, 415–6 (9th Cir. 1957).

[137] P. J. Buckley and M. Casson, 'Joint Ventures', in P. J. Buckley and J. Michie, *Firms, Organizations and Contracts: A Reader in Industrial Organization* (1996), pp. 423–4.

[138] See *Khan* v. *Miah* [2001] 1 WLR 2123.

[139] Muchlinski, *Multinational Enterprises and the Law*, p. 67.

[140] R. Baldwin, M. Cave, and M. Lodge, *Understanding Regulation: Theory, Strategy, and Practice* (2nd edn., 2012), p. 165.

in return for a fee'.[141] In the typical case, the agreement encompasses 'a complete business format'.[142] 'The franchisor will seek to ensure through contract the adoption of uniform standards of product presentation, pricing and marketing.'[143] The franchise agreement authorises operations by the franchisee for a limited period of time and within a specific geographical location.[144] The several cooperating businesses that constitute the franchise adopt a unitary persona for marketing purposes.[145] The 'dominant business hub ... acts like the parent company in a group of companies by issuing instructions to the nodes of the network'. Like subsidiary companies, franchisees are expected to comply with their instructions. The reason for the high degree of centralisation is that 'pure contractual arrangements cannot fulfil the co-ordination requirements demanded by a distribution system' of some complexity.[146] Yet, at the same time, franchisees are expected to 'be autonomous, and to accept sole responsibility for their own actions'.[147] The advantage of the agreement to the franchisee is the ability quickly to develop a market for its product.[148] Although it is important to note the existence of franchise agreements, to date these have not been prominent in businesses undertaking risky activities that give rise to mass-torts causing personal injuries, which are the subject matter of this book. They have tended to be adopted in the services sector instead.[149]

Business licensing involves entry into agreements for the manufacture and distribution of products. Once again, it entails the transfer of resources, patented technology, and/or know-how to the local manufacturer, typically situated in a low-cost jurisdiction.[150] Given this combination of characteristics, business 'licensing is an option open only where a suitable local producer can be found, and where the risk of damaging interference by third parties in the patented technology and secret know-how is small'. (If these conditions cannot be met, it is likely that the

141 Baldwin, Cave, and Lodge, *Understanding Regulation*, p. 165.
142 Muchlinski, *Multinational Enterprises and the Law*, p. 53.
143 Jones, *Multinationals and Global Capitalism*, p. 129.
144 Baldwin, Cave, and Lodge, *Understanding Regulation*, p. 165.
145 Teubner, *Networks as Connected Contracts*, pp. 115–16.
146 Teubner, *Networks as Connected Contracts*, p. 137.
147 Teubner, *Networks as Connected Contracts*, p. 67.
148 Jones, *Multinationals and Global Capitalism*, p. 129.
149 For examples of businesses adopting this form, see, e.g., Jones, *Multinationals and Global Capitalism*, p. 129.
150 Jones, *Multinationals and Global Capitalism*, p. 5; Muchlinski, *Multinational Enterprises and the Law*, p. 54.

producer will have little alternative other than to set up a manufacturing subsidiary company abroad.)[151] Licensing is appropriate also when a business does not want to invest in a large managerial or financial commitment to a particular venture.[152] Business licensing agreements can be quite sophisticated in their operation and might extend into the medium and long term, resulting in the development of international consortia.[153] 'At their most complex international consortia can act as integrated international production enterprises, hardly distinguishable in economic terms from equity based international groups.'[154] An example is the joint development and production of commercial aircraft by Airbus and ATR.[155] Given the attraction of business licensing to manufacturers, this form of network has the potential to give rise to mass-torts and to the insolvent entity problem with which this book is concerned.

A strategic alliance is a less formal mechanism for business cooperation. At its heart is cooperation with respect to 'specific facets of the business of two or more firms'. Such cooperation is designed to enhance 'the effectiveness of the competitive strategies of the participating firms by providing for the mutually beneficial trade of technologies, skills, or products based on them'.[156] More specifically, strategic alliances are entered into between independent businesses in order to create economies of scale by the pooling of resources, in order to gain access to the knowledge or ability of another business, to create legitimacy, and to reduce risks in large undertakings.[157] They permit a 'more rapid means of establishing a competitive position than through replication or internal development'.[158] The costs of achieving such a competitive position are likely to be lower than they otherwise would be.[159] The degree of cooperation involved is not so extensive as to require the setting up of a joint venture. There is no transfer of ownership rights and resources, meaning that the business combination can be dismantled relatively easily and without major expense.[160] Strategic alliances were formerly

151 Muchlinski, *Multinational Enterprises and the Law*, p. 54.
152 Jones, *Multinationals and Global Capitalism*, p. 157.
153 Muchlinski, *Multinational Enterprises and the Law*, p. 54.
154 Muchlinski, *Multinational Enterprises and the Law*, p. 54.
155 Muchlinski, *Multinational Enterprises and the Law*, p. 54.
156 M. Y. Yoshino and U. Srinivasa Rangan, *Strategic Alliances: An Entrepreneurial Approach to Globalization* (1995), pp. 4–5.
157 A. C. Inkpen, 'Strategic Alliances', in A. M. Rugman (ed.), *The Oxford Handbook of International Business* (2nd edn., 2009), p. 392.
158 Inkpen, 'Strategic Alliances', 393. 159 Inkpen, 'Strategic Alliances', 394.
160 Inkpen, 'Strategic Alliances', 394.

of importance in the pharmaceutical industry, which was characterised in the 1980s and 1990s by increasing research and development costs and by increased complexity in obtaining regulatory approvals for products. These alliances were followed by a wave of mergers and acquisitions,[161] which have continued to the present day.[162] A major drawback of strategic alliances is that it is difficult to achieve the degree of coordination that arises within a single business. Frequently, they prove to be unstable arrangements and termination rates are high.[163]

This leads to more general observations about the disadvantages of operating a large-scale business through a corporate network. For all their flexibility and responsiveness, networks can be difficult to organise and sustain. There are several reasons for this. First, networks involve coordination between two or more separate businesses, each with its own objectives, mode of operation, and culture. Second, these businesses must engage in joint decision-making, which can slow down progress.[164] Third, each network participant must cede significant levels of control to the others, which means that high levels of trust are required.[165] Indeed, trust is important in addressing the problem of long-term contracting, which entails gaps in contract terms, and provides opportunities to cheat.[166] Cheating most frequently occurs in the misuse of intellectual property.[167] Even where risks of cheating are low, there is a need to monitor adherence to network agreements, the expense of which reduces the competitiveness of this business form.[168] Fourth, there is the potential always for disputation between the parties, who act primarily in their own interests.[169] Fifth, the conduct of a business through a corporate network can compromise the longer-term research and development, engineering, and manufacturing capabilities of a company as a stand-alone

161 Jones, *Multinationals and Global Capitalism*, p. 105. 162 See Chapter 4.

163 Inkpen, 'Strategic Alliances', 397.

164 Micklethwait and Wooldridge, *The Company*, p. 177. Jennejohn gives the example of Boeing, which decided to build the 787 passenger jet in cooperation with a range of major suppliers with which it shared business risks. Fifteen tier-one subcontractors were appointed, meaning that 'coordination problems quickly overwhelmed' design and construction, leading to costly delays: Jennejohn, 'The Private Order of Innovation Networks', 287–8.

165 Teubner, *Networks as Connected Contracts*, p. 11.

166 Jones, *Multinationals and Global Capitalism*, p. 161. Contracts between network participants will be 'relational' in nature: Teubner, *Networks as Connected Contracts*, p. 8.

167 Jennejohn, 'The Private Order of Innovation Networks', 290 and 317.

168 Jennejohn, 'The Private Order of Innovation Networks', 299; Geis, 'The Space between Markets', 140.

169 Teubner, *Networks as Connected Contracts*, p. 6.

entity.[170] All of these problems will be multiplied when a business is involved in several network collaborations.[171] These are some of the reasons for which corporate networks frequently have not achieved their goals and/or collapsed.[172]

2.3.3 Advantages of the Corporate Group Form

While the form of business adopted depends upon 'factors such as scale, scope, knowledge intensity', and the competitive and institutional environments,[173] there are reasons for which the corporate group remains the predominant form of large-scale business.[174] These include the economic advantages of divisionalisation considered previously, such as the separation of business strategy from operations, the division of business activities along functional lines, the severance of higher management from day-to-day operational concerns, and greater accountability of individual operating units. There are other, more practical reasons, including the logistical ease that accompanies transactions involving individual companies. First, separate incorporation means that the parent company can determine an appropriate level of shareholding in each business. The parent company, for example, might 'share the risks' involved in the operation of a business such as pharmaceutical development, and thus invite outside equity participation. Second, separate incorporation permits better understanding of different businesses by external parties, including credit-rating agencies, financial institutions, and potential suitors. This can be advantageous when seeking loan capital and other forms of finance.[175] Third, local regulatory laws might compel the incorporation of separate businesses. This is the case, for example, when financial services are provided not only 'in-house', but also to third parties. In such a case it might be impossible to submit a division of a single company to regulation while keeping other divisions free of it.[176] Alternatively, 'the domestic law of particular countries in which the group wishes to conduct business may require local businesses to be

170 Jennejohn, 'The Private Order of Innovation Networks', 287–8.
171 Jennejohn, 'The Private Order of Innovation Networks', 320.
172 Jones, *Multinationals and Global Capitalism*, pp. 151–3. See also Teubner, *Networks as Connected Contracts*, 102.
173 Whittington and Mayer, *The European Corporation*, p. 182.
174 See, generally, Micklethwait and Wooldridge, *The Company*, p. 176.
175 Palmer, Jennings, and Zhou, 'Late Adoption', 122. See also ibid., 124.
176 J. J. White, 'Corporate Judgment Proofing: A Response to Lynn LoPucki's The Death of Liability' (1998) 107 *Yale Law Journal* 1363, 1390.

conducted through separate entities.'[177] Finally, it is much easier to sell a business that is operated in a separate corporate shell because usually it is more tax-effective to transfer the shares of a group company to the purchaser, rather than to sell discrete assets.[178]

Again, the corporate group has not stayed still during the rise of corporate networks. It has developed too and 'has learned an adaptability that allows it to introduce the flexibility and integration of contemporary networks while keeping its essential principles intact'.[179] In many instances, we have witnessed 'the emergence of a new flatter, more co-operative version' of the corporate group termed the 'network multidivisional'.[180]

2.3.4 Control in Corporate Groups

Equity ownership provides the parent company with the ability to exercise control over its subsidiaries. But this capacity to control should not be confused with its actual exercise. Many writers on the insolvent entity problem assume that parent companies inevitably assert a high degree of control over their subsidiaries.[181] And control is seen as an important factor in both the regulation of business activity and the imposition of liability for wrongdoing. In part, this is because the basic theory underlying traditional notions of legal responsibility is the 'will theory' (considered in Chapter 9), which involves consideration of the moral quality of an agent's action and is grounded in fault. In the corporate context, the exercise of control often serves as a proxy for findings of fault.

A number of observations can be made about the exercise of control in corporate groups. Parent companies exercise different levels of control.[182] However, the M-Form group is predicated (as noted) upon general strategic decision-making by the parent company, rather than upon the exercise of detailed operational control.[183] The parent company

[177] UNCITRAL, 'Legislative Guide on Insolvency, Part Three: Treatment of Enterprise Groups in Insolvency' (2012), p. 12.
[178] UNCITRAL, 'Legislative Guide', p. 12.
[179] Whittington and Mayer, *The European Corporation*, p. 69.
[180] Whittington and Mayer, *The European Corporation*, p. 83.
[181] E.g., J. E. Antunes, *Liability of Corporate Groups: Autonomy and Control in Parent–Subsidiary Relationships in US, German and EU Law* (1994), p. 5.
[182] See models of corporate group operation set out in R. Winkelmolen and W. C. Buss, 'Developments of Strategic Parenting Models in Small Holding Companies: A Research Agenda' (2013) 8 *Global Conference on Business and Finance Proceedings* 236.
[183] See earlier discussion, and Palmer, Jennings, and Zhou, 'Late Adoption', 103.

determines global business strategy about markets and products and allocates funding and resources.[184] It is likely to make decisions on acquisitions and restructuring.[185] The parent company sets yearly performance targets, and might indicate the level of dividends it expects to receive from its subsidiaries. However, beyond this, the M-Form is characterised by decentralised operations. Each subsidiary has the ability to decide how targets are to be met and retains a great deal of control over its own day-to-day operations.[186] The parent company is unlikely to be familiar with all events taking place at the operational level or to have the technical competence to direct the taking of specific actions. Indeed, attempts to do the latter would undermine the benefits of decentralisation.

Organisation theory about the exercise of control is confirmed by such empirical studies as have been undertaken. Richard Cyert and James March found that 'most organizations most of the time exist and thrive with considerable latent conflict of goals ... there is no internal consensus.' Although procedures exist for dealing with conflicts, they cannot 'reduce all goals to a common dimension or even make them obviously internally consistent'.[187] This suggests the strong possibility that there will be real differences of view in the pursuit of goals as between parent company and subsidiary. Cyert and March also came to the perhaps surprising conclusion that much more managerial focus within a 'firm' is expended upon internal management issues than upon the firm's interactions with the external world.[188] This hints at the substantial challenges that arise in managing a company or corporate group of any size. Commentators on corporate groups should not be misled by impressive marketing and branding efforts into believing that parent companies exercise consistent, pervasive, and effective control over each of their subsidiaries.

Massimo Colombo and Marco Delmastro undertook an empirical study of decentralisation within manufacturing 'business organizations'.[189] They found that the number of hierarchic levels beneath top management significantly affects the allocation of authority to make

[184] Antunes, *Liability of Corporate Groups*, pp. 73 and 80.
[185] Antunes, *Liability of Corporate Groups*, p. 195.
[186] This is the 'strategic planner' model in Winkelmolen and Buss, 'Developments of Strategic Parenting Models', 238.
[187] R. M. Cyert and J. G. March, *A Behavioural Theory of the Firm* (2nd edn., 1992), p. 164.
[188] Cyert and March, *A Behavioural Theory of the Firm*, pp. 205–6.
[189] Colombo and Delmastro, 'Delegation of Authority', 54.

decisions. In particular, 'more complex organizational structures are characterized by decentralization of authority.' One reason for this is that complexity brings 'rapid increases in top management's information costs'. As such, 'being close to operations seems a key factor for optimality of decision-making activity in complex organizations.' Moreover, as the size of an organisation increases, the tendency to delegate authority becomes greater.[190] These findings about the organisation are of direct pertinence to corporate groups, in which delegation and decentralisation are more pronounced than in single companies.

Further evidence undermining the idea that parent companies exercise operational control over subsidiaries comes from the literature on mergers and acquisitions. The evidence is that 'most medium-to-large size firms today have grown through acquisitions.'[191] But acquired businesses are not always integrated within the group. This might be for reasons related to the strategic need to maintain independence, and/or the difficulty of achieving integration. The acquirer might preserve the independence of the acquired unit when it has a 'winning formula' or when key personnel threaten to leave.[192] Integration might be difficult to achieve with respect to a business unit operating in new areas of activity and/or in new markets,[193] where the acquirer does not have sufficient skill or expertise, where the acquisition has impacted negatively upon motivation and discipline, and/or where there are differences in organisational culture. Evidence suggests that it takes five to twelve years fully to integrate acquired business units.[194] But many mergers and acquisitions (especially in conglomerate groups) do not get that far, ending in divestment instead.[195]

Ironically, whereas the parent company in the M-Form group is likely to eschew the exercise of significant control over subsidiaries, the lead participant in a network *might* exercise quite detailed control over other

[190] Colombo and Delmastro, 'Delegation of Authority', 69.

[191] D. Faulkner, S. Teerikangas, and R. J. Joseph, 'Introduction', in D. Faulkner, S. Teerikangas, and R. J. Joseph (eds.), *The Handbook of Mergers and Acquisitions* (2012), p. 9.

[192] D. Angwin, 'Merger and Acquisition Typologies: A Review', in D. Faulkner, S. Teerikangas, and R. J. Joseph (eds.), *The Handbook of Mergers and Acquisitions* (2012), pp. 57 and 59.

[193] See *Thompson* v. *The Renwick Group plc* [2015] BCC 855, [37]–[38].

[194] Faulkner, Teerikangas, and Joseph, 'Introduction', 7.

[195] G. Silverman, 'Corporate Break-Ups Should Make Us Happy', *Financial Times*, 10 October 2014, available at: www.ft.com//cms/s/0/7d295cac-4e3f-11e4-bfda-00144feab7de.html.

participants. Control might be exercised through sheer economic muscle – through the fact that much of the market is in the hands of either a single firm or an oligopoly,[196] creating dependency in business operations – or through the fact that 'dedicated resources (asset-specific investments) have few alternative uses'.[197] Alternatively, a network participant might exercise control through detailed contractual specification of planned activities, use of intellectual property rights, brand management, standardisation, and/or training. These types of 'control' are evident, for example, in most franchising relationships. The exercise of control has been evident also in parts of the high-tech sector, such as in smartphones, cloud computing, integrated systems management, and chip-making.[198]

These are initial reasons for which this book asserts that control, while a seductive criterion of liability, can prove quite unsatisfactory. The evidence is that control is not always present where writers on the insolvent entity problem expect it to be. But it is present sometimes where they do not expect it to be. In later chapters, we encounter further problems with the idea of control as a basis for liability in corporate groups.

2.4 International Dimension

This chapter has set out reasons for which businesses seek to grow, and some of the most important forms of business available. We now consider the international dimensions of large business operations. Businesses expand their operations internationally for reasons which include each of the economic reasons for growth already surveyed. Indeed, as 'technology has improved, the efficient scale of more and more industries has become larger than any one market, even those of the largest industrial nations, can absorb'.[199] Large scale is required in order, for example, to support the financing of research and development so as to sustain technological leadership in fast-changing markets.[200] Multinational enterprises (MNEs) enjoy the benefits of bringing international transactions in house also.[201] The most successful MNEs are

[196] Muchlinski, *Multinational Enterprises and the Law*, p. 308.

[197] Fruin, 'Business Groups and Interfirm Networks', 255.

[198] Fruin, 'Business Groups and Interfirm Networks', 255; Jones, 'Globalization', 150.

[199] S. B. Tallman and G. S. Yip, 'Strategy and the Multinational Enterprise', in A. M. Rugman (ed.), *The Oxford Handbook of International Business* (2nd edn., 2009), p. 313.

[200] M. Wolf, 'Why China Will Not Buy the World', *Financial Times*, 9 July 2013, available at: www.ft.com/cms/s/0/28d1a4a8-e7ba-11e2-babb-001444feabdc0.html.

[201] A. M. Rugman, A. Verbeke, and Q. T. K. Nguyen, 'Fifty Years of International Business Theory and Beyond' (2011) 51 *Management International Review* 755, 760.

those that offer goods and services at a lower cost than can be obtained by contracting for inputs in the marketplace.[202] 'The great strength of the MNE is that it replaces exogenous coordination systems prevailing in external markets (usually with pricing at their core) by coordination through a balanced mix of hierarchical control, socialization and internal prices.'[203] The increasing prevalence of MNEs in some industries is a consequence also of the decreasing costs of organising productive effort across international boundaries[204] due to competition in international transportation and to advances in computing and telecommunications.

However, international expansion involves complexity, and businesses have further matters to take into account when considering this strategy. Experience demonstrates that manufacturers seek overseas markets: when they possess 'ownership advantages' relating to superior technologies protected by patents, as well as superior management skills; when locational advantages make it more profitable for them to exploit their assets in foreign locations rather than at home; and if they can exploit these advantages through internalisation.[205] (By contrast, service-based businesses expand internationally when they enjoy ownership advantages inherent in 'softer' features, such as knowledge, information, and human relationships.)[206] Indeed, international expansion might be unavoidable when competitors engage in the arbitrage of location benefits by moving activities so as to take advantage of lower costs. Under a sophisticated business model, businesses undertake high-end product and service development in advanced nations, move production and distribution to newly industrialising nations, and/or use profit sanctuaries in order to protect accumulated revenues.[207]

Businesses expand beyond home markets for additional reasons not inherent to business, but which relate to the surrounding politico-legal environment. Increasingly, they migrate from one jurisdiction to another on the basis of 'regulatory arbitrage', comparing regulatory and tax

[202] Hennart, 'Theories of the Multinational Enterprise', 130.

[203] Rugman, Verbeke, and Nguyen, 'Fifty Years', 760.

[204] See Hennart, 'Theories of the Multinational Enterprise', 139.

[205] Jones, *Merchants to Multinationals*, p. 5. See also Rugman, Verbeke, and Nguyen, 'Fifty Years', 759.

[206] Jones, *Merchants to Multinationals*, p. 6. Presumably, it is the absence of such factors that has made it difficult for retail banks to expand across borders: e.g., M. Arnold and C. Hall, 'Big Banks Give Up on Their Global Ambitions', *Financial Times*, 19 October 2014, available at: www.ft.com/intl/cms/s/95bed102-5641-11e4-bbd6-00144feab7de.html.

[207] Tallman and Yip, 'Strategy and the Multinational Enterprise', 316.

treatment in various jurisdictions and locating accordingly.[208] Relevant regulation includes corporate governance, competition, labour,[209] and environmental laws.[210] This kind of arbitrage was evident in the asbestos industry. Asbestos manufacturers shut down production in advanced nations and commenced or increased production of dangerous products in the developing world.[211] It is seen in the pharmaceutical industry today. For example, the majority of clinical trials for drugs for which Food and Drug Administration (FDA) approval is sought are undertaken outside the United States. This is explained, in part, by the fact that the FDA is sixteen times less likely to inspect foreign trial operators than they are to inspect US-based operators. The result is that 'US drug companies may conduct ethically problematic research more easily abroad than domestically.'[212] Some governments have responded to regulatory arbitrage by lowering regulatory and other standards in order to retain local manufacturing output and employment.[213] This gives rise to the potential for a 'race to the bottom', where few real standards are imposed upon corporate activity and risks to employee health and welfare and of environmental damage increase accordingly.[214]

Health and safety aside, competition law rules provide another regulatory burden which businesses seek to escape through expansion into overseas production. Competition law rules might be applied in ways

208 Roach, 'A Primer on Multinational Corporations'. See also Hennart, 'Theories of the Multinational Enterprise', 127.

209 E.g., ability to use so-called zero hours contracts in the United Kingdom: J. McDermott, 'Zero-Hours Work for Britain's Zero-Hours Economy', *Financial Times*, 6 August 2013, available at: www.ft.com/cms/s/0/929a41fc-fe8e-11e2-97dc-00144feabdc0.html.

210 See, e.g., *Sithole* v. *Thor Chemical Holdings Ltd* [1999] All ER (D) 102 (relocation of mercury compound extraction from the United Kingdom to South Africa); P. Nygh, 'The Liability of Multi-national Corporations for the Torts of Their Subsidiaries' (2002) 3 *European Business Organization Law Review* 51, 56–7.

211 J. McCullough and G. Tweedale, *Defending the Indefensible: The Global Asbestos Industry and its Fight for Survival* (2008), pp. 230–1. The asbestos industry is examined in Chapter 4. 'Certainly in the United Kingdom, Cape [Industries plc] had to operate under far more stringent safety standards than abroad – standards that were never applied, for example, in South Africa': G. Tweedale and L. Flynn, 'Piercing the Corporate Veil: Cape Industries and Multinational Corporate Liability for a Toxic Hazard, 1950-2004' (2007) 8 *Enterprise and Society* 268, 290.

212 L. Treadaway, 'Big Pharma's Heart of Darkness: The Alien Tort Statute and Preventing Clinical Trial Colonialism' (2012) 43 *Georgetown International Law Journal* 1419, 1428.

213 Eroglu, *Multinational Enterprises and Tort Liabilities*, p. 34. Where governments cannot satisfactorily reduce regulatory burdens, companies withdraw – e.g., with many high-profile businesses withdrawing from India: J. Crabtree, 'BHP Billiton to Back Away from India Exploration Projects', *Financial Times*, 21 October 2013, available at: www.ft.com/cms/s/0/39ddd7c6-3a1c-11e3-9243-00144feab7de.html.

214 Roach, 'A Primer on Multinational Corporations', 35–6.

which prevent businesses from obtaining economies of scale and scope and prevent them reducing transaction costs through domestic mergers and acquisitions. The US antitrust policy, for example, was an explanation for expansion by US companies abroad in the 1950s and 1960s.[215] It has been hypothesised, further, that some US companies have moved business activity overseas in order to avoid veil-piercing by courts (a matter discussed in Chapter 10).[216]

Companies seek to reduce their tax liabilities[217] by moving abroad[218] or otherwise skewing their revenue-earning activities to lower tax jurisdictions, including 'tax havens'.[219] This has resulted in nation states competing with each other in order to set corporate tax rates that are attractive to businesses.[220] Many modern mergers and acquisitions are 'tax-inversions', by which a company from a higher-tax country (for example, the United States) acquires a company from a lower-tax country (for example, Ireland) and then re-domiciles to the latter.[221] This has been evident especially in the pharmaceutical industry. Nine of the ten largest pharmaceutical companies have operations in Ireland.[222] Major companies otherwise make regular use of tax havens through which they funnel revenues.[223]

215 J. H. Dunning, 'The Key Literature on IB Activities 1960-2006', in A. M. Rugman (ed.), *The Oxford Handbook of International Business* (2nd edn., 2009), p. 52.

216 C. L. Boyd and D. A. Hoffman, 'Disputing Limited Liability' (2010) 104 *Northwestern University Law Review* 853, 859.

217 A US court has ruled that there is no 'directors' duty to minimise tax': *Seinfeld* v. *Slager* (Del Ch, 29 June 2012)(unreported), 8–9 (Glassock VC). Matters of tax are seen as falling within the business judgment rule.

218 'In the decade to 2008, 6 per cent of multinationals have relocated, partly for tax reasons': V. Houlder, K. Carnie, and C. Nevitt, 'Tax Reduction Jargon Explained', *Financial Times*, 10 June 2013, available at: www.ft.com/cms/s/0/e0c8317c-ceaf-11e2-8e16-00144feab7de.html. See, generally, UNCITRAL, 'Legislative Guide on Insolvency', p. 13.

219 '[H]alf of the global trade passes through and one-third of the world's wealth is "parked" in tax havens': L-C Wolff, 'Offshore Holdings for Global Investments of Multinational Enterprises: Just Evil?' [2015] *Journal of Business Law* 445, 453.

220 E.g., twenty countries lowered their corporate tax rates in 2004: Eroglu, *Multinational Enterprises and Tort Liabilities*, p. 34.

221 A. Sakoui and J. Politi, 'US Acquirers Cut Taxes by Relocating to Europe after Mergers', *Financial Times*, 12 August 2013, available at: www.ft.com/xms/s/0/a4a88402-033a-11e3-9a46-00144feab7de.html.

222 V. Houlder, V. Boland, and J. Politi, 'Tax Avoidance: The Irish Inversion', *Financial Times*, 29 April 2014, available at: www.ft.com/cms/s/2/d9b4fd34-ca3f-11e3-8a31-00144feabdc0.html.

223 J. Ball, 'FTSE 100's Use of Tax Havens – Get the Full List', *The Guardian*, 12 May 2013, available at: www.theguardian.com/news/datablog/2013/may/12/ftse-100-use-tax-havens-full-list; G. Wilkins, 'Top Firms' Tax Haven Links Revealed', *The Age*, 25 May 2013, available at: www.theage.com.au/business/top-firms-tax-haven-links-revelaed-20130524-2k719.html.

Differences between national tax rates give rise to the problem of transfer price manipulation, by which the prices of inputs and outputs moving between group companies are set so that they attract the lowest overall tax burden. In corporate groups, it is the parent company's attitude towards taxation which determines whether subsidiaries are tax-compliant or not.[224] But transfer price manipulation seems to be an inevitable consequence of vertical integration strategies.[225] By internalising the market for inputs, a business can more readily control prices (whether for physical inputs, intellectual property rights, or services) and subsequent liability to taxes and tariffs.[226] Issues of transfer pricing are acute in e-commerce. A typical ploy has been the use of low-tax jurisdictions from which to make internet sales, marked-up goods merely being 'distributed' by subsidiaries in high-tax jurisdictions rather than being subject to value-enhancing (and taxable) activity.[227] Corporate groups can reduce tax bills also by the manipulation of service fee payments among constituent companies – by engineering payments (such as management fees, cost-sharing agreements,[228] and insurance premiums) which reduce profits in high-tax jurisdictions and increase them in low-tax jurisdictions.

Moreover, multinationals have been 'centralising' intangible assets such as intellectual property rights in low-tax jurisdictions.[229] A typical strategy involves vesting IP rights in a low-tax jurisdiction (for example, the Netherlands) subsidiary, this subsidiary then charging high royalty fees from other, higher-tax jurisdiction subsidiaries, thereby reducing (if not eliminating) taxable profits in the latter.[230] As another example, Apple Inc.

224 TNS BMRB, 'Exploring Large Business Tax Strategy Behaviour' (2015), p. 23.

225 R. Paz-Varga, 'International Transfer Pricing and Subsidiary Performance: The Role of Organizational Justice' (2009) 51 *Thunderbird International Business Review* 219, 220.

226 Muchlinski, *Multinational Enterprises and the Law*, pp. 28–9.

227 E.g., J. Ball, 'Marks and Spencer under Fire over Online Tax Arrangements', *The Guardian*, 19 May 2013, available at: www.theguardian.com/business/2013/may/19/marks-spencer-tax-arrangements-europe; I. Griffiths and S. Bowers, 'Fresh Questions for Amazon over Pittance it Pays in Tax', *The Guardian*, 16 May 2013, available at: www.theguardian.com/technology/2013/may/15/amazon-tax-bill-new-questions.

228 'A cost sharing agreement typically includes a "buy-in" payment from the affiliate, which supposedly compensates the parent for transferring intangible assets to the affiliate and for incurring the initial costs and risks undertaken in ... developing or acquiring intangible assets': US Senate Permanent Subcommittee on Investigations, 'Offshore Profit Shifting and the US Tax Code – Part 2 (Apple Inc.)' (21 May 2013), p. 8.

229 Houlder, Carnie, and Nevitt, 'Tax Reduction Jargon Explained'.

230 A. Barker, J. Smyth, and M. Steinglass, 'Brussels Probes Multinationals' Tax Deal', *Financial Times*, 11 September 2013, available at: www.ft.com/cms/s/0/bc045306-1afa-11e3-b781-00144feab7de.html. In late 2014, Starbucks 'transferred its IP rights to the UK following a

has research-and-development cost-sharing agreements with subsidiaries incorporated in Ireland, which are licensees of Apple IP outside the Americas. Profits are booked in Ireland, which is a low-tax jurisdiction. The problem with respect to IP rights is particularly acute for governments, given the difficulties encountered in independently valuing new inventions.[231] According to the US Senate Permanent Subcommittee on Investigations, 'the bulk of Apple's R&D efforts, the source of the intangible value of its products, is conducted in the United States, yet under the cost sharing agreement a disproportionate amount of the resulting profits remain outside the United States', thereby reducing liability to US taxation.[232]

MNEs are known today to engage in *negotiations* with tax authorities over appropriate rates of taxation, and/or about amounts to be paid against their liabilities.[233] For example, Apple Inc. subsidiaries in Ireland paid less than 2 per cent tax over a number of years following 'negotiations with the Irish government'. This is a figure well below the 'already relatively low statutory rate of 12 per cent'.[234] Similar agreements were entered into between the Luxembourg authorities and Amazon, Fiat, and other multinational companies,[235] and between the Netherlands and Starbucks.[236] As a result of such agreements, the European Commission investigated Ireland, Luxembourg, and the Netherlands for provision of unlawful state aid brought about by the artificial lowering

row over tax avoidance': J. Aglionby and V. Houlder, 'Starbucks Relocates European Headquarters to London', *Financial Times*, 16 April 2014, available at: www.ft.com/cms/s/0/9ea7220c-c53b-11e3-a7d4-00144feabdc0.html.

231 US Senate Permanent Subcommittee on Investigations, 'Offshore Profit Shifting', p. 8.

232 US Senate Permanent Subcommittee on Investigations, 'Offshore Profit Shifting', p. 28.

233 E.g., European Commission, 'Alleged Aid to Apple', State Aid SA.38373 (2014/C), [53], [58], and [69]; J. Croft, 'UK High Court Rules Goldman Sachs Tax Deal Lawful', *Financial Times*, 16 May 2013, available at: www.ft.com/cms/s/0/f0aa6338-be03-11e2-bb35-00144feab7de.html.

234 US Senate Permanent Subcommittee on Investigations, 'Offshore Profit Shifting', p. 20; J. Ford, 'All Carrot, No Stick', *Financial Times* (23–24 March 2013), 9; J. Stiglitz, 'Globalisation Isn't just about Profits. It's about Taxes Too', *The Guardian*, 27 May 2013, available at: www.theguardian.com/commentisfree/2013/may/27/globalisation-is-about-taxes-too (example of General Electric's involvement).

235 D. Robinson and S. Wagstyl, 'Berlin Takes Aim at Luxembourg Tax Deals', *Financial Times*, 12 November 2014, available at: www.ft.com/intl/cms/s/0/2e194acc-6a88-11e4-a038-00144feabdc0.html.

236 E.g., European Commission, 'Commission Decides Selective Tax Advantages for Fiat in Luxembourg and Starbucks in the Netherlands Are Illegal under EU State Aid Rules' (Press Release, 21 October 2015).

of effective tax rates.[237] In each case, state aid was found to have been provided and preference given to the named businesses.[238]

These are but a few of the ways in which corporate groups seek 'tax-efficient' outcomes in their operations. These practices have become more pronounced in a changing, globalised economy, with the relative decline of manufacturing, and the rise of service-based industries as well as the 'digital economy'. The result has been a sharp reduction in the tax base of advanced nations[239] and a distortion of competition in the favour of multinational (as opposed to single-jurisdiction) businesses. Although taxation rules on controlled foreign companies reduce the problem of offshoring,[240] and international tax guidelines and bilateral tax treaties attempt to deal with the complexities of transfer pricing,[241] tax authorities cannot always ensure compliance – in part because of the complexity of structured business activities.

Tax avoidance practices have spurred intense debate about the operation, ethics, and legality of MNE activities. Such is the disquiet that governments around the world have begun to take more active steps to reduce tax evasion. The Organisation for Economic Co-operation and Development launched a fifteen-point 'action plan' to increase tax transparency and to force MNEs to pay their 'fair share'. The plan is said to 'mark a turning point in the history of international tax co-operation'[242] because it seeks to 'align tax with substance, forcing companies to pay tax where sales and profits are made'.[243] Group of Twenty (G20) nations have agreed upon the automatic sharing of tax

237 Treaty on the Functioning of the European Union OJ [2012] C 326/01, Art 107(1). See, e.g., European Commission, 'Alleged Aid to Apple', concerning agreement between Apple and the Republic of Ireland about the treatment of transfer pricing.

238 E.g., European Commission, 'Alleged Aid to Amazon by Way of a Tax Ruling' (COM (2014) 7156).

239 E.g., in the United Kingdom, the proportion of total taxes constituted by corporate tax fell by 11 per cent from 2007 to 2014: V. Houlder, 'Corporation Tax Falls as a Proportion of Big UK Companies' Levies', *Financial Times*, 26 November 2014, available at: www.ft.com/intl/cms/s/0/0ccca76a-74ab-11e4-8321-00144feabdc0.html.

240 Wolff, 'Offshore Holdings', 451.

241 See OECD, 'Articles of the Model Convention with Respect to Taxes on Income and Capital' (2003); OECD, 'Transfer Pricing Guidelines for Multinational Enterprises and Tax Administrations' (2010). See also Wolff, 'Offshore Holdings', 453.

242 J. Moore, 'G20 Think Tank Plans Global Crackdown on Corporate Tax Avoidance', *The Independent*, 19 July 2013, available at: www.independent.co.uk/news/business/news/g20-think-tank-plans-global-crackdown-on-coporate-tax-avoidance-8719988.html.

243 Moore, 'G20 Think Tank Plans'. See also HMRC, 'Tax Administration: Large Businesses Transparency Strategy' (2015).

information.[244] In addition, the United Kingdom and other jurisdictions have adopted 'diverted profits taxes' for businesses utilising offshore companies in order to avoid home state taxation;[245] and the United Kingdom has widened the range of persons who can be charged with offences relating to tax evasion, including companies themselves where they cause professional advisors to put in place offending arrangements.[246]

Having introduced the international dimension of large-scale business operation, it is convenient to return to a continuing issue in this book – the exercise of control within corporate groups. When companies expand their operations abroad, they tend to take controlling stakes in their foreign businesses,[247] consistent with the economic benefits of internalisation. But this does not necessarily entail the exercise of a high degree of operational control. Within all corporate groups, there is an inevitable struggle to 'find the appropriate balance between centralization and local responsiveness'.[248] Just as with purely domestic groups, a 'spectrum' of control exists among MNEs. This is reflected in various models of MNE parent–subsidiary relationships:[249] first, there is a model under which direct control is exercised, typified by a weak subsidiary board, and reporting by subsidiary line managers to their counterparts in the parent company. Usually, the parent company requires extensive and regular financial reporting.[250] Second, there is the 'advisory board' model, which features a subsidiary board that takes advantage of local knowledge and connections and advises the parent of appropriate strategies. However, the parent company retains control and makes most business decisions

244 S. Phua, 'Convergence in Global Tax Compliance' [2015] *Singapore Journal of Legal Studies* 77, 91.

245 V. Houlder, 'New "Google" Tax Targets 100 Multinationals', *Financial Times*, 20 September 2016, available at: www.ft.com/content/5600f746-7f40-11e6-bc52-0c7211ef3189.html; J. Smyth, 'Australia Cracks Down on Tax Avoidance', *Financial Times*, 3 May 2016, available at: https://next.ft.com/content/21f1e7d7-4df9-3468-907a-500fac45345a.

246 See Criminal Finances Act 2017, Part 3; HMRC, 'Tackling Tax Evasion: Government Guidance for the Corporate Offence of Failure to Prevent the Criminal Facilitation of Tax Evasion' (Draft Guidance, October 2016); HMRC, 'Tackling Tax Evasion: Legislation and Guidance for a Corporate Offence of Failure to Prevent the Criminal Facilitation of Tax Evasion' (July 2016).

247 Hennart, 'Theories of the Multinational Enterprise', 127.

248 Jones, *Multinationals and Global Capitalism*, p. 292.

249 G. C. Kiel, K. Hendry, and G. J. Nicholson, 'Corporate Governance Options for the Local Subsidiaries of Multinational Enterprises' (2006) 14 *Corporate Governance* 568.

250 Kiel, Hendry, and Nicholson, 'Corporate Governance Options', 572.

itself.[251] Third, there is a 'dual reporting' model under which management decision-making is shared, although this is subject to the parent company's override. The subsidiary board has a greater role in setting business strategy, making use of local knowledge of markets and business conditions. The subsidiary's chief executive officer reports to both the parent company and the local board.[252] Fourth, there is the 'local board' model, under which the subsidiary company operates as an autonomous business and is accountable to the parent company as a shareholder. Typically, the parent is not informed enough about local operations to exert control, so that the subsidiary board exerts tight control over those operations.[253]

In most cases, research suggests, the position of the subsidiary lies between the first and the last of these models 'in that there is a requirement to operate within certain product/market/resource constraints, but management are still able to take developmental initiatives within those constraints'.[254] More control is exercised by the parent company within MNEs when there is a high level of intra-group trade (the parent company exercising control over transfer pricing of business inputs in order to minimise tax burdens),[255] when subsidiaries are in early stages of development, and when they operate in underdeveloped markets.[256] However, outside these situations, foreign subsidiaries have a high degree of autonomy in their operations. Control is exercised by regional centres and is 'multi-centred' in nature.[257] Local subsidiaries have responsibility for local product lines and other business activities.[258]

The question arises why MNE parent companies eschew a high level of control over foreign subsidiaries. As adumbrated, business history points to the difficulty parent companies experience when attempting to maintain day-to-day operational control over foreign subsidiaries. In addition to the problems of exercising control that apply to purely domestic groups, the following are encountered: first, there are problems in translating parent company edicts on account of language and cultural differences. Second,

251 Kiel, Hendry, and Nicholson, 'Corporate Governance Options', 574–5.
252 Kiel, Hendry, and Nicholson, 'Corporate Governance Options', 572–3.
253 Kiel, Hendry, and Nicholson, 'Corporate Governance Options', 577–8.
254 J. Birkinshaw and T. Pedersen, 'Strategy and Management in MNE Subsidiaries', in A.M. Rugman (ed.), *The Oxford Handbook of International Business* (2nd edn., 2009), p. 376.
255 Paz-Varga, 'International Transfer Pricing', 219.
256 Dunning, *Multinational Enterprises and the Global Economy*, pp. 225–6.
257 Eroglu, *Multinational Enterprises and Tort Liabilities*, p. 53.
258 Eroglu, *Multinational Enterprises and Tort Liabilities*, p. 53.

> many firm resources and capabilities are actually developed at the subsidiary level. And a key feature of these capabilities is that they are system-dependent or 'embedded' to such an extent that they cannot be easily disentangled from their local context. Furthermore, the ability to nurture and develop such capabilities is clearly the responsibility of subsidiary managers, as they have the local contacts and the intimate knowledge of local activities, not the people at HQ.[259]

Third, subsidiaries are subject to local laws,[260] business practices, and market conditions, with respect to which they are in the best position to respond. Finally, the parent company is likely to experience difficulty in 'observing behaviour across distances' and in 'setting up rules specifying the behaviour of foreign subsidiary managers (because headquarters has insufficient knowledge of foreign environments)'. So oversight of foreign subsidiaries is undertaken by setting financial performance targets, rather than by the kinds of behavioural constraints that could be imposed on managers of domestic subsidiaries.[261]

In summary, parent companies in MNEs exercise less hierarchical control than many writers on this matter assume.[262] Indeed, business historians have argued that MNEs might best be viewed, not as monolithic hierarchies, but as 'differentiated networks'.[263] Modern MNEs fit within a complex 'network of vertical and horizontal intra- and inter-firm connection[s]'.[264] Several case studies on the exercise of control in MNEs fortify these conclusions. US MNEs have exercised a greater degree of control over foreign subsidiaries than have their European counterparts, but even among US businesses there has been some variation over time.[265] Parent companies found control more difficult to exercise in the early decades of industrialisation, when travel times were long and communication more difficult. As these factors have become more favourable, and as business has become more cutthroat and competitive, control has tended to increase. This is the case especially when language and culture are not barriers,[266] but the ability to

259 Birkinshaw and Pedersen, 'Strategy and Management in MNE Subsidiaries', 379.
260 Chiappetta and Tombari, 'Perspectives on Group', 267–8.
261 Hennart, 'Theories of the Multinational Enterprise', 139.
262 Cf. Eroglu, *Multinational Enterprises and Tort Liabilities*, p. 53.
263 Rugman, Verbeke, and Nguyen, 'Fifty Years', 764.
264 Eroglu, *Multinational Enterprises and Tort Liabilities*, p. 38.
265 Jones, *Multinationals and Global Capitalism*, p. 177.
266 See C. A. Bartlett and S. Ghoshal, 'The Transnational Organization', in D. S. Pugh (ed.), *Organization Theory: Selected Classic Readings* (5th edn., 2007), p. 68.

exercise control is subject always to institutional and managerial constraints.[267]

For much of the twentieth century, parent companies in branded, packaged goods did not exercise great control over their foreign subsidiaries: 'Because coordination of purchasing, production, and marketing was achieved most effectively at local levels, there was little need for tight home-office control over management in these subsidiaries. They operated autonomously, gently supervised by the executives of the parent company's international division.'[268] As an example, Unilever exerted minimal control over the operations of its foreign subsidiaries. 'While they were free to draw on product technology, manufacturing capabilities, and marketing experience developed at the cent[re], they were not required to do so, and most units chose to develop, manufacture, and market products as they thought fit.'[269] This can be illustrated by reference to the operations of Unilever's African subsidiary UAC:[270]

> From its formation until the mid-1980s UAC operated as a virtually independent company with minimum control by Unilever ... UAC retained its own autonomous board, and ... an arm's length agreement was reached between UAC and Unilever. Under the terms of this agreement, UAC had some priority as a supplier of Unilever raw materials, but not a monopoly ... The lack of integration of UAC into Unilever was curious, but not exceptional.[271]

Although Unilever moved towards more centralised control through the 1990s, since then it has returned to decentralised operations.[272]

Similar patterns of operation can be found in other types of industry.[273] Evidence from the asbestos industry (a major case study in this book) is consistent with the decentralised M-Form group of companies. UK asbestos manufacturing group Turner & Newall exhibited 'a highly devolved structure in which board policy was delegated to local managements with a high degree of independence'.[274] One of the reasons for which foreign subsidiaries had poor health records was 'that decentralized structures

[267] Bartlett and Ghoshal, 'The Transnational Organization', 75.
[268] Chandler, *Scale and Scope*, p. 161.
[269] Bartlett and Ghoshal, 'The Transnational Organization', 67.
[270] Jones, *Merchants to Multinationals*, p. 106.
[271] Jones, *Merchants to Multinationals*, p. 106.
[272] A. Hill, 'Too Big to Manage', *FT Weekend* (28 February–1 March 2015), 11.
[273] E.g., Jones, *Multinationals and Global Capitalism*, p. 177 (example of IBM).
[274] G. Tweedale, *Magic Mineral to Killer Dust: Turner and Newall and the Asbestos Hazard* (2000), p. 219.

allow poor health conditions to flourish unchecked'.[275] Geoffrey Tweedale describes the group health policy of Turner & Newall as laissez faire: 'its overseas operations, holding companies, and decentralized UK administration provided a perfect breeding ground for the future asbestos health problem.'[276] Indeed, a director of the company, Harry Hardy, who eventually took an interest in the matter, was described as not having known in 1972 of 'the occupational health status of any of the firm's overseas factories and mines'.[277] Canadian subsidiary Atlas Asbestos Company had 'an atrocious asbestosis record, which was the worst in Canada'.[278] The situation in Turner & Newall's extensive mining and manufacturing subsidiaries in southern Africa was no better.[279] Indeed, no better could be expected, given that there were no laws regulating dust control in the region until the 1970s. The absence of regulatory standards in foreign jurisdictions would have been seen as good for business and not to be complained about. Ironically, the lack of knowledge, let alone exercise of control over health and safety standards by Turner & Newall, has presented a problem in proving parent company liability in asbestos cases (a matter considered in Chapters 5 and 10).

2.5 Conclusions

This chapter has examined economic reasons for the growth of large-scale businesses, including economies of scale, economies of scope, and internalisation. It has surveyed various business forms available to those engaging in large-scale commercial activity. Reasons have been given for the attractiveness of the corporate form and for the formation of corporate groups. However, detailed explanation has been given of the corporate network because this is a major competitor form to that of the corporate group. Moreover, in the course of this book we shall come to appreciate that liability decisions made with respect to corporate groups need to take into account the ability of large-scale businesses to move to the corporate network form in order to escape or reduce the prospect of liability. This chapter has demonstrated that businesses structure their operations so as to avoid regulation and tax and to increase profits. This is an indication of a certain behavioural pathology. We see in the next

[275] Tweedale, *Magic Mineral to Killer Dust*, p. 293.
[276] Tweedale, *Magic Mineral to Killer Dust*, p. 220.
[277] Tweedale, *Magic Mineral to Killer Dust*, p. 220.
[278] Tweedale, *Magic Mineral to Killer Dust*, p. 222.
[279] Tweedale, *Magic Mineral to Killer Dust*, p. 223.

chapter that this behaviour extends to the protection of group assets and to the avoidance of liability to external parties, such as injured tort claimants. The discussion of business form was accompanied by an initial consideration of the exercise of 'control' within corporate groups, given that this is an important element in both existing and proposed liability rules aimed at resolving the insolvent entity problem. It was found that the usual assumption of parent company control of corporate subsidiaries is of doubtful validity. There are many examples of corporate groups in which parent companies do not exercise day-to-day control over subsidiary operations. A parent company is even less likely to exercise operational control over its foreign subsidiaries than over its domestic subsidiaries.

3

Structuring of Corporate Group Relations

3.1 Introduction

This chapter examines the legal building blocks of corporate groups, these being separate legal personality, the capacity of the company to transact with all comers (including its controlling shareholder), and the limited liability of shareholders. It will become apparent that the extension of limited liability to corporate shareholders leads to problems. This is because of the ability of the parent company to structure relations between group companies in order to protect major assets from the reach of creditors. This chapter highlights how the 'insolvent entity problem' (explained in Chapter 1) arises through such structuring in corporate groups that are *otherwise solvent*. A similar problem is caused by structuring relations in networks. A key aim of this book will be to determine how this problem can be addressed. The need for a solution is all the more pressing given the vulnerability of tort victims. This chapter highlights their vulnerability by pointing to the poor bargaining power of tort victims compared to contract creditors and inadequacies in insurance cover.

3.2 Separate Legal Personality

There was no general right to incorporate in the United Kingdom until the Joint Stock Companies Registration, Incorporation, and Regulation Act 1844.[1] The Act established the registered company as a legal person separate from its shareholders and controllers, which could own property, enter into contracts, become subject to other legal obligations, and

[1] P. I. Blumberg, 'Limited Liability and Corporate Groups' (1986) 11 *Journal of Corporation Law* 573, 581ff. The UK Act followed earlier legislation in the United States achieving the same purpose. The first example was An Act Relative to Incorporations for Manufacturing Purposes 1811 (NY). See S. E. Howard, 'Stockholders' Liability under the New York Act of March 22, 1811' (1938) 46 *Journal of Political Economy* 499.

enjoy perpetual succession.[2] The recognition of the company as a legal person with these characteristics is the basis for 'entity law'. Unless empowered to do so by legislation, judges cannot ignore the separate legal personality of the company created by registration[3] and must deal with the company on its own terms. In *Prest* v. *Petrodel Resources Ltd*, Lord Sumption explained that 'limited companies have been the principal unit of commercial life for more than a century. Their separate personality and property are the basis on which third parties are entitled to deal with them and commonly do deal with them.'[4] In other words, the company is a mechanism for conducting business used by a variety of people to arrange their affairs and transactions.[5] Interfering with its use has the potential to create uncertainty in commercial life. This is a simple reason for difficulty in arguing for the application of veil-piercing doctrine (considered in Chapter 10), which would permit extension of the legal obligations of subsidiary companies to parent companies and/or other shareholders.

Prior to the mid-nineteenth century, it was believed to be beyond the legal power ('ultra vires') of a company to own shares in *another* company.[6] However, from that point in time, English law enabled shareholdings by companies because the definition of 'shareholder' in the Companies Clauses Consolidation Act 1845, section 3, explicitly encompassed both natural and corporate persons. Subsequent legislation continued this practice,[7] and the old 'Table A' Articles of Association permitted companies to appoint proxies to vote on their behalf.[8] So long as a company's Memorandum of Association permitted it to acquire shares in other companies, their acquisition was treated as lawful.[9] However, it seems that, early on, there was little appreciation that this might lead to the acquisition by one company of *substantially all* of the

2 For affirmation of these principles, see *Prest* v. *Petrodel Resources Ltd* [2013] 2 AC 415, [8].
3 Under Companies Act 2006, s. 16, a company comes into existence upon registration.
4 [2013] 2 AC 415, [8].
5 UNCITRAL, 'Legislative Guide on Insolvency, Part Three: Treatment of Enterprise Groups in Insolvency' (2012), p. 5.
6 J. E. Antunes, *Liability of Corporate Groups: Autonomy and Control in Parent–Subsidiary Relationships in US, German and EU Law* (1994), pp. 32–3.
7 A. Muscat, *The Liability of the Holding Company for the Debts of its Insolvent Subsidiaries* (1996), p. 155.
8 Companies Act 1862, sch. 1, cl. 49. See P. Lipton, 'The Mythology of *Salomon*'s Case and the Law Dealing with the Tort Liabilities of Corporate Groups: An Historical Perspective' (2014) 40 *Monash University Law Review* 452, 474.
9 E.g., *In re Barned's Banking Company* (1867) 3 LR Ch 105, 112–13.

shares in other companies.[10] One of the reasons for this failure was the simple assumption that companies were intended to be vehicles by which groups of individuals would participate in business endeavours. This was prior to acceptance, in *Salomon* v. *A Salomon and Co Ltd*, of the proposition that a single person might hold the vast majority of shares in a company and be its absolute controller.[11]

Although English law on this matter developed earlier in time, the corporate group became a reality upon the enactment of the Public Laws of New Jersey, Chapter 269, in 1888, which permitted one company to hold shares in another.[12] This resulted in a rush of re-incorporations in New Jersey, especially by large companies affected by antitrust laws.[13] Other US states followed New Jersey in permitting shareholdings by companies,[14] although the corporate group form only started to become apparent in numbers in the early twentieth century.[15] This was when companies began to develop ambitions to operate nationally[16] and internationally.[17] By the 1920s or 1930s, the balance of economic power shifted from individual companies to corporate groups,[18] and the legal problems of corporate groups started to appear in case law on both sides of the Atlantic.[19] In the present day, larger companies are characterised by their many subsidiary companies. The fifty largest UK companies have, on average, 230 subsidiaries, sub-sub-subsidiaries, and so on, extending up to eleven removes from the parent.[20]

[10] Muscat, *The Liability of the Holding Company*, p. 156. [11] [1897] AC 22.

[12] P. I. Blumberg, *The Multinational Challenge to Corporation Law* (1993), p. 56. Corporate groups began to appear in England in the following decade: Lipton, 'The Mythology of *Salomon*'s Case', 474–5.

[13] Blumberg, *The Multinational Challenge to Corporation Law*, pp. 56–7.

[14] Cf. F. Freedland, 'History of Holding Company Legislation in New York State: Some Doubts as to the "New Jersey First" Tradition' (1955) 24 *Fordham Law Review* 369.

[15] Muscat, *The Liability of the Holding Company*, p. 2.

[16] M. Roe, 'Corporate Strategic Reaction to Mass Tort' (1986) 72 *Virginia Law Review* 1, 47.

[17] Lipton, 'The Mythology of *Salomon*'s Case', 475.

[18] Antunes, *Liability of Corporate Groups*, p. 37.

[19] I. Mevorach, *Insolvency within Multinational Enterprise Groups* (2009), p. 11.

[20] R. T. Wieser, *Liability within Corporate Groups* (2013), pp. 9–10; D. D. Prentice, 'Some Aspects of the Law Relating to Corporate Groups in the United Kingdom' (1999) 13 *Connecticut Journal of International Law* 305, 306. A similar situation obtains in other advanced economies: e.g., R. Squire, 'Strategic Liability in the Corporate Group' (2011) 78 *University of Chicago Law Review* 605, 619–20; I. M. Ramsay and G. P. Stapledon, 'Corporate Groups in Australia' (2001) 19 *Company & Securities Law Journal* 7, 9–10. See also B. Reinschmidt, 'The Law of Tort: A Useful Tool to Further Corporate Social Responsibility?' (2013) 34 *Company Law* 103, 104, asserting that in 2006, '78,441 parent corporations operated through 777,647 foreign affiliates worldwide.'

The mere fact that one company owns the majority of the shares in a subsidiary is not treated as compromising the subsidiary's separate legal personality or as providing a basis for parent company liability.[21] Indeed, separate legal personality is not compromised by the fact of overlapping directorships between the parent company and its subsidiaries either. Courts are prepared to accept that common directors, when sitting on the subsidiary's board, wear their 'subsidiary hat', and not that of the parent.[22] This is to say that the mere formation of a corporate group is no basis for extensions of liability among constituent companies. Unlike the position under the German *Konzernrecht*, which takes a sceptical view of the group form, UK and other common law jurisdictions impose liability on a behavioural basis only.[23] Liability follows the *doing* of something that causes injury to another, and is not attached to mere relationship or status.

The parent–subsidiary relationship is attended by the legal power of control that the former has over the latter. The holding of a majority of the shares in the subsidiary enables the appointment of a majority of the directors to the subsidiary board. In many cases (as noted), there will be some overlap in the identity of parent company and subsidiary company directors. Should subsidiary directors not perform in a way that is satisfactory to the parent company, they can be removed immediately, and replaced with more compliant individuals.[24] This can be done through the general meeting, which, at the subsidiary level, might be (but is not invariably) a rubber-stamping body.[25] But control is possible even without the ability to appoint the majority of directors to the board of the subsidiary (as we saw in Chapter 1). Frequently, effective control arises simply because many (if not most) minority shareholders in a company do not vote their shares (a kind of 'rational apathy', because those shareholders do not expect their votes to make any difference to outcomes). In other cases, effective control accompanies the 'parent' acting in concert with other shareholders.[26] But the ability to influence

[21] See *The Gramophone and Typewriter Ltd* v. *Stanley* [1908] 2 KB 89 (affirming [1906] 2 KB 856).

[22] *BHP Billiton Finance Ltd* v. *Commissioner of Taxation* (2009) 72 ATR 746, [100].

[23] Wieser, *Liability within Corporate Groups*, pp. 42–3.

[24] Companies Act 2006, s. 168.

[25] *Lewis Holdings Ltd* v. *Steel & Tube Holdings* [2015] 2 NZLR 831, [26]; Antunes, *Liability of Corporate Groups*, pp. 100–1.

[26] See Companies Act 2006, s. 1159 (definitions of 'holding company' and 'subsidiary company'). Outside the United Kingdom, control can be exercised through such devices as golden shares or multiple-voting shares: see Antunes, *Liability of Corporate Groups*, pp. 118–19.

the outcome of subsidiary board decisions aside, it seems that parent companies frequently have the practical ability to exercise control over subsidiaries through direct edicts issued by their managers. This is to say that, where formal approval by the subsidiary board is not required, senior parent company executives might make decisions and convey them directly to subordinates in those subsidiaries.[27]

So the parent company has the power to control the actions of its subsidiaries. However, this is different from saying that such control invariably *is exercised*. We have already noted (in Chapter 2) that the parent company often does not exercise day-to-day control over its subsidiaries – especially as regards the operations of foreign subsidiaries and those domestic subsidiaries with businesses respecting which the parent lacks competence to make detailed decisions. Alternatively, control might be exercised earlier in time in order to 'structure' relations within the group (a matter considered later) and relaxed later in time when risky operations are undertaken. The parent might refrain from exercising control *in order* to ensure that it avoids control-based liability to creditors.

3.3 Corporate Capacity

As we have seen, the company has the capacity to enter into and discharge legal obligations (for example, through contract). But, in the corporate group context, another important capacity must be recognised. The doctrine of separate legal personality would mean nothing without the existence of a presumption about dealings between parent companies and their subsidiaries. This is the presumption that we see in *Salomon* v. *Salomon & Co Ltd*[28] and in *Lee* v. *Lee's Air Farming*,[29] both of which were concerned with small ('one-person') companies. The presumption is that the controlling shareholder does not dominate the investee company in such a way as to negate the latter's own decision-making ability. The investee company is competent, from day one, to deal with its controlling shareholder.[30] This presumption is necessary, as a practical matter, so that the controlling shareholder's contractual and other legal relations

[27] *Australian Competition and Consumer Commission* v. *April International Marketing Services Australia Pty Ltd (No 6)* [2010] FCA 704, [42]; Muscat, *The Liability of the Holding Company*, pp. 50–1; Antunes, *Liability of Corporate Groups*, pp. 91 and 103.

[28] [1897] AC 22. [29] [1961] AC 12.

[30] See M. A. Pickering, 'The Company as a Separate Legal Entity' (1968) 31 *Modern Law Review* 481, 502.

with the investee company can be treated as prima facie good and enforceable – so that they cannot be overturned on the simple basis of control by the shareholder over the investee company. The same presumption applies in the corporate group context and is difficult to overcome in that context through use of doctrines such as veil-piercing (considered in Chapter 10).

3.4 Limited Liability

One of the major benefits of the company law regime is the ability of corporators to elect to incorporate companies with limited liability, which allows those who invest to limit their potential losses and thus protects their personal asset holdings. Ordinarily, investors acquire their shares fully paid, so that no further amount is owed, after acquisition, towards satisfaction of the debts of their investee companies when insolvency strikes.[31] A creditor cannot reach into shareholders' personal assets and satisfy the debts of a company from those assets. This has been described as 'defensive asset partitioning', and is said to be the 'primary business advantage' of the corporate form.[32]

It is interesting to examine the context in which this state of affairs came about. Traders were long protected against liabilities to their customers by the rule of caveat emptor.[33] The buyer was to beware and would have to shoulder responsibility for defects in goods resulting in their lack of utility and/or causation of personal injury.[34] This was so unless either the buyer had a cause of action in trespass[35] or the contract with the vendor permitted a claim based on breach of warranty.[36]

[31] E.g.: Insolvency Act 1986, s. 74(2)(d); Model Business Corporation Act § 6.22(b)(3d ed. Supp. 1997); Delaware Code, Title 8, § 102(b)(6)(2002); Corporations Act 2001 (Cth), s. 516.

[32] R. Kraakman et al., *The Anatomy of Corporate Law: A Comparative and Functional Approach* (2004), p. 9; H. Hansmann and R. Kraakman, 'The Essential Role of Organizational Law' (2000) 110 *Yale Law Journal* 387, 395–6.

[33] This was 'the policy of the law': T. F. T. Plucknett, *A Concise History of the Common Law* (5th edn., 1956), p. 665. See also D. G. Owen, 'The Evolution of Products Liability Law' (2007) 26 *Review of Litigation* 955.

[34] E.g., *Chandler* v. *Lopus* (1603) Cro Jac 4; 79 ER 3; *Seixas* v. *Woods* 2 Cai 48 (NY Sup Ct 1804).

[35] D. Ibbetson, *A Historical Introduction to the Law of Obligations* (1999), p. 90 (example of detinue).

[36] 'Generally speaking, the common law did not impose liability on a seller, in the absence of warranty, if his wares turned out to be of poor quality': J. H. Baker, *An Introduction to English Legal History* (4th edn., 2007), p. 357.

However, buyers were hindered by the burden of proof regarding and the strict construction of contractual warranties.[37] It was only with judicial development of the implied term as to merchantability[38] (codified in the Sale of Goods Act 1893) that the law became more favourable.[39] But third parties, not privy to contracts of sale, had no right to compensation for injuries caused by defective products until this was established in the tort of negligence early in the twentieth century.[40] Traders and merchants had another protection from losses in the laws of bankruptcy, which initially were available to them alone.[41] These laws permitted exemption of tools of the trade and other items necessary for conducting their businesses from being apprehended in order to pay commercial debts.[42] These rules have been extended since to allow greater protection of debtors, including corporate debtors, and the making of a fresh start.[43] In these ways, common law jurisdictions have long subsidised commerce by permitting various losses arising from defective goods and services to lie where they fall.[44] This situation continues to the present day, in a different form, through the law of limited liability.

In the early days of the chartered corporation, stockholder liability was limited only when the charter specified that this was to be so. The default rule was that liability ended three years after a stockholder's shares were transferred to another.[45] However, it became common for Parliament to ordain limited liability for chartered corporations, and this became the assumed Parliamentary intention.[46] Joint stock 'companies' (the predecessors to registered companies, which were based upon trust mechanisms) purported to limit stockholder liability by the use of the term 'limited' in

37 Ibbetson, *A Historical Introduction*, pp. 84–5.

38 E.g., *Holcombe* v. *Hewson* (1810) 170 ER 1194; *Gardiner* v. *Gray* (1815) 4 Camp 144.

39 Baker, *An Introduction to English Legal History*, pp. 358–9. See also Owen, 'Evolution of Products Liability Law', 962 (US position).

40 *MacPherson* v. *Buick Motor Co* 111 NE 1050 (NY 1916); *Donoghue* v. *Stevenson* [1932] AC 562.

41 Statute of 13 Elizabeth (1570), ch. 5. See M. Cole, 'Limiting Liability through Bankruptcy' (2002) 70 *University of Cincinnati Law Review* 1245.

42 Cole, 'Limiting Liability through Bankruptcy', 1262.

43 R. Goode, *Principles of Insolvency Law* (4th edn., 2011), ch. 1.

44 'The privity requirement was an effective instrument of social policy for a nation bent on promoting the development of infant industries': Owen, 'Evolution of Products Liability Law', 963–4.

45 C. A. Cooke, *Corporation, Trust and Company: An Essay in Legal History* (1951), p. 110. See also S. M. Bainbridge and M. R. Henderson, *Limited Liability: A Legal and Economic Analysis* (2016), p. 30.

46 Bainbridge and Henderson, *Limited Liability*, pp. 28 and 30.

their contracts and general business documentation,[47] but this was a method of doubtful efficacy. In fact, stockholders were required to meet leviations imposed upon them in order to satisfy company debts.[48] 'Buying just one share in an unlimited company laid [the stockholder] open to a call to pay money sufficient to discharge all the debts of the company.'[49] So stockholders could avoid liability only after transferring their stock to others.[50]

The reasons for passage of a law limiting the liability of shareholders in the new registered company were many and varied and accumulated over time.[51] These included a decline in the attractiveness of undertaking business in England after competitor jurisdictions had begun to offer protection to shareholders, the desire to facilitate 'freedom of association' in business, demands for a suitable form of investment vehicle for middle- and lower-class savers, and continual pressures to permit the raising of capital in large amounts in order to fund the major infrastructure projects of the day. Limited liability was seen as a key means by which to achieve many social and business objectives, because this was a way of enticing investment by individuals who were (and remain) risk-averse[52] and who worried about their lack of control over investee companies. Limited liability was given effect by the Limited Liability Act 1855, and the Joint Stock Companies Act 1856 which succeeded it. While the 1855 Act contained protections against abuse of the rule (including disclosure requirements, and a rule of personal liability of directors if they paid dividends knowing their companies to be insolvent, or if they permitted loans to members), the protections disappeared from the 1856 Act.[53]

Today, Companies Act 2006, section 3(1), enables UK companies to adopt limited liability status, and this is given effect by Insolvency Act 1986, section 74(d). The limited liability rule is indifferent to the origin of company debts, whether arising from statute, contract, or tort law[54]

47 Blumberg, 'Limited Liability and Corporate Groups', 582.

48 Bainbridge and Henderson, *Limited Liability*, p. 30; R. McQueen, *A Social History of Company Law* (2009), p. 32.

49 A. Diamond, 'Corporate Personality and Limited Liability', in T. Orhnial (ed.), *Limited Liability and the Corporation* (1982), p. 33.

50 Blumberg, 'Limited Liability and Corporate Groups', 583.

51 See, generally, McQueen, *A Social History of Company Law*, chs. 2–4.

52 Muscat, *The Liability of the Holding Company*, p. 163.

53 McQueen, *A Social History of Company Law*, p. 49; P. Muchlinski, 'Limited Liability and Multinational Enterprises: A Case for Reform?' (2010) 34 *Cambridge Journal of Economics* 915, 916–17.

54 Although limited liability might be thought controversial in tort cases, it has been long established. See, e.g., *Heacock & Lockwood* v. *Sherman* 14 Wend 58, 60 (NY Sup Ct 1835); G. Skinner, 'Rethinking Limited Liability of Parent Corporations for Foreign Subsidiaries'

(as discussed later). Limited liability is said to facilitate 'risk-sharing' between shareholders and the external parties with whom the company interacts.[55] If the company fails, losses are partly externalised because they fall upon creditors (many of which will be companies that enjoy limited liability also), these creditors often having no further recourse.

As already stated, by the mid-nineteenth century it was accepted in English law that one company could acquire shares in another company. This position obtained prior to the passage of the Limited Liability Act 1855, but remained a novelty for some time. When the 1855 Act was passed, it appears not to have been contemplated that the benefits of limited liability might thus *inure to companies themselves*.[56] The result was that, in the absence of contracts creating additional rights, the creditors of B Co, a group subsidiary, could look only to that company for payment of their debts. They could not look to the parent company, A Co, much less to the sibling C Co.[57] The effect was to create in individual shareholders in the parent company a *second layer of protection* against liability. Over time, these layers of protection would multiply as corporate groups became ever more complex and parent company shareholders were removed completely from the woes of the lowest-level subsidiaries.

A question arises as to the desirability of parent companies' ability to enjoy limited liability. Arguably, it was not necessary to extend limited liability to protect company assets because companies themselves are not inherently risk-averse, and would not be deterred by the risk of liability simply because this derived from being shareholders in other companies, rather than from their own activities. This book will consider potential statutory exceptions to limited liability, as well as the use of tort actions which would bypass it. In advance of the discussion of these topics, it is appropriate to consider a range of economic arguments in favour of the extant rule of limited liability.

Limited liability is said to be justified on a basis beyond mere concern for the personal assets of investors. These justifications point to the economic significance of limited liability as an inducement to capital raising.[58] Thus,

Violations of International Human Rights' (2015) 72 *Washington & Lee Law Review* 1769, 1793–4.

55 C. Witting, 'Liability for Corporate Wrongs' (2009) 28 *University of Queensland Law Journal* 113, 113.

56 Muscat, *The Liability of the Holding Company*, pp. 154–6; Blumberg, 'Limited Liability and Corporate Groups', 607.

57 *Industrial Equity Ltd* v. *Blackburn* (1977) 137 CLR 567, 577.

58 See, generally, F. Easterbrook and D. Fischel, 'Limited Liability and the Corporation' (1985) 52 *University of Chicago Law Review* 89.

limited liability is said to facilitate the separation of ownership and control. This separation enables professional managers to run a business, reducing the need for shareholders to monitor the performance of the company.[59] Limited liability is said also to negate the need for shareholders to monitor *each other* because the personal liability of each shareholder is invariant to the wealth of other shareholders.[60] This, in turn, ensures that shares are homogenous commodities, allows for their easy transfer,[61] and promotes the operation of public securities markets.[62] Limited liability is said, further, to shift some of the costs of monitoring the company from shareholders to credit providers because of the risks that they must bear when dealing with companies. Creditors are 'more likely than they otherwise would be to scrutinize closely – both before and after extending credit – the likely fortunes of the firm and the behavior of the firm's managers'.[63] Each of the advantages so far mentioned permits shareholders to function as passive owners of the company.[64] Limited liability also permits shareholders to diversify their holdings in a larger number of companies.[65] Diversification reduces the risks of investing in any particular type of business, leaving the shareholder vulnerable primarily to swings in the economic cycle.[66] For these reasons, limited liability is seen as a 'key element in the growth of the industrial economy'.[67] Courts the world over have been reluctant to undermine it.[68]

59 Easterbrook and Fischel, 'Limited Liability and the Corporation', 94–5.

60 Easterbrook and Fischel, 'Limited Liability and the Corporation', 95.

61 T. Kaisanlahti, 'Extended Liability of Shareholders?' (2006) 6 *Journal of Corporate Law Studies* 139, 143.

62 P. Halpern, M. Trebilcock, and S. Turnbull, 'An Economic Analysis of Limited Liability' (1980) 30 *University of Toronto Law Journal* 117.

63 Hansmann and Kraakman, 'The Essential Role of Organizational Law' (2000), 425. Note that shareholders might be content with this monitoring role because the alternative is that they would have to monitor the wealth of individual shareholders under a regime of personal liability: S. M. Bainbridge, 'Abolishing Veil Piercing' (2001) 26 *Journal of Corporation Law* 479, 492–3.

64 L. E. Ribstein, 'Limited Liability and Theories of the Corporation' (1991) 50 *Maryland Law Review* 80, 102.

65 Easterbrook and Fischel, 'Limited Liability and the Corporation', 95; H. M. Markowitz, 'Portfolio Selection' (1952) 7 *Journal of Finance* 77.

66 Kaisanlahti, 'Extended Liability of Shareholders?', 147.

67 R. Posner, *Economic Analysis of Law* (4th edn., 1990), pp. 393–98; Halpern, Trebilcock and Turnbull, 'An Economic Analysis', 117–20; S. Presser, 'Thwarting the Killing of the Corporation: Limited Liability, Democracy, and Economics' (1992) 87 *Northwestern University Law Review* 148, 155–6.

68 W. O. Douglas and C. Shanks, 'Insulation from Liability through Subsidiary Corporations' (1929) 39 *Yale Law Journal* 193, 193, the authors noting that limited

Assumptions made about the fundamental economic significance of limited liability have not been the subject of rigorous empirical analysis and, on that account alone, are open to questioning and possible refutation.[69] Phillip Blumberg, for one, is of the opinion that there is no conceptual reason to equate the corporate form with limited liability.[70] As an historical matter, this is correct. The corporate form predates the rule of limited liability for shareholders. But, even if limited liability turns out to be very important for attracting investment by individuals, there are reasons to believe that it does not hold the same importance for investment *by companies*. In what follows, the position of both parent companies *qua* shareholders and individual shareholders is considered. The position of the latter group is important because they are so central to rationales for limited liability.

The first assumption about limited liability relates to the separation of ownership and control, which allows professional managers to manage the company so that shareholders do not have to monitor company performance. This is an important condition for investment by individuals. But the same cannot be said for parent companies, which have financial incentives continually to monitor their subsidiaries.[71] Although parent companies exercise different levels of control over their subsidiaries, typically they provide strategic direction and exercise high-level managerial oversight over group operations (as we saw in Chapter 2). Senior managers of the parent company are accountable for overall group operations. Indeed, the parent company's own financial performance depends upon the performance of its subsidiary companies. It is likely that group accounts will be prepared, and these provide a framework for assessing that performance. Minority shareholders (where they exist), who currently desist from taking a monitoring role, would not

liability is 'ingrained in our economic and legal systems'. Reluctance to impinge upon the doctrine has puzzled some corporate lawyers. Thus, it has been observed that a 'major object of the law of torts is to shift the financial burden of the loss from the victim to the person whose activity caused the damage. There is no reason why a company . . . should not be held liable to pay compensation for harm flowing from civil wrongs in the course of its activities if a natural person in similar circumstances would have been liable': R. P. Austin and I. M. Ramsay, *Ford's Principles of Corporations Law* (12th edn., 2005), 807. See also Chapter 11.

69 H. Hansmann and R. Kraakman, 'Towards Unlimited Shareholder Liability for Corporate Torts' (1991) 100 *Yale Law Journal* 1879, 1880; Blumberg, 'Limited Liability and Corporate Groups', 611.

70 Blumberg, 'Limited Liability and Corporate Groups', 604.

71 I. Ramsay, 'Allocating Liability in Corporate Groups: An Australian Perspective' (1999) 13 *Connecticut Journal of International Law* 329, 343.

necessarily feel compelled to become more proactive with the scaling back of limited liability. This is because a number of stakeholders, other than the parent company, already monitor corporate performance in medium- and larger-size companies – including regulators, credit-rating agencies, and creditors.[72]

The second assumption about limited liability is that it negates the need for shareholders to monitor *each other*. Shareholders might have incentives to monitor each other under a rule of *joint* unlimited liability. This is because each shareholder's susceptibility to ruinous personal liability would depend upon the wealth of fellow shareholders, which determines their ability to contribute upon the winding-up of the company. Shareholders of modest means would be less able to help meet the debts of the insolvent company, so that the burden would fall upon wealthier shareholders.[73] For an asset-rich parent company, joint unlimited liability would encourage it to seek out wealthy co-investors and/or to divest of subsidiaries undertaking particularly risky activities. However, none of these problems would arise were the unlimited liability rule to mandate *pro-rata contribution* to the unpaid debts of the investee company. For this reason, Chapter 9 will argue in favour of *pro-rata* unlimited liability in cases of death and personal injury. Liability under such a rule would not depend upon the level of each shareholder's wealth.

The third assumption about limited liability is that it facilitates the displacement of a proportion of the costs of shareholder monitoring of managers onto external credit providers.[74] Under this assumption, the removal of limited liability from the shareholders of small companies

[72] R. Booth, 'Limited Liability and the Efficient Allocation of Resources' (1994) 89 *Northwestern University Law Review* 140, 147; Presser, 'Thwarting the Killing of the Corporation', 159. Only large and sophisticated creditors, such as banks, might be willing and effective monitors of companies to which they extend credit: J. Freedman, 'Limited Liability: Large Company Theory and Small Firms' (2000) 63 *Modern Law Review* 317, 330. Note also that the efficacy of credit rating agencies has been questioned: Securities Industry and Financial Markets Association, 'Recommendations of the Securities Industry and Financial Markets Association Credit Rating Agency Taskforce' (July 2008), available at: www.sifma.org/capital_markets/docs/SIFMA-CRA-Recommendations.pdf; International Organisation of Securities Commissions, 'The Role of Credit Rating Agencies in Structured Finance Markets: Final Report' (May 2008), available at: http://iosco.org/library/pubdocs/pdf/IOSCOPD270.pdf.

[73] Even if monitoring became necessary, some commentators deride its importance in the context of tort claims: e.g., Booth, 'Limited Liability', 147.

[74] Insurers are likely to fulfil a similar role: M. A. Cohen, M. Gottlieb, J. Linn, and N. Richardson, 'Deepwater Drilling: Law, Policy, and Economics of Firm Organization and Safety' (2011) 64 *Vanderbilt Law Review* 1853, 1900.

would be problematic, because creditors would lose the financial incentive to monitor, so that the burden would shift back to shareholders. But this problem is more apparent than real for two reasons. First, shareholders in small companies are likely to be involved in the operation of those companies (for example, as managers) so that a change in the law would make no difference to them. Many invest all of their time and a large proportion of their wealth in these business ventures.[75] Even when their businesses mature, small company shareholders will remain keen to monitor their performance closely.[76] Second, the significance to shareholders in small companies of limited liability vanishes almost completely when normal practices regarding creditor demands for personal guarantees for company debts are taken into account.[77] In many cases, limited liability is no comfort for shareholders in small companies.

The argument in favour of limited liability is stronger for the shareholders of medium- and larger-size companies, because the vast majority are not paid managers and do not extend personal guarantees. They hold their shares as passive investors. However, this is not to say that a move to unlimited liability would change everything for them. Contrary to the assumption made by the law and economics commentators, there is a reasonable argument that contract creditors would engage in *greater* monitoring of debtor companies under such a rule – if it is accompanied by priority in winding-up for tort creditors over contract creditors.[78] Chapter 9 argues for such a rule. With or without a change in the priorities rule, it is true that a greater level of shareholder monitoring of managers could be expected.[79] But the real point is that (regulators and credit-rating agencies to one side) much of the monitoring of medium- and large-size companies today is done by a particular kind of shareholder – the institutional shareholder – and their appointed corporate advisory firms (discussed in Chapter 9). Monitoring costs incurred by institutional shareholders are likely to be justified by the size of their

[75] Freedman, 'Limited Liability', 332; Ribstein, 'Limited Liability', 103–6.

[76] This point applies even under a limited liability regime: Freedman, 'Limited Liability', 332.

[77] Freedman, 'Limited Liability', 332.

[78] Ramsay, 'Allocating Liability in Corporate Groups', 374. But note practical difficulties that accompany creditor monitoring, given the exigencies of trade and the potential loss of competitiveness for those that would undertake it: A. Keay, 'Wrongful Trading and the Liability of Company Directors: A Theoretical Perspective' (2005) 25 *Legal Studies* 431, 452–3.

[79] M. K. Patterson, 'Is Unlimited Liability Really Attainable? Of Long Arms and Short Sales' (1995) 56 *Ohio State Law Journal* 815, 851, and 897.

investments. But, in many cases, they delegate the monitoring to proxies, who vote in annual general meetings.[80] Such monitoring helps to reduce the amount of injury-producing corporate activity.[81]

These points weaken the argument about the costs to shareholders of monitoring management under a rule of pro-rata unlimited liability. However, the argument is of no real concern at all in the corporate group context. This is because, as already demonstrated, parent companies have every incentive to monitor the performance of their subsidiaries and are unlikely to rely upon external creditors to do so. Indeed, their incentives to monitor will increase along with their potential liability for subsidiary company debts – and this would be a positive development for reasons just given.

The fourth assumption about limited liability is that it facilitates investors in diversifying their holdings of securities, which reduces their exposure to isolated corporate failures. This argument has been seen as crucial to investment by risk-averse individual investors. The problem with unlimited liability is that it threatens to increase the risks of individual insolvency with each investment made in a new company[82] – and this is a valid point. But, once again, this book will propose a rule of *pro-rata* unlimited liability, and *not joint* unlimited liability. Pro-rata unlimited liability would not necessarily reduce opportunities to diversify risks. Individual shareholders could be expected to curtail investments in corporate groups engaged in injury-producing activities (at least where the risks are foreseeable) and to focus on alternative investments. In fact, shareholders would retain their present ability to invest across a broad range of asset classes, including debt instruments, real estate, commodities, and cash.[83] Such diversification reduces the chances of losses from particular investments in risky companies, and reduces the chances of losses stemming from downturns in the economic cycle too.[84] Shareholders could protect themselves also by taking out swaps contracts (discussed in Chapter 9).

[80] I. Anabtawi and L. Stout, 'Fiduciary Duties for Activist Shareholders' (2008) 60 *Stanford Law Review* 1255.

[81] Note, however, that doubt exists about this kind of practice: V. Finch, 'Security, Insolvency and Risk: Who Pays the Price?' (1999) 62 *Modern Law Review* 633, 654.

[82] D. Leebron, 'Limited Liability, Tort Victims, and Creditors' (1991) 91 *Columbia Law Review* 1565, 1597.

[83] Leebron, 'Limited Liability', 1596. See also Hansmann and Kraakman, 'Towards Unlimited Shareholder Liability', 1904.

[84] This is not to say that diversification across asset classes eliminates system-wide risks: see Ribstein, 'Limited Liability', 103.

Even so, the argument about the need for limited liability in order to facilitate diversification is simply less important with respect to parent companies than to individual shareholders because the former are more likely than the latter to be risk-neutral than to be risk-averse.[85] The reality is that companies invest in projects, even if risk-laden, when those projects have positive net present values.[86] Net present value is calculated *before* tort and other liabilities crystallise,[87] but is based on various scenarios which incorporate a best estimate of the likely costs and benefits of projects, including liability costs. As long as projects under consideration have positive net present values, the incentives will be to pursue them. Only in cases of very risky projects, especially where insurance is unavailable or prohibitively costly, will the prospect of unlimited liability make a difference and create a disincentive to invest. (More is said about this scenario in what follows.)

Of course, when considering the desirability of current limited liability rules, it is important to take a wider view than that which focuses solely upon the position of shareholders. Looking at things more broadly, the sad fact is that limited liability in the corporate group context has been positively *harmful* in permitting over-investment in various risky business activities.[88] Because limited liability externalises costs, a company's investments in risky projects can 'have positive value for its shareholders even if its net present value to society is negative'.[89] This is to say that limited liability has provided the wrong incentives to invest in some risky activities – such as those which will be considered in case studies involving asbestos manufacture and distribution and the manufacture of defective pharmaceutical products.

In sum, the arguments against the application of rules of separate legal personality *and* limited liability in favour of the parent company are that: there is no clear separation of ownership and management as between the parent company and those who manage subsidiary companies; there is no need to save the parent company from monitoring its subsidiaries – and every reason to encourage it; there is no need to save the parent company from monitoring minority shareholders in its subsidiaries, because the parent's liability is invariant to changes in the wealth of

[85] Hansmann and Kraakman, 'Towards Unlimited Shareholder Liability', 1882ff.
[86] Muscat, *The Liability of the Holding Company*, p. 167.
[87] Leebron, 'Limited Liability', 1570ff.
[88] T. P. Glynn, 'Beyond "Unlimiting" Shareholder Liability: Vicarious Tort Liability for Corporate Officers' (2004) 57 *Vanderbilt Law Review* 329, 371.
[89] Muscat, *The Liability of the Holding Company*, p. 168.

minority shareholders; and there is no need to facilitate the diversification of parent company investments through limited liability because incentives to diversify would remain unaltered (especially under a rule of pro-rata unlimited liability). These are not the only factors relevant to the issue. Other potential consequences of a move to a modified rule of limited liability will be considered in Chapter 9. But, for the moment, it can be concluded that there are no overwhelming economic reasons against reconsidering the application of limited liability within corporate groups. Of course, any proposals for reform need to be considered carefully; they need to be 'sophisticated and nuanced',[90] so that risks to the economy are thought through and dealt with in an appropriate way. Any modification to the rule will have advantages and disadvantages.

3.5 Judgment-Proofing and Malpractice

In Chapter 2, it was noted that corporate groups are likely to adopt a divisionalised, M-Form structure. Each subsidiary in the group has a different function – whether this be management, manufacturing, distribution, or marketing. Divisionalisation facilitates the setting of performance targets and the monitoring of performance. It facilitates also access to finance for separate businesses and the ability to join with outside investors in those businesses, as well as their sale. Maintenance of separate corporate entities might be important, further, in protecting the goodwill attaching to each business. The evidence suggests that the M-Form is the prevalent business form, not only among large groups, but among medium- and small-size groups as well.[91] Although companies increasingly engage in business through corporate networks, these are not yet predominant in the industrial and manufacturing sectors which give rise to mass-torts causing personal injuries.[92]

Parent companies incorporate subsidiaries for reasons that go beyond ease of management and control. Even without limited liability, separate incorporation reduces the risk that the liabilities of one subsidiary in the group will infect others. However, limited liability improves the position of the parent company because its assets are specifically protected from subsidiary liabilities. The ability to incorporate a subsidiary and to confine the risks of developing a new product or offering a particular service

[90] P. L. Davies and S. Worthington, *Gower and Davies' Principles of Modern Company Law* (9th edn., 2012), p. 245.

[91] Muscat, *The Liability of the Holding Company*, p. 3. [92] See Chapter 2.

encourages parent company investment in innovation, which frequently is accompanied by risk. But there is a dark side to the ability to incorporate subsidiaries at will, while the parent company is protected by limited liability. The parent company has the ability deliberately to *structure* group relations so as to protect the group's main assets and deny creditors access to them. Where the prospect of large liabilities arises, the parent company might be tempted to incorporate multiple subsidiaries *in order* to defeat liability[93] – a practice known as 'judgment-proofing'.[94] The structuring of group relations in order to judgment-proof can take a number of dimensions. In what follows, a general explanation of this practice is given before we move on to consider more specific issues involving multinational enterprises, debt-financing, secured creditors, and strategic use of the insolvency process itself.

In the archetypal judgment-proofing scenario, the parent company, A Co, exists as a holding company ostensibly with no substantial management capability.[95] Its subsidiary B Co owns valuable plant and equipment, while C Co undertakes risky activities that injure.[96] C Co, as the operating subsidiary, has access to necessary plant and equipment through leasehold arrangements with B Co, but might have no substantial assets of its own. The parent company provides capital as and when this is convenient to it.[97] Where necessary in order to obtain credit from external sources or convenient in order to keep the costs of credit down, contract debts are incurred against cross-guarantees within the group.[98] When the parent company decides to move assets from one subsidiary to another,[99] perhaps because of the threat of large tort liabilities, this might

[93] L. M. LoPucki, 'The Death of Liability' (1996) 106 *Yale Law Journal* 1, 20.

[94] For a general overview of means by which companies seek to escape from or to reduce the size of successful tort claims, see Roe, 'Corporate Strategic Reaction to Mass Tort'.

[95] E.g., *Okpabi* v. *Royal Dutch Shell plc* [2017] EWHC 89 (TCC)(Royal Dutch Shell plc, apart from setting overall group business strategy and business principles, was little more than an investment vehicle).

[96] See J. Birkinshaw and T. Pedersen, 'Strategy and Management in MNE Subsidiaries', in A. M. Rugman (ed.), *The Oxford Handbook of International Business* (2nd edn., 2009), 378; LoPucki, 'The Death of Liability', 28; Muscat, *The Liability of the Holding Company*, p. 90; Antunes, *Liability of Corporate Groups*, p. 6.

[97] Muscat, *The Liability of the Holding Company*, 314. If transactions are properly recorded, the basic facts regarding subsidiary capitalisation, etc. should be apparent in the group accounts required by Companies Act 2006, s. 399.

[98] Squire, 'Strategic Liability in the Corporate Group', 606 and 614–15.

[99] This is more likely to occur when the parent does not own all of the shares in the subsidiary: V. Atanasov, A. Boone, and D. Haushalter, 'Is There Shareholder Expropriation in the United States? An Analysis of Publicly Traded Subsidiaries' (2010) 45 *Journal of Financial and Quantitative Analysis* 1, 4.

be done in a number of ways, including: the imposition of management and other fees,[100] the payment of dividends to the parent, the withdrawal of finance support by the parent, the unwarranted extension by the subsidiary of guarantees to other group companies, disadvantageous transfer pricing, the commingling of the subsidiary's assets with other companies in the group, and so on.[101] While strategies such as these are vulnerable to being overturned under various statutory provisions considered in Chapter 6, the point is that C Co is likely to be inadequately financed when tort liability threatens. This means that it will have little margin for the accumulation of losses.[102] In cases where a subsidiary is underperforming and risks declining into insolvency, the parent company might encourage the subsidiary to take greater than normal business risks. This is likely to be so where the parent company's equity interest has diminished to negligible levels, and it prefers not to extend unsecured loans. In such cases, there is a well-recognised moral hazard. The parent company might take a bet on higher-risk business transactions undertaken through the subsidiary. If the gamble is successful, the parent reaps the rewards; if the gamble fails, it loses very little in equity terms.[103]

Judgment-proofing is unlikely to occur among companies dealing with each other at arm's length. In arm's-length transactions, 'each company will seek independent gain ... [N]o company will give up value without demanding equivalent value in return'.[104] Moreover, a 'subsidiary's creditors may possess leverage sufficient to force the parent to reach some compromise requiring the parent's contributions to help satisfy ... liabilities. For instance, the parent and the subsidiary may have many of the same suppliers'.[105] However, groups undertaking physical processes with the potential to cause significant physical injuries might

100 J. H. Farrar, 'Legal Issues Involving Corporate Groups' (1998) 16 *Company & Securities Law Journal* 184, 189.

101 Muscat, *The Liability of the Holding Company*, 76–83. Note that commingling is probably rare due to the need for companies to keep proper records of their assets and liabilities under company and tax legislation: ibid., p. 291.

102 E.g., *Lungowe* v. *Vedanta Resources plc* [2016] BCC 774.

103 See, e.g., T. Rapakko, *Unlimited Shareholder Liability in Multinationals* (1997), p. 172.

104 S. Schwarcz, 'The Inherent Irrationality of Judgment Proofing' (1999) 52 *Stanford Law Review* 1, 3.

105 B. B. Erens, S. J. Friedman, and K. M. Mayerfield, 'Bankrupt Subsidiaries: The Challenges to the Parent of Legal Separation' (2008) 25 *Emory Bankruptcy Developments Journal* 65, 70. The authors make the point also that banks and other lenders might charge higher interest rates to group companies if they perceive group companies as a risk: ibid., 70–1.

deploy this strategy.[106] In the chemical, asbestos, and tobacco industries,[107] judgment-proofing has been a late-stage strategy used to protect group assets. There is evidence also that judgment-proofing occurs routinely in smaller groups, which are not reliant upon capital markets, are not subject to significant external monitoring,[108] and the activities of which are less likely to gain publicity. Thus, it has been noted that 'the level of concern with preserving the group corporate image tends to decline as the scale of the enterprise diminishes. The smaller the enterprise the lower is the incentive to bail out a sinking subsidiary.'[109] For these reasons, it appears that 'a large proportion of the small [companies] created over [recent decades] in hazardous industries were created in order to limit tort liability'.[110]

In multinational groups, judgment-proofing might involve various further actions.[111] For example, a parent company might incorporate subsidiaries in low-regulation jurisdictions, which permit exclusion in employment contracts of liability for death and personal injuries.[112] Even in the absence of this 'benefit', the parent company might locate risky physical processes in low-regulation jurisdictions, typically developing countries because they have the double advantage of fewer rules and lower damages awards.[113] In other cases, especially when tort liability threatens, parent companies might keep valuable assets offshore. While some assets are more mobile than others, in Chapter 2 we saw that it has become commonplace for parent companies to transfer intellectual property rights to subsidiaries in low-tax jurisdictions. Although this does not necessarily mean that such assets are beyond reach, they become more difficult to access because of the need to enforce judgments in

106 White, 'Corporate Judgment Proofing', 1366. See also Birkinshaw and Pedersen, 'Strategy and Management in MNE Subsidiaries', 378.

107 Antunes, *Liability of Corporate Groups*, 271; Roe, 'Corporate Strategic Reaction to Mass Tort', 39–40. See Chapter 4 for examples in the asbestos industry.

108 Farrar, 'Legal Issues Involving Corporate Groups', 189. See case studies in H. Anderson, 'Pressing the Right Buttons: Australian Case Studies in the Protection of Employee Entitlements against Corporate Insolvency' (2014) 153 *International Labour Review* 117.

109 Muscat, *The Liability of the Holding Company*, p. 15.

110 M. Dearborn, 'Enterprise Liability: Reviewing and Revitalizing Liability for Corporate Groups' (2009) 97 *California Law Review* 195, 198.

111 Leading writers have asserted that there are distinct patterns of judgment-proofing behaviour: e.g., Hansmann and Kraakman, 'Towards Unlimited Shareholder Liability', 1881. Only the simplest of examples are given in the text.

112 *Newton-Sealy* v. *ArmorGroup Services Ltd* [2008] EWHC 233 (QB), [36].

113 *Sithole* v. *Thor Chemicals Holdings Ltd* 2000 WL 1421183 (Court of Appeal, 28 September 2000).

foreign courts (considered further later). 'If the foreign legal system will not enforce liability against the assets of the debtor, removal achieves much more than hindrance and delay; it bars recovery.'[114]

Another way of structuring group relations so as to protect assets is by financing subsidiaries with debt rather than equity. In this scenario, the parent extends finance for the operation of subsidiaries not primarily by way of share capital, but by the extension of loans, whether or not secured against subsidiary assets.[115] This type of 'thin capitalisation'[116] is encouraged by the tax deductibility of interest payments on debt.[117] In the case of subsidiary insolvency, the parent might attempt to recoup loan funds in competition with external creditors. The taking of security prima facie entitles repayment of the parent in priority to unsecured external creditors. However, this practice is improper where funds extended to the subsidiary, in reality, are at-risk capital rather than genuine loans (as we see in Chapter 8). But the availability of the strategy reveals the asymmetric nature of risks of insolvency faced by the parent company on the one hand and by creditors on the other. If the business is successful, the parent scoops up the profits, while creditors are repaid their fixed-interest loans. If the business fails, the parent might be first in line to realise its security, while unsecured creditors are left to recover a minor proportion of the funds extended to the subsidiary – or nothing at all.[118] 'To the extent that the distribution of corporate assets to the [parent company upon insolvency] reduces payment to external creditors, external creditors absorb the risk of loss ordinarily suffered by the shareholders.'[119]

Yet another way of structuring group relations so as to protect assets is by giving security for debts to particular classes of contract creditor with market power.[120] Ordinarily, these creditors are suppliers of goods, services, and finance. Providing security to them is in the interest of the

[114] LoPucki, 'The Death of Liability', 32.

[115] Muscat, *The Liability of the Holding Company*, pp. 87–8.

[116] Muscat, *The Liability of the Holding Company*, p. 317. Note that minimum capital requirements do prevail in the European Union, but are confined to public companies and financial institutions: see, esp., Companies Act 2006, s. 763, and Companies (Authorised Minimum) Regulations 2009 (SI 2009/2425), reg. 2 (establishing the minimum at € 57,100). Moreover, applicable requirements are modest and there is no way of ensuring that they are maintained: Muscat, ibid., pp. 327–32.

[117] A. R. Admati, P. Conti-Brown, and P. Pfleiderer, 'Liability Holding Companies' (2012) 59 *UCLA Law Review* 852, 869.

[118] Muscat, *The Liability of the Holding Company*, p. 317.

[119] Muscat, *The Liability of the Holding Company*, p. 318.

[120] See, esp., Finch, 'Security, Insolvency and Risk'.

group itself. It secures credit at lower cost (because the creditors need undertake little, if any, monitoring of the debtor company)[121] and ensures the continuing availability of necessary inputs – perhaps even after subsidiary insolvency. However, the impact of insolvency then falls disproportionately upon unsecured creditors, including tort victims; often there will be no assets left from which their claims can be satisfied. In a variation upon this theme, *major contract creditors* might come to exercise significant power over the corporate group, and its structure. This can be achieved through the use of guarantee provisions in several, interrelated ways. First, a contract creditor might require that multiple companies in the group cross-guarantee a loan made to a group company (the primary loan). Second, the creditor might impose multiple loan conditions, such as the treatment of default on any debt due to it by a group company as a default on the primary loan.[122] Recourse to guarantees might not only threaten guarantor companies with insolvency, but have a knock-on effect in the group as a whole.[123] The creditor can enforce guarantees or waive breaches, according to taste. In the circumstances, the ability selectively to exercise enforcement options creates considerable power over the group.[124] A major contract creditor might have the ability either to gain significant control of the group (for example, by insisting on management changes)[125] and its assets after a default, or else extract assets ahead of involuntary creditors by triggering cross-guarantees and/or acceleration clauses (so that moneys are paid back more quickly).[126] Even where no individual contract creditor has such power over the operations of a group, cooperation among major creditors would permit them to do many of the same things.[127]

In English law, structuring of group relations in order to escape *existing* liabilities is largely impermissible following the enactment of several statutory prohibitions on asset-depleting transfers to be considered in Chapter 6.[128] Indeed, there are good reasons why parent companies ought not to walk away from existing subsidiary company debts

121 Finch, 'Security, Insolvency and Risk', 649–51.

122 A. J. Casey, 'The New Corporate Web: Tailored Entity Partitions and Creditors' Selective Enforcement' (2015) 124 *Yale Law Journal* 2680, 2689.

123 Antunes, *Liability of Corporate Groups*, p. 94.

124 Casey, 'The New Corporate Web', 2685.

125 Casey, 'The New Corporate Web', 2723.

126 Casey, 'The New Corporate Web'.

127 Casey, 'The New Corporate Web', 2691–2.

128 See, e.g., *Sithole* v. *Thor Chemicals Holdings Ltd* 2000 WL 1421183 (Court of Appeal, 28 September 2000)(order under Insolvency Act 1986, s 423 dealing with transactions defrauding creditors).

(including the need for continued credit by other group companies, as well as reputational concerns).[129] However, it is more feasible to engage in such strategic behaviour (in one or more of the ways outlined) in order to avoid the incurrence of *future* liabilities. In *Adams* v. *Cape Industries plc*,[130] the English Court of Appeal asserted that group companies are to be treated as separate entities with their own legal obligations, and that it is impermissible for a court to 'lift the corporate veil as against a defendant company which is the member of a corporate group merely because the corporate structure has been used so as to ensure that the legal liability (if any) in respect of particular future activities of the group ... will fall on another member of the group rather than the defendant company'.[131] In the case of contract liabilities, it is reasoned that counterparties will have notice of where future liabilities are to fall. However, the position of tort victims is different (as discussed later).

The opportunities for structuring relations within corporate groups and for removing assets from creditors do not end with the strategies discussed so far. We now move on to consider ways in which groups engage in malpractice *after* insolvency arises. 'Strategic insolvency' involves the use of insolvency procedures 'in order to transform ties with other institutions or groups of individuals'.[132] The potential exists for their use in ways that are detrimental to some or all of the group's creditors. The scope for wrongdoing in this context has increased with the advent of the 'rescue culture' in modern insolvency law.[133]

One danger accompanies the use of pre-packaged administration. In the typical case, the 'pre-pack' involves a plan to sell the business or assets of the insolvent company to an arranged purchaser by agreement with major creditors.[134] In the United Kingdom, pre-packs entail finding a buyer for the company after its independent valuation.[135] The agreement is held in escrow until an administrator is appointed.[136] Once appointed,

[129] B. Hannigan, *Company Law* (4th edn., 2016), p. 61. [130] [1990] Ch 433.

[131] [1990] Ch 433, 544. This is consistent with the explanation of veil-piercing given in *Prest* v. *Petrodel Resources Ltd* [2013] 2 AC 415, examined in Chapter 10. For a similar approach in the United States, see, e.g., *Craig* v. *Lake Asbestos of Quebec Ltd* 843 F 2d 145 (3rd Cir. 1988).

[132] P. Spender, 'Blue Asbestos and Golden Eggs: Evaluating Bankruptcy and Class Actions as Just Responses to Mass Tort Liability' (2003) 25 *Sydney Law Review* 223, 249–50.

[133] See Goode, *Principles of Corporate Insolvency Law*, pp. 31–2; Spender, 'Blue Asbestos and Golden Eggs', 247.

[134] Goode, *Principles of Corporate Insolvency Law*, p. 34.

[135] Goode, *Principles of Corporate Insolvency Law*, p. 60.

[136] Goode, *Principles of Corporate Insolvency Law*, p. 60.

the administrator can sell the business without either creditor approval or court sanction (unlike the case in the United States).[137] The benefits of pre-packs include less disruption to the business (its operations, brand, and value) and its employees from the sale.[138] More troubling is the fact that, in two-thirds of all cases, pre-packs result in the same managers controlling the business[139] – although the new business entity is freed from (much) of its debt legacy. Unsecured creditors fare worse than they would with ordinary business sales.[140] This is a process that might be repeated again and again.[141] In more specific terms, Roy Goode notes a range of problems with pre-packs:

> pre-packs have attracted a degree of negative publicity on the ground that unsecured creditors have no voice in the process, which lacks transparency with a consequent lack of accountability, that they are presented with a fait accompli, that pre-packs may be unacceptably biased towards the interests of secured creditors ... and that the business may be sold off at an under-value, particularly if there is a proposed management buy-out and the management has a close relationship with the intended administrator.[142]

In order to address some of the problems, the English and Welsh Statement of Insolvency Practice 16 (which is an element of self-regulation by the profession, and only indirectly binding) now requires administrators to perform their functions in the interests of creditors as a whole;[143] but there continues to be no mandatory oversight by an independent body, there being instead a voluntary procedure by which assessments can be obtained by persons from a pool of experts.[144] However, neither of these measures is likely to be very effective in complex cases.[145]

137 *Re Transbus International Ltd* [2004] 1 WLR 2654; Goode, *Principles of Corporate Insolvency Law*, p. 60.

138 House of Commons Library, 'Pre-pack Administrations' (CBP5035, January 2016), 3.

139 B. Adebola, 'Proposed Feasibility Oversight for Pre-pack Administration in England and Wales: Window Dressing or Effective Reform?' [2015] *Journal of Business Law* 591, 592–4. See also *Capital For Enterprise Fund A LP* v. *Bibby Financial Services Ltd* [2015] EWHC 2593 (Ch), [62]; Goode, *Principles of Corporate Insolvency Law*, pp. 34–5, citing R3, 'Pre-packaged Sales ("Pre-packs"): A Survey of R3 Members' (May 2009).

140 They 'almost invariably get nothing from the process and know nothing about it until after the event': *Capital for Enterprise Fund A LP* v. *Bibby Financial Services Ltd* [2015] EWHC 2593 (Ch), [63]. See also Goode, *Principles of Corporate Insolvency Law*, p. 413.

141 Adebola, 'Proposed Feasibility Oversight', 592.

142 Goode, *Principles of Corporate Insolvency Law*, p. 413.

143 R3, 'Statement of Insolvency Practice 16' (2015), [4].

144 R3, 'Statement of Insolvency Practice 16'; House of Commons Library, 'Pre-pack Administrations', 3.

145 Adebola, 'Proposed Feasibility Oversight', 603.

In the United States, greater ostensible protection is provided for creditors than in the United Kingdom under the Bankruptcy Code Chapter 11 procedure applicable to pre-packs, although problems remain. Under the Chapter 11 procedure, existing management remains in office subject to the superintendence of the court and creditors.[146] Approval of a pre-pack sale, whether or not to connected persons, requires that all creditors vote on the proposed reorganisation plan, 'with half of the creditors by number who collectively have at least two-thirds of the dollar value of claims outstanding required for approval'.[147] In some cases, there have been claims about impropriety in the way that creditor approval has been obtained,[148] and about the ability of secured creditors to collude with management in engineering sales on terms that favour them over unsecured creditors.[149] There are concerns, moreover, about the ability of courts properly to assess the feasibility of reorganisation plans.[150] In the usual case (as we see in Chapter 4), pre-packaged bankruptcy disposals have been approved alongside the creation of trust structures for payment of compensation to injured tort victims. The award of channelling injunctions ensures no further recourse against reorganised businesses.[151] A potential problem is that creditors and the court might approve a plan which does not provide adequate funding of the trust, as has occurred on many occasions.[152] This has been a particular problem with respect to asbestos companies which have used pre-pack procedures, because of the inherent difficulty in valuing future claims.[153] Indeed, many applications have involved presently solvent companies with good revenues. These companies have been able to shed their asbestos liabilities and leave claimants to an uncertain future.[154] For all of these reasons, it has been

[146] Goode, *Principles of Corporate Insolvency Law*, p. 64.

[147] US Code, Title 11, Bankruptcy, §1126(c); S. J. Carroll et al., *Asbestos Litigation* (2005), p. 119. A 'super-majority' of 75 per cent is required in asbestos cases: 11 USC § 524(g), considered in Chapter 8.

[148] E.g., *In re Combustion Engineering Inc* 391 F 3d 190 (3d Cir. 2004). See also R. Barliant, D. G. Karcazes, and A. M. Sherry, 'From Free-Fall to Free-for-All: The Rise of Pre-packaged Asbestos Bankruptcies' (2004) 12 *American Bankruptcy Institute Law Review* 441, 467.

[149] S. Ben-Ishai and S. J. Lubben, 'Involuntary Creditors and Corporate Bankruptcy' (2012) *University of British Columbia Law Review* 253, 276.

[150] Adebola, 'Proposed Feasibility Oversight', 601.

[151] US Code, Title 11, Bankruptcy, § 524(g).

[152] Carroll et al., *Asbestos Litigation*, pp. 119–20.

[153] Barliant, Karcazes, and Sherry, 'From Free-Fall to Free-for-All', 454.

[154] Barliant, Karcazes, and Sherry, 'From Free-Fall to Free-for-All', 451–3. See also Cohen, Gottlieb, Linn, and Richardson, 'Deepwater Drilling', 1893; M. P. Weingarten, 'Asbestos Litigation from an American Perspective' [2009] *Journal of Personal Injury Law* 253, 259.

asserted that the reorganisation process needs rethinking in order to ensure that it 'is being used to maximize the value of the debtor's assets, and not merely to transfer wealth among claimants'.[155]

This leads to a wider point about the Chapter 11 procedure, under which bankruptcy is not a prerequisite. The latent nature of harms caused by many modern products and industrial processes means that potential defendants have the ability to liquidate before crippling liabilities arise.[156] In the circumstances, Marcus Cole has argued that 'bankruptcy law is a limited liability device.'[157] This is because the discharge it affords 'acts as a temporal asset partition that limits a debtor's liability to those claims that arose before the impenetrable veil of bankruptcy falls'.[158] The bankruptcy order 'limits a debtor's liability on past and present claims to an artificially fixed and static, current pool of assets. It also prevents claimants on that pool from reaching the debtor's future assets or going concern value unless they exchange their past positions for new ones'.[159] Moreover, 'the capping and disposition of tort claims through Chapter 11 has become de rigueur for solvent companies facing unmanageable mass tort exposure and litigation.'[160]

The parent company's control over corporate group structures means that the risks of judgment-proofing are especially high in that business form. The law needs to develop more effective extended liability rules in order to deal with the risks. But the problem goes further. In Chapter 2, it was observed that businesses can combine in ways that do not rely upon equity holdings. The network form of business is formed through contractual agreements between participating businesses. This form has become more important in a business world where flexibility and speed are required in order to adapt to changes in the marketplace. Just as in corporate groups, network relationships can be used in 'strategic' ways in order to separate participants from liability-causing production and distribution activities. There will be a cost to this,[161] but the risk premium payable to subcontractors might be attractive to companies with valuable assets to protect from creditors. Arguably, this type of risk allocation is evident in franchising agreements, which have standard forms protective

[155] Ben-Ishai and Lubben, 'Involuntary Creditors and Corporate Bankruptcy', 276.
[156] Hansmann and Kraakman, 'Towards Unlimited Shareholder Liability', 1884.
[157] Cole, 'Limiting Liability through Bankruptcy', 1247.
[158] Cole, 'Limiting Liability through Bankruptcy', 1248.
[159] Cole, 'Limiting Liability through Bankruptcy', 1248 and 1254.
[160] Cole, 'Limiting Liability through Bankruptcy', 1274.
[161] See Schwarcz, 'The Inherent Irrationality', 3.

of franchisors.[162] It is evident also in companies which outsource product testing, manufacture, and distribution to the developing world, where regulatory standards are modest,[163] claims by injured persons are difficult to sustain and damages payouts comparatively low.

To date, the law has responded benignly to the problems created by the structuring of relations by network companies. Yet there have been cases of 'extreme negative externalities'.[164] Indeed, there are several reasons for which network liabilities might be significant. First, we saw in Chapter 2 that networks can be difficult to coordinate, so that they 'suffer from insufficient internal oversight and evince substantial dysfunctionality'.[165] This means that 'external risks are intensified by typical co-ordination errors within network[s].'[166] Second, network relationships, as adumbrated, frequently are structured so as to protect the assets of economically stronger participants, whether a large pharmaceutical company, a mining company, or a franchisor. The business structure adopted puts these parties at one or more removes from participants undertaking physical processes and creates the potential for significant externalisation of losses. Under 'general principles of private law, only the member of the network that has directly caused the damage to the outsider will generally be liable for the breach of the contract or a tortious wrong. As independent businesses' to which the claimant outsider is only indirectly related, 'other members of the network will not be held responsible on grounds of agency or vicarious liability.'[167] Third, because economically powerful and solvent companies are insulated from risks and are unlikely to suffer from reputational damage should liabilities be left uncompensated, there are few incentives to ensure proper coordination of activities and adoption of proper health and safety standards in participants undertaking physical processes.[168] Indeed, the intention might be to avoid responsibility for such matters. For this and other reasons, there have been calls for greater social and legal attention to networks.[169] Indeed, as explained in Chapter 1, in order to maintain 'business form neutrality', an

[162] G. Teubner, *Networks as Connected Contracts* (ed. H. Collins; tr. M. Everson)(2011), pp. 5 and 11.
[163] Teubner, *Networks as Connected Contracts*, pp. 241–2.
[164] Teubner, *Networks as Connected Contracts*, p. 103.
[165] Teubner, *Networks as Connected Contracts*, pp. 102 and 106.
[166] Teubner, *Networks as Connected Contracts*, p. 265.
[167] Teubner, *Networks as Connected Contracts*, p. 64.
[168] Teubner, *Networks as Connected Contracts*, p. 64.
[169] Teubner, *Networks as Connected Contracts*, p. 103.

appropriate principle for extending liability within corporate networks must be developed. This is a matter discussed in Chapters 5 and 11.

3.6 Multinationals and Private International Law

Difficulties created by separate legal personality, limited liability, and structuring of legal relations within corporate groups and networks are compounded (as adumbrated) by the fact that many larger businesses operate beyond a single nation's borders. Now-familiar reasons for this include the search for new markets, the desire to achieve lower labour and other production costs, the preference for 'business-friendly' regulatory regimes, and protection of assets from creditors.[170] Under rules examined in this book, it might be possible to extend liability from an insolvent company in one jurisdiction to a solvent company in another jurisdiction. But in order to succeed, the claimant must be able to bring his or her claim in that other jurisdiction. In the typical scenario, persons injured at the hands of a subsidiary in a less-developed country will be dissatisfied with the legal remedies available to them because local laws are not sufficiently protective of their interests, damages levels are too low (perhaps exemplary damages are not available), and/or the local subsidiary is insolvent.[171] In this scenario, the claimant will want to pursue the parent or some other group company in a more-advanced country, such as the United Kingdom.[172] This is the problem with which this section of this book is concerned. This section outlines major issues which face tort claimants in the position described; but readers seeking detailed guidance will need to refer to specialist works on the subject.[173]

As a general proposition, a court entertaining a tort suit must have both personal and subject-matter jurisdiction in the matter.[174] Under EU law, national courts have personal jurisdiction over companies domiciled within their jurisdiction.[175] Domicile includes the place where the company has its 'seat' (is incorporated), its central administration, or its

[170] For an example giving rise to private international law issues (involving the Cape group of companies), see P. Nygh, 'The Liability of Multi-national Corporations for the Torts of Their Subsidiaries' (2002) 3 *European Business Organization Law Review* 51, 54–5.

[171] M. Eroglu, *Multinational Enterprises and Tort Liabilities* (2008), p. 97.

[172] See Reinschmidt, 'The Law of Tort', 105–6.

[173] See Lord Collins et al., *Dicey, Morris and Collins: The Conflict of Law* (15th edn., 2012).

[174] A. Burrows (ed.), *English Private Law* (3rd edn., 2013), p. 1190.

[175] Recast Brussels Regulation, Council Regulation 1215/2012, OJ 2012 No L351/1, Art. 4(1).

principal place of business.[176] These rules permit suits in the case where the company has committed a tort itself. The domicile 'peg' might support also the joinder of parties from outside the jurisdiction where necessary in order to try the issues in a way that avoids potentially irreconcilable judgments.[177] Thus, a claim validly brought against the parent company can establish also the jurisdiction of a UK court over a foreign subsidiary, even if the factual basis of the action against the subsidiary arises almost exclusively in the foreign state.[178] This rule might be useful in actions discussed in Chapters 11 and 12.

But there are potential difficulties in bringing actions against multinational corporate groups. Let us assume the case in which a tortfeasor subsidiary company in a less-developed jurisdiction has become insolvent and cannot meet claims against it. The question is whether the UK parent or other group company can be sued for a tort it has committed, perhaps jointly, with the subsidiary. Under the Recast Brussels Regulation (concerning jurisdiction in civil and commercial matters), a foreign claimant can bring a tort action in the 'courts for the place where the harmful event occurred or may occur'.[179] This phrase has been interpreted to extend beyond the place where the damage occurred and to include the place where the *event giving rise to the damage* occurred.[180] This means that, where a UK-based company defectively designs machinery that causes injury to persons in Guyana, the UK company could be sued in either the UK or Guyanese courts.[181] But the mere fact that a UK parent company exercised control over a foreign, now-insolvent subsidiary is insufficient to create jurisdiction to sue the parent company[182] unless, perhaps, the UK company acted as *agent* for the foreign company.[183]

[176] Recast Brussels Regulation, Council Regulation 1215/2012, OJ 2012 No L351/1, Art. 63.

[177] Recast Brussels Regulation, Council Regulation 1215/2012, OJ 2012 No L351/1, Art. 8(1).

[178] *Lungowe* v. *Vedanta Resources plc* [2016] BCC 774; E. Aristova, 'Jurisdiction of the English Court over Overseas Human Rights Violation' [2016] 75 *Cambridge Law Journal* 468, 468. The court in *Lungowe* held that the matter is decided by reference to: whether it is reasonable for the court to try the issue; whether the defendant subsidiary is a necessary or proper party to the claim against the parent company; and whether England is the proper place in which to bring the claim: [2016] BCC 774, [97].

[179] Recast Brussels Regulation, Council Regulation 1215/2012, OJ 2012 No L351/1, Art. 7(2).

[180] Case 21/76 *Handelskwekerij GJ Bier BV* v. *Mines de Potasse d'Alsace SA* [1976] ECR 1735; [1978] QB 708.

[181] J. Zerk, *Multinationals and Corporate Social Responsibility* (2006), p. 117; cf. Burrows, *English Private Law*, p. 1199 (dubitante).

[182] Zerk, *Multinationals and Corporate Social Responsibility*, p. 86.

[183] Zerk, *Multinationals and Corporate Social Responsibility*, p. 118, referring to *Adams* v. *Cape Industries plc* [1990] Ch 433.

Under the doctrine of forum non conveniens, a defendant argues that an action brought against it should be stayed. According to *Spiliada Maritime Corporation* v. *Consulex Ltd*, a stay of proceedings can be granted on the ground of forum non conveniens 'where the court is satisfied that there is some other available forum, having competent jurisdiction, which is the appropriate forum for the trial of the action, i.e., in which the case may be tried more suitably for the interest of all the parties and the ends of justice'.[184] In the past, forum non conveniens inevitably would be pleaded in cases involving the causation of loss or damage in a foreign jurisdiction,[185] and would likely succeed unless there was injustice to the claimant in requiring him or her to bring action in the alternative jurisdiction.[186] However, in *Owusu* v. *Jackson*, the Court of Justice of the European Union held that the doctrine is not available to decline jurisdiction in cases where personal jurisdiction has been established under the rules of the former Brussels I Regulation, even where the alternative jurisdiction is not an EU Member State.[187]

Having said as much, the doctrine of forum non conveniens continues to apply in other common law countries and might prove an obstacle to suits involving group companies.[188] The presumption is that the claimant is entitled to proceed in the local forum, but this is subject to rebuttal. The Australian rule is quite favourable to claimants, the court asking whether the Australian jurisdiction chosen is 'clearly inappropriate'.[189] The US rule turns on whether the alternative forum is adequate to hear the case and upon a balancing of the interests of the parties and the public interest in the matter.[190] An alternative forum is considered adequate if the parties will not be deprived of meaningful remedies or treated unfairly.[191] As regards the interests of the parties, courts assess such matters as the parties' residence, the location of evidence and witnesses,

[184] [1987] AC 460, 476.

[185] Zerk, *Multinationals and Corporate Social Responsibility*, p. 120. See, e.g., *Lubbe* v. *Cape plc* [2000] 1 WLR 1545; *Connelly* v. *RTZ Corp plc (No 2)* [1998] AC 854.

[186] Burrows, *English Private Law*, p. 1205.

[187] Case C-281/02 *Owusu* v. *Jackson* [2005] ECR I-1383. See Burrows, *English Private Law*, p. 1203. This is now subject to Recast Brussels Regulation, Council Regulation 1215/2012, OJ 2012 No L351/1, Arts. 33 and 34.

[188] See Reinschmidt, 'The Law of Tort', 105–6.

[189] *Voth* v. *Manildra Flour Mills Pty Ltd* (1990) 171 CLR 538.

[190] *Piper Aircraft Co* v. *Reyno* 454 US 235 (1981); American Law Institute, Restatement (Fourth) of the Foreign Relations Law of the United States: Jurisdiction (TD No 2, 2016), § 304.

[191] *Reid-Walen* v. *Hansen*, 933 F 2d 1390, 1393 (8th Cir. 1991).

the compellability of witnesses, and ability to enforce judgments.[192] The public interest element relates to the interests and burdens which would be placed upon the courts.[193]

Assuming that a UK court will hear a claim involving a tort which resulted in loss or damage outside the United Kingdom, the next question is whether it will apply English law or the law of the foreign state from which the claimant brings suit in order to resolve the issue. In the European Union, this question is governed by the Rome II Regulation (regarding civil and commercial matters), Article 4(1) of which provides that 'the law applicable to a non-contractual obligation arising out of a tort/delict shall be the law of the country in which the damage occurs irrespective of the country in which the event giving rise to the damage occurred and irrespective of the country or countries in which the indirect consequences of that event occur.' However, an exception is created by Article 4(3), which provides that, where 'it is clear from all the circumstances of the case that the tort/delict is manifestly more closely connected with a country other than that indicated in paragraph [1], the law of that other country shall apply. A manifestly closer connection with another country might be based in particular on a preexisting relationship between the parties, such as a contract, that is closely connected with the tort/delict in question'.[194]

The UK court will have to consider the strength of the connection between the foreign jurisdiction and the cause of action pleaded.[195] In straightforward cases, where all of the elements of the tort occur within one jurisdiction, liability will be determined by the law of that jurisdiction (*lex loci damni*).[196] In more complicated cases, the court will have to consider where each element of the cause of action, such as the tort, arose so as to determine whether there is sufficient connection to the jurisdiction to justify application of that country's law. This can give rise to a contentious issue in some cases involving corporate groups,

[192] Eroglu, *Multinational Enterprises and Tort Liabilities*, pp. 110–11.

[193] Restatement (Fourth) of the Foreign Relations Law of the United States: Jurisdiction (TD No 2, 2016), § 304, Reporters' Note 5. See, e.g., *In re Union Carbide Corporation Gas Plant Disaster at Bhopal, India in Dec 1984*, 809 F 2d 195 (2nd Cir. 1987) (no substantial managerial links between US shareholder and subsidiary; claimants, witnesses, and evidence predominantly based in India).

[194] Note that product liability cases are the subject of Rome Regulation II, Council Regulation 864/2007, OJ 2007 No L199/40, Art. 5. This is regarded as a particularly murky provision: Burrows, *English Private Law*, p. 1231.

[195] Burrows, *English Private Law*, pp. 1184–5.

[196] Thanks to Professor Richard Garnett for informing me of the terminology here.

where a number of group companies contribute to the causation of injury.[197] A parent company or some other company in a more-advanced jurisdiction might have had a real responsibility for the commission of a tort in a less-developed jurisdiction. However, in cases where both tortious act and the causation of injury occur in the foreign jurisdiction, it is likely that the law of that foreign jurisdiction will be applied.[198]

A final conflict of laws issue is the enforcement of judgments involving multinational companies. Assume, once again, that a claimant has obtained a judgment in a foreign court over a foreign subsidiary which has become insolvent, and suit is brought against the UK parent company. Still 'the corporate separation between parent and subsidiary in a multi-national corporate group could be used as a justification by the courts of the home state for refusing to enforce a judgment issued against a subsidiary in a foreign host jurisdiction, with the aim of holding its parent liable.'[199] Indeed, it has been noted that 'international private law imposes significant hurdles to the enforcement of a foreign judgment against a parent company.'[200]

This is just a snapshot of some relevant private international law rules that affect the European Union (and, at present, the United Kingdom), but the requirements will differ from country to country. On these and related issues, readers are referred to specialist works on the subject.[201]

3.7 Position of Tort Creditors

Most large corporate groups would be reluctant to take advantage of their ability to engage in judgment-proofing and other abusive practices to the disadvantage of tort creditors. In the United Kingdom, listed companies, which typically have multiple subsidiaries, are subject to the enhanced governance and other requirements of the Listing Rules. They are subject

197 Reinschmidt, 'The Law of Tort', 107.

198 Eroglu, *Multinational Enterprises and Tort Liabilities*, pp. 131–2.

199 Muchlinski, *Multinational Enterprises and the Law*, p. 161.

200 Reinschmidt, 'The Law of Tort', 106. See *Adams* v. *Cape Industries plc* [1990] Ch 433.

201 For Australia, see Australian Government, Attorney-General's Department, 'Private International Law' (2017), available at: www.ag.gov.au/Internationalrelations/PrivateInternationalLaw/Pages/default.aspx; R. Mortensen, R. Garnett, and M. Keyes, *Private International Law in Australia* (3rd edn., 2015). For the United States, see American Law Institute, Restatement (Fourth) of the Foreign Relations Law of the United States: Jurisdiction (TD No 2, 2016).

also to scrutiny by the financial community and the press.[202] Larger groups understand the reputational damage that would follow publicity of improper practice. However, this is not to say that it never happens. Indeed, we have seen that – at the other end of the spectrum – it has become prevalent in smaller groups operating in some types of industry. Tort victims are particularly vulnerable to judgment-proofing. We see this in two ways: in their inability to bargain in the manner that contract creditors can and in the shortcomings of the insurance market.

The arguments in favour of the rule of shareholder limited liability are strongest with respect to contract debts and financial losses. Limited liability facilitates risk-sharing with respect to such losses.[203] In theory, creditors enter into contracts by agreeing to their terms and are treated as 'voluntary creditors'.[204] Frequently, such persons can protect their financial interests by examining creditworthiness, taking security on goods sold,[205] and obtaining guarantees. Experience demonstrates that contract creditors with bargaining power often do insist upon guarantees – personal guarantees from directors and others.[206] However, the extent to which contract creditors can strike truly voluntary bargains depends upon a number of factors (especially relative bargaining power, transaction value, and practicability).[207] Where, in theory, it might be possible for creditors to seek credit reports about counterparties or demand security for debts, this is not always practicable – especially when the costs of doing so are high and/or where competitor

[202] Muscat, *The Liability of the Holding Company*, pp. 97–8.

[203] This is not to say that there is no controversy at all: see, e.g., J. Farrar, *Corporate Governance: Theories, Principles, and Practice* (2nd edn., 2006), p. 26.

[204] B. Cheffins, *Company Law: Theory, Structure, and Operation* (1997), p. 501. Theory does not always correspond to reality: H. Anderson, 'Creditors' Rights of Recovery: Economic Theory, Corporate Jurisprudence and the Role of Fairness' (2006) 30 *Melbourne University Law Review* 1, 8–9; M. Whincop, 'Overcoming Corporate Law: Instrumentalism, Pragmatism and the Separate Legal Entity Concept' (1997) 15 *Company & Securities Law Journal* 411, 430.

[205] For a summary of actions that a creditor might take involving secured finance, see: P. L. Davies, *Introduction to Company Law* (2002), pp. 70–1. For some of the problems that arise, see Finch, 'Security, Insolvency and Risk' (discussing, e.g., problems faced by unsecured, non-adjusting creditors).

[206] Kraakman et al., *The Anatomy of Corporate Law*, p. 99; Davies, *Introduction to Company Law*, p. 69; Halpern, Trebilcock, and Turnbull, 'An Economic Analysis', 135. Where groups are concerned, 'it is common for creditors to require security on a group basis': Companies and Securities Advisory Committee, 'Corporate Groups Final Report' (2000), p. 17. This means the entering into of cross-guarantees between group members: ibid., 47. See Chapter 7.

[207] Muscat, *The Liability of the Holding Company*, p. 186.

businesses do not insist upon them.[208] The point is that many contract creditors injured by corporate wrongdoing are employees and ordinary consumers who do not have any real ability to bargain.[209] In this sense, they ought to be equated with involuntary creditors and might require legal protection – whether under statute or in tort.

Whereas risk-sharing between shareholders and contract creditors is capable of justification, justification disappears substantially when the costs of business failure fall upon tort victims, especially those seeking compensation for personal injuries. Tort victims are recognised as a vulnerable group of claimants. Most tort claims arise from wrongdoing or 'accidents' that are not predictable in advance. There can be little informed bargaining about the potential consequences of those accidents. This is the case with employees who must work in order to survive and with consumers undertaking ordinary household purchases. The vulnerability of involuntary tort creditors is exacerbated by judgment-proofing within corporate groups.[210] On account of this practice, Lynn LoPucki has asserted that the tort liability system has begun to fail.[211] Deserving claimants are not being compensated as they should be. This is both an inevitable and an accelerating process – accelerating because enterprises that fail to judgment-proof themselves are at a competitive disadvantage.[212] The ability to externalise costs reduces companies' incentives to take care in the conduct of their activities. More persons are injured than otherwise would be. It is clear, therefore, that significant legal protection of tort claimants is required against corporate wrongdoers.

However, common law courts continually have fallen back upon statutory rules of limited liability in order to prevent extensions of

[208] Note also that what might appear to be truly voluntary agreement between parties can be undermined by vitiating factors such as any misrepresentation. This can affect even large, trade creditors: see H. A. Anderson, 'Veil Piercing and Corporate Groups – An Australian Perspective' [2010] *New Zealand Law Review* 1, 12–13.

[209] 'By choosing employment in a particular industry, the tort victim may tacitly agree to share the risk that the industry will fail financially and that he will lose his job as a result; but he cannot reasonably be said to have assumed the risk of any injury a supplier of that industry might foist upon him.' By contrast, the shareholder 'has agreed explicitly to share the debtor's business risks and has voluntarily entered into a relationship with the debtor': M. Lyle, 'Mass Tort Claims and the Corporate Tortfeasor: Bankruptcy Reorganization and Legislative Compensation versus the Common-Law Tort System' (1983) 61 *Texas Law Review* 1297, 1304–5 and 1307. See also Muscat, *The Liability of the Holding Company*, p. 34.

[210] LoPucki, 'The Death of Liability', 20.

[211] LoPucki, 'The Death of Liability', 4.

[212] LoPucki, 'The Death of Liability', 4.

liability within corporate groups.[213] This is despite the fact that, when the UK Parliament was considering passage of the first Limited Liability Bill, there was no debate about the impact that limited liability would have upon tort creditors.[214] One probable reason for this is that the volume of tort litigation at the time was modest: 'torts that could bankrupt a company were apparently unheard of.'[215] Indeed, since that time, all sorts of social measures have been implemented which reduce the impact of accidents and personal injuries, such as the UK's National Health Service and similar schemes elsewhere, as well as ad hoc statutory schemes dealing with certain egregious modern industrial diseases and afflictions (commented upon in Chapter 1).

Of course, the problems of judgment-proofing and corporate insolvency might be less pressing if tort claims could be met by private insurance cover. Normally, businesses undertaking risky activities will have insurance cover.[216] As we saw in Chapter 1, under the Employers' Liability (Compulsory Insurance) Act 1969, UK employers must acquire and maintain insurance in respect of liability to employees for causation of bodily injury and disease. Responsible manufacturers take out product liability insurance.[217] However, insurance is not always the answer to the insolvent entity problem. One reason for this is that insurers are unwilling to cover excessive product-related and other risks. This was apparent

[213] E.g., *Williams* v. *Natural Life Health Foods Ltd* [1998] 1 WLR 830, discussed in C. Witting, 'What Are We Doing Here? The Relationship between Negligence in General and Misstatements in English Law', in K. Barker, R. Grantham, and W. Swain (eds.), *The Law of Misstatements: 50 Years on from Hedley Byrne v Heller* (2015), ch. 9.

[214] Muscat, *The Liability of the Holding Company*, p. 178.

[215] B. Pettet, 'Limited Liability – A Principle for the 21st Century?' (1995) 48 *Current Legal Problems* 125, 152; Muscat, *The Liability of the Holding Company*, p. 180.

[216] The discussion here is limited to third-party liability insurance – that is, the kind of insurance taken out by defendants in mass-tort cases.

[217] See, e.g., Association of British Insurers, 'Product Liability Insurance' (2014), available at: www.abi.org.uk/Insurance-and-savings/Products/Business-insurance/Liability-insurance/Product-liability-insurance. Tort claimants who establish liability against an insolvent subsidiary *can*, upon winding-up of the subsidiary, bring claims directly against the subsidiary's liability insurer: Third Parties (Rights against Insurers) Act 2010. Without the benefit of this legislation, insurance moneys payable under the policy would form part of the insolvent estate, and would be distributed pari passu between the general creditors of the company: see D. Milman, 'Promoting Distributional Justice on Corporate Insolvency in the 21st Century', in J. Steele and W. H. van Boom (eds.), *Mass Justice: Challenges of Representation and Distribution* (2011), p. 181. Under the Act, it is no longer necessary for claimants to prove their liability against the subsidiary in judicial or arbitral proceedings or by way of enforceable agreement. This can be done through declaration by a court. Thus, claimants need bring only one set of proceedings.

in asbestos cases from an early stage. From 1918, certain insurance companies began to refuse cover for asbestos-related disease.[218] Although the insurer Metlife did not withdraw from covering asbestos-related claims, in the 1930s it increased premiums by 40 per cent[219] – which would have discouraged many businesses from insuring. Where insurance was taken out, it has been difficult sometimes to trace the insurers of since-insolvent companies.[220] In the early 2000s, major re-insurers such as Munich-Re also attempted to limit their potential liabilities for asbestos-related payouts.[221] Today, insurers are especially keen to avoid the prospect of payouts in cases involving the potential for mass-tort claims.[222] As liability for mass-torts has widened in some areas, insurance cover has been withdrawn – such as with liability for environmental clean-up under the US Comprehensive Environmental Response, Compensation, and Liability Act 1980 (considered in Chapter 8).[223]

A second reason for which insurance is not always the answer to mass-tort claims is that many insurance policies are of the claims-made variety. Under claims-made insurance, the insurer offers cover for all claims made within the year of insurance – no matter when the risk-creating conduct occurred. Under this type of insurance, it is very easy for the insurer to withdraw cover in a subsequent year when it predicts that claims levels will increase so as to substantially impact on profits.[224] To the extent that insurance is available, its cost will increase with increases in risk. Thus, early on in the history of asbestos manufacture (discussed in Chapter 4), the leading UK manufacturer,

218 J. McCulloch and G. Tweedale, *Defending the Indefensible* (2008), p. 175; A. McKenna, 'An Overview of the Legal Landscape of Negligently-Inflicted Asbestos Related Conditions' [2011] *Journal of Personal Injury Law* 205, 208.

219 McKenna, 'An Overview of the Legal Landscape', 208.

220 *Fairchild* v. *Glenhaven Funeral Services Ltd* [2003] 1 AC 32; McKenna, 'An Overview of the Legal Landscape', 206.

221 C. Aldred, 'UK Asbestos Exclusions Likely to Spread' (2003) 37 *Business Insurance* 37.

222 From 2008 to 2015, insurers 'contested nine out of every 20 claims described as "large" or "strategically significant" by the company making them': A. Gray, 'Companies Warned to Read Small Print as Insurance Revamp Nears', *Financial Times*, 29 March 2015, available at: www.ft.com/content/4c0ac5fa-cbeb-11e4-beca-00144feab7de. See also D. Lenckus, 'Asbestos Still No 1 among Mass Tort Risks' (2007) 41 *Business Insurance* 11.

223 K. S. Abraham, 'Catastrophic Oil Spills and the Problem of Insurance' (2011) 64 *Vanderbilt Law Review* 1770.

224 Finch, 'Security, Insolvency and Risk', 654–5; Kaisanlahti, 'Extended Liability of Shareholders?', 153; LoPucki, 'The Death of Liability', 78; Panel of Eminent Persons, *Review of the Law of Negligence: Final Report* (2002), p. 31; P. Cane, 'Reforming Tort Law in Australia: A Personal Perspective' (2003) 27 *Melbourne University Law Review* 649, esp. 658ff.

Turner & Newall, objected to the premiums required for cover of asbestos diseases and became a self-insurer[225] until 1948, when many claims for asbestos-related disease were brought within the Industrial Injuries Disability Benefit scheme (discussed in Chapter 1).[226] From 1972, Turner & Newall was required to insure its employees once again under the legislation already mentioned.[227]

There are several other problems with the private insurance solution. Insurance policies include excess (or co-payment) clauses that seek to align the interests of insurer and insured,[228] and insured amounts are capped (that is, subject to claims limits) so that there is always a risk that assureds must endure losses above these amounts.[229] Companies exposed to large asbestos claims, such as Johns-Manville and Dow Corning, were underinsured.[230] Moreover, in modern times, insurers increasingly are careful about the circumstances in which they accept liability to cover losses, seeking to avoid cover on bases such as failures to disclose or the operation of exceptions.[231] 'In mass tort cases where the liability is in the hundreds of millions or billions of dollars, the insurers commonly deny coverage and litigate'[232] – as Dow Corning's insurers did when faced with the prospect of large payments for rupturing breast implants.[233] In the asbestos industry, Turner & Newall's insurers disputed their liability to cover its asbestos claims (on the basis of insufficient disclosure of the extent of asbestos health hazards),[234] but the policies were honoured eventually.[235] Figures suggest that approximately 60 per cent of asbestos-related claims are covered by insurance, although not all of these claims are paid out.[236] Finally, there is always the risk of insurer (and/or

[225] G. Tweedale, *Magic Mineral to Killer Dust* (2000), p. 71.

[226] A. Boggio, *Compensating Asbestos Victims: Law and the Dark Side of Industrialization* (2013), p. 82.

[227] *In re T & N Ltd and ors (No 4)* [2007] Bus LR 1411, 1417; Boggio, *Compensating Asbestos Victims*, p. 110.

[228] J. D. Hanson and K. D. Logue, 'The First-Party Insurance Externality: An Economic Justification for Enterprise Liability' (1990) 76 *Cornell Law Review* 129, 142.

[229] Finch, 'Security, Insolvency and Risk', 654–5.

[230] LoPucki, 'The Death of Liability', 46.

[231] The UK Supreme Court has noted a shift in mesothelioma litigation towards disputes between insurers and responsible parties: *Zurich Insurance plc* v. *International Energy Group Ltd* [2016] AC 509, [1].

[232] LoPucki, 'The Death of Liability', 46.

[233] LoPucki, 'The Death of Liability', 46, n. 202.

[234] *In re T & N Ltd and ors (No 4)* [2007] Bus LR 1411, 1417.

[235] Tweedale, *Magic Mineral to Killer Dust*, pp. 264–5.

[236] D. Landis, 'The Smoldering Threat of Asbestos', *Kiplinger's Magazine*, 28 May 2002, 48. Note that, in the United Kingdom, when an insurer becomes insolvent, liabilities might

underwriter) insolvency in the case of large catastrophes and mass-torts. On several occasions, the combined weight of asbestos claims has called into question the solvency of insurance providers.[237]

Shortfalls in the availability of suitable insurance cover have resulted in some kinds of business becoming self-insurers, in the way that Turner & Newall did for a temporary period. This is the case, for example, with respect to many of the liabilities that arise in the US oil business.[238] 'The risk of pollution-related harm [such as from oil spills] is a prime example of a low-probability risk with catastrophic potential magnitude if it materializes.'[239] BP plc has met the cost of most claims arising from the *Deepwater Horizon* oil disaster of 2010 from its own resources. It is obvious, however, that BP's ability to meet claims stems from operational successes that might not characterise defendants responsible for the 'next catastrophe'. Self-insured businesses are not protected from the special risks of mass-torts in the way that insurance companies are through their re-insurance of risks.

In the words of LoPucki, the overall picture that emerges about liability insurance is that it 'is a valuable adjunct to the working of an otherwise sound liability system, but it can neither save nor replace an unsound one'.[240] The law needs to ensure that creditors without full redress from insolvent group subsidiaries and their insurers have available to them satisfactory means of extending liability to other, solvent group companies.

3.8 Conclusions

This chapter has considered the legal building blocks of corporate groups and the problems that have arisen from the ability of parent companies to use rules of separate legal personality and limited liability in order to reduce their exposure and the exposure of valuable group assets to claims by creditors such as tort victims. These problems are intensified in the multinational corporate group, with respect to which the rules of private international law must be negotiated. Although many examples of the problems caused by the structuring of legal relations within groups have

be met by the Financial Services Compensation Scheme. This scheme is facing 'massive asbestos claims': R. Merkin and J. Steele, 'Historic Asbestos Exposure and Liability Insurance: Issues of Aggregation and Reinsurance', in J. Steele and W. H. van Boom (eds.), *Mass Justice: Challenges of Representation and Distribution* (2011), p. 223, n. 17.

237 McCulloch and Tweedale, *Defending the Indefensible*, pp. 176 and 178.

238 Abraham, 'Catastrophic Oil Spills'. 239 Abraham, 'Catastrophic Oil Spills', 1787.

240 LoPucki, 'The Death of Liability', 72. '[T]he insurance market does not offer non-limited cover when that is not imposed [upon it] by law': Kaisanlahti, 'Extended Liability of Shareholders?', 153.

been adverted to, it remains for us to examine some real-life case studies that will put flesh on the bones of our understanding. In the next chapter, we examine the insolvent entity problem as it has become manifest in cases of asbestos and defective pharmaceuticals, and as it is likely to arise in the 'next catastrophe'. Before doing so, it should be reiterated that what has been said in this chapter is sufficient to question the defensibility of the present position of tort victims faced with the insolvent entity problem. The economic arguments in favour of limited liability have little application to corporate groups. Indeed, the ability of parent companies to judgment-proof themselves means that they have inadequate incentives to take responsibility for properly organising group activities and for ensuring appropriate standards of conduct. Undoubtedly, this means that too much injurious activity takes place.[241]

[241] D. Millon, 'Piercing the Corporate Veil, Financial Responsibility, and the Limits of Limited Liability' (2007) 56 *Emory Law Journal* 1304, 1324–5.

4

Insolvent Entity Case Studies

4.1 Introduction

In this chapter, practical examples of the insolvent entity problem are given arising from the asbestos, pharmaceuticals, and other industries. These case studies feature several themes. First, there is the frequent use of high technology in the development of new products, which are found, eventually, to be toxic or dangerous to humans in some other way. Second, the use of such technologies is becoming more pervasive – meaning that persons are exposed to an ever-greater array of products that have the potential to cause harm. 'Given the tremendous number of new chemicals, pharmaceuticals, and other synthetic substances' being introduced into our lives, 'the probability that some of these substances may produce future injuries seems high.'[1] Third, the harmful effects of these products might become apparent over the medium or long term only, which gives rise to the potential for commission of torts on a mass scale. Fourth, parent companies in high-tech industries and network participants often take advantage of various ways of structuring legal relations (or judgment-proofing), so as to reduce the threat that liability claims pose to their assets. Fifth, the problems created by corporate groups and network participants undertaking modern, industrial processes giving rise to injuries on a mass scale frequently have been the subject of ex post government action designed to alleviate crises caused by shortfalls in recoveries. This demonstrates the need for better alignment of industrial activities and their full social costs and for better ways of achieving tort goals of compensation and deterrence. In sum, the mass-tort case studies in this chapter affirm the need to think through the insolvent entity problem and issues of extended liability as a matter of urgency.

[1] D. R. Anderson, 'Financing Asbestos Claims: Coverage Issues, Manville's Bankruptcy and the Claims Facility' (1987) 54 *Journal of Risk and Insurance* 429, 449. See also G. Vairo, 'Mass Torts Bankruptcies: The Who, the Why and the How' (2004) 78 *American Bankruptcy Law Journal* 93, 129. One reason for which the probability of future mass injury is high is that businesses discount future values: M. J. White, 'Asbestos and the Future of Mass Torts' (2004) 18 *Journal of Economic Perspectives* 183, 202.

4.2 Case Study I: Asbestos Claims

The case studies begin with the most significant product to have given rise to the insolvent entity problem – asbestos. Asbestos-related injury claims have been a prominent feature of the modern, industrial landscape – the 'mass tort that dwarfs all others'.[2] The numbers speak for themselves. In the United States alone, around thirty million people have been exposed occupationally. There have nearly one million claims for personal injury, suits against more than 8,400 businesses, 100 declared bankruptcies, and compensation of at least US$64 billion has been paid with provision made for payment of another $36 billion.[3] Approximately 107,000 persons worldwide die every year from exposure to asbestos.[4] It has been estimated that more than half a million persons could die from asbestos-related diseases in Europe between the years 1995 and 2030.[5] And yet mining and processing continue. Approximately 2.3 million tonnes of asbestos is produced annually.[6] Asbestos continues to be mined and/or used in building and manufacturing in Russia,[7] Kazakhstan, India, China,[8] and Mexico.[9] In India, approximately 100,000 workers are employed in the asbestos industry,[10] and tens of thousands are involved in other countries. But the problem of asbestos-related disease is only starting to emerge in the developing world.[11] It has been estimated that a total of five to ten million people might die worldwide before asbestos is banned everywhere and exposure to it ceases.[12]

[2] D. Hensler and M. Peterson, 'Understanding Mass Personal Injury Litigation: A Socio-legal Analysis' (1993) 59 *Brooklyn Law Review* 961, 1004.

[3] B. Mattock, A. Sackett, and J. Shipp, 'Clearing Up the False Premises Underlying the Push for Asbestos Trust "Transparency"' (2014) 23 *Widener Law Journal* 725, 735; E. F. Sherman, 'The Evolution of Asbestos Litigation' (2014) 88 *Tulane Law Review* 1021, 1023; J. Sanders, 'Risky Business: Causation in Asbestos Cancer Cases (and Beyond?)' in R. Goldberg (ed.), *Perspectives on Causation* (2011), pp. 12–13; A. Gray, 'Insurers Face Extra $15bn Asbestos Bill', *Financial Times*, 29 November 2016, available at: www.ft.com/content/00adf2a4-b5ae-11e6-961e-a1acd97f622d.

[4] D. Ryle, 'Killer Dust' (2014), available at: https://mosaicscience.com/story/killer-dust.

[5] J. McCulloch and G. Tweedale, *Defending the Indefensible* (2008), p. 11.

[6] McCulloch and Tweedale, *Defending the Indefensible*, p. 269.

[7] A. Boggio, *Compensating Asbestos Victims: Law and the Dark Side of Industrialization* (2013), p. 4 (Asbest City producing 25 per cent of the chrysotile asbestos used worldwide).

[8] McCulloch and Tweedale, *Defending the Indefensible*, pp. 12 and 238–44.

[9] J. Morris and A. Avila, 'Disturbing Epidemic in US and Mexico', BBC News Online, 21 July 2010, available at: www.bbc.co.uk/news/world-10633083.

[10] M. Dutta, 'The Indian Government's Complicity in the Asbestos Scandal', in D. Allen and L. Kazan-Allen (eds.), *India's Asbestos Time Bomb* (London, International Ban Asbestos Secretariat, 2008), p. 15.

[11] McCulloch and Tweedale, *Defending the Indefensible*, pp. 10–11.

[12] McCulloch and Tweedale, *Defending the Indefensible*, p. 11.

'Asbestos' is a generic term referring to six types of fibrous mineral with various properties that have proven attractive in large-scale industrial usage. Asbestos combines lightness of weight, flexibility, and toughness with resistance to fire and heat. The material can be used commercially in a number of important ways – especially for building products (such as roofing, walls, insulation, and cement sheeting), and for friction products (such as car brakes, clutches, and transmissions).[13] The fire-retardant qualities of asbestos have ensured that it has been used extensively in buildings, cars, and ships the world over.[14]

Asbestos is mined and then fed into crushers at a mill before being sorted. The processes of mining, milling, and manufacturing asbestos-based products cause the release of dust.[15] Frequently in the past, UK workplaces undertaking these processes were enveloped in asbestos haze and asbestos workers were exposed to the dust. But, given its widespread applications, most of the workers who came into contact with asbestos were second-wave victims employed outside the asbestos industry itself, in industrial settings such as oil refineries, building sites, shipyards, and car repair businesses.[16] Because asbestos has been used so widely, a third wave of exposure has arisen through building demolition and renovation works[17] and through occupation of buildings and structures containing it. Dust from all of these sources might be brought unwittingly into ordinary homes, often on workers' clothing – thus coming to be inhaled by all householders. In addition, there is a level of asbestos ambient in the general urban environment. Electron microscope studies show that 'the lungs of nearly all adult urban dwellers contain[] asbestos fibres',[18] although these low levels are not thought to be harmful.[19]

Asbestos fibres can 'penetrate deep into the most sensitive areas of the lungs . . . where they can trigger pathological reactions'.[20] Indeed, 'the fibres can continue to divide in the lungs and also migrate through the tissue.'[21] Asbestos-related claims encompass three diseases: asbestosis,

13 US Government Accountability Office, 'Asbestos Injury Compensation: The Role and Administration of Asbestos Trusts' (2011), pp. 6–7.

14 G. Tweedale, *Magic Mineral to Killer Dust* (2000), p. 5.

15 Tweedale, *Magic Mineral to Killer Dust*, p. 12.

16 McCulloch and Tweedale, *Defending the Indefensible*, p. 34.

17 D. S. Jackson QC, 'Report of the Special Commission of Inquiry into the Medical Research and Compensation Fund' (2000), p. 59.

18 McCulloch and Tweedale, *Defending the Indefensible*, p. 193.

19 Jackson, 'Report of the Special Commission, Annexure "J"', p. 119.

20 Tweedale, *Magic Mineral to Killer Dust*, p. 13.

21 Tweedale, *Magic Mineral to Killer Dust*, p. 13.

which is a chronic lung fibrosis that places an increasing strain upon the lungs; mesothelioma, which involves a virulent malignancy of the lining of the lungs or abdomen; and lung cancer.[22] Each of these diseases usually causes the death of the sufferer, either by itself or in combination with other hazards such as cigarette smoking.[23] Each of the diseases has a long latency period, meaning that there is a long time period (usually between twenty and forty years) between exposure and the onset of diagnosable illness.[24] Little was done about the problem of asbestos until the numbers of victims became hard to ignore. This is one of the reasons for which the number of asbestos-related disease cases has climbed so high, reaching epidemic levels.[25]

Many stories could be told about asbestos manufacturing and its consequences, some better documented than others. Turner & Newall was a major UK producer.[26] It assumed multinational status when it integrated backwards by taking control of a Rhodesian company, which was in the process of buying asbestos mines.[27] The group went on to acquire multiple foreign subsidiaries engaged in mining and manufacturing of asbestos products.[28] It expanded quickly, developing into a multi-divisional group by the early 1930s. By the end of the 1930s, Turner & Newall controlled 20 per cent of the global asbestos market and was paying its shareholders consistently good dividends.[29] For decades, the company was the largest importer of asbestos fibre. By 1970, it had an international workforce of 36,775, and profits of more than £7 million per annum.[30]

At the beginning of the twentieth century, official concern had arisen in the United Kingdom about the potential dangers of asbestos. The Chief Inspector of Factories and Workshops' Annual Report for 1906

[22] Tweedale, *Magic Mineral to Killer Dust*, p. vii.

[23] Tweedale, *Magic Mineral to Killer Dust*, p. 141.

[24] *In re T & N Ltd* [2006] 1 WLR 1728, 1742.

[25] *In re T & N Ltd* [2006] 1 WLR 1728, 1739.

[26] For the history of asbestos elsewhere, see: for Europe, Boggio, *Compensating Asbestos Victims*; for Australia, G. Haigh, *Asbestos House: The Secret History of James Hardie Industries* (2006); D. S. Jackson QC, 'Report of the Special Commission of Inquiry into the Medical Research and Compensation Fund' (2004); for the United States, S. J. Carroll et al., *Asbestos Litigation* (2005), and Sherman, 'The Evolution of Asbestos Litigation', 1021.

[27] Tweedale, *Magic Mineral to Killer Dust*, p. 5.

[28] Tweedale, *Magic Mineral to Killer Dust*, p. 8. '[D]uring the golden years of asbestos production, [Turner & Newall] owned and operated 14 plants in GB and owned 16 businesses overseas': Boggio, *Compensating Asbestos Victims*, p. 81.

[29] Tweedale, *Magic Mineral to Killer Dust*, p. 9.

[30] Tweedale, *Magic Mineral to Killer Dust*, p. 10.

recorded that asbestos dust seemed to be causing the premature deaths of workers.[31] It came to be accepted that there was a need for proper ventilation of buildings in which asbestos was handled, although much of the industry remained beset by poor practices for decades.[32] By the late 1920s, a dozen medical publications featured reports about asbestosis.[33] In 1928, the UK government commissioned a study of worker health in the industry. The resulting publication by Merewether and Price, 'Report on Effects of Asbestos Dust on the Lungs and Dust Suppression in the Asbestos Industry' (1930), found a strong correlation between exposure to asbestos dust and asbestosis. Of those workers in the asbestos industry with twenty years' or more experience, four out of five suffered from pulmonary fibrosis.[34] In response, the UK government determined that health regulation was required and passed the Asbestos Industry Regulations 1931. The Regulations dealt with the main manufacturing processes and required the taking of precautions such as the use of masks and ventilation at workplaces and proper cleaning.[35] Moreover, the asbestos industry was brought within the ambit of the Workmen's Compensation Act 1925, injured workers being entitled to industry-funded compensation for asbestosis, as were their dependants after death.[36] Compensation claims increased steadily over time, eventually numbering in the tens of thousands.[37]

Unfortunately, the substantive provisions and implementation of the Asbestos Industry Regulations 1931 reflected a significant degree of regulatory capture. The Regulations had been drafted after 'negotiation' with industry: the UK government 'had acquiesced in the industry's wish to confine regulation to asbestos fibre alone in its dry and raw state and to certain dusty manufacturing processes. Many workers outside the scheduled areas were excluded from dust protection'.[38] And companies like Turner & Newall took advantage of their ability to lobby the Home Office for exemptions from the Regulations, so that many of their operations

[31] Tweedale, *Magic Mineral to Killer Dust*, p. 17.
[32] Tweedale, *Magic Mineral to Killer Dust*, pp. 23–4.
[33] Tweedale, *Magic Mineral to Killer Dust*, p. 17. [34] Haigh, *Asbestos House*, p. 23.
[35] Tweedale, *Magic Mineral to Killer Dust*, pp. 27–8.
[36] Workmen's Compensation (Silicosis and Asbestosis) Act 1930; Asbestos Industry (Asbestosis) Scheme 1931. See A. McKenna, 'An Overview of the Legal Landscape of Negligently-Inflicted Asbestos Related Conditions' [2011] *Journal of Personal Injury Law* 205, 207; Tweedale, *Magic Mineral to Killer Dust*, p. 21. Lung cancer did not become compensable under the Act until the 1980s.
[37] Tweedale, *Magic Mineral to Killer Dust*, p. 276.
[38] Tweedale, *Magic Mineral to Killer Dust*, p. 28.

continued to be unregulated.[39] Even with respect to those aspects of manufacture that were covered by the Regulations, Turner & Newall's 'board and the unit companies did what they could to limit the scope and cost of the Regulations'.[40] This was to be the constant pattern, not only with respect to that company's compliance with externally imposed standards, but with respect to the industry's compliance as a whole.

By 1947, the link between asbestos and lung cancer was established, and the Chief Inspector of Factories published scientific data to this effect in his Annual Report.[41] These data were confirmed by the American Medical Association in 1949,[42] and in a study undertaken at the request of Turner & Newall in 1953.[43] By the 1950s, it was known also that asbestos could cause changes in the pleura (the lining of the chest), such as thickening, adhesions, and the formation of plaques.[44] The link between asbestos and mesothelioma was confirmed in a 1960 scientific paper.[45] The crucial point about mesothelioma was that its causation was now thought to be unrelated to dosage – so that a single asbestos fibre might cause it to develop. Indeed, individuals have developed the disease after exposures of less than a day.[46] These facts undermined the value of the Asbestos Industry Regulations, which had been predicated on the idea that the cleaner the air, the lower the dust count, and the lower the chances of disease contraction.[47]

During the 1950s and 1960s, the health implications of exposure to asbestos were obvious. It was understood that workers returning home from mines or factories would bring asbestos into the home, thereby endangering other householders.[48] Simply living in the vicinity of an asbestos factory created significant risks of contracting asbestos-related

[39] Tweedale, *Magic Mineral to Killer Dust*, p. 32.
[40] Tweedale, *Magic Mineral to Killer Dust*, p. 32.
[41] Tweedale, *Magic Mineral to Killer Dust*, pp. 146–7.
[42] Editorial, 'Asbestosis and Cancer of the Lung' (1949) 140 *Journal of the American Medical Association* 1219–20.
[43] Published as R. Doll, 'Mortality from Lung Cancer in Asbestos Workers' (1955) 12 *British Journal of Industrial Medicine* 81.
[44] Tweedale, *Magic Mineral to Killer Dust*, p. 152.
[45] J. C. Wagner et al., 'Diffuse Pleural Mesotheliomas and Asbestos Exposure in the North-Western Cape Province' (1960) 17 *British Journal of Industrial Medicine* 260.
[46] McCulloch and Tweedale, *Defending the Indefensible*, p. 6. But see now Chapter 11.
[47] Tweedale, *Magic Mineral to Killer Dust*, p. 180.
[48] McKenna, 'An Overview of the Legal Landscape', 223; M. L. Newhouse and H. Thompson, 'Mesothelioma of Pleura and Peritoneum Following Exposure to Asbestos in the London Area' (1965) 22 *British Journal of Industrial Medicine* 261.

diseases.[49] Yet mining of asbestos fibre and production of various products based upon it continued.[50]

In 1969, the UK government introduced new regulations to protect against the known health dangers of asbestos, reducing permissible dust concentrations.[51] However, compliance with the law was 'extremely variable'[52] (as was compliance with relevant laws in Europe as a whole).[53] One reason for this was that the taking of costly precautions in order to lower dust concentrations reduced the profitability of asbestos milling and product manufacture.[54] Another reason was that the regulatory system was itself deeply flawed.[55] Thus, the Factory Inspectorate was chronically understaffed, given its large workload. Until the 1970s, few inspectors had specialist skills. Moreover, the Factory Inspectorate preferred to deal with problems through dialogue with industry, which was not always an effective means of protecting people. After the commencement of the Asbestos Regulations 1969, the Factory Inspectorate prosecuted Turner & Newall for breaching the statutory exposure intensity limits, but this was an exceptional case.[56]

The passage of the Health & Safety at Work Act 1974 marked a more definite turning point. The legislation sought to ensure safe working conditions for all workers. It imposed obligations upon employers, including the exercise of environmental control over noxious substances.[57] Manufacturers were obliged to ensure that their products were safe. This led to the labelling of risky products. The Asbestos (Licensing) Regulations 1984 banned importation into the United Kingdom of two kinds of asbestos and again reduced permissible asbestos air concentration levels. As a result of the ban, the volume of asbestos imports fell rapidly.[58] The 1984 Regulations were followed by the passage of the EC Product Liability Directive 1985, implemented in the United Kingdom by the Consumer Protection Act 1987. This legislation created 'strict' liability for the supply of defective products and permitted actions against a number of actors in the chain of supply (as to which, see Chapter 7). A modest proportion of

49 Newhouse and Thompson, 'Mesothelioma of Pleura'.
50 Tweedale, *Magic Mineral to Killer Dust*, p. viii.
51 Tweedale, *Magic Mineral to Killer Dust*, pp. 11 and 207.
52 Tweedale, *Magic Mineral to Killer Dust*, p. 162.
53 McCulloch and Tweedale, *Defending the Indefensible*, p. 109.
54 McCulloch and Tweedale, *Defending the Indefensible*, p. 120.
55 Tweedale, *Magic Mineral to Killer Dust*, pp. 162–3.
56 Tweedale, *Magic Mineral to Killer Dust*, p. 213.
57 Tweedale, *Magic Mineral to Killer Dust*, p. 239.
58 Tweedale, *Magic Mineral to Killer Dust*, p. 256.

claims made against Turner & Newall have been product liability claims,[59] brought mostly by non-employees.[60]

Various developments contributed to a rise in the number and size of legal claims brought against Turner & Newall and other asbestos manufacturers. One was an amendment in 1963 to the Limitation Act 1939, which formerly required claims for personal injury to be brought within six years of the commission of a tort, but which now extended the time available to one year from *discovery* of illness.[61] Unions began to support workers in their claims for compensation.[62] Legal Aid became available as well.[63] Moreover, the proof of claims became easier as medical advances facilitated the diagnosis of disease and understanding of its aetiology.[64] Between 1973 and 1976, both claim numbers and the average costs of settlement doubled.[65] Insurers began to push for use of alternatives to asbestos.[66] The growing publicity of its dangers resulted in users switching to alternatives products, such as when British Rail announced that it would substitute fibreglass for asbestos insulation.[67] The switch to safer materials combined with reduced UK manufacturing activity to lower demand for asbestos-based products.[68] Because asbestos manufacturing had been such an important part of Turner & Newall's operations, the collapse in the market reduced its profitability and led to large losses. In 1982, the company had to reorganise in insolvency.[69] By 1995, the UK parent had relinquished asbestos cement and mining interests in India and Africa.[70] In 1997, Turner & Newall disappeared as an independent entity after being taken over by Federal Mogul, Inc., a US engineering firm.[71]

The European Union banned the importation and use of all asbestos products in 2005.[72] However, much asbestos-based material remains in

[59] T & N UK Asbestos Trust, 'Trustees' Annual Report 2013' (2013), p. 5.
[60] Boggio, *Compensating Asbestos Victims*, p. 110.
[61] Tweedale, *Magic Mineral to Killer Dust*, pp. 180–1. See now Limitation Act 1981, ss. 11-11A.
[62] Boggio, *Compensating Asbestos Victims*, p. 88. Claims generally were settled, and at reasonable levels of compensation: ibid., p. 94.
[63] Tweedale, *Magic Mineral to Killer Dust*, pp. 180–1.
[64] Tweedale, *Magic Mineral to Killer Dust*, p. 181.
[65] Tweedale, *Magic Mineral to Killer Dust*, p. 233.
[66] Tweedale, *Magic Mineral to Killer Dust*, p. 215.
[67] Tweedale, *Magic Mineral to Killer Dust*, p. 187.
[68] Tweedale, *Magic Mineral to Killer Dust*, p. 256.
[69] Tweedale, *Magic Mineral to Killer Dust*, p. 258.
[70] Tweedale, *Magic Mineral to Killer Dust*, p. 260.
[71] Tweedale, *Magic Mineral to Killer Dust*, p. 275.
[72] Commission Directive 1999/77/EC of 26 July 1999 on the marketing and use of certain dangerous substances and preparations, OJ 1999 No. L207/18.

the United Kingdom and other advanced countries. It is to be found still in buildings, including offices, schools, and private residences.[73] Tradespersons and others are at risk if they interfere with it. Indeed, a 'striking' proportion of those claiming for asbestos-related diseases comprise construction workers, electricians, plumbers, and painters.[74] Such diseases have appeared also in building maintenance personnel and building custodians.[75] No general call for remediation has been made yet in the United Kingdom. But whereas the dangers of the substance have been fully acknowledged in much of the Western world,[76] this is not the case everywhere.

There seems to be little doubt that manufacturers were at fault in the ways in which they continued to handle, process, promote, and distribute asbestos products despite growing awareness of the risks to health and well-being. A key date in ascertaining fault was the passage of the Asbestos Industry Regulations in 1931, which was 'official recognition of asbestos manufacture as a "dangerous trade"' and signalled a real problem for the asbestos-producing companies.[77] Following passage of the Regulations, fault became evident in a number of ways, such as: industry lobbying of the Home Office for exemptions from the Regulations,[78] argument that jobs such as spraying asbestos material onto walls and ceilings were outside their ambit,[79] and the continued use of sloppy practices. Thus, Turner & Newall continued repairing ships' boiler matrasses without the use of dust extractors in direct contravention of the Regulations.[80] A dust extraction system used at its Armley plant was not effective in safeguarding workers; it was found to have made only a modest 'contribution' to reducing dust.[81] Again, although Turner & Newall was advised by the Factory Inspectorate in 1962 to find a replacement for the asbestos used in insulation materials, the company significantly delayed exploration of alternatives.[82]

[73] Seventy-five per cent of UK schools feature buildings with asbestos: All-Party Parliamentary Group on Occupational Health and Safety, 'Asbestos in Schools: The Need for Action' (2012), p. 2.

[74] McCulloch and Tweedale, *Defending the Indefensible*, p. 211.

[75] McCulloch and Tweedale, *Defending the Indefensible*, p. 219.

[76] See, e.g., Asbestos Safety and Eradication Agency Act 2013 (Cth), providing for a new government body to oversee the Asbestos Safety and Eradication Agency, 'National Strategic Plan on Asbestos Awareness and Management 2014–2018' (2014).

[77] Tweedale, *Magic Mineral to Killer Dust*, p. 70.

[78] Tweedale, *Magic Mineral to Killer Dust*, p. 35 (exemption as to the work of laggers).

[79] Tweedale, *Magic Mineral to Killer Dust*, p. 37.

[80] Tweedale, *Magic Mineral to Killer Dust*, p. 33.

[81] Tweedale, *Magic Mineral to Killer Dust*, p. 126.

[82] Tweedale, *Magic Mineral to Killer Dust*, p. 139.

Compliance with modern standards of practice was better at UK-based companies than at Turner & Newall's foreign subsidiaries. This was apparent at a number of stages. After the passage of the 1931 Regulations, conditions in UK factories improved to some extent, but there was no change at either Canadian or southern African mines. Indeed, while UK manufacturers ceased importing blue asbestos in 1970, mining continued in South Africa until 1996.[83] As government regulation of asbestos manufacture and use in developed countries became more pervasive, there was a shift in activity to second- and third-world countries.[84] This is consistent with the idea that corporate groups involved in the manufacture of asbestos have engaged in regulatory arbitrage and the exploitation of regulatory gaps in order to profit – even at the expense of life and health.

Although Turner & Newall was statutorily bound to pay compensation for asbestos-related injuries, it tried to escape liability when it could or to reduce amounts payable. Thus, medical opinions were challenged, responsibility was denied, and/or legal actions were vigorously defended.[85] What is even more disturbing is that Turner & Newall, along with many other companies in the industry,[86] strove to ensure that as little information as possible about the true dangers of asbestos was disseminated. '[K]knowledge was kept from the workers, customers and the local community until it was forced out of the company by other parties.'[87] In the meantime, asbestos companies funded 'research' bodies to conduct studies that sought to downplay the facts. 'The global industry [established] a number of professional and semi-autonomous associations to defend work conditions in mines and factories, conduct medical research, and assuage public fears.'[88] Bodies such as the Asbestos Research Council in the United Kingdom and the Industrial Hygiene Foundation in the United States argued the case for the use of asbestos and for delaying regulation.[89] During the 1960s and 1970s, they painted a picture of asbestos as a product which enhanced industrial safety and which had no substitute[90] – both of these claims being incorrect.

[83] McCulloch and Tweedale, *Defending the Indefensible*, pp. 227 and 237.
[84] McCulloch and Tweedale, *Defending the Indefensible*, pp. 230ff.
[85] Tweedale, *Magic Mineral to Killer Dust*, p. 104.
[86] McCulloch and Tweedale, *Defending the Indefensible*, pp. 53ff.
[87] R. C. Warren, 'The Enforcement of Social Accountability – Turner and Newall and the Asbestos Crisis' (1997) 5 *Corporate Governance* 52, 55.
[88] McCulloch and Tweedale, *Defending the Indefensible*, p. 59.
[89] McCulloch and Tweedale, *Defending the Indefensible*, pp. 59–60 and 75.
[90] McCulloch and Tweedale, *Defending the Indefensible*, pp. 114–15.

It is arguable that, as time progressed, what might be called 'negligence' or carelessness in the manufacture and distribution of asbestos products became recklessness – that is to say, that a subjective disregard of the real risks to health of the use of asbestos was evident.[91] As Geoffrey Tweedale asserts, Turner & Newall's 'attitude towards matters of health over so many years [w]as strikingly irresponsible'.[92] Indeed, well after the first evidence of the connection between asbestos exposure and disease emerged, manufacture of asbestos products *increased*. Between 1960 and 1980, worldwide production of asbestos products entered its fastest period of growth.[93] It seems clear also that governmental efforts in the United Kingdom and elsewhere to protect workers, consumers, and others were inadequate. Regulatory failure manifested itself, for example, in UK Home Office agreements to exemptions from regulations and in under-enforcement by the Factory Inspectorate.[94] Although union activism might have reinforced official efforts undertaken to ameliorate the risks of working with asbestos, unions were not active on this issue until comparatively late in UK production history.[95] The overall effect of governmental failure was to shift many of the costs of asbestos production to workers and to the state itself.[96]

In Chapter 3, the practice of structuring legal relations (judgment-proofing) within corporate groups was explained at the theoretical level. This practice has been evident in the asbestos industry, as groups have become aware, not merely of the risks to health of asbestos, but of the potential scale of their liabilities. Although strategic reorganisations have been attempted in the United Kingdom, they have not been very successful in freeing asbestos companies from their liabilities.[97] However, Cape plc managed to achieve two relative 'success' stories.[98] Cape plc was able

[91] D. Rosenberg, 'The Dusting of America: A Story of Asbestos – Carnage, Cover-Up, and Litigation' (1986) 99 *Harvard Law Review* 1693, 1695. This reckless attitude continues today on the part of asbestos industry bodies, such as the International Chrysotile Association: see www.chrysotileassociation.com/en/.

[92] Tweedale, *Magic Mineral to Killer Dust*, p. 279.

[93] McCulloch and Tweedale, *Defending the Indefensible*, p. 84.

[94] In Australia, there were advance notifications to mine owners of government inspections of asbestos mines: S. Engel and B. Martin, 'Union Carbide and James Hardie: Lessons in Politics and Power' (2006) 20 *Global Society* 475.

[95] McCulloch and Tweedale, *Defending the Indefensible*, p. 63.

[96] McCulloch and Tweedale, *Defending the Indefensible*, p. 82.

[97] Jackson, 'Report of the Special Commission', p. 19.

[98] See *Lubbe* v. *Cape plc* [2000] 1 WLR 1545, 1549; P. Nygh, 'The Liability of Multi-national Corporations for the Torts of Their Subsidiaries' (2002) 3 *European Business Organization Law Review* 51, 54–5.

to separate itself from asbestos-related claims arising from foreign operations in both South Africa and the United States of America. From 1893, its predecessor, Cape Asbestos Co Ltd, operated blue asbestos mines in the Northern Cape Province of South Africa. In 1948, the company restructured by transferring hitherto directly operated mines to a new South African subsidiary, Cape Blue Mines (Pty) Ltd, and vested the shares in most of its South African subsidiaries in an intermediary South African holding company (Cape Asbestos South Africa (Pty) Ltd (CASAP)). Thus, the UK parent that became known as Cape plc was twice removed from the South African companies that undertook the mining and processing of asbestos. Between 1979 and 1989, Cape plc sold its asbestos businesses in South Africa to unrelated third parties. By the time the litigation in *Lubbe* v. *Cape plc*[99] commenced in 1997, Cape plc no longer had any assets at all in South Africa, meaning that tort victims had to find a basis for suit in the United Kingdom in order to access assets held there (as to which, see Chapter 11).

Cape plc was successful also in separating itself from US liabilities.[100] Its liabilities were most closely identified there with North American Asbestos Corporation (NAAC), a fully owned subsidiary incorporated in Illinois in 1953 in order to continue the work of Cape's former US agent. NAAC marketed South African-mined asbestos products for several decades, being remunerated by way of 'commission' on sales. Employees of the Pittsburgh Corning Corporation were exposed to asbestos dust from Cape products and thousands of actions were brought against NAAC. In anticipation of the large number of suits that could affect it, Cape plc devised an 'exit strategy'.[101] Part of this strategy involved selling NAAC's assets and transferring shares in NAAC to a newly incorporated shell company called Cape International and Overseas Ltd. A new Illinois corporation was registered, Continental Products Corporation (CPC), and its shares were transferred to the former vice president of NAAC, Gerry Morgan. Sales of asbestos were procured thereafter from a Liechtenstein-based company, AMC, which was wholly owned by the local lawyer who represented Cape businesses. CPC acted as AMC's agent in the United States, but with no authority contractually to bind AMC. Subsequently, Cape plc chose not to defend lawsuits brought against it in the United States (having removed all of its

[99] [2000] 1 WLR 1545.

[100] See A. Boggio, 'Linking Corporate Power to Corporate Structures: An Empirical Analysis' (2012) 22 *Social and Legal Studies* 107, 117–18.

[101] Boggio, 'Linking Corporate Power', 117.

assets from that jurisdiction), and claimants successful in US courts found that they were unable to enforce judgments obtained against Cape plc in the United Kingdom because the English Court of Appeal ruled that Cape plc had not been 'present' in the United States at the time of the exposures.[102]

Elsewhere in the world, further notable attempts have been made at judgment-proofing group assets from asbestos liabilities. The James Hardie group of companies developed an elaborate judgment-proofing scheme. This group dominated the manufacture of asbestos products in Australia. Two subsidiary companies, James Hardie and Company Pty Ltd (Coy) and Jsekarb Pty Ltd (Jsekarb), were involved in its manufacture.[103] These companies failed to meet proper standards of asbestos handling, so that workers and others were exposed to asbestos fibres.[104] This was despite the fact that the company had been alerted to the report by Merewether and Price and that, by the early 1930s, 'the signs, symptoms, radiological appearance and pathology of asbestosis [were] well-understood' in Australia.[105] By 1939, a Victorian Department of Health official recommended that asbestos workers be informed of risks.[106] But Hardie took action to reduce dust exposure only in 1961,[107] and its products did not carry health warnings for another eighteen years.[108] In common with other asbestos producers, Hardie was accused of covering up the risks. In 1977, its insurer, QBE, accused it of having 'adopted a course of deliberately attempting to conceal facts known to it relating to asbestos hazards'.[109] Although Hardie stopped manufacturing asbestos products in 1987, the 'long tail' of injuries meant that Hardie companies' estimated liabilities grew dramatically during the late 1990s.[110] The retention of its asbestos 'legacy' came to be seen as a threat to the

[102] *Adams* v. *Cape Industries plc* [1990] Ch 433, discussed in Chapter 10 (veil-piercing); S. Baughen, 'Multinationals and the Export of Hazard' (1995) 58 *Modern Law Review* 54, 58.

[103] See Jackson, 'Report of the Special Commission'.

[104] McCulloch and Tweedale, *Defending the Indefensible*, p. 109.

[105] Haigh, *Asbestos House*, pp. 27–8. It has been held judicially that James Hardie had been aware of the dangers of asbestos since 1938: *State Rail Authority (NSW)* v. *Wallaby Grip Ltd* (1999) 18 NSWCCR 193.

[106] Haigh, *Asbestos House*, p. 73. [107] Haigh, *Asbestos House*, p. 86.

[108] I. Verrender, 'Hardie's Legal Marathon Ends with Statement of the Bleeding Obvious', *The Age*, 5 May 2012, available at: www.theage.com.au/business/hardies-legal-marathon-ends-with-statement-of-the-bleeding-obvious-20120504-1y4c5.html.

[109] Haigh, *Asbestos House*, pp. 139–40.

[110] It is estimated that 55,000 Australians will die from asbestos-related diseases by 2020: Verrender, 'Hardie's Legal Marathon'.

commercial viability of the group.[111] These liabilities impeded its ability to raise capital and to obtain loan funds at competitive rates.[112]

James Hardie's response was to restructure the group with the intention of minimising the impact upon its assets of liabilities for asbestos-related harms.[113] This was done by diverting business opportunities away from former asbestos-producing subsidiaries[114] and by divesting them of remaining operations.[115] By 1995, Coy was largely inactive, yet it was paying the parent James Hardie Industries Ltd (JHIL) annual fees of A$20 million for the 'management' of its assets. But JHIL intended to put most of those assets beyond the reach of asbestos claimants.[116] Coy sold its intellectual property rights to a new group company, James Hardie Research, and also sold its own controlled companies. It then had cash and other assets worth A$385 million, from which $144.8 million was paid over in dividends to JHIL. The effect of these transactions was to reduce Coy's ability to meet future asbestos-related liabilities.[117]

Subsequently, the Medical Research and Compensation Fund Ltd (MRCF), a company limited by guarantee, was incorporated and severed from the group. Shares in the 'legacy' companies (both Coy and Jsekarb) were transferred to the ownership of the MRCF. The MRCF became the trustee of the MRCF Trust. The total assets available to it, including those of its subsidiaries, were valued at A$293 million. JHIL issued a press release asserting that these funds were sufficient to meet expected liabilities,[118] although the actuarial figures upon which this statement was based did not include new claims against the group and greatly understated the size of expected liabilities.[119] JHIL was to make certain

[111] Another purported aim of the restructure was to reduce the withholding tax liability on dividends paid from the United States to Australia. However, this aim was undermined by a subsequent amendment to Australian tax laws: Jackson, 'Report of the Special Commission', [2.46] and [25.25].

[112] Jackson, 'Report of the Special Commission', p. 8.

[113] *Australian Securities and Investments Commission* v. *Hellicar* (2012) 247 CLR 345, [184] and [201].

[114] Jackson, 'Report of the Special Commission', p. 98.

[115] Haigh, *Asbestos House*, pp. 172–3.

[116] Jackson, 'Report of the Special Commission', p. 129.

[117] Jackson, 'Report of the Special Commission', p. 127.

[118] Jackson, 'Report of the Special Commission', p. 9.

[119] Jackson, 'Report of the Special Commission', pp. 30 and 260–1. Successful actions were later commenced by the Australian Securities and Investments Commission against former directors of James Hardie for breach of their directors' duties to the company to act with care and diligence: see *Australian Securities and Investments Commission* v. *Hellicar* (2012) 247 CLR 345.

payments to Coy and Jsekarb in order to discharge its obligations to claimants. In return, the MRCF agreed to indemnify JHIL against future asbestos-related suits.[120] This meant that asbestos liabilities no longer needed to be reported as annual expenses of the group.[121]

The New South Wales Supreme Court subsequently approved a scheme of arrangement under which James Hardie Industries NV (JHINV), based in the Netherlands, became the new group holding company. Under a share-swap, JHINV became the holder of all shares in JHIL. The scheme proposal included the issue of partly paid shares held by JHINV in JHIL,[122] which would have enabled JHIL to raise a further A$1.9 billion, if necessary, in order to meet its liabilities. After the relocation and the transfer of significant assets to JHINV by way of a reduction of capital and a large dividend payment by JHIL,[123] the partly paid shares were cancelled. Moreover, JHIL entered into an agreement with JHINV not to make any asbestos-related claims against it and to indemnify JHINV for losses arising from asbestos-related claims as well.[124] Although said to be for tax reasons,[125] the move to the Netherlands was inspired by the desire to separate group assets from liability claims[126] – the Netherlands having no treaty with Australia for the enforcement of judgments.[127] In the words of one commentator, the 'legal picture which emerges from the conglomerate restructuring is both frightening and depressing: what was once the parent company of subsidiaries that had dealt in asbestos for more than half a century became a company estranged from the conglomerate, with no operating business, and negligible assets'.[128]

The MRCF was nearing exhaustion when the New South Wales government stepped in to negotiate its renewal. By mid-2004, future asbestos claims had a minimum net present value of A$1.5 billion, although the

120 Jackson, 'Report of the Special Commission', p. 28.
121 Jackson, Report of the Special Commission, p. 12.
122 H. Anderson, 'Veil Piercing and Corporate Groups – An Australian Perspective' [2010] *New Zealand Law Review* 1, 7.
123 S. H. C. Lo, *In Search of Corporate Accountability: Liabilities of Corporate Participants* (2015), p. 48; Boggio, 'Linking Corporate Power', 113.
124 Lo, *In Search of Corporate Accountability*, p. 51.
125 Jackson, 'Report of the Special Commission', pp. 11 and 33. The company ended up paying more tax after the redomicile and has since moved to Ireland: Verrender, 'Hardie's Legal Marathon'.
126 E. Sexton, 'Dust to Dust', *Sydney Morning Herald*, 14 March 2009, available at: http://business.smh.com.au/business/dust-to-dust-20090323-8xww.html.
127 Boggio, 'Linking Corporate Power', 114.
128 Boggio, 'Linking Corporate Power', 114.

Jackson Commission of Inquiry, set up to examine the circumstances which led to the MRCF's deficiency, estimated that A$2.24 billion might have been required adequately to fund it.[129] Were it not for government intervention, it is likely that thousands of tort claimants would have gone without compensation. Agreement on a compensation plan was achieved after six years of concerted effort by unions, victims' groups, and the NSW government.[130] The plan provided for payments into the fund that could be worth A$3–4 billion over its lifetime.[131] However, replenishment of the fund remains dependent upon the availability of free cash flows from James Hardie, and the 2014 Trustees' Report indicated that the Fund had just over A$65 million of assets from which to meet immediate claims.[132] From 2017, it was expected to be unable to meet claims as and when they fall due.[133] In the meantime, James Hardie Industries NV relocated to Ireland, this time more clearly for tax reasons.[134]

Many companies previously involved in asbestos product manufacture and associated processes either have been forced into insolvency or have sought to reorganise. In part, this has been the result of the long latency of disease and larger-than-expected claim numbers, the great expense of treating asbestos-related diseases,[135] and inadequate insurance cover.[136]

[129] Jackson, 'Report of the Special Commission', pp. 7, 56, and 62.

[130] Anon., 'James Hardie Compensation Battle Finally Over', *The Age*, 8 February 2007, available at: www.theage.com.au/news/business/james-hardie-compensation-battle-finally-over/2007/02/08/1170524196283.html. See also James Hardie Industries NV and New South Wales Government, 'Amended and Restated Final Funding Agreement', 21 November 2006, available at: www.ir.jameshardie.com.au/jh/asbestos_compensation.jsp. The agreement, establishing the Asbestos Injuries Compensation Fund, excludes claims for property damage and financial loss: ibid., pp. 91–2; and the State of NSW is not to alter by legislation the common law applicable to the determination of dust disease compensation cases: ibid., p. 114.

[131] Anon., 'James Hardie Shareholders to Vote on Asbestos Compo Deal', ABC Online, 1 February 2007, available at: www.abc.net.au/news/newsitems/200702/s1837633.htm.

[132] The fund can borrow a maximum of A$320 million in order to meet shortfalls: Asbestos Injuries Compensation Fund, 'General Purpose Financial Report' (March 2014), pp. 6–7, available at: www.aicf.org.au/docs/AICF%202014%20Financial%20Accounts.pdf.

[133] Anon., 'James Hardie Faces Asbestos Payout Shortfall', *Financial Times*, 15 September 2014, available at: www.ft.com/intl/fastft/206022/james-hardie-faces-asbestos-payout-shortfall.

[134] Boggio, 'Linking Corporate Power', 116.

[135] 'Even a few such suits can lead to significant damage awards, and numerous suits can tax the financial assets of even large corporations': T. A. Gormley and D. A. Matsa, 'Growing Out of Trouble? Corporate Responses to Liability Risk' (2011) 24 *Review of Financial Studies* 2781, 2786.

[136] See Chapter 3.

In some cases, insolvency has resulted from the structuring of legal relations in order to protect group assets. The 'strategic' use of insolvency and bankruptcy processes in order to confine asbestos and other tort liabilities to undercapitalised operating companies was the subject of initial observations in Chapter 3, which noted that such processes have become another means of 'limiting liability'. The Scheme of Arrangement in the James Hardie case was an egregious example. Let us turn to illustrations of further, common strategies.

In the United States, actions against manufacturers and others involved in the production and distribution of asbestos products were boosted by developments in products liability laws (examined in Chapter 8), which often approximated rules of strict liability.[137] Although liability rules were favourable to claimants, procedural rules were more problematic. Attempts to manage mass asbestos claims by way of class actions failed, due to courts' lack of confidence in the trade-offs sought to be made between class members actually suffering from asbestos-related diseases and future claimants.[138] The US Supreme Court in *Ortiz* v. *Fibreboard*[139] ruled against class-certification of asbestos claims, one reason for this being a concern about the adequacy of safeguards for future claimants in reaching the proposed settlement. In these circumstances, a high proportion of asbestos companies have resorted to the US Bankruptcy Code Chapter 11 procedure in order to reorganise (that is, restructure their debt commitments).[140] Frequently, this is on the basis that, although companies could meet present liabilities, they would be unable to meet future liabilities, given the anticipated number of medium- to long-term claims. This was the case with the Manville Corporation, which, when it filed for bankruptcy protection in 1982, had a net worth of US$1.1 billion and was very profitable. The problem

[137] See Boggio, *Compensating Asbestos Victims*, p. 152. Most of the claims by employees against their responsible employers were barred by state workers' compensation legislation, creating exclusive remedy provisions: ibid., p. 157. However, this still left room for suits by consumers and third parties. See Chapters 8 and 11.

[138] See *Amchem Products Inc* v. *Windsor* 521 US 591 (1997); *Ortiz* v. *Fibreboard Corp* 527 US 815 (1999). See also R. A. Nagareda, 'Mass Resolution of Mass Torts: Emerging Issues in the United States and the Global Future', in J. Steele and W. H. van Boom (eds.), *Mass Justice: Challenges of Representation and Distribution* (2011), esp. pp. 36–7.

[139] 527 US 815 (1999).

[140] At least 100 companies have entered bankruptcy under Chapter 11: US Government Accountability Office, 'Asbestos Injury Compensation: The Role and Administration of Asbestos Trusts' (2011), p. ii. See also Sherman, 'The Evolution of Asbestos Litigation', 1026–7.

was that Manville anticipated future asbestos claims of $2 billion and sought the consolidation and settlement of those claims.[141]

US companies seeking to reorganise in bankruptcy can do so by either the traditional route, whereby the debtor files a petition and negotiates thereafter with creditors, or the 'pre-pack' route (explained in Chapter 3). Asbestos manufacturers typically have opted for pre-packs,[142] and have sought to separate their liabilities by the establishment of trust structures into which debtor company shares (typically 50 per cent of equity), future company profits, insurance company settlements, and other assets are paid.[143] In the case of asbestos claims, settlements must be approved by a 'supermajority' of claimholders by number and dollar amount.[144] Future, unascertained claimants are given representation in settlement proceedings so that their interests are taken into account.[145] The advantage for the debtor company is that, as long as the requisite majority agrees, all other claimants are subordinated in a 'cram-down'.[146] This provides 'certainty' for the restructured businesses.[147] Under the terms of the typical trust, liability for certain kinds of injury is accepted by debtor companies[148] so that claims thereafter can be settled on the basis of administrative procedures,[149] or by alternative dispute resolution when claims are disputed.[150] Once outcomes are approved, the bankruptcy court will issue a channelling injunction to ensure that personal injury claimants are required to proceed against the trust for compensation – rather than directly against

141 Anderson, 'Financing Asbestos Claims', 439. See also Mattock, Sackett, and Shipp, 'Clearing Up the False Premises' (2014), 737. Note that, whereas it is not necessary for a company under Chapter 11 protection to be insolvent, this is a requirement for an administration order under Insolvency Act 1986 UK, s 123.

142 Vairo, 'Mass Torts Bankruptcies', 106–7.

143 McCulloch and Tweedale, *Defending the Indefensible*, 179; Carroll et al., *Asbestos Litigation*, p. xxiii; Vairo, 'Mass Torts Bankruptcies', 101–2; D. Landis, 'The Smoldering Threat of Asbestos', *Kiplinger's Magazine*, 28 May 2002, 48. Sixty such trusts have been created to deal with asbestos claims. They have dealt with 3.3 million claims and have paid out more than US$17.5 billion: US Government Accountability Office, Asbestos Injury Compensation, p. 16.

144 Under US Code, Title 11, Bankruptcy, § 524(g), 75 per cent of claimants whose claims are addressed by the trust must approve the reorganisation.

145 Mattock, Sackett, and Shipp, 'Clearing Up the False Premises', 741–2.

146 Nagareda, 'Mass Resolution of Mass Torts', 39.

147 B. B. Erens, S. J. Friedman, and K. M. Mayerfield, 'Bankrupt Subsidiaries: The Challenges to the Parent of Legal Separation' (2008) 25 *Emory Bankruptcy Developments Journal* 65, 135.

148 US Government Accountability Office, Asbestos Injury Compensation, p. 8.

149 Carroll et al., *Asbestos Litigation*, pp. xxxi–xxxii.

150 Anderson, 'Financing Asbestos Claims', 442.

the manufacturer or other tortfeasors.[151] This reduces litigation costs and ensures that a great proportion of ring-fenced funds is available to meet the costs of injury.[152] Claims are accepted upon proof of exposure to asbestos and the suffering of a compensable disease.[153]

Trustees review payment schedules periodically and adjust payment rates according to the ability of the trusts to meet anticipated claims.[154] However, many of the asbestos trusts have proved under-funded.[155] Depending on the assets available, claims are paid out usually at a proportion of full value, more serious claims having a greater payout rate than less serious claims.[156] In 2011, the US Government Accountability Office found that asbestos trusts paid out between 1.1 and 100 per cent of the value of claims made. The median payment was 25 per cent.[157] The Manville Plan, for example, had anticipated fewer than 100,000 claims would be filed. However, within twelve years of its establishment more than 240,000 claims had been filed against the trust.[158] The result was that early claimants were overpaid[159] and subsequent payments had to be reduced to a limit of 5 per cent of their full value.[160]

Restructuring in bankruptcy has been a 'successful' strategy for US debtor companies. Most asbestos claimants are paid out of trusts, only a comparatively small percentage obtaining compensation through litigation.[161] Debtor companies have been able to offload or quarantine liabilities, and thus we can say that restructuring has proven (as Cole asserted) a 'liability limiting' device.[162] Apart from the externalisation of tort-related costs of business operation, use of bankruptcy procedures by US companies has had a number of unattractive features. First, the suspension of claims against debtor companies during the period of

[151] US Code, Title 11, Bankruptcy, § 524(g). See Carroll et al., *Asbestos Litigation*, pp. 6 and 111.
[152] Anderson, Financing Asbestos Claims, pp. 439–40.
[153] M. P. Weingarten, 'Asbestos from an American Perspective' [2009] *Journal of Personal Injury Law* 253, 260.
[154] US Government Accountability Office, 'Asbestos Injury Compensation', pp. 21–2.
[155] Carroll et al., *Asbestos Litigation*, p. xxix.
[156] US Government Accountability Office, 'Asbestos Injury Compensation', p. 17.
[157] US Government Accountability Office, 'Asbestos Injury Compensation', p. 21.
[158] Vairo, 'Mass Torts Bankruptcies', 104–5.
[159] Sherman, 'The Evolution of Asbestos Litigation', 1026–7.
[160] Carroll et al., *Asbestos Litigation*, pp. 114–15.
[161] Mattock, Sackett, and Shipp, 'Clearing Up the False Premises', 752.
[162] See M. Cole, 'Limiting Liability through Bankruptcy' (2002) 70 *University of Cincinnati Law Review* 1245, 1247; discussed in Chapter 3.

restructuring means that shareholders with residual equity can sell out.[163] Shareholders who choose not to sell usually retain a significant part of their equity holdings after confirmation of the plan. This is seen by many to 'offend bankruptcy priorities'.[164] Yet restructuring plans often have failed to work to the advantage of tort claimants, because (as adumbrated) the number of future claims has been underestimated. This has reflected the weak, compromised position of future claims representatives, who have insufficient incentive to bargain hard for future claimants.[165] Although the creation of trusts for the satisfaction of claims creates certainty for debtor companies, it creates also the potential for future windfalls: 'if a debtor is able to fully recover after confirmation of a plan, perhaps becoming wildly successful, it has no duty to pay pre-petition creditors.'[166]

Following the Chapter 11 reorganisation in the United States of its parent company Federal Mogul, Turner & Newall group companies entered administration in the United Kingdom in 2001.[167] Settlement of a broad set of claims was reached in 2005.[168] Court-approved schemes of arrangement were agreed between fifty-eight Turner & Newall group companies, their insurers, and creditors.[169] Scheme creditors include employees and former employees of debtor companies who have or in the future might have claims for damages for personal injuries, as well as dependants and relatives of such employees who have or in the future might have claims under the Fatal Accidents Act 1976 and equivalent legislation.[170] Contributories to the trust created pursuant to the schemes include group companies, their employers' liability insurers, and other insurers. Under the schemes, any claims available against the insurers[171]

[163] P. Spender, 'Blue Asbestos and Golden Eggs: Evaluating Bankruptcy and Class Actions as Just Responses to Mass Tort Liability' (2003) 25 *Sydney Law Review* 223, 225.

[164] E.g., Spender, 'Blue Asbestos and Golden Eggs', 228.

[165] Y. Listokin and K. Ayotte, 'Protecting Future Claimants in Mass Tort Bankruptcies' (2004) 98 *Northwestern University Law Review* 1435, 1448–9.

[166] G. Zipes, 'After *Amchem* and *Ahern*: The Rise of Bankruptcy over the Class Action Option for Resolving Mass Torts on a Nationwide Basis, and the Fall of Finality?' [1998] *Detroit College of Law at Michigan State University Law Review* 7, 50. 'For example, since 2010, Owens Corning, which originally filed for bankruptcy in 2000, has earned nearly $1.2 billion of net profits on more than $15 billion worth of sales': Mattock, Sackett, and Shipp, 'Clearing Up the False Premises', 725, 740.

[167] Spender, 'Blue Asbestos and Golden Eggs', 253.

[168] *In re T & N Ltd* [2006] 1 WLR 1728, 1737. The largest creditor was the Trustee of the T & N pension scheme: ibid. See also *In the Matter of Cape plc* [2006] 3 All ER 1222.

[169] See *In re T & N Ltd and ors (No 4)* [2007] Bus LR 1411.

[170] *In re T & N Ltd and ors (No 4)* [2007] Bus LR 1411, 1417.

[171] These could be directly asserted under the Third Parties (Rights against Insurers) Act 1930. See now Third Parties (Rights against Insurers) Act 2010.

can no longer be asserted against them directly.[172] By contrast, the schemes embody no compromise between group companies and injured employees (so that claims against the former can still be made directly by the latter).[173] At the time of court approval of class meetings under the schemes, the T & N UK Asbestos Trustee Company was expected to respond to claims for at least forty years from its establishment.[174] Under the terms of the trust, eligible claimants are paid a percentage of the value of their claims, which is fixed from time to time according to the size of the fund, projected investment returns, assessment of the value of present and future claims, and projected administration costs.[175] At the time of judicial sanction of the class meetings, actuaries estimated that the trust would pay 75 per cent of the value of claims.[176] At the time of writing, the trust was paying between 25 and 50 per cent of scheduled injury values.[177] Up to the end of 2013, after seven years of operation, the trust had paid compensation to about 1,800 claimants, and had approximately seventy outstanding claims (but with new claims being filed each year).[178] Many of the criticisms levelled at US bankruptcy procedures could be levelled at UK administration procedures under which asbestos trusts have been created.

Further ways in which those injured by asbestos-related products in the United Kingdom can obtain medical assistance, government benefit payments, and special scheme payments for asbestosis and mesothelioma were considered briefly in Chapter 1.

4.3 Case Study II: Pharmaceutical Claims

The widespread death and human suffering caused by asbestos-related diseases represents the paradigm insolvent entity problem. The lessons of asbestos are important because similar problems are likely to arise in the future in other industries. Problems of insolvent entities and mass-torts are potentially significant, for example, in the pharmaceuticals industry.[179] There are a number of reasons for this, including the large scale of

[172] *In re T & N Ltd and ors (No 4)* [2007] Bus LR 1411, 1418.
[173] *In re T & N Ltd and ors (No 4)* [2007] Bus LR 1411, 1432.
[174] *In re T & N Ltd and ors (No 4)* [2007] Bus LR 1411, 1420.
[175] *In re T & N Ltd and ors (No 4)* [2007] Bus LR 1411, 1420.
[176] *In re T & N Ltd and ors (No 4)* [2007] Bus LR 1411, 1420.
[177] See the trust website, available at: http://tandnasbestos.org.uk/claims/how-much-could-my-claim-be-worth/.
[178] T & N UK Asbestos Trust, 'Trustees' Annual Report' 2013, p. 3.
[179] N. Sheiner, 'DES and a Proposed Theory of Enterprise Liability' (1978) 46 *Fordham Law Review* 963, 1003.

the industry, shortcomings in the way in which drugs are developed, tested, and approved, the potential for long latency in the manifestation of injury, the novel means by which pharma groups are identifying new drug compounds, and the structuring of legal relations with start-ups and other companies. The most important of these issues will be explored in this section. Another frequent difficulty is in obtaining adequate insurance for injuries caused by defective drugs. This has resulted in a measure of self-insurance within the pharmaceuticals industry,[180] which might prove inadequate when disaster strikes (a matter considered in Chapter 3).

The pharmaceuticals industry is very large, highly concentrated, and very profitable for many companies involved.[181] Profitability depends, to a great extent, on the ability of pharma companies both to innovate and to have their intellectual property (IP) protected. IP rights are protected by exclusive patents, which allow patent-holders either to produce themselves or else to licence to others the production of drugs and related products. True breakthroughs take many years of development and testing, and the costs are extremely high.[182] A development programme might begin with 10,000 different compounds and take a number of years before several usable compounds are identified and readied for testing in humans.[183] It might take fifteen years before a drug is approved finally for sale.

In recent decades, a 'flood' of patents for valuable 'blockbuster' drugs has expired,[184] and pharma companies have encountered difficulty in

180 Sheiner, 'DES and a Proposed Theory', 1004.

181 Earlier this decade, US industry profits were said to be $700 billion annually: L. Treadaway, 'Big Pharma's Heart of Darkness: The Alien Tort Statute and Preventing Clinical Trial Colonialism' (2012) 43 *Georgetown International Law Journal* 1419, 1436. See also C. E. Bagley and C. D. Tvarnø, 'Pharmaceutical Public-Private Partnerships: Moving from the Bench to the Bedside' (2014) 4 *Harvard Business Law Journal* 373, 377–8.

182 J. J. Li, *Blockbuster Drugs* (2013), p. 169. Costs for US pharma companies have been estimated to be around US$800 million per drug: J. M. Weigand, 'Vioxx: How Strong Is the Case against Merck?' (2007) 11 *Michigan State University Journal of Medicine and Law* 145, 146. Another estimate is US$2.6 billion per drug: A. Kazmin, 'Gilead Combats Wider Distribution of Cheap Drugs from EM', *Financial Times*, 12 April 2015, available at: http://ft.com/intl/cms/s/0/ce7f059a-d86c-11e4-d86c-00144feab7de.html. For a detailed account of development and testing, see T. M. Jacobsen and A. I. Wertheimer (eds.), *Modern Pharmaceutical Industry: A Primer* (2010).

183 S. P. Gelone, 'Clinical Research', in T. M. Jacobsen and A. I. Wertheimer (eds.), *Modern Pharmaceutical Industry: A Primer* (2010), p. 122.

184 K. Jaeger, 'Generic Drugs', in T. M. Jacobsen and A. I. Wertheimer (eds.), *Modern Pharmaceutical Industry: A Primer* (2010), p. 278; H. L. Feldman, 'Pushing Drugs:

developing profitable replacements. '[T]he low-hanging fruits have been harvested, and it is becoming more and more challenging to bring novel drugs to the market, especially the ones that are "first-in-class" medicines.'[185] Given that competitor companies produce copies (generics) of successful drugs immediately after innovators lose patent protection,[186] the failure to innovate is a major problem.[187] Unless patented drugs can be replaced with new products, market share and profits will be lost. One can appreciate this from the fact that 63 per cent of total prescriptions dispensed in the United States are for generic drugs.[188] These have much lower profit margins than comparable products under patent.[189]

One way that pharma companies try to maintain profitability in the absence of new blockbusters is by taking existing drug compounds and modifying them into 'biosimilars'.[190] Such drugs might 'copy' not only existing molecules, but also their defects.[191] Another strategy involves marketing drugs and treatments which are not responsive to pressing illnesses or conditions, but which are said to enhance users' 'lifestyles'. Pharma companies turn ordinary ailments into medical problems, 'seeing mild symptoms as serious, treating personal problems as medical, seeing risks as diseases, and framing prevalence estimates to maximize market potential'.[192] Examples of products falling into this category include Viagra and other drugs responsive to 'sexual

Genomics and Genetics, the Pharmaceutical Industry, and the Law of Negligence' (2003) 42 *Washburn Law Journal* 575, 581.

185 Li, *Blockbuster Drugs*, p. 169.

186 Note, however, that pharma groups might enter into 'pay-for-delay' deals with other pharma companies in order to extend their ability to profit: A. Ward, 'AstraZeneca Wins Ruling on "Pay-for-Delay" Deals', *Financial Times*, 6–7 December 2014, 13. However, these have been found unlawful under competition rules: see UK Government, 'CMA Fines Pharma Companies £45 Million' (2016), available at: www.gov.uk/government/news/cma-fines-pharma-companies-45-million/.

187 D. Crow, 'Pharmaceuticals: Staying Power', *Financial Times*, 22 August 2016, available at: www.ft.com/content/d7b1c59e-65fb-11e6-a08a-c7ac04ef00aa/.

188 Jaeger, 'Generic Drugs', 271.

189 Jaeger, 'Generic Drugs', 271.

190 B. Goldacre, *Bad Pharma* (2013), p. 111. The US government encourages the development of biosimilars because they help to reduce the cost of healthcare: see A. Ward, 'Novartis Launches First Biological Copycat Drug in US', *Financial Times*, 3 September 2015, available at: www.ft.com/cms/s/0/62e7950-5219-11e5-b029-b9d50a74fd14.html#axzz3kesiOx12.

191 Sheiner, 'DES and a Proposed Theory', 976 (pointing to the example of DES).

192 R. Monihan et al., 'Selling Sickness: The Pharmaceutical Industry and Disease Mongering' (2002) 324 *British Medical Journal* 886, available at: www.bmj.com/content/324/7342/886.1. See W. T. Champion, 'The Vioxx® Litigation Paradigm: The Search for Smoking Guns' (2006) 31 *Thurgood Marshall Law Review* 157, 161; Feldman, 'Pushing Drugs', 576–7.

dysfunction'.[193] While these drugs do not address medical problems, they can have serious side effects. Viagra has been found to cause visual problems, including, in the worst cases, blindness.[194] The result of this kind of market expansion by pharma companies is an increasing medicalisation of various aspects of life,[195] which increases the existing risks of things going wrong and of mass-torts.[196]

Pharmaceuticals have inherent risks; few are completely safe. This is because our bodies treat them as foreign and potentially toxic agents. Given that, sometimes, there is 'a fine line between efficacy and toxicity, a fine line between risk and benefit',[197] all drugs must be approved prior to consumption. In the usual case, regulatory approval is given on the basis of efficacy after short- to medium-term testing. However, clinical trials are limited in what they test for. They cannot screen for every circumstance in which a drug will be used, whether in the short or long term.[198] 'The size and length of the trials, as well as the similarity of clinical patients [to each other] needed to determine efficacy, limit the ability to predict the risk when used by the wider population.'[199] There is a sense, then, in which 'on-market drugs have an experimental quality, since pre-approval testing cannot detect all the risks the user will face.'[200] On the positive side, the benefits of various drugs and related treatments are undeniable – having saved lives and prevented disease, adverse medical conditions, pain, and so on in countless people. On the negative side, it is estimated that 100,000 persons die annually in the United States alone from drug toxicity-related causes,[201] while another 2.2 million suffer from other adverse reactions.[202] Not all deaths and injuries are the result of torts, but many of them are.

The pharmaceuticals industry has been criticised extensively for practices employed in development, testing, and approval processes. It is worthwhile saying something about them. As adumbrated, new drugs must be tested through clinical trials. The first problem lies in the modest

[193] S. Z. Rahman et al., 'Lifestyle Drugs: Concept and Impact on Society' (2010) *Indian Journal of Pharmaceutical Sciences* 409.

[194] Goldacre, *Bad Pharma*, p. 160.

[195] D. Hely, *Pharmageddon* (2013), p. 11.

[196] Feldman, 'Pushing Drugs', 578.

[197] P. McDonnell, 'Drug Safety and Pharmacovigilance', in T. M. Jacobsen and A. I. Wertheimer (eds.), *Modern Pharmaceutical Industry: A Primer* (2010), p. 200.

[198] M. Gilhooley, 'Vioxx's History and the Need for Better Procedure and Better Testing' (2007) 37 *Seton Hall Law Review* 941, 955.

[199] Gilhooley, 'Vioxx's History', 955.

[200] Gilhooley, 'Vioxx's History', 954.

[201] M. Freeman, 'The Tort Mess', *Forbes Magazine*, 13 May 2002, available at: www.forbes.com/forbes/2002/0513/090.html.

[202] Feldman, 'Pushing Drugs', 591.

objective of clinical testing. The objective is not to prove that new drugs are superior to the most effective existing drugs or treatments. The objective is to demonstrate, rather, that the drug in question is superior to the use of a placebo – a placebo being a non-treatment, for example, a sugar tablet.[203] Indeed, a study of drugs approved by the European Medicines Agency between 1999 and 2006 found that only half had been tested against *other treatments*.[204] Moreover, clinical trials have known limitations. Participant numbers usually are such that only the most frequently occurring adverse drug reactions (ADRs) are detected.[205] To give an example: if the threshold for safety is set to a confidence interval of 99 per cent that a serious ADR would occur with an incidence of no more than one in 10,000 patients, the study would need to have 46,000 participating patients.[206] Many clinical trials essentially test for short- to medium-term side effects only. The long-term side effects might become evident only after months or years of patient use.[207] This underlines the importance of post-marketing drug safety surveillance programmes.[208]

A second problem with industry practices is that much testing of new drugs is undertaken either by pharma companies themselves or by sub-contractors answerable to them. This creates obvious conflicts of interest and impacts upon the integrity of studies. In fact, there is evidence of repeated manipulation of data by pharma companies,[209] for example by the simple withholding of 'inconvenient' clinical trial results.[210] Trial information withheld by patent-owner Roche, which was released to researchers after years of resistance, proved critical in determining the doubtful efficacy of the Tamiflu antiviral.[211] Where new drugs are tested against other treatments, experiments might be rigged either by comparing against known, ineffective products or by departing from recommended doses.[212] These are the tricks of the trade, and they indicate that

[203] Goldacre, *Bad Pharma*, pp. 131–2.
[204] S. W. Glickman et al., 'Ethical and Scientific Implications of Globalization of Clinical Research' (2009) 360 *New England Journal of Medicine* 816, available at: www.nejm.org/doi/full/10.1056/NEJMsb0803929#t=article.
[205] McDonnell, 'Drug Safety and Pharmacovigilance', 197.
[206] McDonnell, 'Drug Safety and Pharmacovigilance', 197.
[207] Goldacre, *Bad Pharma*, pp. 184–5.
[208] McDonnell, 'Drug Safety and Pharmacovigilance', 198.
[209] Hely, *Pharmageddon*, pp. 99–103.
[210] Goldacre, *Bad Pharma*, p. 5.
[211] A. Ward, 'Big Pharma: Storehouse of Trouble', *Financial Times*, 11 April 2014, available at: www.ft.com/cms/s/0/10bb1972-c170-11e3-83af-00144feabdc0.html.
[212] Goldacre, *Bad Pharma*, p. 182; Treadaway, 'Big Pharma's Heart of Darkness', 1421–2 (example of projected blockbuster Trovan).

pharma companies regularly develop and market products which they know to be inferior to others in the marketplace. The ability to manipulate data is increased when subcontractors conduct trials in developing countries. 'There have been cases where trial results from developing countries have produced positive results, while those conducted elsewhere [with the same drug] showed no benefit.'[213]

In other cases, trials are undertaken by independent researchers, but are industry-funded. Frequently, the results obtained in such tests are skewed towards finding efficacy in the sponsor's products. One systematic review found that industry-funded trials are four times more likely to report positive results for sponsor drugs than are government-funded trials.[214] Skewing arises because it is 'normal for researchers and academics conducting industry-funded trials to sign contracts subjecting them to gagging clauses which forbid them to publish, discuss or analyse data from the trials they have conducted, without the permission of the funder'.[215] In cases where researchers are prepared to publish results that are not favourable to the sponsor, pressure might be placed upon them either to desist or to alter their conclusions.[216] The potential result of these practices is misleading information about new drugs – which might turn out to be harmful to patients.[217] Although legislation now exists requiring the publication of clinical trial data in both Europe and the United States,[218] this has been honoured more in the breach than the observance.[219] A reason for this seems to be the lack of enforcement by the relevant regulatory agencies.[220]

The problems of the pharma industry extend beyond development and testing. Often, pharma companies seek to 'place' favourable research about their products in academic or industry journals. In a typical case, they do this by providing research findings to a professional writer who

213 Goldacre, *Bad Pharma*, p. 115.

214 J. Lexchin et al., 'Pharmaceutical Industry Sponsorship and Research Outcome Quality: Systematic Review' (2003) 326 *British Medical Journal* 1167, available at: www.bmj.com/content/326/7400/1167.

215 Goldacre, *Bad Pharma*, p. 39.

216 Goldacre, *Bad Pharma*, p. 112.

217 Goldacre, *Bad Pharma*, p. 19.

218 Clinical Trials Regulation, Council Regulation 536/2014, OJ L158/1; US Code, Title 42, Public Health and Welfare, § 282.

219 A. P. Prayle et al., 'Compliance with Mandatory Reporting of Clinical Trial Results on ClinicalTrials.gov: Cross Sectional Study' (2012) 344 *British Medical Journal* 7373, available at: www.bmj.com/content/344/bmj.d7373.

220 That is, the European Medicines Agency and the Federal Drug Administration. See Goldacre, *Bad Pharma*, p. 54.

puts together an article. The pharma company then looks for an academic to check the paper and invites him or her to be named as an author.[221] This gives the paper a degree of weight and respectability. The professional writer might be acknowledged in the footnotes or not acknowledged at all.[222] The reality is that such publications are little more than 'covert advertising'.[223] A study examining articles considering the performance of pharmaceutical products published in six leading medical journals indicated that 8 per cent were ghost-written.[224] If anything, this seems to be a gross underestimate[225] and underlines the extent to which pharma companies are willing to influence prescribing habits so as to grow the market for their products. The pharma industry contributes much funding and organisational effort also to continuing medical education, the effect of which is to propagate favourable opinions about drugs subject to discussion.[226]

Another, quite serious problem is that drugs frequently are used 'off-label' – in the sense that doctors prescribe them for unapproved uses.[227] In fact, drug companies have been known to *encourage* off-label prescription because this increases sales.[228] However, this practice is harmful to patients when drugs turn out to be unsafe for either their original and/or their other applications. Large fines have been imposed on US drug manufacturers employing this practice, some of these companies having 'trained their sales force[s] to disregard the law'.[229]

These related problems demonstrate that the pharma industry is rife with various tricks of the trade designed to promote its products. The result is not only a lack of integrity in the development, testing, and marketing of products, but a compromised system which is bound to propagate harmful or inferior remedies. This increases the risks of mass-scale injuries, mass-torts, and the insolvent entity problem with which this book is concerned.

221 See, e.g., W. J. Thomas, 'The Vioxx Story: Would it Have Ended Differently in the European Union?' (2006) 32 *American Journal of Law and Medicine* 365, 370 (example of the Merck drug Vioxx, considered later).

222 Goldacre, *Bad Pharma*, p. 303.

223 Goldacre, *Bad Pharma*, p. 247.

224 J. S. Wislar et al., 'Honorary and Ghost Authorship in High Impact Biomedical Journals: A Cross Sectional Survey' (2011) 343 *British Medical Journal* 6128, available at: www.bmj.com/content/343/bmj.d6128.

225 Goldacre, *Bad Pharma*, p. 292.

226 Goldacre, *Bad Pharma*, p. 323.

227 Goldacre, *Bad Pharma*, pp. 56–7.

228 Feldman, 'Pushing Drugs', 583 and 587 (example of Neurontin, 80 per cent of prescriptions being off-label). See now Access to Medical Treatments (Innovation) Act 2016 (encouraging off-label uses).

229 Goldacre, *Bad Pharma*, p. 350.

Indeed, it is 'estimated that deaths from drugs rank among the top 10 causes of death in the United States', and there is little reason to think that the situation is different in other advanced nations.[230] Millions of people will either die or suffer serious injury as a result of defective drugs or their improper usage. Over the next few pages, we examine examples of drugs that have failed and caused deaths or injury on a mass scale.

Thalidomide was a sedative used to ameliorate morning sickness in pregnant women. The drug was marketed aggressively. One advertisement promised that it could be taken 'with complete safety to pregnant women'.[231] It was manufactured in England from 1958 until it was withdrawn from sale in 1961.[232] The reason for its withdrawal was the mounting evidence that Thalidomide caused serious damage to embryos. It had terrible consequences for affected children. They were born with phocomelia, which gave the appearance of limbs similar to seal flippers.[233] Nearly 500 claims were made against Distillers Company (Biochemicals) Ltd.[234] Many thousands of claims were made elsewhere. The lesson from this early case was that 'the scale of mass-production of drugs is such that a single error can affect vast numbers of people throughout the world and that there is no guarantee that a given company will be able to insure against, or even obtain coverage for, such an eventuality.'[235]

The Thalidomide tragedy was a milestone in pharmaceuticals regulation. In the United States (where Thalidomide was never authorised for marketing), the tragedy was the catalyst for passage of the Kefauver-Harris Act 1962. This legislation required that the US Food and Drug Administration (FDA) be satisfied that pharma companies can demonstrate both the safety and efficacy of drugs before marketing approval is given.[236] From 1963, European governments began to address issues of drug safety and efficacy.[237] In 1965, the European Economic Community enacted the Directive on pharmaceuticals, which established a framework for centralised approval of pharmaceutical products.[238] These were to be assessed by reference to

230 McDonnell, 'Drug Safety and Pharmacovigilance', 200.

231 H. Teff, 'Products Liability in the Pharmaceutical Industry at Common Law' (1974) 20 *McGill Law Journal* 102, 121.

232 Teff, 'Products Liability', 116.

233 McDonnell, 'Drug Safety and Pharmacovigilance', 190.

234 Teff, 'Products Liability', 116–17.

235 Teff, 'Products Liability', 121.

236 McDonnell, 'Drug Safety and Pharmacovigilance', 190.

237 Thomas, 'The Vioxx Story', 374.

238 Council Directive 65/65/EEC of 26 January 1965 on the approximation of provisions laid down by Law, Regulation or Administrative Action relating to proprietary medicinal products, OJ 1965 No. P369, 9 February 1965.

safety, efficacy, and quality factors.[239] The Thalidomide tragedy was a prime factor behind the passage of the European Community Directive on product liability,[240] which was transposed into UK law in the Consumer Protection Act 1987 (examined in Chapter 8).

A more recent example of a mass-tort in the pharmaceuticals industry involved Vioxx. Vioxx was a prescription pain reliever manufactured by Merck and marketed in more than eighty countries.[241] It was designed as a COX-2 enzyme inhibitor, which would avoid the potential side effect called 'gastropathy' caused by other, non-steroidal anti-inflammatory drugs (NSAIDs).[242] Initial clinical trials were conducted on the basis of a comparison between Vioxx and a placebo, rather than an existing NSAID.[243] Vioxx was given a priority regulatory review by the FDA, based upon surrogate endpoints (meaning that the actual results obtained in trials were not important, but were believed to be predictive of important outcomes).[244] Further testing was required in order to prove its gastrointestinal benefit.[245] Post-approval trials suggested elevated risks of heart attacks and certain forms of stroke, but Merck never undertook clinical testing to confirm this.[246] When this evidence came to light, Merck continued advertising Vioxx in a manner which 'minimized any link between Vioxx and cardiovascular events' – leading the FDA to warn it about misleading consumers.[247] In keeping with the practices of other pharma companies faced with negative information about their products, Merck moved to 'control the dissemination of Vioxx-related information'.[248] Merck's medical writers even went so far as to delete data recording three heart attacks from a paper published in the *New England Journal of Medicine*.[249] Yet, eventually, Vioxx was proven to suppress prostacycline, which caused the clumping of blood platelets and led to cardiovascular events.[250] Marketed over a five-year period from 1999 and supplied under 105 million prescriptions,[251] Vioxx was withdrawn voluntarily by the manufacturer in 2004.[252] An estimated 27,000

239 Thomas, 'The Vioxx Story', 374.
240 S. Whittaker, *Liability for Products: English Law, French Law, and European Harmonization* (2005), p. 568.
241 Thomas, 'The Vioxx Story', 366.
242 McDonnell, 'Drug Safety and Pharmacovigilance', 189.
243 Gilhooley, 'Vioxx's History', 945.
244 Gilhooley, 'Vioxx's History', 942.
245 Gilhooley, 'Vioxx's History', 945–6.
246 Gilhooley, 'Vioxx's History', 949.
247 Thomas, 'The Vioxx Story', 366.
248 Thomas, 'The Vioxx Story', 369.
249 Thomas, 'The Vioxx Story', 367.
250 Thomas, 'The Vioxx Story', 368.
251 Thomas, 'The Vioxx Story', 365–6.
252 McDonnell, 'Drug Safety and Pharmacovigilance', 189.

cardiovascular-related deaths and heart attacks over this period could have been avoided had an alternative pain reliever been prescribed.[253] Early estimates of the value of claims against Merck varied from US$12 billion to more than $50 billion.[254] Settlement of claims against Merck took the novel form of a contractual agreement between the company and law firms representing the bulk of claimants, designed to minimise any inference of wrongdoing on Merck's part.[255] Ultimately, 33,000 claimants out of 50,000 settled their claims.[256]

Up to the present day, mass-torts in the pharma industry have arisen typically from adverse reactions in persons to specific chemical compounds. In the future, problems might arise with respect to modes of delivery. This brings us to a rapidly developing area of technology called 'nanotechnology', which makes use of very small particles of various substances called 'nanoparticles'. Pharma and other companies are exploring the usage of nanoparticles for the targeted delivery of drugs to specific sites within the body. 'Therapeutic agents can be attached to nanoparticles by encapsulation, absorption, or chemically, allowing the therapeutic agent to be delivered to its target destination (e.g., tumor). This in turn may improve therapeutic effectiveness of drugs and cause even fewer side effects.'[257] Whereas a treatment for cancer, such as chemotherapy, causes damage to surrounding organs and tissue, it is hoped that treatment with nanoparticles will avoid this.[258] The theory is that nanoparticles can be cleared from the body quite rapidly through the liver and spleen.[259]

However, there are potentially grave risks in this kind of drug delivery. One risk is that nanoparticles will enter unintended parts of the body. This risk arises, for example, from their ability to breach the blood–brain barrier, and to cross membranes that other potential pathogens are incapable of crossing.[260] A second risk is that certain nanoparticles, such as metal particles, are not capable of clearance from the body, so

253 Champion, 'The Vioxx® Litigation Paradigm', 164 and 175.

254 Thomas, 'The Vioxx Story', 367.

255 See Nagareda, 'Mass Resolution of Mass Torts', 44. See also J. T. Grabill, 'Judicial Review of Private Mass Tort Settlements' (2012) 42 *Seton Hall Law Review* 123.

256 Grabill, 'Judicial Review', 145.

257 T. Jacobsen and A. Wertheimer, 'Future Industry Trends', in T. M. Jacobsen and A. I. Wertheimer (eds.), *Modern Pharmaceutical Industry: A Primer* (2010), p. 300.

258 S. McNamee, 'The Regulatory and Liability Implications of Nanoscale Drug Delivery in the Human Body' (2014) 11 *Nanotechnology Law & Business* 48, 51.

259 Jacobsen and Wertheimer, 'Future Industry Trends', 300.

260 McNamee, 'The Regulatory and Liability Implications', 58.

that they accumulate and possibly interfere with biological processes.[261] At this point in time, these risks cannot be confirmed. Indeed, research into the effects of nanoparticles is complicated because they vary enormously in their 'surface characteristics, charge, shape, base material and size'.[262] A third risk is that nanoparticles used in drug delivery 'might carry charges which interfere with or react with healthy cells'.[263] A final risk is that, over time, persons will be exposed to nanoparticles from a range of different treatments or non-medical applications, giving rise to adverse reactions.[264] In these circumstances, it has been suggested that nanoparticles might become the 'new asbestos'.[265] Indeed, initial murine testing suggests that the exposure of a mouse's mesothelial lining to carbon nanotubes 'results in asbestos-like, length-dependent, pathogenic behaviour'.[266]

Having provided some examples of previous and potential future mass-torts involving the pharmaceuticals industry, something more should be said now about the way in which the industry is organised.[267] Pharma groups have moved away from a business model under which all aspects of development, testing, marketing, and distribution are carried out 'in house'. The reasons for this include more detailed regulation of activity (see later), the extremely high costs of development and approvals processes, and increasing losses on investments in innovation,[268] coupled with fierce competition in the industry. Additionally, pharma groups have sought to reduce the great risks of development failure.[269] This has been attempted through a number of strategies, including mergers and acquisitions (facilitating the diversification of product lines),[270] biotech in-licensing,

261 McNamee, 'The Regulatory and Liability Implications', 54.
262 McNamee, 'The Regulatory and Liability Implications', 54.
263 McNamee, 'The Regulatory and Liability Implications', 55.
264 McNamee, 'The Regulatory and Liability Implications', 77.
265 McNamee, 'The Regulatory and Liability Implications', 56.
266 C. A. Poland et al., 'Carbon Nanotubes Introduced into the Abdominal Cavity of Mice Show Asbestos-Like Pathology in a Pilot Study' (2008) 3 *Nature Nanotechnology* 423, 423. See also N. Gilbert, 'Nanoparticle Safety in Doubt' (2009) 460 *Nature News* 937 (report of deaths from inhaling nanoparticles).
267 See also Chapter 2.
268 Bagley and Tvarnø, 'Pharmaceutical Public-Private Partnerships', 379.
269 Approximately 90 per cent of phase I trials fail: B. Elder, 'About that AstraZeneca Bid Defence . . . ' *Financial Times*, 6 May 2014, available at: http://alphaville.ft.com/2014/05/06/1844642/about-that-astrazeneca-bid-defence/.
270 E.g., G. Viña, 'AstraZeneca Walks Tightrope of Drugs Trials', *Financial Times*, 9 October 2016, available at: www.ft.com/content/626c73e0-a5a9-11e6-8b69-02899e8bd9d1/ (Pfizer has 'boosted pipeline of new drugs by making acquisitions'). By contrast, AstraZeneca has taken a 'big bet' on its own development of cancer-fighting drugs: ibid.

and outsourcing of critical processes to 'drug discovery' firms.[271] The latter two strategies, adopted by other high-technology industries as well, entail finding 'new products and capabilities not internally, but in other companies' through 'rapidly expanding use of ... "differentiated networks" of formal and informal alliances'.[272]

The use of 'drug discovery' firms involves the search for specialist biotech companies or start-ups developing promising new products, and the provision of non-equity funding to them so that they can continue development.[273] As the prospects of a successful discovery increase, so does the pharma group's funding of the start-up. A typical agreement might see the pharma group obtain a licence to market and distribute the product and share in the profits, without ever owning the patents or having had a hand in development and testing.[274] An alternative agreement might see the pharma group patent a drug, but have it developed and tested by agreement with a separate company. The pharma group then manufactures and distributes.[275] The latter is called the 'development contract', or 'spin-off'.[276] In other cases, pharma groups engage in subcontracting of aspects of testing and/or manufacturing[277] while they retain overall responsibility and control of these processes. In an industry with flat-lining revenues, this strategy has been adopted in order to reduce costs and maintain profitability.[278] 'For example, estimates

[271] Bagley and Tvarnø, 'Pharmaceutical Public-Private Partnerships', 381.

[272] S. B. Tallman and G. S. Yip, 'Strategy and the Multinational Enterprise', in A. M. Rugman (ed.), *The Oxford Handbook of International Business* (2nd edn., 2009), p. 326.

[273] See Jacobsen and Wertheimer, 'Future Industry Trends', 300–1.

[274] E.g., A. Ward, 'AstraZeneca in $232m Asthma Drug Deal', *Financial Times*, 12 June 2014, available at: www.ft.com/cms/s/0/a0f46e50-f229-11e3-ac7a-00144feabdc0.html. See also Bagley and Tvarnø, 'Pharmaceutical Public-Private Partnerships', 399 (example of Pfizer partnering with universities).

[275] R. Kraakman, 'Corporate Liability Strategies and the Costs of Legal Controls' (1984) 93 *Yale Law Journal* 857, 872.

[276] M. Roe, 'Corporate Strategic Reaction to Mass Tort' (1986) 72 *Virginia Law Review* 1, 50. But Roe believes that these legal manoeuvers might be difficult to engineer or sustain: 'Development, production, and marketing of a new chemical, for example, usually requires experience; an organization of chemists, engineers, and support staff; and a distribution network of marketing and sales people. Economies of scale and scope thus may often preclude a spin-off or development contract that leaves no substantial contact with the base firm ... Prohibitive costs could make these strategies economical only in the face of an imminent risk of mass tort liability': ibid., 50–1.

[277] Jacobsen and Wertheimer, 'Future Industry Trends', 295. Fifty-seven per cent of clinical trials for drugs for which FDA marketing approval is sought are conducted outside the United States: Treadaway, 'Big Pharma's Heart of Darkness', 1426.

[278] C. Liu, 'Leaving the FDA Behind: Pharmaceutical Outsourcing and Drug Safety' (2012) 48 *Texas International Law Journal* 1, 3.

indicate that outsourcing clinical trials to India can decrease the cost ... by fifty to sixty per cent' compared to conducting them in the United States.[279] Each strategy involves the move to a risk- and profit-sharing model.[280]

Some speculate that the process of outsourcing will reduce 'big pharma' to little more than virtual companies: 'If we extend these trends, it is likely that we will find pharma companies in the United States [and Europe] as virtual companies with most tasks outsourced offshore to independent subcontracting companies or to their own foreign subsidiaries. The principal task maintained by the corporations will be promotion and marketing.'[281] However, there is likely to be a natural limit to the process of 'virtualising' or disaggregation, given the difficulties and costs which arise from attempts to coordinate business activities with external parties (considered in Chapter 2).[282]

Whether this proves to be true or not, the structuring of legal relations among pharma companies (both within and beyond the corporate group) can make it more difficult for those injured by defective pharmaceuticals on a mass scale to claim compensation. If pharma groups do not undertake the crucial processes of drug development and testing themselves, it might be difficult to prove fault against them when liability rules require this.[283] Again, it might be difficult to extend liability beyond insolvent subsidiaries because of the difficulty of proving duties of care owed by parent companies to injured parties, in proving fault in either parents or other solvent companies in the group, and in bringing claims against foreign affiliates. Product liability laws reduce these problems to some extent, by incorporating elements of strict liability and permitting suits against multiple parties in the chain of manufacture and supply. But, as we will see in Chapter 8, these laws are no panacea.

As in cases involving asbestos, mass-tort claims in the United States occasionally have seen pharma groups making use of Chapter 11 bankruptcy procedures in order to reorganise and to create trust structures to determine claims on an administrative basis. This was the case, for example, with Dow Corning, which faced large claim numbers regarding

[279] Treadaway, 'Big Pharma's Heart of Darkness', 1426.

[280] A. Jack, 'Pfizer Chief Looks to Joint Ventures to Bolster Drug Development', *Financial Times*, 6 June 2013, available at: www.ft.com/cms/s/0/9e22f9e6-ceb5-11e2-ae25-00144feab7de.html.

[281] Jacobsen and Wertheimer, 'Future Industry Trends', 295.

[282] Bagley and Tvarnø, 'Pharmaceutical Public-Private Partnerships', 382–3.

[283] See, e.g., *Nash* v. *Eli Lilly & Co* [1993] 4 All ER 383, 387.

silicone gel breast implants that caused an autoimmune disease.[284] AH Robins Corporation sought Chapter 11 bankruptcy protection also, because of the large number of claims made against it for harms caused by the inter-uterine device known as the 'Dalkon Shield'.[285] The plan for reorganisation involved the sale of AH Robins to American Home Products, with a payout to trade creditors and funding of the Dalkon Trust in the amount of $2.255 billion.[286] The Dalkon Trust established three payment options for claimants. They could take advantage of: a quick low-claim option; an option for those with proof of Dalkon Shield use and injury, but lingering issues about causation; and an option for those with serious and provable injuries. Claimants who rejected option three offers could commence litigation.[287] This seems to have been a successful plan. The trust paid out all victims and was terminated in the year 2000. However, the same danger remains as that which affected the asbestos industry: that pharma groups will separate from their liabilities and that trust funds will prove inadequate in the compensation of future claimants.

In cases of defective pharmaceuticals and related products, as in other cases of mass-torts, there is a concern that regulation has failed. Typically, regulatory agencies such as the US Food and Drug Administration are under-resourced, making it difficult for them to fulfil their many responsibilities. Yet such agencies increasingly are required to meet tight timetables for approval of drugs and other tasks.[288] Many new drugs are put through an accelerated approval process, whereby necessary clinical trials are to be conducted *after* approval. Here a 'serious problem' exists,[289] in that many post-approval studies are never completed.[290] Where trials are completed and important information is supplied to regulators, this might be withheld from interested researchers and from medical practitioners. Thus, the European Medicines Agency has been accused, in the past, of withholding information about the success or otherwise of clinical trials, in order to protect commercial sensitivities, and of maladministration.[291] The same accusation of withholding data while patients

284 See *In re Dow Corning Corp* 456 F 3d 668 (6th Cir. 2006); Nagareda, 'Mass Resolution of Mass Torts', 38.

285 Anderson, 'Financing Asbestos Claims', 449.

286 Vairo, 'Mass Torts Bankruptcies', 117.

287 Vairo, 'Mass Torts Bankruptcies', 118–20.

288 K. Stephens, 'Regulatory Affairs', in T. M. Jacobsen and A. I. Wertheimer (eds.), *Modern Pharmaceutical Industry: A Primer* (2010), p. 138.

289 Goldacre, *Bad Pharma*, p. 141.

290 US Government Accountability Office, 'New Drug Approval' (2009).

291 Goldacre, *Bad Pharma*, pp. 74–5.

have been using harmful medicines has been made against the FDA.[292] This potentially reflects undue defensiveness on the part of pharmaceuticals regulators, which seem very concerned about the release of information evidencing their own shortcomings.

The FDA has been caught out also for conflicts of interest. In the Vioxx case, there were several examples of this. During the approvals process, 'the regulated and the regulator conferred' in a manner described as essentially 'corrupt'.[293] Later, the FDA meeting about how to respond to growing concerns about risk was attended by ten members with conflicts of interest (out of thirty-two attending), and 'nine of those ten voted to keep the drug[] on the market, compared with the 60/40 split among the remainder of the committee'.[294]

Another shortcoming with regulation concerns the lack of post-marketing surveillance and lack of responsiveness to growing awareness of risks of approved medicines. One reason for this, applicable to the FDA, has been the 'shortage of experts in the area of drug safety and public health'.[295] Failure to act in a quick and decisive manner was a feature of the Vioxx case, in which it 'took fourteen months of intense negotiation before a warning was added to labelling, which cautioned [] use by those with heart disease'.[296] Finally, it has been noted that 'regulators that have approved a drug are often reluctant to take it off the market, in case that is seen as an admission of their failure to spot problems in the first place.'[297] Again, in the Vioxx case, the failures of the FDA 'led to a loss of public confidence in the agency and a debate about the regulatory system'.[298]

Another set of problems exists with respect to the many pharma groups which undertake clinical testing and manufacturing in developing countries and other low-cost jurisdictions. This type of outsourcing creates difficulty in ensuring compliance with the standards of practice adopted in importing countries. Much manufacturing activity takes place in China. It has been estimated that it would take the FDA eighteen years to inspect all the Chinese sites at which drugs bound for the United States are manufactured.[299] Understanding the difficulty in ensuring compliance, the FDA has sought to enter into agreements with foreign regulators (including the Chinese) to cooperate in compliance and enforcement matters. This has led to the accusation that the 'FDA is outsourcing its

[292] Goldacre, *Bad Pharma*, p. 92. [293] Thomas, 'The Vioxx Story', 372.
[294] Goldacre, *Bad Pharma*, p. 127.
[295] McDonnell, 'Drug Safety and Pharmacovigilance', 198–9.
[296] Gilhooley, 'Vioxx's History', 941. [297] Goldacre, *Bad Pharma*, p. 163.
[298] Gilhooley, 'Vioxx's History', 941. [299] Liu, 'Leaving the FDA Behind', 4.

regulatory power to other countries, some of which are highly susceptible to corrupt regulatory practices and counterfeit production'.[300]

These are just some of the reasons for which writers in this area conclude that the 'tort system will be called upon to play its traditional role in correcting wrongful injuries caused by pharmaceutical manufacturers'.[301]

4.4 Case Study III: 'The Next Catastrophe'

The insolvent entity problem can arise in many ways. A variation on this theme involves a one-off, large-scale industrial accident – 'The Next Catastrophe' of which Charles Perrow writes.[302] Here we speak of catastrophes like the explosion of a chemical plant or of an oil installation. This type of accident has become a feature of the modern world, and the reasons for it are not hard to find. Part of the explanation was discussed in Chapter 2, which outlined the reasons for which businesses pursue growth strategies. Businesses need to grow in size in order to achieve economies of scale and scope, and/or do so in the process of internalising market transactions. The impetus to growth is clear in the chemical industry, for example, where a doubling in the capacity of a plant is achievable upon a mere 60 per cent increase in fixed costs.[303] Globalisation has been a force for growth and consolidation, in many cases increasing the minimum efficient scale of industry. This creates the problem which Perrow identifies: large industrial businesses with giant plants and storage facilities, which in many cases are located in close proximity to large cities, and the mass transportation of hazardous materials. Frequently, industrial processes are 'tightly coupled', meaning that they are closely integrated in geographic and operational terms.[304] The result of large scale, tight coupling, mass transportation or supply, and large populations at risk of injury is the potential for major accidents. Prior examples include the Bhopal chemical plant catastrophe of 1984 and the *Deepwater Horizon* explosion and oil spill of 2010.

In Chapter 1, it was observed that those of us in the advanced world are exposed to the substantial risks that 'synthetic living' brings. Many of these risks arise from the use of chemicals, and it is no surprise to find it predicted 'that a chemical will become the next asbestos'.[305] The Bhopal

300 Liu, 'Leaving the FDA Behind', 4. 301 Feldman, 'Pushing Drugs', 599.
302 C. Perrow, *The Next Catastrophe* (2007). 303 Perrow, *The Next Catastrophe*, p. 182.
304 Perrow, *The Next Catastrophe*, pp. 6–7.
305 Gormley and Matsa, 'Growing Out of Trouble', 2782.

catastrophe fell just short of that mark. It involved a chemical plant operated by Union Carbide India Ltd (UCIL), a subsidiary that was 50.9 per cent owned by Union Carbide Corporation. The plant had been inadequately designed and constructed. Cheap but unproven technological features were employed. The plant was used to manufacture pesticides, the principal ingredient of which was methyl isocyanate. That chemical is especially toxic when it comes into contact with water. An independent expert concluded that the proximity of the chemical plant's gas storage tanks to the water-cooling system was unsafe.[306] Moreover, because the plant came to be unprofitable, UCIL management treated it as a low priority. 'That assumption of unimportance set in motion a self-confirming vicious circle in which worker indifference and management cost-cutting became mutually reinforcing and resulted in deteriorating conditions that became more dangerous.'[307] Managers were provided with scant resources to maintain the plant. On the night of the explosion, important safety mechanisms designed to prevent a chemical leak failed.[308] Personnel were supervised inadequately and were untrained to deal with the emergency.[309] Thus a warning siren was not activated until gas started to leak into the atmosphere. Even then, it was turned off after five minutes and not restarted for ninety minutes.[310] The gas was blown by the wind over heavily populated parts of Bhopal. Up to 20,000 people were killed, while between 120,000 and 150,000 others were severely injured.[311] Overall, up to half a million persons suffered health problems.[312] The water table from which residents drew was contaminated for twenty years after the accident. The chemical plant site, now owned by the Madhya Pradesh government, remains un-remediated at the time of writing.[313] UCIL was insufficiently capitalised to satisfy claims for injury, which, following the passage of special legislation, were taken

306 Baughen, 'Multinationals and the Export of Hazard', 62.

307 K. E. Weick, 'Enacted Sensemaking in Crisis Situations', in D. S. Pugh (ed.), *Organization Theory: Selected Classic Readings* (5th edn., 2007), p. 409.

308 Engel and Martin, 'Union Carbide and James Hardie'.

309 Weick, 'Enacted Sensemaking in Crisis Situations', 404–5.

310 Weick, 'Enacted Sensemaking in Crisis Situations', 406.

311 Engel and Martin, 'Union Carbide and James Hardie'. By early 1987, 487,000 claims had been received pursuant to the Bhopal gas leak disaster (Processing of Claims) Act 1985 (Ind): A. C. Seward III, 'After Bhopal: Implications for Parent Company Liability' (1987) 21 *International Lawyer* 695, 696.

312 V. Mallett, 'Legal Wrangles Remain 30 Years after Bhopal', *Financial Times*, 9 November 2014, available at: www.ft.com/cms/0/9a181746-6595-11e4-aba7-00144feabdc0.html.

313 Mallett, 'Legal Wrangles Remain'.

over by the Indian government.[314] In US proceedings, Union Carbide Corporation argued against its own liability to injured claimants on the basis that it had had limited control only over UCIL and that its input into the design of the Bhopal plant had been modest.[315] After the US case was dismissed on the basis of forum non conveniens (as to which, see Chapter 3), the Indian High Court held that Union Carbide Corporation was 'prima facie liable', and would have to pay compensation of US$192 million, the bulk of which was paid upon settlement.[316]

The *Deepwater Horizon* oil well explosion occurred during an attempt by BP plc (which leased the oil rig of that name and operated the oil and gas prospect)[317] temporarily to shut down and cap the Macondo oil well, situated off the coast of Louisiana. The well had been sunk into fragile sandstone deep below the ocean surface. This meant that a large amount of debris accumulated around the base of the well. The presence of the debris led to several problems, including a breach in the 'shoe-track', which should have guided cement into the well annulus.[318] Halliburton was the contractor nominated to supply cementing services.[319] It was unsuccessful in its attempts to seal the well in order to prevent the flow of hydrocarbons.[320] Given the known risks of a failure properly to place the cement in the well, it was 'obvious' that the parties should have conducted a cement bond log test. BP decided not to undertake this test in order to save money. If the test had been undertaken, it would have demonstrated that the cement was not where it should have been.[321] Another contractor, Transocean, owned the oil rig and was responsible for drilling the well. It conducted a negative pressure test in order to determine whether the cement casing was intact and not leaking. Both

[314] Bhopal Gas Leak Disaster (Processing of Claims) Act 1985 (Ind). See Seward, 'After Bhopal', 696.

[315] *Bhopal I* 634 F Supp 842 (SDNY 1986); aff'd 809 F 2d 195 (2nd Cir. 1987).

[316] J. J. White, 'Corporate Judgment Proofing: A Response to Lynn LoPucki's The Death of Liability' (1998) 107 *Yale Law Journal* 1363, 1392, citing *Union Carbide Corp* v. *Union of India*, 26/88 (Madhya Pradesh HC, 4 April 1988).

[317] For ease of discussion, several different BP entities are referred to here by reference to the group as a whole. Transocean and Halliburton entities will be referred to in the same manner. More detail on the parties involved in the case can be found in H. M. Osofsky, 'Multidimensional Governance and the BP *Deepwater Horizon* Oil Spill' (2011) 63 *Florida Law Review* 1077, 1085.

[318] *In re Oil Spill by Oil Rig 'Deepwater Horizon' in the Gulf of Mexico, on April 20, 2010*, 21 F Supp 3d 657, [159]–[161] (ED La 2014)(rehearing denied *In re Deepwater Horizon* 775 F 3d 741 (5th Cir. 2015)).

[319] 21 F Supp 3d 657, [16]–[27]. [320] 21 F Supp 3d 657, [71].

[321] 21 F Supp 3d 657, [194]–[196].

Transocean and BP misinterpreted the results and erroneously declared the test a success.[322] At this point, the parties began to remove mud from the bottom of the pipeline. But this mud was the only barrier between the hydrocarbons and the seawater. The mud was removed without properly investigating several anomalies in pressure readings.[323] Gas then began to rise up through the pipeline and to deposit mud on the rig floor.

At this point, with disaster looming, the Transocean drill crew attempted to activate the blowout preventer (manufactured by Cameron International Corporation), and then to cause the blind shear rams to cut off the pipeline. However, both procedures were unsuccessful – the latter because the ram's batteries had been running low to the knowledge of Transocean, which had failed to replace them.[324] Finally, the master of the *Deepwater Horizon* failed to activate the emergency disconnect sequence (EDS), even as the rig began to shake, and it became obvious that a blowout was about to occur. Reasons for this failure included the lack of clarity in Transocean's policies about what constituted an emergency and about the transition of control over operations from the offshore installation manager to the master.[325] As a result of the failure to activate the EDS, the rig remained attached to the oil pipeline instead of detaching and floating away from it. The escape of gas from the well caused several explosions, which took eleven lives. The *Deepwater Horizon* burned for days, after which it capsized and sank. This caused the collapse of the oil pipeline, and oil was discharged for eighty-seven days. More than three million barrels of oil escaped before the Macondo well was capped.[326] The catastrophe need never have happened and could have been prevented at a number of stages. However, the cumulative failures of the several parties involved combined to cause the explosions, fire, escape of oil, loss of life, and other damage.

More than 3,000 lawsuits were brought against BP and its contract partners, by more than 100,000 named claimants seeking damages for losses including wrongful death, personal injury, damage to property, and purely financial losses.[327] Many actions were consolidated in multi-district litigation heard in the US District Court for the Eastern District of Louisiana.[328]

[322] 21 F Supp 3d 657, [234], [236], and [247]–[248].
[323] 21 F Supp 3d 657, [251], and [335].
[324] 21 F Supp 3d 657, [342], [346]–[348], [391], and [412].
[325] 21 F Supp 3d 657, [440], [442], and [444].
[326] 21 F Supp 3d 657, [3], and [5]–[7].
[327] 21 F Supp 3d 657, [8].
[328] See C. M. Sharkey, 'The BP Oil Spill Settlements, Classwide Punitive Damages, and Societal Deterrence' (2015) 64 *DePaul Law Review* 681.

A court-appointed claimant steering committee began negotiating with the defendants whilst preparing for trial.[329] Eventually, a 'class-wide settlement' was reached, which conceded class certification for the purposes of settlement only.[330] The settlement resulted in a consent judgment by Barbier J, *In re Oil Spill by Oil Rig 'Deepwater Horizon'*.[331] His Honour recorded that there had been negligence or worse in the conduct of each of the major parties. BP had been reckless in several decisions that it took, which demonstrated a lack of concern for process safety,[332] and was motivated primarily by the desire to save money.[333] Transocean was negligent in its testing (or failure to test) conditions in the well at several stages, and in its failure properly to maintain the blowout preventer.[334] Halliburton was negligent in its supervision of the placement of the cement and in monitoring the well.[335] The BP class settlement made use of a claims grid that compensated class members based on formulae for different categories of damages, such as property damage and financial loss.[336]

Prior to the settlement, BP had established a trust designed to deal with claims for compensation on an administrative basis (as has been common in the asbestos field). This was the Gulf Coast Claims Facility (GCCF), and it paid out more than US$6.5 billion to more than 220,000 claimants.[337] However, as is evident from the previous paragraph, not all claimants opted to submit their claims to the GCCF. Many claimants, such as commercial fishermen, oyster farmers, business owners and their employees, and coastal property owners opted to file claims in court – in part because of the potential for the award of punitive damages.[338] Indeed, while the GCCF was able to deal with many claims in a 'streamlined and efficient manner', BP ultimately decided to move away from it in resolving its liabilities. This was for various reasons, which

329 Sharkey, 'The BP Oil Spill Settlements', 693.
330 Sharkey, 'The BP Oil Spill Settlements', 697.
331 *In re Oil Spill by Oil Rig 'Deepwater Horizon' in the Gulf of Mexico, on April 20, 2010*, 21 F Supp 3d 657 (ED La 2014).
332 J. Ray, 'Offshore Safety and Environmental Regimes: A Post-Macondo Comparative Analysis of the United States and the United Kingdom' (2014) 33 *Mississippi College Law Review* 11, 20. The author believes, in addition, that there was an unhelpful element of 'groupthink' among the contracting parties: ibid., 21.
333 21 F Supp 3d 657, [195], [480], [499], and [518].
334 21 F Supp 3d 657, [335], [412], and [542]–[543].
335 21 F Supp 3d 657, [558].
336 Sharkey, 'The BP Oil Spill Settlements', 698.
337 Sharkey, 'The BP Oil Spill Settlements', 691.
338 Sharkey, 'The BP Oil Spill Settlements', 691–2.

included the lack of finality in awards made[339] and concern over the rigour with which awards were made.[340] The result was a successful 'class settlement' which involved the payment of 'peace premiums' to bring finality and also brought transparency and consistency of approach.[341] The GCCF was replaced by a court-supervised claims resolution facility.[342]

BP's total liabilities for the *Deepwater Horizon* oil spill have been estimated at US$55 billion, which includes the $18.7 billion settlement with federal, state, and local governments.[343] Most of BP's liability payments have been met from its own resources – given the lack of suitable insurance for the type of low-risk, high-damage catastrophe that the blowout involved (an issue explored in Chapter 3). However, a concern arises about the potential for similar types of accident in the future involving a defendant (or defendants) without the same capacity to pay (the 'insolvent entity problem').[344] The potential for another large-scale accident is real. This is for a number of reasons. First, studies concerning the oil and similar industries indicate a large degree of substandard practice. Long before *Deepwater Horizon*, experts had been warning about the shortcomings of blowout preventers used on offshore oil rigs.[345] This concern about risk is reflected in events occurring in the decade prior to *Deepwater Horizon*, which featured scores of losses of well control and the uncontrolled loss of hydrocarbons. Moreover, with some 4,000 deep-water wells 'already drilled and more pending, there will be a substantial number of additional opportunities for environmental

339 S. Issacharoff and D. T. Rave, 'The BP Oil Spill Settlement and the Paradox of Public Litigation' (2014) 74 *Louisiana Law Review* 397, 399–400 and 402–3.

340 J. Collinridge, 'BP Warns over Millions of Dollars of "Fictitious" Compensation Claims for the 2010 Gulf of Mexico Oil Spill', *The Independent*, 16 May 2013, available at: www.independent.co.uk/news/uk/home-news/bp-warns-over-millions-of-dollars-of-fictitious-compensation-claims-for-the-2010-gulf-of-mexico-oil-8618423.html.

341 Issacharoff and Rave, 'The BP Oil Spill Settlement', 402–3.

342 Issacharoff and Rave, 'The BP Oil Spill Settlement', 401–2.

343 A. Parker, 'BP Bolstered by $18.7bn Settlement over Gulf Spill', *Financial Times*, 4–5 July 2015, 14.

344 See W. K. Viscusi and R. J. Zeckhauser, 'Deterring and Compensating Oil-Spill Catastrophes: The Need for Strict Two-Tier Liability' (2011) 64 *Vanderbilt Law Review* 1717, 1718. Even BP has failed fully to reform, there being evidence that it is 'not paying sufficient attention to . . . critical safety measures': T. Burgis, 'Leaked BP Report Reveals Risks of Lethal Accidents', *Financial Times*, 13 December 2016, available at: www.ft.com/content/a62438fc-be36-11e6-8b45-b8b81dd5d080.

345 National Academy of Engineering and National Research Council, 'Macondo Well – Deepwater Horizon Blowout: Lessons for Improving Offshore Drilling Safety' (2011), 40.

disasters' involving loss of life and personal injuries.[346] Second, companies operating in highly risky industries, where insurance cover might be either too expensive or not available at all, have the usual incentives to engage in judgment-proofing behaviour. The evidence is that large chemical companies frequently are connected to each other by small, local companies with limited capacity to satisfy mass-tort claims. This problem has been addressed in the United States and elsewhere by a 'responsible care' regime, under which larger companies are expected to maintain 'a chain of stewardship for their chemicals upstream and downstream'.[347] In the US oil industry, moreover, the risk of such behaviour is ameliorated, in part, by special legislative schemes of great interest to us, including that under the Oil Pollution Act 1990 (examined in Chapter 8). However, neither of these initiatives negates the problem completely.

Returning to a more general point, *Deepwater Horizon* illustrates the continuing dangers of modern, tightly coupled industrial processes. Writing of the processes observed in the *Deepwater Horizon* case, J. B. Ruhl observes that the connections existing between risk nodes create systemic or 'networked risks'. These can be highly problematic because of the 'potential for cascading', meaning that even a localised initial failure in care could have disastrous effects and cause unbounded damage.[348] 'As system organization becomes more complex, even slight perturbations could have cascading and ultimately catastrophic consequences through the tightly interconnected system.'[349] The dangers become all the greater when costs are cut. Cost-cutting seems to be a systemic problem in the oil industry, given that declining oil wells can be made more profitable by cutting back on maintenance and other costs.[350] It is notable that, prior to *Deepwater Horizon*, US regulatory authorities had not addressed these and other dangers of catastrophe.[351]

Finally, *Deepwater Horizon* illustrates the type of business organisation found in some types of large-scale project. Several major, industrial

[346] Viscusi and Zeckhauser, 'Deterring and Compensating', 1762. 'This is not to mention the fact that "close calls are thousands of times more prevalent" than actual disasters': Perrow, *The Next Catastrophe*, p. xxvii.

[347] J. Braithwaite, *Regulatory Capitalism* (2008), p. 22.

[348] J. B. Ruhl, 'Managing Systemic Risk in Legal Systems' (2014) 89 *Indiana Law Journal* 559, 563.

[349] Ruhl, 'Managing Systemic Risk', 588.

[350] J. Bakan, *The Corporation* (2004), p. 82. See also Perrow, *The Next Catastrophe*, pp. xviii and xxi.

[351] Ruhl, 'Managing Systemic Risk', 587–8.

companies cooperated through a network of contracts to install, operate, and remove the oil rig. These parties failed properly to coordinate their operations in a safe way, and Barbier J found that each had acted 'negligently or worse'. An academic study of the case considered whether incentives were aligned properly between BP as lease operator and its subcontractors, such as the drilling contractor Transocean.[352] The authors make the point that incentives to operate safely might be different as between different network participants. Public-facing companies, such as BP, might have more at stake, in reputational terms, than subcontractors known only in the industry, such as Transocean. While the authors point to the fact that BP is likely to address such issues in its contracts (for example, by specifying service standards), this means that capacity to compensate depends (in part) upon private contractual allocations of responsibility for the incurrence of losses[353] – that is, unless statute law or tort law would facilitate an extension of liability. Once again, the Oil Pollution Act 1990 does enable this within certain limits. And this book looks at other ways in which an extension of liability can be accomplished.

4.5 Legal Responses

As discussed in Chapter 1, regulation and the creation of proper standards of conduct is seen, today, as requiring a multipronged approach. One prong involves traditional, command-and-control regulation. Such regulation is important in designing proactive systems and mechanisms of accountability. This is so especially when companies engage in projects on a large scale, with closely integrated operations and the potential for widespread destruction.[354] Time and again, however, command-and-control regulation has proven inadequate in the industrial setting. It is appropriate to catalogue (or reiterate) some of the reasons for this. First, as demonstrated in the pharmaceuticals case study, regulation is a finite resource. Regulatory bodies are subject to inevitable personnel and budgetary constraints, meaning that they face trade-offs in fulfilling their stated objectives.[355] This might be reflected at a higher level in poor policy-making, which is reactive to events rather than principled in nature. It might be reflected, at the

352 M. A. Cohen, M. Gottlieb, J. Linn, and N. Richardson, 'Deepwater Drilling: Law, Policy, and Economics of Firm Organization and Safety' (2011) 64 *Vanderbilt Law Review* 1853.
353 Cohen, Gottlieb, Linn, and Richardson, 'Deepwater Drilling', 1885.
354 Perrow, *The Next Catastrophe*, pp. 302–3.
355 C. R. Sunstein, *Risk and Reason* (2002), pp. 19ff.

operational level, in the fact that regulators can obtain from site inspections and reading of documentation no more than 'isolated glimpses' of regulated activities.[356] They have limited timeframes within which to conduct assessments and file reports. Second, regulators are not as close to the action as operating companies, their employees, and agents. Regulatory bodies inevitably operate at a remove from local factors that affect the use of standard procedures and equipment. They are not familiar with working styles and individual workers. They might not be up to speed with innovations that necessarily impact upon understandings of all of the above. Third, members of regulatory teams are likely, at best, to be expert in operational and technical matters, with limited insight into effective organisational design. This means that problems are not dealt with effectively on a company-wide basis. Fourth, the last two problems mean that regulatory agencies become too reliant upon regulated companies for information and demonstrations of safety.[357] Each organisation will have to work closely with the other and relations might become over-friendly. 'Regulators, being human beings, tend to establish personal relationships with the regulated – they get to like the people they oversee and come to sympathize with their problems on a personal level – and this sometimes compromises their ability to identify, report or sanction violations.'[358] Fifth, safety and other standards might not be ambitious enough or appropriate to the activities in question. Standards that are in place might not be properly enforced.[359] Some of these problems are evident in the case studies in this chapter.

One of this book's key messages is that the imposition of appropriate liability upon risk-taking companies, parent companies, other shareholders, and/or network partners can induce appropriate precautions in risk-taking companies. In economic terms, the imposition of liability upon responsible parties means that costs of wrongs are 'internalised' within companies, groups of companies, and networks, which provides the incentive to avoid their future occurrence. In slightly different language, the imposition of liability helps to deter responsible parties from injury-causing conduct. This book explores two kinds of ex post legal response to mass-torts that cause risk-taking companies to be unable to meet their liabilities. First, it examines an appropriate statutory response, which would see the introduction of an exception to limited liability in the case of personal injury claims. Second, it examines ways in which tort

356 J. Reason, *Managing the Risks of Organizational Accidents* (1998), ch. 8.
357 Reason, *Managing the Risks of Organizational Accidents*, p. 171.
358 Reason, *Managing the Risks of Organizational Accidents*, p. 174.
359 This is seen as 'endemic': Bakan, *The Corporation*, p. 152.

law currently assists in extending liability beyond the insolvent company to other entities within the group and the network and ways of developing individual torts so as to make the tort regime more effective.

4.6 Conclusions

This chapter completes the first part of this book, which sets out the business and legal context in which the insolvent entity problem arises. The chapters in this part have dealt with business history, organisation theory, the legal building blocks for corporate groups and networks, structuring of relations so as to protect the assets of the group or network participants, and case studies involving the commission of mass-torts. As stated in the introduction to this chapter, the problems created by corporate groups and network participants undertaking modern, industrial processes giving rise to injuries on a mass scale often have been subject to ex post government action designed to alleviate crises. This demonstrates the need for better alignment of industrial activities and their full social costs and for better ways of achieving tort goals of compensation and deterrence. In sum, the examples of mass-torts in this chapter illustrate (once again) the need to think through issues of extended liability as a matter of urgency. The next chapter begins this process by exploring essential characteristics of corporate groups and networks, which might be salient in grounding their liability.

PART II

Theory

5

Conceptions of Group and Network Liability

5.1 Introduction

In order to develop effective forms of extended liability in resolution of the insolvent entity problem, this book seeks to obtain a deep understanding of corporate groups and networks. Prior chapters have set out the business and legal contexts in which those business forms operate. But there is a further, important perspective on the subject matter to be taken into account – a more philosophical perspective. This chapter seeks to understand what philosophers, sociologists, and more theoretically inclined lawyers identify as the important features of corporate groups, corporate networks, and their activities. This chapter proceeds by examining each of the building blocks of corporate groups and networks. It starts with simple groups of individuals. We then move on to consideration of the company, which is a type of group in organisational form, before finally considering corporate groups and networks. This chapter identifies the importance of the relationships between persons that are at the heart of all business forms and the potential for action that these relationships create. In sum, these relationships establish the basic deterrability of organisations. Liability can be extended within complex organisational forms without the need for either the exercise of control or fault at the activity or transactional level. The final section of this chapter will determine whether, in seeking to extend liability beyond an insolvent subsidiary, it is better to take an 'enterprise' or an 'entity' approach. It is concluded that the enterprise approach is inconsistent with the way in which responsibility arises in law. Any workable liability regime must treat the corporate entity as the basic unit of accountability.

5.2 Theorising the Group of Persons

The social pervasiveness of 'groups' and of group membership has given rise to concerted efforts to identify their most important attributes – in terms of what defines them, holds them together, and permits them to be held responsible when things go wrong. This first section of this chapter provides the 'collective wisdom' about groups, drawing on the work of well-known philosophers and sociologists. The focus is on groups of persons, taken as generic phenomena, and on commonly found group attributes such as coordination, commitment, reproachfulness, and responsibility. The point of the exercise is to consider ways in which groups are conceptualised outside the law and to examine their operation within the wider, social context. The perspectives provided are important in how we, as lawyers, should conceive of the company and the corporate group or network of which it forms part.

The literature on groups provides a rigorous set of criteria for their identification.[1] It is not suggested that each of the criteria need be present in order to identify a group; however, the more of them that are present, the more certain we can be that we have identified a group. We begin with the observation that virtually all natural persons (or 'individuals') are *social beings*, meaning that they live and work in various groups within society. For most individuals, living and working in groups is necessary because they are not self-sufficient – they cannot create all of the circumstances necessary to live their lives in the modern world. Individuals must cooperate with others in order to obtain such things as food and shelter, sexual relations, and fraternity.[2] The typical individual is a member of a number of different and overlapping social groups – the family, the church, the sports team, and so on.[3] Each of these groups helps to fulfil one or more of the individual's needs. A large proportion of individuals participates in the activities of one or more companies with respect to which they will be either investors and/or have an employment relationship.

Our ability to organise in groups is facilitated by our ability to communicate verbally and to conceptualise the state of the world and various relationships between individuals. According to John Searle, by prior mental conceptualisation and by subsequent utterance through 'speech acts', we can imbue individuals with statuses recognised by others and assign them certain functions to perform. These 'status functions' are of importance because of the 'deontic powers' attaching to them, such as

[1] See, likewise, R. Sanchez Brigido, 'Collective Intentional Activities and the Law' (2009) 29 *Oxford Journal of Legal Studies* 305, 305 (most accounts of collective intentional activities are too demanding).

[2] R. Tuomela, *The Philosophy of Sociality: The Shared Point of View* (2007), p. 192.

[3] See M. Gilbert, *A Theory of Political Obligation* (2006), p. 95.

rights, permissions, and duties.[4] Deontic powers 'have a unique trait' in that, 'once recognized, they provide us with reasons for acting that are independent of our inclinations and desires.'[5] With these tools of conceptualisation, language, status functions, and deontic powers, individuals can create their own organisational reality – create the office of the president, a company, or a game.[6] Searle takes a specific interest in the ways in which persons use a type of speech act – the declaration – to facilitate the creation of companies.[7] '[T]he whole point of doing this is to create a rather elaborate set of power relationships between actual people; indeed, the corporation consists of such relationships.'[8] The very point of the company – as with any other organisation – is that it is an *enabling device* that increases human power and allows persons to do an extended range of things.[9]

So what are the important features of the 'group'? In terms of numbers, it seems difficult to argue with the idea that a group need comprise no more than two individuals.[10] A theory of groups requiring any greater number of participants would be arbitrary. Indeed, the idea that groups are enabling and that they facilitate the ability of individuals to do things is consistent with group membership of two persons. A group of two individuals is capable of displaying each of the important features of groups now to be identified.

One simple, but important feature of the group is that, when undertaking tasks, it can be distinguished from persons who are acting not together, but simply in parallel.[11] The very idea of a group entails individuals doing things together in a *coordinated* way; they work with each other in undertaking tasks. This leads to a second attribute of groups, which is that they are formed for various purposes. Group purposes might be modest, such as taking a walk.[12] Individuals taking a walk together might have further, more specific, private purposes, such as exercising, catching up on gossip, or heading towards a mutual engagement. One individual's private purposes need not be identical to those of the others with whom they coordinate. The private purposes for which

[4] J. R. Searle, *Making the Social World: The Structure of Human Civilization* (2010), pp. 8–9.

[5] Searle, *Making the Social World*, p. 9.

[6] Searle, *Making the Social World*, p. 17.

[7] Searle, *Making the Social World*, pp. 97ff.

[8] Searle, *Making the Social World*, p. 98.

[9] Searle, *Making the Social World*, p. 105.

[10] Thus, see, e.g., Gilbert, *A Theory of Political Obligation*, p. 100.

[11] T. Isaacs, *Moral Responsibility in Collective Contexts* (2011), p. 44; Sanchez Brigido, 'Collective Intentional Activities', p. 306.

[12] Gilbert, *A Theory of Political Obligation*, pp. 102ff.

individuals join the group and partake of its activities need not be known to each other at all. While this might be the subject of agreement amongst philosophers, a question arises as to whether each member of the group should know and understand the purposes of the group itself. On one view, the participants should know of the group purposes and of their own functions within the group.[13] The common purpose is part of what it means to be a group in the first place. The common purpose binds participants together. But, in Christopher Kutz's slightly looser view, it is enough that group participants actually and sufficiently overlap in the conception of the collective end to which they intentionally contribute.[14]

Many philosophers go further than Kutz and identify among the members of each group a *commitment* to group endeavours. The individual's decision to commit 'need not be the result of any deliberative process, of any weighing of reasons for and against'. It is not required, either, that one be *morally* committed to the course of action 'in light of its nature or expected consequences'.[15] The requisite commitment is a commitment 'together to constitute, as far as possible, a single body that believes that such-and-such'.[16] The commitment arises from decision-making by each group participant. Each makes a decision to adopt a particular goal for the group. In this way, rationality requires that the participant act in conformity with his or her decision.[17] According to Margaret Gilbert, decisions, once made, 'stand as guides to action until they are wilfully undone. Thus, they may be said to "bind" their subjects'.[18] Raimo Tuomela sees joint commitment to group endeavours as of importance too. Each group participant must

> be committed (bound) to performing actions that further the group's ethos and other matters that the group is pursuing. Indeed, the members should be collectively committed, namely, committed as group members, to participating in group activities. Their collective commitment involves them also being 'socially' committed (that is, directly committed to other group members) to each other to act in the right group ways. Collective commitment has two basic, intertwined roles here. First, it 'glues' the members together around an ethos. This gives the foundation for the unity and identity of the group. Second, collective commitment serves to

13 Tuomela, The *Philosophy of Sociality*, p. 5.

14 C. Kutz, *Complicity: Ethics and Law for a Collective Age* (2000), p. 90.

15 Gilbert, *A Theory of Political Obligation*, p. 127.

16 Gilbert, *A Theory of Political Obligation*, p. 138.

17 Gilbert, *A Theory of Political Obligation*, p. 128.

18 Gilbert, *A Theory of Political Obligation*, p. 130.

> give joint authority to the group members to pursue ethos-related action.[19]

Given these preconditions to the formation of groups, including (on the stronger view) knowledge of the purposes of the group, commitment to group endeavours, and coordination of activities, a certain level of conformity *can* be expected among participants. '[W]hen people have a collective goal, . . . the underlying joint commitment gives each sufficient reason to direct his forces in a particular way. More precisely, each has a sufficient reason to coordinate his behaviour with that of the others in pursuit of the goal in question.'[20] Tuomela writes that 'the group members are collectively committed to satisfying their joint intention and are also socially committed to each other to performing their parts of the joint action that the intention is about. The collective commitment serves to keep the members together as a unit.'[21] Indeed, being a member of a group has an impact upon attitude: 'there often is a conformist attitude such as that I want you to regard me as a good person or as a good group member. Satisfying this pro-attitude may require conforming – adopting a certain attitude or acting in a certain way.'[22]

There might well be *pressure* to conform to group purposes or to the group ethos, which can be a powerful force. This might arise, for example, because it is important that group participants present a 'single face' to the outside world. Even if there has been debate within the group, the group presents itself as acting as one – which is an aspect of group power. When conformity is not forthcoming, action might be taken to secure it. Thus the attitudes and performance of individuals can be modulated through adjustments to organisational structures and/or culture, 'thereby inducing individuals to develop more group-minded preferences or behavioural dispositions'.[23] Indeed, pressure to conform might be applied in ways that are quite direct and confrontational. The pressure to conform and to present a united front might mean that the true attitudes of the participants are not merely marginalised, but suppressed. Thus appearances might become deceptive when those conforming to group attitudes 'appear

[19] Tuomela, *The Philosophy of Sociality*, p. 5.

[20] Gilbert, *A Theory of Political Obligation*, p. 146. Indeed, List and Pettit believe that what is required from members of a group, acting together as group agent, is a certain *coherence* and *rationality*. If there is inconsistency in the attitudes expressed, the conclusion must be that something is amiss and that the inconsistency should be rectified: C. List and P. Pettit, *Group Agency: The Possibility, Design, and Status of Corporate Agents* (2011), p. 39.

[21] Tuomela, *The Philosophy of Sociality*, p. 86.

[22] Tuomela, *The Philosophy of Sociality*, p. 68.

[23] List and Pettit, *Group Agency*, p. 126.

themselves to have the belief at issue'.[24] The pressures of conformity will 'involve, to a large extent, acting as if one personally wanted the goal to be achieved by virtue of the activity of each of the members'.[25]

When a group member fails to conform to group expectations, this might create a right in other participants to reproach him or her. In Gilbert's view, the fact of joint activity gives each group participant standing with respect to each other participant. This standing is special because it is not shared by persons generally; it arises from their joint activity.[26] Group participants are expected to monitor each other and to control recalcitrant fellow participants through criticism, reproach, and even sanctions.[27] This ability to reproach each other is likely to be reciprocal in each participant.[28] It suggests that 'those engaged in a joint activity have rights against one another to action appropriate to the joint activity and correlative obligations towards one another, rights and obligations that are somehow grounded in the joint activity.'[29] This is a theme confirmed by Christian List and Philip Pettit, who observe:

> In domains where relevant obligations rule, the parties can address claims to others; expect others to comply; and in case of non-compliance, have a complaint others must endorse, on pain of having to reject the conventions. And in such domains, parties must acknowledge that others occupy a reciprocal status: they too may address claims, expect compliance, and make compelling complaints about failures.[30]

The adoption of group purposes, pressures to conform, and the practice of reproaching aberrant group participants mean that, to some extent, the group *extinguishes individual autonomy*.[31] This effect is magnified where the individual fulfils a function within a group that is open to competition, so that he or she can be replaced. Indeed, in certain group situations, the individual might *lose aspects of his or her personhood*. The individual becomes depersonalised because he or she adopts the group ethos to matters and fulfils his or her role as a mere 'cog in the wheel'. The larger the group is, the more likely that this will be the case. The cog-in-the-wheel analogy is taken to an extreme by

[24] Gilbert, *A Theory of Political Obligation*, p. 137.
[25] Gilbert, *A Theory of Political Obligation*, p. 138.
[26] Gilbert, *A Theory of Political Obligation*, p. 104.
[27] Gilbert, *A Theory of Political Obligation*, p. 115.
[28] Tuomela, *The Philosophy of Sociality*, p. 176.
[29] Gilbert, *A Theory of Political Obligation*, p. 115.
[30] List and Pettit, *Group Agency*, p. 173.
[31] Tuomela, *The Philosophy of Sociality*, p. 57.

Meir Dan-Cohen, who writes that 'organizational position-holders are not only treated as cogs but are actually becoming ones: by fully internalizing the organizational point of view, individuals are espousing an instrumental self-definition that pervades their entire being, shaping their social interactions and moulding their world view.'[32]

The result of these attributes of the group, involving group purposes, joint commitment, coordination, and conformity, is that the power of the individuals who constitute the group is magnified – potentially many times over. Groups enable the doing of things that are not possible when attempted by individuals acting alone. Participants coordinate with each other so that things can be done more enjoyably, more skilfully, more quickly, in bigger numbers, and so on. Indeed, it seems that simple membership of the group encourages persons to strive harder to reach certain goals.[33] The motivating aspect of group participation manifests itself in the 'corporate ladder' and other conceptual structures which enable participants to be rewarded for performance through promotions that bring higher prestige and pay. Other attributes of the group further contribute to its power:

> A group's power derives from its financial assets, the network of clients it can summon in its support, the degree of dependency it can create in those who rely on it as an employer, customer, or financier, its mortality-free time-horizon, and the fact that it need not suffer any anxiety or related emotions.[34]

A final point about groups follows from what we have learned already. Groups can be utilised in ways that enable the commission of wrongs that have a significant impact upon society. It has been observed that 'groups cultivate a special social identity. This identity often encourages risky behaviour, leads individuals to behave against their self-interest, solidifies loyalty, and facilitates harm against non-members.'[35] Larger groups can enjoy the functional advantages gained by the diffusion of responsibility for tasks necessary to carry out common goals. Groups thus permit the subversion of social norms 'through strategies that disaggregate' complex tasks,

[32] M. Dan-Cohen, *Rights, Persons, and Organizations: A Legal Theory for Bureaucratic Society* (1986), p. 202.

[33] Tuomela, *The Philosophy of Sociality*, p. 55. [34] List and Pettit, *Group Agency*, p. 183.

[35] N. K. Katyal, 'Conspiracy Theory' (2003) 112 *Yale Law Journal* 1307, 1312. See also B. Fisse and J. Braithwaite, *Corporations, Crime and Accountability* (1993), p. 22; T. J. Leach, 'Civil Conspiracy: What's the Use?' (1999) 54 *University of Miami Law Review* 1, 28–9.

'playing on the idea that little bad acts are excusable'.[36] Successful group endeavours have the potential to cascade into multiple such endeavours.[37] This is because the 'very formation of a joint enterprise generates a mutual commitment to [relevant wrongdoing], supplementing and reinforcing the resolve of an individual' compared to what it would be were he acting alone.[38] As we have seen, wrongdoing might arise on a very large scale, involving mass injuries. All of this entails that the legislature, regulators, and courts have special reasons to be vigilant when it comes to groups.

Having examined important attributes of groups, we can turn to a preliminary consideration of responsibility. We begin by considering responsibility from the philosophical perspective. Notice, first, how groups and the individuals who comprise them operate at *different levels*. 'These are two separate realms in terms of goal possession',[39] and external parties interact differently with each of them. When dealing with the group, the external party does not need to 'look at everything that happens at the individual level'.[40] This idea is explored by Tracy Isaacs, who seeks to defend a 'two level theory of moral responsibility' regarding the actions of groups – a theory 'that recognizes responsibility at the individual and collective level'.[41] Isaacs says that the 'responsibility of collectives is not the blameworthiness and praiseworthiness of their members.'[42] She explains that:

> The individuals who contribute to the outcome [of a collective action] do not – actually cannot – perform or intend the whole act even if they may share the collective goal and contribute to its achievement. The collective intends and performs the action. Therefore, in relation to the act as a whole – that is, in relation to the collective act – only the collective as such is morally responsible.[43]

Consistent with this, Isaacs does not automatically equate the responsibility of the group with the responsibility of individual participants.[44]

[36] Katyal, 'Conspiracy Theory', 1327. This practice can work against the achievement of the common end because of the bounded knowledge of individuals about the overall nature of the enterprise: ibid., 1353.

[37] Katyal, 'Conspiracy Theory', 1335.

[38] A. Simester, 'The Mental Element in Complicity' (2006) 122 *Law Quarterly Review* 578, 599–600.

[39] Gilbert, *A Theory of Political Obligation*, p. 123.

[40] List and Pettit, *Group Agency*, p. 5.

[41] Isaacs, *Moral Responsibility in Collective Contexts*, p. 7.

[42] Isaacs, *Moral Responsibility in Collective Contexts*, p. 53.

[43] Isaacs, *Moral Responsibility in Collective Contexts*, p. 55.

[44] Isaacs, *Moral Responsibility in Collective Contexts*, p. 61.

The responsibility of individuals must be established separately. They are responsible and blameworthy not for collective actions, but for their contributions to such actions.[45] Having said this, there is an undoubted 'interaction between the collective and individual levels of agency' because 'collective action lends shape and form to the obligations of individuals.'[46] Individuals can be called blameworthy, therefore, 'in a particular and morally significant way that cannot be articulated independently of the collective action context in which they participate'.[47]

Individuals and groups do not exhaust the levels at which actions take place and at which responsibility arises. According to Tuomela, 'social institutions in their core sense are norm systems obeyed in accordance with relevant social practices, often highly routine practices accountable in terms of "collective pattern-governed behaviours".'[48] This is to say that individuals participate in groups and groups participate in society in patterned ways, the smaller components being nested within larger entities.[49] Groups perform functions which are necessary to the operation of wider society, creating order and guiding individual action.[50] The patterning of behaviours, the infusion of social norms into groups, and the impact of those norms on individual participants are of importance in thinking through issues of both accountability and responsibility. Groups should not be permitted to act in ways that are detrimental to society as a whole; they should strive to be socially useful and contribute to the flourishing of society as a whole.[51] Where groups act in ways that are detrimental to society, they need to be reformed and wrongdoing needs to be dealt with.

List and Pettit believe there to be three important criteria in imposing responsibility on individual actors or 'agents', including 'group agents'. These are that the 'agent faces a normatively significant choice, involving the possibility of doing something good or bad, right or wrong'; that the 'agent has the understanding and access to evidence required for making normative judgments about the options'; and that the 'agent has the control required for choosing between the options'.[52] They believe that

[45] Isaacs, *Moral Responsibility in Collective Contexts*, p. 83.
[46] Isaacs, *Moral Responsibility in Collective Contexts*, p. 10.
[47] Isaacs, *Moral Responsibility in Collective Contexts*, p. 11.
[48] Tuomela, *The Philosophy of Sociality*, p. 11. [49] List and Pettit, *Group Agency*, p. 40.
[50] Tuomela, *The Philosophy of Sociality*, pp. 183 and 192. 'The order aspect obviously involves that people will obey the norms, which typically are supposed to serve basic human needs and interests': ibid., p. 192.
[51] Tuomela, *The Philosophy of Sociality*, p. 195.
[52] List and Pettit, *Group Agency*, p. 155.

group agents can fulfil these conditions. The second condition is fulfilled when groups take decisions according to their decision-making procedures. Where such procedures appear not to exist, society has a right to insist that they be established.[53] The greater difficulty is with the third condition. Those who directly cause wrongs, the 'enactors', will be responsible. So will 'designers', who 'determine the group's procedures for forming its beliefs and desires and taking its actions'.[54] Other group participants might have responsibility that varies with their roles.[55] The group itself will be responsible also because it maintains 'procedures for the formation and enactment of its attitudes, arranging things so that some individuals are identified as the agents to perform a required task and others are identified as possible back-ups'.[56]

The question arises whether group-level responsibility is *redundant* in the face of the responsibility of individuals – particularly the responsibility of 'enactors' and 'designers' as List and Pettit describe them. These writers believe group-level responsibility to be very important. They identify circumstances in which, say, a group applies a policy in a routine way so that group responsibility arises without any necessary individual responsibility. No individual might have behaved in a way which is identifiable as substandard.[57] Thus the responsibility of the group might be all the responsibility there is.[58] The imposition of responsibility provides encouragement for the group to learn and to transform itself when required. 'By finding the group responsible, we make clear to members that unless they develop routines for keeping their [company, etc.] in check, they will share in member responsibility for what is done by the group and may also have a negative form of enactor responsibility for allowing it to be done.'[59] The need for group responsibility is confirmed by the literature on organisational design.[60]

Having identified these features of groups and their eligibility to be made responsible, List and Pettit ask, furthermore, whether we should treat groups as persons on par with individuals. Answering in the negative, they say that 'individuals enjoy a privileged position'. 'Group persons are deserving only of a lesser range of rights, and should be disciplined in an especially strict manner.'[61] This is because groups have an instrumental

[53] List and Pettit, *Group Agency*, p. 159. [54] List and Pettit, *Group Agency*, p. 164.
[55] List and Pettit, *Group Agency*, p. 164. [56] List and Pettit, *Group Agency*, p. 163.
[57] P. A. French, *Collective and Corporate Responsibility* (1984), p. 15.
[58] List and Pettit, *Group Agency*, p. 166. [59] List and Pettit, *Group Agency*, p. 169.
[60] J. Reason, *Managing the Risks of Organizational Accidents* (1998), p. 36.
[61] List and Pettit, *Group Agency*, p. 180.

value; they are created to serve individual needs. 'Whether or not a group person should exist, and whether it should function within this or that regime of obligation, ought to be settled by reference to the rights or benefits of the individuals affected, members and non-members alike.'[62] This is similar to Dan-Cohen's views that '[w]hile the Kantian notion of individual autonomy is closely-linked to the perception of individuals as ends, formal organizations exist only as means. As such, they are not equal members of the Kantian kingdom of ends, and they do not deserve or admit of the special kind of respect that gives rise to the individual's [autonomy rights].'[63] The thing about these autonomy rights is that they 'embody and protect important aspects of personhood'. They are 'infused with special worth associated with the person, which is the unique, non-marketable worth that is dignity'.[64]

5.3 Theorising the Organisation

Organisations are particular kinds of group which incorporate the ordinary features of groups of persons (just discussed) and further noteworthy features. Important additional features identified in the operation of these sorts of groups, but rarely articulated in either court judgments or the company law literature, are hierarchy, structure, functional separation of roles and responsibilities, and formalised decision-making. These features facilitate the coordination of organisation constituents, and are reasons for which 'organisations are indispensable tools for concerted action.'[65] They are mechanisms for bringing together groups of persons 'in a managed and rationalized structure' so that 'purposive collective action' can be undertaken.[66]

Let us examine these important, additional features of organisations. In larger groups, personal relations and mutual cooperation give way to hierarchy and structure. In the most formal of organisations, this entails high-level, long-term, and strategic decision-making at the top,[67] decisions

[62] List and Pettit, *Group Agency*, p. 182.
[63] Dan-Cohen, *Rights, Persons, and Organizations*, p. 61.
[64] Dan-Cohen, *Rights, Persons, and Organizations*, p. 96.
[65] W. R. Scott, *Institutions and Organizations* (4th edn., 2014), p. 90.
[66] J. W. Meyer, G. S. Drori, and H. Hwang, 'World Society and the Proliferation of Formal Organization', in G. S. Drori, J. W. Meyer, and H. Hwang (eds.), *Globalization and Organization: World Society and Organizational Change* (2006), p. 25.
[67] P. R. Lawrence and J. W. Lorsch, 'High-Performing Organizations in Three Environments', in D. S. Pugh (ed.), *Organization Theory: Selected Classic Readings* (5th edn., 2007), p. 120.

which run down the chain of command, and an organisational chart that indicates where individuals are placed within the decision-making and command structure.[68] Hierarchy and structure help to specify how decisions should be made and tasks allocated.[69] However, while many large organisations have a chain of command, experience indicates that, often, this is more important in its latent form than as a means for the actual exercise of control over subservient employee activity.

Larger, organised groups are likely to be structured along functional lines[70] (as we saw in Chapter 2), meaning that discrete teams of persons, or 'branching hierarchies', undertake specialised functions. This is an extension of the basic division of labour, and it manifests itself in departments (for example, production, purchasing, and marketing) efficiently servicing the organisation as a whole.[71] Decision-making powers in each functional unit are delegated to middle managers.[72] Middle managers have oversight of limited numbers of individuals, and their main responsibility is to coordinate work.[73] Individuals working within each functional unit are likely to specialise in their tasks. These individuals fully understand the work that others within their team are doing and coordinate activities with them. Branching hierarchies facilitate collective learning and memorisation. This is because the organisation has not only the benefit of what has been learned by teams and by individual team members, but also 'the awareness of who knows what'.[74] Branching hierarchies facilitate learning from mistakes and adoption of corrective procedures. The successful implementation of new practices in one part of the organisation can infiltrate others and bring about larger organisational change.[75]

Hierarchy and structure facilitate formalised decision-making procedures. At higher- and middle-management levels, decision-making often is deliberative, being undertaken by committee (for example, the board of directors or subcommittees thereof). Effective committees take advantage of diverse viewpoints and of the combined knowledge

[68] M. J. Hatch, *Organization Theory: Modern, Symbolic, and Postmodern Views* (3rd edn., 2013), pp. 92–3 and 242; Isaacs, *Moral Responsibility in Collective Contexts*, p. 98.

[69] Hatch, *Organization Theory*, p. 93.

[70] A. D. Chandler, *Scale and Scope: The Dynamics of Industrial Capitalism* (1990), p. 230.

[71] Hatch, *Organization Theory*, pp. 91–2.

[72] D. S. Pugh, 'Does Context Determine Form?', in D. S. Pugh (ed.), *Organization Theory: Selected Classic Readings* (5th edn., 2007), p. 34.

[73] S. M. Bainbridge, 'Why a Board? Group Decisionmaking in Corporate Governance' (2002) 55 *Vanderbilt Law Review* 1, 7.

[74] Bainbridge, 'Why a Board?', 20.

[75] Hatch, *Organization Theory*, p. 309.

of their members.[76] They produce solutions to problems that no single individual would be capable of.[77] At lower organisational levels, especially in the manufacturing sector, tasks are undertaken according to written procedures or established routines (for example, in the use of production schedules).[78] These procedures constrain action in a rational way, ensuring that it conforms to organisational objectives. They 'greatly reduce the discretion of most participants so that they make few choices and are circumscribed in the choices they do make'.[79] Written procedures and established routines facilitate uniform and measurable outcomes, which allows monitoring of work and detection of deviations from established standards.[80] They create efficiencies in training also, and in passing on relevant knowledge. More informal norms or expectations further assist in constraining conduct, so that organisation members think and act as a group. These features permit members 'to know what is expected of them in a wide variety of situations, including how to coordinate their behavior with that of others in acts of organizing', and might cover matters such as when to call attention to problems, how to dress, and when to display emotion.[81]

Hierarchy, structure, specialisation, and routine create conditions in which control, although latent, need *not* be exercised actively in order to achieve group purposes. This gives rise to an apparent paradox: that in larger organisations, day-to-day operations become *highly decentralised.* Especially in the manufacturing sector (which forms much of the background to this book), structuring of activity means that things tend to run themselves, and monitoring is routine rather than invasive in nature: 'when the responsibilities of specialized roles are laid down, and activities are regulated by standardized procedures and records, top management can afford to decentralize because the organizational machine will run as it has been set to run, and decisions will be made in the way that they were intended with less need to refer to the top.'[82] Thus a leading organisation studies scholar states that the facts of organisation 'do not confirm the common assumption that large organizations and the routines that go with them "pass the buck" upwards for decision'.[83]

Having said as much, structure, specialisation, and routine are less apparent in the service sector, in creative industries, and when market

[76] List and Pettit, *Group Agency*, p. 86. [77] C. Sunstein, *Infotopia* (2006), pp. 54–5.
[78] Hatch, *Organization Theory*, p. 151. [79] Scott, *Institutions and Organizations*, 24.
[80] Scott, *Institutions and Organizations*, 59; Tuomela, *The Philosophy of Sociality*, p. 192.
[81] Hatch, *Organization Theory*, p. 170. [82] Pugh, 'Does Context Determine Form?', 24.
[83] Pugh, 'Does Context Determine Form?', 22.

conditions are unstable. In unstable market conditions, for instance markets with constantly changing customer requirements, top managers do not behave as though they are omniscient and able to make decisions without consultation and feedback from the wider organisation. 'The definitive and enduring demarcation of functions becomes impossible. Responsibilities and functions, and even methods and powers, have to be constantly redefined through interaction with others participating in common tasks or in the solution of common problems.'[84] Much of this interaction takes place on a footing of equality and respect, rather than of command and control, 'communication between people of different ranks tend[ing] to resemble "lateral" consultation'.[85] This is interesting because it reflects the way that many corporate networks (considered later) operate when faced with similar market conditions.

Hierarchy, structure, and formalised decision-making give rise to conditions under which companies can and ought to be made responsible for their injurious conduct. This responsibility arises in a manner only indirectly related to the responsibility of the particular individuals who participate in organisational decision-making or who take actions on the organisation's behalf.[86] In the view of one influential group of philosophers, the key to *corporate* responsibility is the company's ability to make decisions which represent its own intentions, points of view, and attitudes. In his seminal work, Peter French identified the corporate internal decision (CID) structure as providing this ability. This structure enables the company to form reasons and to act for those reasons, which means that it can be treated as an intentional actor and as a moral person.[87] The CID structure is reflected in the organisational flow chart, which indicates where power is located within the company, and in the corporate-decision recognition rule that specifies when a decision has been made validly. French says that 'when the corporate act is consistent with an instantiation or an implementation of established corporate policy, then it is proper to describe it as having been done for corporate reasons, as having been caused by a corporate' intention.[88] An extension of French's work emphasises that, ordinarily, intentions form as part of forward-looking plans. These intentions involve commitments to action, allow for the coordination

[84] T. Burns, 'Mechanistic and Organismic Structures', in D. S. Pugh (ed.), *Organization Theory: Selected Classic Readings* (5th edn., 2007), pp. 103–4.

[85] Burns, 'Mechanistic and Organismic Structures', 104.

[86] French, *Collective and Corporate Responsibility*, p. 40.

[87] French, *Collective and Corporate Responsibility*, p. 38.

[88] French, *Collective and Corporate Responsibility*, p. 44.

of activities,[89] and direct company employees to adopt appropriate actions.[90]

In developing her two-tier structure of responsibility in the collective context (considered earlier), Isaacs asserts that the decision-making processes of organisations and other group actors are important in normative terms. Organisations, she notes, 'are highly-structured collectives with formal mechanisms for making decisions, articulating the collective's goals and interests, and outlining the positions of individuals within the structure'.[91] Isaacs believes the most significant feature of French's analysis to be 'that in order to understand the organizational intention there is no need to refer to the intentions of individuals':[92]

> Compromise is frequently the rule in group decision-making, mandating courses of action that would not be pursued if any one individual were in a position to make an executive decision. Even in cases in which an individual is authorized to make executive decisions, such that that individual's decisions are the organization's, the decisions she or he makes [in] the organizational role are not always consistent with decisions that would reflect the pursuit of her or his personal interests.[93]

Apart from picking out the importance of formalised decision-making structures, Isaacs' portrayal of organisations is significant in the process of looking backwards, after injury has been caused, in establishing 'intentionality' and in ascribing responsibility. More importantly from the present writer's perspective, she recognises the salience of formalised decision-making structures in explaining the importance of a *forward-looking* capacity for avoiding wrongdoing. The obligation of a group, such as an organisation, is to ensure that its constituents fulfil their stated functions and avoid wrongdoing.[94]

Although the present writer does not subscribe to the theory of free will that underlines the analysis of corporate intentionality by French and Isaacs (as to which, see Chapter 10), their views of organisational decision-making processes are helpful in explaining why organisations are *deterrable*. The ultimate aim of our consideration of the attributes of organisations, such as

[89] D. G. Arnold, 'Corporate Moral Agency', in P. A. French and H. K. Wettstein (eds.), *Shared Intentions and Collective Responsibility* (2006), p. 286.
[90] Arnold, 'Corporate Moral Agency', 289.
[91] Isaacs, *Moral Responsibility in Collective Contexts*, p. 98.
[92] Isaacs, *Moral Responsibility in Collective Contexts*, p. 29.
[93] Isaacs, *Moral Responsibility in Collective Contexts*, p. 30. See also, along similar lines, M. Dan-Cohen, 'Sanctioning Corporations' (2010) 19 *Journal of Law and Policy* 15, 25–7.
[94] Isaacs, *Moral Responsibility in Collective Contexts*, pp. 132 and 137.

companies, is to help construct a liability regime that is appropriate to them. An underlying premise is that legal liability is useful, not only in compensating injured persons, but in bringing about positive change in the conduct of risky activities. This is a matter of *deterrability*. Although a more formal discussion of this issue takes place in Chapter 11, it is useful to draw upon the business organisation literature at this point in order to explain courts' enhanced ability to deter wrongful conduct by imposing liability on companies and other organisations. Deterrability results from the forward-looking nature of organisational decision-making, the structures through which decisions are implemented, the ability to compel managers, employees, and agents to comply with decisions reached higher in the organisational hierarchy, and the ability to create uniform standards of conduct and consistent norms of behaviour. All of these things mean that organisations can bring about change that 'reverberates through the system'.[95]

Let us expand on some of these matters. First, courts have a significant role in developing standards of interaction between legal persons because they determine disputes on a case-by-case basis and receive evidence as to the actual workings of organisations. Tort decisions which respond to organisational failures typically outline the appropriate standards of interaction which should be achieved and have a signalling effect. The organisation is likely to have an enhanced capacity to interpret and learn from tort judgments and the norms of conduct that they promote. This is because organisations are advised by lawyers and have the technical expertise to determine proper responses to the imposition of liability. Organisations are likely to want to learn from court judgments against them so that they are seen as good corporate citizens worthy of continuing custom and respect. French describes the capacity to learn from past mistakes as one of 'reactive adaptation',[96] while Fisse and Braithwaite refer to 'responsive organisational change'.[97] This follows from the regulative nature of organisations. Organisations 'deal with collective action problems' and regulate behaviour in ways already examined.[98]

Second, while there is debate about the deterrability of individual wrongdoers, it is undoubted that organisations typically are deterrable and will respond constructively to tort liability decisions. Organisations are more likely than individuals to have the capability to make proper

95 Dan-Cohen, *Rights, Persons, and Organizations*, p. 130. See text that follows.
96 French, *Collective and Corporate Responsibility*, p. 162.
97 Fisse and Braithwaite, *Corporations, Crime and Accountability*, p. 40. See also Dan-Cohen, *Rights, Persons, and Organizations*, p. 134.
98 Scott, *Institutions and Organizations*, p. 81.

decisions about precautions to avoid harm in their interactions with others.[99] This capacity arises from their expertise, institutional memory, and the formalised decision-making structures noted earlier, employed to respond to changes in the external environment (including new legal directives) through processes of sense making,[100] risk assessment, and forward planning. 'Sanctioning the corporation involves direct deterrence when we envisage the sanction, in impersonal terms, as a "disturbing event" in the corporation's environment which serves to alert its decision making process to the existence of a certain dysfunction, triggering some standard operating procedure into taking remedial action consisting in some structural, or systemic change.'[101] Managers take the information they have about such disturbing events and formulate strategic responses with the assistance of advisors.[102] Organisations can take action, for example, by devising appropriate systems and procedures, investing in infrastructure and safety devices, determining which functional units and individuals shall undertake tasks (perhaps after training), monitoring performance, and terminating relationships with those employee/agents unable to perform adequately.[103] Given the ability of organisations to promote the development of group attitudes among members and to ensure conformity with group values and reproachability amongst members, groups have the potential to be especially effective in implementing their decisions.

Third, change brought about in one organisation can influence practice in the remainder of the industrial sector in which it operates. This means that the power of a judicial signal to bring about change is magnified. It follows from organisations being 'nested' within society. Organisation and interconnection together mean that there is the potential for many people to be affected by court decisions. 'A decision concerning an organization is accordingly more likely than one pertaining to an individual to reverberate through the system, affecting in various ways other organizations and, through them, multitudes of individuals.'[104] So

[99] Dan-Cohen, *Rights, Persons, and Organizations*, p. 134.

[100] Scott, *Institutions and Organizations*, pp. 237–8.

[101] Dan-Cohen, 'Sanctioning Corporations', 29–30. See also J. Pfeffer and G. R. Salancik, 'The Design and Management of Externally Controlled Organizations', in D. S. Pugh (ed.), *Organization Theory: Selected Classic Readings* (5th edn., 2007), pp. 138–9.

[102] M. T. Hannan and J. Freeman, 'The Population Ecology of Organizations', in D. S. Pugh (ed.), *Organization Theory: Selected Classic Readings* (5th edn., 2007), pp. 184–5.

[103] J. H. Arlen and W. B. MacLeod, 'Beyond Master-Servant: A Critique of Vicarious Liability', in M. S. Madden (ed.), *Exploring Tort Law* (2005), p. 120.

[104] Dan-Cohen, *Rights, Persons, and Organizations*, p. 130.

a disturbing event that leads to change in one organisation can lead to changes in industry norms.[105] This is a proven phenomenon which results from mimicry by one organisation so it conforms to the best practice established by another. Mimicry arises by the dissemination of best practice through a variety of channels. These channels include organisational publicity, movement of staff between organisations, adoption of new practices by professional and trade associations, and so on.[106] Such processes have been witnessed, for example, in improvements in safety and environmental protection made in the US chemical and petroleum industries.[107]

Organisations embody all of the basic attributes of groups of persons (coordination, commitment, conformity to group purposes, and reproachability among group participants), as well as those of hierarchy, structure, and formalised decision-making processes just discussed. In examining the latter feature, we noted that organisations might make decisions that no individual working for them would make. What impact does this have upon notions of individual responsibility? This is an important issue about which something should be said. Points made here will be relevant especially when we come back to the issue of shareholder liability in Chapter 8. The basic argument is to reaffirm that individuals retain responsibility for the parts that they play within their organisations.

One of the most advanced treatments of this topic is Christopher Kutz's 'Complicity Principle'. Under this principle, the law should take seriously the individual's intention to participate in a collective endeavour. Participation is an emanation of individual agency, the individual's intentions being reflected also in the idea that other individuals will play their parts in realising the collective purpose.[108] This is not to say that the individual is responsible only when others play their parts exactly as envisaged. Kutz explains that the 'possibility of expanding our powers (or rewards) through cooperation entails the risk that the resulting act will not align with our' preconceived interests.[109] However, those who participate in collective endeavours understand this risk. 'When we act together, we must expect

[105] M. A. Eisenberg, 'Corporate Law and Social Norms' (1999) 99 *Columbia Law Review* 1253, 1269–70.

[106] P. J. DiMaggio and W. W. Powell, 'Institutional Isomorphism', in D. S. Pugh (ed.), *Organization Theory: Selected Classic Readings* (5th edn., 2007), pp. 443 and 445.

[107] A. J. Hoffman, *From Heresy to Dogma: An Institutional History of Corporate Environmentalism* (1997).

[108] Kutz, *Complicity*, p. 141. [109] Kutz, *Complicity*, p. 156.

that the group act may have aspects we do not know about but with which we will have to reckon.'[110] This explains why individuals retain their complicity in collective actions which cause unintended harm. When the participant's position is compared to that of an outsider, it is not acceptable for him or her to plead that he or she was just a 'cog in the wheel' or 'just doing my job'. In the premises, to 'do one's job is to be responsive to norms and directives internal to an organization; it is to accept the relevance of collective, institutional norms to one's action'.[111] The reality with which the law works is that 'marginally effective actors' play their parts in activities that cause harm, even if their specific actions do not make the difference.[112]

Under the 'Complicity Principle', there is no doubt that key decision-makers in a company are liable for wrongs committed by the company, including directors, executives, and other executive committee members.[113] However, liability would not stop there. The principle supports the idea that even ostensibly 'innocent' group participants contribute to losses caused by injury to outsiders. Kutz says (and the present writer agrees) that 'the claim of victims to compensation has lexical priority over the claims of organizational members to fairness.'[114] This ought to be kept in mind when we consider the potential responsibility of shareholders, both directly under statute (Chapter 9) and indirectly for the torts of their investee companies (Chapters 11 and 12).

5.4 Theorising the Corporate Group

Up to now, this chapter has examined important attributes of groups of persons, including organisations, which help us see why they can be made responsible for the wrongs they commit and for injuries they cause.[115] Now we come to the much more under-theorised and difficult subject of corporate groups. The law tells us that each company is a separate legal entity and that each is responsible, prima facie, for its own debts only. In Chapter 2, we saw that M-Form groups operate in a decentralised manner, so that there might be little interaction between subsidiaries. The question

[110] Kutz, *Complicity*, p. 156. [111] Kutz, *Complicity*, p. 162.

[112] Kutz, *Complicity*, p. 138.

[113] See Isaacs, *Moral Responsibility in Collective Contexts*, pp. 107–9.

[114] Kutz, *Complicity*, p. 201.

[115] The list corresponds well with that derived in a different way by G. Teubner, 'Unitas Multiplex: Corporate Governance in Group Enterprises', in D. Sugarman and G. Teubner (eds.), *Regulating Corporate Groups in Europe* (1990), pp. 71–2. Compare G. M. Gulati, W. A. Klein, and E. M. Zolt, 'Connected Contracts' (2000) 47 *UCLA Law Review* 887, 896 (futility of mapping out bounds of many modern 'ventures').

is: what is it about corporate groups that allows us to view each company as part of a meaningful 'group' ('group' being used here in a generic organisational sense), and potentially to extend liability from an insolvent subsidiary to some other element within the group? In this section, it will be argued that corporate groups demonstrate the requisite 'groupness'. Eventually, we will see how the attributes of 'groupness' help to establish a basis for extended liability that depends upon neither fault in each liable party nor the exercise of control.

Perhaps the place to begin consideration of the 'groupness' issue is with internalisation theory (examined in Chapter 2). Internalisation is an important explanation of the formation of corporate groups. In Günther Teubner's view, the corporate group lies 'between Market and Organization'[116] – a conclusion that is consistent with our earlier findings. Aspects of the market are reintroduced within corporate groups, intra-group transactions 'simulating' those that occur in the market.[117] A potential problem with marketisation is that participants usually 'act only for their own advantage' and there is no 'centre of agency beyond the individual'.[118] However, corporate groups do not recreate the market *fully*. Instead of being coordinated by a genuine price mechanism, the internal market within the group is coordinated in large measure through the decision-making mechanism. Referring specifically to the M-Form group, Teubner observes that the control mechanisms employed are 'strategic planning of group policy, coordination by defining top personnel policy and indirect profit'.[119] The present writer's list of the attributes of the typical corporate group overlaps with Teubner's. This section will discuss attributes that include: the structure of corporate groups; decision-making direction within the group; coordination of group operations; and economic unity (which distinguishes group companies from arms'-length actors in the marketplace).

First, the corporate group is characterised by structure. We saw in Chapter 2 that the corporate group reflects the M-Form ideal. It is organised in a functional way, so that discrete business activities are conducted in separate corporate entities. Alfred Chandler provided the example of the industrial group, featuring a parent company and distinct subsidiaries undertaking manufacturing operations, distribution, marketing, and so on.[120] The M-Form facilitates the setting of financial and operating targets and the monitoring of the performance of separate

[116] Teubner, 'Unitas Multiplex', 82. [117] Teubner, 'Unitas Multiplex', 83.
[118] List and Pettit, *Group Agency*, p. 13. [119] Teubner, 'Unitas Multiplex', 83.
[120] See Chapter 2.

businesses. It facilitates also risk assessment by creditors such as financial institutions, as well as ease of valuation of the separate businesses units and the disposal of those units. In these ways, the structuring of groups makes business sense – and cannot be seen as a mere device for attracting limited liability for the ultimate parent and other parent companies within the group. However, we saw in Chapter 3 that the ability to structure the group might move beyond the dictates of function to abusive practice. The parent company might structure group relations so that operating entities are undercapitalised, while the important assets of the group are protected in non-operating subsidiaries. The parent might engage also in transactions which diminish the asset base of at-risk subsidiaries, for example by transfer pricing, shuttling of assets, denial of business opportunities, and so on.[121] The point about the corporate group structure is that it can be manipulated to the ends of the ultimate parent company.

Second, the corporate group, embodying a hierarchical structure, is characterised by downward decision-making direction. Strategic decisions and broad performance goals are set by the parent company and transmitted down the hierarchy to subsidiary companies. In some cases, no doubt, decision-making direction will be quite clear because the parent company exercises day-to-day control. The parent company might determine in detail what business operations are to be conducted by the subsidiary, sums to be invested in business undertakings, managers and employees to be hired, the payment of dividends, and so on.[122] When day-to-day control is present, it creates enhanced susceptibility in the parent company to liability for the wrongs of controlled subsidiaries. However, day-to-day control is not typical in corporate groups (as we saw in Chapter 2),[123] and might not even be possible (because the parent company and subsidiary are in different lines of business, are based in different jurisdictions, etc.). In such cases, subsidiaries are *expected simply to conform* to performance and other objectives set by the parent company. There is no need for the exercise of day-to-day control because subsidiary managers know where they sit in the group organisational hierarchy, and understand that their companies must act in conformity to group objectives and parent company wishes. The important idea is that of the downward direction of decision-making (or expectation-setting) by

[121] A. Muscat, *The Liability of the Holding Company for the Debts of its Insolvent Subsidiaries* (1996), esp. ch. 6.

[122] Muscat, *The Liability of the Holding Company*, p. 66.

[123] Or desirable: see G. Morgan, 'Imaginization: On Spider Plants', in D. S. Pugh (ed.), *Organization Theory: Selected Classic Readings* (5th edn., 2007), pp. 525, 530, and 534.

the parent company, through the subsidiaries, rather than that of the exercise of day-to-day control.

Third, the corporate group is characterised by coordination on group projects. In the usual case, group companies work in conjunction with – and not in opposition to – each other. This is the case in M-Form groups, which comprise a parent company and subsidiaries operated on functional lines. A vertically integrated corporate group is the prime example. In the typical case, an upstream subsidiary supplies raw materials to the manufacturing subsidiary, and the manufacturing subsidiary sells finished goods to a downstream subsidiary, which markets and distributes them. In medium- and small-size groups of companies especially, coordination is achieved by the parent company taking on a managerial role. This occurs when subsidiaries 'appoint' the parent company to act *on their behalf* as 'agent' in undertaking managerial functions.[124] In theory, the parent company does as the *subsidiary requires* (rather than exercising control itself). This type of arrangement avoids duplication of functions in smaller subsidiaries and reduces the overall costs of management. But not all corporate groups are highly coordinated in this way. Thus there would be little need for coordination, for example, between a car manufacturer and a medical technology company owned by a conglomerate. Again, little coordination would be expected among subsidiaries operating in disparate regions of the world, or in cases where the parent company exists as mere passive investor.[125]

Fourth, the corporate group is characterised by economic unity – which is to be distinguished from simple economic *interdependence*. The raison d'être of any commercial company is to earn profits through the sale of goods or services needed by others in an interdependent economy. However, this gets us only so far in identifying the economic unity of the group. The shared profit motive is important, as are the functional parts played by each company in earning that profit. To them we need to add three key elements already discussed: hierarchy, structure, and decision-making direction. These elements are accounted for in the proposition that major strategic and other decisions move down from the parent to the subsidiaries. But there is another dynamic at play. While the strategic

[124] *Federal Commissioner of Taxation* v. *BHP Billiton Finance Ltd* (2010) 182 FCR 526, [14]; *CSR Ltd* v. *Young* [1998] Aust Torts Reports 81–468, at 64,952–64,953; P. I. Blumberg, *The Multinational Challenge to Corporation Law: The Search for a New Corporate Personality* (1993), pp. 144–5.

[125] Muscat, *The Liability of the Holding Company*, p. 51. Cf. *Thompson* v. *Renwick Group plc* [2015] BCC 855 (discussed in Chapter 11).

decision-making direction is downwards, profits move upwards. Profits move up the group hierarchy to the ultimate shareholders. As long as the group as a whole is profitable, it might not matter that a particular subsidiary company is unprofitable – that is, so long as the unprofitable company serves its intended function. Given the tendency for structuring of legal relations in the group, it might make strategic sense to sacrifice the interests of one or more subsidiaries to ensure overall profitability. As a corporate lawyer observes:

> There may be powerful commercial or fiscal incentives for a parent company to allow one or more group members to operate at a loss, or to deny them economic opportunities, or to undercapitalise them, or to adopt integrated financing techniques characterised by the shuffling of assets (particularly funds) and liabilities between them as the need arises.[126]

Fifth, the corporate group is characterised by a common group identity (or 'group persona'). Many groups go to great lengths in order to emphasise this group identity to consumers, business partners, and group employees. This can be achieved through a variety of techniques, such as the use of common trade names, logos, symbols, colour schemes, and so on.[127] The promotion of the activities of one entity within the group serves naturally to cross-promote others. As a result of this, outside parties dealing with a particular subsidiary might not appreciate the legal distinction between that entity and others within the group. Of course, some groups feel no need for *overt* demonstrations of group identity. As a result, rank-and-file employees might feel little affiliation to other group companies. Outside observers might not be able to connect them to each other at all. However, this is not necessarily of great importance in conceptualising the corporate group. This is because there is likely still to be significant interaction among group companies at higher, managerial levels. As adumbrated, top managers in each company will have a strong conception of their company's place within the corporate group. Amongst these top managers, who ensure (where relevant) the coordination of group activities, there is likely to be a high degree of commitment to the group, conformity to the group ethos and performance goals, and reproachability when things go wrong.[128]

[126] A. Nolan, 'The Position of Unsecured Creditors of Corporate Groups: Towards a Group Responsibility Solution which Gives Fairness and Equity a Role' (1993) 11 *Company & Securities Law Journal* 461, 484–5.

[127] Muscat, *The Liability of the Holding Company*, p. 416.

[128] See R. Whittington and M. Mayer, *The European Corporation: Strategy, Structure, and Social Science* (2000), p. 68.

5.5 The Network: A Brief Contrast

The attributes of corporate groups just outlined indicate that there is a reality to their 'groupness' that is normatively significant for the purposes of extending liability from an insolvent subsidiary to other companies in the group. Companies in a corporate group are bound to each other in meaningful ways. The bonds between them create a basis for arguing that liability should be extended from an insolvent subsidiary to other companies in the group. Of course, corporate networks are part of the insolvent entity problem too, and there might be good reasons for imposing incentives upon network participants to adhere to proper standards of safety and general business conduct.[129] A question similar to that asked about groups can be asked here – namely, what is it about the corporate network that would allow us to view each company as part of a meaningful 'group' (used in its generic, organisational sense), and to extend liability from an insolvent company to some other company in the network?

In brief, our examination of corporate network structures and operation in Chapter 2, in conjunction with literature on networks, indicates that groups and networks share several features that indicate 'groupness'. A network agreement prima facie entails the coordination of future activity between participating companies (including distribution of functions and planning), commitment to common objectives, and conformity to those objectives. However, it is clear that, in the typical case, certain features characteristic of the corporate group either are not present at all or are present to a limited degree only. These include a hierarchical command structure, downward decision-making direction, economic unity,[130] and common group identity. These features might be present to some extent within a joint venture subsidiary, but will be less apparent where there is no organisational 'shell' to house the individuals engaged in network activity. Indeed, one of the defining characteristics of the corporate network is its 'boundarilessness',[131] which impedes the development of strong group attributes among the different participants. Each corporate participant within the network has its own way of working and its own culture.

[129] See, e.g., M. A. Cohen, M. Gottlieb, J. Linn, and N. Richardson, 'Deepwater Drilling: Law, Policy, and Economics of Firm Organization and Safety' (2011) 64 *Vanderbilt Law Review* 1853.

[130] Contra Teubner, *Networks as Connected Contracts* (ed. H Collins; tr. M Everson) (2011), p. 158.

[131] Hatch, *Organization Theory*, p. 181.

Indeed, substantial differences between corporate groups and networks indicate the *relative* weakness of networks in terms of their 'groupness'. First, the strength of the ties *between companies* participating in a network, while variable, is likely to be much weaker than those found in corporate groups. These companies are bound by agreements, often of limited duration, and often the network can be disassembled relatively quickly and easily.[132] In this sense, 'groupness' in networks is (and is understood to be) contingent in nature. Second, the individuals who do the work in carrying out network agreements ultimately are likely to be loyal to their employer or 'home' companies, rather than to the network. This is the case for both front-line employees and their managers. Indeed, managers are likely to be clear about the gritty, commercial objectives of participating in networks. Frequently, managers attempt to cheat other network participants and/or engage in disputation with them – which underlines the inevitable tensions that exist in that business form (points which were considered in Chapter 3).[133]

What does this mean for us? The preliminary view taken here is that the corporate group and the corporate network are different in significant ways, which impacts upon their respective amenability to the imposition of extended liability. The companies and individuals that work together in the corporate group are part of a 'group' in a much stronger and more enduring sense than are the companies and individuals that work within corporate networks (joint venture subsidiaries to one side). Often, this means that the reasons for extending liability from an insolvent company in a network to other network participants will be weak and un-compelling. This leads to the further conclusion that 'something more' is required in order to justify extensions of liability from one participating company to another in a network. That 'something' might be actual fault, suitable attributions of fault, or deemed responsibility based upon connection and deterrability. In Chapter 11, we ascertain how such a prerequisite can be satisfied.

[132] E.g., N. Nohria, D. Dyer, and F. Dalzell, *Changing Fortunes: Remaking the Industrial Corporation* (2002), p. 97; W. M. Fruin, 'Business Groups and Interfirm Networks', in G. Jones and J. Zeitlin (eds.), *The Oxford Handbook of Business History* (2007), p. 256; G. Jones, *Multinationals and Global Capitalism: From the Nineteenth to the Twenty-First Century* (2005), pp. 104–5; R. E. Miles and C. C. Snow, 'Organizations: New Concepts for New Forms', in P. J. Buckley and J. Michie (eds.), *Firms, Organizations and Contracts: A Reader in Industrial Organization* (1996), p. 433.

[133] Teubner, *Networks as Connected Contracts*, p. 6; M. Jennejohn, 'The Private Order of Innovation Networks' (2016) 68 *Stanford Law Review* 281, 290; Jones, *Multinationals and Global Capitalism*, p. 161.

5.6 Entity or Enterprise Approach?

This chapter has now explored attributes of corporate groups (and networks) that might be normatively significant in a regime of extended liability. We have seen that responsibility for wrongdoing can arise at different levels – at the level of the individual participant in a group and at the organisational level. This must be kept in mind when, in later chapters, we come to discuss specific liability regimes. But to conclude this chapter (focussed, as it is, on matters of theory), we must consider a very important, related issue – whether to recognise the individual company or the corporate group as the basic unit of responsibility in the liability of corporate groups. As we will see, arguments in favour of an enterprise approach ordinarily are made by reference to a subset of the features of corporate groups just discussed (economic unity and control). The question is whether the presence of these features alone provides justification for departing from the entity approach to group companies. The argument will be that they do not provide such justification.

In Chapter 3, we considered a number of the building blocks of company law. These include separate legal personality, corporate capacity, and limited liability of shareholders. These concepts evolved with the company as a stand-alone entity, this entity facilitating economic activities by groups of individuals. The concepts were not intended to enable one company to own shares in another company; indeed, there was no such thing as the corporate group in the mid-nineteenth century. However, by the turn of the twentieth century, corporate groups formed with several layers of subsidiary to protect the ultimate, individual shareholders, and legal relations among group companies eventually were structured so as to protect group assets. In responding to the challenges which the modern corporate group presents for the law, Phillip Blumberg opines that '[l]egal theory of the corporation still concerned with the small, local corporation of the nineteenth century must catch up with the reality of the modern world of giant, multinational groups.'[134] He goes on to say that:

> with the application of traditional entity law to corporate groups, the older concept of the legal entity no longer matches the reality of the economic entity. The traditional law no longer reflects the society that it seeks to order, and implementation of the underlying policies in the law inevitably is gravely impaired.[135]

[134] Blumberg, *The Multinational Challenge to Corporation Law*, p. ix.
[135] Blumberg, *The Multinational Challenge to Corporation Law*, p. ix.

The question is whether the entity approach should be displaced when dealing with corporate groups, so that the law would make determinations of liability by reference to the group concept. A possible response to the insolvency of a subsidiary company with unpaid creditors, advocated by Blumberg, is to extend liability to other companies within the group on the basis of 'enterprise liability'. This is different from piercing the corporate veil because enterprise liability can extend to any company in a group;[136] it is not limited to corporate shareholders. It is different from veil-piercing, moreover, because there is no suggestion that it should extend to individual shareholders.[137] However, as shall be demonstrated, what enterprise liability does have in common with veil-piercing is a paucity of satisfactory standards of liability.

The conception of the company and its constituents as pursuing business projects as 'an enterprise' can be traced back to the early twentieth century, following implementation of statutory workers' compensation laws in the United Kingdom. Worker injuries were viewed as an unfortunate and inevitable cost of large-scale business operations, which employers were in a position either to absorb through reductions in profits or to spread through insurance or marginal increases in product prices.[138] Imposing the initial burden upon the enterprise was a powerful idea that encouraged movement in US courts towards strict liability doctrines in the common law of tort.[139] In time, scholars and courts began to question the *inevitability* of industrial accidents and to see the deterrent potential of tort law. Industrialisation was understood to have created a world of long-run production and recurrent risks, which were not discrete and random, but

[136] *Premier Building and Consulting Pty Ltd (rec apptd)* v. *Spotless Group Ltd* (2007) 64 ACSR 114, 191; *James Hardie & Co Pty Ltd* v. *Hall* (1998) 43 NSWLR 544, 579; K. A. Strasser, 'Piercing the Veil in Corporate Groups' (2005) 37 *Connecticut Law Review* 637, 646 ff.

[137] The two doctrines are treated separately, e.g., in *Adams* v. *Cape Industries plc* [1990] Ch 433.

[138] J. C. P. Goldberg, 'Twentieth-Century Tort Theory' (2003) 91 *Georgetown Law Journal* 513, 542; G. L. Priest, 'The Invention of Enterprise Liability: A Critical History of the Intellectual Foundations of Modern Tort Law' (1985) 14 *Journal of Legal Studies* 461, 466; F. James Jr, 'Social Insurance and Tort Law: The Problem of Alternative Remedies' (1952) 27 *New York University Law Review* 537, 538; Y. B. Smith, 'Frolic and Detour' (1923) 23 *Columbia Law Review* 444, 454. The apparent conflict between goals of internalisation and loss distribution has been noted: e.g., R. Flannigan, 'Enterprise Control: The Servant-Independent Contractor Distinction' (1987) 37 *University of Toronto Law Journal* 25, 28.

[139] G. C. Keating, 'The Theory of Enterprise Liability and Common Law Strict Liability' (2001) 54 *Vanderbilt Law Review* 1285, 1287, and 1290.

the result of planned processes. This fostered incentives to take precautions against 'characteristic' risks in those who controlled production, ex post impositions of liability on the individuals more immediately involved being viewed as less effective in minimising accident levels.[140] 'Characteristic' risks are those that inhere in an enterprise's long-run business activities (despite the taking of reasonable precautions),[141] although redress is required only in cases of risks which are 'different from those attendant on the activities of the community in general'.[142] Enterprises were viewed as having the ability to anticipate those accidents that issue from their characteristic risks, take steps in advance to minimise their incidence, and disperse their costs after accidents occur.[143] The imposition of liability upon the enterprise without the need to prove which individual employee was causally responsible was to the obvious advantage of injured persons.[144] The theory of the company and actors connected to it as 'enterprise' has been used to explain several types of liability rule. These include the stricter aspects of US products liability law,[145] and the UK and US law of vicarious liability[146] (considered in Chapters 8 and 12, respectively).

Some writers have applied the theory of enterprise liability to questions of extended liability involving corporate groups, and even networks. The common theme is that the law should downplay the separate legal personality of companies involved in joint business projects and impose liabilities based upon the reality and normative significance of their functional integration and economic cohesion. Functional integration arises when each company plays a part in the supply of a product or service. 'Separate firms may, for example, handle different aspects of the refinement, transportation and sale of gasoline, but their activities form a relatively well-organised whole . . . What counts here is

140 Keating, 'The Idea of Fairness in the Law of Enterprise Liability' (1997) 95 *Michigan Law Review* 1266.

141 Keating, 'The Idea of Fairness', 1279.

142 Keating, 'The Idea of Fairness', 1290. This idea is critiqued in N. Garoupa and T. S. Ulen, 'The Economics of Activity Levels in Tort Liability and Regulation', in T. J. Miceli and M. J. Baker (eds.), *Research Handbook on Economic Models of Law* (2014), ch. 2.

143 Keating, 'The Idea of Fairness', 1354.

144 L. A. Kornhauser, 'An Economic Analysis of the Choice between Enterprise and Personal Liability for Accidents' (1982) 70 *California Law Review* 1345, 1370. See also K. Graham, 'Strict Products Liability at 50: Four Histories' (2014) 98 *Marquette Law Review* 555, 568–9.

145 E.g., *Vandermark* v. *Ford Motor Co* 391 P 2d 169 (Cal 1964). See discussion in Chapter 8.

146 E.g., *Mohamud* v. *Wm Morrison Supermarkets plc* [2016] AC 677, [40]; D. Tan, 'Internalising Externalities: An Enterprise Risk Approach to Vicarious Liability in the 21st Century' (2015) 27 *Singapore Academy of Law Journal* 822.

not corporate form but economic substance – not whether activities are formally integrated, but whether they are functionally integrated.'[147] The enterprise is viewed as well-situated both to take precautions against causing injuries and, when accidents occur, either to absorb the losses or to spread them among customers, insurance pools, and (if necessary) shareholders.

In this section, we assess the cogency of enterprise liability as applied to groups of companies and networks. The conclusion reached is that, although enterprise liability has a role to play in explaining the imposition of product liability and vicarious liability upon *individual* companies conducting risky operations, it cannot be used sensibly in order to merge the identities of companies within corporate groups or networks. Entity law must prevail, and liability must be extended from an insolvent company using methods that are compatible with entity law.

The genesis of enterprise liability as a response to the insolvent entity problem in *corporate groups* was a paper by Adolf Berle, which noted the growth of the 'enterprise' consisting of a 'large-scale business' operated through 'a constellation of corporations controlled by a central holding company'.[148] Berle advocated legal recognition of the *reality* of the corporate group as enterprise,[149] and believed the appropriate approach was reflected in legal cases in which 'several corporations became in effect a single enterprise and merged their operations, their several entities were disregarded and their respective assets and liabilities were pooled in a common pot which represented, substantially, the actual enterprise of which they were parts'.[150]

The most influential proponent of the enterprise approach to corporate groups has been Phillip Blumberg.[151] Although the modern multinational group takes the legal form of a multitude of separate companies, in Blumberg's view it comprises a business 'conducted collectively by interlinked companies under common ownership and control'.[152] This is true of vertically and horizontally integrated groups, which grow in order

[147] Keating, 'The Idea of Fairness', 1337.

[148] A. A. Berle, 'The Theory of Enterprise Entity' (1947) 47 *Columbia Law Review* 343, 343.

[149] Berle, 'The Theory of Enterprise Entity', 344.

[150] Berle, 'The Theory of Enterprise Entity', 349.

[151] Blumberg, *The Multinational Challenge to Corporation Law*. A summary of his position is available in P. I. Blumberg, 'The Transformation of Modern Corporation Law: The Law of Corporate Groups' (2005) 37 *Connecticut Law Review* 605.

[152] Blumberg, *The Multinational Challenge to Corporation Law*, pp. viii–ix. For similar views, see also I. Mevorach, *Insolvency within Multinational Enterprise Groups* (2009), pp. 217–19.

to benefit from the internalisation of transactions that would otherwise take place in the market.[153] Blumberg believes it to be sufficiently true of conglomerates as well, because they are characterised by financial and administrative interdependence.[154] Thus, Blumberg opines that 'by including conglomerate corporations and partly owned subsidiaries within the firm, the economists provide support for the similar inclusion of such subsidiaries within the enterprise for legal purposes in those cases where enterprise principles have otherwise been deemed desirable.'[155] Indeed, Blumberg finds that:

> In a growing number of areas of the law – of which statutory law is the leading example but also including tort law and areas of procedural and bankruptcy law – . . . American law is moving from the universal, indiscriminate reliance on entity concepts to formulating and utilizing new concepts of enterprise or group law where required to implement the underlying policies and objectives of the law in the area.[156]

Blumberg argues that enterprise law has developed in a selective way and does not wholly displace entity law.[157] It is utilised when helpful in

[153] See Chapter 2.

[154] Blumberg, *The Multinational Challenge to Corporation Law*, p. 146.

[155] Blumberg, *The Multinational Challenge to Corporation Law*, p. 236. Blumberg's proposals do not extend to the liability of individuals, even when they are controlling shareholders: see M. Dearborn, 'Enterprise Liability: Reviewing and Revitalizing Liability for Corporate Groups' (2009) 97 *California Law Review* 195, 250–1; P. Nygh, 'The Liability of Multi-national Corporations for the Torts of Their Subsidiaries' (2002) 3 *European Business Organization Law Review* 51, 73.

[156] Blumberg, *The Multinational Challenge to Corporation Law*, p. ix. See also C. Stone, 'The Place of Enterprise Liability in the Control of Corporate Conduct' (1980) 90 *Yale Law Journal* 1, 46. Antunes summarises the factors required in US enterprise liability cases in areas including labour and taxation law as: 'organization (to what extent the subsidiary corporation maintains an independent administrative and financial structure . . .), market (what is the extent of the horizontal or vertical integration of the businesses conducted through the various group affiliates; what is the extent of integration of the various functional areas of group affiliates, such as sales, marketing, production and finances) and public posture (to what extent is the group "held out" to the public as a single integrated enterprise)': J. Antunes, *Liability of Corporate Groups: Autonomy and Control in Parent–Subsidiary Relationships in US, German and EU Law* (1994), p. 470. For examples of enterprise liability beyond US law, see UNCITRAL, 'Legislative Guide on Insolvency Law, Part Three: Treatment of Enterprise Groups in Insolvency' (2012), p. 17.

[157] Thus Blumberg notes that enterprise principles rarely confer rights upon a parent company. Instead, they are used to impose liabilities: Blumberg, *The Multinational Challenge to Corporation Law*, p. 237.

meeting pressing legal objectives[158] and provides a basis for disregarding rules of separate legal personality and limited liability within group companies. The precise circumstances necessary for the application of enterprise principles differ according to the 'fundamental jurisprudential problem before the court'.[159] However, in the common law jurisprudence, courts look for 'highly intertwined operational and economic relationships between parent and subsidiary corporations', parent company 'control' over subsidiaries, and the need to meet pressing legal objectives.[160] For Blumberg, sufficient control arises from parent company ownership of 'voting stock' in subsidiaries.[161] 'Economic interrelationship comprises not only vertical and horizontal integration . . ., but also such additional elements as administrative and financial interdependence of the affiliated corporations, integration of employee relationships, and use of a common group persona.'[162] He says that 'these factors are the hallmark of a unitary enterprise that has been fragmented among the affiliated corporations as a matter of legal form, with the companies continuing in the collective conduct of the business under a central, coordinated control.'[163] Enterprise liability principles permit the imposition of 'collective group, rather than individual subsidiary, responsibilities'[164] (although it has not been used to impose liability upon *individual* shareholders).[165] The effect of enterprise liability is intended to be both immediate, in providing avenues of redress for unpaid creditors, and systemic because it forces the parent company to absorb the externalities of group activity 'by purchasing insurance or adequately capitalizing the subsidiary'.[166]

Blumberg believes that enterprise liability principles have application beyond the hierarchical relations of the corporate group – that they can be extended to network relationships between franchisors and franchisees, licensors and licensees, and contractors and subcontractors. This is on the basis that sufficient de facto control might be present, stemming

158 Blumberg, *The Multinational Challenge to Corporation Law*, p. ix. For a similar approach to use of this concept in insolvency, see Mevorach, *Insolvency within Multinational Enterprise Groups*, esp. p. 61 (summary of approach).
159 Blumberg, *The Multinational Challenge to Corporation Law*, p. 120.
160 Blumberg, *The Multinational Challenge to Corporation Law*, p. 92.
161 Blumberg, *The Multinational Challenge to Corporation Law*, p. 245.
162 Blumberg, *The Multinational Challenge to Corporation Law*, p. 246.
163 Blumberg, *The Multinational Challenge to Corporation Law*, p. 246.
164 Blumberg, *The Multinational Challenge to Corporation Law*, p. 232.
165 Blumberg, *The Multinational Challenge to Corporation Law*, p. 123.
166 Dearborn, 'Enterprise Liability', 212.

from power imbalances between parties bound together by contract. 'Contract may provide one party with the ability to direct, in important respects, the business and affairs of another party that may be entirely unrelated insofar as ownership is concerned.'[167] (However, as explained earlier, such relationships do not feature a key attribute of corporate groups – which is that the economic interests of group companies are *unified* with the interests of the parent company. In networks, each company has incentives to cheat in order to gain economic advantage.)

A European liability regime applicable to anti-competitive agreements largely conforms to Blumberg's explanation of enterprise liability (which is based on his views of US law, much of which is considered in Chapters 8, 10, and 12). Under the Treaty on the Functioning of the European Union articles 101 and 102, concerning anti-competitive agreements and abuse of dominant position, the basic unit of accountability is the 'undertaking'. Companies form undertakings through their economic unity.[168] In *Viho Europe BV* v. *Commission of the European Communities*, the General Court of the European Union stated that 'for the purposes of the application of the competition rules, the unified conduct on the market of the parent company and its subsidiaries takes precedence over the formal separation between those companies'.[169] This will be so when 'decisive influence' is exercised by the parent company over its subsidiaries. Any anti-competitive agreements entered into by such companies with a third party (or any abuse practised by such companies) go to make both the controlled and controlling companies jointly and severally liable.[170] The rules on undertakings apply in vertical control relationships, where decisive influence over the activity of the subsidiary in question can be either presumed (in cases of 100 per cent or 'near 100 per cent' ownership) or proven on the evidence.[171] A

[167] Blumberg, *The Multinational Challenge to Corporation Law*, p. 247. See also T. P. Glynn, 'Beyond "Unlimiting" Shareholder Liability: Vicarious Tort Liability for Corporate Officers' (2004) 57 *Vanderbilt Law Review* 329, 346.

[168] See Cases C-201/09 and C216/09, *Arcelormittal Luxembourg SA* v. *European Commission* [2011] 4 CMLR 21, [95]; P. Hughes, 'Competition Law Enforcement and Corporate Group Liability – Adjusting the Veil' (2014) 35 *European Competition Law Review* 68, 68.

[169] Case T-102/92, [1995] ECR II-17, [50].

[170] Hughes, 'Competition Law Enforcement', 69.

[171] Case C-97/08P, *Akzo Nobel NV* v. *Commission of the European Communities* [2009] ECR I-8237. The view is taken by some that this presumption, while rebuttable in theory, is very difficult, if not impossible, to rebut in practice: L. La Rocca, 'The Controversial Issue of the Parent Company Liability for the Violation of EC Competition Rules by the Subsidiary' (2011) 32 *European Competition Law Review* 68, 73. Moreover, the exercise of negative control is sufficient, 'in the sense that the parent . . . could only prevent, rather

50 per cent stake in a joint venture is sufficient to bring the shareholder company and joint venture company into an undertaking relationship,[172] but lesser stakes are not.[173] Where a company has been dissolved, liability for competition law breaches can be extended to successor companies on the basis of 'economic continuity'.[174] Any individual can bring action in a national court for breach of article 101 and seek compensation for losses, including economic losses, where the prohibited agreement restricts EU interstate trade, and is not otherwise exempt.[175] These expansive rules have been deemed necessary in order to ensure the effectiveness of competition law rules in the corporate group context.[176] But, again, there is little evidence that individual shareholders have been targeted.[177] Moreover, the enterprise approach adopted in European competition law cases is exceptional; in no other area of European law do the courts so readily merge the identities of group companies.

Most of those who advocate an enterprise liability approach to corporate group problems, including Blumberg, argue in favour of control as a central justification for parent company liability. Meredith Dearborn, by contrast, thinks the control criterion is 'legally and economically problematic'.[178] In making her argument, Dearborn contrasts two different kinds of enterprise liability regime: a control-based regime and a regime imposed 'solely on the economic fact of the enterprise' ('true enterprise liability').[179] She says about control-based liability that 'there has not been sufficient clarity about what "control" means, and which instances of control liability would be more likely to prevent torts.'[180] Moreover,

than insist on, the subsidiary adopting certain business decisions': Hughes, 'Competition Law Enforcement', 79, citing Case T-77/08, *Dow Chemical Co* v. *European Commission* [2012] 4 CMLR 19, [92].

172 Case C-172/12 P, *EI du Pont Nemours & Co* v. *European Commission* [2014] 4 CMLR 7; S. Mobley, D. Mourkas, and G. Murray, 'Parent Liability for Joint Venture Parents' (2014) 35 *European Competition Law Review* 499.

173 Hughes, 'Competition Law Enforcement', 69 and 77.

174 Case T-117/07, *Areva* v. *European Commission* [2011] 4 CMLR 26, [66] (reversed in part, [2014] 4 CMLR 31); G. De Stefano, 'General Court Rules on Successor Liability and Apportionment of Group Liability in the Gas Insulated Switchgear Cartel' (2011) 2 *Journal of European Competition Law & Practice* 344, 345.

175 Hughes, 'Competition Law Enforcement', 70.

176 *Cooper Tire & Rubber Co Europe Ltd* v. *Dow Deutschland Inc* [2010] EWCA Civ 864, [34].

177 Hughes, 'Competition Law Enforcement', 76. All of this is in stark contrast to US law: see Mobley, Mourkas, and Murray, 'Parent Liability for Joint Venture Parents', 500, and Chapter 11.

178 Dearborn, 'Enterprise Liability', 201.

179 Dearborn, 'Enterprise Liability', 215.

180 Dearborn, 'Enterprise Liability', 248.

imposing liability for the exercise of control (as previously observed in this book) reduces incentives in parent companies and others to try to influence safety in subsidiary activities and products.[181] Dearborn prefers 'true enterprise liability', which is concerned simply with collective economic action,[182] and facilitates application of a stable exception to limited liability.[183] It would apply in certain contexts only – within 'the parent-subsidiary relationship or within the corporate family – not for individual shareholders'.[184] The claimant, it seems, would have to prove only that he or she has been injured in a mass-tort, and that there is some business connection between the insolvent company that causes injury and the liability target. It would not be for the claimant to prove functional and economic integration, but for the defendant company to disprove it, and thus disprove the existence of enterprise.[185]

This book argues against enterprise liability as the basis for extending liability from insolvent companies to other companies within a group or network. In fact, utilisation of enterprise liability would mark a profound shift in corporate law.[186] It would make it unnecessarily difficult to ascertain, ex ante, the true extent of parent company liabilities, and would unduly upset existing recovery rights of unsecured creditors.[187] This is the problem that we will encounter in Chapter 7, which examines statutory pooling and contribution powers. There we see that an order in favour of pooling or contribution might assist the petitioning creditors of B Co, but it does not assist the creditors of other companies in the group, such as those of C Co. They will have fewer assets from which to draw in order to satisfy their demands – and so enterprise liability upsets creditor expectations. Even beyond such concerns, enterprise liability is not attractive in providing a general measure of redress for the unpaid creditors of insolvent subsidiaries. A major problem is that the criteria specified by Blumberg, even when applied in specific case categories, do not provide clear standards for

[181] Dearborn, 'Enterprise Liability', 249.

[182] Note that the extent to which this scheme departs from those based on control seems dubious, given that Dearborn indicates the importance of internalising the costs of 'economic decisions made at the nerve centre of the corporat[e group]': Dearborn, 'Enterprise Liability', 251. See also ibid., 254.

[183] Dearborn, 'Enterprise Liability', 199.

[184] Dearborn, 'Enterprise Liability', 211. See also ibid., 254.

[185] Dearborn, 'Enterprise Liability', 252–3.

[186] A fact noted in Companies and Securities Advisory Committee, 'Corporate Groups Final Report' (2000), p. 22.

[187] Companies and Securities Advisory Committee, 'Corporate Groups Final Report', p. 24.

intervention.[188] This book has criticised control as a basis for liability on a number of occasions, and agrees with Dearborn's conclusions on this matter.

A further problem is that no determination of economic integration could be made without extensive evidence and expert opinions thereon (which is required in the competition law cases already noted).[189] Even then, the 'boundaries of an "enterprise" are far from clear, and attributing liability to such ill-defined "units" would produce "intolerable" uncertainty'. In the circumstances, an '"enterprise" approach would not yield the identifiable, stable boundaries that all investment, insurance (etc.) decisions presuppose'.[190] Liability would be stretched too far if enterprise liability were to encompass corporate networks[191] or go beyond them and encompass all economically connected parties.[192] This is because economic and 'contractual webs extend throughout the economy'.[193] Although Blumberg refines his idea by insisting upon the exercise of control by one company upon another as a precondition to extended liability, the peril is one of over-penalising 'marginally effective participants' in an enterprise. 'If business leaders believe that tort outcomes have little to do with their own behavior, then there is no reason for them to shape their behavior so as to minimize tort exposure.'[194] The present writer's proposal for a conspiracy-based tort liability among network

[188] Blumberg himself recognises the 'complex' nature of the task and the necessarily 'untidy' results: Blumberg, *The Multinational Challenge to Corporation Law*, pp. 115 and 120. See also M. E. Kors, 'Altered Egos: Deciphering Substantive Consolidation' (1998) 59 *University of Pittsburgh Law Review* 381, 437–8 (describing the level of uncertainty in such a test as 'intolerable').

[189] P. Muchlinski, 'Limited Liability and Multinational Enterprises: A Case for Reform?' (2010) 34 *Cambridge Journal of Economics* 915, 924; P. Muchlinski, *Multinational Enterprises and the Law* (2nd edn., 2007), p. 320. Note that the degree of integration might change over time: J. Dine, *The Governance of Corporate Groups* (2000), p. 62. Although such investigations are made when determining issues of competition law, these are conducted by well-resourced bodies such as the European Commission's Directorate-General for Competition.

[190] J. Morgan, 'Vicarious Liability for Independent Contractors?' [2015] *Professional Negligence* 235, 241.

[191] See Blumberg, *The Multinational Challenge to Corporation Law*, pp. 247–8.

[192] L. M. LoPucki, 'The Essential Structure of Judgment Proofing' (1998) 51 *Stanford Law Review* 147, 156–7.

[193] LoPucki, 'The Essential Structure of Judgment Proofing', 158. See also Muscat, *The Liability of the Holding Company*, p. 397.

[194] S. J. Carroll et al., *Asbestos Litigation* (2005), p. xxix. See also R. Flannigan, 'Enterprise Control: The Servant-Independent Contractor Distinction' (1987) 37 *University of Toronto Law Journal* 25, 34.

companies (discussed in Chapter 11) is tied to the deterrent potential of such liability and, as will be submitted, creates a type of liability which network companies can both understand and actively guard against.

Dearborn's proposal for enterprise liability, based upon 'the economic fact of enterprise' as it exists within corporate groups or 'corporate families', can be rejected on similar grounds. In the end, it does not seem to differ much from Blumberg's conception of enterprise liability because Dearborn must (as she admits) confine it to preconceived notions of corporate groups or corporate 'families'. She does not specify exactly how courts would identify such collectives, but refers to criteria including functional integration and subsidiary purpose. If Dearborn wanted more clearly to distinguish her position from Blumberg's, she would need to do more to indicate how liability could be both extended to companies within the enterprise *and confined to them as well.* On the positive side, she is right to emphasise the importance of the forward-looking aspect of liability rules, as well as the 'incentive structure in the corporate conglomerate' which can be used to advantage in order to reduce the risks of future torts being committed.[195]

Theory aside, it is unsurprising that courts prefer to work with established legal concepts in the regulation of corporate groups, assigning especial importance to the concept of separate legal personality. English courts have resisted attempts to utilise an economic integration argument to extend liability in corporate groups. In *Adams* v. *Cape Industries plc*, the Court of Appeal quoted with approval a prior dictum that the fundamental distinction between law and economics cannot be bridged so as to create liability in the parent simply because it is economically integrated with one or more subsidiaries.[196] In *Re Polly Peck International (in administration)*, Robert Walker J adopted a similar analysis, stating that the maintenance of 'the separate legal existence of group companies is particularly important when creditors become involved'.[197] These statements are reinforced by the UK Supreme Court decision in *Prest* v. *Petrodel*,[198] where the veil-piercing doctrine was rendered a virtual dead letter (as discussed in Chapter 10). Again, Australian courts have refused to adopt enterprise liability principles in group situations, using more specific veil-piercing 'techniques' instead.[199] The Full Federal Court of Australia in *Federal*

[195] Dearborn, 'Enterprise Liability', 248 and 251.

[196] [1990] 1 Ch 433, 538, quoting *Bank of Tokyo Ltd* v. *Karoon (note)* [1987] AC 45, 64.

[197] [1996] 2 All ER 433, 448. See also *Ord* v. *Belhaven Pubs Ltd* [1998] 2 BCLC 447, 457.

[198] [2013] 2 AC 415.

[199] Pervasive enterprise liability principles have not been adopted in any common law jurisdiction: Companies and Securities Advisory Committee, 'Corporate Groups Final

Commissioner of Taxation v. *BHP Billiton Finance Limited* observed that the 'conflation of the activities of separate entities into some fictional "group" or single entity is impermissible'.[200] Even in the United States, proponents of enterprise liability have been accused of overestimating the influence of enterprise reasoning in the courts; economic integration is never more than a factor which courts take into account in applying veil-piercing rules.[201]

5.7 Conclusions

This chapter has examined characteristic features of companies, corporate groups, and networks. This exercise has been important in demonstrating the potential strength of the ties that bind these collectives, and provides a basis both for their regulation and for the imposition of responsibility. This chapter has examined, also, the entity-enterprise debate. In effect, it has argued that the whole edifice of private law relations is constructed upon the importance of the individual and its functional equivalent, the incorporated entity. The law does not easily accommodate movement away from the entity approach through the application of enterprise liability (whether in the veil-piercing context, in product liability, or in vicarious liability). Enterprise liability is not a reliable basis for extending liability in either the corporate group or the network. It is too uncertain a mechanism for doing so. The law must work with the entity approach.[202] Exceptions to the application of entity principles must be tightly controlled. The challenge then becomes one of considering how liability might be extended within both the corporate group and the network, so as to provide a solution to the insolvent entity problem. The arguments for extending liability from one company in a corporate group to another are stronger than the arguments

Report', p. 157. For attempted use of enterprise liability in Australia, see, e.g., *Premier Building and Consulting Pty Ltd (rec apptd)* v. *Spotless Group Ltd* (2007) 64 ACSR 114. See also *Briggs* v. *James Hardie & Co Pty Ltd* (1989) 5 NSWLR 549, 576–7.

200 (2010) 182 FCR 526 [37]. Indeed, it has been observed that it might not be open to any court below the High Court of Australia to adopt such a theory, given what was said in *Industrial Equity Ltd* v. *Blackburn* (1977) 137 CLR 567, according to the New South Wales Court of Appeal in *Briggs* v. *James Hardie & Co Pty Ltd* (1989) 5 NSWLR 549, 576. See also *Walker* v. *Wimborne* (1976) 137 CLR 1, 6–7. The Companies and Securities Advisory Committee recommended against the introduction of enterprise liability principles to deal with tort claims: Companies and Securities Advisory Committee, 'Corporate Groups Final Report', ch. 4.

201 Muscat, *The Liability of the Holding Company*, pp. 407 and 410.

202 A point emphasised in *Premier Building and Consulting Pty Ltd (rec apptd)* v. *Spotless Group Ltd* (2007) 64 ACSR 114, 192.

for doing so in a corporate network. The strong features of corporate groups help in arguing the case for strict liability of shareholders for personal injury claims made against insolvent subsidiaries (as to which, see Chapter 9). However, the extension of liability in corporate networks might be justifiable also – where some special factor is present in relations between a company that injures and the targeted company. This is a matter to which we shall return in Chapter 11.

PART III

Statute

6

General Protections for Creditors

6.1 Introduction

This chapter examines statutory regimes of general application to companies which protect creditors in the face of corporate insolvency. The laws in question are aimed at protecting creditors from conduct falling short of outright fraud, but which is abusive nevertheless.[1] They encompass ex ante protections, which are applicable throughout the life of the company, subsisting in the capital maintenance doctrine and in rules against transactions at an undervalue and unfair preferences. To some extent, these provisions help to prevent the insolvent entity problem from arising in the first place. Should it arise, they can be used in order to claw back assets and to inflate the insolvent estate. In this way, the provisions permit extensions of liability in the way that other rules considered in this book do. Further relevant provisions include ex post protections, applicable once a company has become insolvent, in particular the rule against insolvent trading. Taken together, the rules discussed in this chapter are of assistance primarily in cases involving corporate groups, but have some role to play in the network context as well. Following consideration of these rules, Chapter 7 goes on to examine group-specific statutory protections for creditors, while Chapter 8 examines statutory causes of action in tort which facilitate the compensation of creditors. Chapter 9 argues for a statutory exception to limited liability applicable in cases of insolvent subsidiary companies with personal injury liabilities that cannot be satisfied fully.

6.2 Ex ante Protections for Creditors

The creditors of a company, including tort creditors, prima facie have ability to obtain redress only from the debtor company's own assets, and

[1] Whether or not exceptional in the commercial world, cases of fraud are difficult to prove and entail a low likelihood of recovery. For England and Wales, see Insolvency Act 1986, ss. 213 and 423.

not from those of other parties, such as the company's shareholders (as seen in Chapter 3). This means that the preservation and protection of debtor company assets is important to the fairness of the company law regime. The provisions examined in the first part of this chapter create ex ante protections, applicable throughout the life of the company, which encourage the preservation of corporate assets. The provisions do this by making unlawful certain abusive practices by which corporate assets might be run down to the disadvantage of creditors. Although this section focusses on English law, most of the provisions have counterparts in other common law jurisdictions.

6.2.1 *Capital Maintenance*

The Companies Act 2006 requires that dividends to shareholders be paid out of accumulated profits.[2] The relevant profits are those of the individual subsidiary, rather than those of the group as a whole.[3] Where this provision is breached, dividends paid out unlawfully are liable to be recouped from any shareholder who either knows or has reasonable grounds for believing that they were paid without lawful authorisation.[4] This rule is more likely to catch out a parent company than an individual shareholder. In addition, the directors responsible for the payment of dividends have what appears to be a strict liability obligation to restore funds wrongfully paid out.[5] While these rules set out an important prohibition, the capital maintenance doctrine is acknowledged to be of little assistance in protecting the interests of creditors,[6] including personal injury claimants. There are two simple reasons for this: first, it must be recognised that '[n]o aspect of the doctrine in fact seeks to ensure that the company is provided with sufficient funds to enable it to stand a fair chance of success' in its business life.[7] Second, in cases of mass-torts, especially those involving the causation of personal injuries which initially are latent in nature, the true scale of liabilities might not become apparent to company directors until injuries

[2] Companies Act 2006, s. 830; *Trevor* v. *Whitworth* (1887) 12 App Cas 409. This is the general rule, but the matter is more complicated. See, e.g., P. L. Davies and S. Worthington, *Gower and Davies' Principles of Modern Company Law* (9th edn., 2012), ch. 12.

[3] Companies Act 2006, s. 836(2). [4] Companies Act 2006, s. 847.

[5] *Re Paycheck Services 3 Ltd* [2011] 1 BCLC 141, [45]–[47], [124], and 146.

[6] Minimum capital rules apply only to UK *public* companies: Council Directive 2006/49/EC of 14 June 2006 on capital adequacy of investment firms and credit institutions, OJ 2006 No L177/201; Companies Act 2006, ss. 761 and 763.

[7] A. Muscat, *The Liability of the Holding Company for the Debts of its Insolvent Subsidiaries* (1996), p. 345.

have started to manifest themselves. This means that insolvency might arise years after dividends have been paid out, when it is too late to claw them back.

6.2.2 Transactions at an Undervalue and Unfair Preferences

Within a corporate group, there is always a risk that, when insolvency looms, the parent company will direct that transactions be undertaken which are protective of valuable assets or which favour connected parties such as senior executives.[8] This is one manifestation of the judgment-proofing problem. In response to this problem, insolvency laws typically contain 'provisions that apply retroactively from a particular date (such as the date of application for, or commencement of, insolvency proceedings) for a specified period of time (often referred to as the "suspect" period) and are designed to overturn those past transactions to which the insolvent debtor was a party or which involved the debtor's assets where they' reduce its net worth or upset the principle of equal sharing between creditors of the same rank.[9] Typically, three broad types of transaction are characterised as avoidable. These are 'transactions intended to defeat, hinder or delay creditors from collecting their claims; transactions at an undervalue; and transactions with certain creditors that could be regarded as preferential'.[10] Given constraints of space, this chapter focusses upon the latter two types of provision, which have a wider operation than the first.[11] The provisions have implications not only for company insiders, but for external parties that might benefit from avoidable transactions: the provisions

[8] R. P. Austin and I. M. Ramsay, *Ford's Principles of Corporations Law* (12th edn., 2005), p. 497; I. Mevorach, 'Transaction Avoidance in Bankruptcy of Corporate Groups' (2011) 8 *European Company and Financial Law Review* 235, 247–8.

[9] UNCITRAL, 'Legislative Guide on Insolvency Law' (2005), pp. 135–6.

[10] UNCITRAL, 'Legislative Guide on Insolvency Law', p. 141. In addition, see rules on related party transactions – e.g., Financial Conduct Authority, 'Handbook', Listing Rules, LR 11.1.

[11] In the first category, see Insolvency Act 1986, s. 423 (transactions entered into in order to place assets outside the reach of creditors); Corporations Act 2001 (Cth), s. 588FE(5) (defeating, delaying, or interfering with rights of creditors); US Code, Title 11, Bankruptcy, §548(a)(1)(A), and Uniform Voidable Transactions Act 1984, § 4(a)(1) (transactions with actual intent to hinder, delay, or defraud any creditor, often known as fraudulent conveyance law (see C. J. Tabb and R. Brubaker, *Bankruptcy Law Principles, Policies, and Practice* (3rd edn., 2010), ch. 9)). See K. C. Kettering, 'The Uniform Voidable Transactions Act; or, the 2014 Amendments to the Uniform Fraudulent Transfer Act' (2015) 70 *Business Lawyer* 777; UNCITRAL, 'Legislative Guide on Insolvency Law', p. 142.

have 'a deterrent effect, discouraging creditors from pursuing individual remedies in the period leading up to insolvency if they know that these may be reversed or their effects nullified on commencement'.[12] But such provisions are of real effect only when enforced. Factors relevant to enforcement decisions include the difficulty of proving the elements of the statutory actions, cost and delay, and prospects of recovery.[13]

In the United Kingdom, the Insolvency Act 1986 contains provisions on transactions at an undervalue and on unfair preferences. These operate once a company enters into either winding-up or administration, and where impugned transactions result in the diminution of assets available to the general body of creditors. A key factor in determining whether assets have been diminished in the relevant way is the 'absence or inadequacy of new value' in the transactions.[14] The company must have been unable to pay its debts, either at the time of the impugned transactions or as a consequence of them. The provisions facilitate the adjustment of concluded transactions and return to the company of payments made or property transferred.[15] The intention behind the provisions is 'first to inflate the pool of assets available for distribution amongst the creditors; second, to secure parity of treatment as between the creditors; and third, to deter managerial malpractice'.[16]

Insolvency Act 1986, section 238[17] on transactions at an undervalue operates on the basis that an insolvent company should not engage in

[12] UNCITRAL, 'Legislative Guide on Insolvency Law', p. 137. See also R. Mangano, 'The Role of Fraudulent Transfer Rules in Corporate Insolvency' (2008) 5 *European Company and Financial Law Review* 193, 200.

[13] UNCITRAL, 'Legislative Guide on Insolvency Law', p. 137.

[14] R. Goode, *Principles of Corporate Insolvency Law* (4th edn., 2011), p. 527.

[15] Goode, *Principles of Corporate Insolvency Law*, esp. pp. 519–20.

[16] Muscat, *The Liability of the Holding Company*, pp. 219–20. See also Mevorach, 'Transaction Avoidance in Bankruptcy', 236–7.

[17] See also Pensions Act 2004, ss. 52–6 (transactions at an undervalue and powers of pensions regulator); Corporations Act 2001 (Cth), s. 588FE; Companies Act 1993 (NZ), s. 297; US Code, Title 11, Bankruptcy, § 548(a)(1)(B)(i)–(ii)(constructive fraud); Uniform Voidable Transactions Act 1984, § 4(a)(2) and 5(a)(constructive fraud)(see Tabb and Brubaker, *Bankruptcy Law Principles*, ch. 9). Note also that the European Union has announced plans to amend Council Directive 2007/36/EC of 11 July 2007 on the exercise of certain rights of shareholders in listed companies, OJ 2007 No. L184/17 in order to '[e]nhance transparency and shareholder oversight on related party transactions': European Commission, 'Proposal for a Directive of the European Parliament and of the Council Amending Directive 2007/36/EC as Regards the Encouragement of Long-Term Shareholder Engagement and Directive 2013/34/EU as Regards Certain Elements of the Corporate Governance Statement' (COM 2014/0121), p. 2. The latter proposal arises because of the Commission's view that 'shareholders do not have access to sufficient

transactions that deplete its assets, and thereby prejudice creditors. Prohibited transactions include those for which no consideration[18] was obtained, or for which the company obtained 'significantly less than the value, in money or money's worth, of the consideration provided by the company'.[19] Where a party has provided speculative consideration to the insolvent company, the onus is upon it to establish the value of that consideration.[20] Transactions involving persons connected with the company are caught where they were entered into within two years of the onset of insolvency, and the statute adopts the rebuttable presumption that the company was or became unable to pay its debts because of the transactions.[21] A person is 'connected' with a company where he or she is a director or shadow director, an associate of a director or shadow director, or an associate of the company.[22] The term 'associate' has an expansive meaning, which encompasses cases of common control of companies, and cases where a person (A) has control of one company and persons who are associates of A have control of another company.[23] It goes without saying that 'most companies in a group will be associates of each other and hence connected parties',[24] but the provisions reach beyond the confines of the group to other qualifying relationships between commercial parties.

Most avoidable transactions falling within the provisions involve 'the transfer of property, the provision of services or the payment of money by the company in exchange for some money or property'.[25] Examples include the purchase or lease of assets at inflated prices and overpayment for services received.[26] The provisions apply to intra-group loans, and to guarantees without sufficient benefit to the guarantor company, despite

information ahead of the planned transaction and do not have adequate tools to oppose abusive transactions': ibid. 'The [proposed] article 9c will require listed companies that [intend to pursue] related party transactions representing more than 5% of the companies' assets or transactions which can have a significant impact on profits or turnover to submit these transactions to the approval of shareholders and may not unconditionally conclude [them] without their approval': ibid., pp. 8–9.

18 Consideration is said to include the receipt of property or rights by the company, or the satisfaction of an antecedent debt. It does not include benefits received by a third party: Muscat, *The Liability of the Holding Company*, p. 227.

19 Insolvency Act 1986, s. 238(4).

20 B. Hannigan, *Company Law* (3rd edn., 2012), p. 662.

21 Insolvency Act 1986, s. 40.

22 Insolvency Act 1986, s. 249.

23 Insolvency Act 1986, s. 435. See D. Pollard, 'Who Is "Connected" or "Associated" within the Meaning of the Insolvency Act 1986' (2009) 22 *Insolvency Intelligence* 33.

24 Pollard, 'Who Is "Connected" or "Associated"', 39.

25 Muscat, *The Liability of the Holding Company*, p. 227.

26 Goode, *Principles of Corporate Insolvency Law*, p. 531.

these being only contingent liabilities that might never materialise.[27] It might be very difficult to distinguish these transactions from ordinary, intra-group transactions.[28] Especially complex issues arise in characterising guarantees given by a subsidiary to the parent or other group companies, including whether they were given for the purpose of carrying on the subsidiary's own business. This might be so when the subsidiary is dependent upon the welfare of the parent or other group companies, or when it gains simply from being part of a financially sound group.[29] Another issue arises in calculating the value of the guarantees, which will depend on the financial health of the companies to which they are extended.[30]

Section 238 takes hold when the company enters into administration in insolvency or into insolvent liquidation. Where the provision is breached, the court can 'make such order as it thinks fit for restoring the position to what it would have been if the company had not entered into that transaction'.[31] Amounts recovered are held on statutory trust for unsecured creditors.[32] But no order can be made in respect of a transaction at an undervalue when the court is satisfied 'that the company which entered into the transaction did so in good faith and for the purpose of carrying on its business', and 'that at the time it did so there were reasonable grounds for believing that the transaction would benefit the company'.[33] In Muscat's view, this exemption undermines the efficacy of the rules because it saves 'many transactions entered into by a subsidiary, such as the granting of upstream or cross-stream guarantees'.[34]

Insolvency Act 1986, section 239[35] on unfair preferences is 'designed to preserve the sanctity of the pari passu principle by which creditors in a

27 Muscat, *The Liability of the Holding Company*, p. 227.

28 K. J. Hopt, 'Groups of Companies: A Comparative Study on the Economics, Law and Regulation of Corporate Groups', ECGI Law Working Paper no 286/2015 (2015), pp. 14–15.

29 Muscat, *The Liability of the Holding Company*, pp. 232–3.

30 Muscat, *The Liability of the Holding Company*, p. 229.

31 Insolvency Act, s. 241.

32 *Re Oasis Merchandising Services Ltd, Ward* v. *Aiken* [1997] 1 BCLC 689, 689–700. This is subject to payment of winding-up expenses and preferential debts.

33 Insolvency Act 1986, s. 238(5). A presumption arises against the presence of good faith in the circumstances outlined in s. 241(2A).

34 Muscat, *The Liability of the Holding Company*, p. 223.

35 See also Corporations Act 2001 (Cth), s. 588FE; Companies Act 1993 (NZ), s. 292; US Code, Title 11, Bankruptcy, § 547; Uniform Voidable Transactions Act 1984, § 5 (see Tabb and Brubaker, *Bankruptcy Law Principles*, ch. 9; B. B. Erens, S. J. Friedman, and K. M. Mayerfield, 'Bankrupt Subsidiaries: The Challenges to the Parent of Legal Separation' (2008) 25 *Emory Bankruptcy Developments Journal* 65).

winding up share rateably in the assets available for distribution'.[36] The provision reflects the fact that it is unfair for an insolvent company to prefer certain creditors at the expense of the general body of creditors, for example where this would advance the position of parties connected to corporate controllers. The Act provides for a wide definition of 'person connected', the intention being 'to catch all of those whose relationship with the company is such that they either play a role in the company's management or may be privy to information about its affairs not available to outsiders'.[37] Connected persons include companies under common control.[38]

An unfair preference is given to a connected person when that person is one of the company's creditors, or a surety or guarantor for company debts or other liabilities, and where 'the company does anything or suffers anything to be done which . . . has the effect of putting that person into a position which, in the event of the company going into insolvent liquidation, will be better than the position he would have been in if that thing had not been done'.[39] Examples of preferential transactions include 'payment or set-off of debts not yet due; performance of acts that the debtor was under no obligation to perform; granting of a security interest to secure existing unsecured debts; [and] payment of a debt of considerable size in comparison to the assets of the debtor'.[40]

A breach of section 239 occurs when the company, in giving the preference, was influenced by a desire to produce the advantage to the connected person. 'A company which has given a preference to a person connected with the company (otherwise than by reason only of being its employee) at the time the preference was given is presumed, unless the contrary is shown, to have been influenced in deciding to give it by such a desire.'[41] Preferences involving persons connected with the company are caught when they were entered into within two years of the onset of insolvency, and it is proven that the company was unable, or became unable because of the preference, to pay its debts.[42] In order to rebut the presumption applicable to such persons, the court must be satisfied that the insolvent company was acting solely according to proper commercial

36 Goode, *Principles of Corporate Insolvency Law*, p. 575.
37 Goode, *Principles of Corporate Insolvency Law*, p. 593.
38 Insolvency Act 1986, s. 435(6). 39 Insolvency Act 1986, s. 239(4).
40 UNCITRAL, 'Legislative Guide on Insolvency Law', p. 144.
41 Insolvency Act 1986, s. 239(6). In other cases, the existence of the desire is to be inferred from the circumstances of the case: Hannigan, *Company Law*, p. 665.
42 Insolvency Act 1986, s. 40.

considerations when making the payment.[43] Section 239 takes hold when the company enters into administration in insolvency or into insolvent liquidation. Where the provision is breached, the court can 'make such order as it thinks fit for restoring the position to what it would have been if the company had not given that preference'.[44] Amounts recovered are held on statutory trust for unsecured creditors.[45]

The avoidance provisions create incentives in the parent company and directors to engage in proper financial management of the corporate group and, therefore, discourage some abusive conduct.[46] This reduces the risk of subsidiary insolvency. But the provisions will not always be effective in preventing abuse – especially where managers are amenable to risk-taking. Managers might flout them in the hope that their transgressions will not be discovered. Moreover, the provisions have been criticised for deficiencies, including the two-year period within which transactions must have occurred prior to the onset of insolvency, which might prevent the recoupment of substantial assets (although the limitation does not apply in cases of fraud),[47] and the fact that those transactions should have taken place at a time when the subsidiary either was insolvent or became insolvent as a result of them.[48] The effect of the latter requirement is that '[n]othing will stop the dissipation of the subsidiary's resources until it is in dire financial straits' (even taking into account the presumption in section 238).[49] Another potential problem subsists in the time and cost of identifying and unravelling intra-group transactions: 'the costs associated with avoidance proceedings must be weighed against the likelihood of recovering assets and the overall benefit to the estate in the circumstances of each case.'[50]

A problem specific to the prohibition on transactions at an undervalue is that of determining what constitutes fair value. This makes it difficult, for example, for the liquidator or administrator to impugn guarantees given by one company in a group in favour of another. 'In practice, it is unlikely that a guarantee will be impeached as a transaction at an undervalue except where it is clearly of no benefit to the surety company.'[51]

43 *Wills* v. *Corfe Joinery Ltd* [1997] BCC 511, 517. 44 Insolvency Act 1986, s. 239(3).
45 *Re Oasis Merchandising Services Ltd, Ward* v. *Aiken* [1997] 1 BCLC 689, 689–700. This is subject to payment of winding-up expenses and preferential debts.
46 Muscat, *The Liability of the Holding Company*, p. 234. 47 Insolvency Act 1986, s. 240.
48 Insolvency Act 1986, ss. 238(3) and 239(3).
49 Muscat, *The Liability of the Holding Company*, p. 235.
50 UNCITRAL, 'Legislative Guide on Insolvency Law', p. 48.
51 Goode, *Principles of Corporate Insolvency Law*, p. 551.

Andrew Muscat believes that the provisions suffer from the fact that they 'target particular transactions and not a course of conduct generally'.[52] This entails the need for a claimant to be able to adduce evidence about the improvident nature of each transaction entered into. Thus, the law is thought to be 'far too mono-transactional in its approach' to be effective in combating abuse of group assets to the disadvantage of creditors.[53] (This is in contrast to the US approach under the Bankruptcy Code, chapter 11, section 548, which permits examination of a whole course of conduct.)[54]

6.3 Ex post Protections for Creditors

The 'wrongful trading' provisions are designed to discourage directors from allowing their companies to slide into insolvency, thereby creating the insolvent entity problem. Should that problem arise, actions are available to unsecured creditors against directors and shadow directors. Although the provisions are intended to induce a high standard of corporate management, rarely do they result in successful suits against directors. They are yet to feature prominently in cases involving insolvent subsidiaries.

6.3.1 Wrongful Trading

Insolvency Act 1986 sections 214 and 246ZB respond to the fact (noted in Chapter 3) that when approaching insolvency, directors might take greater-than-normal risks in conducting company business because shareholders have little to lose from failed strategies. 'If the risk-taking pays off, then the shareholders will see their wealth maximised, but if it does not, then they have lost nothing more' because their personal assets are protected by limited liability. In the event, 'it is the creditors who will bear the cost.'[55] The provisions aim to ensure that directors engage in 'rigorous monitoring of their companies' health' and, where relevant, take actions necessary to prevent them from sliding into

[52] Muscat, *The Liability of the Holding Company*, p. 202.

[53] Muscat, *The Liability of the Holding Company*, p. 202.

[54] Muscat, *The Liability of the Holding Company*, p. 238, referring to what is now 11 US Code § 548 (fraudulent transfers and obligations), and associated case law.

[55] A. Keay, 'Wrongful Trading and the Liability of Company Directors: A Theoretical Perspective' (2005) 25 *Legal Studies* 431, 434. See also Davies and Worthington, *Principles of Modern Company Law*, p. 230.

insolvency.[56] Should directors fail in these tasks, the provisions facilitate actions by liquidators and administrators for 'wrongful trading'.[57]

The provisions create the threat of personal liability in company directors. The term 'director' includes a 'shadow director'.[58] Under Insolvency Act 1986, section 251, a shadow director is 'a person in accordance with whose directions or instructions the directors of the company are accustomed to act', and the term is accepted to include companies such as parent companies[59] because of their ability to exercise 'real influence in the

[56] Keay, 'Wrongful Trading and the Liability of Company Directors', 432.

[57] For similar provisions elsewhere, see Companies Act 1990 (Ireland), s. 138; Corporations Act 2001 (Cth), ss. 588G–588Y; Companies Act 1993 (NZ), ss. 135–6. In Australia, Corporations Act 2001 (Cth) s. 588V applies to vertical holding company–subsidiary relationships, but does not encompass the control exercised by other companies, for example in heterarchical groups (discussed in Chapter 2): I. M. Ramsay, 'Holding Company Liability for the Debts of an Insolvent Subsidiary: A Law and Economics Perspective' (1994) 17 *University of New South Wales Law Journal* 520, 544. However, companies which are not holding companies might still be liable for insolvent trading if they are shadow directors of an insolvent company, and otherwise fall within the provision applicable to directors (s. 588G): see *Ho* v. *Akai Pty Ltd (in liq)* (2006) 24 ACLC 1526. But courts have interpreted s. 588V to be restricted to 'liability to debts which a company incurs voluntarily with the result that tort liabilities are excluded': *Geraldton Building Co Pty Ltd* v. *Woodmore* (1992) 8 ASCR 585, 590; P. Lipton, 'The Mythology of *Salomon*'s Case and the Law Dealing with the Tort Liabilities of Corporate Groups: An Historical Perspective' (2014) 40 *Monash University Law Review* 452, 481, n 156; Ramsay, ibid., 543. Thus, the provision is seen to be of very limited scope: N. Coburn, *Coburn's Insolvent Trading* (2nd edn., 2003), p. 128. While the United States does not have legislation equivalent to the wrongful trading provisions, courts in some jurisdictions have applied a not dissimilar doctrine known as 'deepening insolvency'. The factors required to support an action by the trustee in bankruptcy against directors are not fully established, but seem to comprise the insolvency of the debtor company, managerial concealment of this state of insolvency, the incurring of new loans which have prolonged the operation of the company, and the causation of a loss to creditors: J. Tully, 'Plumbing the Depths of Corporate Litigation: Reforming the Deepening Insolvency Theory' [2013] *University of Illinois Law Review* 2087, 2100. One court has doubted that any true losses can arise from such actions because they entail the prolonged life of the debtor company – which is a benefit to it and, potentially, to creditors: *In re Greater Southeast Community Hospital Corp* 333 BR 506 (Bankr. DDC 2005). There has been dispute over the theoretical basis for this doctrine – in particular whether it is to be treated as an independent tort or doctrine, or else just a basis for the award of damages under an action in fraud: Tully, ibid., 2088; Erens, Friedman, and Mayerfield, 'Bankrupt Subsidiaries'. The Delaware Court of Chancery has rejected such a cause of action: *Trenwick America Litigation Trust* v. *Ernst & Young* 906 A 2d 168, 174 (Del. Ch. 2006) aff'd sub nom. *Trenwick America Litigation Trust* v. *Billett* 931 A 2d 438 (Del. 2007); it is liable also to defeat under the business judgment rule: Erens, Friedman, and Mayerfield, ibid.

[58] Insolvency Act 1986, ss. 214(7) and 246ZB(7).

[59] See P. Muchlinski, *Multinational Enterprises and the Law* (2nd edn., 2007), p. 332.

corporate affairs of the company'.[60] In the case of parent companies that exercise detailed control over the day-to-day operations of subsidiaries ('subservient subsidiaries'), the inference can be drawn usually that the parent company is acting as shadow director.[61] (The same cannot be said of the individual directors of the parent company, except perhaps in extraordinary circumstances.)[62] But the 'directions or instructions do not have to extend over all or most of the corporate activities of the company'.[63] By contrast, the parent company is unlikely to be made liable where it simply approves decisions made in the first instance by its subsidiary's board of directors.[64] Where the parent is a shadow director of its subsidiary, the wrongful trading provisions create the potential for a form of statutory veil-piercing, or extension of liability.

Sections 214 and 246ZB apply when a company has gone into either insolvent liquidation or insolvent administration,[65] and at some time prior to this the director in question 'knew or ought to have concluded that there was no reasonable prospect that the company would avoid' this result.[66] In determining the knowledge of the director and the steps which ought to have been taken, the court will apply an objective test by reference to the reasonably diligent person having both 'the general knowledge, skill and experience that may reasonably be expected of a person carrying out the same functions as are carried out by that director', and 'the general knowledge, skill and experience that that director has'.[67] This means that it is not necessarily sufficient

60 *Secretary of State for Trade and Industry* v. *Deverell* [2001] Ch 340, 354 (construing analogous provision in Company Directors Disqualification Act 1986, s. 22(5). Note that, in the United States, there is no concept of shadow directorship. However, parent companies, as controlling shareholders, do owe fiduciary duties to creditors of their controlled companies when in the vicinity of insolvency: see *Federal Deposit Insurance Corporation* v. *Sea Pines Company* 692 F 2d 973 (4th Cir. 1982)).

61 Muscat, *The Liability of the Holding Company*, p. 215. By contrast, the parent is not a shadow director merely because it imposes operational guidelines on the conduct of the subsidiary, imposes budgetary restraints, and/or requires that certain decisions require approval of the parent company: Goode, *Principles of Corporate Insolvency Law*, p. 645.

62 *Re Hydrodan (Corby) Ltd* [1992] BCC 161, 164.

63 *Secretary of State for Trade and Industry* v. *Deverell* [2001] Ch 340, 355 (construing the analogous provision in the Company Directors Disqualification Act 1986, sub-s 22(5)).

64 *Re Hydrodan (Corby) Ltd* [1992] BCC 161, 165. Cf. K. Yeung, 'Corporate Groups: Legal Aspects of the Management Dilemma' [1997] *Lloyd's Maritime and Commercial Law Quarterly* 208, 230.

65 Under this provision, 'insolvency' must be assessed by reference to a balance sheet test: see Insolvency Act 1986, s. 214(6).

66 Insolvency Act 1986, ss. 214(2)(b) and 246ZB(2)(b).

67 Insolvency Act 1986, ss. 214(4) and 246ZB(4).

that the director in question met the minimum expectations imposed upon all directors; the 'director must also meet such higher standard as is appropriate to his own general knowledge, skill and experience'.[68] In determining solvency, the director would be expected to consider factors including: any loss of contracts, the availability (or not) of fresh contracts, the demands of creditors whose debts are due, loss of major suppliers, the withdrawal of bank support, and ability (or not) to pay taxes when due.[69]

Where the requisite knowledge exists, the court has power to impose upon the director such liability to contribute to the insolvent company's assets as it thinks proper, unless it is satisfied that, after knowledge arose, 'the person took every step with a view to minimising the potential loss to the company's creditors' as ought to have been taken.[70] The language used in the statute is intended to create 'a high hurdle for directors to surmount'.[71] The standard of care demanded of a parent company in exercising control over the subsidiary is potentially very high, given the knowledge, skill and experience (not to mention the resources) that it could bring to the shadow director role.

A contribution order can be made under section 214 only where it is proved that the company was worse off, on a net basis, upon commencement of the winding-up than it was at the time the directors ought to have ceased trading, and that this was because of the directors' deficient conduct.[72] In this way, the provisions make available an action which permits the restoration of 'the financial position of the company to what it would have been had the wrongful trading not occurred'.[73] Recovered sums are held on statutory trust exclusively for unsecured creditors.[74] Apart from making an order that the parent company make contribution to the assets of the subsidiary, in the case of parent company mismanagement in the vicinity of the subsidiary's insolvency the court exercising power under

68 Goode, *Principles of Corporate Insolvency Law*, p. 673.

69 A. R. Keay, 'Wrongful Trading: Problems and Proposals' [2014] *Northern Ireland Law Quarterly* 63, 73.

70 Insolvency Act 1986, ss. 214(3) and 246ZB(3).

71 *Grant* v. *Ralls* [2016] All ER D 113, [245].

72 *Re Continental Assurance Co of London plc* [2007] 2 BCLC 287, 294, 296, and 413; *Re Marini Ltd* [2004] BCC 172, 197–8.

73 *Grant* v. *Ralls* [2016] All ER D 113, [245].

74 See D. Milman, 'Promoting Distributional Justice on Corporate Insolvency in the 21st Century', in J. Steele and W. H. van Boom (eds.), *Mass Justice: Challenges of Representation and Distribution* (2011), p. 173.

section 215(4) can order that the debts the subsidiary owes to the parent be deferred to debts of other creditors.[75]

Sections 214 and 246ZB have not been used frequently in cases against individual directors.[76] A practical reason for the paucity of actions is the difficulty typically faced by claimants in obtaining funding to bring claims,[77] although new provisions in the Insolvency Act 1986, which permit the insolvency practitioner to assign the benefit of claims, should reduce the extent to which this is a problem.[78] When claims have been brought, courts have been reluctant to second-guess directors in their commercial decision-making,[79] which might take place in less than ideal circumstances that do not permit the formation of any clear view of the future of the company.[80] Courts require convincing evidence that the requirements of the provisions have been met. Claimants have succeeded in clear cases only where directors have engaged in conduct which is 'most irresponsible', such as in ignoring clear signs of inevitable insolvency.[81] As adumbrated, the wrongful trading provisions have been used even less frequently when seeking to access the assets of parent companies.[82] There are a number of reasons for this. First, there is the question whether the parent company was exercising such control over the operations of the subsidiary that it could be said that the subsidiary was accustomed to acting in accordance with its directions. Second, there is the question whether a court would be prepared to cast aside the doctrine of limited liability in order to extend liability to a parent company.[83] Given the doubts, it appears that section 214 'does not achieve what was intended when introduced, for it does not provide the liquidator with an effective weapon in recovering

[75] See Mevorach, *Insolvency within Multinational Enterprise Groups*, pp. 309–10.

[76] Reforms to the Insolvency Act 1986, effected by the Small Business, Enterprise and Employment Act 2015, are not expected to change this situation very much: R. Williams, 'What Can We Expect to Gain from Reforming the Insolvent Trading Remedy?' (2015) 78 *Modern Law Review* 55.

[77] A. Keay and M. Murray, 'Making Company Directors Liable: A Comparative Analysis of Wrongful Trading in the United Kingdom and Insolvent Trading in Australia' (2005) 14 *International Insolvency Review* 27, 53.

[78] Insolvency Act 1986, ss. 176ZB and 246ZD.

[79] Keay, 'Wrongful Trading and the Liability of Company Directors', 440.

[80] Keay, 'Wrongful Trading: Problems and Proposals', 67ff.

[81] Keay, 'Wrongful Trading: Problems and Proposals', 68, referring to *Re Continental Assurance Co of London plc* [2007] 2 BCLC 287.

[82] Most successful cases have been against the directors of private companies: Keay, 'Wrongful Trading and the Liability of Company Directors', 446.

[83] Davies and Worthington, *Principles of Modern Company Law*, p. 233.

funds for the benefit of creditors and it fails as a mechanism that will encourage directors to minimise losses to creditors'.[84]

Assuming these issues away, let us consider the case of a parent company engaging in abusive practices, such as the diversion of corporate opportunities away from the subsidiary, failing to collect debts due to it from other group companies, and draining its funds through techniques like transfer pricing. In such cases, there is the potential for liability under sections 214 and 246ZB, but this is unlikely to arise. A deliberate strategy of this kind is likely to cease in the vicinity of insolvency. Thus Muscat states that 'subservient conduct would usually be carried out as part of a group profit maximisation policy at a time when no immediate threat to the subsidiary's creditors is thereby occasioned and when there is no reason to conclude that the company was approaching insolvent liquidation.'[85]

Next, let us take a case more typical of those with which this book is concerned. Cases of mass-torts arising from asbestos exposure or defective pharmaceuticals, for example, often involve latent injuries caused over an extended period of time. The scale of the liabilities will not be apparent until injuries have started to manifest themselves. In such circumstances, it might be difficult to prove the knowledge of insolvency requirement in sections 214 and 246ZB. Even then, the question arises as to what the directors should do when they have actual or imputed knowledge. The obligation of the directors is to take 'every step with a view to minimising the potential loss to the company's creditors'. It might not be wise for the directors to close down the business because anticipated revenue streams might provide hope that tort victims can be paid the compensation owed to them. Indeed, the prospect of a structured settlement might cloud the issue of whether the subsidiary is insolvent at all. Furthermore, the parent company might fully intend to support the subsidiary in meeting its liabilities up until such time as the parent's own ability to operate is threatened. Counsel Assisting the James Hardie Inquiry was of the view that the Australian equivalent of section

[84] Keay, 'Wrongful Trading: Problems and Proposals', 64. It has been said that 'the focus of s 214 is arguably too narrow and it should be broadened to deal with situations where the parent conducts itself in a manner that allows a creditor, dealing with the subsidiary, to reasonably infer that the parent will stand behind its subsidiary. In other words, a determinant of liability would be the conduct of the parent in relation to creditors of its subsidiary': D. D. Prentice, 'Some Aspects of the Law Relating to Corporate Groups in the United Kingdom' (1999) 13 *Connecticut Journal of International Law* 305, 326–7.

[85] Muscat, *The Liability of the Holding Company*, p. 217.

214 creates a very narrow form of liability, dependent upon 'the resolution of factual issues that are costly and risky to litigate'.[86]

6.4 Conclusions

The provisions considered in this chapter provide company directors with incentives to ensure that the capital of the company is maintained, that assets are preserved for payment of creditors and for other company purposes, and that companies do not continue to trade when in the vicinity of insolvency. These provisions reduce the probability of insolvency and of the insolvent entity problem. In the case of insolvency, the provisions make available certain causes of action which would assist an insolvency practitioner to inflate insolvent estate assets for payment of creditors. However, the provisions are no guarantee against the insolvent entity problem. This means that there is a need to consider what can be done in addition to bringing the causes of action mentioned in this chapter. The chapters that follow consider further actions of assistance in dealing with the insolvent entity problem, Chapter 7 being concerned with group-specific statutory protections for creditors.

[86] D. Jackson QC, 'Report of the Special Commission of Inquiry into the Medical Research and Compensation Fund' (2004), Annexure 'T', p. 417.

7

Group-Specific Protections for Creditors

7.1 Introduction

This chapter turns to ways in which statute and common law specifically address a range of issues involving corporate groups. It examines ways in which corporate groups are recognised under EU and UK statutory provisions about transparency of ownership and control and presentation of group accounts. These provisions help creditors for two reasons: first, the compulsory provision of information has a dampening effect on temptations to engage in misconduct;[1] and, second, information about control might assist creditors in bringing actions for compensation, such as those considered in this book, against responsible parties after insolvency strikes.

This chapter goes on to examine methods by which creditor claims are dealt with in administration and insolvency. This includes consideration of UK statutory provisions on schemes of arrangement, which facilitate the reorganisation of companies through compromises with creditors. It includes, further, consideration of special statutory and judicially created regimes adopted in various common law jurisdictions, which permit the pooling of assets, making of contribution orders, equitable subordination of debts owed to group creditors, and re-characterisation of debt as equity.

This chapter demonstrates that lawmakers are cognisant of the ways in which the corporate form is being misused, and that modest measures have been implemented to counteract misuse.

7.2 Statutory Recognition of Groups

In certain specific circumstances, UK company and insolvency law recognises that companies in corporate groups are under common control and

[1] L. Gullifer and J. Payne, *Corporate Finance Law: Principles and Policy* (2nd edn., 2015), pp. 528–9.

have common financial interests.[2] For example, Companies Act 2006, section 1159 (considered in Chapter 1), defines the term 'subsidiary company' by reference to the voting rights held in it and control exercised over it by another company, its parent company.[3] This definition is of importance in calculating various types of tax liability, and in the world of commercial contracting.[4] Section 1173 of the 2006 Act is a related provision, which defines the term 'parent company' and is considered in the text that follows. Another prominent example of statutory recognition of groups for tax purposes subsists in the Income and Corporation Taxes Act 1988, chapter IV. Relevant provisions permit profits in one company in a corporate group to be off-set against losses in another group company, the group being defined by reference to majority ownership interests.[5] Two further examples of the recognition of groups, now to be considered, concern rules about transparency and group accounts.

7.2.1 Transparency Rules

Concerns have arisen in the European Union both about misuse of the corporate form by controlling parties and about the need for market participants to be provided with minimal levels of information about the issuers of regulated securities. These concerns have resulted in the passage of two significant EU Directives, and amendments to the Companies Act 2006 and other UK legislation. The legislation facilitates the publication of a high level of information about ownership and control of relevant companies. As adumbrated, this information might prove useful in the application of rules which would extend liability from insolvent companies to others in the corporate group and, as such, the legislation is of relevance to the insolvent entity problem.

The EU Transparency Directive (as amended)[6] responds to concerns about opacity in share ownership in Europe, a great proportion of

[2] I. Mevorach, *Insolvency within Multinational Enterprise Groups* (2009), p. 26.

[3] The statute uses the term 'holding company', but for present purposes nothing turns on this.

[4] *Enviroco Ltd* v. *Farstad Supply A/S* [2011] 1 WLR 921, [4].

[5] For further examples of the way in which the law might deal with taxation matters arising from group activities, see UNCITRAL, 'Legislative Guide on Insolvency, Part Three: Treatment of Enterprise Groups in Insolvency' (2012), pp. 12–13.

[6] Council Directive 2004/109/EC of 15 December 2004 on the Harmonisation of Transparency Requirements in Relation to Information about Issuers Whose Securities Are Admitted to Trading on a Regulated Market, OJ 2004 No. 390/38 ('Directive on the Harmonisation of Transparency Requirements').

shares in listed companies being held indirectly through nominees. This means that searches of company share registers often yield little useful information about interests held in those companies.[7] The Directive was enacted in order to improve the level of market information about issuers of securities admitted to trading on EU-regulated markets, and to help protect investors in such securities.[8] It mandates that EU Member States set out rules for issuers so that issuers are required to disclose key information about shareholdings. Under article 9, a Member State 'shall ensure that, where a shareholder acquires or disposes of shares of an issuer whose shares are admitted to trading on a regulated market and to which voting rights are attached, such shareholder notifies the issuer of the proportion of voting rights of the issuer held by the shareholder as a result of the acquisition or disposal where that proportion reaches, exceeds or falls below' various specified thresholds. Courtesy of amendments to the Directive, holdings of financial instruments having an economic effect similar to shares and entitlements to acquire shares must be disclosed as well. This follows from an extended definition of 'financial instrument', which aims to uncover previously hidden controllers and holders of significant voting power.[9] 'This is crucial since hidden ownership makes it possible to acquire a large controlling stake in a target company, without public disclosure.'[10] The provisions enable identification of corporate group structures and other instances in which companies can exercise significant voting power over other companies. These other instances include cases involving 'a chain of controlled undertakings through which voting rights are effectively held',[11] and voting power that arises directly or indirectly through interests in various financial instruments.[12] In the United Kingdom, the provisions of this Directive have been transposed into the Financial Services and Markets Act 2000 and subordinate legislation, the exact provisions of which need not be examined here.[13]

[7] See Gullifer and Payne, *Corporate Finance Law*, pp. 552–3.

[8] Mazars, 'Transparency Directive Assessment Report' (2009), p. vi.

[9] Directive on the Harmonisation of Transparency Requirements (2004/109/EC), arts. 13 and 13a.

[10] K. Vanneste, 'Decoupling Economic Rights from Voting Rights: A Threat to the Traditional Corporate Governance Paradigm' (2014) 15 *European Business Organization Law Review* 59, 71–3.

[11] Directive on the Harmonisation of Transparency Requirements (2004/109/EC), art. 12.

[12] Directive on the Harmonisation of Transparency Requirements (2004/109/EC), art. 13a.

[13] See Financial Services and Markets: The Transparency Regulations (SI 2015/1755), inserting amending provisions into the Act.

The European Union's Fourth Anti Money Laundering Directive[14] imposes transparency requirements with respect to credit and financial institutions and other legal persons dealing in large cash payments.[15] These requirements have been adopted in order to combat tax evasion, money laundering, corruption, and other abuses of the financial system.[16] When establishing a business relationship, and when completing significant transactions, the Directive requires that institutions undertake customer due diligence.[17] Under article 13, customer due diligence measures shall comprise: identification of the customer and verification of the customer's identity; identification of the beneficial owner and the taking of reasonable measures to verify that person's identity, so that the obliged entity is satisfied that it knows who the beneficial owner is, all the while taking reasonable measures to understand the ownership and control structure of the customer; obtaining information on the purpose and intended nature of the business relationship and assessment of this; and the conduct of ongoing monitoring of the business relationship, including scrutiny of transactions undertaken throughout the course of that relationship. These requirements are subject to exceptions, including those covering lower-risk business relationships and transactions.

The Directive provides that '[i]dentification and verification of beneficial owners[18] should, where relevant, extend to legal entities that own other legal entities, and obliged entities should look for the natural person(s) who ultimately exercises control through ownership or through other means of the legal entity that is the customer.' Control 'through other means' includes control obtained through a shareholders' agreement, the exercise of dominant influence, and/or the power to appoint senior management.[19] Under article 30, Member States must ensure that corporate and other legal entities incorporated within their territories obtain and hold adequate, accurate, and current information on their ownership. Member States must ensure that those entities provide, in addition to information about their legal owners, information on the beneficial owners to obliged entities when the obliged entities are taking customer due diligence measures. Member States

[14] Council Directive 2015/849 of 20 May 2015 on the Prevention of the Use of the Financial System for the Purposes of Money Laundering or Terrorist Financing, OJ 2015 No L141/73 ('Fourth Anti Money Laundering Directive').

[15] Fourth Anti Money Laundering Directive (2015/849), art. 2.

[16] Fourth Anti Money Laundering Directive (2015/849), art. 1.

[17] Fourth Anti Money Laundering Directive (2015/849), art. 11.

[18] See definition in Fourth Anti Money Laundering Directive (2015/849), art. 3(6).

[19] Fourth Anti Money Laundering Directive (2015/849), preamble 13.

shall require that the information be accessible in a timely manner by competent authorities; to this end, each Member State must establish a central register of beneficial ownership.

Companies Act 2006, Part 21A anticipated the latter requirements of the Anti Money Laundering Directive. It mandates that UK-registered companies maintain a publicly searchable register identifying persons with significant control in those companies[20] (although exemptions apply, including one for companies already subject to the Financial Conduct Authority's Disclosure and Transparency Rules Sourcebook, ch. 5).[21] The purpose of Part 21A is to 'increase the accountability of companies by making it easier to see who owns or controls them and who might be making decisions about how they are run'.[22] This is intended to have a deterrent effect in countering tax evasion and money laundering.[23] Relevant information must be supplied to Companies House,[24] which keeps a Register of People with Significant Control.[25] Schedule 1A to the Act provides a definition of 'people with significant control'. A person falls within it where one or more of the following circumstances applies – that is, where the person: holds 25 percent or more of the shares in a company; holds 25 per cent or more of its voting rights (whether directly or indirectly); holds the right to appoint or remove the majority of the directors of the company (whether directly or indirectly); or has the right to exercise or actually exercises significant influence or control over the company.[26] A person with significant control might be a company or other legal entity.[27] Department for Business, Innovation and Skills 'Statutory Guidance'[28] indicates that control arises where a person can

[20] Companies Act 2006, ss. 790M–N. [21] Companies Act 2006, s. 790B(1).

[22] Department for Business, Innovation and Skills, 'The Register of People with Significant Control' (June 2015), p. 3.

[23] Department for Business, Innovation and Skills, 'The Register of People with Significant Control', p. 4. Cf. K. J. Hopt, 'Groups of Companies: A Comparative Study on the Economics, Law and Regulation of Corporate Groups', ECGI Law Working Paper no 286/2015 (2015), pp. 14–15 (temptations to abuse ownership interests will continue to exist).

[24] Companies Act 2006, ss. 831I and 831L.

[25] Department for Business, Innovation and Skills, 'The Register of People with Significant Control', p. 3.

[26] Companies Act 2006, s. 790C(2)–(3) and Schedule 1A, items 2–5. See also the Draft Register of People with Significant Control Regulations 2016, esp. regs. 9–13 (additional matters).

[27] Companies Act 2006, sub-ss. 790C(6)–(7).

[28] Department for Business, Innovation and Skills, 'Statutory Guidance on the Meaning of "Significant Influence or Control" over Companies in the Context of the Register of People with Significant Control' (April 2016).

'direct the activities' of a company, and that a person has significant influence over a company where that person can ensure that the company 'generally adopts the activities which they desire'.[29] The Guidance affirms that the 'right to exercise significant influence or control over a company may result in that person being a PSC in relation to the company regardless of whether . . . they actually exercise that right'.[30]

7.2.2 Group Accounts and Cross-Guarantees

Further statutory provisions which recognise corporate groups are of potential assistance to creditors having interactions with them. The EU Accounting Directive[31] mandates that EU Member States enact legislation requiring larger corporate 'undertakings' to prepare consolidated group accounts and management reports. The Directive does not limit undertakings to equity-based control relationships. That term is defined more widely and permits Member States (should they so desire) to impose accounting requirements relating to controlled entities, no matter the basis of control.[32] 'Consolidated financial statements should present the activities of a parent undertaking and its subsidiaries as a single economic entity.'[33] They should include information on all assets and liabilities, and on income and expenditure of group undertakings.[34] (As an aside, there are proposals to amend the Accounting Directive so as to impose country-by-country tax reporting requirements on multinational enterprises with a worldwide turnover of more than EUR 750 million per annum.[35] Directors would have collective responsibility for

[29] Department for Business, Innovation and Skills, 'Statutory Guidance on the Meaning of "Significant Influence or Control"', 1.22. This ties in with the definition of 'shadow director' in Companies Act 2006, s. 251: see ibid., 3.3. Nominee shareholders are irrelevant to the inquiry: Department for Business Innovation and Skills, 'Register of People with Significant Control: Guidance for Companies, Societates Europaeae and Limited Liability Partnerships' (2016), [7.4.1] and [7.4.13].

[30] Department for Business, Innovation and Skills, 'Statutory Guidance on the Meaning of "Significant Influence or Control"', 2.4.

[31] Council Directive 2013/34/EU of 26 June 2013 on the Annual Financial Statements, Consolidated Financial Statements and Related Reports of Certain Types of Undertakings, OJ 2013 No. L182/19 ('Accounting Directive').

[32] Accounting Directive (2013/34/EU), arts. 2 and 22(2).

[33] Accounting Directive (2013/34/EU), preamble 31.

[34] Accounting Directive (2013/34/EU), art. 24(7) and preamble 34.

[35] European Commission, 'Proposal for a Directive Amending Directive 2013/34/EU as Regards Disclosure of Income Tax Information by Certain Undertakings and Branches' (COM (2016) 198).

ensuring compliance with reporting requirements.[36] These proposals follow on from policy adopted by G20 governments[37] (discussed in Chapter 2), and seek to create transparency in reporting on tax payments – which should assist in the fight against tax base erosion and profit shifting.)

The Accounting Directive has been transposed into UK law by various provisions in the Companies Act 2006. As a preliminary, we should note that, under section 1173, a parent company means a company that is a parent undertaking pursuant to section 1162. According to section 1162(2), an undertaking is a parent undertaking in relation to another undertaking, a subsidiary undertaking, if: it holds a majority of the voting rights in the undertaking; or it is a member of the undertaking and has the right to appoint or remove a majority of its board of directors; or it has the right to exercise a dominant influence over the undertaking by virtue of provisions contained in the undertaking's articles, or by virtue of a control contract; or it is a member of the undertaking and controls alone, or pursuant to an agreement with other shareholders or members, a majority of the voting rights in the undertaking.[38] According to section 1162(3), for the purposes of subsection (2) an undertaking shall be treated as a member of another undertaking if any of its subsidiary undertakings is a member of that undertaking, or if any shares in that other undertaking are held by a person acting on behalf of the undertaking or any of its subsidiary undertakings. Under section 1162(4), an undertaking is a parent undertaking, also, in relation to another undertaking, a subsidiary undertaking, if it has the power to exercise, or actually exercises, dominant influence or control over it, or it and the subsidiary undertaking are managed on a unified basis. Under subsection (5), a parent undertaking shall be treated as the parent undertaking of undertakings in relation to which any of its subsidiary undertakings are or are to be treated as parent undertakings.

Under Companies Act 2006, Part 15, Chapter 4, group accounts must be presented in consolidated form. Under section 399(2), where a company is a parent company at the end of the financial year, the directors, as well as preparing individual company accounts for the year, must prepare group accounts unless the company is exempt. Under section 404, group accounts must comprise both a consolidated balance sheet dealing with the state of affairs of the parent company and its subsidiary undertakings,

36 European Commission, 'Proposal for a Directive Amending the Accounting Directive' (COM (2016) 198), [10].

37 OECD, 'Transfer Pricing Documentation and Country-by-Country Reporting, Action 13 – 2015 Final Report' (2015).

38 Terms used in this provision are explained in Companies Act 2006, sched. 7.

and a consolidated profit and loss account dealing with the profit or loss of the parent company and its subsidiary undertakings. The accounts must give a true and fair view of the state of affairs as at the end of the financial year, and profit or loss for the financial year, of the undertakings included in the consolidation as a whole. Section 405(1) requires that, where a parent company prepares group accounts, all the subsidiary undertakings of the company are included in the consolidation.

Under Companies Act 2006, section 479A, a company is exempt[39] from group accounting requirements if it is a subsidiary undertaking, its parent undertaking is established under the law of a European Economic Area State, and all of the following conditions apply: all members of the company agree to the exemption; the parent undertaking provides a guarantee under section 479C; the company is included in the consolidated accounts by the parent undertaking; and the directors of the company have delivered to the registrar certain documents, including the consolidated accounts and an auditor's report. Under section 479C, a guarantee is given by a parent undertaking when the directors of the subsidiary company deliver to the registrar a statement by the parent undertaking that it guarantees the subsidiary company's debts. A guarantee has the effect that the parent undertaking guarantees all outstanding liabilities to which the subsidiary company is subject at the end of the financial year to which the guarantee relates, until they are satisfied in full, and the guarantee is enforceable against the parent undertaking by any person to whom the subsidiary company is liable in respect of those liabilities. As at the time of writing, it was not 'clear to what extent parent companies have taken advantage of this option'.[40]

In Australia, Commonwealth law allows for a similar type of exemption. Under the Corporations Act 2001 (Cth), Part 2 M.6, the Australian Securities and Investments Commission has the power to relieve corporate group subsidiaries of the requirement to prepare individual financial accounts, so that only consolidated group accounts need be prepared. This relief is available when group companies, including the 'holding company', have entered into a deed of cross-guarantee with each other.[41] 'Under the deed each group company included in the deed covenants to pay in full any provable debt of the other group companies in a winding

[39] This is subject to certain exceptions set out in Companies Act 2006, s. 479B, including that related to quoted companies.

[40] B. Hannigan, *Company Law* (4th edn., 2016), p. 64.

[41] This power has been exercised under ASIC Class Order 98/1418.

up.'[42] On the face of it, Part 2 M.6 is attractive because it ameliorates the insolvent entity problem by creating automatic recourse to other group companies, at the same time as it reduces the 'accounts and audit burden on corporate groups'.[43] However, the scheme is voluntary in nature. It is unlikely that parent companies engaged in deliberate structuring of group relations so as to avoid potential tort liabilities will want to provide cross-guarantees for their at-risk subsidiaries. Moreover, cross-guarantees are not required to and often do not encompass all group companies.[44] In Jennifer Hill's view: 'It is simply not true to say that creditor protection is enhanced through the presence of cross guarantees. Rather, the position of some creditors will be advanced to the detriment of others throughout the group.'[45] No doubt, the UK exemption rules might be argued to suffer from similar shortcomings.

7.2.3 Summary

Although the provisions examined in this section indicate legislatures' increasing awareness of and interest in corporate groups, they have had a limited impact to date. The consequence of the limited recognition of and power over corporate groups is that there are few mechanisms available to UK courts that offer a direct response to the insolvent entity problem in the group context. Most mechanisms are not targeted specifically at corporate groups and offer an indirect response to group problems only.[46] In subsequent chapters, this book will make recommendations for addressing this omission.

7.3 Protections in Administration and Insolvency

This chapter now moves on to consider selected methods of addressing creditor claims against corporate groups in administration and insolvency. As adumbrated, this chapter examines UK provisions on schemes of arrangement, which facilitate the reorganisation of companies through compromises with creditors. It examines special statutory and judicially

[42] M. Wyburn, 'Pooling as a Response to the Competing Interests in Corporate Group Collapse in Australia' (2010) 19 *International Insolvency Review* 65, 80.

[43] Wyburn, 'Pooling as a Response', 80. [44] Wyburn, 'Pooling as a Response', 80–1.

[45] J. Hill, 'Corporate Groups, Creditor Protection and Cross Guarantees: Australian Perspectives' (1995) 24 *Canadian Business Law Journal* 321, 346.

[46] Wyburn, 'Pooling as a Response', 72–3 (discussing Australian law; but a comment even more applicable to the United Kingdom).

created regimes also, which facilitate the pooling of assets, contribution orders, equitable subordination of debts owed internally to group creditors, and re-characterisation of debt as equity. This survey indicates not only the variety of ways in which creditors can seek recovery against corporate groups, but reveals the limitations of each regime too. Courts remain wary of exercising their powers to inflate the assets available to satisfy creditor claims, in part because they recognise that such orders undermine the separate legal personality doctrine and can have adverse effects on recoveries by third-party creditors.

7.3.1 Reorganisations

Various statutory provisions give courts power to sanction company reorganisations.[47] Reorganisation involves agreement between a debtor company and its creditors about the status of subsisting claims. Generally, they are predicated on the continuing viability of the debtor business:[48] 'unsecured creditors will be able to obtain a greater proportion of their claims if the debtor continues as an ongoing business capable of generating a stream of payments in the future than if the debtor liquidates immediately. That is, the value of the debtor as an ongoing enterprise is greater than the value of its assets sold piecemeal.'[49] Reorganisation might entail a compromise involving debt reduction and a repayment plan, setting up a trust to administer payments, conversion of debt into equity in the debtor company,[50] or variations on these themes. In the usual case, reorganisation is undertaken by a scheme of arrangement, which involves court approval of the plan, and agreement by the required majorities of affected creditors.[51] While scheme processes are quite flexible, an alternative to a court-sanctioned reorganisation is a more informal 'workout' which can achieve the same kinds of result (but where the threat of resort to judicial procedures remains).[52]

Parties in ongoing commercial relationships are those most likely to agree upon a reorganisation plan because the debtor company and/or its major investors must continue working with creditors (especially trade

47 Esp. Companies Act 2006, Part 26 (schemes of arrangement). See also Insolvency Act 1986, Part 1 (company voluntary arrangements).
48 R. Goode, *Principles of Corporate Insolvency Law* (4th edn., 2011), p. 476.
49 M. Lyle, 'Mass Tort Claims and the Corporate Tortfeasor: Bankruptcy Reorganization and Legislative Compensation versus the Common-Law Tort System' (1983) 61 *Texas Law Review* 1297, 1321–2.
50 Lyle, 'Mass Tort Claims and the Corporate Tortfeasor', 1320–1.
51 Companies Act 2006, Part 26, esp. ss. 897 and 899.
52 Goode, *Principles of Corporate Insolvency Law*, p. 482.

suppliers and banks) in order to stay in business. There is less incentive for agreement where debts are owed to tort claimants – although this is possible and has been seen in some mass-torts cases, including UK asbestos cases. In *In re Cape plc*,[53] for example, the former asbestos producer Cape plc was facing a large but uncertain number of present and future claims of personal injury by employees. In order to be able to continue trading, the company sought court sanction for a compromise with these creditors that involved the creation of a new entity, Cape Claims Services plc (CCS), which would be funded by Cape and respond to all personal injury claims against the group. The Chancery Division approved the proposed scheme of arrangement as the only realistic way of preserving Cape businesses and funding claims on a sustainable basis. The approved scheme ranked all creditors, present and future, equally in their claims against CCS.[54]

But there are concerns about the use of schemes of arrangement in order to reorganise. One problem, which we encountered in Chapter 4, is the tendency to underestimate the number and size of future claims involving some types of toxic product, such as asbestos. This problem was dealt with in *In re Cape plc* by making provision for future alteration of the scheme.[55] But, ordinarily, compromises lead to the externalisation of significant tort losses onto injured claimants. This is because tort claimants who enter into compromises with their injurers (or with the injuring group of companies) receive less than full compensation. That is the 'price' they pay for some degree of certainty about the likelihood of obtaining compensation. Other problems with reorganisations are that, frequently, they fail to entice all creditor classes to vote in favour of proposed plans, meaning that debtor companies must deal separately with the 'holdouts', and that, in the personal injuries sphere, they undermine accident prevention policies.[56]

[53] [2006] 3 All ER 1222. See also J. Townsend, 'Schemes of Arrangement and Asbestos Litigation: *In re Cape plc*' (2007) 70 *Modern Law Review* 837.

[54] [2006] 3 All ER 1222, [37]. [55] [2006] 3 All ER 1222, [53]ff.

[56] 'The response that comes closest to maintaining safety incentives while at the same time retaining the tortfeasor's viability is a corporate reorganization proceeding in which all equity in the tortfeasor corporation is transferred to the tort victim creditors and the corporation continues to exist. The approach would maximize shareholder incentive to put pressure on management to see that such overwhelming tort liability is not incurred . . . But if tort creditors become shareholders of the reorganized corporation in lieu of receiving monetary payments, corporate management will probably be retained to run the reorganized corporation; thus, practical disincentives will not operate as strongly on corporate decision-makers': Lyle, 'Mass Tort Claims and the Corporate Tortfeasor', 1319.

While corporate reorganisations constitute an important topic, not the least because they provide compensation mechanisms for tort victims, they will not be the subject of further discussion here for two reasons: first, the basic problem with which this book deals is the *insolvent* entity, which cannot satisfactorily settle its debts. It cannot or will not reach a compromise which is satisfactory to creditors. Second, entry into a compromise with creditors avoids the formal insolvent entity problem. In the circumstances, we must go on to consider mechanisms available in insolvency and in the general law for *extending* the liability of the insolvent subsidiary to other entities in the group.

7.3.2 Pooling of Group Assets

Various common law jurisdictions have statutory provisions empowering courts to make orders augmenting assets available to satisfy insolvent subsidiary debts with assets from elsewhere in the corporate group. These powers are found either in specific legislation on the matter or arise as a by-product of powers to order reorganisations and/or windings-up. The provisions in question facilitate the making of 'pooling' orders and 'contribution orders'. John Farrar describes them as creating exceptions to the 'limited liability/*Salomon* principle'.[57] We will see, however, that the power to make such orders does not provide a complete answer to the insolvent entity problem. Indeed, courts have been cautious in using their powers to make orders – in part because such orders give rise to considerable problems of fairness as between creditors.

In the usual case, a pooling order is made where two or more subsidiaries within a corporate group are insolvent. Under typical provisions, the assets and liabilities of group companies are aggregated, and intra-group claims are eliminated by setting off corresponding debt claims and obligations against each other.[58] 'In essence, the rights of creditors against particular insolvent debtor companies are transformed into rights, together with other unsecured creditors of all of the other

[57] J. H. Farrar, 'Legal Issues Involving Corporate Groups' (1998) 16 *Company & Securities Law Journal* 184, 185 (referring to *Salomon* v. *A Salomon & Co Ltd* [1897] AC 22). See discussion of separate legal personality and limited liability in Chapter 3.

[58] See H. Anderson, 'Parent Company Liability for Asbestos Claims: Some International Insights' (2011) 31 *Legal Studies* 547, 553.

insolvent companies in the group, against the pool of assets of the entire group.'[59] Group creditors are paid from the common pool.

Pooling is used to deal with intermingled assets and accounts. Intermingling can be found even in large and seemingly respectable corporate groups. Managers 'often conduct the business of a corporate group as a single commercial entity by shifting assets and funds between [elements] of the group without proper accounting or arm's length commercial terms'.[60] When intermingling occurs, creditors might be 'misled into believing that they have claims against the entire group'.[61] Thus pooling enables courts to fulfil the expectations of creditors. By reducing the complexity of the administration of claims against group companies through elimination of the need for extensive tracing of intra-group transactions,[62] pooling also reduces the costs of administration and maximises returns to creditors from available funds.

New Zealand provides a well-known example of pooling provisions. The provisions (along with those on contribution orders, considered later) were enacted in response to situations where group controllers shuttled assets across group companies so as to avoid creditors.[63] They apply when two or more related companies[64] are in liquidation.[65] Where it is just and equitable to do so, corporate assets are brought together in a common pool to meet the claims of unsecured creditors. In considering whether to exercise the power, the New Zealand Court of Appeal noted in *Steel & Tube Holdings Ltd* v. *Lewis Holdings Ltd* that section 271 of the Companies Act 1993 (NZ) 'requires the Court to balance two policy considerations: First, respect for the separate corporate identity of the company in liquidation. Second, avoiding the mischief that can result from an overly strict application of separate corporate identity'.[66] The legislation sets out various factors by which to determine whether it

[59] J. Harris, 'Corporate Group Insolvencies: Charting the Past, Present and Future of "Pooling" Arrangements' (2007) 15 *Insolvency Law Journal* 78, 80.
[60] Harris, 'Corporate Group Insolvencies', 79.
[61] Harris, 'Corporate Group Insolvencies', 80.
[62] Anderson, 'Parent Company Liability for Asbestos Claims', 553.
[63] *Mountfort* v. *Tasman Pacific Airlines of NZ Ltd* [2006] 1 NZLR 104, 120; Farrar, 'Legal Issues Involving Corporate Groups', 195. Legislation in Ireland is similar and will not be discussed separately. See Companies Act 1990 (Ire), s. 141.
[64] Defined in Companies Act 1993 (NZ), s. 2(3) and including cases where the businesses of the companies have been carried on in such a way that the separate business of each company, or a substantial part of it, is not readily identifiable.
[65] Companies Act 1993 (NZ), s. 271(1)(b).
[66] [2016] NZCA 366, [27].

would be just and equitable to make an order.[67] These are: the extent to which any of the companies took part in the management of any of the other companies; the conduct of the companies towards the creditors of any of the other companies; the extent to which the liquidation of any of the companies is attributable to the actions of any of the other companies; the extent to which the businesses of the companies have been combined; and such other matters as the court thinks fit. However, the 'fact that creditors of a company in liquidation relied on the fact that another company is, or was, related to it is not a ground for making an order'.[68]

Pooling orders have been made in cases such as: *Steel & Tube Holdings Ltd* v. *Lewis Holdings Ltd*,[69] where the parent company STH was extensively involved in the management of its subsidiary Stube and extracted value from it in various ways before abandoning it; *Mountfort* v. *Tasman Pacific Airlines of NZ Ltd*,[70] where an airline parent company obtained loan funds from its subsidiary so that it could finance its own operations, the parent being perennially loss-making and dragging the subsidiary into insolvency as well; and in *Re Pacific Syndicates (NZ) Ltd*,[71] where two investment companies had intermingled funds in one account that could not subsequently be traced to specific investments and where there were multiple intra-group transactions to deal with.[72] Despite the breadth of the New Zealand legislation, that country's courts have made relatively few pooling orders.[73]

In Australia, pooling has been available under various forms of external administration,[74] such as schemes of arrangement.[75] The problem had been in successfully obtaining court approvals.[76] Dedicated provisions in the Corporations Act 2001 (Cth)[77] now better facilitate the

[67] Companies Act 1993 (NZ), s. 272. [68] Companies Act 1993 (NZ), s. 272(3).

[69] [2016] NZCA 366. [70] [2006] 1 NZLR 104. [71] (1989) 4 NZCLC 64,757.

[72] A. Nolan, 'The Position of Unsecured Creditors of Corporate Groups: Towards a Group Responsibility Solution which Gives Fairness and Equity a Role' (1993) 11 *Company & Securities Law Journal* 461, 490.

[73] Companies and Securities Advisory Committee, 'Corporate Groups Final Report' (2000), [6.64].

[74] *Dean-Willcocks* v. *Soluble Solution Hydroponics Pty Ltd* (1997) 24 ACSR 79, 85; *Mentha* v. *GE Capital Ltd* (1997) 27 ACSR 696; *Re Charter Travel Co Ltd* (1997) 15 ACLC 1685; *Re Switch Telecommunications Pty Ltd (in liq); Ex parte Sherman* [2000] NSWSC 794.

[75] Corporations Act 2001 (Cth), Part 5.1.

[76] Courts have been concerned about the position of dissenting creditors and about distributions which are not pari passu. See Harris, 'Corporate Group Insolvencies', 91.

[77] Part 5.6, Division 8. See J. Dickfos, C. Anderson, and D. Morrison, 'The Insolvency Implications for Corporate Groups in Australia – Recent Events and Initiatives' (2007) 16 *International Insolvency Review* 103.

pooling of corporate group assets. This can be done through either voluntary pooling or court-ordered pooling, the latter being of greater relevance to the problems dealt with in this book. Court-ordered pooling is available upon application of the liquidator[78] where a number of conditions are fulfilled. First, the court must be satisfied that each company in the group is being wound up and that there is a relevant connection between them,[79] for example that each company is a related body corporate of each other company in the group or that the companies jointly own or operate particular property that was used in connection with an undertaking carried on jointly. On being satisfied of these matters, if just and equitable to do so, the court may make an order determining that the group is a pooled group. Second, in determining whether it is just and equitable to pool assets, the court must have regard to various matters,[80] including: the extent to which a company in the group was involved in the management or operations of any of the other companies in the group; the conduct of a company in the group towards the creditors of any of the other companies in the group; the extent to which the circumstances that gave rise to winding-up are attributable to the acts or omissions of any other companies in the group; the extent to which the activities and business of the companies in the group have been intermingled; and any other relevant matters. The court must refrain from making a pooling order if satisfied[81] that the order would materially disadvantage an eligible unsecured creditor of a group company, and the eligible unsecured creditor has not consented to the making of the order; or all of the following conditions are satisfied: a company in the group is being wound up under a members' voluntary winding-up; the court is satisfied that the order would materially disadvantage a member of that company; the member is not a company in the group; and the member has not consented to the making of the order. When a pooling order is made, intra-group debts are extinguished and each group company is taken to be jointly and severally liable for each claim against group companies.[82] Secured creditors are excluded from claiming against the pool, unless they forfeit their securities.[83]

[78] Corporations Act 2001 (Cth), s. 579E(11).
[79] Corporations Act 2001 (Cth), s. 579E(1).
[80] Corporations Act 2001 (Cth), s. 579E(12).
[81] Corporations Act 2001 (Cth), s. 579E(10).
[82] Corporations Act 2001 (Cth), s. 579E(2). This subsection does not apply to a debt payable by or a claim against a company in the group unless the debt or claim is admissible to proof against the company: s. 579E(4). This creates problems in making provision for unascertained future creditors.
[83] Corporations Act 2001 (Cth), s. 571(6)(b).

The Australian provisions do not assist creditors of insolvent companies where one or more group companies remains solvent;[84] thus, they do not assist creditors of an insolvent subsidiary of a solvent parent company. Helen Anderson comments that the legislation adopts 'the most conservative approach ... [B]y not allowing solvent companies to form part of a reorganisation through pooling, it deprives the tort creditors of the undoubted opportunity of increasing their returns'.[85]

Pooling provisions operate against the background of the principles of separate legal personality and shareholder limited liability examined in Chapter 3, the premise being that creditors share in risks of corporate failure.[86] A major concern of pooling is that it 'overturns the principle of the separate legal identity of each group [company], which is often used to structure an enterprise group to respond to various business considerations ... If the courts routinely agreed to [pooling orders], many of the benefits to be derived from' the ability to incorporate subsidiaries would be lost.[87] The determination whether to order pooling needs to be made with this concern in mind and with the aim of avoiding commercial uncertainty where possible.[88]

While creditors of weaker group companies benefit from gaining access to the assets of stronger group companies, creditors of the latter lose out.[89] Some creditors might object to a proposed pooling order, therefore, because the assets of their own debtor company would yield a better return to them than they would achieve from the pooled fund.[90] The court's power to order pooling of group company assets can be exercised, therefore, only after consideration of the arguments against

[84] This is to protect the solvent company's shareholders: Explanatory Memorandum to Part 4 Facilitating Pooling in External Administration, Corporations Amendment (Insolvency) Bill 2007 (Cth), 53: see Anderson, 'Parent Company Liability for Asbestos Claims', 555.

[85] See Anderson, 'Parent Company Liability for Asbestos Claims', 565. See also H. Anderson, 'Veil Piercing and Corporate Groups – An Australian Perspective' [2010] *New Zealand Law Review* 1, 25.

[86] *Mountfort* v. *Tasman Pacific Airlines of NZ Ltd* [2006] 1 NZLR 104, 113.

[87] UNCITRAL, 'Legislative Guide on Insolvency Law', p. 60.

[88] *Mountfort* v. *Tasman Pacific Airlines of NZ Ltd* [2006] 1 NZLR 104, 122.

[89] See Anderson, 'Parent Company Liability for Asbestos Claims', 565.

[90] Nonetheless, in cases of extensive intermingling of assets and intra-group claims, creditors might be unaware whether they will gain or lose from the pooling of the group's assets: Mevorach, *Insolvency within Multinational Enterprise Groups*, p. 218.

this move, including any claims of unfairness to individual creditors.[91] 'The courts have . . . stated that the cost savings to be gained through the pooling must be balanced against any prejudice accruing to particular creditors, with the former not necessarily more important than the latter as the basis of the [insolvency] rule is to attempt to provide a result that is in the best interests of the creditors as a whole, not merely the majority of creditors.'[92]

In the United Kingdom, there is no express legislation permitting pooling of group assets. However, it has been permitted in cases of extreme intermingling of assets amongst group companies where it is not merely inconvenient, but extremely difficult and costly to separate them.[93] In rare cases, the scheme of arrangement provisions[94] can be used to eliminate intra-group claims and to pool individual company assets. However, English courts are wary of exercising powers available to them in favour of schemes because of the potential for unfairness to specific creditors in the way already considered.[95] Therefore, applications to use a scheme of arrangement to implement the pooling of assets bear the risk that, where there are dissenting creditors, the court will refuse to approve them.[96] Schemes might prove impractical to achieve also if there are multiple classes of creditor, each of which needs to meet separately and agree to the proposals.[97] Given the general problems associated with the use of schemes, such as the need for court approval and the associated cost, they are used rarely to pool group assets.[98]

Considering the challenges that arise with the use of pooling orders, tort law actions might provide a superior solution to the problem of the insolvent subsidiary because of the more direct link those actions make

[91] No solution to the problems created by insolvent subsidiaries is going to be perfect: Nolan, 'The Position of Unsecured Creditors', 501.

[92] Harris, 'Corporate Group Insolvencies', 80.

[93] See, e.g., *Re Bank of Credit and Commerce International SA* (No 3) [1993] BCLC 1490; *Taylor* v. *Morris* [1992] BCC 440. Mere inconvenience in separating the assets and liabilities of insolvent companies is not a sufficient reason to order pooling: *Re Kriegel, Waring and Co; Ex parte Trotman* (1893) 68 LT 588.

[94] Companies Act 2006 (UK), ss. 899 and 900.

[95] Goode, *Principles of Insolvency Law*, pp. 23–4.

[96] See Harris, 'Corporate Group Insolvencies', 84.

[97] Indeed, it was for this reason that the Court of Appeal in *Re Bank of Credit and Commerce International SA (in liq)(No 3)* [1993] BCLC 1490 approved a different approach; it affirmed the exercise of the power under Insolvency Act 1986, s. 167(1) and sched. 4 to sanction a compromise between the parties resulting in a pooling of assets.

[98] Harris, 'Corporate Group Insolvencies', 83–4.

between wrongdoing and liability. Those actions are to be considered in Chapters 11 and 12.

7.3.3 Contribution Orders

We continue consideration of statutory regimes under which courts can order that the assets available to satisfy the debts of insolvent subsidiaries be augmented by assets from elsewhere in the corporate group. Legislation in a number of jurisdictions facilitates the making of 'contribution orders', which involve less radical treatment of corporate group affairs than occurs by pooling assets. The term 'contribution order' refers to the requirement that a solvent group company contribute to the assets of an insolvent group company for the benefit of the latter's creditors. Orders are available 'particularly where the solvent group [company] has acted improperly towards the insolvent group [company]'.[99] 'Such an order might ... be possible, for example, in cases where the controlled group [company] had incurred significant liability for personal injury.'[100]

Once again, New Zealand provides a well-known example of statutory provisions, which provide courts with wide powers to order companies to contribute to the payment of related company debts.[101] Under Companies Act 1993 (NZ), section 271(1)(a), an applicant seeking a contribution order must prove that the company from which contribution is sought is related to the company in liquidation, and then satisfy the court that it is just and equitable to make an order. In determining whether to do so, the court must take into account several matters, that is to say: the extent to which the related company took part in the management of the company being wound up;[102] the extent to which the winding-up is attributable to the actions of the related company; and its conduct towards creditors.[103] The court is able, furthermore, to consider such other matters as it thinks fit.[104] The mere fact that creditors of a company in liquidation relied on the fact that another company was or is related to the

99 UNCITRAL, 'Legislative Guide on Insolvency Law', p. 58.

100 UNCITRAL, 'Legislative Guide on Insolvency Law', p. 59.

101 Legislation in Ireland is similar and will not be discussed separately. See Companies Act 1990 (Ire), s 140.

102 This was a significant factor in *Steel & Tube Holdings Ltd* v. *Lewis Holdings Ltd* [2016] NZCA 366.

103 Companies Act 1993 (NZ), s. 272(1).

104 Companies Act 1993 (NZ), s. 272(1).

company in liquidation is not a sufficient ground for a contribution order.[105]

The contribution provisions are wide in scope and give courts much discretion in determining group liability to contribute to the debts of insolvent subsidiary companies.[106] But some limits have been imposed. In *Lewis* v. *Poultry Processors*,[107] Tipping J held that a contribution order would be made only with respect to 'the balance of assets in the related company's hands after it has satisfied its bona fide indebtedness'. Moreover, if the size of the contribution sought from a related company threatens that company's solvency, the court must consider the overall equities affecting creditors of that company. These creditors might argue that they had relied on the separate assets of the insolvent company when trading with it, and should not be denied a full payout because of that company's relationship with another company.[108] However, 'it might be possible to order a partial contribution that is limited to certain assets, such as the remaining balance after meeting bona fide obligations' of the contributing company.[109] The contribution payment will go to the liquidator to meet the company's overall debts, rather than to petitioning creditors.[110]

In the United Kingdom, legislation permits the making of contribution orders within corporate groups in cases involving funding shortfalls in occupational pensions. Under Pensions Act 2004, section 38,[111] the Pensions Regulator has power to issue a contribution notice stating that

105 Companies Act 1993 (NZ), s. 272(3).

106 Mevorach, *Insolvency within Multinational Enterprise Groups*, p. 307.

107 (1988) 4 NZCLC 64,508. 108 Farrar, 'Legal Issues Involving Corporate Groups', 197.

109 UNCITRAL, 'Legislative Guide on Insolvency Law', p. 59.

110 Companies and Securities Advisory Committee, 'Corporate Groups Final Report', [6.3].

111 For the United States, see Employee Retirement Income Security Act of 1974 (Pub. L. 93–406, 88 Stat. 829). This statute imposes liability on an employer if it terminates its participation in a retirement plan. Under § 1301(b)(1), 'all employees of . . . businesses (whether or not incorporated) which are under common control shall be treated as employed by a single employer and all such . . . businesses as a single employer.' 'Thus, parent [companie]s are directly and statutorily liable for the ERISA debts of their subsidiaries': M. Dearborn, 'Enterprise Liability: Reviewing and Revitalizing Liability for Corporate Groups' (2009) 97 *California Law Review* 195, 240–1. See also B. B. Erens, S. J. Friedman, and K. M. Mayerfield, 'Bankrupt Subsidiaries: The Challenges to the Parent of Legal Separation' (2008) 25 *Emory Bankruptcy Developments Journal* 65, 110–11. For Australia, see Corporations Act 2001 (Cth), s. 556(1)(e)(priority for certain employee entitlements); H. Anderson, 'Thinking outside the Square – Some Alternative Approaches to the Protection of Employee Entitlements' (2014) 32 *Company & Securities Law Journal* 23.

the addressee (the 'target')[112] is under a liability to pay the sum specified to the trustees of the relevant pension scheme. Such a notice can be issued only when the target was a party to an act or a deliberate failure to act, the main purpose of which was either to prevent the recovery of a debt due from the employer in relation to the scheme or to prevent, otherwise than in good faith, such a debt becoming due. The target must have been, within the relevant time period, the employer in relation to the scheme, or a person connected with or an associate of the employer, and it must be reasonable to impose the liability. In deciding whether it is reasonable to do so, the Regulator must take into account various matters, such as the degree of involvement of the target, the relationship which the target had with the employer (including, where the employer is a company, whether the target had control of the employer), any connection or involvement which the target had with the scheme, all the reasons for the act or failure to act, and the target's financial circumstances. The sum specified in a contribution notice may be either the whole or a specified part of the pension shortfall.[113] Where the contribution notice so specifies, the target is to be treated as jointly and severally liable for the debt with any persons specified in the notice who are persons to whom corresponding contribution notices are issued.[114]

Under section 43 of the 2004 Act, further power is given to the Pensions Regulator to issue a financial support direction when the employer is a service company or is insufficiently resourced. An employer is a 'service company' where it is a member of a group of companies, and its turnover is principally derived from amounts charged for the provision of the services of its employees to other members of that group.[115] A financial support direction is a direction requiring the target to secure that (an unspecified amount of) financial support for the scheme is put in place. The Regulator may issue such a direction only when the target is the employer, an associate of an individual who is the employer, or a person other than an individual who is connected with or an associate of the employer, and it is reasonable to impose the direction. In deciding whether it is reasonable to impose the direction upon a target, the Regulator must have regard to various matters, including the relationship which the target had with the employer, the value of any benefits received from the employer, any connection or involvement which the target had with the scheme, and

[112] This term is not used in the Act, but was convenient in the explanation of the provisions in *In re Nortel GmbH (in admin)* [2014] AC 209.

[113] Pensions Act 2004, s. 39.

[114] Pensions Act 2004, s. 40.

[115] Pensions Act 2004, s. 44.

the target's financial circumstances.[116] 'Financial support' for a scheme might include an arrangement whereby, at any time when the employer is a member of a group of companies, all the members of the group are jointly and severally liable for the whole or part of the employer's pension liabilities, or whereby, at any time when the employer is a member of a group of companies, a company, which meets prescribed requirements and is the holding company of the group, is liable for the whole or a part of the employer's pension liabilities.

Where the target fails to comply with a financial support direction, and when reasonable to do so, section 47 of the 2004 Act permits the Pensions Regulator to issue a notice that the target is under a liability to pay to the trustees of the scheme the sum specified in the notice. In determining whether it is reasonable to do so, the Regulator must have regard to matters including whether the target took reasonable steps to secure compliance with the financial support direction, the target's relationship with the employer, the value of any benefits received from the employer, the target's relationship with the parties to any arrangements put in place in accordance with the direction, any involvement the target had with the scheme, and the target's financial circumstances.[117] Under section 49, the Regulator may, on behalf of the trustees of the scheme, exercise powers to recover the debt.

The provisions that have been considered in this section are concerned, most obviously, with orders that courts can make to ensure satisfaction of ordinary commercial obligations, as well as pension liabilities. Each of the provisions is limited in nature, operating in narrowly defined circumstances. As such, it is clear that they do not pose any major threat to ordinary principles of separate legal personality and limited liability. A reason for the limited operation of the provisions is the potential for defeated expectations and inequity in the treatment of the creditors of different companies in affected corporate groups.[118] A notable feature is that the provisions do not (in the way that general insolvency law does not) create any special priority for the repayment of

[116] Given that a direction might undermine the financial stability of group companies, Pensions Act 2004, s. 46(2) permits curtailment of support where it would not be reasonable to impose the requirements of a financial support direction on the applicant: *In re Nortel GmbH (in admin)* [2014] AC 209, [24].

[117] See also I. Fletcher and G. Squires, 'Pensions Again – "Just When You Thought it Was Safe to Go into Administration"' (2014) 27 *Insolvency International* 59, 62 (listing further factors potentially relevant to s 47).

[118] UNCITRAL, 'Legislative Guide on Insolvency Law', 55.

personal injury claims ahead of other unsecured debts. Indeed, they make no specific provision in relation to personal injury claims. This is a matter that needs to be addressed specifically in legislation (as to which, see Chapter 9).

7.3.4 Substantive Consolidation

In the United States, courts exercising jurisdiction under the Bankruptcy Code, section 105, can make orders for substantive consolidation[119] during the course of either Chapter 7 liquidation or Chapter 11 reorganisation. Substantive consolidation involves 'pooling the assets of, and claims against, the two or more entities [in a group], elimination of inter company claims and satisfying liabilities from the resulting common fund'.[120] Pooled assets are distributed on a pari passu basis,[121] all creditors of the pooled companies sharing equally. The rights of secured creditors are unaffected.[122] Large corporate reorganisations often make use of this procedure,[123] which has the potential (like the pooling provisions considered previously) to work in favour of some or all unsecured creditors by reducing the complexity and the cost of untangling the affairs of corporate groups.[124]

Substantive consolidation presents a potentially useful, flexible remedy in cases of corporate wrongdoing. While doctrines such as veil-piercing typically involve '"upstream" claims by corporate creditors against shareholders', the direction of the claim does not matter in substantive consolidation: 'through a request for substantive consolidation, creditors of a

[119] US Code, Title 11, Bankruptcy, § 105(a) provides that a 'court may issue any order, process, or judgment that is necessary or appropriate to carry out the provisions of this title.' However, the status of this provision as the basis for ordering substantive consolidation has been disputed: see *In re Cyberco Holdings Inc* 431 BR 404 (Bankr. WD Mich 2010), Hughes J holding that orders should be made under 11 USC §§ 502(j) and § 542(a)) (aff'd 734 F 3d 432 (6th Cir. 2013) without adopting this reasoning). See also § 1123(a)(5)(c) (Chapter 11 plan can be implemented through consolidation of debtor and other persons).

[120] *Union Savings Bank* v. *Augie/Restivo Baking Co Ltd* (*In re Augie/Restivo Baking Co Ltd)* 860 F 2d 515, 518 (2nd Cir. 1988).

[121] A. Muscat, *The Liability of the Holding Company for the Debts of its Insolvent Subsidiaries* (1996), p. 458.

[122] *In re Augie/Restivo Baking Co Ltd* 860 F 2d 515, 517 (2nd Cir. 1988); *Federal Deposit Insurance Corporation* v. *Hogan* (*Re Gulfco Investment Corp*) 593 F 2d 921, 926–7 (10th Cir. 1979).

[123] W. H. Widen 'Corporate Form and Substantive Consolidation' (2007) 75 *George Washington Law Review* 237, 238.

[124] Widen, 'Corporate Form and Substantive Consolidation', 246–7.

parent may seek to direct a claim against assets of a subsidiary (a downstream move), creditors of a subsidiary may seek a direct claim against assets of a parent (an upstream move), or creditors of one subsidiary may seek a direct claim against assets of another sister subsidiary (a lateral move).'[125] It is possible for substantive consolidation to take place between both solvent and insolvent companies.[126] Furthermore, substantive consolidation can be partial in nature; it need not encompass all companies within the group or all individual company debts.[127]

At present, no generally agreed criteria exist by which US courts determine whether to order substantive consolidation of group companies.[128] However, the substance of successful claims for substantive consolidation appears to inhere in the following: first, there should be a failure by companies in the corporate group to maintain their separate entity status, in that their operations were substantially combined.[129] This is demonstrated by taking account of such matters as: common corporate headquarters, common directorships, overlap of business functions, commingling of assets or transfers without observing formalities, and extensive intra-group loans and guarantees.[130] When there is a failure to maintain corporate separateness, creditors might be able to demonstrate 'contractual expectations ... that they were dealing with debtors as one indistinguishable entity', and reasonable reliance on this fact.[131]

125 Widen, 'Corporate Form and Substantive Consolidation', 270–1.

126 See *In re Crabtree* 39 Bankr. 718 (Bankr. ED Tenn 1984); *In re 1438 Meridian Place, NW, Inc* 15 Bankr. 89 (Bankr. DDC 1981); S. Bowmer, 'To Pierce or Not to Pierce the Corporate Veil – Why Substantive Consolidation Is Not an Issue under English Law' (2000) 15 *Journal of International Banking Law* 193, 193.

127 P. I. Blumberg et al., *Blumberg on Corporate Groups* (2005) vol. 2, § 88.04.

128 'Substantive consolidation lacks the solid foundation one usually expects of doctrines so firmly embedded in day-to-day practice. The US Supreme Court has never formally embraced the concept': D. Baird, 'Substantive Consolidation Today' (2005) 47 *Boston College Law Review* 5, 15. See also Widen, 'Corporate Form and Substantive Consolidation', 246–7.

129 *Drabkin* v. *Midland-Ross Corp (In re Auto-Train Corp)* 810 F 2d 270, 276 (DC Cir. 1987).

130 See *In re Augie/Restivo Baking Co Ltd* 860 F 2d 515, 518 (2nd Cir. 1988); Widen, 'Corporate Form and Substantive Consolidation', 268–9; Muscat, *The Liability of the Holding Company*, p. 460.

131 *In re Owens Corning* 419 F 3d 195, 212 (3rd Cir. 2005); W. C. Blasses, 'Redefining into Reality: Substantive Consolidation of Parent Corporations and Subsidiaries' (2008) 24 *Emory Bankruptcy Developments Journal* 469, 493. The clearest case in favour of substantial consolidation is said to be judgment-proofing: S. Schwarcz, 'The Inherent Irrationality of Judgment Proofing' (1999) 52 *Stanford Law Review* 1, 37, citing *In re Murray Industries Inc* 119 BR 820, 828 (Bankr. MD Fla. 1990).

Second, consolidation should yield a substantial benefit to the greater preponderance of creditors.[132] This is most likely to arise because of the 'practical impossibility of reconstructing the financial records of the debtors to determine intercorporate claims, liabilities and ownership of assets' or,[133] when reconstruction is possible, on the basis of the significant cost savings to be made by avoiding this complicated exercise. There are different expressions of the strictness of this requirement. In *Chemical Bank New York Trust Co* v. *Kheel*, the US Court of Appeals for the Second Circuit indicated that it would be prepared to make an order when the potential costs of unscrambling transactions would 'threaten the realization of any net assets for all the creditors',[134] while in *In re Auto-Train Corp Inc*, the District of Columbia Circuit merely sought 'benefits offsetting the harm' that would be inflicted.[135]

Third, the bankruptcy court will examine factors weighing against substantive consolidation. A typical argument is that particular creditors, who would suffer reduced awards should a consolidation order be made, 'relied on the separate credit of one of the entities' in the group.[136] In such circumstances, the court takes account of the fact that creditors 'structure their loans according to expectations regarding that borrower' and calculate loan interest rates and other terms accordingly.[137] When reliance of this nature is pleaded, a court will order substantive consolidation only if 'the demonstrated benefits "heavily" outweigh the harm'.[138] Where a bankruptcy court is prepared to invoke substantive consolidation principles, typically it will not order

[132] *In re Auto-Train Corp* 810 F 2d 270, 276 (DC Cir. 1987). Mere ease of administration is insufficient: see *In re Owens Corning* 419 F 3d 195, 211 (3rd Cir. 2005).

[133] *Flora Mir Candy Corp* v. *RS Dickson & Co* 432 F 2d 1060, 1063 (2nd Cir. 1970); *Chemical Bank New York Trust Co* v. *Kheel* 369 F 2d 845, 847 (2nd Cir. 1966).

[134] 369 F 2d 845, 847 (2nd Cir. 1966). See also *In re Augie/Restivo Baking Co Ltd* 860 F.2d 515, 518–19 (2nd Cir. 1988).

[135] *In re Auto-Train Corp* 810 F 2d 270, 276 (DC Cir. 1987).

[136] *In re Auto-Train Corp* 810 F 2d 270, 276 (DC Cir. 1987). The problem with substantive consolidation is said to be that because every entity within a group 'is likely to have a different debt-to-asset ratio, consolidation almost invariably redistributes wealth among the creditors of the various entities': ibid., 276. However, against this, it has been noted that 'in case[s] where assets and debts are intermingled and inter-corporate liabilities are untraceable, it would be impossible to claim to what extent there is redistribution and even if there is any at all (without first going through the costs of untangling the web of connections)': Mevorach, *Insolvency within Multinational Enterprise Groups*, p. 255.

[137] *In re Augie/Restivo Baking Co Ltd* 860 F 2d 515, 519 (2nd Cir. 1988).

[138] *In re Auto-Train Corp* 810 F 2d 270, 276 (DC Cir. 1987); *James Talcott, Inc* v. *Wharton (In re Continental Vending Machines Corp)* 517 F 2d 997, 1001 (2nd Cir. 1975).

that all relevant transfers of titles actually be executed and intra-group transactions annulled. Rather, the court will conduct a paper exercise and make orders in favour of creditors as though group companies were being consolidated and such preliminary steps undertaken.[139] But this practice has drawn fire from some courts.[140]

Although substantive consolidation has the potential to provide a welcome remedy in cases of wrongdoing within corporate groups, it has been criticised on the basis of its 'ad-hoc balancing', and the uncertainty to which this gives rise.[141] The remedy is seen as 'the most dramatic and far-reaching exception to corporate separateness'.[142] As such, in *In re Owens Corning*, the US Court of Appeals for the Third Circuit indicated that 'the cross-creep of liability' should be restricted where possible and that 'this "rough justice" remedy should be . . . one of last resort'.[143]

7.3.5 *Equitable Subordination*

In the United States, courts exercising jurisdiction under Bankruptcy Code section 510(c) can order equitable subordination of debts arising in corporate groups[144] during the course of either Chapter 7 liquidation, or Chapter 11 reorganisation. This entails the postponement of debts owed

[139] Baird, 'Substantive Consolidation Today', 8–9.

[140] *In re Owens Corning* 419 F 3d 195, 211–12 (3rd Cir. 2005).

[141] T. E. Graulich, 'Substantive Consolidation – A Post-modern Trend' (2006) 14 *American Bankruptcy Institute Law Review* 527, 530; M. E. Kors, 'Altered Egos: Deciphering Substantive Consolidation' (1997) 59 *University of Pittsburgh Law Review* 381, 384.

[142] Graulich, 'Substantive Consolidation', 538. [143] 419 F 3d 195, 211 (3rd Cir. 2005).

[144] US Code, Title 11, Bankruptcy, § 510(c). There is no formal equivalent in Commonwealth jurisdictions: J. H. Farrar, 'Piercing the Corporate Veil in Favour of Creditors and Pooling of Groups – A Comparative Study' (2013) 25 *Bond Law Review* 31, 32. In the United Kingdom, the Cork Report advocated subordination in a limited form, but this recommendation was not implemented: K. Cork, 'Report of the Review Committee on Insolvency Law and Practice' (Cmnd 8558, June 1982), paras 1958–65. Note, however, that there is a degree of subordination of parent company debt in the United Kingdom. Parent companies as shadow directors might be liable for fraudulent or wrongful trading under Insolvency Act ss. 213 and 214, respectively (see Chapter 6). Pursuant to s. 215(4) of the 1986 Act, '[w]here the court makes a declaration under either section in relation to a person who is a creditor of the company, it may direct that the whole or any part of any debt owed by the company to that person and any interest thereon shall rank in priority after all other debts owed by the company and after any interest on those debts.' Also, it is open to companies within a group to agree to defer intra-group indebtedness to the claims of external creditors: *Banque Financière de la Cité* v. *Parc (Battersea) Ltd* [1998] 1 All ER 737. In Australia, there is provision for a creditor voluntarily to subordinate its claim, and this would include parent company claims on subsidiaries: Corporations Act 2001 (Cth) s. 563C (1).

by group debtor companies to group creditors,[145] in favour of claims against the former by external creditors. Orders are made when the group creditor, such as a parent company or other controlling party or affiliate,[146] has acted inequitably. The aim is to deter such parties from the opportunistic use of their positions in order to prioritise their own claims against group debtors ahead of those of external creditors. Equitable subordination can take place even though debts are secured;[147] indeed, there is express power to transfer liens from group creditors to the bankruptcy estate.[148] The power is exercised, ordinarily, in bankruptcies concerning closely held companies and their insiders.[149]

The US Court of Appeals for the Fifth Circuit in *Benjamin* v. *Diamond (in re Mobile Steel Co)* established the general framework for considering claims of equitable subordination.[150] The first requirement is that the group creditor 'must have engaged in some type of inequitable conduct'. Although undercapitalisation frequently will be the foundation of a claim by external creditors, in itself this is insufficient to ground an order because it might signal no more than a company's inability to access capital, business failure, or both.[151] Rather, undercapitalisation must be accompanied by the group creditor company's knowledge in conjunction with conduct such as: causing external creditors to extend new credit to the subsidiary; causing external creditors to abstain from collecting past debts; obtaining a lien on the debtor's assets while failing to stop the subsidiary from incurring further external debts;[152] or imposing excessive management fees on the debtor company and dividend policies designed to strip it of funds.[153] The misconduct in question need not relate to the specific transaction undertaken with the external creditor seeking subordination;[154] it might 'arise out of any unfair act . . . which affects the bankruptcy results to other creditors and so makes it inequitable' to assert

[145] Subordination does not affect the validity of claims: *80 Nassau Associates* v. *Crossland Federal Savings Bank* (*In re 80 Nassau Associates*) 169 BR 832, 837 (Bankr. SDNY 1994). In practical terms, however, it might result in the insider receiving nothing once the claims of other creditors are met.

[146] See US Code, Title 11, Bankruptcy, § 101(31); UNCITRAL, 'Legislative Guide on Insolvency Law', p. 52.

[147] *In re Lifschultz Fast Freight* 132 F 3d 339, 342 (7th Cir. 1997).

[148] US Code, Title 11, Bankruptcy, § 510(c)(2).

[149] *In re Lifschultz Fast Freight* 132 F 3d 339, 343 (7th Cir. 1997).

[150] 563 F 2d 692, 700 (5th Cir. 1977).

[151] *In re Lifschultz Fast Freight* 132 F 3d 339, 345 (7th Cir. 1997).

[152] Erens, Friedman, and Mayerfield, 'Bankrupt Subsidiaries', 81–2.

[153] UNCITRAL, 'Legislative Guide on Insolvency Law', p. 53.

[154] *Benjamin* v. *Diamond* (*In re Mobile Steel Co*) 563 F 2d 692, 700 (5th Cir. 1977).

either a superior or equal ranking claim.[155] Thus, in one case the unfairness allegedly arose out of the company controllers, as directors of the debtor company, awarding themselves large pay rises at a time when bankruptcy was beckoning.[156]

The second requirement set out by the Fifth Circuit in *Mobile Steel* is that the misconduct must have resulted in injury to the external creditors of the bankrupt or conferred an unfair advantage on the group creditor. The third requirement is that the order sought in favour of subordination must not be inconsistent with the provisions of the Bankruptcy Code. Once these matters have been shown, it falls upon the group creditor to prove that the loan was extended in good faith and that its recoupment would be inherently fair.[157] Orders do not permit direct claims against insiders (in the way that veil-piercing does), but 'enhance the relative recoveries of other creditors'.[158] They are intended to be remedial in nature and to 'minimize the effect that the misconduct has on other creditors'.[159] However, if external creditors should have known of the group creditor's claims on the debtor, the bankruptcy court is unlikely to make an order.[160]

Equitable subordination might hinder genuine efforts by a parent company or other controllers or affiliates to save an ailing group company by the provision of new debt capital. When the subsidiary is facing severe financial difficulties, these funds might be all that are available, as external lenders decline to risk extending funds to a failing entity that might have few unencumbered assets.[161] Nonetheless, there are fundamental concerns about the provision of debt capital by shareholders. As explained in *In re Lifschultz Fast Freight*,[162] because shareholders come last in a liquidation of company assets, 'an owner might disguise her

[155] *In re Kansas City Journal-Post Co (Bostian* v. *Shapiro)* 144 F 2d 791, 803–4 (8th Cir. 1944).

[156] *In re Lifschultz Fast Freight* 132 F 3d 339, 354 (7th Cir. 1997); *Spach* v. *Bryant* 309 F 2d 886 (5th Cir. 1962).

[157] *In re Mobile Steel Co* 563 F 2d 692, 701 (5th Cir. 1977).

[158] Graulich, 'Substantive Consolidation', 535.

[159] *In re Kreisler* 546 F 3d 863, 865–6 (7th Cir. 2008); *In re Mobile Steel Co* 563 F 2d 692, 701 (5th Cir. 1977).

[160] *In re N & D Properties, Inc (Estes* v. *N & D Properties, Inc)* 799 F 2d 726, 732–3 (11th Cir. 1986).

[161] See discussion in *In re Lifschultz Fast Freight* 132 F 3d 339, 342 (7th Cir. 1997). Shareholder loans have long been an essential source of finance for small- and medium-sized companies: D. A. Skeel and G. Krause-Vilmar, 'Recharacterization and the Nonhindrance of Creditors' (2006) 7 *European Business Organization Law Review* 259, 280.

[162] 132 F 3d 339, 343 (7th Cir. 1997).

equity claim as debt'. Extending loan capital, rather than further equity capital, might reveal an intention to improve the controlling shareholders' chances of recovering some of their investment should the company succumb to bankruptcy.[163] This justifies the subordination of these claims and the clawing back of amounts repaid pursuant to the loans. 'The doctrine of equitable subordination empowers a bankruptcy court to foil this queue-jumping, by re-ordering the formal rankings of the claimants to restore a just hierarchy.'[164] But when there is no deception in the conduct of the group creditor, there will be little basis for an order, and courts have agreed that '[w]rongful or unpredictable subordination spawns legal uncertainty', which could make investors hesitant to extend funds.[165] As a result of these concerns, equitable subordination is 'an unusual remedy, and is applied by the courts in only very limited circumstances'.[166]

7.3.6 *Re-characterisation of Debt as Equity*

Under the same statutory provision that permits US bankruptcy courts to order equitable subordination,[167] they can make related, yet distinct, orders for the re-characterisation of debt as equity.[168] An order will be appropriate when the court's inquiry reveals that the true character of an ostensible loan was an equity contribution.[169] Then the loan will be treated as equity for distribution purposes.[170] The effect on the parent company in a group is the same as the effect of an order for equitable subordination – the parent company's claims will be paid only after all of the subsidiary's creditors have been paid in full.[171]

[163] A. Cahn, 'Equitable Subordination of Shareholder Loans?' (2006) 7 *European Business Organization Law Review* 287, 288.

[164] *In re Lifschultz Fast Freight* 132 F 3d 339, 343 (7th Cir. 1997).

[165] *In re Lifschultz Fast Freight* 132 F 3d 339, 347 (7th Cir. 1997).

[166] C. J. Tabb and R. Brubaker, *Bankruptcy Law Principles, Policies, and Practice* (3rd edn. 2010), p. 279.

[167] US Code, Title 11, Bankruptcy, § 510(a).

[168] Given that the question in a re-characterisation case is whether a debt exists at all, it is logical that such a case should be determined before an equitable subordination claim, which will call for the subordination of otherwise valid debts: *Cohen* v. *KB Mezzanine Fund II, LP (In re SubMicron Systems Corp)* 432 F 3d 448, 455 (3rd Cir. 2006).

[169] *Bayer Corp* v. *MascoTech Inc (In re Autostyle Plastics Inc)* 269 F 3d 726, 747–8 (6th Cir. 2011).

[170] Graulich, 'Substantive Consolidation', 536.

[171] *In re Autostyle Plastics Inc* 269 F 3d 726, 748 (6th Cir. 2011); Erens, Friedman, and Mayerfield, 'Bankrupt Subsidiaries', 83–4.

In determining whether to re-characterise debt as equity within a corporate group, the undercapitalisation of the subsidiary is a starting point.[172] Unlike the case of equitable subordination, where the focus is on the group creditor's misconduct, 'the focus of the recharacterization inquiry is whether "a debt actually exists", or to put it another way, ... what is the proper characterization in the first instance of the investment.'[173] Courts consider whether the terms of and the circumstances surrounding the making of the loan indicate an arm's-length transaction of a kind that an external party might make. In *Bayer Corp* v. *MascoTech Inc (In re Autostyle Plastics Inc)*,[174] the US Court of Appeals for the Sixth Circuit set out a number of factors to be considered, which revolve around the nature of the transaction between ostensible debtor and creditor, the conduct of the parties with respect to that transaction, and the economic realities.[175] The court will examine such matters as: whether funds are extended at a fixed rate of interest; whether the repayment schedule is adhered to or repayment depends on the success of the business; whether shareholders in the putative debtor company extend funds in proportion to their shareholdings; whether the funds were required to be secured; whether a reasonable creditor would extend funds in similar circumstances; and whether funds were used for daily operational needs or for longer-term investment in plant and equipment.

The re-characterisation doctrine shares some of the shortcomings of substantive consolidation, in that its exercise depends upon the weighing up of a range of factors. Courts have been reluctant to utilise it.[176]

It is interesting to note that, while re-characterisation of debt as equity has no acknowledged place in UK company and insolvency law, at least one prominent case has used it. In *Atlas Maritime Co SA* v. *Avalon Maritime Ltd (No 1)*,[177] the parent company, Marc Rich & Co AG, had extended funds to its subsidiary Avalon Maritime Ltd in order to purchase a vessel, which was later sold. The subsidiary had no other assets. The claimant, Atlas Maritime Co SA, argued successfully that Avalon had

172 Erens, Friedman, and Mayerfield, 'Bankrupt Subsidiaries', 83–4.

173 *In re SubMicron Systems Corp* 432 F 3d 448, 454 (3rd Cir. 2006).

174 269 F 3d 726, 749 et seq (6th Cir. 2011).

175 See also *In re SubMicron Systems Corp* 432 F 3d 448, 456 (3rd Cir. 2006).

176 'A useful gauge of the uncertainty is the steady proliferation of factors courts try to take into account. After surveying the previous case law, the leading case compiled a list of eleven factors; a subsequent case concluded that eleven was not enough, and added two more': Skeel and Krause-Vilmar, 'Recharacterization and the Nonhindrance of Creditors', 265.

177 [1991] 4 All ER 769.

breached a contract for the purchase of the vessel. The Court of Appeal upheld an order for an injunction against Avalon – on grounds that included re-characterisation as equity of the debt owed by Avalon to Marc Rich. Neill LJ said that the court would examine all the circumstances, including the nature of the debt and the identity of the creditor.[178] The close link between Avalon and Marc Rich was a factor to be taken into account in deciding how the interests of the ultimate holding company should be balanced against those of Atlas.[179] He concluded that 'the sum owed to Marc Rich is not a debt incurred in the course of ordinary routine trading.' Stocker LJ agreed:

> The return of the money due to Marc Rich by Avalon will in fact be a payment to the former by its wholly-owned subsidiary and will thus protect the interests of the holding company, at the expense of an established right to damages . . . Although the financing arrangements between Marc Rich and Avalon have not been put into effect for the purpose of defeating any successful claim by a third party against Avalon, that is the consequence if Avalon's argument is well-founded . . . Repayment by Avalon to its holding company would not . . . be 'carrying on business in the ordinary way' or 'in the ordinary course of business'. It would be, in effect, the evasion of the underlying purpose of the Mareva injunction.[180]

Staughton LJ agreed with this. He said that 'it is a case of a defendant who is "seeking to avoid his responsibilities to the plaintiff if the latter should ultimately obtain a judgment" or taking action "designed to ensure that subsequent orders of the court are rendered less effective than would otherwise be the case".'[181]

7.4 Conclusions

This chapter has dealt with Commonwealth group-specific statutory provisions and US bankruptcy law doctrines, which do several things to advance the position of creditors faced with the insolvent entity problem. The rules help to create transparency of ownership and control. They facilitate group accounting and, in some cases, the awarding of cross-guarantees by group companies. Moreover, there is a range of laws facilitating causes of action by creditors against corporate group debtors. When looking at the combined effect of the rules, we see that undoubted advances have been made in the way that misuse of the corporate form is

178 [1991] 4 All ER 769, 777.
179 [1991] 4 All ER 769, 776.
180 [1991] 4 All ER 769, 778.
181 [1991] 4 All ER 769, 780.

addressed in the corporate group context. But the discussion in this chapter reveals also that hopes accompanying the establishment of the rules facilitating extensions of liability (or deferral of intra-group claims) have been no more than half-fulfilled. Courts have been wary about their use, always concerned about the impact upon commercial expectations of rules that permit 'exceptions' to fundamental concepts of separate legal personality and limited liability. Perhaps this reveals the difficulty of finding a solution to the insolvent entity problem internally, within company and insolvency law. Within this area of the law, the fundamental concepts remain close to sacrosanct. Neither legislatures nor courts have been able to think around them with sufficient boldness. In the following chapter, further regimes for the extension of liability in corporate groups are introduced, which originate in statute, but which do not derive from company and insolvency law.

8

Statutory Torts

8.1 Introduction

Whereas the previous two chapters in this book examined company and insolvency laws applicable to companies in general, and to corporate groups in particular, this chapter considers statutory and common law rules from outside that area of law. Its focus is upon special statutory tort regimes that permit extensions of liability from insolvent companies to others in the group and/or the network. The three liability regimes considered are EU and US product liability rules, the US Comprehensive Environmental Response, Compensation, and Liability Act 1980, and the US Oil Pollution Act 1990. Product liability rules are 'strict' (or 'stricter') in nature, meaning that issues of fault are either of no importance or of little importance, and facilitate recovery from different parties in the chain of manufacture and supply of goods. The US polluter-pays statutes contain several innovations, including: financial responsibility provisions aimed at ensuring ex ante that responsible parties have a notional ability to pay for clean-up and damages claims should accidents occur; rules for extending liability beyond owners of oil and other facilities to remote 'operators'; and provisions 'channelling' liability to such parties, which are designed to ensure that they take responsibility for the prevention of accidents.

8.2 Extended Liability: Products

This chapter commences with consideration of product liability rules. These rules are significant in discussion of the insolvent entity problem because many mass-tort cases have involved defective products. In Chapter 4, we considered case studies in which the insolvent entity problem arose or has the potential to arise from defective asbestos and pharmaceutical products. Defects in these products have loomed large in crafting the rules we now consider.

The EU product liability regime not only provides for a tort of (qualified) strict liability directed against manufacturers of defective products, but permits liability to be extended to certain other parties as well: to 'own-branders' and importers into the European Union, which are the primarily liable parties, and to suppliers of products, which are liable on a contingent basis. In this way, the product liability regime reflects an attempt at creating 'network liability' because it creates joint and several liability in companies, however related, that constitute the chain of manufacture and supply. Despite these features, the Product Liability Directive[1] has had modest impact. Reasons for this include the presence of a wide 'development risks' defence and the long-stop limit on bringing actions.

8.2.1 European Regime

Reform to product liability laws in Europe[2] was prompted by the apparent inability of courts to provide remedies to victims of the defective drug Thalidomide.[3] In order to deal with an international problem, while at the same time not wanting to undermine the competitiveness of national industries, national governments deferred to the then-European Economic Community for a legislative solution that would apply across all Member States.[4] The Product Liability Directive, adopted in 1985, contains maximum harmonisation rules.[5] Although it was possible to give direct statutory

[1] Council Directive 1985/374/EEC of 25 July 1985 on the approximation of the laws, regulations, and administrative provisions of the Member States concerning liability for defective products, OJ L210/29 ('Product Liability Directive').

[2] For Australia: see Competition and Consumer Act 2010 (Cth), Sched. 2, containing the Australian Consumer Law Parts 3–5; H. Luntz, D. Hambly, K. Burns, J. Dietrich, and N. Foster, *Torts: Cases and Commentary* (7th edn., 2012), ch. 7; C. Sappideen and P. Vines (eds.), *Fleming's The Law of Torts* (10th edn., 2011), ch. 23; D. Harland, 'The Influence of European Law on Product Liability in Australia' (1995) 17 *Sydney Law Review* 336. Canadian law in this area is based on rules of common law negligence: see, e.g., S. M. Waddams, 'The Canadian Law of Products Liability' (1999) 34 *Texas International Law Journal* 119; J. Mohrbutter, '*Harrington v Dow Corning Corp* and Social Utility: Unfit for Their Purpose within Product Liability Negligence Law' (2012) 75 *Saskatchewan Law Review* 269.

[3] G. Howells (ed.), *The Law of Product Liability* (2nd edn., 2007), p. 267; J. Stapleton, *Product Liability* (1994), pp. 42–6. Norway, Sweden, Finland, and Germany have alternative liability regimes for pharmaceuticals: Howells, ibid., pp. 287 and 417.

[4] Howells, *The Law of Product Liability*, p. 268; S. Whittaker, *Liability for Products: English Law, French Law, and European Harmonization* (2005), p. 432.

[5] Notably, the Court of Justice of the European Union has held that Member States cannot implement rules more stringent than those contained in the Directive (Case C–52/00,

effect to the rules through passage of a Regulation, that was not done. Instead, each EC Member State was required to transpose core Directive requirements into suitable domestic law. In the United Kingdom, effect was given to the Directive by the Consumer Protection Act 1987. When interpretation of the 1987 Act is in doubt, it must be construed in the light of the Directive.[6]

'Products' are defined in the 1987 Act[7] as 'any goods or electricity', and include component parts,[8] certain substances,[9] and agricultural crops. In order to have an action, the claimant must prove that a defect in a product caused his or her injury. Section 3 of the 1987 Act stipulates that there is a defect in a product if its safety is not such as persons generally are *entitled* to expect.[10] In assessing this matter, all the circumstances are to be taken into account, including: the manner in which and the purposes for which the product has been marketed; any instructions for or warnings with respect to doing or refraining from doing anything with or in relation to the product; what might reasonably be expected to be done with or in relation to the product; and the time when the product was supplied by the producer to another. In relation to manufacturing and presentation defects, strict liability often is straightforward to establish. When the manufacturing process breaks down, the product can be characterised as patently defective. Equally, when instructions on use of the product are inadequate, or when warnings as to use fail to make the consumer safe, a defect will be easy to establish.[11] The need to engage in a rigorous examination of the risks and benefits of a product generally is reserved for design defects[12] because such defects have much greater

European Commission v. *France*, [2002] ECR I-3827) and cannot retain pre-existing rules that are more stringent than those in the Directive (Case C–183/00, *Sanchez* v. *Medicina Asturiana SA* [2002] ECR I-3901). For explanation of maximum harmonisation, or 'total harmonisation', see R. Schütze, *European Union Law* (2015), pp. 550–1.

6 See *A* v. *National Blood Authority* [2001] 3 All ER 289, 297.

7 Consumer Protection Act 1987, s. 1(2).

8 The 1987 Act does not cover immovable property – that is, land and fixtures on land. Liability for defectively constructed buildings remains subject to the general rules of negligence and to the Defective Premises Act 1972. But products which become fixtures within immovable property – for example, central heating boilers – are probably within the scope of the Act: see s. 45(1).

9 E.g., blood and blood products: see *A* v. *National Blood Authority* [2001] 3 All ER 289.

10 See *A* v. *National Blood Authority* [2001] 3 All ER 289.

11 If, however, a warning leaflet is lost or a consumer chooses not to replace a lost leaflet, the manufacturer cannot be held responsible: *Worsley* v. *Tambrands Ltd* [2000] PIQR P95.

12 See, e.g., *Abouzaid* v. *Mothercare (UK) Ltd* [2000] All ER (D) 2436, where Pill LJ thought the question for the court was one of whether the public legitimately could expect a higher degree of safety from the product than that which actually was present.

implications for industry.[13] The question of what the defendant could (reasonably or otherwise) have done to eliminate or reduce the risks is largely irrelevant.[14] This negates the need to examine breach factors which form part of the law of negligence, such as the practicality of taking precautions.[15]

There is no need for the claimant to prove the cause of the *defect*.[16] That is for the defendant to investigate and remedy. The claimant need only prove that the 'defect' in the product caused the relevant *injury or damage*.[17] Substantial problems can arise in proof of causation, but these shall be considered in other parts of this book (namely, when examining US market-share liability later in this chapter, and when considering the '*Fairchild* exception' in Chapter 11). For now, we need note only that intermediate examination of the product does not exonerate the manufacturer from liability for defects existing at the time of entry into circulation. That some third party might share liability for the claimant's injury is relevant only to the issue of contribution between tortfeasors.[18]

The Consumer Protection Act 1987, section 4, provides several defences to strict liability, for example where: the defendant did not supply the product to another,[19] which might be the case if it was stolen and sold by the thieves;[20] the defendant did not supply the product in the course of business;[21] the defect did not exist in the product when it was supplied by the defendant to another;[22] and the defendant was a maker of component parts, and the defect

[13] Compensating ten victims of a freak construction defect is a less daunting prospect than compensating the thousands who might have suffered injury before a design defect became patent.

[14] *A* v. *National Blood Authority* [2001] 3 All ER 289.

[15] See P. Giliker, *The Europeanisation of English Tort Law* (2014), pp. 51 and 53.

[16] *Ide* v. *ATB Sales Ltd* [2009] RTR 8, [19].

[17] See the Consumer Protection Act 1987, s. 2(1). The substantive rules of causation (and remoteness) to be applied are for national courts to determine: D. Fairgrieve and G. Howells, 'Rethinking Product Liability: A Missing Element in the European Commission's Third Review of the European Product Liability Directive' (2007) 70 *Modern Law Review* 962, 966. Under English law, causation may be inferred from the facts by a process of eliminating non-causes, as long as the remaining cause is not one which is improbable in nature: *Ide* v. *ATB Sales Ltd* [2009] RTR 8, distinguishing *Rhesa Shipping Co SA* v. *Edmunds* (*'The Popi M'*) [1985] 1 WLR 948.

[18] See Product Liability Directive, art. 8(1). Contribution is not limited to tortfeasors but is available between all persons liable for the same damage: Civil Liability (Contribution) Act 1978.

[19] Consumer Protection Act 1987, s. 4(1)(b).

[20] C. Witting, *Street on Torts* (14th edn., 2015), p. 425.

[21] Consumer Protection Act 1987, s. 4(1)(c).

[22] Consumer Protection Act 1987, s. 4(1)(d).

arose in the finished product and was caused by the faulty design of the finished product or by inadequate installation of the component into the finished product by the manufacturers of that product.[23]

Prior to adoption of the Product Liability Directive, UK industry – most notably the pharmaceuticals industry – persuaded the UK government to push for a 'development risks' defence, despite official reports advising against this.[24] The United Kingdom won the subsequent argument, and an optional defence was included in the text of the Directive as article 7(e).[25] Section 4(1)(e) of the 1987 Act provides, accordingly, that a defendant shall not be liable when able to show 'that the state of scientific and technical knowledge at the relevant time was not such that a producer of products of the same description as the product in question might be expected to have discovered the defect if it had existed in' its products while under its control.[26] This defence is controversial because it undermines the strictness of the liability regime: 'once liability for unforeseen risks is excluded ... it begins to look rather like a negligence regime.'[27] Assuming that defectiveness can be established, the likelihood of liability in design defect cases is reduced, especially those emanating from innovative industries.[28] And this is why the defence was of such importance to the pharmaceutical industry, given that its members make their profits primarily from in-patent drugs (as we saw in Chapter 4). If we imagine a drug developed (as was Thalidomide) to alleviate sickness during pregnancy which causes unforeseen disabilities in subsequently born children, the development risks defence reduces the effectiveness of the 1987 Act, so that it retains only one significant advantage over actions in negligence for the parents of injured babies. In negligence they would have to prove that the defendants should have foreseen the risk. But under the statute, the onus is on the defendants to prove that they could not have anticipated the danger.[29] Yet this reversal of the onus might not mean much because the defendant, with impressive technical and other

23 Consumer Protection Act 1987, s. 4(1)(f).

24 Howells, *The Law of Product Liability*, p. 288.

25 J. Stapleton, 'Products Liability in the United Kingdom: The Myths of Reform' (1999) 34 *Texas International Law Journal* 45, 60.

26 The test is objective: *Richardson* v. *LRC Products Ltd* (2000) 59 BMLR 185. Knowledge must be accessible if it is to ground liability: *A* v. *National Blood Authority* [2001] 3 All ER 289.

27 Howells, *The Law of Product Liability*, p. 420.

28 Howells, *The Law of Product Liability*, pp. 416 and 418; J. Stapleton, 'Restatement (Third) of Torts: Products Liability, an Anglo-Australian Perspective' (2000) 39 *Washburn Law Journal* 363, 382.

29 See Witting, *Street on Torts*, p. 427.

resources at its disposal, might find it comparatively easy to adduce some sort of evidence that there was no reasonably accessible knowledge of risks of a defect. The burden of proof would thus revert back to the claimant.[30]

Actions under Part I of the 1987 Act are subject to the usual limitation periods. But in no circumstances can actions be brought more than ten years from the date on which the defendant supplied its product to another.[31] This is the 'long-stop' time limit, which was legislated for on account of the need to balance the interests of injured claimants against producers subject to a strict liability regime that represents 'a greater burden than [that arising] under a traditional system of liability'.[32] The long-stop time limit is designed to ensure legal certainty, the ability of producers to insure against liability, and continued innovation in industries such as the pharmaceuticals industry.[33] It effectively prevents actions based on defects in asbestos products because of the long latency period that characterises the diseases to which asbestos exposure gives rise. The long-stop time limit would create difficulties also in many actions against the manufacturers of defective drugs. Claims brought before US courts by women who had developed cervical cancer as a result of their mothers having been prescribed DES in pregnancy, therefore, could not have been brought under the 1987 Act.[34]

Whenever a defect in a product wholly or partly causes death or personal injury, the victim or his or her dependants can bring an action.[35] The injured individual need not be a purchaser or even a direct user of the product. Bystanders are eligible to make claims for losses suffered. When a defective product causes prenatal injury to a baby, an action may be brought once the baby is born alive on its behalf for any disabilities.[36] Moreover, although the 1987 Act is aimed primarily at protection against death and personal injuries, consumers can invoke its provisions also when a product causes damage to private property.[37] Damage to the product itself is excluded,[38] as are other forms of purely financial loss.[39]

[30] Howells, *The Law of Product Liability*, p. 430.

[31] As to time of supply, see *O'Byrne* v. *Aventis Pasteur SA* [2010] 1 WLR 1412.

[32] Case C–358/08, *O'Byrne* v. *Aventis Pasteur* (2009) 113 BMLR 1, [41]–[42].

[33] Case C–358/08, *O'Byrne* v. *Aventis Pasteur* (2009) 113 BMLR 1, [41]–[42], and [46].

[34] Stapleton, 'Products Liability in the United Kingdom', 63.

[35] Consumer Protection Act 1987, s. 2(1).

[36] Consumer Protection Act 1987, s. 6(3).

[37] Provided the amount to be awarded to compensate for that damage exceeds £275. See Consumer Protection Act 1987, s. 5(4). By s. 5(3), recovery for property used for business purposes is excluded.

[38] Consumer Protection Act 1987, s. 5(2).

[39] Financial loss consequent upon physical injury or damage to private property, however, in principle should be recoverable.

As adumbrated, liability for defective products is not limited to manufacturers alone. All those involved in primary production and marketing potentially are liable. Liability is imposed on 'producers';[40] and producers are defined as encompassing: manufacturers;[41] in the case of products which are not made, but won or abstracted (for example, coal and minerals) liability is imposed on the person who won or abstracted the product;[42] and, in respect of products that are neither made nor won or abstracted (for example, crops), but where essential characteristics of the product are attributable to an industrial or other process, liability is imposed on the person carrying out that process.[43]

Although the Directive expressly defines makers of component parts as 'producers',[44] the 1987 Act achieves the same end by defining 'product' so as to embrace component parts.[45] The component part maker is liable only when the component supplied to the ultimate manufacturer was defective; the component maker is not liable when the defect arises as a result of the manner in which the ultimate manufacturer used the component.[46] Thus, should defective brakes in a new car fail and cause personal injury, the injured person can sue both the 'producer' of the finished product (the car manufacturer) and the 'producer' of the defective component (the maker of the brakes). Section 1(3) of the 1987 Act, however, provides that a supplier of the finished product shall not be deemed liable for defects in component parts simply because it cannot name the actual maker of each and every component.

In addition to manufacturers, primary liability is imposed upon any person who brand names a product, or by other means holds itself out as producer,[47] and on any company that imports a product into the European Union from outside its borders.[48] The latter provision ensures that claimants do not have to go to the trouble and expense of suing a

[40] Consumer Protection Act 1987, s. 2(2)(a).

[41] Consumer Protection Act 1987, s. 1(2)(a).

[42] Consumer Protection Act 1987, s. 1(2)(b).

[43] Consumer Protection Act 1987, s. 1(2)(c). Designers and inventors are not made liable under this Act; 'such an approach can be justified given that other commercial entities are normally responsible for implementing the design': Howells, *The Law of Product Liability*, p. 320.

[44] Product Liability Directive, art. 3(1).

[45] See Consumer Protection Act 1987, s. 1(2).

[46] Howells, *The Law of Product Liability*, p. 286.

[47] Consumer Protection Act 1987, s. 2(2)(b).

[48] Consumer Protection Act 1987, s. 2(2)(c). Note that a company importing a product into the United Kingdom from another Member State is not made strictly liable under the Act. However, it might be liable in negligence.

manufacturer located outside the European Union. A secondary form of liability is imposed upon suppliers (such as wholesalers and retailers), although this is defeasible. Section 2(3) of the 1987 Act provides that any supplier of a product will be liable to the injured person unless it complies with a request to name, within a reasonable time, the person supplying it with the product. Compliance with the provision does not arise when the supplier confirms merely that it is not the manufacturer without naming either a primarily responsible party or its own supplier.[49] Section 2(3) is helpful to the consumer, who might not know the identity of those higher up a long supply chain.[50] This and other provisions in the 1987 Act aim to channel liability to primary parties.[51]

The problem of structuring relations within corporate groups so as to reduce the availability of group assets (discussed in Chapter 3) was a concern for some Members when the Consumer Protection Bill was debated in Parliament.[52] Yet no special solution to this problem was developed. Ordinary principles of separate legal personality and limited liability apply to questions of extended product liability.[53] In this respect, it is pertinent that, in *O'Byrne* v. *Sanofi Pasteur MSD Ltd*,[54] the Court of Justice of the European Union held upon a reference that, pursuant to articles 3 and 11 of the Directive, it is open to a national court to treat a distributor of goods as the producer when the distributor is both a wholly owned subsidiary of the manufacturer and under the control of the manufacturer in that the latter determines when goods are put into circulation. The Court held that the separate legal status of the two entities was not to 'influence' it, and that 'the fact that the products are invoiced to a subsidiary company and that the latter, like any purchaser, pays the price, is not conclusive.'[55] This would allow a national court, when appropriate, to substitute the parent company for the subsidiary in proceedings commenced on time against the

[49] Case C-358/08, *O'Byrne* v. *Aventis Pasteur SA* (2009) 113 BMLR 1, [57]. See Howells, *The Law of Product Liability*, p. 303.

[50] However, the system might break down if a link in the chain proves uncontactable: Howells, *The Law of Product Liability*, p. 317. In many cases, the failure of the supplier to name an alternative defendant is likely to be 'faulty' in some way: Whittaker, *Liability for Products*, p. 524.

[51] Howells, *The Law of Product Liability*, p. 304.

[52] C. J. Miller and R. S. Goldberg, *Product Liability* (2nd edn., 2004), pp. 275–6, referring to Hansard, HL, vol. 483, col. 752, 19 January 1987.

[53] Miller and Goldberg, *Product Liability*, p. 276.

[54] Case C-127/04, *O'Byrne* v. *Sanofi Pasteur MSD Ltd* (2006) 91 BMLR 175.

[55] Case C-127/04, *O'Byrne* v. *Sanofi Pasteur MSD Ltd* (2006) 91 BMLR 175, [30]–[31] (aff'd C-358/08, *O'Byrne* v. *Aventis Pasteur SA* Case (2009) 113 BMLR 1).

subsidiary but not against the parent. A circumstance in which this might be advantageous for the claimant is where the distributor turns out to be insolvent, but the manufacturer remains solvent.[56] (The UK Supreme Court held later in *O'Byrne* v. *Aventis Pasteur SA* that the UK distributor of a drug was a proper defendant to proceedings brought by an infant claimant, and that there was no need to rely upon the power available under the Limitation Act 1980 to substitute the French manufacturer for the distributor.[57] The court explained that, if the manufacturer, APSA, was in a position to decide when the product was to be distributed, then the distributor, APMSD, 'would be integrated into the manufacturing process and so tightly controlled by APSA that proceedings against APMSD could properly be regarded as proceedings against the parent company, APSA',[58] insolvency not being an issue.)

When more than one defendant is liable for the same damage under the Consumer Protection Act 1987, their liability is joint and several.[59] This means that each defendant is liable for the whole of the damage and must seek contribution from other liable parties (whether under the 1987 Act or on some alternative basis) if they are available to be sued.[60]

The Consumer Protection Act 1987 provides a compromised and unsatisfactory regime of product liability. In many cases, it is not the preferred means of redress for product-related injuries. Employees injured in the course of their duties find it preferable to bring action under the Employer's Liability (Defective Equipment) Act 1969. And consumers who bought goods under contract find it preferable to bring action for breach of statutory warranties under the Consumer Rights Act 2015. These legislative regimes offer a more comprehensive form of strict liability, because there is no exemption for design defects that cause unforeseeable risks of harm.[61] And, as noted already, the 1987 Act is unlikely to be helpful in cases of defective pharmaceuticals and other injurious products giving rise to injuries with long latency.[62] Moreover, although the Act creates joint and several liability in a number of potential defendants, it can offer no guarantee of a solvent defendant. It

[56] The obvious suggestion made in *O'Byrne* v. *Aventis Pasteur SA* [2010] 1 WLR 1412, [35].

[57] [2010] 1 WLR 1412.

[58] [2010] 1 WLR 1412, at [34]. In other words, proceedings against the subsidiary were sufficient for the purposes of the Act.

[59] Consumer Protection Act 1987, s. 2(5). [60] Civil Liability (Contribution) Act 1978.

[61] Whittaker, *Liability for Products*, pp. 554–5.

[62] See also Harland, 'The Influence of European Law', 344.

is little wonder, then, that product liability laws have been thought of as having little practical benefit for injured claimants.[63]

8.2.2 US Regime

Before moving on to consider other types of statutory regime that facilitate extensions of liability beyond insolvent companies, we consider briefly whether US 'products liability' laws provide a better model of extended liability than the EU Product Liability Directive and national laws derived from it. This is of especial interest because US strict liability rules on products were the inspiration for the liability regime eventually adopted in the European Union.[64]

US products liability rules today present a mixed picture. Some states have enacted legislation either creating a comprehensive products liability regime,[65] or else supplementing the common law, while other states rely upon the common law alone. Courts in the latter states have the option of following the model rules set out in either the Restatement (Second) of Torts (1977), or the Restatement (Third) of Torts: Product Liability (1998).[66] In this section, after plotting the development of these rules, we deal with two matters: first, the movement of products liability under the Restatements from a stricter to a more fault-based regime, which reflects concerns about liability rules having become too liberal so as negatively to affect innovation, competitiveness, and commerce in general; second, the limited range of parties capable of being sued under a products liability theory, it being accepted that the producer is primarily responsible, and there having been some retrenchment from the liability of not-at-fault retailers. Nevertheless some states do permit the imposition of products liability on 'successors' to companies which either have become insolvent or been dissolved.

The story of US products liability begins with *MacPherson* v. *Buick Motor Co*,[67] in which the New York Court of Appeals permitted an action in

[63] Giliker, *The Europeanisation of English Tort Law*, pp. 59–60; M. Reimann, 'Product Liability in a Global Context: The Hollow Victory of the European Model' (2003) 7 *European Review of Private Law* 128; Stapleton, 'Products Liability in the United Kingdom', 65.

[64] See Council of Europe, European Convention on Products Liability in regard to Personal Injury and Death (ETS No 91), Strasbourg, 27 January 1977; Whittaker, *Liability for Products*, p. 568. Cf. Stapleton, 'Products Liability in the United Kingdom', 46 (sceptical about aspects of such claims).

[65] E.g., Louisiana Products Liability Act (La Rev Stat Ann § 9:2800.52 (2009)).

[66] See D. G. Owen and M. J. Davis, *Owen and Davis on Products Liability* (4th edn., 2014).

[67] 111 NE 1050 (NY 1916).

negligence by a non-privy owner against the manufacturer of a vehicle with a faulty wheel that caused injury to the owner. While this was an important breakthrough, practical difficulties attended suits in negligence because of the need for the claimant to prove fault in manufacture. The basis for a products liability regime which avoided this problem was sketched out in a series of papers by Fleming James[68] and adopted by William Prosser in his *Handbook of the Law of Torts*, in which he argued that 'the burden of accidental injuries caused by defective chattels [should] be placed upon the producer, since he is best able to distribute the risk to the general public by means of prices and insurance.'[69] In *Escola* v. *Coca Cola Bottling Co*,[70] Traynor J adopted this idea in a concurring judgment and stressed also the ability of the manufacturer to test its products to ascertain safety in ways not available to consumers.[71] Traynor J's minority opinion was adopted by the California Supreme Court in *Greenman* v. *Yuba Power Products, Inc*,[72] which signalled the expansion of 'strict liability' from warranty law to the core of tort law.[73]

One of the animating ideas behind strict products liability is enterprise liability, which requires, in this context, that all of the costs of an economic activity should be borne (or internalised) by those profiting from it.[74] The manufacturer and/or other sellers are made liable in the first instance, but are assumed able to absorb losses (and avoid social dislocation)[75] through reductions in profits, or to spread losses through insurance or marginal increases in product prices.[76] By contrast, injured parties, such as consumers and bystanders, are unlikely to be able to spread their losses. Enterprise liability is designed, furthermore, to counteract a basic problem where complex industrial processes are concerned, this being the difficulty that external claimants have in proving fault in

[68] E.g., F. James Jr, 'Products Liability' (1955) 34 *Texas Law Review* 192. See K. Graham, 'Strict Products Liability at 50: Four Histories' (2014) 98 *Marquette Law Review* 555, 581–2.

[69] W. L. Prosser, *Handbook of the Law of Torts* (1941), § 83.

[70] 150 P 2d 436 (Cal 1944). The majority opinion was founded upon the application of res ipsa loquitur, establishing an inference of negligence: ibid., 439–40.

[71] 150 P.2d 436, 441 (Cal 1944). See also *Sea Pines* v. *United States* 346 US 15, 51–2 (1953).

[72] 377 P 2d 897 (Cal 1963).

[73] Graham, 'Strict Products Liability at 50', 578. The phrase 'strict liability' appears in parentheses because of qualifications to this idea, introduced in the text that follows.

[74] P. I. Blumberg, *The Law of Corporate Groups: Substantive Law* (1987), p. 264.

[75] See G. Calabresi, *The Costs of Accidents* (1970), p. 44.

[76] E.g., *Greenman* v. *Yuba Power Products, Inc* 377 P.2d 897 (Cal 1963). See also Blumberg, *The Law of Corporate Groups*, pp. 264–5.

the manufacturer or other seller of products.[77] Armed with the decision in *Greenman*, Prosser, as reporter to the American Law Institute on this issue, based Restatement (Second) of Torts (1977) provisions on this conception of enterprise liability.[78] Section 402A creates liability in those who sell 'any product in a defective condition unreasonably dangerous to the user or consumer or to his property' for any 'physical harm thereby caused'. Liability for design defects and inadequate warnings is based upon a consumer expectations test,[79] which pays no heed to whether the defendant exercised care.[80] Section 402A was adopted in most US states,[81] sometimes in legislative form.[82]

The potential 'strictness' of products liability law was exemplified by *Beshada* v. *Johns-Manville Products Corp*,[83] in which the New Jersey Supreme Court held that asbestos sold without warning of its hidden dangers was defective, and that its manufacturer was liable for the resulting harm, regardless of the unforeseeability of the risk. However, *Beshada* was the 'high-water mark' of products liability in the United States – and subject to great criticism because of the inherent difficulty of warning about unforeseeable risks.[84] The decision was effectively side-stepped by the same court in *Feldman* v. *Lederle Laboratories*,[85] which involved a claim for injuries resulting from the use of a prescription drug. David Owen describes this case as marking 'the beginning of the decline of true strict liability in warning cases – the point at which the law turned away from a lock-step march toward strict liability, back toward the principle of fault'.[86]

In fact, products liability under section 402A appears to have expanded beyond what its drafters had envisaged. George Priest believes that the reason for this was the preoccupation of the drafters with the problem of simple manufacturing errors, which they expected to dominate claims (in

77 Blumberg, *The Law of Corporate Groups*, p. 265.

78 Graham, 'Strict Products Liability at 50', 581–2.

79 American Law Institute, Restatement (Second) of Torts, § 402A, comment g.

80 See M. P. Weingarten, 'Asbestos Litigation from an American Perspective' (2009) *Journal of Personal Injury Law* 253, 255.

81 J. C. P. Goldberg and B. C. Zipursky, *The Oxford Introductions to US Law: Torts* (2010), p. 271; Graham, 'Strict Products Liability at 50', 578.

82 T. M. Schwartz, 'The Impact of the New Products Liability Restatement on Prescription Products' (1995) 50 *Food & Drug Law Journal* 399, 411.

83 447 A 2d 539 (NJ 1982).

84 D. G. Owen, 'The Evolution of Products Liability Law' (2007) 26 *Review of Litigation* 955, 980.

85 479 A 2d 374 (NJ 1984).

86 Owen, 'The Evolution of Products Liability Law', 979.

terms of number and monetary awards), while it largely was expected that design defect and inadequate warning cases would continue to be determined under more restrictive negligence rules.[87] The flood of claims arguing each type of defect and the high damages awards in defective design cases resulted in what some called a liability 'disaster'.[88] Coinciding with increased globalisation of trade in the 1980s and with consequent pressures on US manufacturers to remain cost-competitive, there was a 'backlash' against liberal products liability rules.[89] The backlash was fuelled by a wider sense that products liability was too favourable to claimants, that the rules imposed indefensible liability on 'innocent' parties, and that damages awards were too high. Efforts at reform were undertaken by a number of state legislatures, which legislated for defences based on the state of the scientific and technological art at the time of a product's manufacture and sale,[90] and/or for several liability.[91] Change was afoot also in the rewriting of the Restatement rules. Given the debate around products liability, this topic was at the forefront of deliberations early in the development cycle of the third-generation Restatements. However, the new rules have not been a complete success. Nearly two decades after their first publication, they have yet to be adopted by a majority of states.[92] Many states have remained committed to strict-ish products liability across each of the types of defect.[93]

Let us now turn to the latest rules. Under the Restatement (Third) of Torts: Products Liability (1998), section 1, a commercial seller[94] or distributor who sells or distributes a defective product is subject to liability for harm to persons or property caused by the defect. The Restatement recognises the three traditional kinds of product defect, but liability is truly strict only in cases of manufacturing defects. Liability arises for manufacturing defects 'even though all possible care was exercised in the

[87] G. L. Priest, 'Strict Products Liability: The Original Intent' (1989) 10 *Cardozo Law Review* 2301, 2303.

[88] Stapleton, 'Restatement (Third) of Torts', 367 and 399.

[89] J. C. P. Goldberg and B. C. Zipursky, 'The Easy Case for Products Liability Law: A Response to Professors Polinsky and Shavell' (2010) 123 *Harvard Law Review* 1919, 1919.

[90] Owen, 'The Evolution of Products Liability Law', 979.

[91] Goldberg and Zipursky, 'The Easy Case for Products Liability Law', 1920.

[92] In this sense, it has been noted that the Third Restatement rules were not a distillation of then-current legal decisions, but went 'beyond the law': *Delaney* v. *Deere & Co* 999 P 2d 930, 945–6 (Kan 2000).

[93] See, e.g., *Aubin* v. *Union Carbide Corporation* 177 So 3d 489, 505–12 (Fla 2015); *Schwartz* v. *Abex Corp* 106 F Supp 3d 626, 633 (ED Penn 2015)(both asbestos cases).

[94] This includes an own-brander: American Law Institute, Restatement (Third) of Torts: Products Liability (1998), § 14.

preparation and marketing of the product'.[95] Liability arises for defects in the design of a product and inadequate warnings only when risks of injury were foreseeable. This indicates that the capacity of the defendant to respond to knowledge of risks is a prerequisite to liability. The provisions call also for comparisons with what precautions would have been reasonable in the circumstances and appear to be firmly negligence-based. Thus, a design is defective when 'the foreseeable risks of harm posed by the product could have been reduced or avoided by the adoption of a reasonable alternative design ... and the omission of the alternative design renders the product not reasonably safe'.[96] Liability can arise also when 'the foreseeable risks of harm posed by the product could have been reduced or avoided by the provision of reasonable instructions or warnings ... and the omission of the instructions or warnings renders the product not reasonably safe'.[97] Liability for defects in design and in warnings is predicated upon a balancing of the utility of the product against its risk, and largely moves away from section 402A's consumer expectations test.[98] The consumer expectations test is seen today as unsuited to cases involving complex products, with which the consumer is unlikely to have much relevant experience.[99]

The Restatement (Third) of Torts: Products Liability (1998) incorporates a separate provision, section 6, concerning the liability of manufacturers for defects in their prescription drugs and medical devices. The rules applicable to manufacturing defects and inadequate warnings are derived from the provisions of section 2 (just considered). However, section 6(c) is different. It provides that prescription drugs and medical devices are defectively designed only when the foreseeable risks of harm posed are sufficiently great in relation to the foreseeable therapeutic benefits that 'no reasonable health care provider, knowing of such foreseeable risks and therapeutic benefits, would prescribe the drug or medical device for any class of patients'. This creates a high hurdle to liability. It has been said to permit of liability only when there is heightened negligence in the manufacturer, so that 'the drug or device should not have been on the market at all'.[100] The intended effect is to 'eliminate

95 American Law Institute, Restatement (Third) of Torts: Product Liability (1998), § 2(a).
96 American Law Institute, Restatement (Third) of Torts: Product Liability (1998), § 2(b).
97 American Law Institute, Restatement (Third) of Torts: Product Liability (1998), § 2(c).
98 *Aubin* v. *Union Carbide Corporation* 177 So 3d 489, 505–7 (Fla 2015); Owen, 'The Evolution of Products Liability Law', 987–9.
99 Sappideen and Vines, *Fleming's The Law of Torts*, pp. 574–5.
100 Schwartz, 'The Impact of the New Products Liability Restatement', 407.

design claims except in the rare cases where a plaintiff can establish no benefits to any patients'.[101] This provision reflects, no doubt, both the risk-taking that is part and parcel of pharmaceuticals development and the political strength of big pharma in looking after its own interests.

Prima facie, ordinary rules of causation apply to products liability claims (discussed with the tort of negligence in Chapter 11).[102] However, courts in some US jurisdictions have developed exceptions to the but-for test in order to ensure compensation for substantial wrongdoing by product manufacturers, suppliers, and others. In asbestos cases, it might be difficult to prove that a known manufacturer's product has been the effective cause of a claimant's injuries. In such cases, courts generally apply the 'substantial factor' test[103] of factual causation.[104] This test can be satisfied by showing that the claimant has been in close proximity to the defendant's asbestos product on a regular basis and over an extended time period. The test has been applied in cases of both divisible injury (asbestosis and lung cancer) and indivisible injury (mesothelioma).[105] More controversially, the Supreme Court of California in *Rutherford* v. *Owens-Illinois, Inc*[106] applied the substantial factor test in a lung cancer case where there were multiple sources of asbestos fibre. The claimant was able to succeed on causation by proving that his disease was the result of many separate exposures, each constituting a 'substantial factor', that contributed to the aggregate amount of asbestos inhaled or ingested. The claimant was not required to connect specific fibres with the defendant manufacturer. Liability for damages under *Rutherford* is either several or joint and several, according to relevant state legislation.[107] In states with a rule of several liability, recoveries of damages are likely to be modest.[108]

[101] Schwartz, 'The Impact of the New Products Liability Restatement', 409. But note the existence of a compensation scheme for defective vaccines: National Vaccine Injury Compensation Program under US Code, Title 42, Public Health and Welfare, §§ 300aa-10 to -34. This creates a no-fault alternative to litigation: see www.hrsa.gov/vaccinecompensation/.

[102] American Law Institute, Restatement (Third) of Torts: Products Liability (1998), § 15.

[103] See American Law Institute, Restatement (Second) of Torts (1977), § 431.

[104] *Lohrmann* v. *Pittsburgh Corning Corp* 782 F 2d 1156 (4th Cir. 1986).

[105] See S. Steel, *Proof of Causation in Tort Law* (2015), pp. 251–2; J. Sanders, 'Risky Business: Causation in Asbestos Cancer Cases (and Beyond?)', in R. Goldberg (ed.), *Perspectives on Causation* (2011), pp. 18–19; J. Stapleton, 'Two Causal Fictions at the Heart of US Asbestos Doctrine' (2006) 122 *Law Quarterly Review* 189, 192.

[106] 941 P 2d 1203 (Cal 1997). [107] Sanders, 'Risky Business', 30.

[108] Sanders, 'Risky Business', 30. This rule has become commonplace: for criticism, see Stapleton, 'Two Causal Fictions', 192.

In cases involving the generic drug DES, a well-known exception to but-for causation rules has been applied. DES was used to prevent miscarriages, but its consumption resulted in ovarian cancer in the daughters of women who used it, which appeared only after puberty. Because of the long time lag between supply and manifestation of injury, it was not possible for individual claimants to prove which of several hundred manufacturers had supplied injurious products.[109] What was clear, however, was that DES was inherently defective, so that each manufacturer inevitably was responsible for injuring some of the injured women. In *Sindell* v. *Abbott Laboratories*, the Supreme Court of California applied a rule whereby causal contribution to injury was determined according to the manufacturers' share of sales in the relevant market.[110] Under market-share liability, prima facie attribution of liability means that each manufacturer bears the burden of disproving causation. Liability can be defeated when the defendant manufacturer proves that it 'could not have made the product which caused the plaintiff's injuries'.[111] In most cases, liability for damages is several, rather than joint and several.[112] Despite the ability to escape causal attribution, market-share liability is controversial, and not all US jurisdictions adopt it.[113] Courts have refused to apply it in cases involving other generic drugs or asbestos.[114]

Products liability claims brought on the basis of design defects and inadequate warnings are defeasible (as adumbrated) where evidence suggests that the 'state of the art' of scientific and technical knowledge at the time of supply was insufficient to permit knowledge of the dangers.[115] Under the approach in a majority of states that recognise this defence,[116] the state of the art is but one factor which goes to determine

[109] See A. Ripstein and B. C. Zipursky, 'Corrective Justice in an Age of Mass Torts' in G. J. Postema (ed.), *Philosophy and the Law of Torts* (2001), p. 215.

[110] 26 Cal 3d 588 (1980). See also A. Porat and A. Stein, *Tort Liability under Uncertainty* (2001).

[111] *Sindell* v. *Abbott Laboratories* 26 Cal 3d 588, 612 (Cal 1980). Escape by this means was not permitted in *Hymowitz* v. *Eli Lilly Co* 539 NE 2d 1069 (NY 1989).

[112] See *Brown* v. *Superior Court* 751 P 2d 470 (Cal 1988). However, there are exceptions: e.g., *Abel* v. *Eli Lilly & Co* 343 NW 2d 164 (Mich 1984).

[113] E.g., *Smith v. Eli Lilly & Co, Inc* 560 NE 2d 324 (Ill 1990).

[114] E.g., *Celotex Corp v. Copeland* 471 So 2d 533 (Fla 1985). See Sanders, 'Risky Business', 33.

[115] Goldberg and Zipursky, *Torts*, p. 299. The knowledge of one manufacturer was taken to be the knowledge of all others: e.g., *Karjala* v. *Johns-Manville Products Corp* 523 F 2d 155 (8th Cir. 1975).

[116] As noted, such a doctrine undermines the strictness of products liability. This has been a reason for some courts refusing to adopt it: C. E. Cantu, 'The Useful Life Defense:

whether products are defective.[117] In a minority of states, compliance with then-existing state-of-the-art standards constitutes a positive defence.[118] However, the defence will be of limited value when subsequently available knowledge about risk gives rise to a duty to warn.[119] While the state-of-the-art defence proved an impediment to some early claims of injury caused by asbestos, its potency waned after it was found that Raybestos-Manhattan, Inc had covered up evidence of asbestos toxicity in the 1930s.[120] Depending upon the facts, the defence has a greater chance of success in cases involving injuries arising from defective pharmaceutical products.

Moreover, actions brought outside the long-stop period set by many states will be barred. The typical long-stop is ten years from the date of sale[121] – which seriously affects the ability of claimants to bring claims involving long-latent injuries. However, statutes of repose provide various exceptions for asbestos claims.[122]

Products liability actions are available to both injured users of products (including those injured in the workplace)[123] and bystanders.[124] The Restatement (Third) of Torts: Products Liability (1998) expressly creates the potential for liability in 'sellers', 'distributors', and 'successors in title'.[125] Sellers include manufacturers, wholesalers, and retailers.[126] Manufacturers are the 'central targets' of products liability law,[127] and

Embracing the Idea That All Products Eventually Grow Old and Die' (2001) 80 *Nebraska Law Review* 1, 9.

117 E.g., *O'Brien* v. *Muskin Corp* 463 A 2d 298 (NJ 1983). See also American Law Institute, Restatement (Third) of Torts: Products Liability (1998), § 2(b) (inquiry into available alternatives, discussed previously).

118 E.g., Arizona Revised Statutes Annotated, Title 12, Courts and Civil Proceedings, § 12–684. See D. E. Stuby, 'Status and Trends in State Product Liability Law: State of the Art Evidence' (1987) 14 *Journal of Legislation* 261, 262. The pharmaceutical industry lobbied for such legislation: Hon S. G. Pollock, 'Introductory Remark' (1999) 30 *Seton Hall Law Review* 202, 205.

119 Goldberg and Zipursky, *Torts*, p. 299.

120 A. Boggio, *Compensating Asbestos Victims: Law and the Dark Side of Industrialization* (2013), p. 159.

121 E.g., Indiana Code, Title 34, Civil Law and Procedure, Art. 20, ch. 3, § 1(b)(2). See D. G. Owen, 'Special Defenses in Modern Products Liability Law' (2005) 70 *Missouri Law Review* 1, 46.

122 Owen, 'Special Defenses', 47. Other, more minor defences are assumption of risk and claimant misuse of the product: Weingarten, 'Asbestos Litigation', 258.

123 *Borel* v. *Fibreboard Paper Products Corp* 493 F 2d 1076 (5th Cir. 1973).

124 Goldberg and Zipursky, *Torts*, p. 275.

125 American Law Institute, Restatement (Third) of Torts: Products Liability (1998), § 12.

126 American Law Institute, Restatement (Third) of Torts: Products Liability (1998), § 20(a).

127 Goldberg and Zipursky, *Torts*, p. 274.

liability has been channelled towards them.[128] Wholesalers and retailers are prima facie liable because of their ability to insure against losses and to obtain recovery from manufacturers.[129] The liability of these non-manufacturing suppliers has been controversial.[130] Indeed a majority of states now *precludes* actions against non-manufacturing defendants, such as wholesalers and retailers. This is the case, typically, where the non-manufacturing supplier has not contributed to the defectiveness of the product and/or the responsible manufacturer is solvent.[131] However, this does create a risk that claimants will be left with no redress if the time for bringing actions expires and the manufacturer becomes insolvent thereafter.[132] Where the liability of non-manufacturing suppliers is not precluded, these defendants might be protected by contractual indemnities with the manufacturer,[133] or else have their share of liability reduced under apportionment/contribution rules.[134] Of course, contribution might be unavailable when other liable parties have become insolvent.

In contrast to the position under EU law,[135] US products liability law features a distinct doctrine of successor liability.[136] Under Restatement (Third) of Torts: Products Liability (1998), section 12, a successor company that acquires the assets of a predecessor is subject to liability for harm caused by a defective product sold or otherwise distributed commercially by the predecessor if the acquisition meets one of several conditions, including cases where: there is an agreement to assume such liability; the reality is that the companies have merged; or the successor is rightly considered the continuation of the predecessor.[137] The latter two situations are designed to deal with potential sham

[128] See Owen, 'The Evolution of Products Liability Law', 969; Cantu, 'The Useful Life Defense', 4 (noting the ultimate right of non-manufacturing suppliers to indemnities).

[129] See *Vandermark* v. *Ford Motor Co* 391 P 2d 168 (Cal 1964); American Law Institute, Restatement (Third) of Torts: Products Liability (1998), § 2, comment a.

[130] Stapleton, 'Restatement (Third) of Torts', 401.

[131] See American Law Institute, Restatement (Third) of Torts: Products Liability (1998), § 1, comment e; A. Feeney, 'In Search of a Remedy: Do State Laws Exempting Sellers from Strict Product Liability Adequately Protect Consumers Harmed by Defective Chinese-Manufactured Products?' (2009) 34 *Journal of Corporation Law* 567.

[132] See American Law Institute, Restatement (Third) of Torts: Products Liability (1998), § 1, comment e.

[133] Goldberg and Zipursky, *Torts*, pp. 275 and 288.

[134] Goldberg and Zipursky, *Torts*, pp. 360–7.

[135] See Howells, *The Law of Product Liability*, p. 321; D. D. Prentice, 'Veil Piercing and Successor Liability in the United Kingdom' (1996) *Florida Journal of International Law* 469, 481.

[136] See J. H. Matheson, 'Successor Liability' (2011) 96 *Minnesota Law Review* 371.

[137] These grounds derive from *Leannais* v. *Cincinnati Inc* 565 F 2d 431 (7th Cir. 1977).

transactions that otherwise would cleanse a manufacturer of its liabilities.[138] Such transactions are not only unfair to tort claimants, but undermine legal incentives to invest in safety.[139] Successor liability is justified also on the basis that the successor should take both the benefit and the burden of acquisitions, and that it, like other defendants, has the ability to spread the costs of liability.[140] Successor liability appears to have been especially important in cases involving long-tail liabilities.[141]

US products liability rules are not designed for and often have no particular implications for corporate groups. However, there have been cases in which they have been applied so as to extend liability from insolvent subsidiaries to parent companies in circumstances where the parents were not active in manufacture or supply. This has been the case where subsidiaries have manufactured and/or sold defective products in the name of the group, so that consumers have been 'invited to rely' upon the good reputation of the group.[142] However, fudging the rules in this way appears to be the exception, and recent cases have been characterised by a desire to restrict the range of liable parties. But even when the exception applies, the 'reliance' cases do not represent any true exception *to limited liability*. Companies in corporate groups are treated in exactly the same way as companies in networks.

In summary, the development of US products liability law has been an historical milestone and assisted countless numbers of claimants in obtaining compensation for injuries. This has included claimants in asbestos and pharmaceuticals cases. The history of products liability claims demonstrates that judge-made law can both be innovative and radically change the way in which companies operate. However, it has to be acknowledged that strict products liability has created extreme tensions, which inspired the American Law Institute both to retrench on the liberalness of rules on

[138] A concern lingers that the rules can be avoided by piecemeal sales of assets: H. Hansmann and R. Kraakman, 'Toward Unlimited Shareholder Liability for Corporate Torts' (1991) 100 *Yale Law Journal* 1879, 1884–5.

[139] See American Law Institute, Restatement (Third) of Torts: Products Liability (1998), § 12, comment a. Matheson believes that the rule can operate unfairly against a successor who 'has had no part in creating the injurious product and has no ability to limit future injuries resulting from prior defects': Matheson, 'Successor Liability', 409. He points to alternatives, including the possibility of making liable the shareholders in the dissolved corporation: ibid., 411.

[140] *Ray* v. *Alad* 560 P 2d 39 (Cal 1977). [141] Matheson, 'Successor Liability', 410.

[142] E.g., *Kasel* v. *Remington Arms Co* 24 Cal App 3d 711 (Cal 1972). See Blumberg, *The Law of Corporate Groups*, pp. 265–73. The rules have not been extended so as to create liability in inactive co-subsidiaries: ibid., pp. 275–6.

design defects and inadequate warnings and virtually to preclude liability in pharmaceutical cases under the Restatement (Third) of Torts: Products Liability (1998). For those states that have adopted the Third Restatement, the National Vaccine Injury Compensation Program has only partly filled the liability void in pharmaceuticals cases.[143] This is very unsatisfactory. There have been attempts, further, by a majority of states to cut back on the extent to which non-manufacturing suppliers are liable for defective products to which they have not contributed. In this way, there has been a considerable retrenchment from the notion of network liability. However, this retrenchment has been far from uniform.

8.3 Extended Liability: Polluter-Pays Legislation

This chapter now moves on to consider two related US statutory regimes that facilitate extensions of liability for damage caused by hazardous waste and oil spills (collectively termed the 'polluter-pays legislation'). As mentioned earlier, these statutory regimes feature several innovations in confronting the insolvent entity problem, in that they: impose financial responsibility requirements on industry participants; extend liability beyond owners of oil and other facilities to remote 'operators', so that these parties take responsibility for the prevention of accidents; provide authority to levy taxes on industries causing hazardous waste and oil spills; and authorise trust funds that facilitate clean-up operations. In these ways, the polluter-pays legislation presents some sort of model for extended liability regimes. However, courts have been conservative applying their provisions, heads of recoverable damages are restricted, and actual funding for environmental clean-up has been inadequate.

8.3.1 Comprehensive Environmental Response, Compensation and Liability Act 1980

The Comprehensive Environmental Response, Compensation and Liability Act 1980 (CERCLA)[144] was enacted following the Love Canal

[143] See Chapter 1.

[144] US Code, Title 42, Comprehensive Environmental Response, Compensation and Liability, §§ 9601–75. For the European Union, see Council Directive 2004/35/EC of 21 April 2004 on environmental liability with regard to the prevention and remedying of environmental damage (2004) OJ L143/56; L. Bergkamp, The Environmental Liability Directive and Liability of Parent Companies for Damage Caused by Their Subsidiaries ('Enterprise Liability') (2016) 13 *European Company Law* 183 (explaining the limitations

environmental waste disaster[145] in order to facilitate the remediation of land contaminated by hazardous substances and pollutants.[146] CERCLA has a broad remedial goal.[147] The Environmental Protection Agency (EPA), which administers it,[148] may finance clean-up of contaminated sites[149] and bring suits[150] to recover its costs against various legal persons,[151] including those who: currently own or operate facilities where hazardous substances have been released into the environment; formerly owned or operated facilities from which hazardous substances were disposed of; or generated or arranged for disposal or treatment of hazardous substances that were released into the environment. Private parties can bring actions for remediation costs against the same persons.[152]

As adumbrated, an innovative feature of CERCLA is that it introduces financial responsibility requirements for owners and operators of 'facilities' and 'vessels' in the production, treatment, storage, transportation, or disposal of hazardous substances.[153] Financial responsibility can be established by proof of any one or any combination of insurance, guarantees, surety bonds, or self-insurance. Failure to demonstrate financial responsibility results in the revocation of operating licences. Following a release of hazardous waste or pollutants giving rise to response costs and damage, claims for remediation costs can be made against guarantors who provide evidence of financial responsibility, subject to limited defences.

of the Directive). For Canada, see, e.g., Environmental Protection Act RSO 1990, esp. ss. 91 and 99.

145 A. R. Light, 'The *Deepwater Horizon* Oil Spill Trust and the Gulf Coast Claims Facility: The "Superfund" Myth and the Law of Unintended Consequences' (2011) 5 *Golden Gate University Environmental Law Journal* 87, 89.

146 'Hazardous substance' is defined broadly, and includes most relevant chemicals and metals; but it does not include petroleum or natural gas: 42 USC § 9601(14). For discussion of petroleum and natural gas cases, see text that follows.

147 The statute is not itself regulative: L. A. Silecchia, 'Pinning the Blame & Piercing the Veil in the Mists of Metaphor: The Supreme Court's New Standards for the CERCLA Liability of Parent Companies and a Proposal for Legislative Reform' (1998) 67 *Fordham Law Review* 115, 124.

148 States have their own equivalents of CERCLA and/or can conduct many of the same enforcement activities: see C. D. Thomas, 'Tomorrow's News Today: The Future of Superfund Litigation' (2014) 46 *Arizona State Law Journal* 537, 538.

149 42 USC § 9604(a)(1). 150 42 USC § 9607(a). 151 42 USC § 9607(a).

152 42 USC § 9604(a)(1). Thus there is no ability to recover for personal injury, diminution of property value, or lost profits: see A. B. Klass, 'CERCLA, State Law, and Federalism in the 21st Century' (2012) 41 *Southwestern Law Review* 679, 685.

153 42 USC § 9608.

Potentially liable 'persons' under CERCLA include individuals, firms, corporations, and other business entities.[154] Most litigation has involved director and 'responsible officer' liability.[155] Although the statute does not refer specifically to corporate groups, the potential for parent company liability for the defaults of its subsidiaries has been established judicially. In *United States* v. *Bestfoods*,[156] the US Supreme Court ruled that parent company liability under CERCLA arises by way of exception to the ordinary rule that the parent is not liable for the defaults of its subsidiaries – which is considered a 'bedrock principle'.[157] Parent company liability arises where the parent was the owner of a facility, operator of a facility, or arranger of transportation or disposal. Let us consider each of these possibilities in turn.

In the *Bestfoods* case, the Supreme Court held that CERCLA does not purport to upset ordinary common law rules about when a parent company as owner should be made liable for the debts of subsidiaries.[158] The presumption is 'strongly in favour of preserving the limited liability of the parent corporation'.[159] A parent could be held liable as the owner of a subsidiary under corporate veil-piercing principles only.[160] The court emphasised that CERCLA does not create any new ground for piercing the corporate veil, but is founded upon existing grounds (considered in Chapter 10).[161] Few cases have succeeded under this head of liability.[162]

Frequently, the parent company will not be the actual owner of the facility in question; ownership will reside with a subsidiary or some other party. In such cases, CERCLA liability turns on whether the parent company was an operator.[163] In the *Bestfoods* case, the Supreme Court held that an operator is 'someone who directs the workings of, manages, or conducts the affairs of a facility'.[164] It specified that, in the present

154 42 USC § 9601(21).

155 Individuals have been held liable, e.g. in *Browning-Ferris Industries* v. *Ter Maat* 195 F 3d 953 (7th Cir. 1999)(operator liability); *United States* v. *TIC Investment Corp* 68 F 3d 1982 (8th Cir. 1996)(arranger liability, discussed in text that follows).

156 524 US 51; 118 S Ct 1876 (1998).

157 524 US 51; 118 S Ct 1876, 1885 (1998).

158 524 US 51; 118 S Ct 1876, 1885 (1998).

159 C. A. Schipani, 'The Changing Face of Parent and Subsidiary Corporations: Enterprise Theory and Federal Regulation' (2005) 37 *Connecticut Law Review* 691, 700.

160 524 US 51; 118 S Ct 1876, 1885–6 (1998).

161 524 US 51; 118 S Ct 1876, 1885–6 (1998).

162 Schipani, 'The Changing Face', 714.

163 42 USC § 9607(a)(1); or as 'arrangers', as to which see later in this chapter.

164 524 US 51; 118 S Ct 1876, 1887 (1998). The court distinguished this from operation *of the subsidiary*: ibid., 1887.

context, the operator would be involved in the management or direction of 'operations specifically related to pollution, that is, operations having to do with the leakage or disposal of hazardous waste, or decisions about compliance with environmental regulations'.[165] This 'fault-based standard' focuses on the degree to which the parent company was actively involved in conduct that caused the hazardous substance or pollutant to be released.[166] But, in some cases, courts have extended liability to those who had the capacity to control the operations of the relevant facility, despite the absence of direct participation in the breach.[167] In this way, liability under the Act is seen as strict in nature (arising regardless of fault).[168]

The final basis for parent company liability is as an 'arranger', that is as a person who arranged for disposal or treatment or arranged for transport for disposal or treatment of hazardous substances which they owned or possessed.[169] In *United States* v. *TIC Investment Corp*,[170] the US Court of Appeals for the Eighth Circuit found that a parent company would be liable as an 'arranger' when it exercised substantial control, either directly or indirectly, over the subsidiary's 'arrangement for disposal' or its off-site disposal of the subsidiary's hazardous substances.[171]

Although CERCLA has given rise to controversy in the corporate group context, it should be noted that it is applicable also to extend liabilities in corporate networks when its requirements are satisfied. This is the case where the ownership and operation of facilities are allocated to independent companies that cooperate with each other in commercial ventures.

CERCLA provides an affirmative defence for defendants able to prove that a prohibited release was caused solely by an act or omission of an unrelated third party, and that its own conduct was not negligent. In order to avail itself of the defence, the defendant must prove that the third party has no contractual relationship with it.[172] This emphasises the regime's applicability in the network context. However, the liability of

[165] *United States* v. *Bestfoods* 524 US 51, 67–8; 118 S Ct 1876, 1887 (1998).
[166] M. Dearborn, 'Enterprise Liability: Reviewing and Revitalizing Liability for Corporate Groups' (2009) 97 *California Law Review* 195, 235–6.
[167] *United States* v. *Kayser-Roth Corp* 272 F 3d 89 (1st Cir. 2001).
[168] *United States* v. *Cello-Foil Products Inc* 100 F 3d 1227, 1231 (6th Cir. 1996).
[169] 42 USC § 9607(a)(3). [170] 68 F 3d 1082 (8th Cir. 1995).
[171] 68 F 3d 1082, 1091–2 (8th Cir. 1995). See J. J. White, 'Corporate Judgment Proofing: A Response to Lynn LoPucki's The Death of Liability' (1998) 107 *Yale Law Journal* 1363, 1404.
[172] 42 USC 9607(b)(3).

an owner, operator, or other responsible person for each incident involving release of a hazardous substance is capped to specified sums.[173] But these caps do not apply when the release resulted from wilful misconduct or wilful negligence, or when its primary cause was a violation of federal safety, construction, or operating standards or regulations.[174] The latter exception would appear to be quite wide; thus it has been said that, 'if a violation, no matter how trivial, is discovered the cap is removed.'[175]

It was formerly thought that liability under CERCLA was 'joint and several' in all cases.[176] However, the US Supreme Court has held that apportionment of liability is possible on the basis of Restatement rules[177] – a result which has the potential to 'cut away' at the government's and taxpayers' ability to recover clean-up costs from polluters.[178] When liability is found against multiple parties, damages are apportioned prima facie as follows. There will be: individual liability for each responsible party when there are separate harms;[179] individual liability for indivisible harms without a reasonable basis for apportionment;[180] and joint and several liability in cases of indivisible harms without a reasonable basis for apportionment.[181] However, it appears that courts rarely permit apportionment of indivisible harms; the presumption is one of joint and several liability.[182]

In addition to facilitating extended liability for contamination by hazardous substances and pollutants, CERCLA authorises the Hazardous Substances Superfund[183] to finance clean-up response costs incurred by the US government or by other persons,[184] and to undertake clean-up also when either no responsible party can be identified or the responsible party

173 42 USC 9607(c)(1). 174 42 USC 9607(c)(2).

175 M. A. Cohen, M. Gottlieb, J. Linn, and N. Richardson, 'Deepwater Drilling: Law, Policy, and Economics of Firm Organization and Safety' (2011) 64 *Vanderbilt Law Review* 1853, 1890 (referring to similar provisions in the Oil Pollution Act 1990, considered later).

176 *United States* v. *Chem-Dyne Corp* 572 F Supp 802, 810–11 (SD Ohio 1983).

177 American Law Institute, Restatement (Second) of Torts (1977), § 433A, applied in *Burlington Northern & Santa Fe Railway Co v. United States* 129 S Ct 1870 (2009).

178 R. Brady, 'CERCLA Apportionment Following *Burlington Northern*: How Joint and Several Liability Still Thrives – To the Surprise of Many' (2014) 4 *Washington Journal of Environmental Law & Policy* 141, 143.

179 *In re Bell Petroleum Services, Inc* 3 F 3d 889, 901–2 (5th Cir. 1993).

180 *Burlington Northern & Santa Fe Railway Co* v. *United States* 129 S Ct 1870 (2009).

181 See A. Gershonowitz, 'The End of Joint and Several Liability in Superfund Litigation: From *Chem-Dyne* to *Burlington Northern*' (2012) 50 *Duquesne Law Review* 83.

182 'CERCLA Apportionment', 175.

183 Established under US Code, Title 26, Hazardous Substance Superfund, § 9507.

184 42 USC § 9611(a).

is unable to pay for clean-up operations.[185] The Superfund typically is accessed to permit remediation of sites contaminated by a complex mix of chemical substances which impacts upon groundwater, surface water, or soil and has the potential to cause serious health problems.[186] In 2014, there were thirty Superfund-nominated sites which featured contamination by asbestos. Although the Superfund was funded initially through taxes on crude oil and certain chemical industries, authority for the imposition of these taxes expired in 1995.[187] Since then, the majority of funding has come from US federal budgetary appropriations.[188] Superfund balances have diminished over time,[189] so that presently it is capable of pursuing only a fraction of necessary remediation work.

Although liability under CERCLA is broad in terms of the persons covered and in terms of the strictness of their liability, the Act is narrower when viewed in light of damages awards that can be made. There is no provision for recovery of important heads of damage, including personal injuries, diminution in private property values, and various financial losses.[190] (By contrast, some US states do permit recovery for these sorts of loss. The Minnesota Environmental Response and Liability Act 1983, for example, permits recovery for personal injury claims.[191]) Moreover, CERCLA has been criticised, in cases of operator liability, for creating liabilities based upon parent company *actions and involvement*, but not for their omissions. In fact, the legislation is said to encourage parent companies to turn a blind eye to the environmental policies and practices of subsidiaries. Thus the law creates a disincentive against parent companies intervening in subsidiary affairs;[192] the prudent and logical advice is that

185 42 USC § 9611(b).

186 US Environmental Protection Agency, 'Fiscal Year 2016: Justification of Appropriation Estimates for the Committee on Appropriations' (Feb. 2015), p. 54. In 2011, approximately 49 million people lived within three miles of a Superfund site: ibid., p. 684. The number of potentially hazardous sites is greater than 40,000: US Government Accountability Office, 'Superfund: Funding and Reported Costs of Enforcement and Administration Activities' (July 2008), p. 1.

187 US Government Accountability Office, Superfund: Funding and Reported Costs, p. 2.

188 US Government Accountability Office, Superfund: Funding and Reported Costs, p. 2.

189 US Government Accountability Office, Superfund: Funding and Reported Costs, pp. 3 and 9.

190 Klass, 'CERCLA, State Law, and Federalism in the 21st Century'. However, this does not prevent recourse to state laws, which might be more accommodative: ibid., 686, n. 26.

191 Minnesota Statutes Annotated, Ch. 114C–116i, Environmental Protection, §§ 115B.05 and 115B.14, discussed in Klass, 'CERCLA, State Law and Federalism in the 21st Century', 686ff. However, the Minnesota statute has its own limits: ibid., 686–7.

192 Silecchia, 'Pinning the Blame', 124. See also Schipani, 'The Changing Face', 704.

they 'shun all unnecessary involvement with their subsidiaries' facilities'.[193] CERCLA has been criticised also for encouraging lawsuits against peripheral parties, thus deflecting responsibility from others that would be primarily liable.[194] Indeed, it has given rise to a 'ponderous litigation-oriented regime with high transaction costs'.[195]

8.3.2 Oil Pollution Act 1990

CERCLA does not apply to environmental incidents involving oil spills; in such cases, the Oil Pollution Act 1990 (OPA) applies instead.[196] This legislation facilitates federal oversight of oil drilling and transportation, and provides important environmental safeguards by: setting requirements for vessel construction, mandating contingency planning, enhancing US federal response capability, broadening enforcement authority, increasing potential liabilities, and imposing broad financial responsibility requirements.[197] The OPA sets out a framework for making claims for damage from vessel- and facility-caused oil pollution occurring in US navigable waters.[198] The framework has many elements in common with CERCLA, but gives rise to more comprehensive protection in terms of losses covered. The OPA imposes strict, joint, and several liability for damage caused by oil spills. The intention was to ensure oil spill costs are internalised within industry.[199] The provisions on vessels are administered by the US Coast Guard, which operates the National Pollution Funds Center, while its provisions on offshore facilities are administered by the Bureau of Ocean Energy Management.[200] OPA liability does not preclude the further imposition of liability under state law.[201]

193 Silecchia, 'Pinning the Blame', 178–9.

194 M. De Blasi, 'Liability of Parent Corporations, Officers, Directors, and Successors: When Can CERCLA Liability Extend beyond the Company?' (2014) 46 *Arizona State Law Review* 481, 481.

195 Light, 'The *Deepwater Horizon* Oil Spill', 88.

196 US Code, Title 33, Chapter 40, Oil Pollution §§ 2701–2761.

197 US Coast Guard, 'Oil Pollution Act of 1990 (OPA)' (2016) available at: www.uscg.mil/npfc/About_NPFC/opa.asp. The need for the legislation is evident in the fact that there have been close to 5,000 relevant oil spills between 1990 and 2015: US Coast Guard, 'Oil Pollution Act Liability Limits in 2015: Report to Congress' (October 2015), p. 5.

198 33 USC § 2702(a).

199 *Rice* v. *Harken Exploration Co* 250 F 3d 264, 266 (5th Cir. 2001).

200 See Bureau of Ocean Energy Management, 'BOEM Governing Statutes' (Undated), available at: www.boem.gov/Governing-Statutes/; J. D. Morgan, 'The Oil Pollution Act of 1990: A Look at its Impact on the Oil Industry' (1994) 6 *Fordham International Law Journal* 1, 13, and 21.

201 Cohen, Gottlieb, Linn, and Richardson, 'Deepwater Drilling', 1889.

In a manner similar to CERCLA, the OPA requires that operators of offshore facilities and of vessels establish financial responsibility prior to commencement of operations.[202] For offshore facilities, for example, the OPA mandates that responsible parties demonstrate the availability of US $35 million, subject to increase by the president up to a maximum of $150 million.[203] Following an oil spill giving rise to response costs and damage, claims can be made against responsible parties and (subject to limited defences) against guarantors that provide evidence of financial responsibility.[204] Ideally, financial responsibility would mandate significant *external* insurance cover, which creates incentives for external monitoring. But many oil industry participants act as self-insurers.[205] 'In this sense, it is fortunate that BP plc, and not a smaller firm, was the responsible party for the *Deepwater Horizon* spill' (considered in Chapter 4). 'Many smaller drilling firms would have been unable to cover the multi-billion dollar liability and would have gone bankrupt.'[206]

The OPA takes hold where there is an oil discharge or a substantial threat of a discharge into US navigable waters or adjoining shorelines, or into its exclusive economic zone.[207] In order to create simplicity in the regime it creates, the OPA 'channels' responsibility to predefined parties. This is important, given that oil-drilling operations typically involve several partners and contractors. Channelling 'creates incentives for a responsible party to select and monitor partners and subcontractors with care, since the responsible party is ultimately responsible for damage claims'.[208] In the case of an oil discharge from a vessel, the OPA defines 'responsible party' as encompassing 'any person owning or operating' the vessel.[209] In this, the Act creates 'a default presumption assigning liability to owners and operators of vessels that discharge oil into the navigable waters of the United States'.[210] In the case of an oil discharge from an offshore facility, the 'responsible party' means the holder of the drilling

[202] 33 USC § 2716. [203] 33 USC § 2716(c)(1)(C).

[204] In the case of external insurers, this reduces the possibility that liability cannot be satisfied because insurers have avoided policies: Morgan, 'The Oil Pollution Act of 1990', 25.

[205] Cohen, Gottlieb, Linn, and Richardson, 'Deepwater Drilling', 1900. Cf. Morgan, 'The Oil Pollution Act of 1990', 15 (expressing doubts about the feasibility of self-insurance).

[206] Cohen, Gottlieb, Linn, and Richardson, 'Deepwater Drilling', 1895.

[207] 33 USC § 2702(a).

[208] Cohen, Gottlieb, Linn, and Richardson, 'Deepwater Drilling', 1889.

[209] 33 USC § 2701(32)(A).

[210] *Bean Dredging LLC* v. *United States* 773 F Supp 2d 63, 86 (DDC 2011).

permit.[211] Responsible parties are liable to compensate for the causation of damage regardless of fault; liability is strict in nature.[212] This is seen as appropriate because of the clear understanding that the predefined parties take responsibility for oil operations, and because it reduces litigation costs.[213] As we have seen, provisions like these have the potential to create liability in parent companies,[214] as well as in relevant network participants. Indeed, while OPA provisions are intended to facilitate straightforward claims by injured parties, they do not preclude legal actions by responsible parties against industry partners.[215] The legislation simply shifts the burden of establishing fault-based liability to responsible parties, who are provided with incentives to protect their legal position through appropriate contractual terms, ongoing monitoring, and/or litigation.[216]

In terms similar to CERCLA, the OPA provides an affirmative defence for responsible parties that can prove that an oil spill was caused solely by an act or omission of an unrelated third party, and that its own conduct was not negligent. The defence applies only where the responsible parties have no contractual relationships with those third parties.[217]

Responsible parties are liable for the full costs of remediating public land, shorelines, inland waterways, and US coastal waters.[218] Claims can be made for the costs of removal of oil spills[219] and for various heads of damages.[220] Damages claims encompass: damage to real and personal property;[221] natural resources losses, including costs of restoring, rehabilitating, or replacing the claimant's natural resources as well as the diminution in value of those resources pending restoration;[222] and purely financial losses such as lost profits.[223] Claims for personal injury are

211 33 USC § 2701(32)(C). 212 Morgan, 'The Oil Pollution Act of 1990', 4.

213 Cohen, Gottlieb, Linn, and Richardson, 'Deepwater Drilling', 1889.

214 See also Morgan, 'The Oil Pollution Act of 1990', 9. 215 33 USC §§ 2712 and 2717.

216 C. McDonell, 'The Gulf Coast Claims Facility and the *Deepwater Horizon* Litigation: Judicial Regulation of Private Compensation Schemes' (2012) 64 *Stanford Law Review* 765, 768–9.

217 33 USC § 2703(a)(3). See Light, 'The *Deepwater Horizon* Oil Spill', 94–5.

218 33 USC § 2702. See Light, 'The *Deepwater Horizon* Oil Spill', 97.

219 33 USC § 2702(a). 220 33 USC § 2702(b). 221 33 USC § 2702(b)(2)(B).

222 33 USC § 2702(b)(2)(A). These are payable to designated 'Natural Resource Trustees' rather than to private parties: see US Coast Guard, 'Oil Spill Liability Trust Fund (OSLTF) Funding for Oil Spills' (January 2006), p. 11.

223 33 USC § 2702(b)(2)(E). See, generally, McDonell, 'The Gulf Coast Claims Facility', 768–9. 'OPA favors restoration and remediation to try to bring the resource back to its pre-spill condition': W. K. Viscusi and R. J. Zeckhauser, 'Deterring and Compensating Oil-Spill Catastrophes: The Need for Strict Two-Tier Liability' (2011) 64 *Vanderbilt Law Review*

precluded.[224] The total amount of damages payable is subject to various caps, depending on the entity responsible for the spill.[225] However, the caps do not apply in situations of gross negligence, wilful misconduct, or violation of applicable federal regulations pertaining to safety, construction, or operation.[226] As already noted with respect to similar provisions in CERCLA, the latter exception would appear to be a wide one because of the great number of relevant rules in existence – meaning that caps apply rarely.[227]

In a manner similar to CERCLA, the OPA provides financing mechanisms for a trust fund,[228] which, in this case, is used to cover the costs of oil spill clean-up and to meet uncompensated private claims up to a value of US$1 billion per oil spill incident.[229] The Oil Spill Liability Trust Fund (OSLTF), which is administered by the National Pollution Funds Center (NPFC),[230] has two components:[231] first, the Emergency Fund, which comprises a sum set aside each year[232] for rapid response to oil spills and which requires no appropriation by Congress. It can be used for oil spill containment, countermeasures, clean-up, and disposal activities. Second is the Principal Fund, which can be used to pay uncompensated private

1717, 1741. The availability of damages for purely financial losses represents a change from pre-existing law: C. M. Sharkey, 'The BP Oil Spill Settlements, Classwide Punitive Damages, and Societal Deterrence' (2015) 64 *DePaul Law Review* 681, 695.

224 Light, 'The *Deepwater Horizon* Oil Spill', 90.

225 33 USC § 2704(a). Arguments have been made for abolition of the caps because of their potential to cause 'moral hazard': e.g., M. Greenstone, 'Liability and Financial Responsibility for Oil Spills under the Oil Pollution Act of 1990 and Related States' (Testimony before House of Representatives Committee on Transportation and Infrastructure)(9 June 2010), available at: www.brookings.edu/research/testimony/2010/06/09-oil-spill-greenstone.

226 33 USC § 2704(c). See Viscusi and Zeckhauser, 'Deterring and Compensating', 1739–40.

227 Cohen, Gottlieb, Linn, and Richardson, 'Deepwater Drilling', 1890; I. Kim, 'Financial Responsibility Rules under the Oil Pollution Act of 1990' (2002) 42 *Natural Resources Law Journal* 565, 566. The caps have been described as 'deceptive': Morgan, 'The Oil Pollution Act of 1990', 7. But where caps *are* applicable, so that the Oil Spill Liability Trust Fund must pay, the numbers do add up. Between enactment and 2015, the trust was required to cover US$1.3 billion in removal costs: US Coast Guard, 'Oil Pollution Act Liability Limits', p. 9.

228 The fund was created prior to passage of the Oil Pollution Act 1990, but was provided with funding only after the *Exxon Valdez* disaster: US Coast Guard, 'Oil Pollution Act Liability Limits', p. 2.

229 US Code, Title 26, Hazardous Substance Superfund, § 9509.

230 National Pollution Funds Center, 'Oil Pollution Act of 1990 (OPA)'.

231 US Coast Guard, 'The Oil Spill Liability Trust Fund (OSLTF)'.

232 This sum has been modest and currently stands at US$50 million per year, with the possibility of obtaining a further $100 million advance from the Principal Fund if necessary: US Coast Guard, 'The Oil Spill Liability Trust Fund (OSLTF)'.

removal costs and, potentially, could satisfy damages claims where a responsible party is not identified, is unable to pay, or has reached the applicable liability limit.[233] While the OSLTF frequently has been used for discharges from ships, in recent times it has been used for discharges at industrial and onshore oil storage and production facilities.[234] The OSLTF has been used almost exclusively to pay for clean-up costs, rather than damages – it not having received sufficient appropriations for the latter.[235] The Principal Fund derives its revenues from several sources, including a nine-cent-per-barrel excise tax on oil, cost recoveries from responsible parties, and criminal penalties and civil fines.[236]

Passage of the Oil Pollution Act 1990 resulted in significant restructuring of parts of the oil industry and insurance provision, reflecting a desire on the part of industry participants to avoid the internalisation of oil spill costs that Congress sought to achieve. Two notable effects were: first, there was significant disaggregation, in that parent companies moved towards subsidiaries with smaller fleets in order to protect group assets,[237] although this does not necessarily defeat the liability of the parent company should it be characterised as a responsible party.[238] Whether this is so or not, subdivision of fleets makes it more difficult to enforce the OPA – especially when the bulk of corporate group assets is held outside the United States.[239] Second, captive insurers refused to provide financial responsibility statements, which would make them liable as guarantors.[240] In this, they demonstrated concern about the stability of OPA liability caps, and about the potential for further liability under state laws.[241] This second change in practice has spawned a sub-insurance market for financial responsibility purposes only.[242] Although internalisation of costs within the industry has been deficient, the presence of external insurers does introduce a level of independent monitoring of industry practices.

[233] US Code, Title 33, Chapter 40, Oil Pollution, § 2708.

[234] US Coast Guard, 'The Oil Spill Liability Trust Fund (OSLTF)'.

[235] Light, 'The *Deepwater Horizon* Oil Spill', 90; L. I. Kiern, 'Liability, Compensation, and Financial Responsibility under the Oil Pollution Act of 1990: A Review of the Second Decade' (2011) 36 *Tulane Maritime Law Journal* 1, 55.

[236] US Coast Guard, 'The Oil Spill Liability Trust Fund (OSLTF)'.

[237] Morgan, 'The Oil Pollution Act of 1990', 8–9.

[238] Kim, 'Financial Responsibility Rules', 568.

[239] Kim, 'Financial Responsibility Rules', 569.

[240] Morgan, 'The Oil Pollution Act of 1990', 14.

[241] Kim, 'Financial Responsibility Rules', 573–4.

[242] Kim, 'Financial Responsibility Rules', 577.

It has been said that the consequences of the OPA's polluter-pays approach have become evident in the aftermath of the *Deepwater Horizon* oil spill (discussed in Chapter 4), 'given that BP quickly accepted designation as the "responsible party" under OPA and committed publicly to pay both for the clean-up and all "legitimate claims"'.[243] BP agreed to waive the $75 million claims limit notionally applicable to it; indeed, total costs for clean-up, penalties, fines, and damages will exceed US$55 billion.[244] Although BP will pay the majority of the costs of the *Deepwater Horizon* oil spill, and thus internalise most of the loss (subject to what is said in what follows), that event highlighted inadequacies in the OPA regime. 'The limited amount of emergency funding available, the low per-incident caps, and the small size of the OSLTF all seem woefully inadequate when compared to the extraordinary costs and potential damages for which it may be responsible in a major oil spill.'[245] Indeed, although *Deepwater Horizon* is the best known, there have been dozens of oil spills in each of which the damages claims have exceeded the liability caps placed on responsible parties, and for which the OSLTF has had to cover the funding deficit.[246] The simple fact is that 'the Fund is the ultimate insurer with respect to oil removal costs and damages when there is a discharge or substantial threat of discharge to navigable waters, adjoining shorelines, or the exclusive economic zone.'[247] It is not surprising that the US Coast Guard believes formal OPA liability caps to be too low for offshore facility incidents.[248] By contrast, drilling firms' exposure to liability is much greater under most state laws.[249] Florida and Texas, for example, permit uncapped liability.[250]

8.3.3 *Summary of Polluter-Pays Legislation*

CERCLA and the OPA demonstrate the ability of legislatures to create potentially useful regimes under which liability for massive environmental clean-up costs can be extended beyond insolvent group and network

[243] Kiern, 'Liability, Compensation', 5–6.
[244] E. Crooks, 'US Court Signs Off on BP's $20bn Oil Spill Settlement', *Financial Times*, 5 April 2016, available at: https://next.ft.com/content/ca842362-faee-11e5-b3f6-11d5706b613b.
[245] Kiern, 'Liability, Compensation', 62.
[246] US Coast Guard, 'Oil Pollution Act Liability Limits', pp. 3–8.
[247] US Coast Guard, 'Oil Pollution Act Liability Limits', p. 12.
[248] US Coast Guard, 'Oil Pollution Act Liability Limits', p. 13.
[249] Cohen, Gottlieb, Linn, and Richardson, 'Deepwater Drilling', 1891.
[250] Cohen, Gottlieb, Linn, and Richardson, 'Deepwater Drilling', 1891.

companies. Indeed, the polluter-pays legislation makes significant inroads into the separate legal personality and limited liability principles protective of parent companies in corporate groups. Moreover, caps on liability, while having assuaged industry participants at the time of the statutes' enactment, have not always applied because of the ease with which breaches of relevant federal laws are committed by responsible parties, these breaches resulting in the disapplication of the caps. Despite the *potential* (on paper) for virtually unlimited parent company liability under these statutes, which has been understood by polluting industries and has led to some evasive action, there have been no notable, enduring, adverse stock market reactions to the extended liability rules.

However, the polluter-pays legislation has its shortcomings. First, courts have been conservative in their application of the statutory liability rules which permit extensions of liability, reflecting continuing nervousness about the position of parent companies. Second, the heads of recoverable damages under both CERCLA and the OPA are restricted in nature, which means that losses are not fully internalised within affected industries. Third, liabilities imposed under the legislation are not as high as the headline figures suggest, again detracting from the goal of internalisation. This is because of the tax-deductibility of many clean-up costs. Thus, while BP plc incurred significant OPA and other statutory liabilities for the *Deepwater Horizon* oil spill, many of its expenses are deductible against taxable income, resulting in savings of billions of dollars.[251] This loss of tax revenue means that taxpayers continue to absorb social losses. Fourth, the trusts which CERCLA and the OPA authorise have not been funded properly, essentially because of a political failure to impose sufficient taxes and levies. This means that remediation work is not being undertaken in all cases where it is necessary. Fifth, the polluter-pays legislation can be no more than a complement to what is really required in order to resolve the insolvent entity problem – that is, a comprehensive means of extending liability in corporate groups and networks for unsatisfied personal injury claims.

8.4 Conclusions

When we consider the various statutes applicable to corporate groups surveyed in Part III of this book, several patterns emerge. First, it is clear

[251] The estimated tax off-set is US$4.6 billion: M. Conathan, 'The True Value of BP's $18.7 billion Settlement' (Alternet, 2015), available at: www.alternet.org/environment/true-value-bps-187-billion-settlement.

that legislatures have, from the second half of the twentieth century, paid increasing attention to the problems presented by corporate groups, including the insolvent entity problem. Corporate groups are subject now to increased transparency requirements relating to ownership and control, they are given reason to consolidate their accounts for reporting purposes, and there is provision in some statutory regimes for the undertaking of cross-guarantees for insolvent company liabilities. Second, statute law seeks to prevent the misuse of the corporate form, through various types of provision aimed at preventing the shuttling of assets and similar abusive practices. These abusive practices need to be prevented because they might endanger creditor interests. Third, various kinds of statutory law exist under which liability can be extended within the corporate group, whether on the basis of abusive transactions (for example, under pooling and contribution provisions), or on the basis of legislative interest in ensuring redress for certain kinds of accident (under products liability, CERCLA, and the OPA). Statutes reviewed in the latter part of this chapter have the added advantage that they largely respect the business form neutrality principle discussed in Chapter 1, which dictates that a liability regime should not unduly penalise the undertaking of business in one form (say, the corporate group) rather than another (the network). These regimes encompass both corporate group and network liabilities. This is all well and good. But something is missing. What is missing is legislative focus upon something other than transaction and industry types. As adumbrated, that something is personal injury. In Chapters 1 and 3, reasons were given for treating this as a special type of injury. The assertion being made here is that statutory and/or common law rules are required to provide satisfactory avenues of redress when companies cause personal injury and the insolvent entity problem arises. This must be done on a consistent basis, rather than on an ad hoc basis. The reality is that personal injuries can arise in a multitude of ways and in virtually any industry. There is something unfair about making provision for those injured by products, for example, but not making provision for those injured in other ways by corporate activity. In the next chapters of this book, an attempt will be made to put some of these things right.

9

Modified Limited Liability

9.1 Introduction

We now commence consideration of ways in which the insolvent entity problem can be addressed on a basis that is consistent, rather than ad hoc, and which adheres to the business form neutrality principle (explained in Chapter 1). This chapter presents the first part of a two-part solution to the problem, which involves extended shareholder liability. It starts from the premise that the legislative policy of promoting entrepreneurship and growth through the use of the corporate form is legitimate. Use of the corporate form entails risk-sharing by economic actors, and the protection of shareholders from ordinary financial losses. However, there is no justification for putting the interests of shareholders ahead of the interests of victims of personal injury who cannot obtain full compensation because of debtor company insolvency.

This chapter considers a range of existing proposals for reform of the rule of limited liability. Many of these proposals treat control as an important criterion of shareholder liability,[1] but this chapter points to several problems with this, and argues that the exercise of control often is used as a proxy for fault-based liability. Argument is made that shareholders are eligible to be made liable for unsatisfied personal injury claims against their investee companies on other grounds. Shareholders have important attributes which make them eligible for extended liability, including: the function they play in arming their investee companies with capital; their role as company insiders, being part of a collective or group called 'the company'; the fact that companies are organised types of group, and shareholders occupy the highest place in the corporate hierarchy; the ability of injured tort victims to identify shareholders with their investee companies; the lower order of importance of shareholders' financial interests in their investee

[1] See R. Kraakman et al., *The Anatomy of Corporate Law: A Comparative and Functional Approach* (2004), p. 92. Cf. C. Kutz, *Complicity – Ethics and Law for a Collective Age* (2000), and discussion that follows in this chapter.

companies compared to the claims of personal injury victims; and the latter's better claim in a comparative contest over responsibility for personal injuries. Additional reasons for creating an exception to limited liability *applicable to parent companies* include: the greater array of assets from which judgments might be satisfied, and, in the case of multinational groups, the procedural benefits of suing the parent company when located within certain jurisdictions, including the ability to bring class actions.[2]

This chapter argues for a statutory modification to the law of limited liability for application in cases of insolvent subsidiaries unable fully to compensate personal injury victims. The proposed rule of 'modified limited liability' would create strict liability in shareholders for such losses. There are good arguments for *statutory* reform in this area. First, current rules of separate legal personality and limited liability are enshrined in statute, and any exception to these two rules should be set out in legislation as well. This is the case, especially, for exceptions that are of a strict liability nature. Second, statutory reform would help courts in overcoming their reluctance to undermine these two rules, this reluctance being a product of concern about the potential consequences that shareholder liability would have upon the operation of the business world. Third, statutory reform would create more certainty about the circumstances in which exceptions to separate legal personality and limited liability were to apply, which would assist the marketplace to price potential liability costs.[3]

Before examining the most important of the proposals for exceptions to limited liability, something explicit should be said about how these proposals might be compared with each other and with the present writer's own suggestion for reform. Commentators have pointed to a number of criteria for assessing rules of extended liability. Although compensating the injured is an important objective, reform should be implemented with a view to retaining 'certainty in the market and promoting economic stability and growth'.[4] The UNCITRAL 'Legislative Guide on Insolvency Law' lists more specific desiderata including: clear rules for ranking of creditor claims, which to the greatest extent possible should be based upon commercial agreements between affected parties;[5] transparency of

2 S. Joseph, *Corporations and Transnational Human Rights Litigation* (2004), p. 129.

3 See also G. Skinner, 'Rethinking Limited Liability of Parent Corporations for Foreign Subsidiaries' Violations of International Human Rights' (2015) 72 *Washington & Lee Law Review* 1769, 1786, and 1849–50.

4 UNCITRAL, 'Legislative Guide on Insolvency Law' (2005), p. 13.

5 UNCITRAL, 'Legislative Guide on Insolvency Law', 9 and 13.

procedures;[6] and the ability of commercial parties to predict the outcome of the process, so that they know how their rights will be affected. Having rules that meet these criteria will allow both creditors and equity investors 'to calculate the economic implications of default by the debtor and so estimate their risks'.[7] This chapter addresses the first and the third of these desiderata in formulating its proposal for modified limited liability.

9.2 Existing Proposals for Reform

Chapter 6 of this book considered enterprise liability as a basis for extending liability within the corporate group, including proposals for reform by Adolf Berle,[8] Phillip Blumberg,[9] and Meredith Dearborn.[10] Enterprise liability was rejected for reasons which include its lack of standards for extending liability to the parent company, the extensive evidence upon which liability would depend, uncertainty about the extent of parent company liabilities, the potential for the rights of existing unsecured creditors to be upset, and the difficulty of preventing unintended spillovers so as to create a form of network liability. The view was taken that the law must adopt the entity as the basic unit of responsibility in the corporate group context. The reasons for this, in short, are that entity principles are fundamental to company law,[11] and that both the legislature and the courts have found it difficult to jettison these principles in the absence of clear legislative guidance. The proposals for extended liability considered in this chapter respect entity law.[12]

Several corporate law experts have conducted studies of corporate groups, and considered how best to accommodate claims for extended liability. Some proposals would create liability in parent companies on the basis of the exercise of control and an element of wrongdoing which

[6] UNCITRAL, 'Legislative Guide on Insolvency Law', 9 and 13.

[7] UNCITRAL, 'Legislative Guide on Insolvency Law', 15.

[8] A. A. Berle, 'The Theory of Enterprise Entity' (1947) 47 *Columbia Law Review* 343.

[9] See, e.g., P. I. Blumberg, *The Multinational Challenge to Corporation Law: The Search for a New Corporate Personality* (1993), and P. I. Blumberg, 'The Transformation of Modern Corporation Law: The Law of Corporate Groups' (2005) 37 *Connecticut Law Review* 605.

[10] M. Dearborn, 'Enterprise Liability: Reviewing and Revitalizing Liability for Corporate Groups' (2009) 97 *California Law Review* 195.

[11] See Chapter 3.

[12] The proposals to be considered apply generally to corporate groups. However, the literature contains also several more specific proposals, such as one related to the oil industry: see W. K. Viscusi and R. J. Zeckhauser, 'Deterring and Compensating Oil-Spill Catastrophes: The Need for Strict Two-Tier Liability' (2011) 64 *Vanderbilt Law Review* 1717.

leads to insolvency in the subsidiary and the accumulation of unpaid debts. Writers adopting this approach include Andrew Muscat and Irit Mevorach. They see the exercise of control as normatively significant and a basis for responsibility.[13] Responsibility would follow from parental decision-making that impacts upon the subsidiary in the form of, for example, excessive undercapitalisation, diversion of business opportunities, asset shifting, and/or artificial integration with other group companies where this action leads to subsidiary insolvency.[14] Muscat argues for liability based on factors such as the extent and duration of parental domination and the extent to which insolvency is attributable to its abusive conduct.[15] A remedy against the parent, available in favour of both voluntary and involuntary creditors,[16] would vest in the subsidiary liquidator, who would pursue claims on behalf of the insolvent estate.[17] This would reduce litigation costs and preserve the 'procedural unity of liquidation proceedings and the collective regime of insolvency'.[18] In addition to this, Mevorach would leave open the potential for substantive consolidation in cases of abusive asset integration.[19] In the view of the present writer, restricting extensions of liability to parent companies that have exercised control is unsatisfactory – for reasons which will be developed in what follows. Moreover, personal injury claimants should not be required to prove wrongdoing by parent companies.

José Antunes offers a proposal for modest reform. He argues for liability of the parent company based on the presence of an insolvent subsidiary company, unpaid debts, parental control over subsidiary management, and a causal relationship between the exercise of control and the unpaid debts.[20] However, because of the difficulty of obtaining detailed evidence about the

[13] I. Mevorach, *Insolvency within Multinational Enterprise Groups* (2009), p. 316.

[14] Mevorach, *Insolvency within Multinational Enterprise Groups*, p. 316. Muscat concentrates on the 'subservient subsidiary situation', in which a parent company dominates decision-making in a subsidiary company to the disadvantage of both the subsidiary and its creditors: A. Muscat, *The Liability of the Holding Company for the Debts of its Insolvent Subsidiaries* (1996), p. 300.

[15] Muscat, *The Liability of the Holding Company*, p. 304.

[16] Muscat, *The Liability of the Holding Company*, p. 303.

[17] Muscat, *The Liability of the Holding Company*, p. 302.

[18] Muscat, *The Liability of the Holding Company*, pp. 302–3.

[19] Mevorach, *Insolvency within Multinational Enterprise Groups*, pp. 316–18.

[20] J. Antunes, *Liability of Corporate Groups: Autonomy and Control in Parent–Subsidiary Relationships in US, German and EU Law* (1994), pp. 396 and 406. A similar proposal would extend liability in cases of personal injury claims only: D. Jackson QC, 'Report of the Special Commission of Inquiry into the Medical Research and Compensation Fund' (2004), Annexure 'T', p. 417.

operation of corporate groups, Antunes proposes a reversal of the onus of proof: 'it should be up to the parent corporation to bring evidence on whether such business decisions have originated from its own control or have been taken autonomously by the subsidiary.'[21] 'It would then be up to the parent corporation itself to prevent its own exposure to a liability burden by taking careful consideration of the degree and the way in which it exerts control over the various group affiliates.'[22] A defence would be available when the parent can demonstrate 'sound and diligent management of group affiliates'.[23] The problems of control aside, a reversal of the onus of proof is a positive feature of Antunes' proposal because external tort claimants are at a disadvantage when forced to prove the inner workings of parent companies (as we saw in Chapter 8).

We now turn to extended discussion of several more ambitious proposals for the extension of liability within corporate groups. These are proposals by Nina Mendelson, Henry Hansmann and Renier Kraakman, and Christopher Kutz. Their proposals move beyond orthodox thinking about shareholders and assist in conceptualising what is submitted to be the appropriate rule.

Nina Mendelson would move away from a liability regime which is confined to parent companies and which is based upon the exercise of control. She argues that all shareholders with the *capacity* to exercise control over the activities of their investee companies should be liable in an unlimited amount.[24] Mendelson explains the importance of equity ownership in a company, which provides the capacity to control. Those who control the company have better access to information than do ordinary shareholders, the ability to influence management decisions, and 'special opportunities to benefit from corporate activity', including the ability to find synergies with associated businesses, to control the payment of dividends, and to write off the losses of one subsidiary against another.[25] 'In general, . . . the controlling shareholder or parent can realize a benefit from a new corporate activity in excess of its pro rata share.' Because of this, such a shareholder 'is more likely to find hazardous activities attractive and to prompt corporate management to approve activities that present the small risk of a large loss'.[26]

21 Antunes, *Liability of Corporate Groups*, p. 401.
22 Antunes, *Liability of Corporate Groups*, p. 389.
23 Antunes, *Liability of Corporate Groups*, p. 410.
24 N. Mendelson, 'A Control-Based Approach to Shareholder Liability for Corporate Torts' (2002) 102 *Columbia Law Review* 1203.
25 Mendelson, 'A Control-Based Approach', 1206.
26 Mendelson, 'A Control-Based Approach', 1258.

In setting out her proposal, Mendelson recognises that key shareholders have a greater capacity to avoid the causation of harm caused by their companies than do tort victims. 'Compared with an individual tort victim, controlling and institutional shareholders both can better monitor the extent of the firm's research into product risks and act on that information to influence the corporation to address the risks.'[27] 'In addition to imposing liability on shareholders exercising actual control over a corporation by virtue of ownership, a "capacity to control" regime would impose vicarious liability for a corporation's torts and statutory violations on those possessing potential control by virtue of ownership of the corporation. A potentially controlling shareholder's attempt to maintain a more passive role would not shield it from liability for risky corporate activity.'[28] The incentive would be to reduce risky activity levels.[29] Liability would be joint and several with a right to contribution if more than one defendant meets the criterion of capacity to control,[30] although (in the view of the present writer) this is likely to be a rare occurrence unless cooperation among significant minority shareholders permits them each to be characterised as having the capacity to control.

We will consider the problems of control-based liability regimes in detail later. Mendelson herself sees the difficulties in determining when the capacity to control subsists in a minority shareholder, and sets out factors relevant to the determination of this issue.[31] But this looks like it would become a far more complicated exercise than determining where control is actually exercised. Mendelson acknowledges also that her proposal has a significant hole in it because it offers no compensation for tort victims where no shareholder has control.[32] 'A control-based liability regime could create an incentive for shareholders to avoid control completely, so that corporations would no longer have controlling shareholders.' Although Mendelson believes this unlikely to happen 'in view of the substantial benefits of possessing control',[33] shareholders would respond to her proposal, in all probability, by either consolidating their control over investee companies, so as to regulate exposure to

27 Mendelson, 'A Control-Based Approach', 1222.
28 Mendelson, 'A Control-Based Approach', 1272–3.
29 Mendelson, 'A Control-Based Approach', 1283.
30 Mendelson, 'A Control-Based Approach', 1271. One potential problem is that this reintroduces the need for costly monitoring by shareholders of management and of each other (discussed in Chapter 3).
31 See Mendelson, 'A Control-Based Approach', 1273.
32 Mendelson, 'A Control-Based Approach', 1280–1.
33 Mendelson, 'A Control-Based Approach', 1292.

liability, or reducing it well below the control threshold, so as to avoid the prospect of liability. In the latter case, Mendelson notes that management would have control itself, and asserts that 'managerial risk aversion would continue to deter these corporations from selecting excessively risky actions.'[34] Indeed, one would expect a level of deterrence, but also occasional cases of reckless risk-taking by managers, such as has been evident throughout corporate history (including in the case studies considered in Chapter 4). Whatever the case might be, Mendelson's proposal leaves a substantial theoretical gap in liability coverage. For this reason alone, it is no answer to the problem.

In their well-known paper, Henry Hansmann and Renier Kraakman assert the primacy of tort law over company law. They argue in favour of pro-rata, unlimited shareholder liability *for the torts* of insolvent investee companies which attaches at the time of knowledge that there are pending claims. (They would retain limited liability for contractual debts.) The reason for extended shareholder liability for the torts of insolvent investee companies is to ensure that 'share prices reflect tort costs'.[35] Lower share prices create pressure on managers to fix problems affecting companies. Such pressure should induce them properly to consider risks and fully to communicate about projects in which they believe investments should be made.[36] This should result in fewer high-risk activities being undertaken. Indeed, 'the infrequency of catastrophic torts suggests that a pro rata rule would impose relatively small expected costs, even on undiversified investors, except when corporate activities are extremely risky – which is precisely when an unlimited liability regime is needed to prevent corporations from externalizing large costs.'[37]

Hansmann and Kraakman argue in favour of pro-rata rather than joint liability because the latter potentially could result in a single shareholder assuming the liabilities of an entire company. Theory suggests that decisions to invest would be made, then, on the basis of the wealth of fellow shareholders, which would reduce the efficacy of the marketplace. The authors anticipate that 'the only effect of a pro rata liability would be a marginal increase in shareholder incentives to monitor the enterprise's expected tort losses. Although this additional monitoring would not differ in kind from what shareholders already do, it would encourage

[34] Mendelson, 'A Control-Based Approach', 1292.
[35] H. Hansmann and R. Kraakman, 'Towards Unlimited Shareholder Liability for Corporate Torts' (1991) 100 *Yale Law Journal* 1879, 1903.
[36] Hansmann and Kraakman, 'Towards Unlimited Shareholder Liability', 1907.
[37] Hansmann and Kraakman, 'Towards Unlimited Shareholder Liability', 1904.

managers to consider the full social costs of investment decisions.'[38] Liability should attach on the basis of knowledge of pending claims in order to avoid a number of problems with the alternatives, including obvious attempts to evade responsibility. 'This information based rule would fix liability before shareholders could evade responsibility for tort damages, without creating the uncertainties and complexities that would attend an occurrence rule.'[39] Moreover, Hansmann and Kraakman expect that a rule of pro-rata unlimited liability would attract a favourable response from insurance markets: 'insurers might offer portfolio insurance to individual investors to supplement the liability insurance carried by the public corporation directly'. Indeed, they anticipate the availability of reasonably priced, unlimited coverage to small shareholders.[40] Hansmann and Kraakman acknowledge that their proposal might operate harshly upon passive shareholders who are held liable for pro-rata shares of vast losses and are uninsured for such liability. They argue that this harshness could be alleviated by the exercise of court discretion in the award of damages.[41]

Hansmann and Kraakman's proposal has been the subject of intense interest, scrutiny, and criticism. A first criticism is that their pro-rata, unlimited liability rule would be easy to evade because foreign shareholders would have little to fear from judgments likely to be unenforceable against them.[42] Yet this criticism is overplayed because foreign shareholdings are not risk-free bets. Problems include: adverse movements in exchange rates which diminish dividend earnings; difficulty in monitoring management from afar; and difficulty in enforcing shareholder claims against investee companies. A second, related criticism is that a pro-rata, unlimited liability rule would bring with it extremely high domestic enforcement costs.[43] Indeed, this looks to be a potential problem for litigants in the United States, where all parties carry their own costs regardless of the outcome of actions.[44] But such a rule does not apply in either the United Kingdom or other Commonwealth countries,

[38] Hansmann and Kraakman, 'Towards Unlimited Shareholder Liability', 1906.

[39] Hansmann and Kraakman, 'Towards Unlimited Shareholder Liability', 1897.

[40] Hansmann and Kraakman, 'Towards Unlimited Shareholder Liability', 1901.

[41] Hansmann and Kraakman, 'Towards Unlimited Shareholder Liability', 1917.

[42] J. Grundfest, 'The Limited Future of Unlimited Liability: A Capital Markets Perspective' (1992) 102 *Yale Law Journal* 387, 393, 395, and 399.

[43] Grundfest, 'The Limited Future of Unlimited Liability', 397–9.

[44] This is acknowledged in H. Hansmann and R. Kraakman, 'Do the Capital Markets Compel Limited Liability? A Response to Professor Grundfest' (1992) 102 *Yale Law Journal* 427, 432.

which adopt a rule that 'costs follow the event'.[45] A third criticism is that a pro-rata, unlimited liability rule might lead to the disaggregation of equity-based groups and to coordination of activities by way of 'independent contract' – that is, movement to the network form of business organisation. Larger companies would be divided up and run as smaller companies linked by contracts, in part because this permits a more effective form of judgment-proofing and creates further enforcement difficulties.[46] In this way:

> A large oil company, rather than continuing to ship its oil in tankers that it owns and operates though subsidiary corporations, might sell each of its tankers to a separate individual who would then contract with the company to ship its oil. Similarly, small firms with only one or a few high-rolling shareholders might replace large drug companies in the development and initial marketing of pharmaceuticals; these small firms would then sell a product line to a large company for mass production and marketing only when it proved safe.[47]

Again, disaggregation is not a risk-free bet. It might be very difficult for any extant group to find buyers for individual, risky businesses. Any independent purchaser of such assets will seek 'independent gain'.[48] And the severed business might become less economically efficient for reasons implicit in our discussion in Chapter 2.[49] 'An incentive for disaggregation in any given case would not arise under unlimited liability unless the resulting inefficiencies, including lost economies of scale or quality of management, were smaller than the private gains from avoiding potential tort liability.'[50] Finally, coordination costs would rise (as seen in Chapter 2), as would risks of opportunism. '[T]here will always be some residual loss from strategic behavior that slips through the net' of coordination efforts.[51]

45 See, e.g., *R* v. *Lord Chancellor Ex p Child Poverty Action Group* [1999] 1 WLR 347; Corporations and Markets Advisory Committee, 'Shareholder Claims against Insolvent Companies: Implications of the *Sons of Gwalia*' (Decision Discussion Paper, 2007), p. 30.

46 L. LoPucki, 'The Death of Liability' (1996) 106 *Yale Law Journal* 1, 64–6.

47 Hansmann and Kraakman, 'Towards Unlimited Shareholder Liability', 1913–14.

48 S. Schwarcz, 'The Inherent Irrationality of Judgment Proofing' (1999) 52 *Stanford Law Review* 1, 3.

49 A. Chandler, *Scale and Scope: The Dynamics of Industrial Capitalism* (1990), pp. 14–18 (noting the general advantages of scale in the manufacturing industry); Hansmann and Kraakman, 'Towards Unlimited Shareholder Liability', 1914 (noting that 'an individually-owned firm with substantial firm-specific assets will have difficulty obtaining debt financing').

50 Hansmann and Kraakman, 'Towards Unlimited Shareholder Liability', 1914. See also Mendelson, 'A Control-Based Approach', 1301.

51 S. M. Bainbridge and M. T. Henderson, *Limited Liability: A Legal and Economic Analysis* (2016), p. 300.

Disaggregation is a risky strategy. However, the threat of disaggregation is not an idle one, because (as Chapter 2 recounts) there has been significant business movement towards the network form. So Hansmann and Kraakman's concern about it is cogent – and gives reason for the adoption of a supplementary liability regime applicable to networks, in order to maintain business form neutrality. As stated, more will be said about this in subsequent chapters.

A more serious objection to Hansmann and Kraakman's proposal concerns the effect that it would have upon investment decisions by ordinary 'mums and dads'. This is an issue that the learned professors acknowledge themselves, suggesting that investment in risky activities might become more attractive to 'high-rollers' than ordinary investors.[52] Timo Kaisanlahti argues that pro-rata unlimited liability creates indeterminacy because 'investors are denied any certainty about their possible maximum liability. In other words, to provide risk-spreading opportunities, an explicit upper cap for potential liability is essential for the stock markets'.[53] Kaisanlahti makes some points also about the difficulty for the parent company or other shareholders in obtaining adequate insurance for potentially unlimited liabilities (discussed in Chapter 3). Premiums might rise steeply from present levels, or insurance might disappear altogether.[54] Indeed, these are serious challenges. However, argument will be made later that these challenges can be overcome, if necessary, by setting outer limits upon liability which are generous to tort claimants yet provide reasonable certainty to markets, and by taking advantage of swaps transactions, which operate in ways similar to insurance.

For these reasons, it is submitted that Hansmann and Kraakman's proposal holds up reasonably well to scholarly criticism. However, the present writer believes that it goes too far in some respects and creates an unnecessarily radical liability regime. First, it treats all tort claims in a similar way and does not prioritise personal injury claims. Yet the reasons for departing from company law rules of separate legal personality and limited liability are not very strong with respect to purely financial losses.

[52] S. Presser, 'Thwarting the Killing of the Corporation: Limited Liability, Democracy, and Economics' (1992) 87 *Northwestern University Law Review* 148, 159. See also T. P. Glynn, 'Beyond "Unlimiting" Shareholder Liability: Vicarious Tort Liability for Corporate Officers' (2004) 57 *Vanderbilt Law Review* 329, 379.

[53] T. H. Kaisanlahti, 'Extended Liability of Shareholders?' (2006) 6 *Journal of Corporate Law Studies* 139, 151.

[54] Kaisanlahti, 'Extended Liability of Shareholders?', 154.

Second, the idea of judges being able to reduce or eliminate the liability of shareholders on the basis that they have been mere passive holders of shares has the potential to defeat the purpose of reform. It is not appropriate for judges to play fast and loose with the tort principle of full compensation.[55] As adumbrated, the better approach is to limit the exposure of shareholders by restricting claims to those for death and personal injury.

Of all the writers considered here, Christopher Kutz presents the most radical proposal for reform of the rule of limited liability. He would impose liability upon all shareholders on the basis of his rejection of certain ordinary assumptions about responsibility. He rejects the 'individual difference' principle. This is the idea that responsibility (generally defined) should flow only in circumstances where the individual has made a difference, in a causal sense, to the outcome of an event.[56] He rejects also the 'control principle', which is the idea that the individual is accountable only for acts and outcomes over which he or she has control.[57] (The present writer agrees with Kutz's stance on these matters, a point to be developed in what follows.) For Kutz, ordinary assumptions about responsibility 'define an individualistic conception of moral agency'.[58] He prefers a collective conception, a key element of which is that responsibility flows from agents' participatory intentions.[59] Such intentions 'generally shape[] agents' normative relations to the consequences of collective action, as well as their relations to other members of the group'.[60] Their actions, when performed, can be seen to stand in a 'certain instrumental relation to the group act'.[61] When agents intentionally contribute to the group's activity by playing their respective parts in that activity, and when their conceptions of their interacting roles sufficiently overlap, they undertake the activity jointly.[62] Participation on these terms means that agents can be accountable for the outcomes attributable to the group as a whole, as well as for those attributable to other members where 'done for the sake of the institution's goals'.[63] In sum, he subscribes to the view that 'marginally effective participants in a collective harm are accountable for the victims' suffering, not because of the individual differences they make, but because their intentional

[55] Amendments to state laws in Australia have been effected which impose thresholds and caps on damages. However, these do not apply, generally, in cases of dust diseases: e.g., Civil Liability Act 2002 (NSW), s. 3B.

[56] Kutz, *Complicity*, p. 3. [57] Kutz, *Complicity*, p. 3. [58] Kutz, *Complicity*, p. 4.

[59] Kutz, *Complicity*, p. 67. [60] Kutz, *Complicity*, p. 69. [61] Kutz, *Complicity*, p. 78.

[62] Kutz, *Complicity*, p. 103. [63] Kutz, *Complicity*, pp. 69 and 107.

participation in a collective endeavour directly links them to the consequences of that endeavour.'[64]

Turning more specifically to the company, Kutz opines that the company is a 'co-operative structure' in which each individual cooperates by contributing either financial or human capital.[65] 'The corporation and its goals exist only in virtue of this participatory structure. Restricting liability to corporate assets only makes sense on the assumption that there is something, the corporation, and no one else' that stands behind it.[66] Kutz believes the law's adherence to limited liability of shareholders to be 'at odds' with 'general practices and norms of moral and legal accountability'.[67] He posits the scenario of a company manufacturing a product that turns out, unforeseeably, to cause harm, but which has no insurance to cover this possibility.[68] The company might be undercapitalised – given that limited liability seems to encourage this in operating companies.[69] The issue becomes what happens when the company cannot meet liabilities to tort claimants. Kutz does not think limited liability is morally justified:

> Corporate torts are consequences, accidental or intended, of profit-seeking enterprises. Ordinarily one might well think that the chief beneficiaries of those enterprises – a group identical with their owners – would have to bear the burden of those consequences – as opposed to their being borne by their unlucky victims. Limited liability also flouts the default presumption of tort law of concerted action [giving rise to joint and several liability].[70]

Kutz believes that shareholders' participatory intentions mean that they can be held accountable for corporate wrongs, even if they are not individually blameworthy.[71] He makes an initial argument in favour of pro-rata shareholder liability for corporate torts (although he recognises that the argument is defeasible, potentially, when there are sufficient countervailing reasons, which might include economic necessity). Taking Johns-Manville as the example, Kutz observes that the 'shareholders did nothing to injure the workers, and their causal contribution to the workers' suffering was hardly

[64] Kutz, *Complicity*, p. 138. [65] Kutz, *Complicity*, p. 253.

[66] Kutz, *Complicity*, p. 253. It has long been recognised that the reality is that 'a corporation is at bottom but an association of individuals united for a common purpose and permitted by law to use a common name': Berle, 'The Theory of Enterprise Entity', 352. This is consistent with the argument presented in Chapter 5.

[67] Kutz, *Complicity*, p. 205. [68] Kutz, *Complicity*, p. 239.

[69] Kutz, *Complicity*, pp. 239–40. See discussion in Chapter 3.

[70] Kutz, *Complicity*, p. 240. [71] Kutz, *Complicity*, p. 246.

greater' than that of persons unconnected to the company.[72] However, this initial view is misleading because shareholders occupy 'a special responsive position, not that of a mere onlooker, but as someone with a "stake in the venture"'.[73] 'Investors who purchase shares in corporations, or who authorize others to purchase shares on their behalf[,] have control over their exposure to the risk that the enterprise's activities will go awry.'[74] If they wish to reduce their exposure to liability, they 'can put pressure on their companies to insure adequately or conduct their businesses even more carefully . . . At the very least, investors might begin to pay more attention to the public reports of their potential investments, refraining from investing in companies engaged in overly risky or socially undesirable activities'.[75]

There are several important elements in this reasoning, capable of being developed. First, Kutz identifies shareholders as insiders. They play a particular function within companies that injure.[76] A 'function' is a role played by the particular part in the operation of a whole system.[77] A part that constitutes a vital function in the operation of a system can be said to be intrinsic to it. A part, which is not necessary in this way, might be significant, nevertheless, in contributing to the overall efficacy of the system.[78] The idea of a person's function is important in certain legal contexts in determining the relationships between legal persons.[79] Kutz is right to believe that the idea is important in relating the shareholder to the company.[80] The very point and purpose of shareholders – from a functional view of the company – is that they arm companies with the funds required to undertake activities that can lead to injury.[81] This is a

[72] Kutz, *Complicity*, p. 245. [73] Kutz, *Complicity*, p. 248. [74] Kutz, *Complicity*, p. 246.

[75] Kutz, *Complicity*, pp. 249–50.

[76] This point has been made also by F. Easterbrook and D. Fischel, 'Limited Liability and the Corporation' (1985) 52 *University of Chicago Law Review* 89, 94.

[77] A. Marmor, *Positive Law and Objective Values* (2001), p. 158. See also, to like effect, J. Levin, 'Functionalism', in *Stanford Encyclopedia of Philosophy* (2004), available at: https://plato.stanford.edu/entries/functionalism/.

[78] Cf. J. Coleman, *The Practice of Principle: In Defence of a Pragmatist Approach to Legal Theory* (2001), pp. 25–31 (discussing functionalism in its causal and 'hermeneutic' senses).

[79] A well-known example from the law concerns the place of a person within an organisation in findings of vicarious liability: see *Stevenson, Jordan and Harrison Ltd* v. *MacDonald and Evans* [1952] 1 TLR 101, 111.

[80] See also P. Cane, *Responsibility in Law and Morality* (2002), p. 42.

[81] Note, in another context, that the financing of terrorist activities is an unlawful function under various instruments: e.g., US Code, Title 18, Providing Material Support or Resources to Designated Foreign Terrorist Organizations, § 2339B, discussed in T. Stacy, 'The "Material Support" Offense: The Use of Strict Liability in the War against Terror' (2005) 14 *Kansas Journal of Law and Public Policy* 461. For an indication of

function that is legally significant and provides a potential basis for responsibility – a matter *fully recognised by the legislature* in its decision to grant shareholders the privilege of limited liability.[82] In passing a provision such as Insolvency Act 1986 section 74(2)(d), the legislature has at once recognised the potential for shareholder liability, and at the same time determined that shareholders should be protected from this prospect. It is the extent of that legislative protection which, it is submitted, requires reassessment.

Second, the company is accountable to shareholders, and shareholders have a right to a proportionate share of the spoils of the company's business successes. Shareholders' fortunes are tied to their investee companies, and they identify themselves, to a greater or lesser extent, with those companies. This identification manifests itself in the shareholder who attends *her* company meeting, or reads the newspaper to see how *his* company's share price is faring. There is an argument that *outsiders* should be able to identify shareholders with their investee companies, just as the shareholders do themselves. To a limited extent, Christian List and Philip Pettit agree. In their view, membership of a group touches upon the identity of the individual members: 'generally our membership in group agents, active or aspirational, provides us with novel channels of identification and self-identification.'[83] But they doubt the extent to which members of economic groups, such as shareholders, identify robustly with the group, and believe that shareholder loyalty usually goes no further than their prospective returns.[84] This reflects Meir Dan-Cohen's views about modern-day shareholders, who are likely to have diversified holdings and are 'less attached to a particular corporation'.[85] Such shareholders display a rational apathy towards active participation in the company's internal decision-making, so that there is little 'incentive for members in large organizations to exercise "voice" in order to remedy deviations by the organization from its pursuit of its stated goals'.[86] Although the argument might appear finely balanced on this issue, it is submitted that shareholders' identification with their investee

further measures taken by the US government, see D. Shetterly, 'Starving the Terrorists of Funding: How the United States Treasury Is Fighting the War on Terrorism' (2006) 18 *Regent Law Review* 327.

[82] See Chapter 3.

[83] C. List and P. Pettit, *Group Agency: The Possibility, Design, and Status of Corporate Agents* (2011), p. 195.

[84] List and Pettit, *Group Agency*, p. 197.

[85] M. Dan-Cohen, *Rights, Persons, and Organizations: A Legal Theory for Bureaucratic Society* (1986), p. 19.

[86] Dan-Cohen, *Rights, Persons, and Organizations*, p. 24.

companies is 'real', even if it is not very strong at this point in time. The potential for shareholder liability would likely increase this sense of identification, because the fortunes of the shareholders more clearly would be attuned to those of their investee companies.

In sum, Kutz sets out a minimalist view of the conditions of shareholder responsibility for the debts of investee companies. In the view of the present writer, he makes a good initial case for liability, which turns on the distinction between insiders who have a functional role in a company and outsiders who are injured by that company. But, in one sense, Kutz is not as radical as might be thought. He does not depart completely from the free-will paradigm of responsibility (examined further later) that he ostensibly rejects. He takes comfort, so it seems, in finding that relevant shareholder 'intentions' exist at the time that shareholders acquire their shareholdings – rather than at the time of investee company wrongdoing. The question is whether such 'intention' is necessary to shareholder liability. This chapter argues for a conception of shareholder liability that does not depend upon any ex ante intention or upon contemporary fault in the person to be made liable. Moreover, Kutz does not deal properly with modern phenomena in the investment world, such as portfolio investment and hedge fund activity. Arguments for identification between those investors and their investee companies are potentially weaker than for ordinary shareholders. However, this is not to say that the argument cannot be strengthened. Indeed, a change in the law on shareholder liability is likely to change investment behaviour, so as to encourage greater monitoring of managerial decisions and greater corporate responsibility – or so it will be argued later.

9.3 Control as the Basis for Shareholder Liability

As will be appreciated from our survey of proposals for reform to limited liability rules, a frequent argument in favour of reform is the exercise of control by shareholders over their investee companies. On a wide view, the 'key elements of control include actual control or capacity to control, either directly or indirectly, financial and operating policy and decision-making.'[87] Where present, the exercise of control might provide a satisfactory basis for the imposition of liability. However, this is a restrictive

[87] UNCITRAL, 'Legislative Guide on Insolvency, Part Three: Treatment of Enterprise Groups in Insolvency' (2012), p. 15.

criterion because the absence of control implies defeat for the injured claimant. Argument will be made in what follows as to why 'modified limited liability' should be imposed without the need to prove shareholder control over their investee companies. Before moving to examine this proposal, several further points about control need to be discussed so that we can put it to one side in considering the preferable rule of extended liability for shareholders.

A philosophical argument about control has been made specifically in response to those, like the present writer, who argue for an exception to limited liability based upon criteria that do not depend on control. Jonathan Crowe has argued that, on corrective justice, non-corrective justice, and consequentialist grounds, the preferable rule is a nuanced rule which, first, requires that controlling shareholders be made liable for corporate wrongs, and, second, that where this is insufficient, liability be extended to ordinary shareholders.[88] Crowe justifies this stance on the basis that, while controlling shareholders have influence over the conduct of a company, permitting them to both foresee and take action to avoid harm to others,[89] so that they should be liable for excessive or preventable injuries,[90] ordinary shareholders have a lesser degree of responsibility because, frequently, they 'do not know a great deal about the company's everyday operations'.[91] Paying heed to the incentivising effect of liability, he states that the nuanced approach 'concentrates the incentives for responsible behaviour on those who control the company, while encouraging ordinary shareholders to adopt a more active role'.[92]

Crowe's argument has a strong internal logic to it. One way or another, it ensures that the parent company is made liable for the torts of its insolvent subsidiaries. In this sense, we need go no further. However, it is important to address a number of Crowe's assumptions. In what follows, something is said about the proper focus of reasoning about liability in tort and wider liability rules and about control, particularly in the corporate group context. This will help to explain why the present writer advocates a simpler rule about shareholder liability than Crowe's nuanced rule and eschews inquiry into the presence of control.

[88] J. Crowe, 'Does Control Make a Difference? The Moral Foundations of Shareholder Liability for Corporate Wrongs' (2012) 75 *Modern Law Review* 159.
[89] Crowe, 'Does Control Make a Difference?', 171.
[90] Crowe, 'Does Control Make a Difference?', 171.
[91] Crowe, 'Does Control Make a Difference?', 165.
[92] Crowe, 'Does Control Make a Difference?', 179.

The philosophical argument in favour of control-based liability is a reflection of will-theory inspired arguments[93] for the liability of individuals in tort, wider liability rules, and the criminal law. This type of theory turns upon the idea that acts can be judged as good or bad only insofar as the individual wills them.[94] Thus the focus of tort liability should be (largely) upon what the defendant intends. However, this view of tort law demonstrates a misplaced emphasis upon one side of the tort relationship – that is, upon the 'agent' or actor who causes harm – and reflects neither the broad range of negligence- and strict-liability torts that exist, nor the way that cases are decided. For Peter Cane, by contrast, an account of responsibility 'that condemns infliction of harm and interference with the interests of others only if they result from the agent's choice, puts far too much weight on our interests, as agents, in freedom of action, and takes far too little account of our interests, as victims, in security of person and property'.[95] Instead, tort law is a two-sided relation which takes into account *both* the quality of the agent's will *and* the impact that injurious conduct has upon the victim. Indeed, 'the basic measure of civil law remedies is the impact of the proscribed conduct on the victim.'[96]

Turning back to the insolvent entity problem, a requirement of control as the critical ingredient of shareholder liability looks like another instantiation of will theory that, ultimately, is unacceptable. There are two broad reasons for this. First, one might question why will theory–based concepts such as intention or the exercise of control, which are easier to identify in individuals and to link to individual 'bad' character, should be imported into the law regarding collective activity. In the corporate context, decision-making is likely to arise at various levels and to be collective in nature (as we saw in Chapter 5). It *might* be difficult to determine exactly who is responsible for a particular decision or action and/or who exercises control. Even if this is not a problem, it might be difficult to characterise collective decisions and actions in uncomplicated moral terms which justify liability. The company's decisions and actions, whenever taken by collective bodies, might not reflect

93 For the origins of the theory, see J. Gordley, *Foundations of Private Law: Property, Tort, Contracts, Unjust Enrichment* (2006), pp. 14–31. It is part of a wider phenomenon of 'methodological individualism': see, e.g., B. Fisse and J. Braithwaite, *Corporations, Crime and Accountability* (1993), p. 18.

94 See, esp., J. Finnis, 'Intention in Tort Law', in D. G. Owen (ed.), *Philosophical Foundations of Tort Law* (1995), ch. 10. For further discussion, see Cane, *Responsibility in Law and Morality*, pp. 95ff.

95 Cane, *Responsibility in Law and Morality*, p. 98.

96 Cane, *Responsibility in Law and Morality*, p. 99.

the preferred approach of any of the individuals involved. As we saw in Chapter 5, company decisions and actions frequently are the result of compromise – about doing what is best for the collective, rather than for individuals. Instead of searching for the true 'moral essence' of collective actions, it appears more coherent to take notice of the collective's power and ability to cause harm. This is Günther Teubner's standpoint, Teubner viewing as a false construct the 'social fiction of a corporate actor' which permits of 'the existence of one and only one center of action and will – the "person" – that has to be conceived as a point of attribution for actions, rights, duties, and liabilities'.[97] It is also Kutz's standpoint, insofar as he rejects both the control and individual difference principles. Second, importation of the control criterion jeopardises claims to recovery by tort victims who suffer personal injury in circumstances where better, alternative liability bases are present.

Moving on from matters of philosophy, there are further reasons for avoiding control as the, or as an important, criterion of shareholder liability. Two reasons are just as applicable to parent companies as they are to individual shareholders. First, it is difficult to define control adequately.[98] It has been said that 'control is an ambiguous concept. A principal ambiguity is that between control in the sense of the ability to impose one's will by coercion despite resistance and control in the sense of the probability that an order will be obeyed. Control, moreover, comes in infinite shades and gradation and can be exercised in different ways.'[99] New provisions in the Companies Act 2006, considered in Chapter 7, overcome some of the difficulties. Part 21A requires that companies maintain a publicly searchable register identifying persons with significant control in the company.[100] Schedule 1A provides a definition of 'people with significant control'. The definition will be satisfied in cases involving parent companies. But, while these provisions assist in providing greater insight into potential control in companies, ownership and other bases of theoretical control do not equate to the actual exercise of control. It is the actual exercise of control which, to this point, has been most relevant in extending liability from insolvent subsidiaries.[101]

97 G. Teubner, 'Unitas Multiplex: Corporate Governance in Group Enterprises', in D. Sugarman and G. Teubner (eds.), *Regulating Corporate Groups in Europe* (1990), pp. 88–9.
98 Mendelson, 'A Control-Based Approach', 1290.
99 Muscat, *The Liability of the Holding Company*, pp. 441–2.
100 Companies Act 2006, ss. 790M-N.
101 See also Glynn, 'Beyond "Unlimiting" Shareholder Liability', 355.

Second, the adoption of control as the basis of extended liability creates a disincentive to active engagement by shareholders in their investee companies.[102] This does lead, and will continue to lead, to attempts at evading whatever type of control courts look for.

It should be noted, further, that a requirement of shareholder control poses particular conundrums in the group context. Control is a concept of limited application that applies only between parent and subsidiary companies in vertically constructed groups. It is more likely to be present in smaller and medium-size groups,[103] where subsidiary companies are functionally dependent, than in larger groups organised along functional lines and with decentralised decision-making.[104] Indeed, business historians demonstrate that parent companies in larger groups have allowed their overseas subsidiaries a high degree of autonomy in their operations, and might be unable to make detailed business decisions with respect to subsidiaries that operate in lines of business different from their own. It might be argued, moreover, that notions of control lose all normative significance in the face of the structuring of legal relations within corporate groups. As we saw in Chapter 3, in the typical case, structuring ensures that assets are held by non-operating companies, that parent companies are not involved in decision-making by operating subsidiaries which are borderline insolvent,[105] and/or that risky activities are outsourced to independent contractors. In cases where this type of structuring occurs, parent companies would like to 'set it and forget it', but the law should not permit this.

To summarise the position we have now reached, this chapter has examined a number of existing proposals for reform of the law of limited liability. The more conventional among them would restrict liability to cases involving the exercise by shareholders of control over insolvent investee companies, or else to cases where there is the capacity to exercise control. This chapter has criticised control as a criterion of shareholder liability, and proposals have been examined which do not rely upon it. Such proposals hold out the potential for creating liability in the 'marginally effective participant'. Key features include the function shareholders play when subscribing to shares in a company, their participation in a

[102] E.g., Skinner, 'Rethinking Limited Liability', 1823.
[103] M. Eroglu, *Multinational Enterprises and Tort Liabilities* (2008), p. 262.
[104] See Chapter 2 for this proposition and others discussed in this paragraph.
[105] See, e.g., Muscat, *The Liability of the Holding Company*, p. 441; Glynn, 'Beyond "Unlimiting" Shareholder Liability', 333.

group activity, and the ability of outsiders to identify shareholders with the group.

In his proposals, Kutz emphasises the importance of shareholders being part of a collective or group of persons. In Chapter 5, we examined important attributes of groups that distinguish them from crowds and from persons acting in parallel. The attributes of 'groupness' strengthen the argument that shareholders are involved in a normatively significant endeavour, whether or not they exercise control. Relevant attributes of all those persons who comprise the company include the existence of group purposes, commitment to those purposes, conformity to group norms, and reproachability for the failures of members of the group to live by those norms. The result of coordinated group activity includes greater power both to achieve goals and to cause harm. In Chapter 5, we saw also that organised groups feature structure and hierarchy. We might note here that, in the traditional conception, shareholders occupy the highest place in the corporate hierarchy, and that directors and managers act as their 'agents'. Thus, when shareholders exercise their 'voices', directors and managers ought to listen. Moreover, shareholders might have a significant role in deterring wrongdoing by their investee companies because, in the usual case, they would pay the ultimate price of corporate liability.

9.4 Modified Limited Liability

We have now identified reasons for which shareholders are eligible to be made liable for unsatisfied personal injury claims brought against their investee companies, regardless of whether they exercise control over those companies. The proposal for a statutory rule of 'modified limited liability' in summary terms is as follows: where a company becomes insolvent, and there are unsatisfied personal injury claims against it, an exception to limited liability would arise. Both corporate and individual shareholders would become liable, pro-rata, in an unlimited amount for those personal injury claims. Shareholder liability would be strict and would crystallise at the time that the reasonable shareholder obtains knowledge of the personal injury claims.

Various aspects of the proposal for modified limited liability have been discussed already, including pro-rata liability, and the point in time when liability crystallises (both of these features being adopted from Hansmann and Kraakman's proposals). The remainder of this chapter deals with important aspects of the proposal which have not been the subject of substantial discussion yet. These are matters regarding: the restriction of the rule to personal injury cases, the desirability of strict shareholder liability, the need for an accompanying alteration to the priorities rule that operates on the winding-up of companies, a possible defence to shareholder liability, and the potential consequences of a rule of modified limited liability for the marketplace and several other things.

9.4.1 *Restriction to Personal Injury Cases*

None of the proposals for reform of the limited liability rule surveyed earlier in this chapter distinguishes between the different kinds of damage for which tort liability would extend to parent companies, corporate controllers, or shareholders in general. This means that these proposals are too wide, when viewed against the background of a corporate law regime that currently *promotes* the imposition by corporators of financial risks upon external parties. Modern economies are characterised by the mutual imposition of such risks, and most people benefit from this to some extent because it encourages entrepreneurial activity and generates income and wealth. However, as adumbrated in Chapter 3, it is unlikely that limited liability was intended to shield shareholders from personal injury claims. This is because, at the time when limited liability rules were established, there were far fewer personal injury actions available in tort, and because tort law burdens were not the concern of legislators. Moreover, fundamental ethical questions arise when companies can 'transfer the cost of wrongful death and injury from the company to the injured themselves – and indirectly to the taxpayer – by utilisation of the interposed entity'.[106]

The proposed rule of modified limited liability would extend the liability of insolvent subsidiaries to their shareholders, but only in cases of unsatisfied personal injury claims. This rule can be justified by the fact that tort law involves a *comparative contest* over liability.[107] When a claimant sues a defendant, judgment on any issue will be for *either* the claimant *or* the defendant – there are no other possibilities. Given that shareholders have some responsibility for corporate activities that injure outsiders, whether based in fault or not, tort theory suggests that claimants' interest in their physical person are worthy of greater protection than shareholders' financial interests.[108] First, tort law protects interests

[106] Jackson, 'Report of the Special Commission, Annexure "T"', p. 423.
[107] S. Perry, 'The Moral Foundations of Tort Law' (1992) 77 *Iowa Law Review* 449, 500.
[108] W. Lucy, *Philosophy of Private Law* (2007), pp. 216ff.

in the body, property, and reputation to a very high degree[109] for the obvious reason that these are the most basic interests required for human survival.[110] This interest is of a higher order than the shareholders' financial interests – as Allan Hutchinson explains:

> For corporate defendants, the cost of accidents is simply that – an economic cost and calculation. For [injured] plaintiffs, the costs of accidents are much more personal, physical and irremediable ... Their injuries remain the same, no matter what the extent of the plaintiff's compensation or even their own insurance; monetary compensation does not alter, even if it cushions the physical effects of their injuries.[111]

Second, the 'victim of a major tort suffers damage to a large part of his wealth and probably to his future earning capacity'.[112] This means that infliction of personal injuries is a double blow to victims, potentially creating great personal hardships for each directly affected individual and their dependants that the law ought, in this context, to take notice of.[113] Shareholders are in a better position to cope when residual losses represented by the shortfall in company assets are shifted to them because they have the ability to diversify against financial losses.[114] When taken together, these points establish the basic defensibility of a system of extended liability which prioritises the personal injury claims of tort victims over the financial interests of company shareholders.

9.4.2 Strict Liability

The proposed rule of modified limited liability for personal injuries would involve a form of strict liability for shareholders, whether corporate or individual, with respect to the wrongs of their investee companies. This is to say that shareholders would be held liable for their investee companies' causation of personal injuries regardless of fault because there would be no inquiry into fault when determining liability.[115]

[109] Cane, *Responsibility in Law and Morality*, p. 130.

[110] See also C. Witting. 'Distinguishing between Property Damage and Pure Economic Loss in Negligence: A Personality Thesis' (2001) 21 *Legal Studies* 481.

[111] A. C. Hutchinson, 'Out of the Black Hole: Toward a Fresh Approach to Tort Causation' (2016) 39 *Dalhousie Law Journal* 651, _. See also D. Leebron, 'Limited Liability, Tort Victims, and Creditors' (1991) 91 *Columbia Law Review* 1565, 1602.

[112] B. Pettet, 'Limited Liability – A Principle for the 21st Century?' (1995) 48 *Current Legal Problems* 125, 154.

[113] See also T. Rapakko, *Unlimited Shareholder Liability in Multinationals* (1997), p. 357.

[114] Pettet, 'Limited Liability', 154.

[115] See Cane, *Responsibility in Law and Morality*, p. 82.

Such a regime would help force each responsible entity or person to consider the full, social costs of corporate activity ex ante in determining the type and level of activity to undertake.[116]

For some observers, the imposition of strict liability upon shareholders for personal injuries is a troubling thought. However, will theory–inspired views of tort law, which insist that acts can be judged as good or bad only insofar as the individual wills them, have been criticised as too simplistic (see earlier). As Cane notes, 'responsibility in civil law is two-sided, concerned not only with agent conduct, but equally with the impact of that conduct on others.'[117] Notions of intention and fault, which reflect a basic commitment to will theory, do not provide the only basis upon which liability can be imposed in tort law.[118] There are substantial arguments for viewing tort liability rules through a wider lens.

In fact, strict liability better coheres with the idea of collective responsibility for harms than does either a negligence or other fault-based standard.[119] Negligence-based regimes are less effective than strict liability because they require merely that *reasonable* action be taken to avoid risks of harm and are not focussed simply on the issue of whether harm occurs or not. The onus is upon the injured claimant, often an outsider, to pinpoint where a failure to take reasonable care took place, whether at the level of the organisation or the individual employee.[120] This might be a daunting exercise when the defendant is a large organisation (or, worse still, a parent company).[121] The evidence of what was done to prevent harm occurring will be more easily ascertained by the defendant company itself: 'Given the information gap between what the company knows and what outside observers can determine, a strict liability standard offers the advantage of overcoming the informational asymmetry problem.'[122]

[116] J. Arlen and R. Kraakman, 'Controlling Corporate Misconduct: An Analysis of Corporate Liability Regimes' (1997) 72 *New York University Law Review* 687, 692.

[117] Cane, *Responsibility in Law and Morality*, p. 50 (emphasis in original).

[118] '[V]olition is one ground of responsibility, but not the only ground': M. Dan-Cohen, 'Responsibility and the Boundaries of the Self' (1992) 105 *Harvard Law Review* 959, 961.

[119] K. Abraham, 'Individual Action and Collective Responsibility: The Dilemma of Mass Tort Reform' (1987) 73 *Virginia Law Review* 845, 854–5.

[120] 'A strict liability standard avoids the task of determining whether the company had been negligent in the training, monitoring and operations procedures': Viscusi and Zeckhauser, 'Deterring and Compensating', 1746.

[121] This is a reason for avoiding overreliance upon liability focussed upon individual directors and officers: see P. Conti-Brown, 'Elective Shareholder Liability' (2012) 64 *Stanford Law Review* 409, 453–4.

[122] Viscusi and Zeckhauser, 'Deterring and Compensating', 1745. The alternative to strict liability would be a reversal in the onus of proof.

So these are some of the arguments in favour of a strict liability regime. The strictness of the proposed liability regime should be fortified by discouraging wasteful litigation. Attempts at evasion could be dealt with through supplementary measures, perhaps involving the use of anti-evasion powers, and/or the imposition of treble damages upon those who contest their liability and yet are found liable.[123]

9.4.3 *Strict Liability, Companies, and Shareholders*

Given the lack of substitutability between personal health and monetary damages,[124] the law should aim for the *prevention* of accidents which cause personal injuries. The law should encourage those contemplating action to be proactive in planning risky activities. Strict liability provides strong incentives for those made responsible either to cease the conduct of particularly risky activity[125] or to put in place policies and procedures that actually work in preventing the occurrence of injury. The preferable rule is one which shifts responsibility for preventing personal injuries to companies and other organisations when they plan new, risky ventures. Let us see why.

Organisations are 'actively engaged in the manufacture of risk';[126] their complexity means that mistakes or misconduct taking place in one part of the organisation might have 'serious repercussions elsewhere; anomalies may be systemic and relate to poor coordination and communication between different parts of' the organisation.[127] Good management means implementing proper processes and procedures to deal with risk. In Chapter 5, we examined various attributes of the company which make this possible. The company is characterised by a hierarchical structure, specialisation of function, and coordination of activity. Company plans are transmitted through the organisation by way of policies, routines, and organisational culture. These constrain the actions of individuals and ensure (as far as possible) that they act in conformity with corporate objectives. The result is that companies are deterrable and will act to

[123] Conti-Brown, 'Elective Shareholder Liability', 461.

[124] '[S]erious injuries reduce the degree to which money enhances well-being': Viscusi and Zeckhauser, 'Deterring and Compensating', 1736.

[125] Cane, *Responsibility in Law and Morality*, p. 84.

[126] B. Hutter and M. Powers (eds.), *Organizational Encounters with Risk* (2005), p. 3, quoting U. Beck, *Risk Society: Towards a New Modernity* (1992).

[127] Hutter and Powers, *Organizational Encounters with Risk*, p. 14. These matters are encapsulated in the idea of 'system interconnectedness': ibid., p. 17.

avoid risks when provided with appropriate incentives.[128] A rule of modified limited liability would provide an incentive (among those that exist already) for shareholders to ensure that their companies' managers take action by putting in place effective policies and procedures for the prevention of harm in the course of risky activities.[129]

We have seen that shareholders have an important function to play in companies, at least in financing their operations. Controlling shareholders and institutional investors have a function that goes further, which necessarily involves some level of monitoring. The position of controlling shareholders such as parent companies was considered in Chapter 3. Here we note the continual rise of the institutional investor. Institutions now own the majority of shares in listed companies in common law jurisdictions such as the United States, Canada, the United Kingdom, Australia, and New Zealand.[130] Given their large stakes, institutional investors often are 'locked in' to their holdings and have incentives to improve corporate governance in investee companies in order to better their own investors' returns.[131] Indeed, there is much evidence of increasing institutional shareholder participation in corporate management.[132] Institutional investors are highly informed about corporate governance issues and have real expertise in influencing corporate decision-making.[133] Such investors might establish their own

[128] Hutter and Powers, *Organizational Encounters with Risk*, p. 9.

[129] Of course, directors and officers often are major shareholders themselves and thus are the 'shareholders most interested in risk management': Conti-Brown, 'Elective Shareholder Liability', 436–7.

[130] E.g., J. Solomon and A. Solomon, *Corporate Governance and Accountability* (2004), pp. 91–2. See also P. Santella, E. Baffi, C. Drago, and D. Lattuca, 'Legal Obstacles to Institutional Investor Activism in the EU and US' [2012] *European Business Law Review* 257, 260.

[131] Solomon and Solomon, *Corporate Governance and Accountability*, pp. 95 and 113.

[132] P. H. Edelman, R. S. Thomas, and R. B. Thompson, 'Shareholder Voting in an Age of Intermediary Capitalism' (2014) 87 *Southern California Law Review* 1359, 1365; Santella, Baffi, Drago, and Lattuca, 'Legal Obstacles', 258–9; J. Hill, 'Changes in the Role of the Shareholder', in R. Grantham and C. Rickett (eds.), *Corporate Personality in the 20th Century* (1998), p. 194. Note also that the Shareholder Rights Directive (Directive 2007/36/EC) will be amended in order to '[i]ncrease the level and quality of engagement of asset owners and asset managers with their investee companies': European Commission, 'Proposal for a Directive of the European Parliament and of the Council Amending Directive 2007/36/EC as Regards the Encouragement of Long-Term Shareholder Engagement and Directive 2013/34/EU as Regards Certain Elements of the Corporate Governance Statement' (COM 2014/0121), p. 2. The proposal will require '[m]andatory transparency of institutional investors and asset managers on their voting and engagement': ibid., p. 5.

[133] Hill, 'Changes in the Role of the Shareholder', 176.

voting policies,[134] which can be used to influence investee company attitudes towards corporate issues. Often this engagement is 'beneficial to the management of companies pointing towards issues or shortcomings which management itself has not been able to settle'.[135]

When an institutional investor believes that corporate performance has been substandard, they are in a position to lobby for change either with a public challenge to management or by engaging in dialogue with management behind the scenes.[136] In addition, institutional investors might seek to interest other shareholders in the issues and, where management is resistant, can either take the lead in seeking change[137] or join with other institutional investors through campaigns orchestrated by corporate advisory firms such as ISS or Glass, Lewis.[138] '[P]roxy advisory firms help to solve the monitoring problem by offering a low-cost way for institutional investors to inform themselves about issues on the corporate ballot and in some cases to cast votes for institutions.'[139] There is evidence to suggest that activist campaigns increase value in targeted companies.[140] Although monitoring by institutions cannot be trusted always to ensure good, socially responsible decision-making (because institutional shareholders potentially are amenable to profiteering from questionable conduct),[141] this does affirm the picture of a corporate incentive structure which, on balance, should assist in avoiding the commission of corporate wrongs which lead to injury.[142]

134 Solomon and Solomon, *Corporate Governance and Accountability*, p. 100.

135 P. Böckli et al., 'Shareholder Engagement and Identification' (European Company Law Experts, 2015), available at: https://europeancompanylawexperts.wordpress.com/papers-of-the-ecle/shareholder-engagement-and-identification-february-2015/.

136 B. R. Cheffins and J. Armour, 'The Past, Present, and Future of Shareholder Activism by Hedge Funds' (2011) 37 *Journal of Corporation Law* 51, 56; Solomon and Solomon, *Corporate Governance and Accountability*, pp. 111–12.

137 Solomon and Solomon, *Corporate Governance and Accountability*, pp. 105–6.

138 J. Eley, 'Be Heard by Companies Whose Shares You Own', *FT Money*, 4–5 May 2013, 11. However, insider trading provisions and the danger of being treated as acting in concert are still potential problems: Böckli et al., 'Shareholder Engagement and Identification'.

139 Edelman, Thomas, and Thompson, 'Shareholder Voting', 1425.

140 Edelman, Thomas, and Thompson, 'Shareholder Voting', 1410. See also K. Reynisson, 'Related Party Transactions: Analysis of Proposed Article 9c of Shareholders' Rights Directive' (2016) 13 *European Company Law* 175, 176.

141 D. Skeel, *Icarus in the Boardroom* (2005), p. 203.

142 It should be acknowledged that shareholders will not always have the ability properly to respond to risks created by their investee companies. This was evident, for example, with respect to shareholders in the UK building products company Turner & Newall – which was a major producer of asbestos-based products. As we saw in Chapter 4, the company did its best to ensure that knowledge of risks of asbestos products was not disseminated

In addition to these ways in which institutional investors can inform themselves of issues, deliberate, and seek beneficial change in the management of investee companies, there are a number of mechanisms today by which *retail* shareholders can achieve similar things. These include campaigns run by organisations representing small shareholders, including the UK Shareholders' Association and ShareSoc. In addition, there have been a number of examples of single-issue shareholder action groups which have sought change in corporate governance or company policy through dedicated websites.[143]

Argument in favour of 'modified limited liability' for shareholders, while based upon the several ways in which shareholders can help to bring about change, specifically rejects the need for the exercise by shareholders of control over corporate activities as the basis of their liability. There is no need to confine liability to those individual shareholders who could have 'made a difference'. Ordinarily, the law does not refrain from imposing responsibility on persons simply because they lack complete control over an activity.[144] 'If responsibility depended on control over all aspects of our conduct and its consequences, we would never be (fully) responsible for anything.'[145] Vicarious liability (examined in Chapter 12), for example, does not depend upon a substantial causal relationship between employment and the commission of a tort. The test for liability is comparatively lax – the tort need merely have a *sufficient connection* with the employment.[146] Indeed, vicarious liability has been imposed in a range of circumstances where employers have done all that is reasonable to prevent employee wrongdoing. The similarity between the kind of shareholder liability proposed in this chapter and vicarious liability is significant – in both cases there is an expectation that the principal, although not directly engaged in the activities in question, will profit from them, and that they should bear the full social costs of those activities.

to stakeholders. '[T]he shareholders of T&N, by being kept in the dark about the risks of [their] investment[s], did not have the opportunity of withdrawing their investments or the opportunity to censure the company executives for their actions': R. C. Warren, 'The Enforcement of Social Accountability – Turner and Newall and the Asbestos Crisis' (1997) 5 *Corporate Governance* 52, 55.

143 Eley, 'Be Heard by Companies', 11.

144 Cane, *Responsibility in Law and Morality*, p. 69. See also J. Fischer and M. Ravizza, *Responsibility and Control: A Theory of Moral Responsibility* (1998).

145 Cane, *Responsibility in Law and Morality*, p. 67.

146 *Lister* v. *Hesley Hall Ltd* [2002] 1 AC 215, [28]. See discussion in Chapter 12.

9.4.4 *Priorities Rule*

Shareholder liability for unsatisfied personal injury claims against insolvent subsidiaries and stand-alone companies will bolster the funds available to meet those claims. However, reform of liability rules will not have its intended effect unless it is accompanied by a change in the rule on priority of payments on winding-up in insolvency.[147] In the United Kingdom, the order of priority of payments is as follows:[148] payment of employee entitlements to unpaid remuneration and pension contributions;[149] payment of the costs and expenses of the winding-up;[150] payment to floating charge-holders less the 'prescribed part', which is an amount set aside for unsecured creditors;[151] tort creditors join the other unsecured creditors in recovering pari passu from what remains;[152] and shareholders receive nothing unless there is a surplus of assets after all of the aforementioned claims have been satisfied. It is evident thus that personal injury victims have a low priority in the final distribution of company assets,[153] which reduces their chances of recovery.

The justifications for allowing the enforcement of security interests before payment of general creditors are that this encourages financial institutions to extend loans when they otherwise would not do so, which

[147] See LoPucki, 'The Death of Liability', 54–5.

[148] Rules elsewhere are similar. For the United States, see Hansmann and Kraakman, 'Toward Unlimited Shareholder Liability', 1884, citing US Code, Title 11, Bankruptcy, § 507 (tort claims not included among priority claims in US bankruptcy).

[149] Insolvency Act 1986, Sched. 6, paras. 5, 8, and 9.

[150] Insolvency Act 1986, s. 176ZA.

[151] Insolvency Act 1986, s. 176A. 'The prescribed part has been calculated so as to offset the gain to the holder of a floating charge resulting from the abolition of Crown preference': R. Goode, *Principles of Corporate Insolvency Law* (4th edn., 2011), p. 210.

[152] Insolvency (England and Wales) Rules 2016 (SI 2016/1024), r.14.12. In the United Kingdom, under Insolvency Rules, rr 14.1–14.2, future tort claimants can be ranked as creditors for purposes of distribution. We have seen, in addition, that future claimants can be taken into account in US bankruptcy proceedings (Chapter 7). This is different from the rule in Australia where future tort claimants are not recognised: Corporations Act 2001 (Cth), s. 553 (definition of 'creditor'); Corporations and Markets Advisory Committee, 'Long-Tail Liabilities: The Treatment of Unascertained Future Personal Injury Claims: Report' (2008), 12–13.

[153] In Australia, 'a small degree of priority' is extended in a winding-up 'to a limited group of tort creditors. Under s 556(1)(f) of the Corporations Act, amounts due in respect of injury compensation rank as a category of preference in a winding up. However, injury compensation ranks behind the payment of employer entitlements, and given that the higher-ranking categories of priority are to be paid in full before lower categories of creditors receive any distribution, it is unlikely that the injured tort creditors will obtain adequate recovery as a result of this priority': H. Anderson, 'Corporate Social Responsibility – The Case for Unsecured Creditors' (2007) 7 *Oxford University Commonwealth Law Journal* 93, 109.

might be helpful in keeping a company going, and that the secured creditor will be able to exercise control over the debtor company in a way that might be beneficial by 'reducing the expected variance of the projects to which the company's business is committed'.[154] These actions reduce the threat of insolvency and are said thus to benefit both secured and unsecured creditors.[155] Secured debt is thought, furthermore, to reduce the aggregate costs of monitoring debtor companies. This is because unsecured creditors benefit from the monitoring activity of secured creditors, and 'subjecting the debtor's major assets to security interests might inhibit the debtor from substituting riskier assets for his original assets because secured creditors would monitor the encumbered assets.'[156]

The priorities rule favours creditors with market power. Banks and other financial institutions, especially, are likely to be at the head of the queue in insolvency, having demanded and obtained 'security in the majority of commercial loan arrangements' that they enter into.[157] Even where no winding-up is sought, 'a major secured creditor is in a strong position of influence when it comes to both the choice of administrator and the approval of proposals he puts forward.'[158] Secured creditors are likely to control the course of events in insolvency. For companies facing large tort claims, the temptation will be to utilise insolvency procedures in a strategic way, so as to facilitate ongoing business relations with secured creditors, while reducing sums to be paid out by way of compensation – especially to future tort claimants.[159] In three-quarters of windings-up, secured creditors exhaust the assets of the insolvent estate so that unsecured creditors receive no distribution.[160] In most other windings-up, unsecured creditors receive

[154] R. J. Mokal, 'What Liquidation Does for Secured Creditors, and What It does for You' (2008) 71 *Modern Law Review* 699, 703.

[155] Mokal, 'What Liquidation Does', 703. Mokal does not see the same benefits as flowing from floating charges: ibid.

[156] C. M. E. Painter, 'Tort Creditor Priority in the Secured Credit System: Asbestos Times, the Worst of Times' (1984) 36 *Stanford Law Review* 1045, 1053.

[157] V. Finch, 'Security, Insolvency and Risk: Who Pays the Price?' (1999) 62 *Modern Law Review* 633, 634.

[158] Goode, *Principles of Corporate Insolvency Law*, p. 81.

[159] Note that various sale arrangements 'operate in practice as security devices', such as reservation of title agreements and sale and lease-back deals: Finch, 'Security, Insolvency and Risk', 635.

[160] Mokal, 'What Liquidation Does', 713. The figure in the United States has been put at 90 per cent for Bankruptcy Code liquidations under Chapter 7: see C. J. Tabb and R. Brubaker, *Bankruptcy Law Principles, Policies, and Practice* (3rd edn., 2010), p. 251.

only a small percentage of what is owed to them.[161] The result is a transfer of 'insolvency wealth from non-adjusting unsecured creditors to secured creditors'.[162]

The pari passu rule provides that unsecured creditors recover in proportion to the size of their admitted claims against the company. The rule is 'based on the notion that losses caused by liquidation should be borne by unsecured creditors equally'.[163] The rule reinforces the collective nature of insolvency proceedings, which are designed to prevent a free-for-all in the race to claim against the insolvent estate, and ensure a degree of order in winding-up its affairs.[164] The problem is that external unsecured creditors, including tort creditors, have to compete not only against contract claimants, but against the insolvent subsidiary's parent company and/or against other group subsidiaries which seek to prove in the winding-up.[165] Personal injury claims have no priority over other unsecured debts. This is a legacy of the pari passu rule having been 'drafted with the assumption that tort claims would appear infrequently ... and that when such claims were presented they would be in the nature of business torts such as conversion or defalcation rather than personal injury'.[166]

The priorities rules (including the pari passu rule) are acknowledged to be problematic. David Milman believes that English law permits 'companies to incur too many secured liabilities', which is 'an inherent weakness' in the insolvency regime.[167] This issue 'needs to be addressed by corrective legislation if respect is to be maintained for the distributional process as a whole'.[168] Moreover, the position of personal injury claimants needs to be improved.[169] Personal injury claimants are more risk-averse than the

[161] Goode, *Principles of Corporate Insolvency Law*, p. 99.
[162] Finch, 'Security, Insolvency and Risk', 668.
[163] Goode, *Principles of Corporate Insolvency Law*, p. 236.
[164] Goode, *Principles of Corporate Insolvency Law*, pp. 7ff.
[165] Inter-company debts might 'represent trading balances from intercompany trading within the group; or they may arise from loans and subventions made by other companies in the group to support continued trading by the borrowing company': Sir K. Cork, 'Insolvency Law and Practice: Report of the Review Committee' (Cmnd 8558) (1982), [1955].
[166] A. Ashwin, 'Tortious Liability of Company in Winding Up: An Analysis' (2005) 26 *Company Lawyer* 163, 168.
[167] D. Milman, 'Promoting Distributional Justice on Corporate Insolvency in the 21st Century', in J. Steele and W. H. van Boom (eds.), *Mass Justice: Challenges of Representation and Distribution* (2011), p. 635.
[168] Milman, 'Promoting Distributional Justice', 183.
[169] See P. Spender, 'Blue Asbestos and Golden Eggs: Evaluating Bankruptcy and Class Actions as Just Responses to Mass Tort Liability' (2003) 25 *Sydney Law Review* 223.

companies that injure them.[170] Generally speaking, such claimants do not agree to share in the risks of business activity. Moreover, when compared with contract creditors, personal injury claimants have a lesser ability to plan for and insure against corporate insolvency.[171] For those tort creditors unlucky enough to suffer serious personal injury, failure to recover might result in considerable personal (and possibly social) dislocation. '[T]he damage goes beyond the injury.'[172] The claimant might be unable to work, might have to undergo physical rehabilitation, relationships might suffer, and so on. Any diminution in their productivity will have wider social costs.[173] Christopher Painter summarises well the overall position:

> The present priority system thwarts the tort law goal of promoting socially desirable conduct. Because there is some likelihood that the debtor can avoid tort claims entirely in bankruptcy and does not have to pay these claimants a premium for their increased risk, the system provides only a diminished incentive for a potential tortfeasor to avoid causing harm or to mitigate the extent of that harm by acting in a reasonably safe manner, or to take other precautions such as purchasing insurance. This reduced incentive increases the possibility of future harm. Moreover, since secured creditors have priority over tort victims, these creditors have no incentive to refuse to provide supplies or capital that enables the defendant to cause the harm, or to insist that the debtor take precautions likely to prevent future harm.[174]

Sums set aside for the costs of the winding-up excepted, tort claimants should rank first in payments out of the insolvent estate. They should rank prior to secured creditors.[175] This is on the basis that compensation for personal injury fundamentally is more important than are the purely financial interests of secured creditors. The same reasoning entails that personal injury claimants rank ahead of other general creditors. Moreover, where personal injury claimants include both outsiders and company employees, the former should have the first opportunity to satisfy their claims from the insolvent estate. This is on the basis that employees readily can be identified with their employer companies and the torts that they commit, given their functional roles within organisations.

There are several reasons beyond simple fairness for altering the priorities rules in the manner argued for.[176] Whereas tort creditors (in

170 Painter, 'Tort Creditor Priority', 1064 and 1070.

171 When faced with the risk of default on debts owed to them, contract creditors will seek a higher return on the credit they extend to compensate them for lower chances of recovery: see Painter, 'Tort Creditor Priority', 1055.

172 Painter, 'Tort Creditor Priority', 1064.

173 Painter, 'Tort Creditor Priority', 1064.

174 Painter, 'Tort Creditor Priority', 1057.

175 Leebron, 'Limited Liability', 1647.

176 LoPucki, 'The Death of Liability', 61–2.

most cases) have no bargaining power against those companies that injure them, contract creditors do have such bargaining power. If they fear subordination to tort claimants, secured creditors will have the same incentives as other contract creditors to monitor risk-creating creditors,[177] to charge higher premiums for risks undertaken,[178] and/or to obtain adequate insurance. The subsequent emphasis upon safety and increases in the costs of risky activities will assist in reducing the incidence of *unjustifiably* risky activities. A diverse portfolio of business investments will ensure the acceptability of residual risks.[179]

9.4.5 Defence

Should policy-makers desire it, a rule of modified limited liability could be accompanied by a defence available to shareholders that have taken steps to publicise corporate decision-making which is likely to give rise to unreasonable risks to life and/or to the health of workers, consumers, or other persons, and/or have taken steps to prevent such activities being conducted – such as writing to the board of directors in opposition to such activities. Such a defence would encourage some shareholders to take a greater interest in corporate strategy, and open up debate about risky activities and products. However, it could result also in the development of regressive corporate strategies which stifle innovation and investment. Such a defence would undermine the strict nature of modified limited liability also, and reduce the extent to which shareholders are required to take responsibility for personal injury claims against insolvent companies. For these reasons, although lawmakers should discuss the possibility of such a defence, it is not argued for here.

9.4.6 Acquired Companies

An issue arises as to the position of parent companies that acquire wrongdoing subsidiaries which become insolvent after acquisition and cannot pay tort claimants in full. Under the proposed rule of modified limited liability, the parent is to be made strictly liable to unsatisfied personal injury

[177] This is subject to the point made in Chapter 3 about the practical limits of the ability to monitor.

[178] I. M. Ramsay, 'Holding Company Liability for the Debts of an Insolvent Subsidiary: A Law and Economics Perspective' (1994) 17 *University of New South Wales Law Journal* 520, 543; Leebron, 'Limited Liability', 1644; Painter, 'Tort Creditor Priority', 1081.

[179] Ramsay, 'Holding Company Liability', 543; Leebron, 'Limited Liability', 1644.

claimants. Liability will be imposed at the time that knowledge arises of claims, and is to be pro-rata (in the case of subsidiaries not wholly owned). But what of the case where the subsidiary engaged in the wrongdoing prior to acquisition by the new parent? The new parent's position will depend, firstly, upon whether it can plead a defence. Its position will depend also upon any agreement as to the allocation of liability made with the vendor parent company. Such agreements should be enforceable when permitting the extension of liability to the vendor, insofar as they widen the ability of personal injury claimants to recover. Such agreements should be unenforceable insofar as they seek to limit or exclude vendor liabilities. Where no agreement has been entered into, or where liability remains in excess of the agreement, a question of contribution will arise. Under normal principles of contribution, liability is apportioned on the basis of what is 'just and equitable having regard to the extent of [the] person's responsibility for the damage in question'.[180] This focusses on such matters as the degree of fault in the parties and their causal contributions to damage. In determining fault, courts could take into account the extent of parent company responsibility for undercapitalisation of subsidiaries (if any)[181] and for abusive practices that have led, for example, to the depletion of the subsidiaries' assets. This would seem to be the appropriate approach, even if the liability of parent companies, as shareholders, is strict (arising without regard to fault). The liability of both former and present parent companies to tort creditors would be joint and several. But the allocation of liability as between these parent companies should proceed on a principled basis.[182]

9.4.7 Networks

This chapter focusses upon corporate groups, in large part because of our concern to ensure that liability for unsatisfied personal injury claims can be extended from insolvent subsidiaries to their parent companies. However, this chapter does not distinguish between corporate and individual shareholders in setting out its proposal for modified limited liability. Here we need to note that this proposal would impact upon corporate networks – not only when group and network forms overlap (such as in the case of joint venture companies which incorporate subsidiaries), but

180 Civil Liability (Contribution) Act 1978, s. 2(1).

181 Muscat, *The Liability of the Holding Company*, p. 454.

182 But note that, in *Viasystems (Tyneside) Ltd* v. *Thermal Transfer (Northern) Ltd* [2006] 2 WLR 428, the Court of Appeal held two vicariously (i.e., strictly) liable employers equally responsible under the contribution rules.

even when they do not. This is to say that the individual shareholders in an insolvent network company would become pro-rata liable in an unlimited amount for unsatisfied personal injury claims. The ability of personal injury claimants to bring suit against individual shareholders would represent a potentially important avenue of recovery and help to resolve the insolvent entity problem in the network context. However, there are likely to be reasons for which this will be less satisfactory than the ability to proceed against a solvent corporate entity such as a parent company. These reasons include the greater difficulty of ascertaining individual shareholder wealth, the greater costs that will be incurred as the number of individual shareholder suits increases, and the difficulties of locating and suing foreign shareholders (noted already). In short, it will not be as *easy* to bring suits against individuals as it will be against a solvent parent company. This means that modified limited liability will be less important in the network context – although it might be very important in some cases. (Further points about the position of individual shareholders are made in what follows.)

9.4.8 Consequences

A question arises as to the likely consequences of a regime of unlimited liability for personal injuries in the marketplace, and in the conduct of commercial relationships more generally. The predictions range across a spectrum – from a minor readjustment to the investment landscape to the collapse of capitalism as we know it. It is suggested that the consequences would not be as drastic as some would assert. There are several reasons for this. First, modified limited liability does not entail a completely new form of liability. David Leebron, for example, is sanguine about the likely consequences of shareholder liability, noting that 'exposure to unlimited liability would not be a phenomenon of a completely new order in our lives . . . we constantly take risks far more drastic than those posed by unlimited liability.'[183]

Second, Leebron observes that investors make their decisions looking forward in time, after assessing potential risks and expected returns on investments. They make their calculations on the basis of projects' positive net present values. As argued in Chapter 3, when considering the economic arguments in favour of limited liability, businesses have every incentive to invest in projects with positive net present values. 'One invests in the belief

[183] Leebron, 'Limited Liability', 1574–5.

that one will derive a profit ... One selects one's investments after having concluded that the investment is one that will *make* money, not *lose* it.'[184] By contrast, investors do not make their decisions in hindsight, with the certainty that tort claims *will* arise. Indeed, one would hope that such claims are avoidable where proper planning is undertaken and precautions put in place.

A third reason for doubting that a rule of modified limited liability would overly deter investment relates to individual investors: the presence of solvent parent companies and/or institutional investors would ensure, in all probability, that individual shareholders were not called upon personally to satisfy claims arising in the group context.[185] However, this possibility cannot be ruled out – and, indeed, needs to be preserved. In proposing a not-dissimilar scheme of liability applicable to banks, Peter Conti-Brown opines that 'not all equity investors will resist payment. Many, perhaps most, investors will take calculated risks, enjoying the upside when the risk cuts their way and footing the bill when the risk does not. Every day in the capital markets, investors admit losses and pay out losing trades.'[186]

Shareholders who are nervous about their potential exposure to modified limited liability will have several options for protecting their position. The most important of these options arises from the derivatives market, which permits persons to 'manage and distribute their risks more effectively and efficiently, be it for hedging or speculative purposes. A firm [or individual] can use derivatives to take the risks it wants to take, and to lay off to others the risks it does not want to take'.[187] The most obviously suitable derivative is the credit default swap, which can be used to pay out on a liability in the event of corporate insolvency impacting upon shareholders personally. For the payment of a premium proportionate to the risk faced, the shareholder obtains a form of insurance.[188] Other more risk-averse individuals would move away from investment in companies engaged in risky activities and into other shareholdings and asset classes. Their shares would likely be acquired by corporate shareholders – because of the extra level of protection that they offer the individual shareholders who stand behind them.[189] However, some

[184] Presser, 'Thwarting the Killing of the Corporation', 159.
[185] Conti-Brown, 'Elective Shareholder Liability', 465.
[186] Conti-Brown, 'Elective Shareholder Liability', 465.
[187] C. Briault, 'Risk Society and Financial Risk', in B. M. Hutter (ed.), *Anticipating Risks and Organising Risk Regulation* (2010), p. 29.
[188] Conti-Brown, 'Elective Shareholder Liability', 439–40.
[189] P. I. Blumberg, 'Limited Liability and Corporate Groups' (1986) 11 *Journal of Corporation Law* 573, 575.

individuals, perhaps 'high-rollers', would be attracted to the new risk propositions created by a modified limited liability rule.[190]

Of course, there might be some risky activities, with the *potential* for catastrophe, that could no longer adequately be insured and for which there would be little investor appetite. An example might be the development, testing, and distribution of certain pharmaceutical products. In these cases, government guarantees, subsidies, or direct investment might become necessary. Typically, government participation would be forthcoming following proper risk assessment, which would include (no doubt) assessment of the political risks in guaranteeing particular projects.[191] Although not encouraged in today's deregulated world, direct government investment in projects of public importance was once the norm,[192] and might be entirely appropriate in a business world more attuned to the importance of industrial safety.

Experience with modified limited liability might (this is not a foregone conclusion) result in the diminished transferability of shares in companies undertaking risky activities. If this occurred because of the need ex ante for information about the maximum potential liability to which a share in a company might give rise,[193] some such figure could be legislated for. Thus the legislature might legislate for a cap on liability equal to (for example) twenty times the value (in real terms) of capital contributed. And if necessary it might limit pro-rata liability to claims incurred during a specified period of time surrounding share ownership – which might be important in a market characterised by automated trading.[194] These measures would allow markets to price risk and would enhance the transferability of equities.[195]

9.5 Conclusions

This chapter has argued in favour of a modification to the existing rule of limited liability that protects shareholders' personal assets. It suggests that it is appropriate to make all shareholders – corporate

190 Presser, 'Thwarting the Killing of the Corporation', 159.

191 Leebron, 'Limited Liability', 1577–8. See also Painter, 'Tort Creditor Priority', 1082.

192 Blumberg, *The Multinational Challenge to Corporation Law*, pp. 10–11.

193 See discussion in Kaisanlahti, 'Extended Liability of Shareholders?', 152–7.

194 Conti-Brown, 'Elective Shareholder Liability', 433–4.

195 '[T]he available evidence is suggestive that . . . multiple liability could function even on current stock markets despite the collection costs and other procedural hurdles that tort plaintiffs would have to overcome to hold shareholders accountable': Kaisanlahti, 'Extended Liability of Shareholders?', 162. See also Painter, 'Tort Creditor Priority', 1083.

and individual – personally liable, pro-rata, for personal injuries inflicted by their investee companies. The proposal preserves the legitimate benefits of risk-sharing by both shareholders and creditors of the company.[196] The desire simply is to ensure that risks are not shared with tort claimants suffering from personal injuries where they need not be. However, it is acknowledged that a system of modified limited liability would not be problem-free for companies, shareholders, or the marketplace. The potential consequences of an alteration to the law have been noted. The point is that we live in a world of the second best. The present regime of limited liability is deeply flawed, and has the potential to operate in ways that offend basic notions of justice. It allows for externalisation of risks of company activity upon tort claimants, and the suggestion is that a more satisfactory and just compromise is available. Amendment to the law would promote a more acceptable pricing of risks, and it would create incentives to ensure that risky activity is conducted only after all appropriate precautions have been taken.

However, the proposal for modified limited liability is not sufficient in itself in dealing with the insolvent entity problem. This is because the insolvent entity problem encompasses not only group companies, but network participants as well. As Chapter 1 argues, in order to achieve business form neutrality in the development of liability rules, where the prospect of liability arises with respect to one business form (here, the corporate group), an off-setting type of liability must be imposed upon alternative business forms (here, the corporate network) so that businesses are not tempted to avoid liability by moving to the alternative. The remaining chapters in this book attempt to determine, inter alia, the best means for extending the liability of insolvent corporate network participants to other network participants. A proposed new tort, called 'multiple entity recklessness', would be applicable to resolve the insolvent entity problem in *both* corporate group *and* network contexts. The proposed tort is based upon the extant tort of conspiracy by unlawful means, but would permit actions upon proof of objective recklessness in the causation of injury. The deemed fault element would provide substantial justification for extensions of liability in the group or network. Were such a tort developed, the amendment of the statutory rule of limited liability argued for in this chapter would be necessary still in providing an

[196] On the importance of risk-sharing, see Easterbrook and Fischel, 'Limited Liability and the Corporation', 101; Kraakman et al., *The Anatomy of Corporate Law*, p. 9.

important measure of redress on a strict liability basis, to encourage action which deters future wrongdoing in investee companies, and in order to signal to courts a new policy direction which moves from the current, zealous adherence to rules of separate legal personality and limited liability and permits consideration of other weighty tort law and social goals.

PART IV

Common Law

10

Veil-Piercing

10.1 Introduction

This last part of this book considers common law rules of potential assistance in extending liability in response to the insolvent entity problem. This chapter examines a remedial doctrine of company law which prima facie provides the means for extending liability beyond insolvent subsidiaries to their parent companies. Veil-piercing has been described as 'the only significant doctrinal concession' to the ordinary operation of the rules of separate legal personality and limited liability.[1] It involves a court examining the relationship between a company and its shareholders in order to determine whether to extend liability to the shareholders, whose assets are protected by limited liability. This doctrine has been used most frequently in cases of individual shareholders and in smaller corporate groups. It has been used infrequently to impose liability on parent companies of any size, and UK court decisions emphasise the narrow confines of its operation. This chapter considers the judicial history and main features of veil-piercing before casting it aside.

10.2 Defining Veil-Piercing

The first difficulty with veil-piercing involves the lack of consensus about what it is and about what it is supposed to achieve. This is a consequence, in part, of the misleading nature of the longer-form expression 'piercing the corporate veil', which implies that something is done *to the company*. Insofar as the company is a legal entity, this is not the case at all. In seeking clarification of the matter, we note also that there are competing definitions of veil-piercing that focus on either separate legal personality, limited liability, or a combination of the two. Moreover, many judges and commentators assume that the doctrine is available to extend liability

[1] P. Muchlinski, 'Limited Liability in Multinational Enterprises: A Case for Reform?' (2010) 34 *Cambridge Journal of Economics* 914, 919.

from an insolvent company to persons *other than its shareholders*. But this would appear to be a mistaken view. Let us see why.

In the UK Supreme Court case of *Prest* v. *Petrodel Resources Ltd*,[2] Lord Sumption stated that, properly speaking, veil-piercing involves 'disregarding the *separate personality* of the company', and other members of the court agreed.[3] Indeed, this statement reflects definitions adopted by eminent works on UK company law.[4] A variation of Lord Sumption's definition of veil-piercing adopts a conjunctive approach, but still emphasises the effect of the doctrine upon separate legal personality. Jonathan Macey and Joshua Mitts say, for example, that:

> limited liability is an implication of the notion that a complete separation of identities exists between investors and the corporations in which they have invested ... [T]he existence of this corporate separateness implies that investors in the corporation – whether they are equity investors or debt investors – have only an attenuated relationship with the people and the companies with whom the corporation interacts. And that relationship does not include personal responsibility or liability for the debts of the corporation on the part of investors. Thus, limited liability derives from the concept of corporate separateness.[5]

Under this approach, veil-piercing reverses the consequences of both separate legal personality *and* limited liability. However, it is submitted that these definitions of veil-piercing are misguided, for a start because they are inconsistent with the effect of legislation creating companies as separate legal persons.[6] A company springs to life fully formed,[7] and has immediate competence in its legal dealings with others, including those

2 [2013] 2 AC 415.

3 [2013] 2 AC 415, [16](emphasis added). See also [35], [91]–[92], and [106]. But Lord Sumption also says that the effect of the doctrine is that 'a person who owns and controls a company is said ... to be identified with it in law by virtue of that ownership and control' [16]. This could be viewed as internally inconsistent because 'identifying with' does not happen by 'disregarding'. In other parts of his judgment, his Lordship speaks not of disregard of separate legal personality but, rather, of the *corporate veil* being disregarded [9] or pierced [27]. See also [83] (Lord Neuberger). Again, this is internally inconsistent because it would seem possible only to do one or the other. There was similar confusion in other judgments.

4 G. Morse (ed.), *Palmer's Company Law*, Volume 1 (Online) (2016), [2.1533]; L. Sealy and S. Worthington, *Sealy and Worthington's Cases and Materials in Company Law* (10th edn., 2013), p. 53.

5 J. Macey and J. Mitts, 'Finding Order in the Morass: The Three Real Justifications for Piercing the Corporate Veil' (2014) 100 *Cornell Law Review* 99, 104–5.

6 See Chapter 3.

7 Just as Athena leaped from Zeus' head fully armed: *Commissioner for Probate Duties (Vic)* v. *Mitchell* (1960) 105 CLR 126, 152.

with its controlling shareholder.[8] Statute provides for the company's perpetual existence and enjoyment of its capacities until it is de-registered.[9] Given the clarity of the statutory position, there would seem to be no power in courts to 'ignore' or apply 'exceptions' to the separate legal personality of the company. There can be no 'exception' to the fact of a company's existence when the legislature has willed its existence, and so the company must be treated prima facie as responsible for all of its legal obligations.[10]

The definition of veil-piercing as involving ignoring or an exception to separate legal personality is expedient for those who consider that the doctrine permits the extension of liability from an insolvent subsidiary to any of the companies in a group (including co-subsidiaries)[11] or, indeed, to directors, corporate officers, and agents. However, this usage elides two distinct issues. First, the existence of the company as an 'artificial' legal person requires rules about ownership and the use of assets. The term 'corporate veil' properly refers to the segregation of company assets from the assets of shareholders and others.[12] Thus, to 'pierce' through the veil entails reaching into assets that belong to somebody else in order to satisfy an obligation of the company. Those assets might belong to the shareholders, or to directors, corporate officers, etc. Second, the only persons whose assets are *protected* by company and insolvency law are shareholders. Limited liability is a rule that specifically protects their hold over their assets. It does not protect either the company or any other party.[13] Indeed, it does not protect shareholders when they owe obligations to others derived from their status as, for example, directors or guarantors. It is for this reason that veil-piercing is controversial; because it reverses a protection specifically given to shareholders qua

[8] *Salomon* v. *A Salomon & Co Ltd* [1897] AC 22. See Chapter 3.

[9] C-H Tan, 'Piercing the Separate Personality of the Company: A Matter of Policy?' [1999] *Singapore Journal of Legal Studies* 531, 542–3.

[10] F. J. Powell, *Parent and Subsidiary Corporations: Liability of a Parent Corporation for the Obligations of its Subsidiary* (1931), p. 85.

[11] E.g., M. F. Khimji and C. C. Nicholls, 'Piercing the Corporate Veil Reframed as Evasion and Concealment' (2015) 48 *University of British Columbia Law Review* 401, 418 (speaking of, inter alia, veil-piercing among 'related' companies).

[12] R. Kraakman et al., *The Anatomy of Corporate Law: A Comparative and Functional Approach* (2nd edn., 2009), p. 6.

[13] S. Worthington, *Sealy and Worthington's Text, Cases and Materials in Company Law* (11th edn., 2016), pp. 64–5; H. Anderson, 'Piercing the Veil on Corporate Groups in Australia: The Case for Reform' (2009) 33 *Melbourne University Law Review* 333, 342. Even the highest courts continue to invoke veil-piercing language when speaking of the potential liability of directors: *Campbell* v. *Peter Gordon Joiners Ltd* [2016] AC 1513.

shareholders. Thus, properly speaking, 'piercing the veil' is an expression used to mean making shareholders liable for what are prima facie the company's obligations. However, many cases of piercing the veil concern, not shareholders *in strictu sensu*, but beneficial owners of shares (those who are 'functionally equivalent' to the legal holders of shares).[14] It seems right that veil-piercing be defined in a way that encompasses extensions of liability to beneficial owners. The point is that veil-piercing properly is seen as 'a doctrine to overcome limited liability rather than the separate legal personality of the company'.[15]

Veil-piercing would not be a coherent doctrine were it to facilitate courts in ignoring the separate legal personality of the company. Indeed, the doctrine makes sense only when the existence of both the company and its obligations is established. 'Cases dealing with the liability of a shareholder for corporate obligations refer to circumstances where a third party seeks to compel the shareholder to satisfy a debt or other obligation that, strictly speaking, is an obligation of the corporation. The shareholder may be an individual or a parent company.'[16] 'Pure veil-piercing enables a plaintiff to reach the personal assets of only a shareholder'[17] or beneficial owner. This is a narrow definition, but it is both accurate and useful in saying something about both the direction and the effect of veil-piercing. The doctrine involves: first, only relations between the company and its (beneficial) shareholders, and, second, the extension of company liabilities upwards to (beneficial) shareholders.[18] In a veil-piercing case arising in the corporate group context, the court simply determines whether to extend liabilities from a subsidiary upwards to the parent company.

14 E.g., *Gilford Motor Co Ltd* v. *Horne* [1933] Ch 935, approved in *Prest* v. *Petrodel Resources Ltd* [2013] 2 AC 415, [29].

15 Anderson, 'Piercing the Veil on Corporate Groups', 342. See also Kraakman et al., *The Anatomy of Corporate Law*, p. 10.

16 M. F. Khimji and C. C. Nicholls, 'Piercing the Corporate Veil in the Canadian Common Law Courts – An Empirical Study' (2015) 41 *Queen's Law Journal* 207, 226. See also I. M. Ramsay and D. B. Noakes, 'Piercing the Corporate Veil in Australia' (2001) 19 *Company and Securities Law Journal* 250, 252.

17 P. Oh, 'Veil Piercing Unbound' (2013) 93 *Boston University Law Review* 89, 102. See also *Atlas Maritime Co SA* v. *Avalon Maritime Ltd (No 1)* [1991] 4 All ER 769, 779; Anderson, 'Piercing the Veil on Corporate Groups', 342; J. H. Matheson, 'The Modern Law of Corporate Groups: An Empirical Study of Piercing the Corporate Veil in the Parent-Subsidiary Context' (2009) 87 *North Carolina Law Review* 1091, 1098.

18 See *The Print Factory (London) 1991* v. *Millam* [2007] ICR 1331, [7].

10.3 Power to Pierce the Veil

Having arrived at a straightforward and workable definition of veil-piercing, the next issue is whether it involves a legitimate judicial practice when not undertaken pursuant to statute. A difficulty in asserting its legitimacy is Insolvency Act 1986, section 74(2)(d) (reflected in Companies Act 2006, section 3(1), and the Model Articles for limited companies),[19] and equivalent provisions elsewhere in the common law world that provide for the limited liability of shareholders. Upon a winding-up of the company, shareholders prima facie need contribute no more than the amounts unpaid on their shares. *Despite* the existence of explicit statutory provisions protecting the personal assets of shareholders, courts have awarded themselves the ability to pierce the veil. It is in this context that, in *Dimbleby & Sons Ltd* v. *National Union of Journalists*, Lord Diplock stated that 'one would expect that any parliamentary intention to pierce the corporate veil would be expressed in clear and unequivocal language.'[20] While legislative exceptions to limited liability do exist (for example, in the wrongful trading provisions considered in Chapter 6), legislative supremacy over the courts and the presence of a clear, protective rule would seem to preclude *judicially crafted* exceptions. Although in *Prest* v. *Petrodel Resources Ltd*, Lord Neuberger thought it unnecessary to decide whether 'there is a principle that it is open to a court, without statutory authority . . . to pierce the veil of incorporation',[21] Mohamed Khimji and Christopher Nicholls opine that 'to pierce the corporate veil, courts must essentially ignore or effectively overrule explicit and unambiguous provisions of corporate legislation. Indeed, this assumed judicial power to overrule Parliament . . . may well be unique to the corporate veil-piercing context.'[22]

However, there is a question whether all kinds of exception to limited liability really are precluded by statute. Certainly, strict liability actions against shareholder assets must be precluded in the absence of a statutory exception, because they involve automatic recourse to those assets and

[19] See B. Hannigan, *Company Law* (4th edn., 2015), p. 94. [20] [1984] 1 WLR 427, 435.

[21] [2013] 2 AC 415, [63].

[22] Khimji and Nicholls, 'Piercing the Corporate Veil Reframed', 401. Similar observations have been made as regards the United States, Glynn noting that 'courts use veil-piercing to extend liability to select shareholders when, in fact, state legislatures have conferred on all shareholders the benefits of limited liability', which is 'both unqualified and universal': T. P. Glynn, 'Beyond "Unlimiting" Shareholder Liability: Vicarious Tort Liability for Corporate Officers' (2004) 57 *Vanderbilt Law Review* 329, 333, 340, and 352. See also C. H. Tan, 'Veil-Piercing – a Fresh Start' [2015] *Journal of Business Law* 20, 29.

this directly contradicts the intention of the legislature.[23] In the absence of further guidance on this matter, the present writer believes that the most sensible boundary line that can be drawn is between liability founded on recognised, fault-based wrongs and those which are either ad hoc or strict liability in nature. This is to say that the law must permit of shareholder liability and access to shareholder assets when the shareholder has committed recognised fault-based wrongs. Fault-based wrongdoing transforms the shareholder from a passive investor to a recognised wrongdoer (a position that would have been apparent to nineteenth-century legislators contemplating passage of the first statutory provisions limiting liability). The problem is that, in UK law at least, there have been few successful veil-piercing cases, so that it is difficult to say that there are established categories of veil-piercing founded on fault-based wrongdoing which permit exceptions to the rule of limited liability. This is one of the reasons for which this book would avoid reliance upon the doctrine as an answer to the problems of insolvent subsidiaries and mass-torts. Further reasons for this position will be developed in what follows.

10.4 Recent History of Veil-Piercing

In the next few paragraphs, brief observations are made about the history of the veil-piercing doctrine in the United Kingdom, before we turn to the pivotal modern authority of *Prest* v. *Petrodel Resources Ltd.*[24] In the section that follows, we review the law concerning veil-piercing in corporate groups, including the eponymous case of *Adams* v. *Cape Industries plc.*[25] The position in the United Kingdom is compared with that in other Commonwealth countries. Following this, we move on to consider the potential bases upon which veil-piercing doctrine can be invoked. A later section of this chapter looks at veil-piercing law in the United States.

It is difficult to identify any example of a UK case in which the claimants have succeeded solely on a veil-piercing argument. Two prominent corporate group cases decided by the Court of Appeal – *DHN Food Distributors Ltd* v. *Tower Hamlets LBC*[26] and *Smith, Stone and*

[23] Similar reasoning is adopted in Chapter 12 when considering the 'vicarious liability' of the parent company for the torts of the subsidiary.

[24] [2013] 2 AC 415. [25] [1990] Ch 433.

[26] [1976] 3 All ER 462. Disposition towards veil-piercing in English law was said to have been at its peak in this case, there having been a sharp decline since then: Sealy and

Knight Ltd v. *Birmingham Corporation*[27] – although often described as involving veil-piercing, do not conform to this book's definition of the doctrine because liabilities were not extended from subsidiary companies *to* shareholders. Indeed, in each case the Court of Appeal conferred a *benefit* on the parent company, ostensibly in conformity with the terms of statutory compensation schemes for land resumption. Other cases, which do conform to the definition of veil-piercing, either have been disapproved by the UK Supreme Court as illegitimate (*Trustor AB* v. *Smallbone (No 2)*,[28] and *Gencor ACP Ltd* v. *Dalby*,[29] in particular)[30] or, if seen as legitimate, nevertheless are susceptible to *alternative and better* explanations (for example, *Gilford Motor Company* v. *Horne*,[31] *Jones* v. *Lipman*,[32] and *Re a Company*[33]). As such, many observers were unsurprised when, in *Prest* v. *Petrodel Resources Ltd*, Lord Neuberger commented that there appears *never* to have been a successful UK veil-piercing case – at any level of the judicial hierarchy.[34] The importance of the *Prest* case was that it sought to determine whether such a doctrine *ought* to be recognised as a part of English law.

Prest v. *Petrodel Resources Ltd*[35] involved a 'corporate group' in the sense that the companies at issue were related because they were each controlled (directly or through intermediate entities) by Mr Prest.[36]

Worthington, *Cases and Materials in Company Law*, pp. 54–5. But the decision in the *DHN* case was not followed on the similar facts in *Woolfson* v. *Strathclyde Regional Council* 1978 SC (HL) 90.

27 [1939] 4 All ER 116, criticised in J. Harris and A. Hargovan, 'Cutting the Gordian Knot of Corporate Law: Revisiting Veil Piercing in Corporate Groups' (2011) 26 *Australian Journal of Corporate Law* 39.

28 [2001] 1 WLR 1177 (offshore company in receipt of funds derived from breach of fiduciary duty), criticised in *Prest* v. *Petrodel Resources Ltd* [2013] 2 AC 415, [35].

29 [2000] 2 BCLC 734 (company in receipt of proceeds of fraud), criticised in *Prest* v. *Petrodel Resources Ltd* [2013] 2 AC 415, [31]–[33].

30 Another pro-liability case, *Creasey* v. *Breachwood Motors Ltd* [1992] BCC 638, was effectively overruled in *Ord* v. *Belhaven Pubs Ltd* [1998] 2 BCLC 447.

31 [1933] Ch 935 (company used as a means of evading a non-compete provision), re-characterised in *Prest* v. *Petrodel Resources Ltd* [2013] 2 AC 415, [71]–[72]; Tan, 'Piercing the Separate Personality', 547 (orthodox agency analysis).

32 [1962] 1 All ER 442 (company used to hold title to land subject to contract for sale to another), re-characterised in Tan, 'Piercing the Separate Personality', 549 (purchase being subject to claimant's equity due to notice of fraud).

33 [1985] BCLC 333 re-characterised in Tan, 'Piercing the Separate Personality', 550 (procuring commission of wrong).

34 [2013] 2 AC 415, [64].

35 [2013] 2 AC 415. I am grateful to my colleague Professor Alan Dignam for illuminating conversations with me about the case.

36 [2013] 2 AC 415, [2].

Some shareholdings were hierarchically arranged – there being various degrees of separation between Mr Prest and the sub-subsidiaries.[37] But there were no independent directors.[38] In general, the directors were relatives of Mr Prest.[39] In each case, they accepted directions from him in fulfilling their roles.[40] PRL was owner of five residential properties, while Vermont was owner of two. In each case, the beneficial ownership in the companies was in Mr Prest.[41] He treated the cash balances and assets of these companies 'as his own and drew on them as he saw fit' in funding his lifestyle.[42] According to the Supreme Court, the legal issue was whether the court had 'the power to order the transfer of these seven properties to the wife given that they legally belong not to him but to his companies'.[43]

A preliminary question is whether *Prest* v. *Petrodel Resources Ltd* involved any issue of veil-piercing, given the understanding that piercing is concerned (as explained) with extending liability *from a company upwards to (beneficial) shareholders*. This is *not* what the case was about; *no liability* was extended from a company to anyone else. Indeed, Lord Sumption stated that the case was about whether to appropriate company 'assets to satisfy a personal liability of its shareholder to his wife'.[44] Because the corporate veil protects neither the company's assets nor shareholders from their personal liabilities, it is here asserted that this case had *nothing* to do with veil-piercing.

This point aside, the *Prest* case stands for several very important obiter dicta: first, the Supreme Court held that there is a limited doctrine of veil-piercing in UK law, which applies primarily in cases of the deliberate 'evasion' of pre-existing legal obligations or restrictions through the use of interposed companies.[45] The court will recognise the relevant obligations to exist in controllers seeking to evade them, or otherwise deprive the controller of the sought-after advantage when acting in evasion.[46] In expressing the principle this way, the court expressed a desire to move away from picturing companies subjected to veil-piercing litigation as mere 'facades' or 'shams'.[47] This seems right, for reasons already traversed. Second, the evasion ground for veil-piercing was said to be different in concept from 'concealment', because the latter 'does not involve piercing the corporate veil at all'.[48] In concealment cases, the

[37] [2013] 2 AC 415, [13]. [38] [2013] 2 AC 415, [12]. [39] [2013] 2 AC 415, [12].
[40] [2013] 2 AC 415, [12]. [41] [2013] 2 AC 415, [4], and [13].
[42] [2013] 2 AC 415, [14]. [43] [2013] 2 AC 415, [2]. [44] [2013] 2 AC 415, [491].
[45] [2013] 2 AC 415, [35], [60], and [81]. [46] [2013] 2 AC 415, [35].
[47] [2013] 2 AC 415, [28]. [48] [2013] 2 AC 415, [28], and [61].

court looks behind the company form in order to identify who the real actors are and to recognise their obligations accordingly.[49] Even so, Lord Sumption acknowledged that cases of evasion and concealment could overlap.[50] Third, the court observed that veil-piercing has been invoked successfully in few cases and represents no wide avenue of redress. (In fact, Lord Neuberger doubted whether there had been *any* true cases of veil-piercing.) Indeed, other, conventional legal principles should be pleaded and exhausted before consideration is given to veil-piercing. Veil-piercing is to be considered only when conventional legal principles do not help.[51] Fourth, the reasons given for the narrowness of the doctrine include: a reluctance to 'step in and undo transactions, save where there is a well-established and principled ground for doing so';[52] the related need to protect genuine creditors of the companies in question; and the desire not to elevate claimants to the level of secured creditors where they have not bargained for such protection.[53]

While agreeing with Lord Sumption that evasion is an example of veil-piercing, other justices of the Supreme Court in the *Prest* case were reluctant to foreclose on further, appropriate categories of veil-piercing. Lady Hale, Lord Mance, and Lord Clarke were each of the view that there *might* be other applications of the doctrine.[54] However, their Lordships treated the issue before them as concerned with precedent and as an analytical exercise in conceptualising an existing doctrine. There was no substantive discussion of the policy reasons for either limited liability or exceptions to it. In the result, the court did not pierce the corporate veil because there was, in Mr Prest's use of group companies, no evasion of a legal obligation owed *by him* to his former wife.[55]

Subsequent academic commentary has noted two important points about *Prest* v. *Petrodel Resources Ltd*: first, the distinction that Lord Sumption drew between veil-piercing on the ground of evasion and the (non-veil-piercing) concealment principle is difficult to appreciate, if not conceptually flawed. Brenda Hannigan, for example, notes that '[c]oncealment is inherent in many evasion cases, indeed, evasion is commonly achieved through concealment.'[56] Second, the veil-piercing doctrine that remains following this case is narrow in scope. It appears designed merely to catch very rare cases that cannot be decided on the

[49] [2013] 2 AC 415, [28]. [50] [2013] 2 AC 415, [28]. [51] [2013] 2 AC 415, [103].
[52] [2013] 2 AC 415, [83]. [53] [2013] 2 AC 415, [41]–[42].
[54] [2013] 2 AC 415, [92], [100], and [103], respectively. [55] [2013] 2 AC 415, [36].
[56] Hannigan, *Company Law*, pp. 54–5. See also Ramsay and Noakes, 'Piercing the Corporate Veil in Australia', 256 (fraud argument dependent upon company being a sham).

basis of conventional legal reasoning – that is, through contract, equity, torts, or any residuum of concealment cases. In *Antonio Gramsci Shipping Corpn* v. *Recoletos Ltd*, the Court of Appeal noted that this leaves very little scope for judicial development of the doctrine.[57] Indeed, it has become 'rather difficult to envisage circumstances in which the application of the evasion principle would be the exclusive determinant of the case';[58] the doctrine might well wither into obsolescence.[59]

10.5 Corporate Groups

Having considered the general development of veil-piercing doctrine in the United Kingdom, this chapter turns now to a more specific consideration of its deployment in corporate group cases. The question is whether courts can pierce the corporate veil so as to extend liability from insolvent subsidiaries to their parent companies. Let us consider the matter, first, at the level of theory. Here we might note that the rule of limited liability was never intended by the legislature to protect *company* assets. This is one argument in favour of veil-piercing, which facilitates extensions of liability from subsidiary companies to their parents. Another argument involves the weakness of the economic case in favour of protecting parent company assets through limited liability.[60] Readers will recall that Chapter 3 established that: there is no clear separation between ownership by parent companies of their subsidiaries and management of those subsidiaries because, in the typical case, parent companies are not content to hold shares as passive investors; there is no need to save parent companies from monitoring their subsidiaries and every reason to encourage such monitoring; there is no need to save parent companies from monitoring minority shareholders in their subsidiaries, because the parents' potential liabilities in case of subsidiary insolvency are invariant to changes in the wealth of minority investors (at least under a rule of pro-rata unlimited liability); and there is no need to facilitate the diversification of parent company investments through the grant of limited liability. Moreover, judicial power to pierce the corporate veil would permit courts to address a basic asymmetry in risk imposition and reward that arises in the group setting:

57 [2014] Bus LR 239, [66]. 58 Morse, *Palmer's Company Law*, [2.1544.8].

59 Hannigan, *Company Law*, p. 58. See, e.g., *Regina* v. *Boyle Transport (Northern Ireland) Ltd* [2016] 4 WLR 63.

60 See Ramsay and Noakes, 'Piercing the Corporate Veil in Australia', 264.

> If limited liability is absolute, a parent can form a subsidiary with minimal capitalization for the purpose of engaging in risky activities. If things go well, the parent captures the benefits. If things go poorly, the subsidiary declares bankruptcy, and the parent creates another with the same managers to engage in the same activities. This asymmetry between the benefits and costs, if limited liability were absolute, would create incentives to engage in a socially excessive amount of risky activities.[61]

Finally, holding parent companies liable for the debts of their subsidiaries would not impose personal liability on individual shareholders.[62] Their ability to enjoy the usual benefits of limited liability is unaffected.[63]

Despite a certain amount of theory favouring removal of the protection of limited liability from parent companies, UK courts have both affirmed its application and restricted the operation of veil-piercing in corporate groups. *Adams* v. *Cape Industries plc*[64] is the most important authority. It is largely but not wholly consistent with the subsequent decision in *Prest* v. *Petrodel Resources Ltd.*[65] The *Adams* case is especially interesting because it arose in a mass-tort context involving the causation of asbestos-related disease and injury. The Cape Group was a multinational enterprise with its parent company, Cape Industries plc, located in the United Kingdom. Subsidiary companies Casap and Egnep mined asbestos in South Africa. Another subsidiary, Capasco, organised the sale of South African asbestos to manufacturers around the world.[66] Asbestos was supplied to an insulation factory in Owentown, Texas. Employees of the manufacturing companies and consumers of asbestos products suffered various types of lung injury. The claimants argued that this asbestos was supplied to the manufacturers without the provision of adequate warnings of dangers to health.[67] Between 1953 and 1978, another Cape subsidiary, North American Asbestos Corporation (NAAC), assisted in the marketing of asbestos in the United States. NAAC was succeeded by Continental Products Corporation (CPC), which was ostensibly an independent company. However, CPC was formed using funds supplied by Cape Industries plc and managed by the same person who had headed NAAC.[68] It was little secret that CPC had been formed in order to ensure

61 F. Easterbrook and D. Fischel, *The Economic Structure of Corporate Law* (1991), p. 56.

62 Easterbrook and Fischel, *The Economic Structure of Corporate Law*, p. 56; H. Anderson, 'Veil Piercing and Corporate Groups – An Australian Perspective' [2010] *New Zealand Law Review* 1, 19.

63 Easterbrook and Fischel, *The Economic Structure of Corporate Law*, p. 56.

64 [1990] Ch 433. 65 [2013] 2 AC 415. 66 [1990] Ch 433, 505.

67 [1990] Ch 433, 506. 68 [1990] Ch 433, 541.

the removal of all Cape Group companies from the United States and from the jurisdiction of US courts.[69]

In the primary action in the *Adams* case, the asbestos claimants brought suit in the United States against NAAC, and that company was held liable. However, NAAC had no substantial assets left in the United States. The issue in the English litigation was whether Cape Industries plc could be held liable for NAAC's torts on a veil-piercing argument, so that it could be said that Cape Industries had been 'present' in the United States, and so that the US judgment could be enforced against it. In the High Court, Wyn Williams J had found that NAAC's business was its own business, and not the business of Cape Industries or Capasco, and dismissed the action.[70] Importantly, NAAC had had no authority to enter into contracts for and on behalf of Cape Group companies.[71] Similar findings were made with respect to CPC.[72]

On appeal to the Court of Appeal, the claimants submitted that: Cape and Capasco constituted a single commercial entity, and,[73] for jurisdictional purposes, NAAC's presence in the United States constituted the presence of Cape and Capasco; Cape and Capasco had been present and carrying on business in the United States in marketing and selling asbestos through NAAC, which had been its agent; and the corporate veil should be pierced as against CPC, to reveal the presence of Cape/Capasco in the United States.[74] The English Court of Appeal rejected each of these arguments. Important steps in its reasoning were as follows: first, the Court of Appeal rejected any attempt to elide the separate legal personalities of each of the companies involved. Slade LJ stated that '[t]here is no general principle that all companies in a group of companies are to be regarded as one',[75] not even so as to achieve substantial justice in the case. On the contrary, the law as it was then (and is now) constituted recognised 'the creation of subsidiary companies, which though in one sense the creatures of their parent companies, will . . . be treated as separate legal entities with all the rights and liabilities which would normally attach to separate legal entities.'[76] In this sense, it was not to the point that Cape ran a single integrated

69 [1990] Ch 433, 541. 70 [1990] Ch 433, 512. 71 [1990] Ch 433, 527.

72 [1990] Ch 433, 527.

73 Occasionally, Commonwealth courts have indicated sympathy with such an approach. See, e.g. *DHN Food Distributors* v. *Tower Hamlets LBC* [1976] 3 All ER 462; *Theosophical Foundation Pty Ltd* v. *Commissioner of Land Tax* (1966) 67 SR (NSW) 70, 75–6.

74 [1990] Ch 433, 531–2. 75 [1990] Ch 433, 532.

76 [1990] Ch 433, 536. See also *Re Polly Peck International plc* [1996] 2 All ER 433, 448.

mining division with little regard to corporate formalities as between members of the group.[77]

Second, the Court of Appeal accepted that Cape Industries plc controlled its subsidiary companies. It 'ran a single integrated mining division'. Moreover, Cape Industries plc enforced 'its power of control over the boards of Egnep, Capasco and NAAC'.[78] It ensured that orders for asbestos mined by the group went through NAAC,[79] and it was responsible for the migration of marketing activities from NAAC to CPC. However, day-to-day control of NAAC had been left to its manager, Mr Morgan.[80]

Third, the evidence did not establish that either NAAC or CPC had acted as Cape Industries plc's agent in a way which would establish Cape's presence in the United States. NAAC's functions included marketing, encouraging sales, and acting as a channel of communication. It played a coordinating role, especially in arranging for deliveries.[81] All of this was of 'great assistance to Cape/Capasco in arranging the sales of their group's asbestos in the United States'.[82] But a substantial part of the business carried on by NAAC was its own business.[83] It had its own creditors and debtors. It declared its own income and paid its own taxes. 'The return to Cape as NAAC's shareholder took the form of an annual dividend passed by resolution of NAAC's board of directors.'[84] There was an agency agreement between Cape Industries plc and NAAC, but it was not of the sort to create an extended liability. Most importantly, 'strictly defined limits' were imposed on the functions that NAAC was authorised to carry out. It had had no general authority to bind Cape/Capasco to contractual obligations.[85] The contention that CPC was an agent was even weaker because CPC was 'independently' owned. CPC carried on its own business and had no authority to bind Cape/Casap.[86]

Finally, the Court of Appeal rejected the contention that it should pierce the corporate veil on the basis that either NAAC or CPC was a 'mere façade'. The court acknowledged that this ground of veil-piercing had been recognised by the House of Lords in *Woolfson* v. *Strathclyde Regional Council*.[87] In determining its applicability, the Court of Appeal held the 'motive' of the defendant to be relevant.[88] In this way, the court was fully prepared to accept that 'Cape's intention was to enable sales of

[77] [1990] Ch 433, 537. [78] [1990] Ch 433, 537. [79] [1990] Ch 433, 538.
[80] [1990] Ch 433, 538. [81] [1990] Ch 433, 546. [82] [1990] Ch 433, 547.
[83] [1990] Ch 433, 545. [84] [1990] Ch 433, 546. [85] [1990] Ch 433, 547.
[86] [1990] Ch 433, 548–9. [87] 1978 SC (HL) 90, 96, noted at [1990] Ch 433, 539.
[88] [1990] Ch 433, 540.

asbestos from the South African subsidiaries to continue to be made in the United States while (a) reducing the appearance of any involvement therein of Cape or its subsidiaries, and (b) reducing by any lawful means available to it the risk of any subsidiary or of Cape as parent company being held liable for US taxation or subject to the jurisdiction of the US courts.'[89] But there was nothing unlawful in any of this, particularly as the scheme was not directed towards depriving anybody of pre-existing claims against Cape companies.[90] The court acknowledged also that CPC's role in the continued marketing of Cape asbestos in the United States was of great assistance to it, and that it had benefitted from Mr Morgan's knowledge and experience.[91] However, CPC was always intended to be – and was in reality – an independent company.[92]

Following on from this last set of findings, one will recall our discussion of *Adams* v. *Cape Industries plc* in Chapter 3, where we saw that the Court of Appeal affirmed the right of companies to engage in the structuring of group relations so as 'to ensure that the legal liability (if any) in respect of particular future activities of the group . . . will fall on another member of the group rather than the defendant company'.[93] This is consistent with the idea from *Prest* v. *Petrodel Resources Ltd*[94] that veil-piercing on the basis of evasion arises as a response to company controllers attempting to evade *pre-existing* legal obligations. While such a distinction is, no doubt, significant as a legal matter, it does not sound so convincing as a moral matter. This is to say that it is morally dubious to permit the structuring of group relations in such a way that operating companies hold negligible assets against which future tort judgments might potentially attach.[95]

The narrow confines of the veil-piercing doctrine enunciated in *Adams* v. *Cape Industries plc* are consonant with the restrictive approach the UK Supreme Court adopted in *Prest*. However, the main ground of veil-piercing – in corporate groups, as elsewhere – is no longer the 'sham' or 'façade' argument (considered further later).[96] Rather, the main ground of veil-piercing in groups is likely now to be evasion. 'The limited circumstances where the courts will pierce the corporate veil do not

[89] [1990] Ch 433, 541. [90] [1990] Ch 433, 544. [91] [1990] Ch 433, 541.
[92] [1990] Ch 433, 541, and 543–4. [93] [1990] Ch 433, 544. [94] [2013] 2 AC 415.
[95] See also P. Lipton, 'The Mythology of *Salomon*'s Case and the Law Dealing with the Tort Liabilities of Corporate Groups: An Historical Perspective' (2014) 40 *Monash University Law Review* 452, 479.
[96] Hannigan, *Company Law*, p. 47.

appear to extend to cases where a holding company quarantines the possible or potential future tort liabilities of a group within a subsidiary because it would be difficult to show there was an existing legal obligation or liability that was deliberately evaded by interposing a controlled company.'[97]

Having outlined the important UK authorities on veil-piercing in the corporate group context, it is interesting to refer to the empirical studies of this company law doctrine. Courts have been reluctant to pierce the veil in corporate groups. This has been said to reflect English law's 'extreme' conceptualism and adherence to the concept of separate legal personality.[98] To the extent that courts use the doctrine at all, piercing occurs less frequently with respect to parent companies than in cases of individual shareholders.[99] Piercing against a parent company is even more unlikely in cases where subsidiaries are not wholly owned – there being less of an alignment between the interests of parent and subsidiaries in such cases.[100] Consistently across the common law world, courts have been most willing to pierce the veil with respect to private companies closely controlled by shareholders managing those companies.[101] This appears to entail the conclusion that veil-piercing is unlikely to be applicable in cases involving larger corporate groups responsible for mass-torts:[102] piercing 'as a means of achieving group liability is a non-starter even in relation to arguably the most deserving case, namely that of the tort victims of a subsidiary company'.[103]

Although this chapter could well end at this point, for the sake of a more comprehensive treatment of the issue, we now go on to consider the ostensible elements of veil-piercing doctrine and the grounds upon which veil-piercing occurs, before turning to a comparison with US law.

[97] Lipton, 'The Mythology of *Salomon*'s Case', 480. See also Sealy and Worthington, *Cases and Materials in Company Law*, p. 73.

[98] J. Dine, *The Governance of Corporate Groups* (2000), p. 43.

[99] C. Mitchell, 'Lifting the Corporate Veil in the English Courts: An Empirical Study' (1999) 3 *Company Financial and Insolvency Law Review* 22. See also Ramsay and Noakes, 'Piercing the Corporate Veil in Australia', 263.

[100] S. Haddy, 'A Comparative Analysis of Directors' Duties in a Range of Corporate Group Structures' (2002) 20 *Company & Securities Law Journal* 138, 150.

[101] Ramsay and Noakes, 'Piercing the Corporate Veil in Australia', 263.

[102] See discussion below on US law, and S. M. Bainbridge, 'Abolishing Veil Piercing' (2001) 26 *Journal of Corporation Law* 479, 523 (noting that piercing is more likely to occur in the case of a single-car taxi company owner than in the case of Union Carbide).

[103] E. Ferran, *Corporate Finance Law* (2008), p. 37.

10.6 Elements of a Veil-Piercing Action

Consistently with the wider veil-piercing jurisprudence, the ostensible control which parent companies exercise over their subsidiaries is seen as a prerequisite for veil-piercing within corporate groups.[104] The basic reason for this arises from the 'misuse' of the corporate form;[105] those principally able to engage in such misuse are company controllers. In the corporate group context, one commentator explains the rationale thus: the parent–subsidiary relationship principally involves one corporate investor, which also acts 'in a managerial role, controlling business and policy direction, determining the [subsidiary] budget and undertaking, or strongly influencing, decision-making processes. The parent company, therefore, is usually aware, informed and in control of the risks undertaken by the subsidiary and in a good position to avoid unnecessary risks'.[106] This contrasts to the passivity of ordinary shareholders.

Leaving aside the problematic invocation of will theory–inspired notions of fault in this analysis, there are reasons to avoid making control the key to veil-piercing liability – and the reason for this lies in the structure of shareholdings in both corporate groups and very small companies. In both of these contexts, the fact that shareholdings are closely held (rather than dispersed) means that majority shareholders are in control.[107] As such, '[u]sing control as the sole test for veil-piercing would be tantamount to removing the veil altogether.'[108] In the words of David Millon: 'While it might make sense as a matter of abstract logic to have shareholder responsibility turn on the extent to which the shareholders caused the corporation to act as it did, a focus on shareholder control and the ends for which control is exercised invites controversy over facts that will be present to some degree in virtually every case involving a closely held corporation or corporate subsidiary.'[109] Finally, if the exercise of control were to be the key to veil-piercing liability, this

[104] See *Antonio Gramsci Shipping Corpn* v. *Recoletos Ltd* [2014] Bus LR 239, [46].

[105] P. B. Oh, 'Veil-Piercing' (2010) 89 *Texas Law Review* 81, 139.

[106] E. Dunn, 'James Hardie: No Soul to Be Damned and No Body to Be Kicked' (2005) 27 *Sydney Law Review* 339, 346. See also R. Thompson, 'Piercing the Veil within Corporate Groups: Corporate Shareholders as Mere Investors' (1999) 13 *Connecticut Journal of International Law* 379, 389.

[107] D. Millon, 'Piercing the Corporate Veil, Financial Responsibility, and the Limits of Limited Liability' (2007) 56 *Emory Law Journal* 1304, 1333.

[108] Anderson, 'Piercing the Veil on Corporate Groups in Australia', 336.

[109] Millon, 'Piercing the Corporate Veil', 1333. For reasons such as this, one may presume, the claimants in *Heytesbury Holdings Pty Ltd* v. *City of Subiaco* (1998) Aust Torts Rep ¶ 81–488 did not succeed despite the presence of control and a number of other factors.

would simultaneously reduce the scope of the doctrine and discourage the future exercise of beneficial control by parent companies.

All of this assumes the simple case of parent companies with full ownership or majority ownership of their subsidiaries as the targets of extended liability claims. But what is to be the position of minority shareholders? Perhaps there would be little difficulty in extending liability under the veil-piercing doctrine to all those shareholders with 'significant involvement in control'.[110] As regards companies with both controlling and non-controlling minority shareholders, one suggestion is that courts should not pierce the corporate veil at all – even as against the controlling shareholders.[111] But this appears to be like throwing the baby out with the bathwater. One must assume that a veil-piercing regime based upon a substratum of shareholder control would permit extensions of liability to controlling shareholders, but exempt the non-controlling minority shareholders.

The real controversy about veil-piercing doctrine has concerned what elements are necessary *in addition* to or beyond the control shareholders exercise over their investee companies.[112] As stated previously, some kind of 'misuse' must be proven,[113] the corporate entity being deployed in a way which could not have been intended or permitted by the legislature. There are a number of frequently cited grounds of veil-piercing, which we will work through in the following sections of this chapter. Some of these grounds appear to be unavailable in the United Kingdom following the decision in *Prest* v. *Petrodel Resources Ltd.*[114] That case restricts veil-piercing to cases of evasion. Indeed, a number of these alternative grounds for veil-piercing are weak foundations for a separate company law doctrine. However, other jurisdictions accept that veil-piercing is permissible on the alternative grounds.

It is useful to consider the position on veil-piercing in other Commonwealth jurisdictions – in part because we will make use of some of their jurisprudence and academic writing as we go forward. The veil-piercing doctrine is recognised in both Canada and

110 Millon, 'Piercing the Corporate Veil', 1361.

111 *Trustor AB* v. *Smallbone (No 2)* [2001] 1 WLR 1177, [14] and [20]; Hannigan, *Company Law*, 52.

112 'Veil-piercing is an enigma of company law. Its existence is almost universally accepted, yet it is not a principle reducible to distinct elements': P. W. Lee, 'The Enigma of Veil-Piercing' (2015) 26 *International Company and Commercial Law Review* 28, 28.

113 In *Ben Hashem* v. *Ali Shayif* [2009] 1 FLR 115, [171], Munby J stated that UK authorities emphasised 'the twin features of control and impropriety'.

114 [2013] 2 AC 415.

Australia,[115] but is not used frequently by their courts. When Commonwealth courts decide to pierce the corporate veil,[116] this seems to occur on the basis of a 'high' degree of control by controlling shareholders over their investee companies.[117] But consistently with the UK position, Commonwealth courts have not accepted the exercise of even day-to-day control as sufficient.[118] In addition, courts invoke various grounds for veil-piercing, the most important being the use of the entity as a façade to conceal the real decision-making of and undertaking of activities by the persons involved.[119] The trend seems to be away from use of the doctrine, the suggestion being that Commonwealth courts prefer to determine cases involving the liability of those associated with the company on orthodox legal grounds involving contract, equity, and tort rules.[120] This is, in part, a result of the lack of authoritative pro-liability decisions by appellate courts.[121]

Consistent, again, with UK case law, veil-piercing in other Commonwealth jurisdictions rarely occurs in corporate groups. The reluctance to extend liability to parent companies by use of this doctrine coheres with the long-standing attitude of the High Court of Australia, which emphasises the need to observe the separate entity principle even within groups of companies. In *Industrial Equity Ltd* v. *Blackburn*,[122] Mason J stated that 'in the absence of contract creating some additional right, the creditors of company A, a subsidiary company within a group, can look only to that company for payment of their debts. They cannot look to company B, the holding company, for payment.'[123] Where veil-piercing is undertaken, it occurs in small, closely held groups rather than in larger

[115] The position in the United States will be considered in a separate section.

[116] Although veil-piercing is comparatively 'rare', there can be no doubt that the doctrine has been utilised in the cases: see empirical studies in Khimji and Nicholls, 'Piercing the Corporate Veil Reframed'; Ramsay and Noakes, 'Piercing the Corporate Veil in Australia'.

[117] Khimji and Nicholls, 'Piercing the Corporate Veil in the Canadian Common Law', 248.

[118] E.g., *Dennis Willcox Pty Ltd* v. *Federal Commissioner of Taxation* (1988) 79 ALR 267, 274; Companies and Securities Advisory Committee, 'Corporate Groups Final Report' (2000), p. 17.

[119] Khimji and Nicholls, 'Piercing the Corporate Veil Reframed', 410–11; Anderson, 'Piercing the Veil on Corporate Groups in Australia', 354.

[120] Sealy and Worthington, *Cases and Materials in Company Law*, pp. 54–5.

[121] Khimji and Nicholls, 'Piercing the Corporate Veil Reframed', 404 (Canada lacks authoritative statement); *Walker* v. *Wimborne* (1976) 137 1 (High Court of Australia asserting the independent obligations of group companies).

[122] (1977) 136 CLR 567. [123] (1977) 136 CLR 567, 577.

groups.[124] There are few recorded cases where veil-piercing has been successful as against the shareholders of public companies.[125]

Before examining the grounds for extending liability, it is worth reiterating that the consequence of a successful claim to pierce the veil is (as defined) an extension of the liability of the company upwards to the shareholder. In the case of a corporate subsidiary, the parent company is made liable *in addition* to that subsidiary. The result is a form of joint and several liability.[126] This means that the claimant can choose to sue one only of these defendants and recover the whole amount from that defendant, while leaving it to seek contribution from other wrongdoing parties.[127]

10.7 Grounds of Veil-Piercing

In addition to control by the shareholder over the company in question, under UK and wider Commonwealth law, some additional factor must be present in order to pierce the corporate veil.[128] We now begin consideration of the grounds on which veil-piercing might be undertaken. The grounds (or potential grounds) considered are statute, fraud, evasion, concealment, and agency. Given the focus of this work on the position of personal injury claimants, no separate consideration will be given to the position in contract. Suffice it to say that, in English law, courts are reluctant to pierce the corporate veil where this would extend contractual obligations to new parties.[129] Although the potential grounds for veil-piercing are dealt with individually, this is for purposes of exposition; in many instances, decided cases appear to be capable of analysis under more than one heading.

124 Khimji and Nicholls, 'Piercing the Corporate Veil in the Canadian Common Law', 242; Ramsay and Noakes, 'Piercing the Corporate Veil in Australia', 263.

125 Khimji and Nicholls, 'Piercing the Corporate Veil in the Canadian Common Law', 232–3; Companies and Securities Advisory Committee, Corporate Groups Final Report, p. 17.

126 *VTB Capital plc* v. *Nutritek International Corpn* [2013] 2 AC 337, [114]–[115].

127 Civil Liability (Contribution) Act 1978. See C. Witting, *Street on Torts* (14th edn., 2015), p. 666ff.

128 *Antonio Gramsci Shipping Corpn* v. *Recoletos Ltd* [2014] Bus LR 239, [46].

129 *VTB Capital plc* v. *Nutritek International Corpn* [2013] 2 AC 337; *Linsen International Ltd* v. *Humpuss Transportasi Kimia* [2012] Bus LR 1649; *British Thomson-Houston Company Ltd* v. *Sterling Accessories Ltd* [1924] 2 Ch 33. See also *MacDonald Dickens & Macklin* v. *Costello* [2012] QB 244 (claimants aware that direct contract would give rise to unwanted tax liabilities for defendants).

10.7.1 Statute

We begin with consideration of veil-piercing on the basis of statute. In *Dimbleby & Sons Ltd* v. *National Union of Journalists*, Lord Diplock stated that the '"corporate veil" in the case of companies incorporated under the Companies Acts is drawn by statute and it can be pierced by some other statute if such other statute' provides for this in clear terms.[130] *Prest* v. *Petrodel Resources Ltd*[131] 'underlines that where a statutory rule is at issue the question is primarily to be resolved by interpretation of the legislation. Although the starting point is that a company is treated as a separate person for legislative purposes, a statute may, even implicitly, require that the corporate veil be disregarded'.[132] Indeed, this is the only ground of veil-piercing which the present writer would regard as consistent with statutory provisions limiting shareholder liability, absent recognised, fault-based wrongdoing.

Genuine statutory exceptions to the ordinary rule of shareholder limited liability arise in provisions such as: Insolvency Act 1986, section 214 and equivalents elsewhere in the Commonwealth, that create liability for wrongful trading, which can be imposed on parent companies when they act as shadow directors; those in the Commonwealth that permit the pooling of assets amongst group companies (considered in Chapter 7); and those in the US Comprehensive Environmental Response Compensation and Liability Act 1980 and the Oil Pollution Act 1990, which impose liability on the owners and the operators of certain facilities that give rise to hazardous pollution (considered in Chapter 8).

10.7.2 Fraud

In the tort of deceit, from which the common law of fraud emanates, a cause of action arises where the defendant makes a representation knowing of its falsity or without belief in its truth, or recklessly, careless as to whether it is true or false, with the intention that the claimant should act in reliance upon the representation, which causes damage to the claimant in consequence of his or her reliance upon it.[133] Under this tort, the relevant representation ordinarily consists of a statement, but any conduct that is intended (etc.) to mislead will suffice.[134] The exact relationship between

130 [1984] 1 WLR 427, 435. 131 [2013] 2 AC 415.

132 S. Bull, 'Piercing the Corporate Veil – in England and Singapore' [2014] *Singapore Journal of Legal Studies* 24, 32.

133 *Derry* v. *Peek* (1889) 14 Cas App 337. 134 Witting, *Street on Torts*, p. 355.

the tort of deceit and veil-piercing on the ground of fraud has never been examined properly by the courts. Yet it appears that veil-piercing on the ground of fraud might have occurred with less rigorous analysis than is apparent in deceit cases.[135] This is not necessarily a problem – as will be argued in Chapter 11, alteration of the elements of a cause of action might be defensible in order to cater to new circumstances.

The fraud head of veil-piercing is concerned with cases in which a company is operated in a manner or an express statement is made regarding it that misleads persons unfamiliar with the true facts. Ordinarily, this conduct is undertaken in order to avoid an existing legal obligation or to further some prohibited conduct. In the seminal veil-piercing case on the ground of fraud, *Re Darby, ex parte Brougham*,[136] the defendant was an undischarged bankrupt who was unable lawfully to act as a company director. He sought to hide his ownership and control over a newly incorporated company, which raised funds from the public. The prospectuses did not reveal the part the defendant played in the company. The company itself engaged in wrong-doing by buying assets from a connected party at a grossly inflated price. The debenture-holders succeeded in their claims against the defendant. Phillimore J observed that what had been done had been done through a company, which had been portrayed as an entity both substantial and respectable in nature and distinct from the defendant himself.[137]

Prima facie, veil-piercing on the ground of fraud would appear to be justifiable. This is on the basis, reaffirmed in *VTB Capital plc* v. *Nutritek International Corpn*, that 'fraud unravels everything'.[138] Yet, despite the comparative laxity of the rules regarding veil-piercing on the ground of fraud (as compared to the tort of deceit), this is a plea that rarely succeeds.[139] This appears, in part, to reflect the aversion of UK courts

[135] See, e.g., *Trustor AB* v. *Smallbone (No 2)* [2001] 1 WLR 1177. Although the allegation was one of fraud (ibid., 1180), it is not clear that there was any relevant representation which was misleading. For similar observations to those in the text, see Millon, 'Piercing the Corporate Veil', 1334.

[136] [1910] 1 KB 95. [137] [1910] 1 KB 95, 101.

[138] *Lazarus Estates Ltd* v. *Beasley* [1965] 1 QB 702, 712, discussed in *Prest* v. *Petrodel Resources Ltd* [2013] 2 AC 415, [18]. But doubt has been cast upon the validity of this statement, given the result in the *VTB* case itself: see Bull, 'Piercing the Corporate Veil', 31.

[139] This assumes that the results of an Australian study reflect the English position: see Ramsay and Noakes, 'Piercing the Corporate Veil in Australia'. A study of veil-piercing in England, Mitchell, 'Lifting the Corporate Veil in English Courts', does not provide specific figures about success rates in relation to particular heads such as fraud.

to make findings of 'fraud' in individuals, which carry a particular stain in the corporate and commercial worlds.

A new difficulty for claimants tempted to plead fraud in the United Kingdom is that veil-piercing doctrine is now seen as a remedy of last resort.[140] This was confirmed in the *VTB Capital* case,[141] in which RAP Co was interested in the purchase of various assets, including dairy companies, offered for sale by Nutritek. RAP needed finance for the purchase and entered into an agreement with VTB. VTB seems to have understood that the assets for sale were inadequate to secure the loan, yet loaned RAP US$225 million nevertheless. It turns out that both RAP and Nutritek were controlled by Mr Malofeev. RAP was unable to repay the loan and the security was deficient. VTB sought to pierce the corporate veil and make the beneficial owner Malofeev liable, based on misrepresentations about Malofeev's true role. One argument was that 'Mr Malofeev used RAP's separate legal status to disguise the ownership and control ultimately exercised over RAP by [Malofeev and Marcap], which disguise duly misled VTB into believing that there was a genuine arm's length transaction at a genuinely negotiated price.'[142] The UK Supreme Court refused to pierce the veil. Lord Neuberger was hesitant about agreeing to any wide proposition about the availability of this doctrine. He noted that the effect of the claimant's argument was that the person controlling a company would be held 'liable as if he had been a co-contracting party', even though this had never been the intention of the parties.[143] But there was no need to extend veil-piercing doctrine this far. Indeed, if the claimant's allegations were sound, there would be an action available against Malofeev for fraudulent misrepresentation, and that would be the better course to take.[144] This is consistent with idea that veil-piercing is a doctrine of last resort, to be relied upon when there is no other appropriate statutory or common law action.

In the United Kingdom, a question now arises as to whether the fraud ground for piercing the veil is sufficiently different from the newly announced evasion ground (to be considered next),[145] so as to justify its continued existence. Although they appear to be wafer-thin, differences might exist in that: first, the evasion ground was not expressed in *Prest* v. *Petrodel Resources Ltd*, to be dependent upon or overtly equated with fraud; and, second, the evasion ground might not require that there

140 Bull, 'Piercing the Corporate Veil', 31. 141 [2013] 2 AC 337.
142 [2013] 2 AC 337, [117]. 143 [2013] 2 AC 337, [132]. 144 [2013] 2 AC 337, [139].
145 In *Prest* v. *Petrodel Resources Ltd*, Lord Neuberger was not sure of the exact relationship intended by Lord Sumption: [2013] 2 AC 415, [83].

be any intention that the claimant rely upon a misrepresentation (whether by words or conduct),[146] which is a requirement in the tort of deceit. Under veil-piercing on the ground of evasion, the intention must be to evade and need not be to induce reliance. But this is a subtle distinction. The argument against drawing such a distinction is, indeed, that veil-piercing on the ground of fraud is *not* to be treated as equivalent to deceit. If this is the position, the fraud ground, because it is wider than the tort of deceit but without substantial difference from the evasion ground, has now been subsumed by the evasion ground.

In fact, a number of commentators have failed to see the point of veil-piercing on the specific ground of fraud. A conceptual problem with it (which might well infect the evasion ground also) is that the presence of 'fraud' does not give rise to any particular issue unique to company law (except that of attributing states of mind to the company for the purpose of making the company itself liable for the wrong). This is to say that shareholders acting 'fraudulently' by their use of a corporate entity take their place alongside all other fraudsters; the presence of a shareholder–company relationship does not seem to give rise to a particular problem to be resolved by company law. Successful cases of veil-piercing on the ground of fraud could be decided on other, more clearly defined grounds.[147]

In summary, the tentative argument being made here is that, in UK law, there is no longer a separate ground of veil-piercing on the basis of fraud. This ground has been subsumed by the evasion ground, and has been proven unnecessary.

10.7.3 Evasion

In *Prest* v. *Petrodel Resources Ltd*, Lord Sumption stated that 'there is a limited principle of English law[148] which applies when a person is under

[146] Thus, it has been observed that the 'company need not be set up for the purpose of evasion, though that is often the case': Hannigan, *Company Law*, p. 51.

[147] E.g., see argument that *Re Darby, ex parte Brougham* [1910] 1 KB 95 could have been decided on the basis that the defendant director had procured an unlawful act: Tan, 'Piercing the Separate Personality of the Company', 549.

[148] In support of this, Lord Sumption relied upon two notoriously shaky authorities: *Gilford Motor Co Ltd* v. *Horne* [1933] Ch 395; *Jones* v. *Lipman* [1962] 1 WLR 832. For criticism of these decisions, see *Antonio Gramsci Shipping Corp* v. *Stepanovs* [2011] 1 Lloyd's Rep 617, at [18](subsequently overruled); R. Cooke, *Turning Points of the Common Law* (1997), p. 13; J. W. Neyers, 'Canadian Corporate Law, Veil-Piercing, and the Private Law Model Corporation' (2000) 50 *University of Toronto Law Journal* 173, 220–2; Tan, 'Piercing the Separate Personality of the Company', 549. The thrust of the criticism is

an existing legal obligation or liability or subject to an existing legal restriction which he deliberately evades or whose enforcement he deliberately frustrates by interposing a company under his control.'[149] The remedy is confined to cases involving a legal obligation that X owed to Y 'independently of the company's involvement', and is not available where the obligation in question, in truth, was the company's own and not X's.[150] Moreover, as Hannigan summarises it the 'motive behind the use (not necessarily the incorporation) of the company must be a deliberate evasion of obligations or liabilities of X or the deliberate frustration of enforcement measures against X'.[151] Where the corporate controller is using the corporate form in this way, the court has the ability to 'pierce the corporate veil for the purpose, and only for the purpose, of depriving the company or its controller of the advantage that they would otherwise have obtained by the company's separate legal personality'.[152] On the facts of the *Prest* case, Lord Sumption noted Mr Prest had not taken part in evasion. Whatever his reasons for vesting residential properties in group companies, 'there is no evidence that he was seeking to avoid any obligation which is relevant in these proceedings. The judge found that his purpose was "wealth protection and the avoidance of tax"'.[153]

A modern case of veil-piercing on the ground of evasion is *Kensington International Ltd* v. *Republic of Congo*.[154] Kensington was assignee of contract claims against the Republic of Congo, but Congo refused to pay its debts in the absence of a restructuring agreement. Kensington sought attachment over a payment due to Congo from a third-party oil purchaser. Société Nationale des Pétroles du Congo (SNPC) was Congo's oil-trading instrumentality[155] and Mr Gokana was its president. Gokana was the ultimate owner and controller of Sphynx Bermuda.[156] Gokana signed contracts for and on behalf of Sphynx Bermuda, which was the intended

that the cases were capable of being decided on other grounds. In this sense, they would fail Lord Sumption's own test for invoking veil-piercing principles. See Khimji and Nicholls, 'Piercing the Corporate Veil Reframed', 428.

149 [2013] 2 AC 415, [35].

150 Hannigan, *Company Law*, p. 51. This is reflected in the obvious concern in *VTB Capital plc* v. *Nutritek International Corpn* [2013] 2 AC 337 about extending contractual obligations to a party never contemplated to bear them.

151 Hannigan, *Company Law*, p. 52.

152 [2013] 2 AC 415, [35].

153 [2013] 2 AC 415, [36].

154 [2005] EWHC 2684 (Comm). Some doubt about the result in this case was expressed by Lord Neuberger in *VTB Capital plc* v. *Nutritek International Corpn* [2013] 2 AC 337, [127] – but the issue was not explored.

155 [2005] EWHC 2684 (Comm), [63].

156 [2005] EWHC 2684 (Comm), [80].

recipient of the money over which the claimant sought attachment.[157] The argument was that the court should 'pierce the veil' of Sphynx Bermuda and treat a debt owed to it as a debt owed to Congo. Kensington pleaded a scheme 'by which the Congo dishonestly sought to defraud its creditors' by selling oil through entities including Sphynx Bermuda 'in a deliberate and dishonest attempt to conceal the true facts of a sale and receipt of proceeds by the Congo, in the hope of preventing the Congo's creditors from attaching the oil or proceeds of sale'.[158] Cooke J found that Sphynx Bermuda was used for such a purpose,[159] and that Gokana controlled its actions:

> Mr Gokana orchestrated the chain of transactions between Sphynx Bermuda and SNPC. He had control over all the entities concerned and directed what should take place, including the creation of contractual documents and invoices which were intended to present the appearance of commercial transactions between independently operated companies ... [T]he structure was designed and operated to conceal the fact that it was the Congo, through SNPC[], which was selling the oil in the international market and receiving the proceeds for it.[160]

Cooke J concluded that Gokana had deliberately put into place a scheme in order to enable SNPC to sell oil to international buyers, without their assets becoming available to meet Congo's existing liabilities.[161] This was a dishonest use of the corporate form.[162] The court pierced the corporate veil and treated the debt owed to Sphynx Bermuda as one owed to the Congo.[163] Because this order did not diminish the assets of Sphynx Bermuda's shareholder, Mr Gokana, it can be treated as a veil-piercing case only on the basis that Congo was in the functional position of shareholder or (in other words) the beneficial owner of the company.

There can be little doubt that the evasion ground for veil-piercing is very narrow in scope and that, in *Prest* v. *Petrodel Resources Ltd*,[164] the UK Supreme Court intended that this should be so. According to Lee Pey Woan, the 'singular focus' of the newly reformulated doctrine 'on the avoidance of a pre-existing legal obligation owed by a company's controller would exclude even egregious wrongdoing'.[165] The suggestion has been made that its operation could be widened, without loss of integrity,

[157] [2005] EWHC 2684 (Comm), [88].
[158] [2005] EWHC 2684 (Comm), [24].
[159] [2005] EWHC 2684 (Comm), [92].
[160] [2005] EWHC 2684 (Comm), [146].
[161] [2005] EWHC 2684 (Comm), [199].
[162] [2005] EWHC 2684 (Comm), [200].
[163] [2005] EWHC 2684 (Comm), [201].
[164] [2013] 2 AC 415.
[165] Lee, 'The Enigma of Veil-Piercing', 30.

by extending it to cases in which a company 'is interposed before the liability came into existence but when it was seriously contemplated'.[166]

10.7.4 Sham and Façade

Further grounds for veil-piercing, of continuing relevance in some parts of the Commonwealth, but apparently not in the United Kingdom, are those based upon a company being a 'sham' with no substantial operation,[167] or a 'façade' intended to hide the true dealings between transacting parties.[168] Although these grounds for veil-piercing have different emphases, they are closely related. In either case, by piercing the veil, courts purport to determine legal rights and liabilities according to the real or substantive underlying transactions, and impose liability upon corporate controllers.[169] In *Woolfson* v. *Strathclyde Regional Council*,[170] the House of Lords appeared to treat this as the main basis upon which veil-piercing occurred, but the strength of this dictum has dissipated over time. The façade argument appears to have been recycled, in *Prest* v. *Petrodel Resources Ltd*, as the 'concealment principle'.[171] But, as adumbrated, Lord Sumption held that this was not to be treated in the United Kingdom as a ground of veil-piercing.[172]

There are a number of problems with the sham and façade grounds of veil-piercing which have contributed to their decline. First, the sham argument often is associated with companies that lack adequate capital and resources for undertaking commercial operations. However, it is difficult to maintain this head of veil-piercing[173] in the absence of

[166] Bull, 'Piercing the Corporate Veil', 30. Cf. *Ord* v. *Belhaven Pubs Ltd* [1998] 2 BCLC 447 (which seems to support a commercially motivated restructure of a group of companies which disadvantages existing creditors, where there is no proven intention to evade the liability).

[167] *Adams* v. *Cape Industries plc* [1990] Ch. 433, 540.

[168] *Adams* v. *Cape Industries plc* [1990] Ch. 433, 539. See also Ramsay and Noakes, 'Piercing the Corporate Veil in Australia', 256.

[169] *ICT Pty Ltd* v. *Sea Containers Ltd* (1995) 39 NSWLR 640, 655–6.

[170] 1978 SC (HL) 90. See also *The Print Factory (London) 1991* v. *Millam* [2007] ICR 1331, [7].

[171] This is consistent with the argument put in Tan, 'Veil-Piercing – a Fresh Start', 25.

[172] [2013] 2 AC 415, [28].

[173] Macey and Mitts, 'Finding Order in the Morass', 108; S. B. Presser, 'The Bogalusa Explosion: "Single Business Enterprise", "Alter Ego", and Other Errors: Academics, Economics, Democracy, and Shareholder Limited Liability: Back towards a Unitary "Abuse" Theory of Piercing the Corporate Veil' (2006) 100 *Northwestern University Law Review* 405, 413; Bainbridge, 'Abolishing Veil Piercing', 520–1. The empirical data confirm that undercapitalisation is not a good indicator of liability: R. B. Thompson,

minimum capital requirements extending beyond public companies.[174] 'Thin capitalization, as a ground for veil-piercing, . . . assumes that it is appropriate for courts to effectively impose ad hoc or ongoing capital requirements upon corporations, even when the legislature has decided that such requirements are neither necessary nor desirable.'[175] Indeed, it would be absurd to have courts rule on *ongoing* capital requirements because 'practical considerations will often lead responsible business owners to prefer debt financing over equity'.[176] Moreover, there is no straightforward relationship between the amount of a company's capital and its ability to pay its debts in a timely manner.[177]

Both the sham and façade arguments suffer from the further problem (considered already) that a sham company or façade is still a real company which the courts cannot properly ignore.[178] In *Federal Commissioner of Taxation* v. *Casuarina Pty Ltd*, Windeyer J stated that '[a] company which speaks with the voice of the person who controls it and which acts as he directs is not necessarily to be called a façade, nor its acts in the law called shams. Its existence as a legal person is not incompatible with its practical obedience to orders.'[179] This was a reason for holding, in *VTB Capital plc* v. *Nutritek International Corpn*, that UK courts are reluctant to employ the sham or façade arguments. Such arguments were said, further, to be of uncertain scope and to give rise to confusion in their application.[180]

Veil-piercing on the ground of sham or façade has been an occasional feature of the jurisprudence in other Commonwealth jurisdictions. An example involving such an argument, arising in the context of a small-scale corporate group, was the Supreme Court of Queensland decision in *Commissioner for Fair Trading* v. *TLC Consulting Services Pty Ltd*.[181]

'Piercing the Corporate Veil: An Empirical Study' (1991) 76 *Cornell Law Review* 1036, 1066–7. Compare Oh, 'Veil-Piercing', 134 (table); J. Freedman, 'Limited Liability: Large Company Theory and Small Firms' (2000) 63 *Modern Law Review* 317, 335–8.

174 Council Directive 2006/49/EC of 14 June 2006 on capital adequacy of investment firms and credit institutions, OJ 2006 No L177/201. See also Companies Act 2006 (UK), ss. 761 and 763.

175 Khimji and Nicholls, 'Piercing the Corporate Veil in the Canadian Common Law', 218.

176 Millon, 'Piercing the Corporate Veil', 1338.

177 Millon, 'Piercing the Corporate Veil', 1338.

178 *VTB Capital plc* v. *Nutritek International Corp.* [2012] 2 CLC 431, at [68].

179 (1970–1) 127 CLR 62, 77. See, to similar effect, *Gas Lighting Improvement Co Ltd* v. *Inland Revenue Commissioners* [1923] AC 723, 740–1; *Hobart Bridge Co Ltd* v. *Federal Commissioner of Taxation* (1951) 82 CLR 372, 385; R. P. Austin and I. M. Ramsay, *Ford's Principles of Corporations Law* (13th edn., 2007), p. 131.

180 [2013] 2 AC 337, [124]. 181 [2011] QSC 233.

Proceedings for contempt were brought against a Ms Dimitrijevski, who had breached an order restraining her from carrying on the business of introduction services by use of interposed corporate entities. Dimitrijevski had been the sole shareholder, director, and company secretary of Southport Central Property Pty Ltd. That company had been, in turn, the sole shareholder of Love Network Qld Pty Ltd (LN). Dimitrijevski appointed directors to LN, but those directors and company employees understood that Dimitrijevski was in charge. It was pleaded that LN was but a sham or device used to avoid obligations arising under court orders.[182] The court held that the corporate veil could be pierced:

> It is one thing for the respondent to have been a shareholder of a company that in turn owned a company that conducted an introduction services business. The Order did not prohibit such indirect engagement. But it was an entirely different matter to circumvent the prohibition contained in the Order by interposing a corporate structure to disguise and conceal the reality revealed by the affidavit material that the respondent was in fact directly engaged in the operation of the business and was its controlling mind.[183]

However this may be, the case is open to the criticism that there was no need to pierce the corporate veil and impugn the 'reality' of LN's corporate existence, because Dimitrijevski had herself 'directly engaged' in prohibited activities.

It has been argued, further, that in many cases of sham or façade, the liability of the shareholder for the acts of the company will be capable of establishment on the basis of agency[184] – our next ground of veil-piercing.

10.7.5 Agency

Although it was long argued that veil-piercing might occur on the basis of a company acting as agent for its shareholder, it is now widely acknowledged that there is no need to resort to veil-piercing in such cases, and that liability on the basis of agency can be established by reference to the

182 [2011] QSC 233, [31]. 183 [2011] QSC 233, [56].

184 Khimji and Nicholls, 'Piercing the Corporate Veil Reframed', 441. It should be noted, though, that the authors take the view that agency does not require piercing the veil – because such a relationship reaffirms the separate legal personality of the company. Although the present author does not believe the veil-piercing is primarily concerned with separate legal personality, he otherwise agrees with this view.

normal principles governing agency agreements.[185] The danger of invoking veil-piercing principles when normal agency rules should apply is the same one that we encountered when considering veil-piercing on the ground of fraud – that is, that shortcuts will be taken to establish liability. The mere fact that one company owns the vast majority of the shares in another company does not make the subsidiary its agent,[186] and neither does the exercise of complete control. *Salomon* v. *A Salomon and Co Ltd*[187] is direct authority against the latter as a basis for a finding of agency.[188] The company must be treated from its registration as competent to deal with all comers,[189] including its controlling shareholder, on terms of equality.[190]

That agency *might* exist as between controlling shareholders and their controlled companies was established shortly after *Salomon*'s case. In *The Gramophone and Typewriter Co Ltd* v. *Stanley*, the Court of Appeal upheld the separate legal personality of a subsidiary company and affirmed that it was responsible for its own tax affairs. However, Cozens-Hardy MR stated also that a sole shareholder 'may cause such an arrangement to be entered into between himself and the company as will suffice to constitute the company his agent for the purpose of carrying on the business, and thereupon the business will become, for all taxing purposes, his business'.[191]

Whether an agency agreement exists is a question of fact as to the intention of the parties to the alleged agreement. This involves establishing an agreement evidencing assent by the agent to act for and on behalf of the principal. Transactions are undertaken as part of the principal's business, and the benefits inure to it.[192] Ordinarily, no such intention will be evident as between the parent company and its subsidiary,[193] and true

185 A. Muscat, *The Liability of the Holding Company for the Debts of its Insolvent Subsidiaries* (1996), p. 120; W. Day, 'Skirting around the Issue: The Corporate Veil after Prest v Petrodel' [2014] *Lloyd's Maritime and Commercial Law Quarterly* 269, 286.

186 *Kodak Ltd* v. *Clark* [1903] 1 KB 505 (98 per cent shareholding). For the US position (not covered in what follows), see American Law Institute, Restatement (Third) of Agency (2006), § 7.03, comment d (3).

187 [1897] AC 22.

188 *JH Rayner (Mincing Lane) Ltd* v. *Department of Trade and Industry* [1989] Ch 72, 189. See also Harris and Hargovan, 'Cutting the Gordian Knot of Corporate Law', 50–1.

189 *In re Wragg Ltd* [1897] 1 Ch 796, 824.

190 See Chapter 3.

191 [1908] 2 KB 89, 96. See also *Rainham Chemical Works Ltd* v. *Belvedere Fish Guano Co Ltd* [1921] AC 465; *Inland Revenue Commissioners* v. *Sansom* [1921] 2 KB 492, 503.

192 Harris and Hargovan, 'Cutting the Gordian Knot of Corporate Law', 50–1. However, the agent committing a tort is liable for its own acts: e.g., *CSR Ltd* v. *Young* (1998) Aust Torts Rep ¶ 81–468, 64,938.

193 Harris and Hargovan, 'Cutting the Gordian Knot of Corporate Law', 45.

examples of an agency relationship are said to be rare.[194] The typical intention of the parent company in incorporating subsidiaries is to avoid liability as a principal for the subsidiaries' acts,[195] in order to protect the parent company's own assets.[196] This is a reason for which subsidiaries are *not* authorised to bind the parent in contract, or under other forms of obligation.[197] The cases reveal that subsidiaries rarely have the ability to bind their parent companies in contract. Parent companies will use their own employees for this purpose.

The surprising thing about agency within corporate groups is that, where it exists, it might be 'the wrong way around'. The subsidiary agrees that the parent company carry out particular functions as the subsidiary's agent. This will be the case when the subsidiary is an operating entity, without substantial managerial and administrative infrastructure. In the Australian asbestos case of *CSR Ltd* v. *Young*,[198] the New South Wales Court of Appeal found that a subsidiary company, Australian Blue Asbestos, had appointed its parent company as its agent to enter into transactions on its behalf in the management of its business and in the sale and distribution of its products. Decision-making by the parent company for the subsidiary was at the behest of the subsidiary and, moreover, was subject to termination by the subsidiary.[199] This was not an unusual case. The nomination of the parent company to act as agent usually reflects a desire to avoid duplication of management roles within the group. Other functions that might be centralised in the parent company include finance, research and development, and/or procurement. This type of arrangement might be found among even the largest corporate groups.[200]

194 '[T]he idea that [the company] is mere machinery for effecting the purposes of the shareholders is a layman's fallacy': *Gas Lighting Improvement Co Ltd* v. *Inland Revenue Commissioners* [1923] AC 723, 741. See also Hannigan, *Company Law*, p. 44.

195 Muscat, *The Liability of the Holding Company*, p. 121; A. Nolan, 'The Position of Unsecured Creditors of Corporate Groups: Towards a Group Responsibility Solution which Gives Fairness and Equity a Role' (1993) 11 *Company & Securities Law Journal* 461, 479.

196 Harris and Hargovan, 'Cutting the Gordian Knot of Corporate Law', 51.

197 P. I. Blumberg, *The Multinational Challenge to Corporation Law* (1993), p. 80; K. A. Strasser, 'Piercing the Veil in Corporate Groups' (2005) 37 *Connecticut Law Review* 637, 648–9.

198 [1998] Aust Torts Reports 81–468.

199 [1998] Aust Torts Reports 81–468, 64,952–65,953.

200 E.g., *Federal Commissioner of Taxation* v. *BHP Billiton Finance Ltd* (2010) 182 FCR 526, [14] (findings of fact).

10.8 US Position

US courts have had much more extensive experience deciding veil-piercing cases than have Commonwealth courts – and the doctrine has been used on many more occasions to extend company liabilities to their shareholders. Given that this is so, we ought to consider whether a comprehensive and coherent approach has been arrived at – which might provide the model for other jurisdictions. A survey of the law and literature reveals that US case law is just as unsatisfactory as Commonwealth case law in this area.

The most widely recognised ground of veil-piercing in the United States is the so-called instrumentality doctrine. The doctrine reflects the fact 'that the directors or executives of the subsidiary do not act independently in the interests of the subsidiary, but take their orders from the holding company in the latter's interest'.[201] The recognised elements of this ground of veil-piercing are: the exercise by the defendant shareholder of dominant control over decision-making and operations in the company; the use of this control for a fraudulent or for some other improper purpose resulting in the commission of a wrong; and resultant injury to the claimant.[202]

In terms of what constitutes sufficient control in the corporate group context, Phillip Blumberg's analysis of the cases suggests the need for the parent company to be heavily engaged in decision-making for the subsidiary, perhaps bypassing subsidiary executives, and issuing instructions directly to subsidiary employees.[203] Courts might insist upon evidence of this level of intrusive control, not only in the general relations between companies, but also with respect to the specific transactions at issue.[204] Courts will insist upon more convincing evidence of the requisite control where the subsidiary is a substantial company than in cases where it is not.[205]

An 'alternative test' for veil-piercing in the United States, the alter ego test, was developed originally by California courts. It applies when there is 'such unity of interest and ownership that the separate personalities of the corporation and the individual no longer exist and that, if the acts are

[201] Muscat, *The Liability of the Holding Company*, p. 260.

[202] These requirements stem from the so-called Powell doctrine – from Powell, *Parent and Subsidiary Corporations*, p. 6. See, e.g., *Freeman* v. *Complex Computing Co* 119 F 3d 1044, 1053 (2nd Cir. 1997)(applying New York law).

[203] P. I. Blumberg, *The Law of Corporate Groups: Substantive Law* (1987), [10.02].

[204] W. J. Rands, 'Domination of a Subsidiary by a Parent' (1999) 32 *Indiana Law Review* 421, 437.

[205] Rands, 'Domination of a Subsidiary by a Parent', 443.

treated as those of the corporation alone, an inequitable result will follow'.[206] This test ostensibly is broader in nature than the instrumentality test. The first requirement has given rise to a multitude of 'laundry lists' used by courts to determine whether shareholders and their investee companies have separate operations,[207] which has the potential for the creation of uncertainty.

The empirical evidence on the success rates of veil-piercing arguments is quite clear. US courts are more amenable to veil-piercing in statutory and contract claims than in tort cases – and this is true no matter whether defendants are companies or individuals.[208] It is explicable, in part, on the basis that claims in contract disputes tend to be more tangible and quantifiable in nature.[209] There has been no veil-piercing in mass-tort cases.[210] When it occurs, veil-piercing in US corporate group cases appears to conform to the requirements of the instrumentality test, in that there must be a high level of control and fraud or misrepresentation practised by controlling shareholders in their use of investee companies.[211] Veil-piercing is less evident in groups on the basis of the alter ego doctrine. The reason for this appears to be that 'commingling of assets and failure to follow corporate formalities' is less frequently encountered in corporate group cases.[212] Veil-piercing occurs less frequently as against parent companies than it does against individual shareholders.[213] Where veil-piercing arguments are successful in the group context, this is against parent companies in closely held groups.[214] Veil-piercing against

[206] *Riddle* v. *Leuschner* 335 P 2d 107, 110–11 (Cal 1959).

[207] J. E. Antunes, *Liability of Corporate Groups: Autonomy and Control in Parent–Subsidiary Relationships in US, German and EU Law* (1994), p. 246 (listing seventeen commonly cited factors).

[208] C. L. Boyd and D. A. Hoffman, 'Disputing Limited Liability' (2010) 104 *Northwestern University Law Review* 853, 895; Oh, 'Veil-Piercing', 141; Matheson, 'The Modern Law of Corporate Groups', 1097 and 1122; R. B. Thompson, 'Piercing the Veil within Corporate Groups: Corporate Shareholders as Mere Investors' (1999) 13 *Connecticut Journal of International Law* 379, 386.

[209] Boyd and Hoffman, 'Disputing Limited Liability', 904.

[210] Bainbridge, 'Abolishing Veil Piercing', 523.

[211] Matheson, 'The Modern Law of Corporate Groups', 1153; T. E. Graulich, 'Substantive Consolidation – A Post-modern Trend' (2006) 14 *American Bankruptcy Institute Law Review* 527, 533; Thompson, 'Piercing the Corporate Veil: An Empirical Study', 1054–6.

[212] Matheson, 'The Modern Law of Corporate Groups', 1114–15.

[213] Matheson, 'The Modern Law of Corporate Groups', 1097 and 1114–15. See also N. Mendelson, 'A Control-Based Approach to Shareholder Liability for Corporate Torts' (2002) 102 *Columbia Law Review* 1203, 1259–60. Contra Boyd and Hoffman, 'Disputing Limited Liability', 904 (finding no evidence for this proposition).

[214] Oh, 'Veil-Piercing', 89–90.

public companies does not arise.[215] One commentator concludes that empirical study 'belie[s] the claims by enterprise liability proponents that courts are more readily viewing this area as one involving corporate groups rather than distinct corporate entities'.[216]

Just as there are major shortcomings in the Commonwealth law on veil-piercing, so are there shortcomings in the US law in this area. A first problem concerns the perennial difficulty of determining what is meant in a particular context by the term 'control', and then assessing whether the facts demonstrate that the requisite level of control existed. In William Rands' view, a 'determination of what constitutes excessive control is a difficult job for a judge because the "separateness" of a parent and subsidiary is formalistic. It is unrealistic to think that a parent and a subsidiary are truly separate, making it hard for a judge to determine when they are not separate.'[217]

A second problem is that, in deciding whether to pierce the veil, '[c]ourts and legislators have chosen to rely on after-the-fact adjudication based on general principles in lieu of more specific standards.'[218] Veil-piercing is undertaken, especially in the alter ego cases, by considering 'a myriad of independent and un-weighted factors'.[219] Many of the items regularly considered in the 'laundry list' are said to be vague. The result is, as adumbrated, that it is difficult to predict when courts will pierce the veil and extend liability to controlling shareholders.[220]

A third problem with US veil-piercing law is that there is insufficient policy guidance about what is and what is not permissible in the ownership and operation of companies.[221] In response to this issue, Mitts and Macey have attempted to isolate the policy factors that courts (sometimes unconsciously) adopt in determining veil-piercing cases. They assert three underlying concerns: first, courts pierce the corporate veil in order to achieve applicable statutory objectives. Second, they do so in order to remedy 'what appears to be fraudulent conduct that does not satisfy the strict elements of common law fraud'. If a court believes that a shareholder has led a contractual counterparty to understand that an obligation is a personal liability rather than merely a corporate debt, then

215 Thompson, 'Piercing the Veil within Corporate Groups', 385; Thompson, 'Piercing the Corporate Veil: An Empirical Study', 1070–1.
216 Matheson, 'The Modern Law of Corporate Groups', 1114–15.
217 Rands, 'Domination of a Subsidiary by a Parent', 443.
218 Thompson, 'Piercing the Corporate Veil: An Empirical Study', 1043.
219 Oh, 'Veil Piercing Unbound', 104.
220 Millon, 'Piercing the Corporate Veil', 1330.
221 Macey and Mitts, 'Finding Order in the Morass', 125; Oh, 'Veil Piercing Unbound', 105.

it might pierce the veil to impose liability on the individual shareholder. Third, courts pierce the corporate veil in order to promote 'bankruptcy values'. In order to maximise the insolvent estate, courts disregard the corporate form in order to prevent fraudulent conveyances and preferential transfers.[222]

Mitts and Macey might well be correct in their identification of key policy concerns. Yet these policy concerns do not reflect the whole gamut of issues that need to be addressed. Mitts and Macey neglect to consider the basic legitimacy of a company enjoying the protections of limited liability. The reasons for doubting the cogency of economic arguments in favour of limited liability for parent companies were considered in Chapter 3 (and summarised earlier in this chapter). These can be summed up here by the observation that the 'parent company as a shareholder in its subsidiary companies is in quite a different economic role and performs quite a different management function [from] individual shareholders, including public shareholders in the parent company itself'.[223] Yet there is hardly a trace of this concern in the cases.[224]

Be that as it may, there is little to suggest that veil-piercing doctrine is of real assistance in the kinds of case with which this book is concerned – that is, in cases of insolvent subsidiaries and mass-torts. In fact, a leading commentator on the US law of veil-piercing tells us to 'banish' the thought from our minds.[225]

10.9 Deficiencies in Veil-Piercing Doctrine

Many of the conclusions about the operation of the veil-piercing doctrine in the United States are equally applicable to the Commonwealth law. Briefly stated, the objections include the following arguments, not all of which have been explicitly mentioned to this point. First, veil-piercing that entails a court 'ignoring' the existence of a validly formed company is highly problematic. The better view is that veil-piercing, if lawful, provides exceptions to limited liability. Shareholders are made liable for debts of the companies in which they invest. Second, apart from those

222 Macey and Mitts, 'Finding Order in the Morass', 101–2.

223 Strasser, 'Piercing the Veil in Corporate Groups', 638–9. See also Bainbridge, 'Abolishing Veil Piercing', 528.

224 '[J]udges seem to be concerned more with the facts and equities of the specific case at bar than with the implications of personal shareholder liability for society at large': Bainbridge, 'Abolishing Veil Piercing', 481.

225 Bainbridge, 'Abolishing Veil Piercing', 523.

with a statutory mandate, exceptions to limited liability are directly at odds with statutory limited liability for shareholders when they arise by way of strict liability rather than from recognised forms of fault-based wrongdoing. Third, courts across the common law world have struggled to provide defensible and consistent rules that govern veil-piercing – with the exception that the doctrine in the United Kingdom now is very narrow, so that it rarely will be of assistance. Where rules have not been properly defined, it becomes difficult to predict when veil-piercing will occur. This creates uncertainty for business, and might well entail little 'meaningful effect on internalizing risk or on increasing firm monitoring' as a result.[226] Fourth, at least one commentator believes that a fundamental problem of veil-piercing doctrine is that, ultimately, it focusses upon the behaviour of corporate controllers, and so liability would be largely explicable on the basis of traditional private law rules.[227] It is for such reasons that Stephen Bainbridge argued that 'veil-piercing brings a shotgun approach to a context in which more carefully targeted solutions are preferred' and that it ought to be abolished.[228] This is an argument with which the present writer has much sympathy.

10.10 Alternatives to Veil-Piercing

There is a growing chorus among courts and commentators to the effect that veil-piercing ought to be either abolished or limited to dealing with exceptional cases that are not capable of resolution by other means. In the United Kingdom, the Supreme Court decision in *Prest* v. *Petrodel Resources Ltd*[229] emphasises the importance of applying ordinary statutory and common law rules in the resolution of creditor claims against corporate controllers. This reflects the fact that UK veil-piercing decisions (of which there are, at best, very few) can be explained better on the basis of those rules. It might be, then, that the practical effect is 'to abolish the veil-piercing jurisdiction'.[230]

As adumbrated, many eminent academic commentators now take this stance. Thus, Tan Cheng-Han has argued for the need to focus upon statutory provisions creating separate personality and limited liability so as to ascertain their proper limits. In this way, he argues that 'the idea of

226 Glynn, 'Beyond "Unlimiting" Shareholder Liability', 349–50. See also Strasser, 'Piercing the Veil in Corporate Groups', 637 and 650.
227 Anderson, 'Piercing the Veil on Corporate Groups in Australia', 335.
228 Bainbridge, 'Abolishing Veil Piercing', 524. 229 [2013] 2 AC 415.
230 Lee, 'The Enigma of Veil-Piercing', 32. See also Day, 'Skirting around the Issue', 271.

abuse (or misuse) of the corporate form is apposite because even if one cannot formulate all the purposes for legislation relating to companies, it is at least possible in certain cases to establish what is clearly not within such legislative intent. Corporations are facilitative instruments and the privilege of incorporation was granted to facilitate legitimate human endeavour. Corporate vehicles were not intended to facilitate dishonesty or acts against public policy.'[231] The present writer would go further and argue for clear legislative guidelines as to when exceptions to limited liability should be utilised, especially in favour of personal injury claimants.[232] Such was the argument in the previous chapter.

The argument in favour of using ordinary common law principles to resolve veil-piercing cases is not new.[233] 'This renewed emphasis on conventional principles is generally a step in the right direction as it encourages consistency and avoids the proliferation of liability through (potentially) unprincipled extensions of the law.'[234] Indeed, Bainbridge notes that his proposals for abolishing veil-piercing are not intended to circumvent appropriate liability decisions. In particular, he notes that 'shareholders who participate in tortious conduct can (and should) be held personally liable.'[235] The present writer would clarify that liability should be extended to all those involved in wrongdoing, whether they be parent companies, directors (including shadow directors), company officers, or others.[236] This would ensure the uniform application to all legal

[231] Tan, 'Veil-Piercing – a Fresh Start', 29.

[232] Note that 'a general concern resulting from holding companies walking away from insolvent subsidiaries leaving creditors of the subsidiaries unpaid, led to the Australian Commonwealth Parliament amending the Corporations Law in 1993 to introduce s 588V': Ramsay and Noakes, 'Piercing the Corporate Veil in Australia', 259.

[233] '[T]he corporate capacity is a legal fact, not a fiction. Problems of responsibility for fraud or for acts of a corporation used as an agent are to be solved not by "disregarding" the corporate personality, but by the application of the usual principles of liability for the acts of other persons or for collusion with them': H. W. Ballantine, 'Separate Entity of Parent and Subsidiary Corporations' (1925–6) 14 *California Law Review* 12, 20. See also S. H. C. Lo, 'Liability of Directors as Joint Tortfeasors' [2009] *Journal of Business Law* 109; C. H. Tham, 'Piercing the Corporate Veil: Searching for Appropriate Choice of Law Rules' [2007] *Lloyd's Maritime and Commercial Law Quarterly* 22; Neyers, 'Canadian Corporate Law', 215ff.

[234] Lee, 'The Enigma of Veil-Piercing', 32.

[235] Bainbridge, 'Abolishing Veil Piercing', 524. Bainbridge suggests the need to think outside the box and consider the application of torts of misrepresentation and doctrines of vicarious liability and joint tortfeasance: ibid., 516.

[236] See, e.g., *Standard Chartered Bank* v. *Pakistan International Shipping Corp (No. 2)* [2003] 1 AC 959 (directors); Lo, 'Liability of Directors as Joint Tortfeasors'; *MCA Records Inc* v. *Charly Records Ltd* [2002] BCC 650, 668 (de facto managing director); R. Flannigan, 'The

persons of policies including compensation for and deterrence of wrongdoing.[237] The next two chapters consider how ordinary tort law principles might be used in order to address the more specific insolvent entity problem. Chapter 11 is concerned with torts permitting direct actions against parent companies and network participants. Chapter 12 is concerned with arguments that the law of vicarious liability and/or cognate principles of joint liability might have a place in the corporate group context.

Personal Tort Liability of Directors' (2002) 81 *Canadian Bar Review* 247, 259–61 (shareholders).

237 This argument, as applied to company directors, is made in Lo, 'Liability of Directors as Joint Tortfeasors', 110.

11

Direct Liability in Tort

11.1 Introduction

The insolvent entity problem involves at least three parties: an insolvent company, another, solvent company in the corporate group or network, and an unsatisfied tort claimant. This chapter examines ways in which tort law allows personal injury claimants in three-party situations to extend liability from the insolvent company to other, solvent companies. This chapter considers tort actions available or potentially available for the causation of personal injuries to employees, consumers, and bystanders. It examines two fault-based torts applicable to three-party cases, namely negligence and unlawful means conspiracy.

This chapter recommends that a new tort, inspired by the existing tort of unlawful means conspiracy, be created in order to facilitate actions against coordinating parties where at least one company has been objectively reckless in the causation of personal injuries. To anticipate what comes next, Chapter 12 complements this chapter on direct liability in tort by considering strict liability rules of vicarious liability and non-delegable duties, which are available, also, in three-party contexts. That chapter concludes by examining how rules of joint liability assist in extending liability from an insolvent company which has caused personal injuries.

In preface to our discussion of these torts and tort doctrines applicable in three-party cases, it is convenient to consider the aims of modern tort law. This will help us to understand why tort law has the potential to be of great assistance in resolving the insolvent entity problem.

Tort law is composed of civil wrongs. Typically, these wrongs are constructed upon elements of loss, causation, and a responsibility base. Responsibility bases are of different kinds. They include intention (a mental state), negligence (not a mental state, but rather a failure to reach a reasonable standard of care), and other bases, such as significant relationships between persons (for example, in vicarious liability). Torts are designed to protect fundamental human interests.[1] These 'interests' comprise natural and other goods and attributes[2] that people need to lead secure, meaningful, and satisfying lives, and which civilised societies recognise as worthy of (some degree of) protection. Tort law identifies which of the many human (and related) interests are so fundamental that the law should impose obligations upon all persons that are designed primarily to protect those interests and, secondarily, to provide remedies when those interests are wrongfully violated by others.

Persons commence tort actions when they have suffered *infringement* of their interests, usually resulting in a measurable loss of some kind. The claimant seeks compensation for the loss – and perhaps brings action for subsidiary reasons involving vindication of his or her sense of rectitude and/or dignity,[3] and the desire to deter future wrongdoing. Just as important are the reasons for which the *state* permits actions in tort law. One basic reason relates to the need to maintain order amongst its citizenry – to prevent persons engaging in their own vendettas with the potential that this might have for blood to be spilt. A second reason relates to the state's instrumentalist desire to create appropriate standards or norms of conduct among persons.[4] Tort law facilitates interactions between persons so that they can undertake their business in the knowledge that certain minimum standards of conduct will be respected. Tort law aims to deter those who do not meet such standards of conduct.[5] A third reason is that tort law permits the state to create and uphold these standards without having to accept complete responsibility for studying coordination problems in advance, and being proactive in the provision of solutions – the system is one of private enforcement, which is a cost-effective way of achieving the state's instrumentalist aims. This is not to

[1] 'Interests' rather than 'rights' because rights talk is potentially misleading, being constructed ordinarily upon the idea of pre-existing entitlements. For problems with tort theories of rights, see P. Cane, 'Rights in Private Law', in D. Nolan and A. Robertson (eds.), *Rights and Private Law* (2012), ch. 2, and G. C. Keating, 'Is the Role of Tort to Repair Wrongful Losses?', ibid., ch. 13.

[2] For a full consideration of what these might be, see, e.g., J. M. Finnis, *Natural Law and Natural Rights* (2nd edn., 2011); N. J. McBride, 'Tort Law and Human Flourishing', in S. G. A. Pitel, J. W. Neyers, and E. Chamberlain (eds.), *Tort Law: Challenging Orthodoxy* (2013), ch. 2.

[3] J. Varuhas, 'The Concept of "Vindication" in the Law of Torts: Rights, Interests, and Damages' (2014) 34 *Oxford Journal of Legal Studies* 253.

[4] On norms, see S. A. Smith, 'The Normativity of Private Law' (2011) 31 *Oxford Journal of Legal Studies* 1.

[5] E.g., *Crawford Adjusters Ltd* v. *Sagicor Insurance Ltd* [2014] AC 366, 403, and 432; *E* v. *English Province of Our Lady of Charity* [2013] QB 722, 745, 751, and 758.

deny that, in more pressing cases, the state will step in and pass legislation that directly addresses the issues – which it occasionally does. In previous chapters of this book, we have considered several ad hoc statutory interventions that result in extended liability of corporate groups and networks.

The problem of uncompensated victims of corporate torts reveals a clash of values between tort law and company law: 'first, the need to ensure sufficient certainty in the law to permit the efficient allocation of risk in a corporate group, whether through the creation of subsidiaries, or through the contractual allocation of rights and duties; secondly, the need to ensure that the resulting allocation of risk in the group does not end in failure to compensate third parties for losses caused by the activities of group members'.[6] Injured claimants unable to obtain full compensation from injuring companies that have become insolvent have been forced to rely either upon the state or upon their own resources in order to obtain treatment and recover their health. This reflects the *externalisation* of tort losses onto both the state and individual victims. In this way, it would seem that the aims of tort law are being subordinated to those of company law, or perhaps more accurately, to the perceived needs of commerce in modern, competitive economies.[7] Adherence to commercial imperatives has manifested itself in repeated, often unthinking applications of rules of separate legal personality and limited liability of shareholders. Thus, tort claimants might go uncompensated, even when the injuring companies are part of viable corporate groups.

The world over, respected company lawyers have argued against the subordination of tort law goals to company law. Henry Hansmann and Renier Kraakman, for example, believe that liability for corporate wrongs should be treated as a question of tort law, rather than of company law.[8] This chapter attempts to identify tort rules which fulfil this mandate and which are attuned to the ways in which corporate groups and networks operate. In thinking through the issues, a number of important points should be kept in mind. The first point was made in the discussion of a proposal for 'modified limited liability' in Chapter 9, which is that, in the typical personal injury case arising from a mass-tort, tort claimants and

[6] P. Muchlinski, *Multinational Enterprises and the Law* (2nd edn., 2007), p. 321.

[7] P. I. Blumberg, *The Law of Corporate Groups: Substantive Law* (1987), p. 162; J. Antunes, *Liability of Corporate Groups: Autonomy and Control in Parent–Subsidiary Relationships in US, German and EU Law* (1994), p. 262.

[8] H. Hansmann and R. Kraakman, 'Towards Unlimited Shareholder Liability for Corporate Torts' (1991) 100 *Yale Law Journal* 1879, 1881.

corporate constituents seek to protect quite different interests. On the one hand, tort claimants suffer physical injuries, and in many asbestos and pharmaceutical cases these injuries cause deaths or ruin lives forever. On the other hand, companies and their shareholders stand to suffer no more than financial losses should they be held liable for the causation of these injuries. Yet rules of separate legal personality and shareholder limited liability prevent recovery from parent companies and other shareholders. The second point is that these rules prevent recovery on contestable grounds. As Chapter 3 explained, economic arguments in favour of limited liability are weak – at least when applied to corporate shareholders. The third point is that, in considering the appropriate extent of tort liability, we need to keep the aims of tort law in mind, and to keep in mind their importance not only in ensuring properly coordinated interactions within communities (free from accidents), but also in fully respecting the value of life and limb.

The aims of tort law have been explained to encompass compensation, vindication, and deterrence. Before bringing this introduction to tort law in the group and network context to a close, something more should be said about the last of these aims. This is because many scholars question the idea that tort law is an effective deterrent of wrongful conduct.[9] The argument to be made in response to this concern is that tort law has the potential to be a relatively effective deterrent of *corporate* misconduct. This is because courts can speak to and act upon companies and other organisations in ways that they cannot do so easily with respect to most *individuals* (professional persons being an exception).[10] In the present writer's view, companies and other organisations are deterr*able* parties. This is evident in several organisational traits identified in various chapters in this book.

Deterrence is seen at work when courts make orders intended to change the future behaviour of wrongdoers. Companies and other organisations are well-placed to absorb the lessons that courts address to them through their orders. This arises from several structural features, which facilitate comprehension, learning, adaptation, and change: first, organisations form because groups are better able to achieve sophisticated aims than

9 E.g., E. Weinrib, *The Idea of Private Law* (1995), pp. 39–42.

10 Professionals are likely to be an exception for a number of reasons: typically, they are highly educated and inculcated with certain standards of conduct; standards are reinforced through the requirements of professional organisations; and insurers of professionals will play an educative role.

individuals are when acting alone.[11] Organisations facilitate the assembly of large-scale resources, planning of complex activities, and the execution of predefined tasks. Coordination among managers, experts, technicians, workers, and others is achieved through the hierarchical nature of organisations, orders originating at the top of the hierarchy, providing direction to subordinates about who should be doing what.[12] In manufacturing especially, work must be structured in these ways in order to deal with the continual flow of physical inputs.[13] Second, organisations have integrating mechanisms for implementing managerial decisions.[14] These mechanisms give them internal effect. They include recording decisions in rule books or policy manuals, holding training days, and developing the organisational ethos or culture. Third, organisations foster commitment to group endeavours,[15] which strengthens the resolve to get things done, and conformity to the group ethos, which ensures that decisions, norms, and policies are given proper effect.[16] The development of organisational values and commitment thereto reduces the need for the use of formal sanctions, as participants are subject to mutual oversight and informal reproach.[17] All of this ensures that commitment to organisational values has the potential to become self-reinforcing. Formal sanctions are applied as a last resort.[18] As indicated, these structural features of organisation make them especially amenable to change brought about by such things as court orders. Indeed, there is an argument in the organisation literature that attributes of organisation, such as those described, are *inherently geared towards*

[11] M. J. Hatch, *Organization Theory: Modern, Symbolic, and Postmodern Views* (3rd edn., 2013), p. 90.

[12] Hatch, *Organization Theory*, pp. 92–3.

[13] D. S. Pugh, 'Does Context Determine Form?', in D. S. Pugh (ed.), *Organization Theory: Selected Classic Readings* (5th edn., 2007), p. 24.

[14] Hatch, *Organization Theory*, p. 101.

[15] E.g., R. Tuomela, *The Philosophy of Sociality: The Shared Point of View* (2007), p. 5; M. Gilbert, *A Theory of Political Obligation* (2006), p. 138.

[16] E.g., Tuomela, *The Philosophy of Sociality*, p. 68; Gilbert, *A Theory of Political Obligation*, p. 146. See also M. A. Eisenberg, 'Corporate Law and Social Norms' (1999) 99 *Columbia Law Review* 1253, 1291–2 ('shifts in obligational norms depend heavily on shifts in belief-systems').

[17] E.g., C. List and P. Pettit, *Group Agency: The Possibility, Design, and Status of Corporate Agents* (2011), p. 173.

[18] Large organisations might have further attributes that make them deterrable, including significant expertise and knowledge, say, on health and safety matters; significant research and development budgets, so that things can be done better in the future; legal and regulatory expertise to guide future activity and ensure conformity with the law; and pressures to conform to law and social expectations which arise from existence in the public eye.

adaptation to external events and to the implementation of norms of behaviour, whether these external events take place in markets, the legal environment, or wider society.[19]

It should be apparent, then, that organisations are deterr*able*. Whether they are deterred in fact by court orders addressed to them will depend upon a number of factors which, it is submitted, are amenable to improvement should they prove problematic. These include the clarity with which judgments are written, the terms of the specific orders that are made against organisational defendants, the priorities of organisational management in dealing with court orders, and the enthusiasm with which management pursues required changes.

All of this is to affirm, then, that tort law has a place in the regulation of conduct, and that it has an especial resonance in the organisational setting with which this book is concerned. The three-party torts to be discussed in this chapter are negligence and unlawful means conspiracy. As will become evident, the tort of negligence has the potential to permit the extension of liability from insolvent subsidiaries in an upward direction towards their parent companies based upon parent company control over their subsidiaries and their role in the causation of injury. But being based upon the exercise of control, negligence liability is capable of application only in vertical parent–subsidiary relationships. This points to a major limitation, and gives rise to the question whether some other tort might prove a useful complement to negligence were it to facilitate the extension of liability from insolvent subsidiaries to other elements in the group – without the need to prove control.

At present, no other three-party tort provides such complementary liability. However, the argument to be made in this chapter is that the tort of unlawful means conspiracy is now at a stage where – in England, Canada, and Australia – it is ripe for development in the corporate context. In order to ensure its appropriate development in the group context, courts will need to lower the degree of fault required to establish liability from intention to injure to objective recklessness, and accept that the tort of unlawful means conspiracy should be available to redress claims of personal injury. It will be submitted that neither of these steps is insurmountable. The resulting tort, tentatively named 'multiple entity recklessness', would be capable of application beyond corporate groups to any

[19] H. Tsoukas and R. Chia, 'On Organizational Becoming: Rethinking Organizational Change' (2002) 13 *Organization Science* 567. See also M. Dan-Cohen, 'Sanctioning Corporations' (2010) 19 *Journal of Law and Policy* 15, 25–7.

commercial relationships, for example among networks which evince objective recklessness in the coordination of activities and which cause personal injuries. In this sense, the tort would have value even if a statutory exception to limited liability (argued for in Chapter 9) were available.

11.2 Tort of Negligence

Although negligence is by far the most important of the torts in terms of the number of claims made in court, only occasionally have successful claims been made against parent companies for injuries suffered by employees, customers, and bystanders interacting with subsidiaries. However, the number of successful claims is growing, and this tort might yet prove an important type of extended liability. The elements of negligence encompass a 'duty of care', which signifies a legal relationship between classes of person such that care must be taken, breach of the standard of conduct applicable to the relevant interaction between the actual parties, and damage of a kind that is reasonably foreseeable. The focus of this section will be upon duty of care and causation, proof of actual causation of damage being required in most cases of negligence but less frequently in cases involving mass-torts. The courts have been required to adapt the duty of care and notions of causation in order to accommodate the special problems that arise in three-party cases involving mass-torts, insolvent subsidiaries, and claims against parent companies. Illustration of some of these problems will be given by reference to cases involving asbestos and defective pharmaceutical products. The assumption underlying the discussion is that loss or injury arises from the defendant's positive acts, such as in the supply of injurious products.[20]

11.2.1 Duty of Care

We begin with the first element of the cause of action in negligence, which is the duty of care. This section discusses the function of the duty of care, the method by which the existence of a duty is determined, and its application in the asbestos context.

The historical origins of the 'duty of care' are consistent with its modern role in signifying that the law recognises certain relationships

[20] There is no specific discussion of failures to warn through demonstration of safe usage or better labelling. For the latter, see C. Witting, *Liability for Negligent Misstatements* (2004), ch. 13.

between classes of person to which onerous obligations of care attach.[21] Whether a new duty category should be recognised depends upon various factors concerning the nature of interactions between the relevant classes of person. UK and Canadian law utilises the concept of 'proximity' to pick out significant features in the interactions between persons, these features creating pathways to harm. The test of foreseeability is used in order to ascertain whether members of the defendant class have a minimal ability to recognise that the proximity existing between the parties has the potential to facilitate injury should care not be taken. Together, proximity and foreseeability constitute the factual basis upon which a duty of care is imposed. Where these sub-elements are present, frequently the law imposes a duty of care as between the interacting classes. However, courts can assess the duty issue on more normative or policy-oriented terms. Policy-based reasons might lead to the denial of a duty of care despite the presence of the requisite factual sub-elements.[22] We turn now to a more detailed consideration of these sub-elements beginning with proximity.

In the seminal UK negligence case of *Donoghue* v. *Stevenson*, Lord Atkin attempted to determine what sorts of relations between persons give rise to duties of care.[23] He concluded that prior courts had used a concept of proximity in examining factual relations between persons, proximity subsisting where persons 'are closely and directly affected' by the acts of others.[24] Lord Atkin's view of proximity is analytically *relational*, concerned with identifying factual features which closely link persons to each other.[25] Proximity appears important because it helps to identify the

[21] See, generally, C. Witting, *Street on Torts* (14th edn., 2015), pp. 26–7. Just as in the United Kingdom, it seems that the key duty concept in Canada is that of proximity of relationship between claimant and defendant: see *Odhavji Estate* v. *Woodhouse* [2003] 3 SCR 263; *Cooper* v. *Hobart* [2001] 3 SCR 537; M. Conway, 'A New Duty of Care? Tort Liability from Voluntary Human Rights Due Diligence in Global Supply Chains' (2015) 40 *Queen's Law Journal* 741, 776. The rules to be described can be contrasted to approaches taken in the United States (see J. C. P. Goldberg and B. C. Zipursky, *The Oxford Introductions to US Law: Torts* (2010), 77–82) and Australia (see *Sullivan* v. *Moody* (2001) 207 CLR 562 on the 'salient features' approach). Steps in the historical evolution of duty are set out in J. Plunkett, *The Duty of Care: A Comparative Common Law Analysis* (DPhil Thesis, University of Oxford, 2015).

[22] See *Caparo Industries plc* v. *Dickman* [1990] 2 AC 605; *Odhavji Estate* v. *Woodhouse* [2003] 3 SCR 263, [52].

[23] [1932] AC 562, 579. [24] [1932] AC 562, 580.

[25] C. Witting, 'Duty of Care: An Analytical Approach' (2005) 25 *Oxford Journal of Legal Studies* 33; D. Tan, 'The Salient Features of Proximity: Examining the *Spandeck* Formulation for Establishing a Duty of Care' [2010] *Singapore Journal of Legal Studies* 459.

potential for the infliction of harm between those persons. In the Australian case of *Jaensch* v. *Coffey*, Deane J explained that proximity extends beyond physical closeness and contemporaneity, and encompasses 'causal proximity'.[26] This term was said to capture the 'closeness or directness of the relationship between the particular act ... and the injury sustained'.[27] This explanation is helpful insofar as it indicates that proximity focusses upon factual relations subsisting between persons *prior* to wrongful interactions. It is used to determine whether the positioning of the claimant vis-à-vis the defendant was such as to involve risk and to enable the causation of harm. However, the phrase 'causal proximity' is unhelpful insofar as it defines proximity in terms of itself. In order to avoid circularity, proximity is better conceptualised as 'pathways to harm'.[28] The pathways idea helps to clarify that courts are concerned with the potential for doing harm that exists prior to harmful interactions subsequently alleged to constitute negligence. The pathways idea clarifies also that proximity exists in *all of the mechanisms* for harm causation that subsist prior to failures in care – and not simply in mechanisms which do cause harm. It is *because of* the presence of proximity, subsisting in one or more pathways to harm, that courts might impose duties of care between persons, which create notional obligations of care.

Given the struggle to conceptualise duty and to specify its exact function in negligence, it is not surprising that there is no definitive list of factual features encompassed by the term 'proximity'. The explanation of proximity given here encompasses a variety of causal pathways arising in cases of physical damage, financial loss, and psychiatric illness. In the cases of physical harm relevant to this book, recognised causal pathways to harm include such things as: the exercise of power or control over the person or property of another;[29] directing the conduct of risky activities by others; the supply of goods subsequently consumed, used, or impacting upon others;[30] and the supply of prescriptions for medicines.[31]

A judicial finding of proximity based on the facts of a particular case is made retrospectively. The court looks back to discover whether proximity arose between the parties to an actual dispute. But a finding of proximity is

26 (1984) 155 CLR 549, 584–5. 27 (1984) 155 CLR 549, 584–5.

28 There is a definite analogy between the pathway to harm in the causal sense and *path*ogenesis as the 'mechanism by which an etiologic agent produces disease': see M. de Villiers, 'Foreseeability Decoded' (2015) 16 *Minnesota Journal of Law, Science & Technology* 343, 347.

29 *Carmarthenshire CC* v. *Lewis* [1955] AC 549.

30 *Donoghue* v. *Stevenson* [1932] AC 562. 31 *Jones* v. *Fay* (1865) 4 F & F 525.

likely to be of importance also for application of duty rules in the future. This is because the particular pathways to harm as found between A and B very often are characteristic of repetitive interactions between the relevant classes of person – that is, between A-class and B-class. Prior cases are concrete illustrations of how proximity arises between persons and provide the basis for ordering future legal relations.[32]

The sub-element of foreseeability focusses upon the reasonable person and his or her assumed capacities, rather than upon the defendant's actual capacities. The focus is upon cognitive capacity and reflects a judgment about the reasonable person's ability, in the circumstances, to appreciate the risks to other persons who might be affected by failures in care.[33] Ordinarily, cognitive capacity is assessed in an intuitive way. However, the assessment can be broken down into logically relevant factors such as: the pathways to harm that characterised the interaction between the parties; the reasonable person's understanding of cause and effect in the relevant realm of action (that is, ability to appreciate 'known or partially known causal regularities');[34] and the reasonable person's beliefs about the frequency with which harmful interactions arise in such circumstances.[35] In *Haley* v. *London Electricity Board*,[36] for example, the House of Lords had to consider a case of physical injury arising when a blind person tripped over a long hammer left in the footpath. Although the hammer was situated so as to alert pedestrians to the excavation, it was foreseeable that blind persons might pass along a particular stretch of pavement and be injured by obstructions because of their inability to detect them in the way that sighted persons can (knowledge of cause and effect). In reaching this conclusion, the House examined evidence about the prevalence of blind persons in London and ordinary experience of them (frequency).[37]

Foreseeability is concerned with whether injury to a member or members of a *class* of person was foreseeable.[38] The court's preoccupation with classes of person, although tested by looking back in time at what was then

[32] See *Home Office* v. *Dorset Yacht Co Ltd* [1970] AC 1004, 1058–9.

[33] A. Dorfman, 'Foreseeability as Re-cognition' (2014) 59 *American Journal of Jurisprudence* 163, 191.

[34] S. R. Perry, 'The Moral Foundations of Tort Law' (1992) 77 *Iowa Law Review* 449, 505. That is, the reasonable person's 'attributed common knowledge and beliefs about possible causal connections between actions and outcomes of the relevant kinds': ibid., 509.

[35] In other words, how typical such harmful interactions are: B. C. Zipursky, 'Foreseeability in Breach, Duty, and Proximate Cause' (2009) 44 *Wake Forest Law Review* 1247, 1264–5.

[36] [1965] AC 778. [37] [1965] AC 778, 791, 798, 804, and 807.

[38] *Alcock* v. *Chief Constable of South Yorkshire Police* [1992] 1 AC 310, 397, and 420. Foreseeability is a component of three aspects of negligence, but the *focus* is different in

foreseeable, pays heed also to the forward-looking nature of duty and the need to address general patterns of interaction among persons. Thus, for example, experience of the general patterns of interaction involving motorists informs the court that motorists are expected to anticipate harm to pedestrians and other motorists, but not necessarily to office workers on the upper floors of nearby buildings. It does not matter whether the claimant was foreseeable as a specific individual.[39] This is because, in the ordinary case, nothing about the individual within a class of persons is analytically significant. Thus, we could say with respect to a case like *Haley*, that some blind persons are tall, some short; some are irascible, others not. These fine-grained attributes generally are not relevant to the causal regularities in play.

Being about future possible consequences of failures in care, foreseeability of harm to persons is *informed by* the kind of damage that might arise.[40] Thus, while establishing the foreseeability of directly caused physical injury frequently is a straightforward exercise, establishing the foreseeability of indirectly caused, non-physical injury can be more difficult.[41] It is easily foreseeable, for example, that failure by a driver to take care will cause bodily injury to persons in the immediate vicinity, such as pedestrians. But is it reasonably foreseeable that a psychiatric illness might be caused to another driver after a minor prang?[42] Is it reasonably foreseeable that the stricken driver's children might no longer be able to attend private schools, and that their future earning power will be diminished? These are questions the answers to which are not so intuitive, and with respect to which matters of reasonableness – of judgment about what is reasonably foreseeable – become important.

Finally, it is important to notice that the sub-element of foreseeability sets a limit upon the defendant's potential liability.[43] Although the limit is a wide one, because the bounds of human cognition and understanding of cause and effect are wide, foreseeability ensures that duties of care are

each case. At the breach stage, the focus is upon *risk* of a specific injury, and at the remoteness stage, upon the *type of injury*.

[39] *Dorset Yacht Co Ltd* v. *Home Office* [1970] AC 1004, 1039.

[40] See also Goldberg and Zipursky, *Torts*, p. 81.

[41] *Dorset Yacht Co Ltd* v. *Home Office* [1970] AC 1004, 1052.

[42] *Page* v. *Smith* [1996] AC 155. See also *Barber* v. *Somerset County Council* [2004] 1 WLR 1089 (foreseeability of psychiatric illness in employees).

[43] See, e.g., S. Balganesh, 'Foreseeability and Copyright Incentives' (2009) 122 *Harvard Law Review* 1569, 1591–602 (survey of foreseeability across areas of law); W. J. Cardi, 'Reconstructing Foreseeability' (2005) 46 *British Columbia Law Review* 921, 938.

concomitant with the reasonable person's agential capacities.[44] The presence of foreseeability speaks of a minimal sense in which the reasonable person can avoid the imposition of unnecessary risks of harm to others.[45] Reasonable road workers in a case like *Haley*, for example, being able to understand the kinds of danger posed to blind persons by their operations in the footpath, had a minimal ability to consider measures to ensure that such persons were protected. The defendant's ability to foresee harm to the claimant class does not, of itself, entail full control over the circumstances that lead to injury (indeed has nothing at all to say about the actual defendant's capacities), but is simply a minimal prerequisite to being held responsible for subsequent actions.[46] When foreseeability is absent, there is no need to go further in considering an obligation to take care. It would not be fair to the defendant to impose an obligation of care towards a claimant class that is unforeseeable because he or she would be incapable of devising appropriate precautions to avoid the causation of harm.

Proximity *informs* what is foreseeable. This is to say that what reasonably can be foreseen by a person in the position of the defendant is best determined *by reference* to how the actual defendant was situated vis-à-vis the claimant prior to their harmful interaction. It is dependent upon whether proximity was physical, whether it arose through a relationship of some kind, its duration, and so on. It is for this reason that we ought to consider proximity first when applying the duty of care framework. A further reason for proceeding in this order is suggested by our characterisation of foreseeability as concerned with the minimal ability of the person in the position of the defendant to avoid harming at-risk persons. It simply is more intelligible to consider this issue when one knows the exact pathways to harm that arose on the facts of a case.

Proof by the claimant of both proximity of relationship and foreseeability of harm is a precondition to the imposition of a duty of care in

44 See Perry, 'The Moral Foundations of Tort Law', 474ff.

45 S. R. Perry, 'Responsibility for Outcomes, Risk, and the Law of Torts', in D. G. Owen (ed.), *Philosophy and the Law of Torts* (2001), p. 93. Another way of expressing it is to say that the agent has the ability to understand how the accident could have been circumvented: W. Lucy, *Philosophy of Private Law* (2007), p. 68. Cf. A. Slavny, 'Nonreciprocity and the Moral Basis of Liability to Compensate' (2014) 34 *Oxford Journal of Legal Studies* 1 (discussing several other meanings of avoidability).

46 Perry refers to both the possibility of control and partial control: Perry, 'The Moral Foundations of Tort Law', 505. His cautiousness reflects the fact that the 'knowledge that we only ever have partial or imperfect control over our interactions with the external world is itself a fundamental aspect of our sense of agency': Perry, 'Responsibility for Outcomes', 83.

negligence. These sub-elements signify that the parties were, as an historical matter, in a significant fact-based relationship prior to the defendant's failure in care. However, the decision whether to recognise a duty is *normative*.[47] The court decides whether to recognise a duty according to what it determines to be the most appropriate rule in the resolution of the type of coordination problem which arose. But the focus of decision-making is not restricted to backward-looking factors. Typically, policy arguments are both forward-looking, and consequentialist.[48] In *Michael* v. *Chief Constable of South Wales Police*, for example, Lord Kerr noted that '[s]ome assessment has to be made of what a judge considers the public interest to be; what detriment would be caused to that interest if liability were held to exist; and what harm would be done to claimants if they are denied a remedy.'[49] A court will need to consider the potential *extent* of negligence liability in determining the duty issue. 'The established method . . . involves examining the decided cases to see how far the law has gone and where it has refrained from going. From that analysis it looks to see whether there is an argument . . . for extending liability to a new situation.'[50] It is at the duty stage that courts have said such things as the 'lawyer likes to draw fixed and definite lines and is apt to ask where the thing is to stop',[51] and 'thus far and no further'.[52] The use of this method has been most obvious in cases of indirectly caused psychiatric injury and financial loss – where the extent of liability is not limited by the laws of inertia. Nevertheless, several policy considerations have informed the limits on the duty of care in personal injury cases, including the supposed need to avoid indeterminate liability, which encompasses 'the needs of commerce [for] some limitation on the extent to which those who engage in commercial activity are liable for foreseeable acts of negligence'.[53]

47 *Dorset Yacht Co Ltd* v. *Home Office* [1970] AC 1004, 1058 ('at bottom a matter of public policy'); *Hedley Byrne & Co Ltd* v. *Heller & Partners Ltd* [1964] AC 465, 536 ('depends ultimately upon the courts' assessment of the demands of society for protection').

48 E.g., *Haley* v. *London Electricity Board* [1965] AC 778, 795; A. Robertson, 'Constraints on Policy-Based Reasoning in Private Law', in A. Robertson and H. W. Tang (eds.), *The Goals of Private Law* (2009), p. 263.

49 [2015] AC 1731, [160].

50 *Michael* v. *Chief Constable of South Wales Police* [2015] AC 1731, [102].

51 *Bourhill* v. *Young* [1943] AC 92, 110.

52 *Frost* v. *Chief Constable of South Yorkshire Police* [1992] 2 AC 455, 500. See also *Donoghue* v. *Stevenson* [1931] AC 562, 577 ('If one step, why not fifty?'); *Alcock* v. *Chief Constable of South Yorkshire Police* [1992] 1 AC 310, 418.

53 *CSR Ltd* v. *Wren* (1997) 44 NSWLR 463, 480.

This section of this book now moves from a general description of the duty of care to its application in asbestos cases (continuing one of this book's thematic case studies). In a small number of cases, courts have imposed duties of care owed by parent companies to persons whose primary interactions were with subsidiaries. The cases can be divided into two groups – those dealing with duties owed to insolvent subsidiary employees, and those dealing with duties owed to third-party consumers and bystanders. Ordinarily, factual features linking the parties so as to create pathways to harm (or proximity) are more easily satisfied in the former than in the latter group of cases. However, the English Court of Appeal has been reticent to accept claims of duty. The tension that exists between ordinary duty principles and the policy of limited liability is a major factor in explaining this reticence.

11.2.1.1 Parent Company to Subsidiary Employees

As a preliminary matter, it should be noted that some jurisdictions curtail common law actions by employees injured at work against negligent *employers* when their claims are covered by a statutory scheme under which employers pay contributions towards liability insurance, social insurance, or a compensation or similar fund.[54] However, even under such schemes, actions by injured employees against *third-party* parent companies or network participants might be available when scheme compensation awards are inadequate.[55] In this section, we consider cases brought in England and Australia after subsidiary employees have been injured in the course of employment and have sought redress against parent companies.[56] The immediate employer is referred to for the sake of clarity as either the 'insolvent subsidiary' (even if the subsidiary has not

[54] For the US sole remedy rule under state workers' compensation legislation, see J. A. Reiter and J. J. Ranta, 'The Exclusive Remedy Provision State-by-State Survey' (2009), available at: http://apps.americanbar.org/labor/errcomm/mw/Papers/2009/data/papers/020.pdf. For restrictions on recovery in Australia, see, e.g., Workplace Injury, Rehabilitation and Compensation Act 2013 (Vic). In New Zealand, no actions are available for personal injury claims: Injury Prevention, Rehabilitation and Compensation Act 2001 (NZ). See failed action in *James Hardie & Co Pty Ltd* v. *Putt* (1998) 43 NSWLR 554.

[55] S. Deakin, A. Johnston, and B. Markesinis, *Markesinis and Deakin's Tort Law* (7th edn., 2013), pp. 542–3.

[56] There has been no appellate decision on whether a parent company in Canada owes a duty of care to the employees, customers, etc. of a subsidiary company – although the suggestion is that such a duty might be constructed from principles established in foreign cases, such as those now to be considered in the text: Conway, 'A New Duty of Care?'. Certain strike-out decisions are consistent with duties of care being owed by parent companies where the usual factors of proximity and foreseeability exist: e.g., *Choc* v.

paid full compensation for reasons other than insolvency, such as statutory preclusion or de-registration) or the 'subsidiary'.

The House of Lords in *Connelly* v. *RTZ Corporation plc*[57] opened the way to argument that a parent company might owe a duty of care to insolvent subsidiary employees affected by exposure to asbestos. The case concerned an application for a stay of proceedings on the ground that England was (under a now-superseded private international law rule) an inappropriate forum.[58] The claimant had been employed at a uranium mine in Namibia and thereafter suffered cancer of the larynx. He claimed that his cancer was caused by inhaling silica uranium and its radioactive decay products. The underlying action was in negligence, the claim being that RTZ had devised its Namibian subsidiary RUL's policy on health, safety, and the environment, and that RTZ supervisors implemented the policy and supervised health, safety, and/or environmental protection at the mine.[59] The House of Lords refused to stay proceedings because it was arguable that substantial justice could not be done in Namibia, where legal aid would not have been available to the claimants.

The leading English case ruling that parent companies might owe duties of care to insolvent subsidiary employees is *Chandler* v. *Cape plc.*[60] Mr Chandler was an employee of Cape Building Products Ltd (CBP) over several periods of time, working outdoors loading bricks. Asbestos was produced in a factory at the site with open sides, and dust from the factory migrated into the area where he worked.[61] Fifty years later, he began to suffer from asbestosis. By this time, CBP had been de-registered and no insurance cover was available.[62] The claimant alleged that Cape plc, as parent company of CBP, had owed him a duty of care when he was CBP's employee. The Court of Appeal accepted this claim.

Arden LJ specified the importance of four proximity factors in establishing a duty owed by a parent company for the health and safety of its subsidiary's employees.[63] First, it was necessary to prove that the parent and subsidiary had had overlapping business operations in respect of the injury-causing activity. On the facts, the evidence was that Cape and CBP

Hudbay Minerals, Inc 2013 ONSC 1414; *United Canadian Malt Ltd* v. *Outboard Marine Corporation of Canada Ltd* (2000) 48 OR (3d) 352.

57 [1998] AC 854. See, to similar effect, *Lubbe* v. *Cape plc* [2000] 1 WLR 1545 (claim of a failure by a parent company to institute proper practices for working with asbestos).

58 For modern rules, see discussion in Chapter 3 and further references cited therein.

59 [1998] AC 854, 864.

60 [2012] 1 WLR 3111.

61 [2012] 1 WLR 3111, [3].

62 [2012] 1 WLR 3111, [4].

63 [2012] 1 WLR 3111, [80]. These factors demonstrate that the case was not one involving an 'omission' as the Court of Appeal had assumed. Far from it.

had been companies in an integrated building materials group with overlapping management,[64] Cape installed the asbestos-producing plant where the claimant had worked,[65] and both companies conducted operations at the same work site. Second, it was necessary to prove that the parent company had or ought to have had superior knowledge about relevant aspects of health and safety 'in the industry'. On the facts, Cape had stipulated how asbestos products were to be manufactured and had conducted research into the risks those products posed.[66] Third, it was necessary to prove that the subsidiary's system of work was unsafe as the parent company knew or ought to have known. On the facts, Cape had been 'fully aware' of 'systemic failures' which resulted in the escape of asbestos dust from the plant, and had known of real risks to the health and safety of employees engaged in the brick-making business and to others.[67] Finally, the claimant had to prove that the parent company knew or ought to have foreseen that the subsidiary or its employees relied on it to use that superior knowledge for the employees' protection.[68] This could be established by evidence that the parent had intervened in the trading operations of the subsidiary, for example in production and funding issues. It would not be necessary to prove that the parent had intervened specifically in the health and safety policies of the subsidiary. On the facts, it was proven that: Cape plc had taken decisions about the expansion of CBP's business;[69] Cape oversaw product development at a central laboratory; Cape had superior knowledge of the asbestos business and made available to CBP certain technical know-how;[70] and Cape undertook health and safety functions impacting upon its subsidiary's employees.[71] In these circumstances, Arden LJ held that it was appropriate for the court to impose a duty of care upon Cape plc, the content (that is, the relevant standard) of which was 'either to advise Cape Products on what steps it had to take in the light of knowledge then available to provide those employees with a safe system of work or to ensure that those steps were taken'.[72]

Although *Chandler* v. *Cape plc* represented an important breakthrough in the application of negligence liability to parent companies in favour of their subsidiaries' employees (perhaps even where subsidiaries are located

[64] [2012] 1 WLR 3111, [8] and [10]. [65] [2012] 1 WLR 3111, [7].
[66] [2012] 1 WLR 3111, [75]. [67] [2012] 1 WLR 3111, [77].
[68] Note that deemed knowledge is not a proximity factor in the present author's opinion. It is not a fact which links the parties creating a pathway to harm.
[69] [2012] 1 WLR 3111, [10] and [28]. [70] [2012] 1 WLR 3111, [14] and [75].
[71] [2012] 1 WLR 3111, [18]–[19]. [72] [2012] 1 WLR 3111, [78].

in foreign jurisdictions),[73] the indications are that courts will adhere closely to its stated proximity requirements and not expand its operation beyond cases where the evidence is clear. This is the message from the subsequent Court of Appeal decision in *Thompson* v. *The Renwick Group plc*. That case underscores the need for both the parent company and the subsidiary to be in the same line of business, meaning that the parent company is more than just a holding company with no substantial business activities of its own.[74] The requirement is that the parent company actually be engaged in risk-creating business activity which overlaps with that of the subsidiary, for example, by involving itself in some stage of the production of asbestos. But, although integration of activity is necessary,[75] such as where the subsidiary is a division of the parent company's own business, this is insufficient because it is commonplace in corporate groups. A court would be interested, further, in proof of superior knowledge and expertise in the parent company about the relevant health and safety matter, and of direct interventions in the risk-creating activity.[76]

Despite the reticence of the Court of Appeal in the *Thompson* case, the duty framework laid out in *Chandler* v. *Cape plc* does not appear to be overly demanding of claimants. It focusses upon overlapping industrial activity, parent company interventions into the affairs of the subsidiary that do not necessarily relate closely to the injuring activity,[77] knowledge of risk to health and safety, and 'reliance' upon the parent company by subsidiary employees. On the facts of *Chandler*, there were both interventions of a high-level, business-management kind by the parent, such as are found frequently in integrated groups of companies, as well as specific interventions which impacted more obviously upon the claimant's working conditions and activities. Although not free from doubt as a matter of proximity-based reasoning, commentators have assumed that it is the latter, more specific type of intervention in risk-creating activities that is relevant in establishing the parent company's duty of care.[78]

[73] *Lungowe* v. *Vedanta Resources plc* [2016] BCC 774.

[74] [2014] PIQR P18, [37]. See also *Okpabi* v. *Royal Dutch Shell plc* [2017] EWHC 89 (TCC). But one commentator believes that this rejection of liability for 'holding companies' will open the way to evasion of negligence liability: W. Day, 'Negligence and the Corporate Veil: Parent Companies' Duty of Care to Their Subsidiaries' Employees' [2014] *Lloyd's Maritime and Commercial Law Quarterly* 454, 455.

[75] [2014] PIQR P18, [37]. [76] [2014] PIQR P18, [37].

[77] See M. Petrin, 'Assumption of Responsibility in Corporate Groups: *Chandler v Cape plc*' (2013) 76 *Modern Law Review* 603, 613.

[78] E.g.: The 'relevant "control test" focuses on the extent to which a parent is somehow in control of the causes of the tort, which will be linked to, but not the same as, the issue of a

A criticism of *Chandler* is that it reduces the incentives for parent companies to take a hands-on approach to the organisation and monitoring of risk-creating activity undertaken by subsidiary companies and thus will reduce the number of interventions into health and safety matters.[79] Parent companies in risky industries will 'maintain "strategic control" but avoid responsibility by delegating operational matters, which are more likely to give rise to tortious consequences'.[80] Such a change in parent company management strategy might well add to the number of employees and others who are injured by negligently conducted risky activities – so that, in the result, the law of negligence would undermine itself in its task of setting proper standards of conduct. Indeed, this is a problem common to control-based forms of liability, as discussed already at several points in this book.

Certain commentators believe that the true effect of *Chandler* v. *Cape plc* is to permit the piercing of the corporate veil and the imposition of the company's own liability upon parent company shareholders.[81] However, this is not correct. The recognition of a duty of care in such a case is in no way derivative from the subsidiary; rather, it is an element going to prove that the parent company *itself* committed a tort,[82] irrespective of any failures in the subsidiary. Indeed, obvious failures in the parent company might not be reflected in any particular failures in the subsidiary – meaning that the liability of the parent is not necessarily duplicative in nature either. Although the liability *result* might be the same as when the court pierces the corporate veil,[83] the analytical route taken is very different. Moreover, it is important to understand that there is no general principle which says that the preclusion of one form of liability in a

parent's control over its subsidiary': S. Joseph, *Corporations and Transnational Human Rights Litigation* (2004), p. 136.

79 T. Bullimore, 'Sins of the Father, Sins of the Son' (2012) 28 *Professional Negligence* 212, 214; Petrin, 'Assumption of Responsibility in Corporate Groups', 618.

80 Joseph, *Corporations and Transnational Human Rights Litigation*, p. 137.

81 E.g., Bullimore, 'Sins of the Father, Sins of the Son', 214.

82 Another view is that '[t]he implied basis for this statement [of Arden LJ] is surely that the existence of the subsidiary company was factually irrelevant to the legal question whether the parent had assumed a duty of care to the employee': W. Day, 'Skirting around the Issue: The Corporate Veil after *Prest v Petrodel*' [2014] *Lloyd's Maritime and Commercial Law Quarterly* 269, 279.

83 P. Lipton, 'The Mythology of *Salomon*'s Case and the Law Dealing with the Tort Liabilities of Corporate Groups: An Historical Perspective' (2014) 40 *Monash University Law Review* 452, 483. See also P. J. Turner, 'Revisiting the Direct Liability of Parent Companies Following *Chandler v Cape Plc*' (2015) 33 *Company & Securities Law Journal* 45.

commercial or other party (say, veil-piercing) entails the preclusion of all other forms of liability (such as negligence) in that party. The imposition of a duty of care upon the parent company *affirms* its existence as a separate legal entity, capable of bearing responsibility in tort law.

None of this is to deny that policy-based arguments of a consequentialist nature *are* relevant to the court's determination of when to recognise duties of care and the scope of those duties. Although there are strong arguments for the protection of bodily integrity in cases of parent company failures in care, arguments might be presented about the potential impact of pro-duty decisions upon such things as the policies behind limited liability rules, including the need for business investment and entrepreneurialism.[84] However, in the view of the present writer, business investment that leads to mass personal injury is hardly likely to be a positive sum game, and its prospect is insufficient to counter a presumption that a duty of care should be owed by the parent company to subsidiary company employees where sufficient proximity exists between those parties, signifying the presence of pathways to harm and the need for care to be taken.

The leading Australian decision holding that parent companies might owe duties of care to insolvent subsidiary employees is *CSR Ltd* v. *Wren*.[85] The New South Wales Court of Appeal held that CSR Ltd, which was the parent company of Asbestos Products Pty Ltd (APL), was liable in negligence to one of APL's employees for failing to take care in making an asbestos-producing factory workplace safe so that he contracted mesothelioma. The evidence indicated that APL's factory had no dust extraction equipment and that, because the building had neither windows nor proper ventilation, the doors were left open so that, on windy days, asbestos fibres would be blown around. As a result, 'there was dust everywhere, it was unbelievable'.[86] No masks were supplied to reduce dust inhalation.[87] The claimant, who had been involved in the physical handling of asbestos slurry for a mere twelve-month period, had had no recourse against APL because that company had been liquidated many years earlier. The crucial holding was that CSR had owed a duty of care to the employee. This was based on the presence of both foreseeability of the risk of harm to workers

[84] E.g., S. H. C. Lo, 'A Parent Company's Tort Liability to Employees of a Subsidiary' (2014) 1 *Journal of International and Comparative Law* 117.

[85] (1997) 44 NSWLR 463. No argument was made at trial about piercing the veil: ibid., 466. See also E. McGaughey, '*Donoghue* v *Salomon* in the High Court' (2011) 4 *Journal of Personal Injury Law* 249.

[86] (1997) 44 NSWLR 463, 468. [87] (1997) 44 NSWLR 463, 467.

and proximity of relationship between the parent company and the claimant. Foreseeability was established by reference to the medical and other literature available in the early 1950s on the link between asbestos and lung diseases. Much of this literature had been available to CSR itself; it had kept a comprehensive library of industry-related books and journals available for consultation by its 'officers'.[88] In addition, lists of relevant articles were circulated within the company on a regular basis. This literature established that asbestos had been a 'known hazard in industry'.[89] Proximity was evident in several factors. There was a complete overlap between CSR and APL management,[90] only the factory personnel being APL's own employees. The CSR-employed management team exercised pervasive influence over the operations of APL beyond that expected in 'holding' company management,[91] including hiring and firing of staff, the purchase of equipment, and the organisation of its work.[92] Powell JA summarised the evidence as follows:

> it was not Asbestos Products Pty Ltd, through its officers or employees, but CSR, through those of its employees – including the factory foreman – which in fact controlled and supervised the factory, the manufacturing processes carried out within it, and the activities of Asbestos Pty Ltd employees – including Mr Wren – who were engaged in carrying out those processes.[93]

CSR's control over APL's operations impacted upon measures taken to minimise dust in the factory and upon other working conditions.[94] By contrast, the Court of Appeal found that there was no similar exercise of control by APL's own board.[95] A duty of care arose because CSR brought itself into a relationship with APL's employees 'by placing its staff in the role of management' of that company.[96] There were no reasons of policy for denying recognition of a duty of care.[97] In fact, the duty CSR owed ran parallel to that which APL owed to its own employees and, as such, would not 'frustrate or restrict commercial activity'.[98] Breach of the relevant standard of care was established also. Although there had been no statutory standards or formal industry guidelines about exposure levels,

[88] (1997) 44 NSWLR 463, 475, and 477. [89] (1997) 44 NSWLR 463, 475.
[90] (1997) 44 NSWLR 463, 469, and 485. [91] (1997) 44 NSWLR 463, 470, and 483–4.
[92] (1997) 44 NSWLR 463, 469–70, and 484. [93] (1997) 44 NSWLR 463, 465.
[94] (1997) 44 NSWLR 463, 484. This is seen as the most important of the proximity factors: Lipton, 'The Mythology of *Salomon*'s Case', 485. See also Muchlinski, *Multinational Enterprises and the Law*, p. 311.
[95] (1997) 44 NSWLR 463, 484. [96] (1997) 44 NSWLR 463, 485.
[97] (1997) 44 NSWLR 463, 485. [98] (1997) 44 NSWLR 463, 485.

the risks of asbestos fibres were known and there had been 'reasonably practicable methods available' to reduce the amount of dust in circulation.[99] No dispute arose over the issue of causation.

CSR Ltd v. *Wren* differs from *Chandler* v. *Cape plc* insofar as the New South Wales Court of Appeal was not as prescriptive about the kinds of proximity factor that would be sufficient to establish the parent company's duty of care towards insolvent subsidiary employees. The evidence was of a higher-level management role exerted by the parent company, but not of the more specific interventions into health and safety that also characterised *Chandler*. Nevertheless, the court was satisfied that the parent company's management role had impacted sufficiently upon the health and safety of the claimant's work environment. The emphasis in the decision upon the importance of control, again, is problematic for reasons already discussed, and indicative of the presently limited nature of duties of care in negligence.

11.2.1.2 Parent Company to Consumers and Bystanders

Courts have held that asbestos producers owe duties of care not only to their employees, but also to residents living nearby factories from which asbestos dust is emitted in significant quantities.[100] Thus, the evidence in *Margereson* v. *JW Roberts Ltd*[101] was that neighbourhood children lived very close to a factory and had been permitted into a loading bay, where they jumped up and down on bags of blue asbestos. In addition, large quantities of asbestos accumulated in the vicinity of the factory and was transported into homes on workers' clothing. The English Court of Appeal held that a duty of care had been owed, at least, to persons who had played in the loading bays as children and who, decades later, had developed mesothelioma. This was on the bases that, by the late 1920s, there had been sufficient knowledge of the dangers of asbestos to the pulmonary system,[102] so that pulmonary injury was foreseeable, and the obvious proximity that existed between the factory owner and the children.

It has been held, further, that *parent companies* might owe duties of care to residents who live in the vicinity of insolvent subsidiary factories when they emit significant amounts of asbestos dust into the neighbouring environment. In *CSR Ltd* v. *Young*,[103] the New South Wales Court of

[99] (1997) 44 NSWLR 463, 490.
[100] For discussion of cases beyond asbestos, see, e.g., J. Zerk, *Multinationals and Corporate Social Responsibility* (2006), pp. 219ff.
[101] [1996] Env LR 304. [102] [1996] Env LR 304, 309.
[103] (1998) Aust Torts Reports ¶ 81–468.

Appeal held that CSR Ltd had owed a duty of care to its subsidiary's (Australian Blue Asbestos Ltd or ABA's) employee's children – in other words, to third parties affected by its failure to take care in the manufacture and distribution of asbestos. The asbestos dust in the remote Australian town of Wittenoom was pervasive, generated 'by vehicles, by pedestrian movement, and by wind. From a distance there was a blue-grey haze over the town from the dust containing asbestos fibres'.[104] As a toddler, the claimant had crawled around in asbestos tailings. As an older child, she had played in a backyard covered in tailings, which were to be found also at the local school, near the hospital, and in the roads. The claimant had been no safer inside her home, having inhaled asbestos dust from her father's clothing. Eventually, she succumbed to mesothelioma and died at age thirty-five. The claim was that both CSR and ABA 'should have warned their employees, and the adult members of their families, that they and their children ran the risk of contracting mesothelioma' as a result of industrial and environmental exposure to blue asbestos.[105]

The court in *Young* recognised a duty of care owed to the claimant based on foreseeability of harm to persons (for reasons similar to those in the *Wren* case),[106] and proximity manifested in the pervasive control and influence which CSR exercised over the entire town of Wittenoom. As regards foreseeability, the court explained that both CSR and ABA had been aware of not far-fetched or fanciful risks to the residents of Wittenoom posed by exposure to blue asbestos. This foreseeable risk was not mitigated on the basis that the concentration of asbestos was much less than that recognised as dangerous to workers at the mines and in the mills because there had been the potential for both highly concentrated exposures for concentrated periods and also for prolonged exposures to low concentrations of asbestos fibres which had accumulated in the surrounds.[107] As regards proximity of relationship between the parties, the Court of Appeal held that, in truth, Wittenoom was '"a company town", existing to serve the working population and families of the mine and mills'.[108] CSR had been conducting *its own operations* through ABA, which it incorporated, and which granted to CSR a comprehensive power to act as its agent.[109] 'CSR

[104] (1998) Aust Torts Reports ¶ 81–468, 64,951.
[105] (1998) Aust Torts Reports ¶ 81–468, 64,931.
[106] (1998) Aust Torts Reports ¶81–468, 64,953–7.
[107] (1998) Aust Torts Reports ¶ 81–468, 64,955.
[108] (1998) Aust Torts Reports ¶81–468, 64,957.
[109] 'On 23 June 1943, an agreement was entered into by which ABA appointed CSR to act as its Managing Agent and Sole Distributor with full and absolute authority to do all things

and ABA had exercised an undoubted role in the establishment, operation and maintenance of Wittenoom.'[110] Moreover, there was no basis for distinguishing 'between the operations at the mines and in the mills and other activities the responsibility for which is said to fall upon ABA alone, most relevantly the distribution of tailings throughout the town', and the failure to warn of the risks they posed.[111] In its obiter holding, the court held that the duty of care that it recognised had been owed to the residents of Wittenoom *as a whole*.[112] Moreover, ABA had been 'in a position to warn Mrs Olson's parents that they and their children were at risk of injury'.[113] There was no appeal against the finding that 'if Mrs Olson's mother had been warned that she and her family were at risk of injury, the family would not have remained at Wittenoom.'[114] There was no dispute that the mesothelioma had been caused by the defendants' breach.[115]

11.2.1.3 Duty of Care in Networks

The duties of care discussed in previous paragraphs were imposed upon parent companies in the asbestos industry in favour of insolvent subsidiary employees or third parties interacting with subsidiaries. An important reason for judicial recognition of such duties is the control parent companies exercise over subsidiaries and their activities. However, proximity can arise on the basis of other kinds of connection (not simply control), including organisation of work, supply of goods, exposure to toxins, and

necessary for the proper management and control of the business and undertaking of [ABA]. The agreement was to operate for five years and thereafter from year to year until terminated on notice, and there was no evidence of termination. CSR's shareholding domination remained at all times, as did the identity of officers of CSR with directors of ABA': (1998) Aust Torts Reports ¶ 81–468, 64,952–64,953.

110 (1998) Aust Torts Reports ¶ 81–468, 64,957.

111 (1998) Aust Torts Reports ¶ 81–468, 64,953.

112 (1998) Aust Torts Reports ¶ 81–468, 64,953.

113 (1998) Aust Torts Reports ¶ 81–468, 64,957.

114 (1998) Aust Torts Reports ¶ 81–468, 64,958.

115 (1998) Aust Torts Reports ¶ 81–468, 64,958. Scholars continue to think through the insolvent entity problem, and there is the possibility of future actions being available in negligence. Chris Riley has been developing an interesting paper which would create a negligence-based liability in shareholders for debts of their insolvent companies: C Riley, 'Shareholder Liability for Company Torts: Should it Be Vicarious or Fault Based?' (paper presented at SLS Conference, Oxford, 7 September 2016). Shareholders would owe a duty 'to take reasonable steps to prevent [their] company committing torts which the company lacks the means to remedy'. The extent of the duty would vary according to the influence of the shareholder in the company so that those with the potential to exercise control would have a more extensive duty. This is not the model of shareholder liability preferred by the present author, as to which see Chapter 9.

inadequate warnings of risk. This creates the possibility of duties of care being owed by multiple companies in a network engaged in common activities.[116] Such cases are encompassed within the discussion of joint liability in the next chapter, but specific mention of the possibility is necessary at this point. Although companies in a network might attempt to channel liabilities to particular parties by use of contract terms, such attempts will be difficult to defend when claimants suffer bodily injury.[117]

11.2.2 Breach of Duty

While arguments about parent company duties of care owed to insolvent subsidiary employees and to third parties connected to subsidiaries can be contentious, breach rules do not give rise to problems of particular note for this book, so that only brief discussion of this element of negligence is warranted. In determining whether the defendant was in breach of its duty to the claimant, the court examines, first, the foreseeability of the risk of harm should care not be taken, an action in negligence being available with respect to reasonably foreseeable risks only.[118] If the risk was reasonably foreseeable, the court goes on to determine the appropriate standard of care owed by the defendant to the claimant, ordinarily expressed as that standard observed by the reasonable person in the position of the defendant. This standard will be formulated after consideration of factual matters concerning the risk of harm that manifested itself and the range of precautions available by way of response.[119]

Case law establishes several specific rules of relevance to determination of the appropriate standard of care in the insolvent subsidiary context. These include rules that: relevant legislation, industry standards, and observed practice inform what the appropriate standard of care should be (without necessarily dictating that standard);[120] employers have an obligation to take care in choosing independent contractors for engagement in risky work

[116] *Morris* v. *Breaveglen Ltd* [1993] ICR 766, 773; *Denham* v. *Midland Employers Mutual Assurance Ltd* [1955] 2 All ER 561.

[117] E.g., Consumer Rights Act 2015, ss 62, 63, 65 and Schedule 2, Part 1; Unfair Contract Terms Act 1977, s. 2.

[118] E.g., *Glasgow Corporation* v. *Muir* [1943] AC 448, 454, and 460. For Australia, see, e.g., Civil Liability Act 2002 (NSW), ss. 3B and 5B.

[119] E.g., *Morris* v. *West Hartlepool Steam Navigation Co Ltd* [1956] AC 552, 574. For Australia, see relevant legislation: e.g., Civil Liability Act 2002 (NSW), ss. 3B and 5B.

[120] *Baker* v. *Quantum Clothing Group Ltd* [2011] 1 WLR 1003; *Ryan* v. *Victoria (City)* [1999] 1 SCR 201, 222; *Jeromson* v. *Shell Tankers UK Ltd* [2001] PIQR P19; Zerk, *Multinationals and Corporate Social Responsibility*, 220–1.

which could injure employees and third parties;[121] and manufacturers, suppliers, and installers of products must takes steps so that they are aware of risks to health and safety and take reasonable precautions to counter them, which might include obligations to warn consumers and others affected by risks to health and safety.[122] Other, more general factors of relevance to determination of the appropriate standard of care include the likelihood of harm arising, the seriousness of the potential harm, the social utility of the defendant's activity, and the cost and practicability of available precautions.[123]

Finally, once the court has formulated the appropriate standard of care that ought to have been observed by the defendant, it will compare that standard with the conduct of the defendant, in order to determine whether the defendant met the standard or fell below it. Discussion of the asbestos cases under the heading of 'duty of care', as given previously, provides some indication of circumstances in which courts have found parent companies to be in breach of obligations that they owed to personal injury claimants.

11.2.3 Causation of Damage

Negligence is actionable only when the claimant suffers a recognised form of damage. For the purposes of this book, 'recognised damage' includes physical injury and validly grounded pure psychiatric injury. However, there have been relatively few cases of the latter type in the insolvent entity context, and they will not be subject to further discussion here. Mere exposure to risk from toxic substances is not sufficient to constitute recognised damage for the purposes of negligence.[124] The risk of injury must become manifest in detrimental physical change. In asbestos cases, for example, the claimant must contract a disease such as mesothelioma, asbestosis, or lung disease. When he or she does suffer physical injury, the claimant will be entitled to consequential damages for psychiatric ills and other losses which *accompany* it.

In addition to the damage requirement, in the usual case of negligence the claimant must be able to prove a causal connection between the defendant's failure to take care and the ensuing damage.[125] There are

[121] E.g., *Wilsons and Clyde Coal Ltd* v. *English* [1938] AC 57.

[122] E.g., *Distillers Co (Biochemicals) Ltd* v. *Thompson* [1971] AC 458; *Vacwell Engineering Co Ltd* v. *BDH Chemicals* [1971] 1 QB 88.

[123] See Witting, *Street on Torts*, pp. 118ff.

[124] *Rothwell* v. *Chemical & Insulating Co Ltd* [2008] 1 AC 281.

[125] For detailed discussion, see, e.g., S. Steel, *Proof of Causation in Tort Law* (2015).

two main causation issues to be examined. The first is 'causation in fact', and the second is 'scope of liability for consequences of breach'. A third issue concerning 'remoteness of damage' might arise if pleaded by the defendant.

The primary issue in the law on causation is whether the defendant's failure to take care was a factual cause of the claimant's loss or harm. In most cases, this can be addressed by applying the 'but-for' test of causation. According to this test, the defendant's breach of the relevant standard of care was a factual cause of the claimant's loss or harm when, but for the breach,[126] the claimant would not have suffered the loss or harm in the way that he or she did.[127] Controlling for background factors, the test identifies whether the breach was a necessary cause of the loss or harm. However, there is a number of exceptional types of case in which the 'but-for' test is not useful. Since courts cannot shy away from deciding hard cases, they have been forced to confront them and have developed some alternative rules. This book examines two important exceptions to but-for causation, these being the '*Fairchild* principle' (to be discussed now) and market share liability (arising in certain product liability cases and discussed in Chapter 8).

By way of introduction to the '*Fairchild* principle', it should be noted that asbestos-induced diseases pose special problems for many claimants because of the long latency periods between exposure and manifestation of injury.[128] This creates two significant problems. The first is in establishing how exposure came about, and the second is in determining which of the range of applicable sources of asbestos exposure were actual causes of injury.[129] While asbestosis and mesothelioma can be caused by exposure to asbestos only, lung diseases have other potential causes, such as cigarette smoking.[130] Happily, many cases involving asbestos can be determined on the basis of a relatively straightforward extension to the ordinary but-for rule. This is the 'substantial contribution to damage' test, which is pertinent to asbestos cases where cumulative exposure is

126 In other words, without the breach.

127 E.g., *Barnett* v. *Chelsea and Kensington Hospital Management Committee* [1969] 1 QB 428; *Resurfice Corporation* v. *Hanke* [2007] 1 SCR 333. For Australia, see, e.g., Civil Liability Act 2002 (NSW), ss. 3B and 5D.

128 Although the minimum length of the period of latency has been revised down several times, and now stands at five years: G. Turton, *Evidential Uncertainty in Causation in Negligence* (2016), p. 169.

129 J. Sanders, 'Risky Business: Causation in Asbestos Cancer Cases (and Beyond?)', in R. Goldberg (ed.), *Perspectives on Causation* (2011), p. 14.

130 Sanders, 'Risky Business', 14.

relevant to the causation of harm, such as with exposures leading to claimant asbestosis.[131] So long as the claimant can prove that the defendant's exposure made a substantial contribution to his or her injury (in other words, that the defendant was a but-for cause of some part of a divisible injury),[132] then he or she can claim damages for that part of it.

However, in *Fairchild* v. *Glenhaven Funeral Services Ltd*,[133] the House of Lords was confronted with a more problematic type of asbestos-induced disease. The principle which has evolved from *Fairchild* applies in cases involving exposure of the claimant to more than one source of asbestos fibres, the claimant eventually suffering from the indivisible disease mesothelioma. Cases have considered situations in which the sources have included a negligent employer, and either another negligent employer,[134] the claimant himself or herself,[135] or the background environment[136] (which, in urban settings, is likely to contain significant quantities of asbestos fibre).[137] The problem for the claimant in such cases has been that medical science does not yet fully comprehend the way in which mesothelioma is caused. Although additional exposure increases the chances that the victim will suffer from mesothelioma,[138] small doses might be sufficient to cause the disease too. Moreover, it was still believed at the time of the *Fairchild* decision that a single fibre might be sufficient.[139] This means that there can be no certainty about the source of the fibres that have caused the claimant's mesothelioma.

The current position in English law is that the claimant can recover from any negligent employer that has exposed him or her to asbestos, as long as the claimant subsequently contracted mesothelioma. This is

[131] E.g., *Holtby* v. *Brigham & Cowan (Hull) Ltd* [2000] 3 All ER 421; Steel, *Proof of Causation in Tort Law*, pp. 243–7; A. Boggio, *Compensating Asbestos Victims: Law and the Dark Side of Industrialization* (2013), p. 102.

[132] Steel, *Proof of Causation in Tort Law*, p. 243; S. Bailey, 'Causation in Negligence: What Is a Material Contribution?' (2010) 30 *Legal Studies* 167.

[133] [2003] 1 AC 32. [134] *Fairchild* v. *Glenhaven Funeral Services Ltd* [2003] 1 AC 32.

[135] *Barker* v. *Corus UK Ltd* [2006] 2 AC 572.

[136] *Sienkiewicz* v. *Greif (UK) Ltd* [2011] 2 AC 229.

[137] J. Stapleton, 'Lords A'Leaping Evidentiary Gaps' (2002) 10 *Torts Law Journal* 276, 277.

[138] Sanders, 'Risky Business', 18 ('the more asbestos fibres in one's lungs, the greater the probability some fibre or set of fibres will cause the genetic damage that generates the disease').

[139] The High Court of Australia rejected this possibility in *Amaca Pty Ltd* v. *Booth* (2011) 283 ALR 461, [79], which held that, on the basis of evidence available to it, the causation of mesothelioma from a single asbestos fibre is not physically possible. See also *Sienkiewicz* v. *Greif (UK) Ltd* [2011] 2 AC 229, [101]–[102]; Turton, *Evidential Uncertainty in Causation in Negligence*, p. 169; S. Green, *Causation in Negligence* (2015), p. 130.

despite the existence of other sources of asbestos fibres to which the claimant was exposed. The negligent employer will be liable fully for the loss,[140] unless able to obtain contribution from another liable party or able to reduce the damages award by successfully pleading contributory negligence. In this way, the risk of an incorrect finding about causation is borne by the negligent employer, rather than by the claimant.[141] The Compensation Act 2006 imposes a presumptive rule of apportionment between joint wrongdoers based on 'the relative lengths of the periods of exposure for which each [tortfeasor] was responsible'.[142] The presumption *can* be overturned, either when some agreement as to responsibility among wrongdoers is reached, or when 'the court thinks that another basis for determining contribution is more appropriate in the circumstances of a particular case'.[143]

The juristic basis for the *Fairchild* principle is uncertain. On one approach, it rests on a combination of justice-based arguments for recovery (especially by 'innocent' sufferers of mesothelioma) in combination with the facts of exposure and subsequent contraction of the disease.[144] Although this might be considered an exception to the but-for test of causation, another way of describing the result is to say that it involves an exception to the need for proof of causation *simpliciter*,[145] because it is not expressed to apply via a reversed onus of proof. Indeed, at this point in time, reversing the onus of proof is futile because there is a 'rock of uncertainty' about the way in which mesothelioma is caused.[146]

The *Fairchild* principle is a narrow exception to the ordinary but-for test of causation applicable in mesothelioma cases. But there has been debate about whether the underlying principle might be applicable in analogous cases of evidential uncertainty and indivisible disease. Use of the principle might be restricted to cases involving exposures to the same causal agent,[147]

140 Compensation Act 2006, s 3.

141 *Fairchild* v. *Glenhaven Funeral Services Ltd* [2003] 1 AC 32, [33].

142 Compensation Act 2006, s. 3(4).

143 Compensation Act 2006, s. 3(4)(a) and (b).

144 See, e.g., *Fairchild* v. *Glenhaven Funeral Services Ltd* [2003] 1 AC 32, [2]; *Durham* v. *BAI (Run Off) Ltd (in scheme of arrangement)* [2012] 1 WLR 867, [58]; A. Ripstein and B. C. Zipursky, 'Corrective Justice in an Age of Mass Torts', in G. J. Postema (ed.), *Philosophy and the Law of Torts* (2001), ch. 6 (justice argument).

145 A. C. Hutchinson, 'Out of the Black Hole: Toward a Fresh Approach to Tort Causation' (2016) 39 *Dalhousie Law Journal* 651, _.

146 *Sienkiewicz* v. *Greif (UK) Ltd* [2011] 2 AC 229, [160]; C. J. Miller, 'Causation in Personal Injury after (and before) *Sienkiewicz*' (2012) 32 *Legal Studies* 410.

147 *Fairchild* v. *Glenhaven Funeral Services Ltd* [2003] 1 AC 32 [170]. See also Green, *Causation in Negligence*, p. 149.

or to exposures to different agents that act in the same way so as to cause disease.[148] Alternatively, the principle might be extended to all cases of evidential uncertainty involving agents that have the potential to cause the same indivisible disease. In *Heneghan v Manchester Dry Docks*,[149] the Court of Appeal effectively opted for the last alternative. It decided that the *Fairchild* principle *is* applicable to cases of negligent exposure by multiple employers to asbestos resulting in lung cancer (an indivisible disease) because a finding had been made that 'the carcinogens were caused by exposure to asbestos fibres' and the court saw no relevant difference from the eponymous case.[150] However, while the *Fairchild* case was concerned with exposure to asbestos only (a 'single agent'), the *Heneghan* case *was different* because it involved exposure to both asbestos and cigarette smoke (two agents), which operate in different ways to cause lung cancer.[151] So, the question arises whether the UK Supreme Court will accept this as a legitimate development.[152] For the moment, the extension to lung cancer cases having been made and, because Compensation Act 2006, section 3 does not apply to them, each defendant is liable *in proportion* to its contribution to the risk of injury.

In Canada, rules on causation in mesothelioma and other asbestos cases have not been fully developed. The material contribution *to risk* test is applicable in mesothelioma cases where it is impossible to apply the but-for test because of the existence of multiple tortfeasors.[153] There might be scope for the extension of the test to cases of a single tortfeasor and additional exposure to background, environmental asbestos, but this has not yet occurred.[154] However, it seems unlikely that courts will depart from the but-for test in cases where one of the sources of asbestos was the claimant him- or herself.[155] Although not free from doubt,[156] it seems

148 *Barker* v. *Corus (UK) plc* [2006] 2 AC 572, [24]. See Steel, *Proof of Causation in Tort Law*, p. 237.

149 [2016] 1 WLR 2036. 150 [2016] 1 WLR 2036, [41] and [48].

151 S. Steel, 'On When *Fairchild* Applies' (2015) 131 *Law Quarterly Review* 363, 366.

152 S. Green '*Fairchild* and the Single Agent Criterion' (2017) 133 *Law Quarterly Review* 25; Steel, 'On When *Fairchild* Applies' (both arguing no causation). See also J. Morgan, 'Causation, Politics, and Law' in Goldberg, *Perspectives on Causation*, p. 80.

153 See *Clements* v. *Clements* [2012] 2 SCR 181, [13], [34], [43], and [46]; *Resurfice Corp* v. *Hanke* [2007] 1 SCR 333, [25]; D. Cheifetz, 'Causation in Negligence: Material Contribution and But-for after *Clements*' (2012) 40 *Advocates' Quarterly* 275, 278.

154 *Clements* v. *Clements* [2012] 2 SCR 181, [42]; Cheifetz, 'Causation in Negligence', 279, n. 15.

155 *Lange* v. *Bennett* [1964] 1 OR 233, [10]–[11]; Cheifetz, 'Causation in Negligence', 284.

156 See Cheifetz, 'Causation in Negligence'.

that ordinary rules on material contribution *to injury* are applicable in asbestos cases involving divisible diseases.[157]

Australian courts have taken a different starting point in their consideration of asbestos cases involving mesothelioma. In *Amaca Pty Ltd* v. *Booth*,[158] the High Court of Australia stated that, based on the evidence presented to it, it was not possible for a single asbestos fibre to cause that disease.[159] The assumption is that mesothelioma requires some cumulative exposure to asbestos, so that cases concerning it can be determined in the same way as asbestosis and lung cancer cases. Accordingly, the High Court has determined asbestos cases by asking separately of each defendant whether it was more probable than not that the negligence of the defendant was a cause of the claimant's injury.[160]

The second main issue regarding causation, which concerns the scope of liability for consequences of breach,[161] arises only when the claimant has succeeded (on whatever basis) on the factual causation issue. Scope of liability is a particular issue in cases where the defendant commits a tort earlier in time, and a second event occurs later in time which gives rise to further damage. The question is whether the defendant is liable for that further damage. This is determined by asking (using the language of metaphor) whether the subsequent event can be regarded as a new intervening cause which severs the 'chain of causation' emanating from breach. A subsequent event of relevance to the insolvent entity problem that might break the chain of causation is gross medical negligence, which gives rise to further injury in the claimant. In a case of gross medical negligence, the original defendant is not liable for the further damage caused by responsible medical staff.[162] Given that such rules pose no special problems in mass-tort cases, they need not be considered further.

11.2.4 Remoteness of Damage

The law does not permit recovery for all damage that can be linked, no matter how tenuously, to a prior tort. Limits are placed on the losses for which any given defendant will be held responsible and required to pay

157 *Athey* v. *Leonati* [1996] 3 SCR 458. 158 (2011) 283 ALR 461.

159 (2011) 283 ALR 461, [79]. 160 *Amaca Pty Ltd* v. *Ellis* (2011) 283 ALR 461, [40].

161 See J. Stapleton, '"Cause-in-Fact" and the Scope of Liability for Consequences' (2003) 119 *Law Quarterly Review* 388 (examining English law). For Australia, see, e.g., Civil Liability Act 2002 (NSW), ss. 3B and 5D; J. Stapleton, 'Factual Causation' (2010) 38 *Federal Law Review* 467, 484.

162 *Wright* v. *Cambridge Medical Group* [2013] QB 312, [111].

compensation. In other words, some forms of loss are regarded as too remote from the defendant's tort for the defendant to be held liable for them. The general test of remoteness in tort law revolves around the extent to which the harm in question was reasonably foreseeable in its general (not specific) type *and* manner of causation. In asbestos cases, it is sufficient to establish liability that the defendant had been able to foresee 'pulmonary injury' or 'lung disease', rather than something more specific (such as mesothelioma).[163] By contrast, future courts might find that particular side effects of new medicines were not reasonably foreseeable in nature – depending on how unusual those side effects happen to be.[164] So negligence claims might fail upon a pleading of remoteness.

11.2.5 US Negligence Rules

Just as in the Commonwealth jurisdictions surveyed previously, the tort of negligence is of occasional assistance in the corporate group context to US claimants[165] seeking to extend liability beyond a subsidiary corporation. Suit against the parent company might be brought either because the subsidiary is insolvent, or because the subsidiary's liability to its own employees is limited to amounts determined under workers' compensation statutes.[166] However, the trend appears to be against this type of liability[167] because of strong concerns that it undermines rules of separate legal personality and limited liability. This section focusses upon the two especially problematic elements of the tort – duty of care and factual causation.

US courts frequently begin their observations in three-party duty of care cases, involving a claim that the parent company owed obligations to the subsidiary's injured employees (or, perhaps, to external parties), by recounting the status of the parent company as a shareholder and its entitlement to a

[163] See *Margereson* v. *JW Roberts Ltd* [1996] Env LR 304, 310; *CSR Ltd* v. *Young* (1998) Aust Torts Rep ¶ 81–468, 64,965, respectively.

[164] E.g., *Christofferson* v. *Kaiser Foundation Hospitals* 15 Cal App 3d 76 (1971).

[165] K. A. Strasser, 'Piercing the Veil in Corporate Groups' (2005) 37 *Connecticut Law Review* 637, 648 (notes that there have been few successful cases).

[166] E.g., *Waste Management, Inc* v. *Superior Court of San Diego* 119 Cal App 4th 105 (Cal 2004), discussed in what follows. Suit against the employer corporation was precluded by the California workers' compensation legislation (California Labor Code, Div 4 Workers' Compensation and Insurance, ch. 3, § 3601), but this did not preclude action against third parties.

[167] Muchlinski, *Multinational Enterprises and the Law*, p. 313.

presumption of no liability.[168] Courts note also that the parent company can be expected, in the ordinary course of business, to exercise control over the subsidiary,[169] and frequently insist that there must be something which goes beyond the exercise of ordinary levels of control in order to ground a duty of care.[170] We examine two contexts in which the issues have arisen – cases of parental control over subsidiary budgets and cases of parental participation in subsidiary activities (although frequently these will be intertwined). Ordinarily, the cases concern actions brought by subsidiary employees or their representatives.

In *Forsythe* v. *Clark USA, Inc*,[171] the use of a substandard maintenance procedure caused fire to erupt at an oil refinery, which led to the deaths of two subsidiary company workers. The claimants' representatives contended that the parent company, Clark USA, had imposed significant budget cuts on its subsidiary, Clark Refining, and had demanded that the latter operate the refinery 'pursuant to an overall business strategy that it knew would adversely affect safety by forcing reductions in training and maintenance'.[172] The claimants argued that this resulted in the use of unqualified employees as maintenance technicians at the time of the accident.[173] The Illinois Supreme Court held that a parent company, which exercises higher than usual levels of control over a subsidiary, and which specifically directs an activity or else mandates a course of action and authorises the manner in which specific activities pursuant to that course of action are undertaken, owes a duty of care to subsidiary employees foreseeably at risk of harm.[174] In an industry with inherent dangers, 'severe cutbacks in staffing, safety, maintenance and training in such industries could lead, with reasonable foreseeability, to the injury of others'.[175]

Clark USA, Inc appears to be an outlier. In the usual case, the exercise of even strict control over the budget of a subsidiary is an insufficient

[168] E.g., *In re Silicone Gel Breast Implants Products Liability Litigation* 837 F Supp 1128, 1134 (11th Cir. 1993); Blumberg, *The Law of Corporate Groups*, p. 318.

[169] *In re Silicone Gel Breast Implants Products Liability Litigation* 837 F Supp 1128, 1134 (11th Cir. 1993).

[170] E.g., *United States* v. *Bestfoods* 524 US 51, 71–2 (1998)(control which is 'eccentric under accepted norms of parental oversight of a subsidiary's facility'); *Forsythe* v. *Clark USA, Inc* 864 NE 2d 227, 237 (Ill 2007)(control beyond the normal incidents of ownership); *Esmark, Inc* v. *National Labor Relations Board* 887 F 2d 739 (7th Cir. 1989)(direct control by way of command and not mere cajoling).

[171] 864 NE 2d 227 (Ill 2007).

[172] 864 NE 2d 227, 232 (Ill 2007).

[173] 864 NE 2d 227, 231 (Ill 2007).

[174] 864 NE 2d 227, 237 (Ill 2007).

[175] 864 NE 2d 227, 238 (Ill 2007).

basis for the recognition of a duty of care in the parent company, even when this control entails a deficiency in funding for health- and safety-related actions. In *Waste Management, Inc* v. *Superior Court of San Diego*,[176] for example, the California Court of Appeals, Fourth District, rejected a claim that a parent company's budgetary decisions impacting upon the ability of the subsidiary to replace and repair 'dangerous' rubbish trucks grounded a duty of care. McConnell PJ stated that negligently controlling a subsidiary's budget 'does not create a duty on the part of the parent corporation to ensure safety or prevent injuries to the subsidiary's employees'.[177] In the usual case, a duty would attach only to foreseeably risky actions of the parent company, which are distinct from activities of the subsidiary. On the facts, there was no separate act, it being the subsidiary which supplied the inadequately maintained truck.

The more secure basis by which a parent company can be held to owe a duty of care to an insolvent subsidiary's injured employee or to an external party is by proof of its 'direct participation' in the injury-causing activity.[178] In the seminal case of *Johnson* v. *Abbe Engineering Company*,[179] the claimants were employed by the subsidiary Tuboscope in making a coating compound and poured flammable solvents into a tank by the prescribed procedure, after which an explosion occurred. The claimants were thrown by the force of the explosion, engulfed in flames, and severely injured. They sued the parent company, AMF, for its role in safety breaches which led to the accident. In a short judgment, the US Court of Appeals for the Fifth Circuit held that a duty of care could be grounded upon AMF's manager of accident prevention and safety training having inspected the area where the accident occurred several times during the years preceding the accident, in the course of safety 'audit[s] of the entire complex'. The inspections inevitably encompassed the procedures used to make the compound. Tuboscope managers relied upon the inspections and would have followed any pertinent safety recommendations made.[180]

The modern US requirements for the imposition of duties of care upon parent companies with respect to health and safety matters affecting subsidiaries are reminiscent of those in UK law (discussed earlier). A

[176] 119 Cal App 4th 105 (2004). See also *The Coastal Corporation* v. *Torres* 133 SW 3d 776 (Tex App 2004)(requirement of 'affirmative conduct' which injures).

[177] 119 Cal App 4th 105, [13] (2004).

[178] E.g., *Esmark, Inc* v. *National Labor Relations Board* 887 F.2d 739, 756 (7th Cir. 1989); Blumberg, *The Law of Corporate Groups*, 324–5.

[179] 749 F 2d 1131 (5th Cir. 1984). [180] 749 F 2d 1131, 1133–4 (5th Cir. 1984).

duty of care more readily attaches to a parent company which undertakes activities that overlap with those of the subsidiary, takes the lead on health and safety matters, and expects compliance with its standards.[181] In *Little* v. *Delta Steel, Inc*,[182] the Texas Court of Appeals held that a claimant must be able to demonstrate that the parent company 'had actual control or a right to control over the specific aspect of the safety and security of the premises that led to' injury.[183] As argued several times by now, the need to prove control in order to ground liability is likely to give rise to mischief in the corporate group context. Consistently with this, it has been said that the 'current law is producing the wrong incentives, because it encourages parents to avoid exerting control over [their] subsidiaries. Competent lawyers are warning managers, "Stay away from the subsidiary, especially safety issues and hazardous waste site problems, or the courts will hold you liable."'[184]

Just as in the United Kingdom, US courts have faced pressures to depart from the rigours of the but-for test of factual causation in mass-tort cases litigated in negligence. As adumbrated, this has occurred in cases involving both asbestos and some types of generic drugs. The exceptions to but-for causation, which operate in cases of both negligence and strict products liability,[185] were discussed in Chapter 8.

11.2.6 Deficiencies in Negligence Rules

The question arises whether current rules of negligence provide an adequate avenue of recovery in resolution of the insolvent entity problem. There are good reasons for believing that this tort is not especially useful at the moment in extending liability in corporate group cases. Two sets of reasons for this revolve around issues of asset ownership and the exercise of control.

First, while the negligence cases have been concerned with vertical relationships between parent companies and their subsidiaries, there is no guarantee that a parent company is any more solvent than a

181 E.g., *Morvant* v. *Oil States International, Inc* 3 F Supp 3d 561, 569 (ED La 2014); *Abdel-Fattah* v. *Pepsico, Inc* 948 SW 2d 381 (Tex App 1997); *Anglo Eastern Bulkships, Ltd* v. *Ameron, Inc* 556 F Supp 1198 (SDNY 1982); *Boggs* v. *Blue Diamond Coal Co* 590 F 2d 655 (6th Cir. 1979).

182 409 SW 3d 704 (Tex App 2013).

183 409 SW 3d 704, 717 (Tex App 2013).

184 W. J. Rands, 'Domination of a Subsidiary by a Parent' (1999) 32 *Indiana Law Review* 421, 454. See also Strasser, 'Piercing the Veil in Corporate Groups', 664.

185 See Steel, *Proof of Causation in Tort Law*, pp. 251–2.

wrongdoing subsidiary. The whole corporate group might be at risk of insolvency. Alternatively, the structuring of relations might mean that the valuable assets of the corporate group are not held directly by the parent, but by non-operating subsidiaries. The natural response is to argue that, when that is so, the parent can be ordered to sell some or all of its shareholdings in those subsidiaries in order to satisfy its debts.[186] However, a forced sale might not yield a satisfactory return in cases where subsidiary assets are specialised in nature (being valuable only in conjunction with other assets held within the group) or subject to fluctuations in value.[187] Creditors might have a better prospect of being paid if the parent company is permitted to retain its assets in its subsidiaries so that the latter can generate future profits out of which creditors can be paid.

Second, potential limitations arise in the application of the tort of negligence when control is used as an important criterion of parent company liability. The parent company might not exercise sufficient control over relevant subsidiary activities so as to owe a duty of care under *Chandler* v. *Cape plc*[188] or equivalent rules elsewhere. While Cape plc and CSR Ltd exercised appreciable control over some aspects of their operating entities' activities, not all parent companies have done the same. Thus, the British asbestos manufacturer Turner & Newall exercised very little supervision over its foreign subsidiaries (as we saw in Chapter 4).[189] In *Thompson* v. *The Renwick Group plc*,[190] the group was engaged mainly in leisure activities, and the defendant was considered little more than a holding company that appointed a director to the board of the subsidiary undertaking the transportation and unpacking of asbestos. Moreover, pharmaceutical companies frequently operate in an arm's-length relationship with their subsidiaries and network collaborators, which undertake developmental and other risky kinds of work (as we saw in Chapter 4). When the exercise of control is absent, negligence law does not provide a remedy. And control-based liability discourages the exercise of beneficial control, as much as it discourages the exercise of harm-inducing control.

[186] A. Muscat, *The Liability of the Holding Company for the Debts of its Insolvent Subsidiaries* (1996), p. 456.
[187] UNCITRAL, 'Legislative Guide on Insolvency Law' (2005), p. 28.
[188] [2012] 1 WLR 3111.
[189] G. Tweedale, *Magic Mineral to Killer Dust: Turner and Newall and the Asbestos Hazard* (1999), p. 293.
[190] [2014] PIQR P18.

11.3 Unlawful Means Conspiracy

More needs to be done in order to provide an appropriate tort liability regime for dealing with the insolvent entity problem. There is a need for the development of 'sideways' liability among corporate group subsidiaries, which is the level at which wrongdoing occurs most frequently and at which assets are held. This book now moves on to consider another tort that might be capable of application or adaptation to the corporate group context in order to create such liability. Indeed, this tort might prove very useful in dealing with another unresolved issue – the insolvent entity problem as it arises in the corporate network. Companies coordinating with each other at the subsidiary level in corporate groups and within networks need to have incentives to monitor each other's conduct and to avoid dealing with entities that display reckless disregard for the safety and well-being of employees, customers, and bystanders.

The tort of unlawful means conspiracy ('conspiracy') might be of future significance in extending liability from insolvent subsidiaries and network participants.[191] There are several reasons for considering its use in this context: first, conspiracy is a tort which does not depend upon the presence of control; it is concerned with agreements between individuals, and has a role to play in a liability regime that takes the separate legal personality of the company seriously. Second, conspiracy ensures that liability is extended *beyond the actor that injures* to those who entered into the agreement and did something to further it. Third, conspiracy actions might be useful when torts are committed in different jurisdictions, enabling separate acts to be linked together for the purpose of extending liability.[192]

However, the current law of unlawful means conspiracy does not facilitate extensions of liability in resolution of the insolvent entity problem. There are two hurdles to overcome. First, unlawful means conspiracy requires intention to injure – which is not present in the typical mass-tort case. Second, courts restrict the operation of this tort to cases of financial losses – although there appears to be no justification for doing so. Argument will be made for adaptation of unlawful means conspiracy so as to create a suitable form of corporate group or network liability. Under the proposed tort, each entity

[191] For the position in Australian law, see C. Witting and J. Rankin, 'Tortious Liability of Corporate Groups: From Control to Coordination' (2014) 22 *Tort Law Review* 91; P. Edmundson, 'Conspiracy by Unlawful Means: Keeping the Tort Untangled' (2008) 16 *Torts Law Journal* 189. For more general comment on Commonwealth law, see P. W. Lee, 'Civil Conspiracy in the Corporate Context' (2016) 23 *Torts Law Journal* 257.

[192] See *Kuwait Oil Tanker* v. *Al Bader* [2000] 2 All ER (Comm) 271, 316, and 319.

having substantial commercial relations with a company acting recklessly would be deemed to have agreed to the risky activity, and would become prima facie jointly liable with the risk-taking company when personal injury ensues. This would ensure that, whether in a corporate group or network of companies, there is the potential for liability to be extended to those entities coordinating their actions with risk-taking companies in a way that causes injury to third parties. It would then be for the prima facie liable parties to prove that they took every step[193] in order to avoid the future causation of personal injury to others by doing such things as blowing the whistle on the risky conduct and ceasing coordination with the risk-creating company. The remainder of this chapter develops a proposal for such a tort. The proposed tort is named 'multiple entity recklessness'.

Let us begin substantive discussion with an overview of the tort of conspiracy. Under current law, conspiracy arises when two or more persons agree upon a course of action with an aim of injuring another, and the latter suffers loss as a consequence of the wrong committed.[194] It comes in two different forms.[195] Conspiracy by *lawful* means arises when persons combine to act with the predominant purpose of injuring another, and when that other is injured as a consequence.[196] Given the requirement of *predominant* purpose, this form of conspiracy rarely will be found in commercial contexts, and nothing more will be said about it. Conspiracy by *un*lawful means is related, but features important differences, the most obvious of which concerns the type of intention necessary to commit the tort. The use of unlawful means results in a lesser requirement that the intention to injure be merely one of the purposes of the conspirators.[197]

11.3.1 Agreement

The first element of unlawful means conspiracy is a relevant combination between the parties,[198] often described as an 'agreement'.[199] While there

193 Readers will recall this language as used in the Insolvency Act 1986, s 214.

194 *Crofter Hand-Woven Harris Tweed Co Ltd* v. *Veitch* [1942] AC 435, 445, and 461; *McKernan* v. *Fraser* (1931) 46 CLR 343, 407. The agreement need be no more than tacit in nature: H. Carty, *An Analysis of the Economic Torts* (2nd edn., 2012), p. 127.

195 There is, however, debate about whether this separation is viable; there might be a 'spectrum' of liability for 'harmful combinations': Carty, *An Analysis of the Economic Torts*, p. 124.

196 *McKernan* v. *Fraser* (1931) 46 CLR 343, 362.

197 *Fatimi Pty Ltd* v. *Bryant* (2004) 59 NSWLR 678, 681. See discussion in Edmundson, 'Conspiracy by Unlawful Means', 189, who notes that 'the tort is not yet at the stage where the precise scope of its elements can be [stated] with confidence.'

198 K. Oliphant (ed.), *The Law of Tort* (3rd edn. 2015), p. 1630.

199 Carty, *An Analysis of the Economic Torts*, pp. 122 and 127.

needs to be a combination, there need be no *explicit* agreement. A court is entitled to examine the conduct of the parties and to infer that they have pursued what is, in substance, a common objective.[200] The parties must be sufficiently aware of the material facts and share the common objective at the time of the acts complained of.[201] There is no need to prove that each conspirator acted upon the agreement, for participation can be either active or passive.[202] The requisite combination has been distinguished from lesser types of coordination, which do not suffice. These include 'mere facilitation' of acts,[203] mere association with the primary tortfeasor,[204] and 'weak and incompetent acquiescence' in what is done.[205]

11.3.2 Fault Element

Unlawful means conspiracy is an intention-based tort, although there have been different formulations of the intention requirement. Under the traditional formulation, the agreement between the parties must be one to injure the particular claimant by the use of acts which constitute unlawful means.[206] The unlawful means utilised must be 'aimed at' or 'directed against' the claimant.[207] In addition, the defendant must have knowledge of the facts which make the proposed conduct unlawful, even if that person does not appreciate their legal significance.[208] Findings of intention and knowledge in corporate defendants are via rules of

200 *CC Containers Pty Ltd* v. *Lee* [2011] VSC 537, at [13].

201 *Kuwait Oil Tanker Co SAK* v. *Al Bader* [2001] 2 All ER (Comm) 271, 312; *Huntly* v. *Thornton* [1957] 1 WLR 321, 353; *EFT Holdings Inc* v. *Marinteknik Shipbuilders (S) Pte Ltd* [2014] 1 SLR 860.

202 *R* v. *Siricusa* (1989) 90 Cr App R 340, 349.

203 Carty, *An Analysis of the Economic Torts*, p. 127.

204 *Sandman* v. *Panasonic UK Ltd* [1998] FSR 651.

205 *Grupo Torras SA* v. *Al Sabah* [1999] CLC 1469, 1583.

206 *Emerald Supplies Ltd* v. *British Airways plc (No 1)* [2016] Bus LR 145, 201; *Baldwin* v. *Berryland Books* [2010] EWCA Civ 1440, at [45] and [48]; *Meretz Investments NV* v. *ACP Ltd* [2008] Ch 244; *Kuwait Oil Tanker Co SAK* v. *Al Bader* [2000] 2 All ER (Comm) 271, [108]. In *Capital for Enterprise Fund A LP* v. *Bibby Financial Services Ltd* [2015] EWHC 2593 (Ch), it was clarified that 'on the current state of the law, it is not a requirement for liability to be established that the claimant proves that the defendant knew that the loss was to be caused by unlawful means but rather it is sufficient if it is proved that the defendant knew of the facts which in the event made the means used unlawful': ibid. [91].

207 *Revenue and Customs Commissioners* v. *Total Network SL* [2008] 1 AC 1174, [44], and [120]; *Lonrho plc* v. *Fayed* [1992] 1 AC 448, 467. See also R. Lewis, 'Economic Torts: Where Are We Now?' [2008] *Business Law Review* 216, 217.

208 *Belmont Finance Corp* v. *Williams Furniture (No 2)* [1980] 1 All ER 393, 404, and 414.

attribution. Under the modern approach,[209] a company demonstrates the requisite state of mind if that state of mind exists in either the board of directors, senior officers of the company, or any other relevant person(s) undertaking the relevant act. However, we must put 'intention' to one side because of its limited relevance to the insolvent entity problem.

The more important issue is whether *recklessness* suffices as the fault element in unlawful means conspiracy. There are opposing views on this issue, but the prevailing opinion is that it does not. On the one hand, the English Court of Appeal in *Baldwin* v. *Berryland Books* stated that intention needs to be grounded in sufficient knowledge of the circumstances in which injury could arise, and held that 'what is required is actual intention or reckless indifference.' Reckless indifference would be evident in 'a conscious decision not to inquire into the existence of a fact'.[210] On the other hand, the same court held in *Meretz Investments NV* v. *ACP Ltd* that unlawful means conspiracy is not committed when two persons act merely with the substantial certainty that a third party will be injured.[211] Again, in *Emerald Supplies Ltd* v. *British Airways plc (No 1)*,[212] Elias LJ stated that 'intention to harm the claimant cannot properly or sensibly be described as a cause of the defendant's conduct if the defendant is not even sure that the claimant will suffer loss at all.'[213] Indeed, there is a fear that a recklessness criterion might dissipate into mere foreseeability.[214] In this way, the utility of the current tort of unlawful means conspiracy is reduced in the corporate group or network context by a restrictive intention requirement.

Another, background reason for which courts have tended to reject the idea that recklessness in the causation of injury suffices for the purposes of unlawful means conspiracy is that it has been treated as an 'economic tort'. Unlawful means conspiracy is reserved for the causation of financial losses resulting from egregious wrongdoing in commercial contexts. Given the lesser protection offered by tort law to purely financial interests, and the

[209] *Bilta (UK) Ltd (in liq)* v. *Nazir* [2015] 2 WLR 1168, esp. [41], [202], and [204].

[210] [2010] EWCA Civ 1440, at [48], citing *OBG Ltd* v. *Allan* [2008] 1 AC 1, [41].

[211] *Meretz Investments NV* v. *ACP Ltd* [2008] Ch 244, [92]. See also *Crofter Hand Woven Harris Tweed Co Ltd* v. *Veitch* [1942] AC 435, 444–5 (case of lawful means conspiracy); *WH Newson Holdings Ltd* v. *IMI plc* [2014] 1 All ER 1132, [35].

[212] [2016] Bus LR 145.

[213] [2016] Bus LR 145, [167]. Australian courts have taken a similar negative view: C. Sappideen and P. Vines (eds.), *Fleming's The Law of Torts* (10th edn., 2011), p. 794 (requirement of intention to injure).

[214] *Emerald Supplies Ltd* v. *British Airways plc (No 1)* [2016] Bus LR 145, [167], [169], and [174].

policy in favour of competition among economic actors, courts have clung to the 'bright line' of an intention standard of fault.[215] For now, it need merely be noted that such reasoning would make no sense were the tort extended to protect bodily integrity. In fact, there are suggestions that the tort ought to be applicable in cases arising beyond the causation of financial losses. This is a matter that we will return to.

11.3.3 Unlawful Means

Whereas the unlawful means conspiracy rules on 'agreement' and intention are restrictive, the same cannot be said about the unlawful means requirement. Indeed, the restrictive nature of the former elements might be said to justify a wider approach to the latter. There are two dimensions to the liberal nature of the rules. First, Commonwealth courts have established that the wrong committed need not be independently actionable by the claimant (that is, actionable outside the conspiracy itself). Thus, to give an example, unlawful means conspiracy might arise where there is no recognised tort, but where a common law crime has been committed[216] or a statutory provision has been breached in a manner that is not actionable against the wrongdoers.[217] This demonstrates the utility of the tort as more than 'a barren iteration of joint tortfeasance'.[218] Second, Lord Walker remarked in *Revenue and Customs Commissioners* v. *Total Network SL* that 'the range of possible conspiracies [is] so wide and varied that it would be unwise to attempt to lay down any general rule' as to the circumstances in which it applies.[219] Wrongs beyond those already identified that might ground a claim include breaches of: directors' duties,[220] competition law rules,[221] administrative regulations,[222]

215 See, e.g., *Meretz Investments NV* v. *ACP Ltd* [2008] Ch 244, [127], and [174].

216 *Revenue and Customs Commissioners* v. *Total Network SL* [2008] 1 AC 1174 (crime of cheating the Revenue).

217 *Canada Cement LaFarge Ltd* v. *British Columbia Lightweight Aggregate Ltd* [1983] 1 SCR 452, 471. For Australia, see e.g., *Dresna Pty Ltd* v. *Misu Nominees Pty Ltd* [2004] FCAFC 169, [16]; *Fatimi Pty Ltd* v. *Bryant* (2004) 59 NSWLR 678; Edmundson, 'Conspiracy by Unlawful Means', 201–3.

218 *Revenue and Customs Commissioners* v. *Total Network SL* [2008] 1 AC 1174, [66].

219 [2008] 1 AC 1174, [96].

220 *Chen* v. *Karandonis* [2002] NSWCA 412, [28]; *Beach Petroleum NL* v. *Johnson* (1993) 43 FCR 1, 22–3. Compare *Terranora Leisure Time Management Ltd* v. *Harris* [2004] 1 Qd R 93, 98–9.

221 *Emerald Supplies Ltd* v. *British Airways plc (No 1)* [2016] Bus LR 145.

222 *Revenue and Customs Commissioners* v. *Total Network SL* [2008] 1 AC 1174, [45], and [95]; Carty, *An Analysis of the Economic Torts*, p. 136.

contract terms,[223] and fiduciary duties.[224] In each case, there must be a causal link between the use of the unlawful means and the infliction of damage.[225]

11.3.4 *Recognised Damage*

Being an action on the case, the tort of unlawful means conspiracy is complete only upon sufferance by the claimant of some form of recognised damage. However, the types of primary damage encompassed by the tort are narrow. In part, this is a result of its conceptualisation as an 'economic tort'. The 'focus of the economic torts from the late Victorian period onwards centred on targeted economic harm, within the context of trade competition'.[226] Indeed, in *Lonrho* v. *Shell Petroleum Co Ltd*, Lord Diplock spoke of the 'civil tort of conspiracy' as an established one permitting redress for injury to 'commercial interests'.[227] Loss of employment, loss of profit through the cancellation of a potentially profitable contract, and general loss of custom all suffice as damage.[228] But neither emotional harm, such as distress,[229] nor injury to reputation can found an action in conspiracy.[230] If the law is to continue to deny recovery for wider forms of damage, then (needless to say) this tort will be of little use in the insolvent entity situation where claimants have suffered physical injury. It will be noted in what follows, however, that some judges and commentators have expressed a more liberal view on this matter.

11.3.5 *Extended Liability*

Where the elements of unlawful means conspiracy are made out, each of the conspirators is liable for recognised damage that eventuates, even if

[223] *Kuwait Oil Tanker Co SAK* v. *Al Bader* [2001] 2 All ER (Comm) 271, 319; *Stanley* v. *Layne Christensen Co* [2006] WASCA 56, [47]. Note, though, that case law places restrictions upon pleading inducing breach of contract against a company and its directors: *Said* v. *Butt* [1920] 3 KB 497; *O'Brien* v. *Dawson* (1942) 66 CLR 18, 32. This is to prevent the creation of an indirect liability in directors for breach of contract: R. P. Austin, H. A. J. Ford, and I. M. Ramsay, *Company Directors: Principles of Law and Corporate Governance* (2005), p. 614.

[224] *Avonwick Holdings Ltd* v. *Castle Investment Fund Ltd*, [2015] EWHC 3832 (Ch), [28].

[225] See Edmundson, 'Conspiracy by Unlawful Means', 197 and 204.

[226] H. Carty, 'The Tort of Conspiracy as a Can of Worms', in G. A. Pitel, J. W. Neyers, and E. Chamberlain (eds.), *Tort Law: Challenging Orthodoxy* (2013), p. 392.

[227] [1982] AC 173, 189. [228] *Lonrho plc* v. *Fayed (No 5)* [1993] 1 WLR 1489, 1501.

[229] *Mbasago* v. *Logo Ltd (No 1)* [2007] QB 846.

[230] *Lonrho* v. *Fayed (No 5)* [1993] 1 WLR 1489, 1509 (lawful means conspiracy); Carty, *An Analysis of the Economic Torts*, p. 136.

only one of their number carries out the unlawful act that directly injures the claimant's interests.[231] In this fact lies a primary advantage of pleading conspiracy: liability can be extended beyond the defendant (including a corporate defendant) that carries out the unlawful act.[232] With respect to the defendant who does not directly employ unlawful means to injure, in order to be liable, that actor must have a purpose of furthering and actually further the agreement in some way.[233] In the *Berryland Books* case,[234] for example, there was a conspiracy to divert business from an established bookseller to a new bookseller. A director of the established business, Mr Selvandam, was held liable for breaching his fiduciary duty in the use of confidential information and corporate opportunities for the benefit of the new bookseller and in the destruction of company records.[235] A business manager was held liable also for various actions in breach of her duty of fidelity to the company.[236] But the Court of Appeal accepted that, although an acquaintance of Mr Selvandam, Mr Navaratnarajah, *had taken sufficient steps* by incorporating the new company and acting as its initial director, he was not liable for unlawful means conspiracy because he had not acted with the intention of diverting book sales. He simply had tried to assist a friend in establishing a new business.[237]

11.3.6 Damages

An advantage of a successful pleading in unlawful means conspiracy is that, unlike the situation in negligence, damages are not limited by a rule of remoteness (requiring that types of damage be foreseeable by a person in the defendant's position). Damages are available for all financial losses flowing directly from the commission of the tort.[238] In an appropriate case, given the presence of intention to injure, an award of exemplary damages might be available.

231 *Credit Lyonnais* v. *ECGD* [1998] 1 Lloyd's L Rep 19.

232 'In the past this facet of unlawful means conspiracy – extending civil liability to a wider circle of defendants – has been seen as its most important feature': Carty, *An Analysis of the Economic Torts*, p. 129. See also N. K. Katyal, 'Conspiracy Theory' (2003) 112 *Yale Law Journal* 1307, 1334; T. J. Leach, 'Civil Conspiracy: What's the Use?' (1999) 54 *University of Miami Law Review* 1.

233 *Credit Lyonnais* v. *ECGD* [1998] 1 Lloyd's LR 19; Carty, *An Analysis of the Economic Torts*, p. 129.

234 [2010] EWCA Civ 1440.

235 [2010] EWCA Civ 1440, at [11].

236 [2010] EWCA Civ 1440, at [37]–[39].

237 [2010] EWCA Civ 1440, at [87].

238 Damages are 'at large': *Lonrho* v. *Fayed (No 5)* [1993] 1 WLR 1489.

11.3.7 US Law of Conspiracy

This completes our review of the existing Commonwealth law on unlawful means conspiracy. No substantive review of the US law on conspiracy need be undertaken for two reasons, which collectively remove it from the present discussion of the insolvent entity problem. The first reason is that, in many US jurisdictions, conspiracy is *not an independent tort*. It is a doctrine which turns upon the commission of a substantive tort (not being conspiracy) by one actor, and permits the extension of liability to others who have acted in concert with that tortfeasor.[239] Thus, conspiracy falls within the rules of joint liability (considered in Chapter 12).[240] Second, many US courts refuse to apply the tort of conspiracy to combinations by companies within the same corporate group. Originally, the 'intra-corporate immunity'[241] was applied in antitrust cases. In *Copperweld Corp* v. *Independence Tube Corp*, the US Supreme Court stated that a 'parent and its wholly owned subsidiary have a complete unity of interest. Their objectives are common, not disparate; their general corporate actions are guided or determined not by two separate corporate consciousnesses, but one'.[242] Although the US Supreme Court in recent times has become more willing to find conspiracy amongst 'independent decision-making centres',[243] perhaps even within the same corporate group, the intra-corporate immunity has spread beyond antitrust law to other areas including the wider law of tort.[244] In general, there can be no claim of conspiracy deriving from the coordinated actions of companies in groups, whether related to each other vertically or horizontally.[245] These

[239] *In re Trilegiant Corporation Inc* 11 F Supp 3d 132, [12]–[14] (D Conn 2014); *Beck* v. *Prupis* 529 US 494 (2000)(reviewing common law); *Satin* v. *Satin* 69 App Div 2d 761 (NY 1979); *Cohen* v. *Bowdoin* 288 A 2d 106, 110 (Me 1972); *Royster* v. *Baker*, 365 SW 2d 496, 499, and 500 (Mo 1963). See American Law Institute, Restatement (Second) of Torts (1979), § 876, comment b. Note, there have been dissents from the majority position: e.g., *Rogers* v. *RJ Reynolds Tobacco Co* 761 SW 2d 788, 797 (Tex App 1988).

[240] See J. Dietrich and P. Ridge, *Accessories in Private Law* (2015), p. 118, n. 106.

[241] Appellation given in *Robertson* v. *Sea Pines Real Estate Companies Inc* 679 F 3d 278, 283 (4th Cir. 2012).

[242] 467 US 752, 771 (1984). A corporation cannot conspire with its employees for similar reasons: *McAndrew* v. *Lockheed Martin Corp* 206 F 3d 1031, 1036 (11th Cir. 2000).

[243] See *American Needle Inc* v. *National Football League* 130 S Ct 2201 (2010). For consideration of how such an issue is decided, see N. G. Menell, 'The *Copperweld* Question: Drawing the Line between the Corporate Family and Cartel' (2016) 101 *Cornell Law Review* 467, 483–4.

[244] J. S. Nelson, 'The Intracorporate Conspiracy Trap' (2015) 36 *Cardozo Law Review* 969, 972. See also T. H. Koenig and M. L. Rusted, 'Reconceptualizing the BP Oil Spill as Parens Patriae Products Liability' (2012) 49 *Houston Law Review* 291, 326.

[245] *Horst* v. *Laidlaw Waste Systems Inc* 917 F.Supp 739 (D Colo 1996).

points mean that, if US courts are to develop a tort like the proposed tort of 'multiple entity recklessness' (to be considered next), they will have to do so on some basis other than the existing law of conspiracy.

11.4 Multiple Entity Recklessness

In Commonwealth jurisdictions, the rules of unlawful means conspiracy apply just as much to companies in a group or network as they do to any other legally recognised persons. Thus, for example, a parent company can combine with a subsidiary, and two subsidiaries can combine with each other, for the purposes of the law of conspiracy.[246] However, two limitations that impede the application of the tort to the insolvent entity problem have been identified. These are the intention requirement and the recognised damage requirement. Argument will be made that each of these requirements can be and should be adapted to deal with the problem of insolvent companies and mass-torts.

Given that conspiracy currently is a tort involving intention to injure, there is an obvious question about why it cannot be applied in cases of personal injury. It would seem that there is good justification for permitting actions against those who act in combination with a purpose of injuring another and where they cause that other person personal injury. Intention is the highest form of fault, and bodily integrity is the most highly protected interest in tort law. In fact, there have been several suggestions that the tort should extend beyond cases of financial loss caused through trade disputes. In *Scala Ballroom (Wolverhampton) Ltd* v. *Ratcliffe*, for example, Hodson LJ stated that he was 'not prepared . . . to say that the interests which can lawfully be protected are confined to the material interests, in the sense of interests which can be exchanged for cash'. Lawful interests, he thought, 'extend further than that'.[247] Indeed, following the decision of the House of Lords in *Revenue and Customs Commissioners* v. *Total Network SL*,[248] a recognised expert in this area, Hazel Carty, believes that Commonwealth courts are now 'prepared to apply the tort outside the paradigm setting for the economic torts (and outside trade competition disputes)'.[249] This does not necessarily entail

246 *Digicel (St Lucia) Ltd* v. *Cable & Wireless plc* [2010] EWHC 774 (Ch), Annex 1, [77].

247 [1958] 1 WLR 1057, 1061. See also *Crofter Hand Woven Harris Tweed Co Ltd* v. *Veitch* [1942] AC 435, 446–7.

248 [2008] 1 AC 1174.

249 Carty, 'The Tort of Conspiracy as a Can of Worms', 399. See also Edmundson, 'Conspiracy by Unlawful Means', 198.

extension beyond cases of financial loss, but it might be the beginning of a wider application of the principles.

Indeed, there is strong reason to believe that unlawful means conspiracy is an appropriate tort by which to protect personal interests. The argument[250] is that this tort is an emanation of what has been called, variously, the tortious 'harm principle', the 'prima facie tort',[251] and the 'abuse of rights' principle.[252] In *Mogul Steamship* v. *McGregor Gow & Co*, Bowen LJ formulated the principle to be that intentionally to injure another, without just cause or excuse, is the commission of a tort.[253] *This* principle is seen in several types of case involving the intentional infliction of physical harm by individuals.[254] It would not be much of a leap to apply it to cases of combined action that, the combination aside, have the same underlying elements. Judicial hesitation in recognising such a principle in the field of trade competition[255] can have no place in cases involving the infliction of personal injury.[256]

So the crucial issue is whether unlawful means conspiracy should be extended to cases of the *reckless* infliction of personal injury. The argument to be presented comprises two parts: first we consider the idea that recklessness is of moral and, potentially, legal equivalence to intention in cases of combined action. Second, we consider the appropriateness of a recklessness standard as an element of a new tort derived from the law of unlawful means conspiracy, but applicable specifically in the insolvent entity situation. The latter argument will be for the establishment of a new tort of 'multiple entity recklessness'.

There are arguments for treating recklessness in the infliction of injury as equivalent to the intentional infliction of injury and as sufficient for incurring liability under unlawful means conspiracy. As we have seen, the

250 C. Witting, 'Of Principle and Prima Facie Tort' (1999) 25 *Monash University Law Review* 295. Although writing about lawful means conspiracy, the reasoning is applicable to unlawful means conspiracy.

251 See K. Vandevelde, 'A History of Prima Facie Tort: The Origins of a General Theory of Intentional Tort' (1990) 19 *Hofstra Law Review* 447.

252 The latter terminology is adopted in J. W. Neyers, 'Explaining the Inexplicable? Four Manifestations of Abuse of Rights in English Law', in D. Nolan and A. Robertson (eds.), *Rights and Private Law* (2012), p. 309, and reflects the civil law doctrine of the same name: ibid., p. 310. See also Carty, 'The Tort of Conspiracy as a Can of Worms', 394.

253 (1889) 23 QBD 598, 613.

254 *Wilkinson* v. *Downton* (1897) 2 QBD 57; *Bird* v. *Holbrook* (1828) 4 Bing 628.

255 Expressed, e.g., in *Allen* v. *Flood* [1898] AC 1.

256 The US prima facie tort doctrine is capable of application to 'loss or detriment in fact of any kind': American Law Institute, Restatement (Second) of Torts (1979), § 870, comment (e).

English Court of Appeal, in at least one case, treated recklessness in the form of conscious indifference to the prospect of injury as sufficient for proof of unlawful means conspiracy.[257] However, this is not the prevailing view of the law – despite the fact that recklessness is equated with intention in the criminal law.[258] The reason in favour of attaching significant consequences to 'subjective recklessness' is that it involves proscribed conduct that is deliberate in nature and a 'mental element' subsisting in knowledge of the probability of injury following the proscribed conduct.[259] 'The relevant standard of conduct' which underlies certain forms of liability 'proscribes the taking of unreasonable risks' which manifest in actual injury.[260]

The alternative to accepting that unlawful means conspiracy should encompass subjectively reckless conduct, because it is morally equivalent to intention to injure, is that a new tort should be developed from it, applicable in cases involving insolvent subsidiaries and network companies. In fact, this is likely to be the better option, given the artificiality of attributing mental states to collectives (discussed in Chapter 5). *Subjective* recklessness might be difficult to prove in companies of real size using the attribution doctrine – the more so because of the common law's aversion to the aggregation of the knowledge of company officers and employees in order to prove corporate fault.[261]

The proposed tort of 'multiple entity recklessness' would be committed when a company (the 'risk-taking company') has engaged in conduct which is objectively reckless in that it gives rise, in a way which would be apparent to any similarly situated party, to an obvious and unreasonable risk of physical injury to persons (whether employees, consumers, or bystanders), and where the risk-taking company nevertheless undertakes

257 *Baldwin* v. *Berryland Books* [2010] EWCA Civ 1440, at [48].

258 A. P. Simester, J. R. Spencer, G. R. Sullivan, and G. J. Virgo, *Simester and Sullivan's Criminal Law: Theory and Doctrine* (5th edn., 2013), p. 126. This is the case also under the US prima facie tort doctrine: American Law Institute, Restatement (Second) of Torts (1979), § 870, comment b (considered earlier).

259 P. Cane, *Responsibility in Law and Morality* (2002), p. 80.

260 Cane, *Responsibility in Law and Morality*, p. 80.

261 See S. Worthington, *Sealy and Worthington's Text, Cases, and Materials in Company Law* (11th edn., 2016), p. 163, citing *Orr* v. *Milton Keynes Council* [2011] EWCA Civ 62 (attribution of liability under Employment Rights Act 1996); *Commonwealth Bank of Australia* v. *Kojic* [2016] FCAFC 186, [101] ('scant support in England and Australia'). See also *In re Apple Computer, Inc* 243 F Supp 2d 1012, 1023 (ND Cal 2002); and B. J. Bondi, 'Dangerous Liaisons: Collective Scienter in SEC Enforcement Actions' (2009) *New York University Journal of Law & Business* 1 (limited support in the United States).

that conduct so that injury is caused.[262] Given the obviousness of the risk-taking company's reckless conduct, the law would be entitled to create a prima facie liability in *any other parties* (the 'participating entities') having significant commercial connections to it and to that conduct. This prima facie liability would be imposed on the basis that the law could *deem* that participating entities *agreed* to the reckless and injurious course of conduct.[263] In this way, the basic form of participating entity liability would be strict, but based upon their conduct and deemed agreement to reckless conduct in the risk-taking company.[264] Each of the parties to the deemed agreement would be jointly and severally liable for resulting injuries.

Several aspects of this proposal require further explanation. First, under the contemplated rule, objective recklessness would arise where it should have been obvious to the risk-taking company that its activities gave rise to an unreasonable risk of personal injury, and where it undertook those activities despite the unreasonable risk. Objective recklessness would be capable of proof without the need for defendant companies to 'target' specific persons (as required under the tort of unlawful means conspiracy); recklessness as to the personal safety of *some* persons would be enough. Second, application of an objective recklessness standard justifies prima facie joint liability in participating entities. This is because, in the usual case, it will have been or should have been obvious to them that the risk-taking company's activities were reckless. In this way, their continued coordination with that company would justify their being deemed to have agreed to that conduct. Third, an obvious attraction of the proposed tort of multiple entity recklessness is that it would provide incentives for participating defendants both to monitor risky conduct

[262] For discussion of a similar concept in criminal law, see Simester, Spencer, Sullivan, and Virgo, *Simester and Sullivan's Criminal Law*, pp. 142–4. The reasons for limiting this type of mens rea in criminal law (unfairness as regards those without capacity) do not apply in the context being discussed in the text. See also American Law Institute, Restatement (Third) of Torts: Liability for Physical and Emotional Harm (2009), § 2 (definition of recklessness).

[263] See suggestion to similar effect in P. W. Lee, 'Civil Conspiracy in the Corporate Context' (2016) 23 *Torts Law Journal* 257. This avoids the potential problem of a conspiracy-based liability arising from 'inadvertence'. It is submitted that the proposed tort meets criteria for liability set out by the Texas Court of Appeals in *Rogers* v. *RJ Reynolds Tobacco Co* 761 SW 2d 788, 797 (Tex App 1988), viz., the defendant 'must consciously and knowingly combine with others to engage in an intended course of conduct and perform acts to implement the intended course of conduct and set it on its way' (or continue it).

[264] This is by contrast to arguments for the vicarious liability of parent companies for the torts of subsidiary employees, considered in Chapter 12.

which could result in personal injuries, and to cease coordinating with the risk-taking company should the latter refuse to modify its conduct. This form of extended liability could be especially important in companies that are taken over and brought within a group. This is because group companies might come together with different ways of operating and of conceptualising risk, different tolerances to risk, and different responses to risk. If group companies are to coordinate their risk-creating activities properly, this will require conscientious planning, monitoring, and follow-up. Fourth, a defence to the proposed tort of multiple entity recklessness in principle should be available to participating entities which took every step to avoid the future causation of personal injury to others by doing such things as blowing the whistle on the risky conduct and ceasing coordination with the risk-creating company. Entities which take 'every step' available to them to avoid injuries should not be liable for injuries caused after their cooperation in the risky activity has ceased. (But liability would still arise for injuries incurred after the date of cessation, for example, where the participating defendant's inputs continue to be incorporated into injury-causing products.)

The attractiveness of the proposed tort of multiple entity recklessness lies in the fact that it would involve relatively small (but justifiable) extensions to two elements of an existing tort, which are tailored to the particular problems found in the insolvent entity context. There would be no need to demonstrate a vertical relationship of control between defendant parties, meaning that the tort could be pleaded in cases going beyond those of parent company and insolvent subsidiary. The new tort would permit comparative flexibility in fashioning liability in the corporate group or network, centred upon coordinated action at whatever level it occurs. It could be used to overcome the structuring of legal relations that is typical of corporate groups and networks. It would operate so as to create liability for coordinated conduct, where several companies each play a functional part in the causation of injury – whether this part be design, development, manufacture, marketing, or distribution. Thus the new tort would fill the gap in the existing liability regime. Because multiple entity recklessness would require proof of a high level of fault in the risk-taking company, it would permit a widening of the net of recovery without overly deterring future investment. Use of the reversed onus of proof would help to create an incentive in companies to monitor the activities of entities with which they coordinate.

One might think the development of the proposed tort of multiple entity recklessness to be entirely within the capacity of the courts, given the historic role of the action on the case in fashioning causes of action when ordinary tort rules are deficient, and when the justice of the case calls for a remedy. Percy Winfield noted that in his day '[n]othing would have astonished the legal profession more than to be told that the scope of actions on the case could not be widened.'[265] Indeed, in *Revenue and Customs Commissioners* v. *Total Network SL*, Lord Walker admitted that the development of the tort of unlawful means conspiracy 'may not yet be complete',[266] and Lord Scott confirmed 'the essential flexibility of the action on the case'.[267] Just as the crime of conspiracy was once developed in the Court of Star Chamber to deal with new problems,[268] it would be apposite for a modern, appellate court to develop the tort of unlawful means conspiracy in a way which is attuned to the working of today's corporate actors.

Having proposed a new tort of multiple entity recklessness, derived from UK law on unlawful means conspiracy, its operation can be illustrated by reference to the well-documented facts of *In re Oil Spill by Oil Rig 'Deepwater Horizon'*.[269] This case, discussed in Chapter 4, involved an example of the network form, complex decision-making by interconnected parties, failures properly to coordinate operations in a fail-safe way, and recklessness on the part of at least two companies. BP plc had been acting in ways which were objectively reckless during the drilling phase and attempted capping of the Macondo well. Transocean had acted negligently 'or worse'. Indeed, its failure to provide the rig's master with emergency management training could have been characterised as reckless. In this way, both BP and Transocean were risk-taking companies within the scope of the tort of multiple entity recklessness. BP's actions (if not Transocean's) gave rise to obvious and unreasonable risks of physical injury to persons, which became manifest in eleven deaths, at least forty cases of personal injury, and the escape of millions of barrels of oil which caused extreme environmental damage.[270] Because the risks taken by BP were (or should have been) obvious to close collaborators in the industry, those collaborators could be deemed to have agreed to the running of

[265] P. Winfield, 'The Foundation of Liability in Tort' (1927) 27 *Columbia Law Review* 1, 5.

[266] [2008] 1 AC 1174, [89]. [267] [2008] 1 AC 1174, [57].

[268] A. Harding, *The Law Courts of Medieval England* (1973), pp. 106–7.

[269] *In re Oil Spill by Oil Rig 'Deepwater Horizon' in the Gulf of Mexico, on April 20, 2010*, 21 F Supp 3d 657 (ED La 2014)(rehearing denied *In re Deepwater Horizon* 775 F 3d 741 (5th Cir. 2015)).

[270] 21 F Supp 3d 657, [3] and [6]; Antin, Ehrlich and Epstein LLP, '*Deepwater Horizon* Worker Reaches Injury Settlement with BP, Others' (7 September 2012), available at: http://aeelaw.com/deepwater-horizon-worker-reaches-injury-settlement-bp-others/.

those risks. (By contrast, there would be no liability in, for example, a catering company supplying the crew of the oil rig with meals because that catering company would not be in a position to assess the riskiness of activities taking place.) This would mean, for example, that the liability of BP could be extended to both Transocean and Halliburton. Each party would be liable according to their degree of responsibility for injuries caused.

11.5 Conclusions

This chapter has considered how torts creating direct liability in wrongdoers might assist in resolving the insolvent entity problem. The tort of negligence can be utilised to create liability in a parent company for its own torts which injure employees and customers of its insolvent subsidiaries. However, this is a narrow kind of liability, which subsists in the context of a vertical relationship. There is no evidence that negligence might be capable of use in horizontal relationships between companies. It is in this context that we considered the potential for the law of conspiracy to fill the liability gap. Analysis of the tort of unlawful means conspiracy reveals that, presently, it is limited by the requirement of intention to injure and its restriction to cases of financial loss. However, argument has been presented that this action on the case can be modified so as to be applicable in both corporate group and network contexts, where companies have combined to undertake activities that involve recklessness, these activities causing personal injuries to third parties. The development of a tort of multiple entity recklessness, facilitating extensions of liability among network participants, would even the scales as between corporate groups and networks. It would discourage the reorganisation of corporate group activities as network activities in order to escape the prospect of extended liability, and help preserve the principle of business form neutrality (discussed in Chapter 1), while ameliorating the insolvent entity problem.

12

Vicarious and Joint Liability in Tort

12.1 Introduction

In this chapter, further *tort doctrines* of potential application to the insolvent entity problem are considered. These are the doctrines of vicarious liability and accessory liability. Prima facie, both should apply to corporate groups, in accordance with the equivalence principle – which is the principle that common law doctrines applicable to individuals should be applicable to corporate entities on similar terms, unless there is a good reason for exemption (explained in Chapter 1). But the equivalence principle has not been given full play in this context. Neither vicarious liability nor accessory liability has been much used in the corporate network context either. This indicates that there is room for their further development in resolution of the insolvent entity problem. Let us consider them in turn, with a brief digression also to consider the operation of non-delegable duties in the corporate group context.

12.2 Vicarious Liability

Vicarious liability is a three-party doctrine that permits the extension to employers of tortfeasor liabilities for wrongs committed so as to create joint liability in those parties. Ordinarily, joint liability arises *within* individual organisations – employer organisations being vicariously liable for the torts of their own employees. However, developments in UK law have inspired the thought that the doctrine might be capable of application so as to make parent companies liable for torts committed by subsidiary employees. This is a matter which now requires consideration.

12.2.1 General Rules

Under the usual formulation of vicarious liability rules, a claimant must prove that a tort was committed by an employee either in the course of employment, or with a sufficient connection to the employment. An employee 'is one who is paid a wage or salary to work under some, if only slight, control of his employer in his employer's business for his employer's business', whereas the 'independent contractor works in and for his own business at his risk of profit or loss'.[1] Ordinarily, the employer is not liable for torts committed by independent contractors.[2]

A tort occurs 'in the course of employment' when committed as part of the activities of the employer and for its benefit.[3] The alternative, 'sufficient connection' test[4] is broader, but of a somewhat indeterminate application. It is applicable especially when the employee's acts were not for the benefit of the employer.[5] A sufficient connection between the employment and the tort arises so long as the nature of the work undertaken has created or significantly enhanced risks of the kind which have become manifest in injury whether because they are inherent in the work,[6] or substantially 'bound up' with it.[7] Courts have held that vicarious liability is capable of application in cases of deliberate wrongdoing under the sufficient connection test.[8] Liability might arise even where the employer has prohibited the specific type of conduct which resulted in commission of a tort.[9] Explaining this, the House of Lords in *Dubai Aluminium Co Ltd* v. *Salaam* stated that 'it is a fact of life, and therefore to be expected by those who carry on businesses, that sometimes their agents may exceed the boundaries of their authority or even defy express instructions. It is fairer to allocate risks of losses thus arising to the businesses than leave those wronged with the sole remedy, of doubtful value, against the individual employees.'[10]

[1] *E* v. *English Province of Our Lady of Charity* [2013] QB 722, [70].
[2] But see discussion of breach of the non-delegable duty in what follows.
[3] *Cox* v. *Ministry of Justice* [2016] AC 660, [23].
[4] Adopted in *Lister* v. *Hesley Hall Ltd* [2002] 1 AC 215.
[5] *Lister* v. *Hesley Hall Ltd* [2002] 1 AC 215, [79].
[6] E.g., *Hawley* v. *Luminar Leisure Ltd* [2006] PIQR P17.
[7] *Mohamud* v. *Wm Morrison Supermarkets plc* [2016] AC 677, [44]–[45]; *Various Claimants* v. *Catholic Child Welfare Society* [2013] 2 AC 1, [88]; C. Witting, *Street on Torts* (14th edn., 2015), pp. 632 and 638–9. Having said as much, there seems no escaping a certain amount of circularity in the statement of this sub-test.
[8] E.g., *Mattis* v. *Pollock* [2003] 1 WLR 2158; *Lister* v. *Hesley Hall Ltd* [2002] 1 AC 215; *New South Wales* v. *Lepore* (2003) 77 ALJR 558; *Bazley* v. *Curry* [1999] 2 SCR 534.
[9] E.g., *Canadian Pacific Railway Company* v. *Lockhart* [1942] AC 591; *Rose* v. *Plenty* [1976] 1 All ER 97.
[10] [2003] 2 AC 366, [22], affirmed in *Mohamud* v. *Wm Morrison Supermarkets plc* [2016] AC 677, [44].

When the conditions for vicarious liability are satisfied, the employer is made jointly liable for the commission of the tort. This means that recovery can be had from either the employer or the employee – and the employer might be able to exercise rights of contribution (or indemnity) against the employee.

The UK rules of vicarious liability have been expanded in two ways, so as to open up the *possibility* of a 'corporate group vicarious liability'. First, courts have permitted findings of 'dual vicarious liability' in cases of workers who undertake tasks for more than one 'employer', so long as the usual criteria of employment are satisfied. This entails the vicarious liability of both employers for the torts of the same employee. Second, courts have widened the types of relationship that support findings of vicarious liability by extending them beyond employment *in strictu sensu* to other relationships which are 'akin to employment'. In this way, the parent company might be said to have a relationship to its subsidiaries' employees which is 'akin to employment'. Let us take each of these possibilities in turn.

12.2.2 Dual Vicarious Liability

First, we consider dual vicarious liability. As the appellation suggests, this form of the doctrine enables two companies or other organisations to be found vicariously liable for the commission of the same tort.[11] The key to its application is that both companies are found to be employers of the tortfeasor who injured the claimant according to ordinary tests. In conformity to the test of employment stated previously, Rix LJ held in *Viasystems (Tyneside) Ltd* v. *Thermal Transfer (Northern) Ltd*[12] that the critical issue is whether the tortfeasor 'is so much a part of the work, business or organisation of both employers that it is just to make both employers answer for the tort'.[13] It might be thought that the likelihood of finding dual vicarious liability is enhanced in the corporate group context,[14] where parent company managers interact with subsidiary

[11] Dual vicarious liability is accepted in the United Kingdom (*Various Claimants* v. *Catholic Child Welfare Society* [2013] 2 AC 1) and Canada (*Blackwater* v. *Plint* (2005) 258 DLR (4th) 275), but has been rejected in Australia (*Oceanic Crest Shipping Co* v. *Pilbara Harbour Services Pty Ltd* (1986) 160 CLR 626; *Day* v. *The Ocean Beach Shell Harbour Pty Ltd* [2013] NSWCA 250).

[12] [2006] 2 WLR 428.

[13] [2006] 2 WLR 428, [16], affirmed in *Various Claimants* v. *Catholic Child Welfare Society* [2013] 2 AC 1, [45].

[14] See P. Morgan, 'Vicarious Liability for Group Companies: The Final Frontier of Vicarious Liability?' (2015) 31 *Professional Negligence* 276, 298–9.

company employees, and so on. However, as at the time of writing, no reported case deals explicitly with this point. Although this form of vicarious liability might prove useful in the odd situation of an insolvent subsidiary with unsatisfied tort claims, this is likely to be a rare thing – not only because the lack of case law attests to this, but because proof of dual employment relationships would require adduction of twice the amount of evidence compared to that required in the ordinary case of a single employer. Usually, the injured claimant will prefer to save time and expense by simply suing the more solvent employer, taking into account its insurance cover (although there is always the risk that this will not be adequate). The same basic point would apply to the injured claimant wanting to bring action against a network participant. There would be no need to sue any party other than the most solvent employer. For these reasons, dual vicarious liability is unlikely to present a major route to recovery in mass-tort cases.

12.2.3 Vicarious Liability of the Parent Company

Next, we consider the argument that the parent company might be liable on a more systematic basis for torts committed by its subsidiaries' employees. This possibility follows from the UK Supreme Court decision that vicarious liability can be imposed in cases 'akin' to employment. In *Various Claimants* v. *Catholic Child Welfare Society* (*CCWS*),[15] actions for sexual abuse involving brother teachers were brought against the Institute of Brothers, an unincorporated association with responsibility for Catholic education. The court held that '[w]here the defendant and the tortfeasor are not bound by a contract of employment, but their relationship has the same incidents, that relationship might give rise to vicarious liability where it is "akin to that between an employer and an employee".'[16] In this, the Court followed the path created by other common law jurisdictions, which have eschewed the doctrine's confinement to strict relationships of employment.[17] On the facts of the *CCWS* case itself, Lord Phillips found several features significant in establishing that the relationship between the Institute and the brothers was akin to

[15] [2013] 2 AC 1.

[16] [2013] 2 AC 1, [47], quoting *E* v. *English Province of Our Lady of Charity* [2013] QB 722, [131]. From here onwards, these kinds of workers will be referred to simply as 'employees'.

[17] See also *Doe* v. *Bennett* [2004] 1 SCR 436; *Nathan* v. *Dollars & Sense Ltd* [2008] 2 NZLR 557.

employment. Most pertinently: the 'Institute was subdivided into a hierarchical structure and conducted its activities as if it were a corporate body'; it placed brother teachers into schools, and those teachers were obliged to conduct themselves in the manner dictated by the Institute's rules.[18]

The *CCWS* case gives rise to a number of questions about what other relationships might be 'akin to employment'. Indeed, it raises the issue whether employment will continue as the paradigm case of vicarious liability, or whether there will be a movement away from this kind of thinking.[19] There are signs that UK and other courts are willing to extend the bounds of vicarious liability to further relationships, examples including the liability of the Ministry of Justice for the negligence of prisoners taking part in rehabilitative work,[20] and the liability of bishops for sexual abuse committed by subordinate priests.[21] Beyond these cases, speculation exists that the *CCWS* case will open the way for suits against professional regulatory bodies in instances of 'regulatory failure',[22] against parent companies for the torts of their subsidiaries,[23] and against franchisors for the torts of franchisees.[24]

An extended argument in favour of the *vicarious liability of the parent company* for torts committed by subsidiary company employees was made in the New Zealand case of *Dairy Containers Ltd* v. *NZI Bank Ltd*[25] – although, ultimately, the High Court held that binding authority in the Privy Council decision of *Kuwait Asia Bank EC* v. *National Mutual Life Nominees Ltd*[26] precluded it. On the facts, the New Zealand Dairy Board (NZDB) was the (statutory) parent corporation, which exercised complete control over its wholly owned subsidiary Dairy Containers Ltd (DCL). DCL's sole role was to make cans, which were supplied to facilitate the sale of NZDB's milk. DCL was not permitted to profit from this

18 [2013] 2 AC 1, [56], [89], and [91].

19 See, e.g., J. O. 'Sullivan, 'The Sins of the Father – Vicarious Liability Extended' (2012) 71 *Cambridge Law Journal* 485, 487. *Woodland* v. *Essex County Council* [2014] AC 537, [3], suggests that the employer–independent contractor distinction remains fundamental. But this position is not inconsistent with greater liability on the basis of other kinds of relationship.

20 *Cox* v. *Ministry of Justice* [2016] AC 660.

21 *E* v. *English Province of Our Lady of Charity* [2013] QB 722.

22 S. Deakin, A. Johnston, and B. Markesinis, *Markesinis and Deakin's Tort Law* (7th edn., 2013), p. 565.

23 M. Petrin, 'Assumption of Responsibility in Corporate Groups: *Chandler v Cape plc*' (2013) 76 *Modern Law Review* 603, 612–13.

24 P. Morgan, 'Vicarious Liability on the Move' (2013) 129 *Law Quarterly Review* 139, 143.

25 [1995] 2 NZLR 30.

26 [1990] 2 Lloyd's Rep. 95; [1990] 3 NZLR 513.

role, its profits being absorbed by NZDB itself. NZDB directly employed DCL's three directors. These gentlemen 'perceived DCL as nothing, or little more, than a manufacturing division of NZDB'.[27] The problem was that they permitted frauds and losses to occur through various management failures. The issue before the High Court concerned NZDB's liability for their defaults. Thomas J made a very strong obiter argument for holding NZDB vicariously liable. He observed that subsidiary company directors are appointed with a clear 'mandate to protect and promote their employer's interests'. Their first loyalty will be to the parent company, to which they report. They undertake their activities as representatives of the parent company, which has a real measure of control over them, and will likely indemnify them for their liabilities. 'Loyalty inspired by their recruitment and confirmed by the confidence which employers repose in their employees is reinforced by the employer's power of dismissal.'[28] All of these features entailed that (were the matter free of precedent) the parent company, as the employer, ought to be made legally responsible for the defaults of their employee directors committed in the course of their employment in the subsidiary.[29]

Phillip Morgan has explored further the suggestion that vicarious liability should be applied to make parent companies liable for torts committed by subsidiary company employees. First, Morgan argues that tort law has a regulatory role to play because it helps to eliminate poor practices and to improve standards of conduct in the commercial world. He sees the potential for vast tort liability awards as a helpful thing because it would drive substandard operators into insolvency.[30] This book takes the same view of tort's regulatory role (as to which, see Chapter 1). Second, Morgan notes the structuring of legal relations, or 'judgment-proofing' problems, that give rise to potential difficulties for claimants seeking compensation from insolvent subsidiaries, and asserts that the 'answers must be found in tort law', given the narrowness of current veil-piercing doctrine in the United Kingdom.[31] Third, he notes developments in the law of vicarious liability (explained earlier), which he believes open up the possibility that it can be deployed to tackle judgment-proofing. He says that 'the justifications that represent the current understanding of the English courts point towards vicarious liability for some group companies.'[32] Fourth, Morgan believes that

[27] [1995] 2 NZLR 30, 80–1. [28] [1995] 2 NZLR 30, 94–5. [29] [1995] 2 NZLR 30, 97.
[30] Morgan, 'Vicarious Liability for Group Companies', 278.
[31] Morgan, 'Vicarious Liability for Group Companies', 279 and 285.
[32] Morgan, 'Vicarious Liability for Group Companies', 289.

moral and economic notions of the enterprise as the beneficiary of risk-creating activity provide reasons to expand vicarious liability in the group context.[33] The ability of the enterprise to spread losses strengthens the case.[34] Fifth, he thinks that the relationship between parent company and subsidiary (including subsidiary employees) is sufficient to satisfy the ordinary characteristics of the employer–employee relationship. These parties have integrated operations, the parent company exercises managerial control over subsidiary productivity and work quality, and the parent company benefits from work done.[35] Morgan concludes that 'the parent company will often have better resources and greater expertise to conduct risk assessments, better planning capabilities, and superior knowledge of industry safety, than any individual subsidiary within the group, alongside the ability to instruct subsidiaries as to precautions.'[36]

Together, the contentions in the *Dairy Containers* case and Morgan's article present an attractive argument for utilising vicarious liability in helping to resolve the judgment-proofing problem. As Morgan notes, the introduction of vicarious liability in the corporate group would cohere with enterprise liability theory, which is the most well-developed theoretical explanation of the doctrine presently available.[37] Enterprise liability is said to justify ordinary (that is, non-group) vicarious liability for reasons related to those explored in Chapters 5 and 8. It aims to ensure that, as between an enterprise and an injured individual, the enterprise bears the initial costs of wrongdoing because it will profit from the activities from which wrongdoing stems. The enterprise is likely to be better able to absorb losses (and avoid social dislocation)[38] through reductions in profits, or to spread losses through either insurance or increases in product prices.[39] Moreover, the

[33] Morgan, 'Vicarious Liability for Group Companies', 291.

[34] Morgan, 'Vicarious Liability for Group Companies', 292.

[35] Morgan, 'Vicarious Liability for Group Companies', 296.

[36] Morgan, 'Vicarious Liability for Group Companies', 293.

[37] This theory has been embraced to a large extent by the courts: see, e.g., *Mohamud* v. *Wm Morrison Supermarkets plc* [2016] AC 677, [40]; *Cox* v. *Ministry of Justice* [2016] AC 660, [22]–[24]; *Limpus* v. *LGO Co* (1862) 1 H & C 526, 539; *671122 Ontario Ltd* v. *Sagaz Industries Canada Inc* [2001] 2 SCR 983, [34]–[35]; *Bazley* v. *Curry* [1999] 2 SCR 534, 548–9; *Scott* v. *Davis* (2000) 175 ALR 217, [253]. See also D. Tan, 'Internalising Externalities: An Enterprise Risk Approach to Vicarious Liability in the 21st Century' (2015) 27 *Singapore Academy of Law Journal* 822, 832, and 834.

[38] '[A]ccidents are a source of some of the most dramatic concentrations of costs in our society': G. Calabresi, *The Costs of Accidents* (1970), p. 44.

[39] *Polygram International Publishing, Inc* v. *Nevada/TIG, Inc* 855 F Supp 1314, 1325 (D Mass 1994). See also Calabresi, *The Costs of Accidents*, pp. 50–1; Y. B. Smith, 'Frolic and Detour' (1923) 23 *Columbia Law Review* 444, 457.

enterprise is in a better position vis-à-vis its employees to organise ongoing, recurrent business activities so as to minimise the risks of future injuries.[40] And strict liability is preferable in circumstances where neither the claimant nor the court would find it easy to identify where wrongdoing arose in the operation of a complex organisation.[41]

Such authority as exists on this matter, including *Dairy Containers Ltd* v. *NZI Bank Ltd*[42] itself, upholds the separate legal personality and limited liability of the parent company.[43] The parent company is not vicariously liable for torts committed by subsidiary company employees. Several persuasive arguments entail this result. First, vicarious liability, being a strict liability doctrine, applies automatically once the relationship of employer and employee is established, and the tort is found to have occurred in the course of employment or with sufficient connection to it. Such automatic liability would be incompatible with shareholder limited liability.[44] As is argued in this book, if there is to be a true exception to limited liability, it needs to be embodied within statute. Second, even if courts were to accept that vicarious liability is capable of application in the group context, there would be a need to consider whether it should result in liability for all kinds of loss, or be restricted to personal injuries (and, perhaps, property damage). The argument, again, is that the availability of vicarious liability for the causation of merely financial losses would be inconsistent with rules of limited

[40] P. Giliker, *Vicarious Liability in Tort: A Comparative Perspective* (2010), p. 238; J. H. Arlen and W. B. McLeod, 'Beyond Master-Servant: A Critique of Vicarious Liability', in M.S. Madden (ed.), *Exploring Tort Law* (2005), p. 118; G. C. Keating, 'The Idea of Fairness in the Law of Enterprise Liability' (1997) 95 *Michigan Law Review* 1266, 1267; K. S. Abraham, 'Individual Action and Collective Responsibility: The Dilemma of Mass Tort Reform' (1987) 73 *Virginia Law Review* 845, 855–8.

[41] B. Fisse and J. Braithwaite, *Corporations, Crime and Accountability* (1993), p. 66; J. H. Arlen and R. Kraakman, 'Controlling Corporate Misconduct: An Analysis of Corporate Liability Regimes' (1997) 72 *New York University Law Review* 687, 692–3; L. A. Kornhauser, 'An Economic Analysis of the Choice between Enterprise and Personal Liability for Accidents' (1982) 70 *California Law Review* 1345, 1351, and 1370.

[42] [1995] 2 NZLR 30.

[43] *R* v. *Waverley Construction Co Ltd* (1972) 30 DLR (3d) 224, 231. See also *Ebbw Vale Urban District Council* v. *South Wales Traffic Area Licensing Authority* [1951] 2 KB 366, 370; Petrin, 'Assumption of Responsibility in Corporate Groups', 613 (UK law); B. Reinschmidt, 'The Law of Tort: A Useful Tool to Further Corporate Social Responsibility?' (2013) 34 *Company Law* 103, 107 (US law).

[44] *Choc* v. *Hudbay Minerals, Inc* 2013 ONSC 1414, [43]; V. Ulbeck and A. Ehlers, 'Tort Law, Corporate Groups and Supply Chain Liability for Workers' Injuries: The Concept of Vicarious Liability' (2016) 13 *European Company Law* 167, 169. See discussion in Petrin, 'Assumption of Responsibility in Corporate Groups', 613.

liability, which were designed to achieve the *sharing* of risks of financial loss between shareholders and those who interact with companies (as explained in Chapter 3). Third, the vicarious liability of a parent company for all of its subsidiaries' employees' torts would create a wide vista of liability. This would cause those controlling corporate groups to reconsider their preference for the group form.[45] It would create a direct incentive to 'disaggregate' and move towards business activity in the network form. Unless this prospect were addressed, corporate group vicarious liability would be, to a greater or lesser extent, self-defeating. The only parent companies left to sue would be those with no assets to protect.

12.2.4 Vicarious Liability in the United States

The US rules on the general law of vicarious liability, as set out in the Restatement (Third) of Agency (2006) sections 7.03 and 7.07, are consistent with those in the United Kingdom, apart from the stricter adherence in the United States to the principle that liability arises only when torts are committed in the 'course of employment'. There has been no acceptance of an 'akin to employment' extension of vicarious liability.[46] However, the Restatement does permit findings of dual employment.[47] Again, consistent with UK law, there has been no real experimentation with the extension of rules of vicarious liability so as to create strict liability in the parent company for torts committed by subsidiary employees.[48] Although such claims have been pleaded in various cases, courts have either denied that the parent company is vicariously liable,[49] or treated the issue as one of veil-piercing[50] and required satisfaction of

45 See discussion in Arlen and MacLeod, 'Beyond Master-Servant'.

46 See American Law Institute, Restatement (Third) of Agency (2006), § 7.07, Comment b.

47 E.g., *Dazo* v. *Globe Airport Security Services* 295 F 3d 934 (9th Cir. 2002). See American Law Institute, Restatement (Third) of Agency (2006), § 7.03, Comment d (2), and Reporter's Note b (2).

48 However, some cases of copyright infringement committed by a subsidiary company come close to imposing vicarious liability on the parent – although successful cases against the parent have been criticised. See J. M. Siegel, 'Reconciling Shareholder Limited Liability with Vicarious Copyright Liability: Holding Parent Corporations Liable for the Copyright Infringements of Subsidiaries' (2007) 41 *University of Richmond Law Review* 535.

49 *Feszczyszyn* v. *General Motors Corp* 248 AD 2d 939 (NY 1998); *Ritter* v. *BJC Barnes Jewish Christian Health Systems* 987 SW 2d 377 (Mo App ED 1999).

50 Even so, these claims usually fail: see, e.g., *Doney* v. *TRW Inc* 39 Cal Rptr 2d 292 (Cal App 6 Dist 1995); *Frazier* v. *Bryan Memorial Hospital Authority* 775 P 2d 281 (Okl 1989); *Gass*

rules on veil-piercing (considered in Chapter 10). There has been no real suggestion (so far as the writer is aware) in the scholarly literature that vicarious liability should be deployed to resolve problems of insolvent subsidiary liability affecting the corporate group. As indicated, this seems to be a perfectly defensible position to take.

12.3 Non-delegable Duties

An exception to the proposition that employers are not liable for the torts of independent contractors applies in cases involving breaches of non-delegable duties.[51] One type of non-delegable duty incorporates an obligation to 'ensure' that employees enjoy a safe workplace and proper equipment.[52] Employers can be made liable where failures to provide these things are the sole fault of independent contractors. Insofar as the employer is made liable for the torts of their independent contractors, the doctrine can operate as one of strict liability (arising regardless of fault in the liable party).[53]

Hugh Collins has suggested that breach of the non-delegable duty might have a role to play in extending liability from insolvent subsidiaries to parent companies.[54] However, consistent with the foregoing discussion, the present writer does not see this as a viable option. First, given the nature of the non-delegable duty as it applies to employers, the cause of action arising for its breach is most likely to be of use *within* organisations, permitting actions by employees against their employers. Employers will be insured against most liability claims. Although employees might suffer injuries on a large scale, so that the insolvent

v. *Anna Hospital Corporation* 911 NE 2d 1084 (Ill App 5 Dist 2009); *McQuade* v. *Draw Tite Inc* 659 NE 2d 1016 (Ind 1995); *Urban* v. *American Legion Post* 184 NW 2d 153 (Minn App 2005).

51 Note that there is continued debate about the legitimacy of this doctrine – the argument being that it exists in order to avoid the limitations of vicarious liability in certain areas where strict liability is otherwise attractive: see, e.g., J. Morgan, 'Vicarious Liability for Independent Contractors?' [2015] *Professional Negligence* 235, 246–7.

52 See, e.g., *McDermid* v. *Nash Dredging & Reclamation Co Ltd* [1987] 3 WLR 212; *Wilsons & Clyde Coal Co Ltd* v. *English* [1938] AC 57; *Kondis* v. *State Transport Authority* (1984) 154 CLR 672. With respect to equipment, see also Employer's Liability (Defective Equipment) Act 1969.

53 *Leichhardt Municipal Council* v. *Montgomery* (2007) 230 CLR 22, noted in C. Witting, 'Non-delegable Duties and Roads Authorities' (2008) 32 *Melbourne University Law Review* 332.

54 H. Collins, 'Ascription of Legal Responsibility to Groups in Complex Patterns of Economic Integration' (1990) 53 *Modern Law Review* 731, 735.

entity problem arises, this book is concerned with mass-torts which affect *both* persons external to the organisation *and* employees. Breach of the non-delegable duty has little to offer the former group of claimants. This is one reason for doubting the utility of the breach of the non-delegable duty in the present context.

Second, claims involving breaches of non-delegable duties are not only likely to be restricted to claims by employees, they have been invoked rarely to make parent companies liable for failures in subsidiary companies' provision of safe workplaces and proper equipment.[55] Some doubt arises as to whether courts might develop the doctrine in such a way. In the Australian case of *New South Wales* v. *Lepore*, Gummow and Hayne JJ were of the opinion that the range of non-delegable duties should not be expanded without the exercise of 'considerable caution'.[56] Indeed, there is a powerful policy reason which stands in the way of the use of breach of the non-delegable duty in order to create parent company liability for torts committed by subsidiary companies. The strict liability nature of the doctrine means that it suffers from the same difficulty as vicarious liability. It is incompatible with statutory provisions which limit the liability of shareholders (including parent companies). As such, it is necessary to create a *statutory exception to limited liability* rather than attempt to extend strict liability doctrines in ways which would have a similar effect as a statutory exception.[57]

12.4 Joint Liability

The final part of this chapter concerns 'joint liability'. Joint liability is a term signifying that two or more persons are legally responsible for the commission of a tort or torts where their actions cause the *same* damage.[58] Co-conspirators are jointly liable for commission of unlawful means conspiracy,[59] and the vicariously liable employer is jointly liable

[55] But see *McDermid* v. *Nash Dredging & Reclamation Co Ltd* [1987] 3 WLR 212.

[56] (2003) 77 ALJR 558, 604. Note, however, that the Supreme Court of India in *MC Mehta* v. *Union of India* 1987 AIR 965 developed a doctrine of strict liability to apply in cases of ultra-hazardous activity.

[57] Recall that this is argued for in Chapter 9.

[58] *Baxter* v. *Obacelo Pty Ltd* (2001) 205 CLR 635, [24]; C. Sappideen and P. Vines (eds.), *Fleming's The Law of Torts* (10th edn., 2011), p. 303. In terms of what constitutes the 'same damage', see *Royal Brompton Hospital NHS Trust* v. *Hammond (No 3)* [2002] 1 WLR 1397. There is no need, in this chapter, to consider the case of tortfeasors causing different lots of damage.

[59] See Chapter 11.

with the employee who commits a tort in the course of employment, or with sufficient connection to it.[60] In each case of joint liability, the claimant in a personal injury action need only bring action against one, usually the most solvent, of the jointly liable parties in order to obtain full damages.[61] If another jointly liable party is worth suing, the defendant to the main action has the ability to bring a further or joined action for 'contribution' against that person.[62] Under the usual formula, contribution is awarded according to what is 'just and equitable' between the parties,[63] having regard to matters including the degree of fault in each of the jointly liable parties, and the causal importance of their respective actions resulting in damage.[64] The rules regarding unlawful means conspiracy and vicarious liability having been examined already, this chapter now turns to a less well-defined type of joint liability which arises on the part of 'accessories' for the commission of torts by the primary wrongdoers. The rules on accessory liability provide another potential avenue of tortious redress against companies in the corporate group or network, beyond the insolvent company which has unsatisfied tort claims against it.

12.4.1 Accessory Liability

Two established heads[65] of accessory liability involve commission of a tort and causation of injury to the claimant arising from situations in which: first, D2 has ordered or procured commission of a tort by D1;[66] and, second, D1 and D2 have engaged in a 'common design'. Both D1 and D2 are liable for injuries they cause. Of the two heads of accessory liability, the common design head is the wider and, therefore, of greater potential application in the corporate group context.[67] It will be discussed here.

60 *Michael* v. *Alestree* (1675) 2 Lev 173; 83 ER 504; American Law Institute, Restatement (Third) of Torts: Apportionment of Liability (2000), § 15, Comment b. See Giliker, *Vicarious Liability in Tort*, p. 15.

61 In some jurisdictions, each jointly liable party is held proportionately liable for property damage and purely financial losses: e.g., Civil Liability Act 2002 (NSW), Pt. 4.

62 E.g., Civil Liability (Contribution) Act 1978, s. 1(1); American Law Institute, Restatement (Third) of Torts: Apportionment of Liability (2000), § 10.

63 E.g., Civil Liability (Contribution) Act 1978, s. 2(2).

64 *Miraflores (Owners)* v. *George Livanos (Owners)* [1967] 1 AC 826, 845. For more detail, see Sappideen and Vines, *Fleming's The Law of Torts*, pp. 311–12.

65 This is not to say that such cases arise frequently in tort because they do not: J. Dietrich and P. Ridge, *Accessories in Private Law* (2015), p. 101.

66 E.g., *Performing Right Society Ltd* v. *Ciryl Theatrical Enterprises Ltd* [1924] 1 KB 1.

67 '[I]f C fails to make out a common design, procurement may be difficult to establish': Dietrich and Ridge, *Accessories in Private Law*, p. 114.

The UK Supreme Court in *Sea Shepherd UK* v. *Fish v Fish Ltd*[68] held that accessory liability on the basis of common design arises when three elements are satisfied. First, D2 must assist D1 in the commission of acts amounting to a tort. D2's act must be substantial (more than merely facilitative) in nature.[69] Second, there must be a 'common design' as between D1 and D2 consisting in agreement of some kind (whether explicit or not) that they should work towards a common end.[70] Third, the primary wrongdoer must commit the tort, regarding which D2's acts of assistance must be at least a contributing cause.[71] The most difficult aspect of this definition concerns the common design element. In the *Sea Shepherd* case, there were various statements about what would suffice. Lord Sumption was of the view that there must be a shared *intention* to commit the acts which prove tortious,[72] while both Lords Toulson and Neuberger would have accepted knowledge in D2 of D1's intention to commit a tort.[73] (On this explication of the rules, what separates accessory liability on the basis of common design from unlawful means conspiracy is that there is no need to prove intention *to injure* on the part of either D1 or D2 in the former, while such intention is crucial to the latter. The accessory is liable as a joint tortfeasor for the commission of, not his or her own, but the primary wrongdoer's tort.[74] By contrast, each co-conspirator is jointly liable for his or her own tort.)

The rules of accessory liability have been justified by a number of considerations. First, the accessory who takes action according to a common design 'enhances' the risk of wrongdoing by the primary

[68] [2015] 2 WLR 694. The law in both Australia and the United States on common design liability is very similar to that described: Dietrich and Ridge, *Accessories in Private Law*, pp. 118–20. For the US position, see American Law Institute, Restatement (Second) of Torts (1979), § 876; Restatement (Third) of Torts: Apportionment of Liability (2000), § 15. For the Australian position, see J. Dietrich, 'The Liability of Accessories under Statute, in Equity, and in Criminal Law: Some Common Problems and (Perhaps) Some Common Solutions' (2010) 34 *Melbourne University Law Review* 106.

[69] [2015] 2 WLR 694, [21], [23], [37], [49], [57], and [58]. See also *CBS Songs Ltd* v. *Amstrad Consumer Electronics plc* [1988] 1 AC 1013; P. W. Lee, 'Accessory Liability in Tort and Equity' (2015) 27 *Singapore Academy of Law Journal* 853, 861. The law in Australia might be 'broader' than this: see Dietrich and Ridge, *Accessories in Private Law*, p. 125.

[70] [2015] 2 WLR 694, [23], [37], and [55]. See also *Unilever plc* v. *Gillette (UK) Ltd* [1989] RPC 583, 609; Dietrich and Ridge, *Accessories in Private Law*, p. 117.

[71] P. S. Davies, *Accessory Liability* (2015), pp. 12–13; Dietrich and Ridge, *Accessories in Private Law*, p. 38.

[72] [2015] 2 WLR 694, [44]. This issues is explored in Lee, 'Accessory Liability in Tort and Equity', 862–4.

[73] [2015] 2 WLR 694, [27] and [60] respectively.

[74] Dietrich and Ridge, *Accessories in Private Law*, p. 12.

wrongdoer by promoting the decision to commit the wrong in the first place, by increasing the capacity of the primary wrongdoer to commit the wrong, or by assisting in the wrongdoing.[75] When this is so, the accessory 'ought not to be able to hide behind the fact that he did not himself commit the primary wrong'.[76] Second, accessory liability is a deterrent to coordinated wrongdoing, and, therefore, should lead to commission of fewer wrongs.[77] 'Deterrence is particularly relevant in this area as the conduct of the accessory is calculated ex ante: a conscious decision is taken by the accessory, so an opportunity to deter the accessory from becoming "involved" in the primary breach clearly exists.'[78] Third, accessory liability permits the extension of liability for the commission of wrongs to promote full recovery of compensation by injured parties.

Paul Davies observes that there has been a long-standing reluctance to deploy rules of accessory liability in tort law when compared to other areas of private law.[79] This is reflected in the relative stringency of the rules on common design liability.[80] Indeed, in the *Sea Shepherd* case, the justices were careful to avoid setting the bar to accessory liability too low so as to create an inappropriately wide sphere of liability.[81] Lord Sumption expressed the 'pragmatic concern to limit the propensity of the law of tort to interfere with a person's right to do things which are in themselves entirely lawful'.[82] The concern of their Lordships to restrict accessory liability arises, in part, from a fear of liability for mere facilitation of infringements of intellectual property rights, given the prominence of such cases in the evolution of the rules.[83] Whether the same concern should infect cases of personal injury is another matter.

12.4.2 Accessory Liability in Groups

Of course, our interest in the rules of accessory liability concerns how they are to apply in the corporate group context. As it happens, the UK Supreme Court decision in the *Sea Shepherd* case serves as some sort of guidance. The case involved a 'network of entities' with a parent company, subsidiary entities, and common directorships.[84] The allegation

75 Dietrich and Ridge, *Accessories in Private Law*, pp. 37 and 122.
76 Dietrich and Ridge, *Accessories in Private Law*, pp. 15–16.
77 Dietrich and Ridge, *Accessories in Private Law*, p. 17.
78 Davies, *Accessory Liability*, p. 16.
79 Davies, *Accessory Liability*, pp. 214 and 280.
80 Davies, *Accessory Liability*, p. 282.
81 [2015] 2 WLR 694, [56].
82 [2015] 2 WLR 694, [39]. See also Lee, 'Accessory Liability in Tort and Equity', 855.
83 [2015] 2 WLR 694, [40].
84 [2015] 2 WLR 694, [6] and [32].

was that the parent company facilitated the commission of both trespass and conversion by the subsidiary company by making available a sea vessel for an environmental campaign aimed at disruption of tuna fishing operations, by recruiting volunteers for the campaign, and by paying the crew and obtaining financial contributions.[85] A bare majority of the Supreme Court allowed an appeal against a finding by the Court of Appeal that the parent had been jointly liable for the commission by the subsidiary of the torts. In the Supreme Court, there was support for the proposition that the parent company had acted pursuant to a common design. The case failed because the parent's acts of assistance were not sufficient to meet the de minimis threshold. The parent company's fundraising efforts were crucial to the success of the claimants' case, but the majority held them to have been insubstantial.[86] However, Lord Neuberger admitted that he might have decided the case differently, and found assistance to be present, if the parent had been more successful in the recruitment of volunteers.[87] That would have made a majority in favour of the parent company's liability as accessory.

The *Sea Shepherd* case follows in the footsteps of other cases which have indicated the potential for accessory liability on the part of parent companies for torts committed by subsidiaries.[88] However, *Sea Shepherd* did not deal with obvious policy issues about the separate legal entity status of each group company, and the limited liability of shareholder companies (most likely because the companies involved were not profit-making).[89] For reasons which have been developed in this book already, holding the parent company liable as an accessory to the commission of a tort would involve no more than the ordinary application of the common law to separate legal persons. This would *reinforce* the legal personhood of group companies and underline their capacity for accepting

[85] [2015] 2 WLR 694, [13]. [86] [2015] 2 WLR 694, [26], [70], and [88].

[87] [2015] 2 WLR 694, [72].

[88] *Intel Corporation* v. *General Instrument Corporation* [1991] RPC 235; *Unilever plc* v. *Gillette (UK) Ltd* [1989] RPC 583. While the potential is there, the application is largely untested: J. Zerk, *Multinationals and Corporate Social Responsibility* (2006), p. 226. See also W. Day, 'Skirting around the Issue: The Corporate Veil after *Prest v Petrodel*' [2014] *Lloyd's Maritime and Commercial Law Quarterly* 269, 288 (arguing for expanded rules).

[89] In the corporate groups context, it has been argued that liability should be restricted to cases of 'the intrusive exercise of control' or 'direct participation': A. Muscat, *The Liability of the Holding Company for the Debts of its Insolvent Subsidiaries* (1996), p. 128. But, given policy preferences of the UK Supreme Court in *Prest* v. *Petrodel* [2013] 2 AC 415 (discussed in Chapter 10) to reduce the scope of the veil-piercing doctrine, and to extend liability to parent companies in other ways, this is a tort doctrine worth further exploring. See Day, 'Skirting around the Issue'.

responsibility. But the exact extent of accessory liability would need serious consideration. Joachim Dietrich and Pauline Ridge observe that the law of accessory liability is flexible in nature, and that relevant liability rules take shape from their surroundings. Liability depends upon 'the primary wrong that has been committed, particularly in light of the purposes and values promoted by the law proscribing that wrong, and the factual context in which that wrong came about'.[90] So far as the factual context is concerned, there is a number of reasons why accessory liability could be a suitable doctrine by which to extend the liability of an insolvent subsidiary to other companies in the group. The context encompasses matters considered in Chapter 5, including top managers of group companies coordinating group activities, commitment to the group as a whole, conformity to the group ethos and performance goals, and reproachability of managers who are not seen as meeting their obligations to the group.

In the corporate group context, there is the potential for the test of accessory liability to produce very different results according to whether a subsidiary undertaking tortious conduct was incorporated by the parent or acquired from another company. In the former case, where the parent incorporates the subsidiary, provides finance, assets, and facilities, mandates the line of business to be undertaken, and appoints representatives to the subsidiary board, there is a much greater potential for fulfilment of the accessory liability conduct requirement than in cases of subsidiaries acquired from other companies and which have engaged in similar sorts of tortious conduct. Although this could lead to potential embarrassment in the application of the laws, such could be avoided by exempting ordinary acts of incorporation from fulfilling the conduct requirement *except* where the common design between group companies was present prior to the subsidiary's existence.

12.4.3 Comparing Multiple Entity Recklessness and Accessory Liability

A question arises as to the difference that would exist between the proposed tort of 'multiple entity recklessness' promoted in this book and the rules of accessory liability just discussed. To recall, multiple entity recklessness would turn upon objective recklessness in the risk-taking company, and deemed agreement by participating entities. The participating entities would be jointly liable for injuries caused unless they could

[90] Dietrich and Ridge, *Accessories in Private Law*, pp. 3–4.

prove that they took every step to avoid the future causation of personal injury to others by doing such things as blowing the whistle on the risky conduct and ceasing coordination with the risk-creating company. The point is that the basic form of liability in participating entities would be strict liability. Accessory liability, by contrast, would arise in circumstances where a relevant tort was committed by the injuring company, which need not be a fault-based tort, the accessory undertaking acts of assistance pursuant to a common design with the primary wrongdoer, for example to engage in acts that breach a statutory obligation. The accessory would be liable only in cases where it is proved to have had the relevant level of culpability.

12.5 Conclusions

This chapter has considered further *tort doctrines* capable of application to the insolvent entity problem. It has dismissed the usefulness of vicarious liability for various reasons, including the problem of its inconsistency with the limited liability of the parent company (in the case of corporate groups), and the futility in many cases of bringing actions against two companies when one action against a solvent defendant will do. This chapter has demonstrated also that the developing rules of accessory liability are of greater potential relevance to the insolvent entity problem – although there are few case illustrations. The overall result of our survey of tort law actions available to extend liability from an insolvent company in both corporate group and network contexts is similar: there is a need further to develop the rules so as to assist personal injury claimants.

13

Conclusions

13.1 The Problem

This book has examined the insolvent entity problem. The problem arises when a company in a corporate group or network becomes insolvent and is unable to satisfy its debts to creditors. The focus of this book has been upon the need to provide appropriate remedies for personal injury claimants.

In the usual corporate group case, claimants seek to extend liability to the parent company. Under current law, the parent is largely protected from extended liability claims by rules of separate legal personality and limited liability. Indeed, groups have been using these rules to their advantage by structuring relations between constituent companies in order to move assets from the reach of creditors. Such behaviour was evident, for example, in the asbestos industry. This book accepts that there are valid reasons for the retention of limited liability, which permits shareholders to share the financial risks of business ventures with creditors. However, risk-sharing is not appropriate when employees, consumers, or bystanders suffer personal injuries but cannot obtain compensation because they have no recourse to shareholder assets.

Relationships between network participants can be structured in order to protect assets from the reach of creditors too. Structuring has become a defining feature, for example, of the pharmaceuticals industry. Frequently, pharmaceuticals companies outsource development and testing programmes – partly in order to reduce their exposure to liability. Yet there are serious shortcomings in drug development, testing, and approvals processes. The 'medicalisation' of everyday life, combined with the possibility of long latency in the development of injury and disease in drug consumers, entails the likelihood of significant mass-tort claims against pharma companies in the future.

13.2 Current Law

This book has examined the circumstances in which liability can be extended from insolvent companies to solvent companies in corporate groups and networks. At present, there are few dependable means by which liability for personal injuries can be extended.

13.2.1 Statute

Legislation in this area does not deal comprehensively with liability for personal injuries, but operates in a piecemeal fashion.

The US Comprehensive Environmental Response, Compensation and Liability Act 1980 (CERCLA) and the Oil Pollution Act 1990 have several innovative features which provide bite in the extension of liability within corporate groups and networks. The statutes extend liability beyond owners of oil and other industrial facilities to operators, so as to encourage them to take responsibility for potential accidents. These polluter-pays statutes contain provisions on financial responsibility also, which are aimed at ensuring that responsible parties have a notional ability to pay for cleanup and damages claims should accidents occur. However, in practice, CERCLA discourages parent companies from taking responsibility for the affairs of their subsidiaries, allowing them to escape allegations that they are operators of subsidiary facilities, and it does not permit recovery for personal injury claims. The Oil Pollution Act 1990 shares many of the same liability features. Although it does permit recovery for a wider range of losses, personal injury claims are precluded and liability caps are set at relatively low levels.

EU-derived product liability law is of assistance to some consumers of defective products in extending liability to solvent companies. The Consumer Protection Act 1987 broadens avenues of recovery in both group and network contexts. It aids the search for a solvent defendant in the chain of manufacture and supply of goods. However, the cause of action that it creates is not as liberal as first appears. One reason for this is the wide development risks defence, applicable, for example, to new types of pharmaceutical. Another reason for the limited effectiveness of the 1987 Act is the long-stop time limit on bringing actions, which denies recovery in cases involving long-latent injuries and many mass-torts.

Several other types of statute assist creditors in extending liability from insolvent companies to other group companies. These include the Companies Act 1993 (NZ), which contains provisions that permit pooling of group assets and the making of contribution orders. However, the provisions have restrictive requirements. And courts have been wary of exercising powers under them in order to inflate assets available to satisfy the claims of creditors, in part because they recognise that such orders both undermine separate legal personality and can have adverse effects on third-party creditors who have interests opposing those of the claimants. Given the potential for unfairness to third-party creditors, common law actions arguably provide a superior solution to the insolvent entity problem because of the more direct link those actions make between wrongdoing and liability awards.

13.2.2 Common Law

Several kinds of common law rule have been examined that might facilitate extensions of liability in three-party cases. Veil-piercing frequently is seen as a useful company law doctrine for dealing with the insolvent entity problem. In this book, veil-piercing is defined as the extension of liability from an insolvent company upwards to one or more of its shareholders (whether corporate or individual). Leaving aside the issue about whether it involves usurpation of the legislature, the application of this doctrine is controversial because it undermines the rule of limited liability and the efficacy of commercial relationships. The newly restated UK law on veil-piercing leaves the doctrine to a narrow area of operation in cases of evasion. These are cases involving attempts by shareholders to avoid pre-existing legal obligations. The cases confirm what many had suspected – that veil-piercing is a doctrine which exists more in the minds of scholars than in actual legal practice.

It appears difficult to find a solution to the insolvent entity problem within company and insolvency law, where fundamental concepts of separate legal personality and limited liability remain sacrosanct. In both the United Kingdom and the wider Commonwealth, there has been a renewed judicial push to have cases involving claims against shareholder assets determined according to *established private law* principles, including those in tort law. Three-party torts and tort doctrines that might be of assistance to creditors wanting to extend liability from an insolvent company to the parent company or network participant include negligence, vicarious liability, and joint tortfeasance. This book's survey of relevant cases reveals that these torts and doctrines rarely have been used in this way.

Although there had been some hope that the tort of negligence might develop so as to permit a greater number of actions against parent companies, courts have not readily found in favour of personal injury claimants. For the moment, duties of care appear to be arguable primarily in cases involving injured subsidiary employees, although there is some scope for claims by injured consumers and bystanders. The four factors required in order to establish proximity between a parent company and subsidiary employees are: overlapping business operations conducted by the parent company and subsidiary; the parent company's superior knowledge about relevant aspects of health and safety in the industry; the parent company's knowledge that the subsidiary's system of work is unsafe; and reliance by the subsidiary or its employees upon the parent company using its superior knowledge for the protection of employees. When duties of care *are* recognised in parent companies (which is rarely the case), claimants can take advantage of relatively generous causation rules.

As an alternative to the tort of negligence, both courts and scholars have considered the possibility of deploying the doctrine of vicarious liability in the corporate group setting. To do so, prima facie, would cohere with the equivalence principle – which states that liability rules should be applicable to all persons recognised by the law, so that rules affecting individuals are applied to corporate entities on similar terms (unless there is a good reason for not doing so). However, the argument against application of vicarious liability in the corporate group context is that it is a doctrine of strict liability and liability arises automatically; it is not based upon recognised *wrongdoing in the defendant*. The imposition of strict liability in the parent company for the wrongs of its subsidiary's employees, absent something more, would be contradictory to the legislative purpose of limited liability.

Most scholars who advocate the greater use of negligence and vicarious liability rules so as to extend liability from insolvent subsidiaries to parent companies believe that the latter can satisfy damages claims. Parent companies, being the ultimate owners of group assets, are assumed to be substantial entities with access to both those assets and outside finance. However, these assumptions are not necessarily correct. The structuring of relations within corporate groups might mean that valuable assets are held not directly by parent companies, but by non-operating subsidiaries. Moreover, it might not be easy for parent companies to sell their shares in group subsidiaries holding valuable assets. Assets might be specialised in nature (being valuable only in conjunction with other assets held within the group) or subject to major fluctuations in their value (as in the oil industry).

We might note, also, that both the tort of negligence and the vicarious liability doctrine arise in vertical, control-based relationships. In this book, it has been demonstrated that control-based torts and doctrines might not be very helpful in confronting the next wave of mass-torts, which are just as likely to spring from network collaborations as they are from corporate groups. One reason for this is that businesses undertaking risky physical processes are more likely today than in the past to outsource product development, testing, and distribution – taking advantage of contract-based network relationships. In such cases, a more flexible tort or tort doctrine is required in order to facilitate horizontal extensions of liability.

This book has considered two potential candidates for extending liability horizontally, one of which subsists in the rules of joint liability. Joint liability arises when two or more persons are made legally responsible for the commission of torts on the basis that their actions cause the same damage in the claimant(s). The advantage to claimants of a successful pleading of joint liability is that they need bring only one action – against the more solvent of the defendants – in order to obtain the full award of damages. If the other jointly liable parties are worth suing, then the defendant to the main action can bring further or joined actions for contribution. This book has considered the utility of a subset of the rules of joint liability concerned with 'common design'. The accessory under the common design head is liable as a joint tortfeasor for the commission of, not his or her own tort, but for the primary wrongdoer's tort. However, courts have set the bar to successful pleas of common design at a high level in order to avoid a wide sphere of liability. A common design arises when D2 has (at minimum) knowledge of D1's intention to commit an act which amounts to a tort, and when D2's acts of assistance are not merely facilitative, but substantial in nature. In the circumstances, the rules have not yet proven their worth in either the corporate group or network contexts. One reason for this might be that no strong conception of wrongdoing underpins the common design rules, so that courts are reluctant to use them.

13.3 Assumptions Underlying the Present Law

Taking stock of the laws that operate in the present context, we might say that attempts at providing a regime of extended liability in order to tackle the insolvent entity problem have been half-hearted. Fundamental change in the law is required in order to resolve the problem. Before recounting the two specific suggestions for law reform that have been made in this book, we ought to reflect in more detail upon a number of assumptions underlying the existing law. These assumptions relate to limited liability, fault, and deterrence.

First, there are assumptions about the need for the limited liability of parent companies as shareholders in their subsidiaries. The economic arguments in favour of limited liability are not convincing when applied to the parent company–subsidiary relationship. Companies are not risk-averse in the way that individuals are, and would not be put off investments with positive net present values simply because their status as shareholders carries liability risks (which most of their own activities do anyway). Indeed, there are strong justice-based arguments that favour the extended liability of parent companies. One such argument involves a simple comparison of the interests at stake in cases involving claims by unsatisfied personal injury claimants against a parent company defendant. Shareholders in the subsidiary company and other group contributories would suffer no more than financial losses should they be made liable for unsatisfied claims. The importance of protecting physical interests in the person must be recognised and weighed against the law's lesser concern for the protection of purely financial interests.

Second, there are assumptions that the parent company should be liable only on the basis of fault. This book argues that, given the importance of protecting personal interests in the individual, the law should move away from (without completely abandoning) the idea that liability within corporate groups ought to be based on fault. Fault-based liability is (it is suggested) an overhang of will theory–inspired views of tort law and wider liability rules that derive from a long-superseded age of individual rather than corporate acts. Such views, which make liability dependent upon the moral quality of the defendant's actions, are not always appropriate when corporate group activities cause mass-torts. Whether or not fault is present in the parent company, the focus of tort law is not upon defendants alone – tort law must take into account the real, practical needs of claimants who come before the courts. Frequently, these claimants have no source of compensation for their injuries other than the corporate groups that cause them. Courts must take into account the position of such persons, and the *two-sided* nature of the tort contest over liability when developing liability rules. As a related matter, when designing corporate group liability, there is a need to move away from (without completely abandoning) the idea that liability in parent and other group companies should be based upon control. Indeed, in many cases control is a proxy for fault and limits unnecessarily the range of defendants to whom recourse can be had.

Moving away from fault-based liability means moving towards strict liability. This is liability that arises regardless of fault. There has been comparatively little discussion in the literature about using strict liability in order to extend liability within the group. Yet strict liability has its uses, and the insolvent subsidiary problem gives rise to one of them. Indeed, the imposition of strict liability upon shareholders is a legitimate way of placing the onus upon them to plan better for the future and to take actions which ensure that company managers reduce risks of personal and other types of injury. Strict-liability torts and doctrines are, by their nature, not backward-looking. They do not focus upon what the defendant has done in the past to avoid causing injury to the claimant. Such torts and doctrines have a forward-looking rationale. Because they place responsibility for avoiding harms upon predefined parties, these torts and doctrines force such parties to take actions now that will prevent harms in the future.

Third, assumptions are made about the relative unimportance of tort law as a deterrent. However, the doubts seem to be misplaced. In this book, argument has been made that threats of liability can be very effective when directed towards organisations. The ability to deter results from the forward-looking nature of organisational decision-making, structures through which decisions are implemented, and the ability to create standards of conduct and consistent norms of behaviour. Organisations, such as companies, have hierarchical structures that facilitate the widespread and effective implementation of decisions. Moreover, formalised decision-making takes advantage of both collective and specialised knowledge in the formulation of appropriate responses to risks. Risk-taking can be controlled through corporate policies, work schedules, and routines.

This book has sought to find a principled basis for extending liability within corporate groups and networks. In determining an appropriate liability regime, the present writer has taken the view that it is important to observe two principles. These are the 'equivalence' principle (already explained), and the 'business form neutrality' principle. The latter principle is concerned to ensure that liability rules do not unduly burden one form of business when another business form can be substituted for it. The particular concern is about the inadvisability of creating liability rules that impact upon corporate groups alone, without taking into account the fact that groups can migrate to the network form. Where liability rules apply only to corporate groups, and not to networks, this drives the insolvent entity problem out of corporate groups and into networks, leaving it unresolved.

13.4 Proposals

So – the question arises as to the type of liability regime (or components of a liability regime) that could operate in a way which is impervious to corporate form. Given the frequently quite different structures of corporate groups and networks, there is no simple solution. Instead, this book argues for a two-pronged approach that involves: first, a statutory alteration to the law on limited liability; and, second, the development of a flexible tort which would permit extensions of liability in the face of coordinated, risky conduct.

13.4.1 Statute

This book argues for modification to the law of limited liability in order to deal with insolvent companies unable fully to compensate personal injury victims. Statutory reform to the rule would help courts to overcome their reluctance to challenge the basic concepts of company law (especially separate legal personality and limited liability), and would help to create clarity for markets about the extent of the exception. The proposal for a rule of 'modified limited liability', which would permit access to shareholders' assets, is based upon several important attributes of shareholders, including: the function they play in arming the company with capital; their role as company insiders, the company enjoying important attributes of 'groupness'; and the lower order of importance of shareholders' financial interests in their investee companies than the interests of personal injury victims.

When a company becomes insolvent and there are unsatisfied personal injury claims against it, an exception to limited liability would be engaged. Both parent company and individual shareholders in the insolvent company would become liable, pro-rata, in an unlimited amount for those personal injury claims. Shareholder liability would be strict and would arise at the time that the reasonable shareholder obtains knowledge of claims. Attempts at evasion could be dealt with through measures such as anti-evasion powers and the imposition of treble damages upon those who unsuccessfully contest their liability. In line with the idea of the deterrable organisation, a rule of modified limited liability would provide incentive for shareholders to ensure that their investee companies' managers take action by putting into place effective policies and procedures for the prevention of harm in the course of risky activities. Much of the necessary work would be done by institutional shareholders, which frequently are locked into their shareholdings in investee companies, and have incentives to improve corporate governance in order to better their own investors' returns.

In order to ensure the efficacy of modified limited liability – and recoveries by personal injury claimants – this book argues for an accompanying change in the rule governing the priority of payments upon winding up. The main point is that personal injury claimants should rank ahead of both secured creditors and all other unsecured creditors whose have claims for ordinary business debts.

No doubt, there is concern that capital markets would react adversely to the prospect of unlimited shareholder liability, especially with respect to individual shareholders. However, it is suggested that such concerns have been overplayed. First, in the corporate group context, individual shareholders would become liable only when the subsidiary has such large personal injury claims against it that assets, insurance cover, and parent company support are inadequate and it is forced into insolvency. Second, shareholders would have the ability to: plan for the future by either monitoring managers in investee companies themselves so as to reduce risks of personal injury, encouraging institutional shareholders to do so, or doing so through corporate advisory firms; obtain their own personal liability insurance (if available); enter into swaps agreements to trade away risk; and/or take the risk that they will become personally liable.

13.4.2 Common Law

Of course, under the proposal for modified limited liability, shareholders in network companies would be liable pro-rata for their investee companies' unsatisfied personal injury claims. But the question arises as to whether there are any other means by which liabilities could be extended to the solvent entities participating in the network. This is an important issue because the insolvent entity problem encompasses not only corporate groups, but networks as well. It has been argued that there is a need for a tort cause of action which could operate horizontally, so as to extend liability at the subsidiary level in corporate groups *and* among network participants.

This book has argued for a modification to the tort of unlawful means conspiracy, the new tort tentatively being named 'multiple entity recklessness'. This tort would apply when a company acts in a way which is objectively reckless in undertaking physical processes which give rise to significant risks of injury. Where personal injury results from objectively reckless conduct, liability could be extended to other companies having significant commercial relationships with the risk-taking company and its reckless conduct. Each would become prima facie jointly liable with the risk-taking company for personal injury claims on the basis of their deemed agreement. It would then be up to the prima facie liable parties to prove that they took every step to avoid the future causation of personal injury to others by doing such things as blowing the whistle on the reckless conduct and ceasing coordination with the risk-creating company. The new tort of multiple entity recklessness would permit comparative flexibility in creating liability in corporate groups and networks, liability being based upon coordinated action rather than upon vertical relationships of control. The idea would be that, given the deterrable nature of organisations, companies coordinating with each other in either the corporate group or the network would have incentives to monitor each other's conduct and to avoid dealing with entities that display a reckless disregard for the safety, and well-being, of employees, customers, and bystanders.

BIBLIOGRAPHY

Books and Theses

Antunes, J. E., *Liability of Corporate Groups: Autonomy and Control in Parent–Subsidiary Relationships in US, German and EU Law* (Deventer, Kluwer Law and Taxation Publishers, 1994)

Austin, R. P., H. A. J. Ford, and I. M. Ramsay, *Company Directors: Principles of Law and Corporate Governance* (Chatswood, NSW, LexisNexis Butterworths, 2005)

Austin, R. P. and I. M. Ramsay, *Ford's Principles of Corporations Law* (12th edn., Chatswood, NSW, LexisNexis Butterworths, 2005)

Bainbridge, S. M. and M. R. Henderson, *Limited Liability: A Legal and Economic Analysis* (Cheltenham, UK, Edward Elgar, 2016)

Bakan, J., *The Corporation* (London, Constable & Robinson Ltd, 2004)

Baker, J. H., *An Introduction to English Legal History* (Oxford, Oxford University Press, 4th edn., 2007)

Baldwin, R., M. Cave, and M. Lodge, *Understanding Regulation: Theory, Strategy, and Practice* (Oxford, Oxford University Press, 2nd edn., 2012)

Blumberg, P. I., *The Law of Corporate Groups: Substantive Law* (Boston, MA, Little, Brown & Company, 1987)

Blumberg, P. I., *The Multinational Challenge to Corporation Law* (Oxford, Oxford University Press, 1993)

Blumberg, P. I., et al., *Blumberg on Corporate Groups* (2nd edn., New York, NY, Aspen Publishers, 2005)

Boggio, A., *Compensating Asbestos Victims: Law and the Dark Side of Industrialization* (Burlington, VT, Ashgate Publishing Company, 2013)

Braithwaite, J., *Regulatory Capitalism* (Cheltenham, UK, Edward Elgar, 2008)

Calabresi, G., *The Costs of Accidents* (New Haven, CT, Yale University Press, 1970)

Carroll, S. J., et al., *Asbestos Litigation* (Santa Monica, CA, RAND Institute for Civil Justice, 2005)

Carty, H., *An Analysis of the Economic Torts* (Oxford, Oxford University Press, 2nd edn., 2012)

Chandler, A. D., *Scale and Scope: The Dynamics of Industrial Capitalism* (Boston, MA, Harvard University Press, 1990)

Cheffins, B., *Company Law: Theory, Structure, and Operation* (Oxford, Oxford University Press, 1997)

Coase, R. H., *The Firm, the Market and the Law* (Chicago, IL, University of Chicago Press, 1988)

Coburn, N., *Coburn's Insolvent Trading* (2nd edn., Pyrmont, NSW, Law Book Co., 2003)

Coleman, J., *The Practice of Principle: In Defence of a Pragmatist Approach to Legal Theory* (Oxford, Oxford University Press, 2001)

Collins (Lord) et al., *Dicey, Morris and Collins: The Conflict of Law* (15th edn., London, Sweet and Maxwell, 2012)

Cooke, C. A., *Corporation, Trust and Company: An Essay in Legal History* (Manchester, Manchester University Press, 1951)

Cooke, R., *Turning Points of the Common Law* (London, Sweet and Maxwell, 1997)

Cyert, R. M. and J. G. March, *A Behavioural Theory of the Firm* (2nd edn., Oxford, Blackwell Publishers Ltd, 1992)

Dan-Cohen, M., *Rights, Persons, and Organizations: A Legal Theory for Bureaucratic Society* (Berkeley, University of California Press, 1986)

Davies, P. L., *Introduction to Company Law* (Oxford, Oxford University Press, 2002)

Davies, P. L. and S. Worthington, *Gower and Davies' Principles of Modern Company Law* (9th edn., London, Sweet and Maxwell, 2012)

Davies, P. S., *Accessory Liability* (Oxford, Hart Publishing Ltd, 2015)

Deakin, S., A. Johnston, and B. Markesinis, *Markesinis and Deakin's Tort Law* (7th edn., Oxford, Oxford University Press, 2013)

Dietrich, J. and P. Ridge, *Accessories in Private Law* (Cambridge, Cambridge University Press, 2015)

Dine, J., *The Governance of Corporate Groups* (Cambridge, Cambridge University Press, 2000)

Dunning, J. H., *Multinational Enterprises and the Global Economy* (Wokingham, UK, Addison-Wesley, 1993)

Easterbrook, F. and D. Fischel, *The Economic Structure of Corporate Law* (Boston, MA, Harvard University Press, 1991)

Eroglu, M., *Multinational Enterprises and Tort Liabilities* (Cheltenham, UK, Edward Elgar, 2008)

Farrar, J., *Corporate Governance: Theories, Principles, and Practice* (2nd edn., South Melbourne, Oxford University Press, 2006)

Ferran, E., *Corporate Finance Law* (Oxford, Oxford University Press, 2008)

Finnis, J. M., *Natural Law and Natural Rights* (2nd edn., Oxford, Oxford University Press, 2011)

Fischer, J. and M. Ravizza, *Responsibility and Control: A Theory of Moral Responsibility* (Cambridge, Cambridge University Press, 1998)

Fisse, B. and J. Braithwaite, *Corporations, Crime and Accountability* (Cambridge, Cambridge University Press, 1993)

French, P. A., *Collective and Corporate Responsibility* (New York, NY, Columbia University Press, 1984)

Gaughan, P. A., *Mergers, Acquisitions and Corporate Restructurings* (4th edn., Hoboken, NJ, John Wiley and Sons, Inc, 2007)

Gilbert, M., *A Theory of Political Obligation* (Oxford, Oxford University Press, 2006)

Giliker, P., *The Europeanisation of English Tort Law* (Oxford, Hart Publishing Ltd, 2014)

Giliker, P., *Vicarious Liability in Tort: A Comparative Perspective* (Cambridge, Cambridge University Press, 2010)

Goldacre, B., *Bad Pharma* (London, Fourth Estate, 2013)

Goldberg, J. C. P. and B. C. Zipursky, *The Oxford Introductions to US Law: Torts* (New York, NY, Oxford University Press, 2010)

Goode, R., *Principles of Corporate Insolvency Law* (4th edn., London, Sweet and Maxwell, 2011)

Gordley, J., *Foundations of Private Law: Property, Tort, Contracts, Unjust Enrichment* (Oxford, Oxford University Press, 2006)

Green, S., *Causation in Negligence* (Oxford, Hart Publishing Ltd, 2015)

Griffin, R. W., *Fundamentals of Management* (8th edn., Mason, OH, South-Western Cengage Learning, 2011)

Gullifer, L. and J. Payne, *Corporate Finance Law: Principles and Policy* (2nd edn., Oxford, Hart Publishing Ltd, 2015)

Haigh, G., *Asbestos House: The Secret History of James Hardie Industries* (Carlton North, Scribe Publications Pty Ltd, 2006)

Hannigan, B., *Company Law* (4th edn., Oxford, Oxford University Press, 2016)

Harding, A., *The Law Courts of Medieval England* (London, Allen and Unwin, 1973)

Hatch, M. J., *Organization Theory: Modern, Symbolic, and Postmodern Views* (3rd edn., Oxford, Oxford University Press, 2013)

Hoffman, A. J., *From Heresy to Dogma: An Institutional History of Corporate Environmentalism* (San Francisco, CA, New Lexington Press, 1997)

Howells, G. (ed.), *The Law of Product Liability* (2nd edn., London, LexisNexis Butterworths, 2007)

Hutter, B. and M. Powers (eds.), *Organizational Encounters with Risk* (Cambridge, Cambridge University Press, 2005)

Ibbetson, D., *A Historical Introduction to the Law of Obligations* (Oxford, Oxford University Press, 1999)

Isaacs, T., *Moral Responsibility in Collective Contexts* (Oxford, Oxford University Press, 2011)

Jacobsen, T. M. and A. I. Wertheimer (eds.), *Modern Pharmaceutical Industry: A Primer* (Sudbury, MA, Jones and Bartlett Publishers, 2010)

Jones, G., *Merchants to Multinationals: British Trading Companies in the Nineteenth and Twentieth Centuries* (Oxford, Oxford University Press, 2000)

Jones, G., *Multinationals and Global Capitalism: From the Nineteenth to the Twenty-First Century* (Oxford, Oxford University Press, 2005)

Joseph, S., *Corporations and Transnational Human Rights Litigation* (Oxford, Hart Publishing Ltd, 2004)

Kraakman, R., et al., *The Anatomy of Corporate Law: A Comparative and Functional Approach* (2nd edn., Oxford, Oxford University Press, 2009)

Kutz, C., *Complicity: Ethics and Law for a Collective Age* (Cambridge, Cambridge University Press, 2000)

Li, J. J., *Blockbuster Drugs* (New York, NY, Oxford University Press, 2013)

List, C. and P. Pettit, *Group Agency: The Possibility, Design, and Status of Corporate Agents* (Oxford, Oxford University Press, 2011)

Lo, S. H. C., *In Search of Corporate Accountability: Liabilities of Corporate Participants* (Newcastle upon Tyne, UK, Cambridge Scholars Publishing, 2015)

Lucy, W., *Philosophy of Private Law* (Oxford, Oxford University Press, 2007)

Luntz, H., D. Hambly, K. Burns, J. Dietrich, and N. Foster, *Torts: Cases and Commentary* (7th edn., Chatswood, NSW, LexisNexis Butterworths, 2012)

Marmor, A., *Positive Law and Objective Values* (Oxford, Oxford University Press, 2001)

McCullough, J. and G. Tweedale, *Defending the Indefensible: The Global Asbestos Industry and its Fight for Survival* (Oxford, Oxford University Press, 2008)

McQueen, R., *A Social History of Company Law* (Burlington, VT, Ashgate Publishing Company, 2009)

Mevorach, I., *Insolvency within Multinational Enterprise Groups* (Oxford, Oxford University Press, 2009)

Micklethwait, J. and A. Wooldridge, *The Company: A Short History of a Revolutionary Idea* (London, Weidenfeld and Nicolson, 2003)

Miller, C. J. and R. S. Goldberg, *Product Liability* (2nd edn., Oxford, Oxford University Press, 2004)

Morse, G. (ed.), *Palmer's Company Law*, Volume 1 (Online) (London, Sweet and Maxwell, 2016)

Mortensen, R., R. Garnett, and M. Keyes, *Private International Law in Australia* (3rd edn., Chatswood, NSW, LexisNexis Butterworths, 2015)

Muchlinski, P. T., *Multinational Enterprises and the Law* (2nd edn., Oxford, Oxford University Press, 2007)

Muscat, A., *The Liability of the Holding Company for the Debts of its Insolvent Subsidiaries* (Aldershot, UK, Dartmouth, 1996)

Nohria, N., D. Dyer, and F. Dalzell, *Changing Fortunes: Remaking the Industrial Corporation* (New York, NY, John Wiley and Sons, Inc, 2002)

Oliphant, K. (ed.), *The Law of Tort* (3rd edn., London, LexisNexis Butterworths, 2015)

Owen, D. G. and M. J. Davis, *Owen and Davis on Products Liability* (4th edn., Thomson Reuters, 2014)

Perrow, C., *The Next Catastrophe* (Princeton, NJ, Princeton University Press, 2007)
Plucknett, T. F. T., *A Concise History of the Common Law* (5th edn., Boston, MA, Little, Brown and Co., 1956)
Plunkett, J., *The Duty of Care: A Comparative Common Law Analysis* (DPhil Thesis, University of Oxford, 2015)
Porat, A. and A. Stein, *Tort Liability under Uncertainty* (Oxford, Oxford University Press, 2001)
Posner, R. *Economic Analysis of Law* (4th edn., Boston, MA, Harvard University Press, 1990)
Powell, F. J., *Parent and Subsidiary Corporations: Liability of a Parent Corporation for the Obligations of its Subsidiary* (Chicago, IL, Callaghan, 1931)
Prosser, WL., *Handbook of the Law of Torts* (St Paul, MN, West Publishing Co., 1941)
Rapakko, T., *Unlimited Shareholder Liability in Multinationals* (The Hague, Kluwer, 1997)
Reason, J., *Managing the Risks of Organizational Accidents* (Burlington, VT, Ashgate Publishing Company, 1998)
Sappideen, C. and P. Vines (eds.), *Fleming's The Law of Torts* (10th edn., Pyrmont, NSW, Thomson Reuters, 2011)
Schütze, R., *European Union Law* (Cambridge, Cambridge University Press, 2015)
Searle, J. R., *Making the Social World: The Structure of Human Civilization* (Oxford, Oxford University Press, 2010)
Simester, A. P., J. R. Spencer, G. R. Sullivan, and G. J. Virgo, *Simester and Sullivan's Criminal Law: Theory and Doctrine* (5th edn., Oxford, Hart Publishing Ltd, 2013)
Skeel, D., *Icarus in the Boardroom* (New York, NY, Oxford University Press, 2005)
Solomon, J. and A. Solomon, *Corporate Governance and Accountability* (Chichester, UK, John Wiley and Sons, Inc, 2004)
Stapleton, J., *Product Liability* (London, Butterworths, 1994)
Steel, S., *Proof of Causation in Tort Law* (Cambridge, Cambridge University Press, 2015)
Sunstein, C. R., *Risk and Reason* (Cambridge, Cambridge University Press, 2002)
Tabb, C. J. and R. Brubaker, *Bankruptcy Law Principles, Policies, and Practice* (3rd edn., New Providence, NJ, LexisNexis, Inc, 2010)
Teubner, G., *Networks as Connected Contracts* (ed. H Collins; tr. M. Everson) (Oxford, Hart Publishing Ltd, 2011)
Tuomela, R., *The Philosophy of Sociality: The Shared Point of View* (Oxford, Oxford University Press, 2007)
Turton, G., *Evidential Uncertainty in Causation in Negligence* (Oxford, Hart Publishing Ltd, 2016)
Tweedale, G., *Magic Mineral to Killer Dust: Turner and Newall and the Asbestos Hazard* (Oxford, Oxford University Press, 2000)

Weinrib, E., *The Idea of Private Law* (Boston, MA, Harvard University Press, 1995)

Whittaker, S., *Liability for Products: English Law, French Law, and European Harmonization* (Oxford, Oxford University Press, 2005)

Whittington, R. and M. Mayer, *The European Corporation: Strategy, Structure, and Social Science* (Oxford, Oxford University Press, 2000)

Wieser, R. T., *Liability within Corporate Groups* (Bad Frankenhausen, Societas Verlag, 2013)

Witting, C., *Liability for Negligent Misstatements* (Oxford, Oxford University Press, 2004)

Witting, C., *Street on Torts* (14th edn., Oxford, Oxford University Press, 2015)

Worthington, S., *Sealy and Worthington's Text, Cases and Materials in Company Law* (11th edn., Oxford, Oxford University Press, 2016)

Yoshino, M. Y. and U. Srinivasa Rangan, *Strategic Alliances: An Entrepreneurial Approach to Globalization* (Boston, MA, Harvard University Business School Press, 1995)

Zerk, J., *Multinationals and Corporate Social Responsibility* (Cambridge, Cambridge University Press, 2006)

Articles, etc.

Adebola, B., 'Proposed Feasibility Oversight for Pre-pack Administration in England and Wales: Window Dressing or Effective Reform?' [2015] *Journal of Business Law* 591

Abraham, K. S., 'Catastrophic Oil Spills and the Problem of Insurance' (2011) 64 *Vanderbilt Law Review* 1770

Abraham, K. S., 'Individual Action and Collective Responsibility: The Dilemma of Mass Tort Reform' (1987) 73 *Virginia Law Review* 845

Admati, A. R., P. Conti-Brown, and P. Pfleiderer, 'Liability Holding Companies' (2012) 59 *UCLA Law Review* 852

Aldred, C., 'UK Asbestos Exclusions Likely to Spread' (2003) 37 *Business Insurance* 37

Anabtawi, I. and L. Stout, 'Fiduciary Duties for Activist Shareholders' (2008) 60 *Stanford Law Review* 1255

Anderson, D. R., 'Financing Asbestos Claims: Coverage Issues, Manville's Bankruptcy and the Claims Facility' (1987) 54 *Journal of Risk and Insurance* 429

Anderson, H., 'Corporate Social Responsibility – The Case for Unsecured Creditors' (2007) 7 *Oxford University Commonwealth Law Journal* 93

Anderson, H., 'Creditors' Rights of Recovery: Economic Theory, Corporate Jurisprudence and the Role of Fairness' (2006) 30 *Melbourne University Law Review* 1

Anderson, H., 'Parent Company Liability for Asbestos Claims: Some International Insights' (2011) 31 *Legal Studies* 547

Anderson, H., 'Piercing the Veil on Corporate Groups in Australia: The Case for Reform' (2009) 33 *Melbourne University Law Review* 333

Anderson, H., 'Pressing the Right Buttons: Australian Case Studies in the Protection of Employee Entitlements against Corporate Insolvency' (2014) 153 *International Labour Review* 117

Anderson, H., 'Thinking outside the Square – Some Alternative Approaches to the Protection of Employee Entitlements' (2014) 32 *Company & Securities Law Journal* 23

Anderson, H., 'Veil Piercing and Corporate Groups – An Australian Perspective' [2010] *New Zealand Law Review* 1

Angwin, H., 'Merger and Acquisition Typologies: A Review', in D. Faulkner, S. Teerikangas, and R. J. Joseph (eds.), *The Handbook of Mergers and Acquisitions* (Oxford, Oxford University Press, 2012), ch. 3

Aristova, E., 'Jurisdiction of the English Court over Overseas Human Rights Violation' (2016) 75 *Cambridge Law Journal* 468

Arlen, J. H. and R. Kraakman, 'Controlling Corporate Misconduct: An Analysis of Corporate Liability Regimes' (1997) 72 *New York University Law Review* 687

Arlen, J. H. and W. B. MacLeod, 'Beyond Master-Servant: A Critique of Vicarious Liability', in M. S. Madden (ed.), *Exploring Tort Law* (Cambridge, Cambridge University Press, 2005), ch. 4

Arnold, D. G., 'Corporate Moral Agency', in P. A. French and H. K. Wettstein (eds.), *Shared Intentions and Collective Responsibility* (Oxford, Blackwell Publishing, Inc, 2006), ch. 17

Ashwin, A., 'Tortious Liability of Company in Winding Up: An Analysis' (2005) 26 *Company Lawyer* 163

Atanasov, V., A. Boone, and D. Haushalter, 'Is There Shareholder Expropriation in the United States? An Analysis of Publicly Traded Subsidiaries' (2010) 45 *Journal of Financial and Quantitative Analysis* 1

Bagley, C. E. and C. D. Tvarnø, 'Pharmaceutical Public-Private Partnerships: Moving from the Bench to the Bedside' (2014) 4 *Harvard Business Law Journal* 373

Bailey, S., 'Causation in Negligence: What Is a Material Contribution?' (2010) 30 *Legal Studies* 167

Bainbridge, S. M., 'Abolishing Veil Piercing' (2001) 26 *Journal of Corporation Law* 479

Bainbridge, S. M., 'Why a Board? Group Decisionmaking in Corporate Governance' (2002) 55 *Vanderbilt Law Review* 1

Baird, D., 'Substantive Consolidation Today' (2005) 47 *Boston College Law Review* 5

Balganesh, S., 'Foreseeability and Copyright Incentives' (2009) 122 *Harvard Law Review* 1569

Ballantine, H. W., 'Separate Entity of Parent and Subsidiary Corporations' (1925–6) 14 *California Law Review* 12

Barliant, R., D. G. Karcazes, and A. M. Sherry, 'From Free-Fall to Free-for-All: The Rise of Pre-packaged Asbestos Bankruptcies' (2004) 12 *American Bankruptcy Institute Law Review* 441

Bartlett, C. A. and S. Ghoshal, 'Beyond the M-Form: Toward a Managerial Theory of the Firm' (1993) 14 *Strategic Management Journal* 23

Bartlett, C. A. and S. Ghoshal, 'The Transnational Organization', in D. S. Pugh (ed.), *Organization Theory: Selected Classic Readings* (5th edn., London, Penguin Books Ltd, 2007), ch. 4

Bartrip, P., 'Changing Attitudes to Risk? Managing Myxomatosis in Twentieth-Century Britain', in B. Hutter (ed.), *Anticipating Risks and Organising Risk Regulation* (Cambridge, Cambridge University Press, 2010), ch. 4

Baughen, S., 'Multinationals and the Export of Hazard' (1995) 58 *Modern Law Review* 54

Ben-Ishai, S. and S. J. Lubben, 'Involuntary Creditors and Corporate Bankruptcy' (2012) *University of British Columbia Law Review* 253

Bergkamp, L., 'The Environmental Liability Directive and Liability of Parent Companies for Damage Caused by Their Subsidiaries ("Enterprise Liability")' (2016) 13 *European Company Law* 183

Berle, A. A., 'The Theory of Enterprise Entity' (1947) 47 *Columbia Law Review* 343

Birkinshaw, J. and T. Pedersen, 'Strategy and Management in MNE Subsidiaries', in A. M. Rugman (ed.), *The Oxford Handbook of International Business* (2nd edn., Oxford, Oxford University Press, 2009), ch. 14

Blasses, W. C., 'Redefining into Reality: Substantive Consolidation of Parent Corporations and Subsidiaries' (2008) 24 *Emory Bankruptcy Developments Journal* 469

Blumberg, P. I., 'Limited Liability and Corporate Groups' (1986) 11 *Journal of Corporation Law* 573

Blumberg, P. I., 'The Transformation of Modern Corporation Law: The Law of Corporate Groups' (2005) 37 *Connecticut Law Review* 605

Böckli, P., et al., 'Shareholder Engagement and Identification' (European Company Law Experts, 2015)

Boggio, A., 'Linking Corporate Power to Corporate Structures: An Empirical Analysis' (2012) 22 *Social and Legal Studies* 107

Bondi, B. J., 'Dangerous Liaisons: Collective Scienter in SEC Enforcement Actions' (2009) *New York University Journal of Law & Business* 1

Booth, R., 'Limited Liability and the Efficient Allocation of Resources' (1994) 89 *Northwestern University Law Review* 140

Bowmer, S., 'To Pierce or Not to Pierce the Corporate Veil – Why Substantive Consolidation Is Not an Issue under English Law' (2000) 15 *Journal of International Banking Law* 193

Boyd, C. L. and D. A. Hoffman, 'Disputing Limited Liability' (2010) 104 *Northwestern University Law Review* 853

Brady, R., 'CERCLA Apportionment Following *Burlington Northern*: How Joint and Several Liability Still Thrives – To the Surprise of Many' (2014) 4 *Washington Journal of Environmental Law & Policy* 141

Briault, C., 'Risk Society and Financial Risk', in B. M. Hutter (ed.), *Anticipating Risks and Organising Risk Regulation* (Cambridge, Cambridge University Press, 2010), ch. 2

Buckley, P. J. and M. Casson, 'Joint Ventures', in P. J. Buckley and J. Michie (eds.), *Firms, Organizations and Contracts: A Reader in Industrial Organization* (Oxford, Oxford University Press, 1996), ch. 15

Bull, S., 'Piercing the Corporate Veil – in England and Singapore' [2014] *Singapore Journal of Legal Studies* 24

Bullimore, T., 'Sins of the Father, Sins of the Son' (2012) 28 *Professional Negligence* 212

Burns, T., 'Mechanistic and Organismic Structures', in D. S. Pugh (ed.), *Organization Theory: Selected Classic Readings* (5th edn., 2007), ch. 6

Cahn, A., 'Equitable Subordination of Shareholder Loans?' (2006) 7 *European Business Organization Law Review* 287

Campbell, A., M. Goold, and M. Alexander, 'Corporate Strategy: The Quest for Parenting Advantage' [1995] *Harvard Business Review* 120

Cane, P., 'Reforming Tort Law in Australia: A Personal Perspective' (2003) 27 *Melbourne University Law Review* 649

Cane, P., 'Rights in Private Law', in D. Nolan and A. Robertson (eds.), *Rights and Private Law* (Oxford, Hart Publishing Ltd, 2012), ch. 2

Cantu, C. E., 'The Useful Life Defense: Embracing the Idea That All Products Eventually Grow Old and Die' (2001) 80 *Nebraska Law Review* 1

Cardi, W. J., 'Reconstructing Foreseeability' (2005) 46 *British Columbia Law Review* 921

Carty, H., 'The Tort of Conspiracy as a Can of Worms', in G. A. Pitel, J. W. Neyers, and E. Chamberlain (eds.), *Tort Law: Challenging Orthodoxy* (Oxford, Hart Publishing Ltd, 2013), ch. 13

Casey, A. J., 'The New Corporate Web: Tailored Entity Partitions and Creditors' Selective Enforcement' (2015) 124 *Yale Law Journal* 2680

Cassis, Y., 'Big Business', in G. Jones and J. Zeitlin (eds.), *The Oxford Handbook of Business History* (Oxford, Oxford University Press, 2007), ch. 8

Champion, W. T., 'The Vioxx® Litigation Paradigm: The Search for Smoking Guns' (2006) 31 *Thurgood Marshall Law Review* 157

Cheffins, B. R. and J. Armour, 'The Past, Present, and Future of Shareholder Activism by Hedge Funds' (2011) 37 *Journal of Corporation Law* 51

Cheifetz, D., 'Causation in Negligence: Material Contribution and But-For after *Clements*' (2012) 40 *Advocates' Quarterly* 275

Chiappetta, F. and U. Tombari, 'Perspectives on Group Corporate Governance and European Company Law' (2012) 3 *European Company and Financial Law Review* 261

Coase, R. H., 'The Nature of the Firm' (1937) 4 *Economica* (NS) 386

Coase, R. H., 'The Nature of the Firm: Influence' (1988) 4 *Journal of Law, Economics & Organization* 33

Coase, R. H. 'The Nature of the Firm: Meaning' (1988) 4 *Journal of Law, Economics & Organization* 19

Coase, R. H., 'The Nature of the Firm: Origin' (1988) 4 *Journal of Law, Economics & Organization* 3

Cohen, M. A., M. Gottlieb, J. Linn, and N. Richardson, 'Deepwater Drilling: Law, Policy, and Economics of Firm Organization and Safety' (2011) 64 *Vanderbilt Law Review* 1853

Cole, M., 'Limiting Liability through Bankruptcy' (2002) 70 *University of Cincinnati Law Review* 1245

Collins, H. 'Ascription of Legal Responsibility to Groups in Complex Patterns of Economic Integration' (1990) 53 *Modern Law Review* 731

Colombo, M. G. and M. Delmastro, 'Delegation of Authority in Business Organizations: An Empirical Test' (2004) 52 *Journal of Industrial Economics* 53

Companies and Securities Advisory Committee, 'Corporate Groups Final Report' (Sydney, NSW, 2000)

Conti-Brown, P., 'Elective Shareholder Liability' (2012) 64 *Stanford Law Review* 409

Conway, M., 'A New Duty of Care? Tort Liability from Voluntary Human Rights Due Diligence in Global Supply Chains' (2015) 40 *Queen's Law Journal* 741

Cork, K., 'Report of the Review Committee on Insolvency Law and Practice' (Cmnd 8558, June 1982)

Corporations and Markets Advisory Committee, 'Long-Tail Liabilities: The Treatment of Unascertained Future Personal Injury Claims: Report' (Sydney, NSW, 2008)

Corporations and Markets Advisory Committee, 'Shareholder Claims against Insolvent Companies: Implications of the *Sons of Gwalia*' (Sydney, NSW, Decision Discussion Paper, 2007)

Crowe, J., 'Does Control Make a Difference? The Moral Foundations of Shareholder Liability for Corporate Wrongs' (2012) 75 *Modern Law Review* 159

Dan-Cohen, M., 'Responsibility and the Boundaries of the Self' (1992) 105 *Harvard Law Review* 959

Dan-Cohen, M., 'Sanctioning Corporations' (2010) 19 *Journal of Law and Policy* 15

Day, W., 'Negligence and the Corporate Veil: Parent Companies' Duty of Care to Their Subsidiaries' Employees' [2014] *Lloyd's Maritime and Commercial Law Quarterly* 454

Day, W., 'Skirting around the Issue: The Corporate Veil after *Prest v Petrodel*' [2014] *Lloyd's Maritime and Commercial Law Quarterly* 269

Dearborn, M., 'Enterprise Liability: Reviewing and Revitalizing Liability for Corporate Groups' (2009) 97 *California Law Review* 195

De Blasi, M., 'Liability of Parent Corporations, Officers, Directors, and Successors: When Can CERCLA Liability Extend beyond the Company?' (2014) 46 *Arizona State Law Review* 481

Demsetz, H., 'The Theory of the Firm Revisited' (1988) 4 *Journal of Law, Economics & Organization* 141

Department for Business, Innovation and Skills, 'The Register of People with Significant Control' (June 2015)

Department for Business, Innovation and Skills, 'Register of People with Significant Control: Guidance for Companies, Societates Europaeae and Limited Liability Partnerships' (2016)

Department for Business, Innovation and Skills, 'Statutory Guidance on the Meaning of "Significant Influence or Control" over Companies in the Context of the Register of People with Significant Control' (April 2016)

De Stefano, G., 'General Court Rules on Successor Liability and Apportionment of Group Liability in the Gas Insulated Switchgear Cartel' (2011) 2 *Journal of European Competition Law & Practice* 344

Diamond, A., 'Corporate Personality and Limited Liability', in T. Orhnial (ed.), *Limited Liability and the Corporation* (London, Croom Helm, 1982), ch. 2

Dickfos, J., C. Anderson, and D. Morrison, 'The Insolvency Implications for Corporate Groups in Australia – Recent Events and Initiatives' (2007) 16 *International Insolvency Review* 103

Dietrich, J., 'The Liability of Accessories under Statute, in Equity, and in Criminal Law: Some Common Problems and (Perhaps) Some Common Solutions' (2010) 34 *Melbourne University Law Review* 106

DiMaggio, P. J. and W. W. Powell, 'Institutional Isomorphism', in D. S. Pugh (ed.), *Organization Theory: Selected Classic Readings* (5th edn., London, Penguin Books Ltd, 2007), ch. 22

Dorfman, A., 'Foreseeability as Re-cognition' (2014) 59 *American Journal of Jurisprudence* 163

Douglas, W. O. and C. Shanks, 'Insulation from Liability through Subsidiary Corporations' (1929) 39 *Yale Law Journal* 193

Dunn, E., 'James Hardie: No Soul to Be Damned and No Body to Be Kicked' (2005) 27 *Sydney Law Review* 339

Dunning, J. H., 'The Key Literature on IB Activities 1960–2006', in A. M. Rugman (ed.), *The Oxford Handbook of International Business* (2nd edn., Oxford, Oxford University Press, 2009), ch. 2

Dutta, M., 'The Indian Government's Complicity in the Asbestos Scandal', in D. Allen and L. Kazan-Allen (eds.), *India's Asbestos Time Bomb* (London, International Ban Asbestos Secretariat, 2008), ch. 2

Easterbrook, F. and D. Fischel, 'Limited Liability and the Corporation' (1985) 52 *University of Chicago Law Review* 89

Edelman, P. H., R. S. Thomas, and R. B. Thompson, 'Shareholder Voting in an Age of Intermediary Capitalism' (2014) 87 *Southern California Law Review* 1359

Edmundson, P., 'Conspiracy by Unlawful Means: Keeping the Tort Untangled' (2008) 16 *Torts Law Journal* 189

Eisenberg, M. A., 'Corporate Groups', in M. Gillooly (ed.), *The Law Relating to Corporate Groups* (Annandale, NSW, Federation Press, 1993), ch. 1

Eisenberg, M. A., 'Corporate Law and Social Norms' (1999) 99 *Columbia Law Review* 1253

Elson, S., 'Legal Liability of Holding Companies for Acts of Subsidiary Companies' [1930] *Commercial Law Journal* 680

Engel, S. and B. Martin, 'Union Carbide and James Hardie: Lessons in Politics and Power' (2006) 20 *Global Society* 475

Erens, B. B., S. J. Friedman, and K. M. Mayerfield, 'Bankrupt Subsidiaries: The Challenges to the Parent of Legal Separation' (2008) 25 *Emory Bankruptcy Developments Journal* 65

European Commission, 'Alleged Aid to Amazon by Way of a Tax Ruling' (COM (2014) 7156)

European Commission, 'Alleged Aid to Apple', State Aid SA.38373 (2014/C)

European Commission, 'Commission Decides Selective Tax Advantages for Fiat in Luxembourg and Starbucks in the Netherlands Are Illegal under EU State Aid Rules' (Press Release, 21 Oct 2015)

European Commission, 'Proposal for a Directive of the European Parliament and of the Council Amending Directive 2007/36/EC as Regards the Encouragement of Long-Term Shareholder Engagement and Directive 2013/34/EU as Regards Certain Elements of the Corporate Governance Statement' (COM 2014/0121)

European Commission, 'Proposal for a Directive Amending Directive 2013/34/EU as Regards Disclosure of Income Tax Information by Certain Undertakings and Branches' (COM (2016) 198)

European Commission, 'Proposal for a Directive Amending the Accounting Directive' (COM (2016) 198)

Fairgrieve, D. and G. Howells, 'Rethinking Product Liability: A Missing Element in the European Commission's Third Review of the European Product Liability Directive' (2007) 70 *Modern Law Review* 962

Farrar, J. H., 'Legal Issues Involving Corporate Groups' (1998) 16 *Company & Securities Law Journal* 184

Faulkner, D., S. Teerikangas, and R. J. Joseph, 'Introduction', in D. Faulkner, S. Teerikangas, and R. J. Joseph (eds.), *The Handbook of Mergers and Acquisitions* (Oxford, Oxford University Press, 2012), ch. 1

Feldman, H. L., 'Pushing Drugs: Genomics and Genetics, the Pharmaceutical Industry, and the Law of Negligence' (2003) 42 *Washburn Law Journal* 575

Finch, V., 'Security, Insolvency and Risk: Who Pays the Price?' (1999) 62 *Modern Law Review* 633

Finnis, J., 'Intention in Tort Law', in D. G. Owen (ed.), *Philosophical Foundations of Tort Law* (Oxford, Oxford University Press, 1995), ch. 10

Flannigan, R., 'Enterprise Control: The Servant-Independent Contractor Distinction' (1987) 37 *University of Toronto Law Journal* 25

Flannigan, R., 'The Personal Tort Liability of Directors' (2002) 81 *Canadian Bar Review* 247

Fletcher, I. and G. Squires, 'Pensions Again – "Just When You Thought it Was Safe to Go into Administration"' (2014) 27 *Insolvency International* 59

Freedland, F., 'History of Holding Company Legislation in New York State: Some Doubts as to the "New Jersey First" Tradition' (1955) 24 *Fordham Law Review* 369

Freedman, J., 'Limited Liability: Large Company Theory and Small Firms' (2000) 63 *Modern Law Review* 317

Fruin, W. M., 'Business Groups and Interfirm Networks', in G. Jones and J. Zeitlin (eds.), *The Oxford Handbook of Business History* (Oxford, Oxford University Press, 2007), ch. 11

Garoupa, N. and T. S. Ulen, 'The Economics of Activity Levels in Tort Liability and Regulation', in T. J. Miceli and M. J. Baker (eds.), *Research Handbook on Economic Models of Law* (Cheltenham, UK, Edward Elgar, 2014), ch. 2

Garrett, B. L., 'The Corporate Criminal as Scapegoat' (2015) 101 *Virginia Law Review* 1789

Geis, G. S., 'The Space between Markets and Hierarchies' (2009) 95 *Virginia Law Review* 99

Gershonowitz, A., 'The End of Joint and Several Liability in Superfund Litigation: From *Chem-Dyne* to *Burlington Northern*' (2012) 50 *Duquesne Law Review* 83

Gilhooley, M., 'Vioxx's History and the Need for Better Procedure and Better Testing' (2007) 37 *Seton Hall Law Review* 941

Gilson, R. J., C. E. Sabel, and R. E. Scott, 'Contracting for Innovation: Vertical Disintegration and Interfirm Collaboration' (2009) 109 *Columbia Law Review* 431

Glickman, S.W., et al., 'Ethical and Scientific Implications of Globalization of Clinical Research' (2009) 360 *New England Journal of Medicine* 816

Glynn, T. P., 'Beyond "Unlimiting" Shareholder Liability: Vicarious Tort Liability for Corporate Officers' (2004) 57 *Vanderbilt Law Review* 329

Goldberg, J. C. P., 'Twentieth-Century Tort Theory' (2003) 91 *Georgetown Law Journal* 513

Goldberg, J. C. P. and B. C. Zipursky, 'The Easy Case for Products Liability Law: A Response to Professors Polinsky and Shavell' (2010) 123 *Harvard Law Review* 1919

Gormley, T. A. and D. A. Matsa, 'Growing Out of Trouble? Corporate Responses to Liability Risk' (2011) 24 *Review of Financial Studies* 2781

Grabill, J. T., 'Judicial Review of Private Mass Tort Settlements' (2012) 42 *Seton Hall Law Review* 123

Graham, K., 'Strict Products Liability at 50: Four Histories' (2014) 98 *Marquette Law Review* 555

Graulich, T. E., 'Substantive Consolidation – A Post-modern Trend' (2006) 14 *American Bankruptcy Institute Law Review* 527

Greenfield, K., 'The Disaster at Bhopal: Lessons for Corporate Law?' (2008) 42 *New England Law Review* 755

Grundfest, J., 'The Limited Future of Unlimited Liability: A Capital Markets Perspective' (1992) 102 *Yale Law Journal* 387

Gulati, G. M., W. A. Klein, and E. M. Zolt, 'Connected Contracts' (2000) 47 *UCLA Law Review* 887

Hadden, T., 'Regulating Corporate Groups: An International Perspective', in J. McCahery, S. Picciotto, and C. Scott (eds.), *Corporate Control and Accountability: Changing Structures and Dynamics of Regulation* (Oxford, Oxford University Press, 1993), ch. 18

Haddy, S., 'A Comparative Analysis of Directors' Duties in a Range of Corporate Group Structures' (2002) 20 *Company & Securities Law Journal* 138

Hall, M. I., 'Theorizing the Institutional Tortfeasor' (2016) 53 *Alberta Law Review* 995

Halpern, P., M. Trebilcock, and S. Turnbull, 'An Economic Analysis of Limited Liability' (1980) 30 *University of Toronto Law Journal* 117

Hannan, M. T. and J. Freeman, 'The Population Ecology of Organizations', in D. S. Pugh (ed.), *Organization Theory: Selected Classic Readings* (5th edn., London, Penguin Books Ltd, 2007), ch. 10

Hansmann, H. and R. Kraakman, 'Do the Capital Markets Compel Limited Liability? A Response to Professor Grundfest' (1992) 102 *Yale Law Journal* 427

Hansmann, H. and R. Kraakman, 'The Essential Role of Organizational Law' (2000) 110 *Yale Law Journal* 387

Hansmann, H. and R. Kraakman, 'Toward Unlimited Shareholder Liability for Corporate Torts' (1991) 100 *Yale Law Journal* 1879

Hanson, J. D. and K. D. Logue, 'The First-Party Insurance Externality: An Economic Justification for Enterprise Liability' (1990) 76 *Cornell Law Review* 129

Harland, D., 'The Influence of European Law on Product Liability in Australia' (1995) 17 *Sydney Law Review* 336

Harper Ho, V., 'Theories of Corporate Groups: Corporate Identity Reconceived' (2012) 42 *Seton Hall Law Review* 879

Harris, J., 'Corporate Group Insolvencies: Charting the Past, Present and Future of "Pooling" Arrangements' (2007) 15 *Insolvency Law Journal* 78

Harris, J. and A. Hargovan, 'Cutting the Gordian Knot of Corporate Law: Revisiting Veil Piercing in Corporate Groups' (2011) 26 *Australian Journal of Corporate Law* 39

Hennart, J.-F., 'Theories of the Multinational Enterprise', in A. M. Rugman (ed.), *The Oxford Handbook of International Business* (2nd edn., Oxford, Oxford University Press, 2009), ch. 5

Hensler, D. and M. Peterson, 'Understanding Mass Personal Injury Litigation: A Socio-legal Analysis' (1993) 59 *Brooklyn Law Review* 961

Hill, C. W. L., 'Oliver Williamson and the M-Form Firm: A Critical Review' (1985) 19 *Journal of Economic Issues* 731

Hill, J., 'Changes in the Role of the Shareholder', in R. Grantham and C. Rickett (eds.), *Corporate Personality in the 20th Century* (Oxford, Hart Publishing Ltd, 1998), ch. 10

Hill, J., 'Corporate Groups, Creditor Protection and Cross Guarantees: Australian Perspectives' (1995) 24 *Canadian Business Law Journal* 321

HMRC, 'Tackling Tax Evasion: Government Guidance for the Corporate Offence of Failure to Prevent the Criminal Facilitation of Tax Evasion' (Draft Guidance, October 2016)

HMRC, 'Tackling Tax Evasion: Legislation and Guidance for a Corporate Offence of Failure to Prevent the Criminal Facilitation of Tax Evasion' (July 2016)

HMRC, 'Tax Administration: Large Businesses Transparency Strategy' (2015)

Hopt, K. J., 'Groups of Companies: A Comparative Study on the Economics, Law and Regulation of Corporate Groups' (ECGI Law Working Paper 286/2015)

House of Commons Library, 'Pre-pack Administrations' (CBP5035, January 2016)

Howard, S. E., 'Stockholders' Liability under the New York Act of March 22, 1811' (1938) 46 *Journal of Political Economy* 499

Hughes, P., 'Competition Law Enforcement and Corporate Group Liability – Adjusting the Veil' (2014) 35 *European Competition Law Review* 68

Hutchinson, A. C., 'Out of the Black Hole: Toward a Fresh Approach to Tort Causation' (2016) 39 *Dalhousie Law Journal* 651

Inkpen, A. C., 'Strategic Alliances', in A. M. Rugman (ed.), *The Oxford Handbook of International Business* (2nd edn., Oxford, Oxford University Press, 2009), ch. 15

International Organisation of Securities Commissions, 'The Role of Credit Rating Agencies in Structured Finance Markets: Final Report' (May, 2008)

Issacharoff, S. and D. T. Rave, 'The BP Oil Spill Settlement and the Paradox of Public Litigation' (2014) 74 *Louisiana Law Review* 397

Jackson QC, D. S., 'Report of the Special Commission of Inquiry into the Medical Research and Compensation Fund' (Sydney, NSW, 2004)

Jacobsen, T. and A. Wertheimer, 'Future Industry Trends', in T. M. Jacobsen and A. I. Wertheimer (eds.), *Modern Pharmaceutical Industry: A Primer* (2010), ch. 17

Jaeger, K., 'Generic Drugs', in T. M. Jacobsen and A. I. Wertheimer (eds.), *Modern Pharmaceutical Industry: A Primer* (Sudbury, MA, Jones and Bartlett Publishers, 2010), ch. 15

James Jr, F., 'Products Liability' (1955) 34 *Texas Law Review* 192

James Jr, F., 'Social Insurance and Tort law: The Problem of Alternative Remedies' (1952) 27 *New York University Law Review* 537

Jennejohn, M., 'The Private Order of Innovation Networks' (2016) 68 *Stanford Law Review* 281

Jones, G., 'Multinationals from the 1930s to the 1980s', in A. D. Chandler and B. Mazlish (eds.), *Leviathans: Multinational Corporations and the New Global History* (Cambridge, Cambridge University Press, 2005), ch. 3

Joskow, P., 'Vertical Integration', in C. Menard and M. Shirley (eds.), *Handbook of New Institutional Economics* (2005), ch. 13

Kaisanlahti, T., 'Extended Liability of Shareholders?' (2006) 6 *Journal of Corporate Law Studies* 139

Katyal, N. K., 'Conspiracy Theory' (2003) 112 *Yale Law Journal* 1307

Keating, G. C., 'The Idea of Fairness in the Law of Enterprise Liability' (1997) 95 *Michigan Law Review* 1266

Keating, G. C., 'Is the Role of Tort to Repair Wrongful Losses?', in D. Nolan and A. Robertson (eds.), *Rights and Private Law* (Oxford, Hart Publishing Ltd, 2012), ch. 13

Keating, G. C., 'The Theory of Enterprise Liability and Common Law Strict Liability' (2001) 54 *Vanderbilt Law Review* 1285

Keay, A., 'Wrongful Trading and the Liability of Company Directors: A Theoretical Perspective' (2005) 25 *Legal Studies* 431

Keay, A. R., 'Wrongful Trading: Problems and Proposals' [2014] *Northern Ireland Law Quarterly* 63

Keay, A. R. and M. Murray, 'Making Company Directors Liable: A Comparative Analysis of Wrongful Trading in the United Kingdom and Insolvent Trading in Australia' (2005) 14 *International Insolvency Review* 27

Kettering, K. C., 'The Uniform Voidable Transactions Act; or, the 2014 Amendments to the Uniform Fraudulent Transfer Act' (2015) 70 *Business Lawyer* 777

Khimji, M. F. and C. C. Nicholls, 'Piercing the Corporate Veil in the Canadian Common Law Courts – An Empirical Study' (2015) 41 *Queen's Law Journal* 207

Khimji, M. F. and C. C. Nicholls, 'Piercing the Corporate Veil Reframed as Evasion and Concealment' (2015) 48 *University of British Columbia Law Review* 401

Kiel, G. C., K. Hendry, and G. J. Nicholson, 'Corporate Governance Options for the Local Subsidiaries of Multinational Enterprises' (2006) 14 *Corporate Governance* 568

Kiern, L. I., 'Liability, Compensation, and Financial Responsibility under the Oil Pollution Act of 1990: A Review of the Second Decade' (2011) 36 *Tulane Maritime Law Journal* 1

Kim, I., 'Financial Responsibility Rules under the Oil Pollution Act of 1990' (2002) 42 *Natural Resources Law Journal* 565

Klass, A. B., 'CERCLA, State Law, and Federalism in the 21st Century' (2012) 41 *Southwestern Law Review* 679

Koenig, T. H. and M. L. Rusted, 'Reconceptualizing the BP Oil Spill as Parens Patriae Products Liability' (2012) 49 *Houston Law Review* 291

Kornhauser, L. A., 'An Economic Analysis of the Choice between Enterprise and Personal Liability for Accidents' (1982) 70 *California Law Review* 1345

Kors, M. E., 'Altered Egos: Deciphering Substantive Consolidation' (1998) 59 *University of Pittsburgh Law Review* 381

Kraakman, R., 'Corporate Liability Strategies and the Costs of Legal Controls' (1984) 93 *Yale Law Journal* 857

Lamoreaux, N. R., D. M. G. Raff, and P. Temin, 'Economic Theory and Business History', in G. Jones and J. Zeitlin (eds.), *The Oxford Handbook of Business History* (Oxford, Oxford University Press, 2007), ch. 3

La Rocca, L., 'The Controversial Issue of the Parent Company Liability for the Violation of EC Competition Rules by the Subsidiary' (2011) 32 *European Competition Law Review* 68

Lawrence, P. R. and J. W. Lorsch, 'High-Performing Organizations in Three Environments' in D. S. Pugh (ed.), *Organization Theory: Selected Classic Readings* (5th edn., London, Penguin Books Ltd, 2007), ch. 7

Lazonick, W., 'Business History and Economic Development', in G. Jones and J. Zeitlin (eds.), *The Oxford Handbook of Business History* (Oxford, Oxford University Press, 2007), ch. 4

Leach, T. J., 'Civil Conspiracy: What's the Use?' (1999) 54 *University of Miami Law Review* 1

Lee, P. W., 'Accessory Liability in Tort and Equity' (2015) 27 *Singapore Academy of Law Journal* 853

Lee, P. W., 'Civil Conspiracy in the Corporate Context' (2016) 23 *Torts Law Journal* 257

Lee, P. W., 'The Enigma of Veil-Piercing' (2015) 26 *International Company and Commercial Law Review* 28

Leebron, D., 'Limited Liability, Tort Victims, and Creditors' (1991) 91 *Columbia Law Review* 1565

Lenckus, D., 'Asbestos Still No 1 among Mass Tort Risks' (2007) 41 *Business Insurance* 11

Levin, J., 'Functionalism', in *Stanford Encyclopedia of Philosophy* (Stanford, CA, Stanford University, 2004)

Lewis, R., 'Economic Torts: Where Are We Now?' [2008] *Business Law Review* 216

Lexchin, J., et al., 'Pharmaceutical Industry Sponsorship and Research Outcome Quality: Systematic Review' (2003) 326 *British Medical Journal* 1167

Light, A. R., 'The *Deepwater Horizon* Oil Spill Trust and the Gulf Coast Claims Facility: The "Superfund" Myth and the Law of Unintended Consequences' (2011) 5 *Golden Gate University Environmental Law Journal* 87

Lipton, P., 'The Mythology of *Salomon*'s Case and the Law Dealing with the Tort Liabilities of Corporate Groups: An Historical Perspective' (2014) 40 *Monash University Law Review* 452

Listokin, Y. and K. Ayotte, 'Protecting Future Claimants in Mass Tort Bankruptcies' (2004) 98 *Northwestern University Law Review* 1435

Liu, C., 'Leaving the FDA Behind: Pharmaceutical Outsourcing and Drug Safety' (2012) 48 *Texas International Law Journal* 1

Lo, S. H. C., 'Liability of Directors as Joint Tortfeasors' [2009] *Journal of Business Law* 109

Lo, S. H. C., 'A Parent Company's Tort Liability to Employees of a Subsidiary' (2014) 1 *Journal of International and Comparative Law* 117

LoPucki, L. M., 'The Death of Liability' (1996) 106 *Yale Law Journal* 1

LoPucki, L. M., 'The Essential Structure of Judgment Proofing' (1998) 51 *Stanford Law Review* 147

Lyle, M., 'Mass Tort Claims and the Corporate Tortfeasor: Bankruptcy Reorganization and Legislative Compensation versus the Common-Law Tort System' (1983) 61 *Texas Law Review* 1297

Macey, J. and J. Mitts, 'Finding Order in the Morass: The Three Real Justifications for Piercing the Corporate Veil' (2014) 100 *Cornell Law Review* 99

Macrae, C., 'Regulating Resilience? Regulatory Work in High-Risk Arenas', in B. Hutter (ed.), *Anticipating Risks and Organising Risk Regulation* (Cambridge, Cambridge University Press, 2010), ch. 7

Mangano, R., 'The Role of Fraudulent Transfer Rules in Corporate Insolvency' (2008) 5 *European Company and Financial Law Review* 193

Markowitz, H. M., 'Portfolio Selection' (1952) 7 *Journal of Finance* 77

Matheson, J. H., 'The Modern Law of Corporate Groups: An Empirical Study of Piercing the Corporate Veil in the Parent-Subsidiary Context' (2009) 87 *North Carolina Law Review* 1091

Matheson, J. H., 'Successor Liability' (2011) 96 *Minnesota Law Review* 371

Mattock, B., A. Sackett, and J. Shipp, 'Clearing Up the False Premises Underlying the Push for Asbestos Trust "Transparency"' (2014) 23 *Widener Law Journal* 725

Mazars, 'Transparency Directive Assessment Report' (2009)

McBride, N. J., 'Tort Law and Human Flourishing', in S. G. A. Pitel, J. W. Neyers, and E. Chamberlain (eds.), *Tort Law: Challenging Orthodoxy* (Oxford, Hart Publishing Ltd, 2013), ch. 2

McDonell, C., 'The Gulf Coast Claims Facility and the *Deepwater Horizon* Litigation: Judicial Regulation of Private Compensation Schemes' (2012) 64 *Stanford Law Review* 765

McDonnell, P., 'Drug Safety and Pharmacovigilance', in T. M. Jacobsen and A. I. Wertheimer (eds.), *Modern Pharmaceutical Industry: A Primer* (Sudbury, MA, Jones and Bartlett Publishers, 2010), ch. 9

McGaughey, E., '*Donoghue* v *Salomon* in the High Court' (2011) 4 *Journal of Personal Injury Law* 249

McKenna, A., 'An Overview of the Legal Landscape of Negligently-Inflicted Asbestos Related Conditions' [2011] *Journal of Personal Injury Law* 205

McNamee, S., 'The Regulatory and Liability Implications of Nanoscale Drug Delivery in the Human Body' (2014) 11 *Nanotechnology Law & Business* 48

Menell, N. G., 'The *Copperweld* Question: Drawing the Line between the Corporate Family and Cartel' (2016) 101 *Cornell Law Review* 467

Merkin, R. and J. Steele, 'Historic Asbestos Exposure and Liability Insurance: Issues of Aggregation and Reinsurance', in J. Steele and W. H. van Boom (eds.), *Mass Justice: Challenges of Representation and Distribution* (Cheltenham, UK, Edward Elgar, 2011), ch. 10

Meyer, J. W., G. S. Drori, and H. Hwang, 'World Society and the Proliferation of Formal Organization', in G. S. Drori, J. W. Meyer, and H. Hwang (eds.), *Globalization and Organization: World Society and Organizational Change* (Oxford, Oxford University Press, 2006), ch. 1

Miles, R. E. and C. C. Snow, 'Organizations: New Concepts for New Forms', in P. J. Buckley and J. Michie (eds.), *Firms, Organizations and Contracts: A Reader in Industrial Organization* (Oxford, Oxford University Press, 1996), ch. 16

Miller, C., J. 'Causation in Personal Injury after (and before) *Sienkiewicz*' (2012) 32 *Legal Studies* 396

Millon, D., 'Piercing the Corporate Veil, Financial Responsibility, and the Limits of Limited Liability' (2007) 56 *Emory Law Journal* 1304

Milman, D., 'Promoting Distributional Justice on Corporate Insolvency in the 21st Century', in J. Steele and W. H. van Boom (eds.), *Mass Justice: Challenges of Representation and Distribution* (Cheltenham, UK, Edward Elgar, 2011), ch. 8

Mitchell, C., 'Lifting the Corporate Veil in the English Courts: An Empirical Study' (1999) 3 *Company Financial and Insolvency Law Review* 22

Mobley, S., D. Mourkas, and G. Murray, 'Parent Liability for Joint Venture Parents' (2014) 35 *European Competition Law Review* 499

Mohrbutter, J., '*Harrington v Dow Corning Corp* and Social Utility: Unfit for Their Purpose within Product Liability Negligence Law' (2012) 75 *Saskatchewan Law Review* 269

Mokal, R. J., 'What Liquidation Does for Secured Creditors, and What it Does for You' (2008) 71 *Modern Law Review* 699

Monihan, R., et al., 'Selling Sickness: The Pharmaceutical Industry and Disease Mongering' (2002) 324 *British Medical Journal* 886

Morgan, G., 'Imaginization: On Spider Plants', in D. S. Pugh (ed.), *Organization Theory: Selected Classic Readings* (5th edn., London, Penguin Books Ltd, 2007), ch. 25

Morgan, J., 'Causation, Politics, and Law: The English – and Scottish – Asbestos Saga', in R. Goldberg (ed.), *Perspectives on Causation* (Oxford, Hart Publishing Ltd, 2011), ch. 4

Morgan, J., 'Vicarious Liability for Independent Contractors?' [2015] *Professional Negligence* 235

Morgan, J. D., 'The Oil Pollution Act of 1990: A Look at its Impact on the Oil Industry' (1994) 6 *Fordham International Law Journal* 1

Morgan, P., 'Vicarious Liability for Group Companies: The Final Frontier of Vicarious Liability?' (2015) 31 *Professional Negligence* 276

Morgan, P., 'Vicarious Liability on the Move' (2013) 129 *Law Quarterly Review* 139

Muchlinski, P., 'Limited Liability and Multinational Enterprises: A Case for Reform?' (2010) 34 *Cambridge Journal of Economics* 915

Nagareda, R. A., 'Mass Resolution of Mass Torts: Emerging Issues in the United States and the Global Future', in J. Steele and W. H. van Boom (eds.), *Mass Justice: Challenges of Representation and Distribution* (Cheltenham, UK, Edward Elgar, 2011), ch. 2

National Academy of Engineering and National Research Council, 'Macondo Well *Deepwater Horizon* Blowout: Lessons for Improving Offshore Drilling Safety' (Washington, DC: The National Academies Press, 2012)

Nelson, J. S., 'The Intracorporate Conspiracy Trap' (2015) 36 *Cardozo Law Review* 969

Neyers, J. W., 'Canadian Corporate Law, Veil-Piercing, and the Private Law Model Corporation' (2000) 50 *University of Toronto Law Journal* 173

Neyers, J. W., 'Explaining the Inexplicable? Four Manifestations of Abuse of Rights in English Law', in D. Nolan and A. Robertson (eds.), *Rights and Private Law* (Oxford, Hart Publishing Ltd, 2012), ch. 11

Nolan, A., 'The Position of Unsecured Creditors of Corporate Groups: Towards a Group Responsibility Solution which Gives Fairness and Equity a Role' (1993) 11 *Company & Securities Law Journal* 461

Nygh, P., 'The Liability of Multi-national Corporations for the Torts of Their Subsidiaries' (2002) 3 *European Business Organization Law Review* 51

OECD, 'Articles of the Model Convention with Respect to Taxes on Income and Capital' (2003)

OECD, 'Transfer Pricing Documentation and Country-by-Country Reporting, Action 13 – 2015 Final Report' (2015)

OECD, 'Transfer Pricing Guidelines for Multinational Enterprises and Tax Administrations' (2010)

Oh, P. B., 'Veil-Piercing' (2010) 89 *Texas Law Review* 81

Oh, P. B., 'Veil Piercing Unbound' (2013) 93 *Boston University Law Review* 89

Osofsky, H. M., 'Multidimensional Governance and the BP *Deepwater Horizon* Oil Spill' (2011) 63 *Florida Law Review* 1077

O'Sullivan, J., 'The Sins of the Father – Vicarious Liability Extended' (2012) 71 *Cambridge Law Journal* 485

Owen, D. G., 'The Evolution of Products Liability Law' (2007) 26 *Review of Litigation* 955

Owen, D. G., 'Special Defenses in Modern Products Liability Law' (2005) 70 *Missouri Law Review* 1

Painter, C. M. E., 'Tort Creditor Priority in the Secured Credit System: Asbestos Times, the Worst of Times' (1984) 36 *Stanford Law Review* 1045

Palmer, D. A., P. D. Jennings, and X. Zhou, 'Late Adoption of the Multidivisional Form by Larger US Corporations: Institutional, Political, and Economic Accounts' (1993) 38 *Administrative Science Quarterly* 100

Panel of Eminent Persons, 'Review of the Law of Negligence: Final Report' (Canberra, ACT, Commonwealth of Australia, 2002)

Patterson, M. K., 'Is Unlimited Liability Really Attainable? Of Long Arms and Short Sales' (1995) 56 *Ohio State Law Journal* 815

Paz-Varga, R., 'International Transfer Pricing and Subsidiary Performance: The Role of Organizational Justice' (2009) 51 *Thunderbird International Business Review* 219

Perry, S. R., 'The Moral Foundations of Tort Law' (1992) 77 *Iowa Law Review* 449

Perry, S. R., 'Responsibility for Outcomes, Risk, and the Law of Torts', in D. G. Owen (ed.), *Philosophy and the Law of Torts* (Oxford, Oxford University Press, 2001), ch. 11

Petrin, M., 'Assumption of Responsibility in Corporate Groups: *Chandler v Cape plc*' (2013) 76 *Modern Law Review* 603

Pettet, B., 'Limited Liability – A Principle for the 21st Century?' (1995) 48 *Current Legal Problems* 125

Pfeffer, J. and P. Nowak, 'Joint Ventures and Interorganizational Interdependence', in P. J. Buckley and J. Michie, *Firms, Organizations and Contracts: A Reader in Industrial Organization* (Oxford, Oxford University Press, 1996), ch. 14

Pfeffer, J. and G. R. Salancik, 'The Design and Management of Externally Controlled Organizations', in D. S. Pugh (ed.), *Organization Theory: Selected Classic Readings* (5th edn., London, Penguin Books Ltd, 2007), ch. 8

Phua, S., 'Convergence in Global Tax Compliance' [2015] *Singapore Journal of Legal Studies* 77

Pickering, M. A., 'The Company as a Separate Legal Entity' (1968) 31 *Modern Law Review* 481

Pollard, D., 'Who Is "Connected" or "Associated" within the Meaning of the Insolvency Act 1986' (2009) 22 *Insolvency Intelligence* 33

Pollock, Hon S. G., 'Introductory Remark' (1999) 30 *Seton Hall Law Review* 202

Prentice, D. D., 'Some Aspects of the Law Relating to Corporate Groups in the United Kingdom' (1999) 13 *Connecticut Journal of International Law* 305

Presser, S. B., 'The Bogalusa Explosion: "Single Business Enterprise", "Alter Ego", and Other Errors: Academics, Economics, Democracy, and Shareholder Limited Liability: Back towards a Unitary "Abuse" Theory of Piercing the Corporate Veil' (2006) 100 *Northwestern University Law Review* 405

Presser, S. B., 'Thwarting the Killing of the Corporation: Limited Liability, Democracy, and Economics' (1992) 87 *Northwestern University Law Review* 148

Priest, G. L., 'The Invention of Enterprise Liability: A Critical History of the Intellectual Foundations of Modern Tort Law' (1985) 14 *Journal of Legal Studies* 461

Priest, G. L., 'Strict Products Liability: The Original Intent' (1989) 10 *Cardozo Law Review* 2301

Pugh, D. S., 'Does Context Determine Form?', in D. S. Pugh (ed.), *Organization Theory: Selected Classic Readings* (5th edn., London, Penguin Books Ltd, 2007), ch. 2

Qu, C. Z., 'Recent German Developments in Company Controllers' Liability in Rescue Situations: A Comparative Evaluation' [2011] *Journal of Business Law* 330

R3, 'Pre-packaged Sales ("Pre-packs"): A Survey of R3 Members' (May 2009)

Rahman, S. Z., et al, 'Lifestyle Drugs: Concept and Impact on Society' (2010) *Indian Journal of Pharmaceutical Sciences* 409

Ramsay, I. M., 'Allocating Liability in Corporate Groups: An Australian Perspective' (1999) 13 *Connecticut Journal of International Law* 329

Ramsay, I. M., 'Holding Company Liability for the Debts of an Insolvent Subsidiary: A Law and Economics Perspective' (1994) 17 *University of New South Wales Law Journal* 520

Ramsay, I. M. and D. B. Noakes, 'Piercing the Corporate Veil in Australia' (2001) 19 *Company and Securities Law Journal* 250

Ramsay, I. M. and G. P. Stapledon, 'Corporate Groups in Australia' (2001) 19 *Company & Securities Law Journal* 7

Ray, J., 'Offshore Safety and Environmental Regimes: A Post-Macondo Comparative Analysis of the United States and the United Kingdom' (2014) 33 *Mississippi College Law Review* 11

Reimann, M., 'Product Liability in a Global Context: The Hollow Victory of the European Model' (2003) 7 *European Review of Private Law* 128

Reinschmidt, B., 'The Law of Tort: A Useful Tool to Further Corporate Social Responsibility?' (2013) 34 *Company Law* 103

Reynisson, K., 'Related Party Transactions: Analysis of Proposed Article 9c of Shareholders' Rights Directive' (2016) 13 *European Company Law* 175

Ribstein, L. E., 'Limited Liability and Theories of the Corporation' (1991) 50 *Maryland Law Review* 80

Richardson, G. B., 'The Organization of Industry', in P. J. Buckley and J. Michie (eds.), *Firms Organizations and Contracts: A Reader in Industrial Organization* (Oxford, Oxford University Press, 1996), ch. 3

Riley, C., 'Shareholder Liability for Company Torts: Should it Be Vicarious or Fault Based?' (paper presented at SLS Conference, Oxford, 7 September 2016)

Ripstein, A. and B. C. Zipursky, 'Corrective Justice in an Age of Mass Torts', in G. J. Postema (ed.), *Philosophy and the Law of Torts* (Cambridge, Cambridge University Press, 2001), ch. 6

Roach, B., 'A Primer on Multinational Corporations', in A. D. Chandler and B. Mazlish (eds.), *Leviathans: Multinational Corporations and the New Global History* (Cambridge, Cambridge University Press, 2005), ch. 1

Robertson, A., 'Constraints on Policy-Based Reasoning in Private Law', in A. Robertson and H. W. Tang (eds.), *The Goals of Private Law* (Oxford, Hart Publishing Ltd, 2009), ch. 11

Roe, M., 'Corporate Strategic Reaction to Mass Tort' (1986) 72 *Virginia Law Review* 1

Rosenberg, D., 'The Dusting of America: A Story of Asbestos – Carnage, Cover-Up, and Litigation' (1986) 99 *Harvard Law Review* 1693

Ruhl, J. B., 'Managing Systemic Risk in Legal Systems' (2014) 89 *Indiana Law Journal* 559

Rugman, A. M., A. Verbeke, and Q. T. K. Nguyen, 'Fifty Years of International Business Theory and Beyond' (2011) 51 *Management International Review* 755

Sanchez Brigido, R., 'Collective Intentional Activities and the Law' (2009) 29 *Oxford Journal of Legal Studies* 305

Sanders, J., 'Risky Business: Causation in Asbestos Cancer Cases (and Beyond?)', in R. Goldberg (ed.), *Perspectives on Causation* (Oxford, Hart Publishing Ltd, 2011), ch. 2

Santella, P., E. Baffi, C. Drago, and D. Lattuca, 'Legal Obstacles to Institutional Investor Activism in the EU and US' [2012] *European Business Law Review* 257

Schipani, C. A., 'The Changing Face of Parent and Subsidiary Corporations: Enterprise Theory and Federal Regulation' (2005) 37 *Connecticut Law Review* 691

Schwarcz, S., 'The Inherent Irrationality of Judgment Proofing' (1999) 52 *Stanford Law Review* 1

Schwartz, T. M., 'The Impact of the New Products Liability Restatement on Prescription Products' (1995) 50 *Food & Drug Law Journal* 399

Seward III, A. C., 'After Bhopal: Implications for Parent Company Liability' (1987) 21 *International Lawyer* 695

Sharkey, C. M., 'The BP Oil Spill Settlements, Classwide Punitive Damages, and Societal Deterrence' (2015) 64 *DePaul Law Review* 681

Sheiner, N., 'DES and a Proposed Theory of Enterprise Liability' (1978) 46 *Fordham Law Review* 963

Sherman, E. F., 'The Evolution of Asbestos Litigation' (2014) 88 *Tulane Law Review* 1021

Shetterly, D., 'Starving the Terrorists of Funding: How the United States Treasury Is Fighting the War on Terrorism' (2006) 18 *Regent Law Review* 327

Siegel, J. M., 'Reconciling Shareholder Limited Liability with Vicarious Copyright Liability: Holding Parent Corporations Liable for the Copyright Infringements of Subsidiaries' (2007) 41 *University of Richmond Law Review* 535

Silecchia, L. A., 'Pinning the Blame & Piercing the Veil in the Mists of Metaphor: The Supreme Court's New Standards for the CERCLA Liability of Parent Companies and a Proposal for Legislative Reform' (1998) 67 *Fordham Law Review* 115

Simester, A., 'The Mental Element in Complicity' (2006) 122 *Law Quarterly Review* 578

Skeel, D. A. and G. Krause-Vilmar, 'Recharacterization and the Nonhindrance of Creditors' (2006) 7 *European Business Organization Law Review* 259

Skinner, G., 'Rethinking Limited Liability of Parent Corporations for Foreign Subsidiaries' Violations of International Human Rights' (2015) 72 *Washington & Lee Law Review* 1769

Slavny, A., 'Nonreciprocity and the Moral Basis of Liability to Compensate' (2014) 34 *Oxford Journal of Legal Studies* 1

Smith, S. A., 'The Normativity of Private Law' (2011) 31 *Oxford Journal of Legal Studies* 1

Smith, Y. B., 'Frolic and Detour' (1923) 23 *Columbia Law Review* 444

Spender, P., 'Blue Asbestos and Golden Eggs: Evaluating Bankruptcy and Class Actions as Just Responses to Mass Tort Liability' (2003) 25 *Sydney Law Review* 223

Squire, R., 'Strategic Liability in the Corporate Group' (2011) 78 *University of Chicago Law Review* 605

Stacy, T., 'The "Material Support" Offense: The Use of Strict Liability in the War against Terror' (2005) 14 *Kansas Journal of Law and Public Policy* 461

Stapleton, J., '"Cause-in-Fact" and the Scope of Liability for Consequences' (2003) 119 *Law Quarterly Review* 388

Stapleton, J., 'Factual Causation' (2010) 38 *Federal Law Review* 467

Stapleton, J., 'Lords A'Leaping Evidentiary Gaps' (2002) 10 *Torts Law Journal* 276

Stapleton, J., 'Products Liability in the United Kingdom: The Myths of Reform' (1999) 34 *Texas International Law Journal* 45

Stapleton, J., 'Restatement (Third) of Torts: Products Liability, an Anglo-Australian Perspective' (2000) 39 *Washburn Law Journal* 363

Stapleton, J., 'Two Causal Fictions at the Heart of US Asbestos Doctrine' (2006) 122 *Law Quarterly Review* 189

Stephens, K., 'Regulatory Affairs', in T. M. Jacobsen and A. I. Wertheimer (eds.), *Modern Pharmaceutical Industry: A Primer* (Sudbury, MA, Jones and Bartlett Publishers, 2010), ch. 7

Stone, C., 'The Place of Enterprise Liability in the Control of Corporate Conduct' (1980) 90 *Yale Law Journal* 1

Strasser, K. A., 'Piercing the Veil in Corporate Groups' (2005) 37 *Connecticut Law Review* 637

Stuby, D. E., 'Status and Trends in State Product Liability Law: State of the Art Evidence' (1987) 14 *Journal of Legislation* 261

Tallman, S. B. and G. S. Yip, 'Strategy and the Multinational Enterprise', in A. M. Rugman (ed.), *The Oxford Handbook of International Business* (2nd edn., Oxford, Oxford University Press, 2009), ch. 12

Tan, C-H., 'Piercing the Separate Personality of the Company: A Matter of Policy?' [1999] *Singapore Journal of Legal Studies* 531

Tan, C-H., 'Veil-Piercing – a Fresh Start' [2015] *Journal of Business Law* 20

Tan, D., 'Internalising Externalities: An Enterprise Risk Approach to Vicarious Liability in the 21st Century' (2015) 27 *Singapore Academy of Law Journal* 822

Tan, D., 'The Salient Features of Proximity: Examining the *Spandeck* Formulation for Establishing a Duty of Care' [2010] *Singapore Journal of Legal Studies* 459

Teff, H., 'Products Liability in the Pharmaceutical Industry at Common Law' (1974) 20 *McGill Law Journal* 102

Teubner, G., 'Unitas Multiplex: Corporate Governance in Group Enterprises', in D. Sugarman and G. Teubner (eds.), *Regulating Corporate Groups in Europe* (Baden Baden, Nomos, 1990), ch. 5

Tham, C. H., 'Piercing the Corporate Veil: Searching for Appropriate Choice of Law Rules' [2007] *Lloyd's Maritime and Commercial Law Quarterly* 22

Thomas, C. D., 'Tomorrow's News Today: The Future of Superfund Litigation' (2014) 46 *Arizona State Law Journal* 537

Thomas, W. J., 'The Vioxx Story: Would it Have Ended Differently in the European Union?' (2006) 32 *American Journal of Law and Medicine* 365

Thompson, R. B., 'Piercing the Corporate Veil: An Empirical Study' (1991) 76 *Cornell Law Review* 1036

Thompson, R. B., 'Piercing the Veil within Corporate Groups: Corporate Shareholders as Mere Investors' (1999) 13 *Connecticut Journal of International Law* 379

TNS BMRB, 'Exploring Large Business Tax Strategy Behaviour' (2015)

Townsend, J., 'Schemes of Arrangement and Asbestos Litigation: *In re Cape plc*' (2007) 70 *Modern Law Review* 837

Treadaway, L., 'Big Pharma's Heart of Darkness: The Alien Tort Statute and Preventing Clinical Trial Colonialism' (2012) 43 *Georgetown International Law Journal* 1419

Tsoukas, H. and R. Chia, 'On Organizational Becoming: Rethinking Organizational Change' (2002) 13 *Organization Science* 567

Tully, J., 'Plumbing the Depths of Corporate Litigation: Reforming the Deepening Insolvency Theory' [2013] *University of Illinois Law Review* 2087

Turner, P. J., 'Revisiting the Direct Liability of Parent Companies Following *Chandler v Cape Plc*' (2015) 33 *Company & Securities Law Journal* 45

Tweedale, G. and L. Flynn, 'Piercing the Corporate Veil: Cape Industries and Multinational Corporate Liability for a Toxic Hazard, 1950-2004' (2007) 8 *Enterprise and Society* 268

Ulbeck, V. and A. Ehlers, 'Tort Law, Corporate Groups and Supply Chain Liability for Workers' Injuries: The Concept of Vicarious Liability' (2016) 13 *European Company Law* 167

UNCITRAL, 'Legislative Guide on Insolvency Law' (United Nations, 2005)

UNCITRAL, 'Legislative Guide on Insolvency, Part Three: Treatment of Enterprise Groups in Insolvency' (United Nations, 2012)

US Coast Guard, 'Oil Pollution Act of 1990 (OPA)' (2016)

US Coast Guard, 'Oil Pollution Act Liability Limits in 2015: Report to Congress' (October 2015)

US Coast Guard, 'Oil Spill Liability Trust Fund (OSLTF) Funding for Oil Spills' (January 2006)

US Government Accountability Office, 'Asbestos Injury Compensation: The Role and Administration of Asbestos Trusts' (2011)

US Government Accountability Office, 'New Drug Approval' (2009)

US Government Accountability Office, 'Superfund: Funding and Reported Costs of Enforcement and Administration Activities' (July 2008)

US Senate, 'Permanent Subcommittee on Investigations, Offshore Profit Shifting and the US Tax Code – Part 2 (Apple Inc)' (21 May 2013)

Vairo, G., 'Mass Torts Bankruptcies: The Who, the Why and the How' (2004) 78 *American Bankruptcy Law Journal* 93

Vandevelde, K., 'A History of Prima Facie Tort: The Origins of a General Theory of Intentional Tort' (1990) 19 *Hofstra Law Review* 447

Vanneste, K., 'Decoupling Economic Rights from Voting Rights: A Threat to the Traditional Corporate Governance Paradigm' (2014) 15 *European Business Organization Law Review* 59

Varuhas, J., 'The Concept of "Vindication" in the Law of Torts: Rights, Interests, and Damages' (2014) 34 *Oxford Journal of Legal Studies* 253

de Villiers, M., 'Foreseeability Decoded' (2015) 16 *Minnesota Journal of Law, Science & Technology* 343

Viscusi, W. K., 'Pricing Lives for Corporate Risk Decisions' (2015) 68 *Vanderbilt Law Review* 1117

Viscusi, W. K. and R. J. Zeckhauser, 'Deterring and Compensating Oil-Spill Catastrophes: The Need for Strict Two-Tier Liability' (2011) 64 *Vanderbilt Law Review* 1717

Waddams, S. M., 'The Canadian Law of Products Liability' (1999) 34 *Texas International Law Journal* 119

Warren, R. C., 'The Enforcement of Social Accountability – Turner and Newall and the Asbestos Crisis' (1997) 5 *Corporate Governance* 52

Weick, K. E., 'Enacted Sensemaking in Crisis Situations', in D.S. Pugh (ed.), *Organization Theory: Selected Classic Readings* (5th edn., London, Penguin Books Ltd, 2007), ch. 20

Weigand, J. M., 'Vioxx: How Strong Is the Case against Merck?' (2007) 11 *Michigan State University Journal of Medicine and Law* 145

Weingarten, M. P., 'Asbestos Litigation from an American Perspective' [2009] *Journal of Personal Injury Law* 253

Westney, D. E. and S. Zaheer, 'The Multinational Enterprise as an Organization', in A.M. Rugman (ed.), *The Oxford Handbook of International Business* (2nd edn., Oxford, Oxford University Press, 2009), ch. 13

Whincop, M., 'Overcoming Corporate Law: Instrumentalism, Pragmatism and the Separate Legal Entity Concept' (1997) 15 *Company & Securities Law Journal* 411

White, J. J., 'Corporate Judgment Proofing: A Response to Lynn LoPucki's The Death of Liability' (1998) 107 *Yale Law Journal* 1363

White, M. J., 'Asbestos and the Future of Mass Torts' (2004) 18 *Journal of Economic Perspectives* 183

Widen, W. H., 'Corporate Form and Substantive Consolidation' (2007) 75 *George Washington Law Review* 237

Williams, R., 'What Can We Expect to Gain from Reforming the Insolvent Trading Remedy?' (2015) 78 *Modern Law Review* 55

Williamson, O. E., 'The Modern Corporation: Origins, Evolution, Attributes' (1981) 19 *Journal of Economic Literature* 1537

Williamson, O. E., 'Transaction Cost Economics and Business Administration' (2005) 21 *Scandinavian Journal of Management* 19

Williamson, O. E., 'Transaction-Cost Economics: The Governance of Contractual Relations', in P. J. Buckley and J. Michie (eds.), *Firms Organizations and Contracts: A Reader in Industrial Organization* (Oxford, Oxford University Press, 1996), ch. 6

Winfield, P., 'The Foundation of Liability in Tort' (1927) 27 *Columbia Law Review* 1

Winkelmolen, R. and W. C. Buss, 'Developments of Strategic Parenting Models in Small Holding Companies: A Research Agenda' (2013) 8 *Global Conference on Business and Finance Proceedings* 236

Witting, C., 'Distinguishing between Property Damage and Pure Economic Loss in Negligence: A Personality Thesis' (2001) 21 *Legal Studies* 481

Witting, C., 'Duty of Care: An Analytical Approach' (2005) 25 *Oxford Journal of Legal Studies* 33

Witting, C., 'Liability for Corporate Wrongs' (2009) 28 *University of Queensland Law Journal* 113

Witting, C., 'Non-delegable Duties and Roads Authorities' (2008) 32 *Melbourne University Law Review* 332

Witting, C., 'Of Principle and Prima Facie Tort' (1999) 25 *Monash University Law Review* 295

Witting, C., 'What Are We Doing Here? The Relationship between Negligence in General and Misstatements in English Law', in K. Barker, R. Grantham, and W. Swain (eds.), *The Law of Misstatements: 50 Years on from Hedley Byrne* v. *Heller* (Oxford, Hart Publishing Ltd, 2015), ch. 9

Witting, C. and J. Rankin, 'Tortious Liability of Corporate Groups: From Control to Coordination' (2014) 22 *Tort Law Review* 91

Wolff, L-C., 'Offshore Holdings for Global Investments of Multinational Enterprises: Just Evil?' [2015] *Journal of Business Law* 445

Wyburn, M., 'Pooling as a Response to the Competing Interests in Corporate Group Collapse in Australia' (2010) 19 *International Insolvency Review* 65

Yeung, K., 'Corporate Groups: Legal Aspects of the Management Dilemma' [1997] *Lloyd's Maritime and Commercial Law Quarterly* 208

Zeitlin, J., 'The Historical Alternatives Approach', in G. Jones and J. Zeitlin (eds.), *The Oxford Handbook of Business History* (Oxford, Oxford University Press, 2007), ch. 10

Zipes, G., 'After *Amchem* and *Ahern*: The Rise of Bankruptcy over the Class Action Option for Resolving Mass Torts on a Nationwide Basis, and the Fall of Finality?' [1998] *Detroit College of Law at Michigan State University Law Review* 7

Zipursky, B. C., 'Foreseeability in Breach, Duty, and Proximate Cause' (2009) 44 *Wake Forest Law Review* 1247

INDEX

Abuse of rights, 390
Accessory liability
  overview, 396, 406–7, 412, 417
  common design, based on, 407–9, 417
  control and, 410
  of corporate groups, 409–11
  deterrence and, 409
  direct participation and, 410
  incentive to reduce injuries and, 408–9
  justification of, 408–9
  multiple entity recklessness compared, 411–12
  in UK, 408, 409–10
Advisory board model, 58–59
Agency as ground for veil-piercing, 336–38
Agency costs, 29
A.H. Robins Corp., 134–35
Airbus, 45
Alter ego test, 339–40, 341
Amazon, 56–57
American Law Institute, 246, 253–54
American Medical Association, 107
AMF, 378
Anacor Pharmaceuticals, 41
Anderson, Helen, 219
Antunes, José, 178, 271–72
APMSD, 243
Apple, 41, 55–56
APSA, 243
Arm's-length transactions, judgment-proofing in, 81–82
Asbestos industry
  generally, 6
  in Australia, 114–18, 375
  in Canada, 111, 374–75
  causation and, 371–75
  in China, 103
  control in, 61–62
  duty of care in, 360–62
  employment in, 103
  in EU, 109
  harmful effects of, 104–5, 107–8
  in India, 103, 109
  insurance and, 97–98
  in Ireland, 117
  judgment-proofing in, 112–22, 413
  in Kazakhstan, 103
  in Mexico, 103
  negligence in, 112
  in Netherlands, 116
  production of, 104
  recklessness in, 112
  regulatory arbitrage in, 52–53
  in Russia, 103
  in South Africa, 111, 112–14
  statistics, 103
  in UK, 104, 105–11, 371–75
  in US, 103, 118–21
Asbestos Products Ltd., 364–66
Asbestos Research Council, 111
AstraZeneca, 132
Atlas Asbestos Co., 62
Atlas Maritime Co. SA, 232–33
ATR, 45
Austin, R.P., 73–74
Australia
  asbestos industry in, 114–18, 375
  Australian Securities and Investments Commission, 211–12
  causation in, 375
  Companies and Securities Advisory Committee, 185
  Corporations Act 2001, 211–12, 217–18, 228, 295

Australia (cont.)
duty of care in, 353–54, 358, 364–68
enterprise liability in, 184–85
equitable subordination in, 228
forum non conveniens in, 92–93
group accounts in, 211–12
institutional shareholders in, 292
Jackson Commission of Inquiry, 116–17, 202–3
liability rules in, 15
non-delegable duties in, 406
pooling orders in, 217–19
priorities rule in, 295
regulation of corporate groups in, 10
unlawful means conspiracy in, 351–52
veil-piercing in, 325–27, 335–36, 338
wrongful trading in, 198
Australian Blue Asbestos, 338, 366–68
Avalon Maritime Ltd., 232–33

Bainbridge, Stephen, 343, 344
Baird, D., 226
Ballantine, H.W., 344
Berle, Adolf, 177, 270
Bhopal explosion, 7, 137–39
Biosimilars, 123–25
Blumberg, Phillip, 74, 174–75, 177–81, 183, 184, 270, 339
Braithwaite, J., 164
Breach of duty, negligence and, 369–70
British Petroleum plc, 32, 100, 139–44, 261, 265, 394–95
Business form, 34–36
Business licensing agreements, 44–45
"But for" causation, 371, 379

Calabresi, G., 3
Canada
asbestos industry in, 111, 374–75
causation in, 374–75
duty of care in, 353, 359–60
institutional shareholders in, 292
unlawful means conspiracy in, 351–52
veil-piercing in, 325–26
Cane, Peter, 284, 290
Capacity
shareholder liability based on, 272–74
of subsidiary companies, 68–69
Capasco, 319–22
Cape Asbestos Co. Ltd., 113
Cape Asbestos South Africa Ltd., 113
Cape Blue Mines Ltd., 113
Cape Building Products Ltd., 360–62
Cape Claims Services plc, 213–14
Cape Industries plc, 319–22, 360–62, 380
Cape International and Overseas Ltd., 113–14
Cape plc, 112–14, 213–14
Capitalisation, limited liability and, 72–73
Care, duty of. *See* Duty of care
Carnie, K., 54
Carty, Hazel, 387
Casap, 319
Case studies
overview, 102
asbestos industry (*See* Asbestos industry)
Deepwater Horizon oil spill, 139–44 (*See also Deepwater Horizon* oil spill)
pharmaceutical industry (*See* Pharmaceutical industry)
Causation
asbestos industry and, 371–75
in Australia, 375
"but for" causation, 371, 379
in Canada, 374–75
causation in fact, 370–71
Fairchild principle, 371–74
material contribution to risk test, 374–75
product liability, 238, 249–50
remoteness of injury and, 370–71, 375–76
scope of liability and, 370–71, 375
in UK, 371–74
CERCLA, 254–60. *See also* Comprehensive Environmental Response, Compensation and Liability Act of 1980 (US)

Chandler, Alfred, 23, 24, 26–27, 31, 35, 168
China
  asbestos industry in, 103
  pharmaceutical industry in, 136–37
Choice of law, 93–94
Claims-made insurance, 98–99
Clark Refining, 377
Clark USA, 377
Coase, Ronald, 23, 27, 28
Cole, Marcus, 12, 88, 120
Collective concept of liability, 278–82, 287
Collins, Hugh, 405
Colombo, Massimo, 49–50
Command-and-control regulation, 8–10, 144–45
Common design, accessory liability based on, 407–9, 417
Common law
  generally, 19
  joint and several liability (*See* Joint and several liability)
  regulation of corporate groups in common law countries, 10
  tort law (*See* Tort law)
  veil-piercing (*See* Veil-piercing)
  vicarious liability (*See* Vicarious liability)
Companies Act 2006 (UK)
  generally, 80, 83
  control under, 285
  corporate groups under, 204–5, 208–9, 210–11
  creditor protection under, 190–91
  limited liability under, 71–72
  veil-piercing under, 313
Compensation
  for personal injuries, 12–15
  tort law and, 347–48
Competition law, 53–54
Complicity principle, 166–67
Component parts, product liability, 241
Comprehensive Environmental Response, Compensation and Liability Act of 1980 (US), 254–60
  generally, 98, 235
  overview, 254–55, 265–66, 414
  arranger liability, 257
  corporate groups and, 256–57
  defences, 257–58
  director liability, 256
  financial responsibility requirements, 255
  Hazardous Substances Superfund, 258–59
  joint and several liability, 258
  networks and, 257
  officer liability, 256
  operator liability, 256–57
  owner liability, 256
  potentially responsible persons, 256
  problems with, 259–60
  veil-piercing and, 256, 328
Concealment, veil-piercing and, 316–17, 334
Conflict of laws, 93–94
Conflicts of interest, 136
Conspiracy. *See* Unlawful means conspiracy
Conti-Brown, Peter, 302
Continental Products Corp., 113–14
Contract law, limited liability in, 95–96
Contribution
  in product liability, 238
  vicarious liability and, 398
Contribution orders, 221–25, 414–15
Control
  accessory liability and, 410
  advisory board model, 58–59
  ambiguity in, 285
  in asbestos industry, 61–62
  in corporate groups, 48–51
  decentralisation and, 49–50
  dual reporting model, 59
  enterprise liability and, 181–82
  extended shareholder liability, rejected as basis of liability in, 294
  incentive to reduce injuries, control-based liability and, 285–86
  local board model, 59
  mergers and acquisitions and, 50
  in MNEs, 58–62
  multidivisional form of business (M-Form) and, 49, 50–51
  negligence and, 378–79, 380, 417

Control (cont.)
organisation theory and, 49
separate legal personality and, 67–68
shareholder liability based on, 272–74
in small and medium-sized businesses, 286
tort law, in context of, 284
veil-piercing and, 324–25, 339, 341
vicarious liability and, 417
weak board model, 58
Copyright infringement, 404
Corporate groups
generally, 19
accessory liability of, 409–11
advantages of, 47–48
business form, 34–36
capacity of, 68–69
CERCLA and, 256–57
circular shareholding in, 4
common group identity in, 171
contribution orders, 221–25, 414–15
control in, 48–51 (*See also* Control)
coordination on group projects in, 170
creditor protection and, 204, 233–34
cross guarantees, 209–12
decentralisation in, 49–50
defined, 3–4
diversification and, 31–32
downward decision-making in, 169–70
economic unity in, 170–71
economies of scale and, 25–26
economies of scope and, 26
enterprise liability in, 176–79
equitable subordination, 228–31
evolution of, 36–39
extended shareholder liability and (*See* Extended shareholder liability)
finance and, 32–33
group accounts, 209–12
"groupness" in, 167–68
growth of, 6
hierarchical shareholding in, 3–4
internalisation and, 26–30, 168
judgment-proofing in, 88–89
liability rules and, 15–16
limited liability of (*See* Limited liability)
mergers and acquisitions in, 50
multidivisional form of business (M-Form) in, 36–39, 48–49, 50–51, 79, 167–71
networks versus, 1, 172–73
pooling orders, 215–21 (*See also* Pooling orders)
problems of, 6–8
product liability and, 253
recharacterisation of debt as equity, 231–33
regulation of, 8–12 (*See also* Regulation of corporate groups)
reorganisations, 213–15
separate legal personality of, 64–68, 413
specialised management and, 33–34
statutory recognition of, 204–5, 212
structure of, 36–39, 168–69
substantive consolidation, 225–28
transparency rules, 205–9
in UK, 204–5
veil-piercing in, 315–16, 318–23
vicarious liability of, 398
Corporate internal decision structure, 162–63
Creditor protection
capital maintenance, 190–91
contribution orders and, 221–25, 414–15
corporate groups and, 204, 233–34
cross guarantees and, 209–12
equitable subordination and, 228–31
ex ante protection, 189–90
ex post protection, 197
group accounts and, 209–12
pooling orders and, 215–21 (*See also* Pooling orders)
priorities rule and, 295–99
recharacterisation of debt as equity and, 231–33
reorganisations and, 213–15
security given to creditors for debt, 83–84

statutory protection generally, 189, 203
substantive consolidation and, 225–28
transparency rules and, 205–9
undervalue transactions, avoiding, 191–94, 196–97
unfair preferences, avoiding, 191–92, 194–96
wrongful trading, 197–203
Cross guarantees, 209–12
Crowe, Jonathan, 283
CSR Ltd., 364–68, 380
Cyert, Richard, 49

Dairy Containers Ltd., 400–1
Dalkon Shield, 134–35
Damages
Oil Pollution Act of 1990, 262–63
unlawful means conspiracy, 387
Dan-Cohen, Meir, 154–55, 159, 281
Davies, Paul, 409
Dearborn, Meredith, 181–82, 184, 270
Debt
financing of subsidiaries through, 83
inter-company debt, 297
recharacterisation as equity, 231–33
security given to creditors for, 83–84
Deceit as ground for veil-piercing, 328–31
Deepwater Horizon oil spill, 139–44
generally, 7
insurance and, 100
multiple entity recklessness and, 394–95
Oil Pollution Act of 1990 and, 261, 265
Defences
CERCLA, 257–58
extended shareholder liability, 299
multiple entity recklessness, 393
Oil Pollution Act of 1990, 262
product liability, 238–39
Defensive asset partitioning, 69
Delmastro, Marco, 49–50
DES, 250
Deterrence
accessory liability and, 409
assumptions regarding, 419
organisations, deterrability of, 163–66, 350, 351
tort law and, 347–48, 349–51
Dietrich, Joachim, 411
Directors
CERCLA, liability under, 256
personal liability of, 17
removal of, 67–68
shadow directorship, 199
Direct participation
accessory liability and, 410
negligence and, 378
Disaggregation, 276–77
Distillers Co. (Biochemicals) Ltd., 129
Diversification, 31–32
corporate groups and, 31–32
limited liability and, 77–78
networks and, 31–32
Domicile, 90–91
Douglas, W.O., 73–74
Dow Corning, 99
Drug-discovery firms, 133–34
Drugs. *See* Pharmaceutical industry
Dual reporting model, 59
Dual vicarious liability, 398–99
Du Pont, 31
Duty of care
overview, 352–59
in asbestos cases, 360–62
in Australia, 353–54, 358, 364–68
breach of duty, 369–70
in Canada, 353, 359–60
foreseeability and, 352–53, 355–58
incentive to reduce injuries and, 363
in networks, 368–69
of parent to consumers and bystanders, 366–68
of parent to subsidiary, 359–66
policy arguments regarding, 364
proximity and, 352–55, 357–58, 416
in UK, 353, 355, 360–64, 366
veil-piercing and, 363–64

Economies of scale, 25–26
Economies of scope, 26
Egnep, 319

Employees
  non-delegable duties, 405–6
  vicarious liability (*See* Vicarious liability)
Enterprise liability
  overview, 174–75
  in Australia, 184–85
  control and, 181–82
  in corporate groups, 176–79
  entity liability versus, 174–75, 177
  in EU, 180–81
  evolution of, 175–76
  extended shareholder liability and, 270
  limited liability versus, 270
  in networks, 176–77, 179–80
  problems with, 182–84
  product liability and, 245–46
  in UK, 175–76, 184
  in US, 178, 185
Entity liability, 174–75, 177
Equitable subordination, 228–31
Equivalence principle, 2, 396, 416
European Commission, Directorate-General for Competition, 183
European Economic Community
  Medicinal Products Directive 1965, 129–30
  Thalidomide in, 129–30
European Medicines Agency, 126, 135
European Union
  Accounting Directive, 209–10
  asbestos industry in, 109
  Brussels I Regulation, 92
  choice of law in, 93
  conflict of laws in, 93
  enterprise liability in, 180–81
  Fourth Anti Money Laundering Directive, 207–8
  group accounts in, 209–10
  Product Liability Directive 1985, 108, 236–37
  Recast Brussels Regulation, 91
  Rome II Regulation, 93
  Shareholder Rights Directive, 292
  Transparency Directive, 205–6
  transparency rules in, 205–8
  undervalue transactions, avoiding in, 192–93
Evasion as ground for veil-piercing, 316–17, 322–23, 331–34
Extended shareholder liability
  overview, 268–70, 287–88, 303–5, 420–21
  acquired companies and, 299–300
  argument for, 1–2
  capacity, based on, 272–74
  collective concept of liability, 278–82, 287
  consequences of, 301–3
  control rejected as basis of liability, 294
  defences, 299
  disaggregation and, 276–77
  enterprise liability and, 270
  equivalence principle and, 2
  as incentive to reduce injuries, 291–92
  institutional shareholders and, 292–94
  negligence standard, rejection of, 290
  networks and, 300–1
  personal injuries, restricted to, 288–89
  possible objections to, 301–3
  priorities rule and, 295–99, 421
  proposal of, 420–21
  pro rata tort liability, 274–78, 420–21
  recommendations regarding, 18–19
  regulation of corporate groups and, 11–12
  strict liability, 289–91, 420–21
  unlawful means conspiracy and, 386–87
External credit providers, limited liability and, 75–77
Exxon, 32

Façade as ground for veil-piercing, 316, 322–23, 334–36
Fairchild principle, 371–74
Farrar, John, 215
Fault
  assumptions regarding, 418–19

unlawful means conspiracy, fault requirement, 383–85
Federal Mogul, Inc., 109, 121
Fiat, 56–57
Finance in corporate groups and networks, 32–33
Fisse, B., 164
Flynn, L., 53
Ford Motor Co., 24
Foreseeability
breach of duty and, 369
duty of care and, 352–53, 355–58
Formation of corporate groups and networks
overview, 23, 62–63
advantages of corporate groups, 47–48
business form, 34–36
control in corporate groups, 48–51 (*See also* Control)
disadvantages of networks, 46–47
diversification and, 31–32
economies of scale and, 25–26
economies of scope and, 26
finance and, 32–33
internalisation and, 26–30
multidivisional form of business (M-Form), 35–36
specialised management and, 33–34
unitary form of business (U-Form), 34–35
Forum non conveniens, 92–93
Foxconn, 41
Franchising agreements, 43–44
Fraud as ground for veil-piercing, 328–31
French, Peter, 162–63, 164

General Electric, 32
General Motors, 33
Germany
regulation of corporate groups in, 10
separate legal personality in, 67
Gilbert, Margaret, 152, 154
Glass, Lewis, 293
GlaxoSmithKline, 41
Glynn, Timothy P., 17, 313
Goode, Roy, 86
Group accounts, 209–12
Group of Twenty (G20), 57–58
Groups of persons
overview, 149–50
autonomy, loss of, 154–55
"cog in the wheel" analogy, 154–55
coherence in, 153
commitment in, 152–53
common purpose in, 151–52
communication and, 150–51
conceptualisation and, 150–51
criteria for identification, 150
individual persons versus, 158–59
power of, 155–56
pressure to conform in, 153–54
rationality in, 153
reproaching in, 154–55
responsibility of, 156–58
social beings, persons as, 150
Gulf Coast Claims Facility, 141–42

Halliburton, 139, 141, 395
Handbook of the Law of Torts (Prosser), 245
Hanningan, Brenda, 317
Hansmann, Henry, 272, 274–78, 348
Hardy, Harry, 62
Harm principle in tort law, 390
Hazardous substances, 255. *See also* Comprehensive Environmental Response, Compensation and Liability Act of 1980 (US)
Holding company form of business (H-Form), 37
Houlder, V., 54
Hutchinson, Allan, 289

Incentive to reduce injuries
accessory liability and, 408–9
control-based liability and, 285–86
duty of care and, 363
extended shareholder liability as, 291–92
multiple entity recklessness and, 392–93
Indemnity, vicarious liability and, 398
India, asbestos industry in, 103, 109
Industrial Hygiene Foundation, 111

Insolvency Act 1986 (UK)
generally, 119
creditor protection under, 191–203
equitable subordination under, 228
limited liability under, 71–72
pooling orders under, 220
shareholder liability under, 281
veil-piercing under, 313, 328
Insolvent entity problem, 1–3. *See also specific topic*
overview, 413
business context, 19
corporate groups versus networks, 1
personal injuries and, 1–2
in small and medium-sized businesses, 1
tort law and, 346
Institutional shareholders, 292–94
Instrumentality doctrine, 339
Insurance
asbestos industry and, 97–98
claims-made insurance, 98–99
Deepwater Horizon oil spill and, 100
Oil Pollution Act of 1990 and, 264
self-insurance, 100
tort law and, 97–100
Intellectual property, MNEs and, 55–56
Internalisation
corporate groups and, 26–30, 168
networks and, 26–30
Ireland
asbestos industry in, 117
intellectual property in, 55–56
tax avoidance in, 56
tax inversions in, 54
Isaacs, Tracy, 156–57, 163
ISS, 293

James, Fleming, 245
James Hardie and Co. Ltd., 114–18
James Hardie Industries Ltd., 115–16
James Hardie Industries NV, 116, 117
James Hardie Research, 115
Jennejohn, M., 46
Johns-Manville, 99
Joint and several liability
accessory liability (*See* Accessory liability)
CERCLA, 258
product liability, 243
Joint ventures, 42–43
Jones, Geoffrey, 23
Jsekarb Ltd., 114
Judgment-proofing
overview, 80–81
in arm's-length transactions, 81–82
in asbestos industry, 112–22, 413
in corporate groups, 88–89
debt financing of subsidiaries, 83
malpractice in, 85
in MNEs, 82–83
in networks, 89–90
in pharmaceutical industry, 134–35, 413
pre-packaged administration, 85–88, 119–20
product liability and, 242–43
security for debt given to creditors, 83–84
strategic insolvency, 85
in tort law, 94–95
in UK, 84–85, 121–22
in US, 118–21, 134–35
vicarious liability and, 401–3
Jurisdiction, 90–91

Kaisanlahti, Timo, 277, 303
Kant, Immanuel, 159
Kazakhstan, asbestos industry in, 103
Kensington International Ltd., 332–33
Khimji, Mohamed, 313
Kraakman, Renier, 272, 274–78, 348
Krause-Vilmar, D.A., 232
Krause-Vilmar, G., 232
Kutz, Christopher, 152, 166–67, 272, 278–82, 285, 287

Leebron, David, 301
Lee Pey Woan, 333
Legal personhood. *See* Separate legal personality
"Legislative Guide on Insolvency Law" (UNCITRAL), 269–70
Liability rules, 15–18
companies versus corporate groups or networks, 15–16

control and, 15
in developed countries, 15
in New Zealand, 15
personal liability of directors or officers, 17
in UK, 15
in US, 15
Limited liability
overview, 69, 78–79, 413
assumptions regarding, 418
capitalisation and, 72–73
in contract law, 95–96
defensive asset partitioning, 69
diversification and, 77–78
enterprise liability versus, 270
evolution of, 69–71
extended shareholder liability (*See* Extended shareholder liability)
external credit providers and, 75–77
justifications for, 72–73
of parents, 72, 79–80
pooling orders and, 219
purposes of, 71
reform proposals, 270–82 (*See also* Reform proposals regarding limited liability)
risk, effect on, 78
as second layer of protection, 72
shareholder monitoring of management and, 74–75
shareholder monitoring of shareholders and, 75
in tort law, 71–72, 96–97
veil-piercing and, 309–12, 323
vicarious liability and, 403–4
List, Christian, 153, 154, 157–58, 281
Local board model, 59
LoPucki, Lynn, 96, 100
Love Canal, 254–55
Love Network Queensland Ltd., 335–36
Luxembourg, tax avoidance in, 56–57
Lyle, M., 96, 214

Macey, Jonathan, 310, 341–42
Malpractice, 85
Manville Corp., 118–19, 120
March, James, 49
Marc Rich & Co. AG, 232–33
Material contribution to risk test, 374–75
Matheson, J.H., 253
Medical Research and Compensation Fund Ltd., 115–17
Mendelson, Nina, 272–74
Merck, 130–31
Merewether, E.R.A., 106, 114
Metlife, 98
Mevorach, Irit, 227, 271
Mexico, asbestos industry in, 103
Millon, David, 324
Milman, David, 296–97
Minority shareholders, 325
Mitts, Joshua, 310, 341–42
Modified limited liability. *See* Extended shareholder liability
Morgan, Gerry, 113–14
Morgan, Phillip, 401–3
Multidivisional form of business (M-Form)
control and, 49, 50–51
in corporate groups, 36–39, 48–49, 50–51, 79, 167–71
formation of corporate groups and networks, 35–36
Multinational enterprises (MNEs)
overview, 51–52
choice of law, 93–94
competition law and, 53–54
conflict of laws and, 93–94
control in, 58–62
domicile and, 90–91
forum non conveniens and, 92–93
intellectual property and, 55–56
international versus domestic expansion, 52–53
judgment-proofing in, 82–83
jurisdiction and, 90–91
regulatory arbitrage and, 52–53
tax avoidance and, 54, 56–58
transfer price manipulation and, 55
in US, 60
Multiple entity recklessness
overview, 391–92, 395, 421–22
accessory liability compared, 411–12

Multiple entity recklessness (cont.)
advantages of, 393
capacity of courts to create cause of action, 393–94
Deepwater Horizon oil spill and, 394–95
defences, 393
elements of, 391–92
incentive to reduce injuries and, 392–93
objective recklessness and, 392
proposal of, 420–21
Munich-Re, 98
Muscat, Andrew, 194, 196–97, 202, 271

Nanoparticles, 131–32
Negligence
overview, 352, 395
in asbestos industry, 112
asset ownership and, 379–80
breach of duty, 369–70
causation (*See* Causation)
control and, 378–79, 380, 417
direct participation and, 378
duty of care (*See* Duty of care)
extended shareholder liability, rejection in, 290
foreseeability and, 352–53, 355–58
injury requirement, 370
presumption against liability, 376–77
problems with, 379–80, 416–17
proximity and, 352–55, 357–58, 416
in US, 376–79
Netherlands
asbestos industry in, 116
tax avoidance in, 56–57
Networks
generally, 19
"boundarilessness" of, 172
business form, 34–36
business licensing agreements, 44–45
CERCLA and, 257
corporate groups versus, 1, 172–73
defined, 5
disadvantages of, 46–47
diversification and, 31–32
duty of care in, 368–69
economies of scale and, 25–26
economies of scope and, 26
enterprise liability in, 176–77, 179–80
evolution of, 39–42
extended shareholder liability and, 300–1
finance and, 32–33
franchising agreements, 43–44
"groupness" in, 172–73
internalisation and, 26–30
joint ventures, 42–43
judgment-proofing in, 89–90
liability rules and, 15–16
in pharmaceutical industry, 40–41
specialised management and, 33–34
strategic alliances, 45–46
structure of, 39–42
Nevitt, C., 54
New England Journal of Medicine, 130
New Zealand
Companies Act 1993, 216–17, 221–22, 414–15
contribution orders in, 221–22, 414–15
Dairy Board, 400–1
institutional shareholders in, 292
liability rules in, 15
pooling orders in, 216–17, 414–15
vicarious liability in, 400–1
"Next catastrophe," 6–7, 137
Nicholls, Christopher, 313
Nissan, 43
Noakes, D.B., 344
Non-delegable duties, 405–6
North American Asbestos Corp., 113–14, 319–22
Nutritek, 330

Objective recklessness, 392
Officers
CERCLA, liability under, 256
personal liability of, 17
Oil Pollution Act of 1990 (US), 260–65
generally, 143, 144, 235
overview, 260, 265–66, 414

"channelling," 261–62
damages, 262–63
Deepwater Horizon oil spill and, 261, 265
defences, 262
insurance and, 264
Oil Spill Liability Trust Fund, 263–64, 265
problems with, 265
responsible parties, 261–62
veil-piercing and, 328
Organisation for Economic Co-Operation and Development (OECD), 57
Organisations
overview, 159
complicity principle, 166–67
corporate internal decision structure, 162–63
decentralisation of, 161
decision-making in, 160–61
deterrability of, 163–66, 350, 351
hierarchy in, 159–60
individual responsibility in, 166–67
responsibility of, 162–63
routine in, 160–61
specialisation in, 160
structure in, 159–60
tort law in organisational setting, 351
in unstable market conditions, 161–62
Owen, David G., 70, 246
Owens Corning, 121

Painter, Christopher, 298
Parents. *See* Corporate groups
Perrow, Charles, 137, 143
Perry, S.R., 357
Personal injuries
in asbestos industry (*See* Asbestos industry)
compensation for, 12–15
extended shareholder liability restricted to, 288–89
incentive to reduce (*See* Incentive to reduce injuries)
insolvent entity problem and, 1–2
in pharmaceutical industry (*See* Pharmaceutical industry)
unlawful means conspiracy, applicability of, 389–90
Personhood. *See* Separate legal personality
Pettit, Philip, 153, 154, 157–58, 281
Pfizer, 132
Pharmaceutical industry
generally, 6
overview, 122–23
approval process, 125
biased research in, 127–28
biosimilars, 123–25
in China, 136–37
clinical testing, 125–27
drug-discovery firms, 133–34
failure of regulation, 135–36
judgment-proofing in, 134–35, 413
nanoparticles, 131–32
networks in, 40–41
off-label use, 128
organisation of, 132–33
outsourcing in, 133–34, 136–37
"pay-for-delay" deals, 124
product liability in, 248–49, 250
spin-offs in, 133–34
start-ups in, 133–34
tax inversions in, 54
in US, 134–37
Piercing of veil. *See* Veil-piercing
Pittsburgh Corning Corp., 113–14
"Polluter pays" legislation
overview, 254, 265–66
CERCLA, 254–60 (*See also* Comprehensive Environmental Response, Compensation and Liability Act of 1980 (US))
Oil Pollution Act of 1990, 260–65 (*See also* Oil Pollution Act of 1990 (US))
Pooling orders, 215–21
overview, 215, 414–15
in Australia, 217–19
insolvent subsidiaries and, 215–16
intermingled assets and accounts and, 216, 219

Pooling orders (cont.)
limited liability and, 219
in New Zealand, 216–17
separate legal personality and, 219
in UK, 220
Prentice, D.D., 202
Pre-packaged administration, 85–88, 119–20
Price, C.V., 106, 114
Priest, George, 246–47
Prima facie torts, 390
Priorities rule, 295–99, 421
Privity, 70
Product liability
overview, 235–36
backlash against, 246–47
causation, 238, 249–50
component parts, 241
contribution, 238
corporate groups and, 253
defences, 238–39
designer liability, 241
development risks defence, 239–40
enterprise liability and, 245–46
inventor liability, 241
joint and several liability, 243
judgment-proofing and, 242–43
in pharmaceutical industry, 248–49, 250
primary liability, 241–42
problems with, 243–44
producer liability, 241
products defined, 237–38
proof required, 238
rules of, 247–48, 251–52
secondary liability, 242
standing, 240
"state of the art," 250–51
statutes of limitations, 240, 251
strict liability, 238, 246
successor liability, 252–53
supplier liability, 242
in UK, 237–44, 414
in US, 244–54
Pro rata tort liability, 274–78, 420–21
Prosser, William, 245, 246
Proximity, duty of care and, 352–55, 357–58, 416

QBE, 114

Ramsay, I.M., 73–74, 344
Rands, William, 341
RAP Co., 330
Recklessness
in asbestos industry, 112
multiple entity recklessness (*See* Multiple entity recklessness)
objective recklessness, 392
subjective recklessness, 391
unlawful means conspiracy and, 384–85, 390–91
Reform proposals regarding limited liability, 270–82
capacity, liability based on, 272–74
collective concept of liability, 278–82
disaggregation and, 276–77
enterprise liability and, 270
extended shareholder liability (*See* Extended shareholder liability)
multiple entity recklessness (*See* Multiple entity recklessness)
pro rata tort liability, 274–78, 420–21
Regulation of corporate groups, 8–12
in Australia, 10
in civil law countries, 10
command-and-control regulation, 8–10, 144–45
in common law countries, 10
defined, 8
extended shareholder liability and, 11–12
in Germany, 10
pharmaceutical industry, failure in, 135–36
in UK, 10
in US, 11
Regulatory arbitrage, 52–53
Remoteness of injury, causation and, 370–71, 375–76
Renault, 43
Reorganisations, 213–15
Restatement (Third) of Agency, 404–5

Restatement (Second) of Torts, 244, 246–47
Restatement (Third) of Torts: Product Liability, 244, 247–49, 251–54
Richardson, G.B., 30
Ridge, Pauline, 411
Riley, Chris, 368
Roche, 126
Roe, M., 133
RTZ Corp. plc, 360
Ruhl, J.B., 143
Russia, asbestos industry in, 103

Scale and Scope: The Dynamics of Industrial Capitalism (Chandler), 24
Scope of liability, causation and, 370–71, 375
Searle, John, 150–51
Security for debt given to creditors, 83–84
Self-insurance, 100
Separate legal personality
 control and, 67–68
 of corporate groups, 64–68, 413
 in Germany, 67
 pooling orders and, 219
 in UK, 64–66, 67
 in US, 66
 veil-piercing and, 309–12, 323
 vicarious liability and, 403–4
Shadow directorship, 199
Sham as ground for veil-piercing, 316, 322–23, 334–36
Shanks, C., 73–74
Shareholders
 capacity, liability based on, 272–74
 circular shareholding in, 4
 collective concept of liability, 278–82, 287
 control, liability based on, 282–87
 extended shareholder liability (*See* Extended shareholder liability)
 hierarchical shareholding in, 3–4
 institutional shareholders, 292–94
 minority shareholders, 325
 monitoring of management by, 74–75
 monitoring of shareholders by, 75
 pro rata tort liability, 274–78, 420–21
 veil-piercing as upward extension of liability to, 312, 316, 327
ShareSoc, 294
Singer Sewing Machine Co., 29
Sloan, Alfred, 33
Société Nationale des Pétroles du Congo, 332–33
South Africa, asbestos industry in, 111, 112–14
Southport Central Property Ltd., 335–36
Specialised management, 33–34
Sphynx Bermuda, 332–33
Standing in product liability, 240
Starbucks, 55–56
Statutes of limitations in product liability, 240, 251
Statutory law
 generally, 19
 overview, 235
 CERCLA, 254–60 (*See also* Comprehensive Environmental Response, Compensation and Liability Act of 1980 (US))
 creditor protection (*See* Creditor protection)
 Oil Pollution Act of 1990, 260–65 (*See also* Oil Pollution Act of 1990 (US))
 product liability (*See* Product liability)
STH, 217
Strategic alliances, 45–46
Strategic insolvency, 85
Strict liability
 assumptions regarding, 418–19
 extended shareholder liability, 289–91, 420–21
 product liability, 238, 246
Structuring of relations. *See* Judgment-proofing
Subjective recklessness, 391
Subsidiaries. *See* Corporate groups
Substantive consolidation, 225–28
"Synthetic living," 7–8

Tamiflu, 126
Tan Cheng-Han, 343–44
T & N Asbestos Trustee Co., 121–22
Tax avoidance by MNEs, 54, 56–58
Tax inversions, 54
Teubner, Günter, 168, 285
Thalidomide, 129–30, 236
Tort law
  overview, 235, 266–67
  abuse of rights, 390
  accessory liability (*See* Accessory liability)
  aims of, 346–48
  causation (*See* Causation)
  CERCLA, 254–60 (*See also* Comprehensive Environmental Response, Compensation and Liability Act of 1980 (US))
  compensation and, 347–48
  control in context of, 284
  creditor protection (*See* Creditor protection)
  deterrence and, 347–48, 349–51
  harm principle in, 390
  insolvent entity problem and, 346
  insolvent subsidiaries and, 97
  insurance and, 97–100
  interests versus rights in, 347
  judgment-proofing in, 94–95
  limited liability in, 71–72, 96–97
  multiple entity recklessness (*See* Multiple entity recklessness)
  negligence (*See* Negligence)
  Oil Pollution Act of 1990, 260–65 (*See also* Oil Pollution Act of 1990 (US))
  in organisational setting, 351
  prima facie torts, 390
  product liability (*See* Product liability)
  pro rata liability, 274–78, 420–21
  recklessness (*See* Recklessness)
  subordination to company law, 348–49
  in UK, 415
  unlawful means conspiracy (*See* Unlawful means conspiracy)
  vicarious liability (*See* Vicarious liability)
  vindication and, 347–48
Transaction costs, 27, 30
Transfer price manipulation, 55
Transocean, 139–40, 144, 394–95
Transparency rules, 205–9
Treaty on the Functioning of the European Union, 180
Tuomela, Raimo, 152–53, 157
Turner & Newall, 61–62, 98–99, 100, 105, 106–7, 108–9, 110–12, 121–22, 293–94, 380
Tweedale, Geoffrey, 53, 62, 112

UAC, 61
UNCITRAL "Legislative Guide on Insolvency Law," 269–70
Undervalue transactions, avoiding, 191–94, 196–97
Unfair preferences, avoiding, 191–92, 194–96
Unilever, 61
Union Carbide Corp., 137–39
Union Carbide India Ltd., 137–39
Unitary form of business (U-Form), 34–35
United Kingdom
  accessory liability in, 408, 409–10
  asbestos industry in, 104, 105–11, 371–74
  Asbestos Industry Regulations 1931, 106, 107, 110
  Asbestos Regulations 1969, 108
  Asbestos (Licensing) Regulations 1984, 108
  British Rail, 109
  Business, Innovation and Skills Department "Statutory Guidance," 208–9
  causation in, 371–74
  Child Maintenance and Other Payments Act 2008, 14
  Civil Liability (Contribution) Act 1978, 238
  Companies Act 2006 (*See* Companies Act 2006 (UK))

Companies Clauses Consolidation Act 1845, 65–66
Companies House, 208
Companies (Authorised Minimum) Regulations 2009, 83
Consumer Protection Act 1987, 108, 129–30, 237–44, 414
Consumer Rights Act 2015, 243
contribution orders in, 222–24
corporate groups in, 204–5
Defective Premises Act 1972, 237
Diffuse Mesothelioma Payment Scheme, 13–14
duty of care in, 353, 355, 360–64, 366
Employers' Liability (Compulsory Insurance) Act 1969, 12–13, 97
Employers' Liability (Defective Equipment) Act 1969, 243
English and Welsh Statement of Insolvency Practice, 86
enterprise liability in, 175–76, 184
equitable subordination in, 228
Factory Inspectorate, 108, 110, 112
Fatal Accidents Act 1976, 121
Financial Services and Markets Act 2000, 206
Financial Services Compensation Scheme, 99–100
group accounts in, 210–11
Health & Safety at Work Act 1974, 108
Income and Corporation Taxes Act 1988, 204–5
Industrial Injuries Disablement Benefit, 12–13, 98–99
Insolvency Act 1986 (*See* Insolvency Act 1986 (UK))
institutional shareholders in, 292
Joint Stock Companies Act 1856, 71
Joint Stock Companies Registration, Incorporation, and Regulation Act 1844, 64–65
judgment-proofing in, 84–85, 121–22
liability rules in, 15
Limitation Act 1939, 109
Limitation Act 1980, 243
Limited Liability Act 1855, 71, 72, 97
Listing Rules, 94
Mesothelioma Act 2014, 13–14
minimum capital rules, 190
National Health Service, 12–13, 97
Pensions Act 2004, 222–24
Pensions Regulator, 222–24
Pneumoconiosis (Workers' Compensation) Act 1979, 14
pooling orders in, 220
pre-packaged administration in, 85–86
priorities rule in, 295, 296–97
product liability in, 237–44, 414
recharacterisation of debt as equity in, 232–33
Register of People with Significant Control, 208
regulation of corporate groups in, 10
reorganisations in, 213–14
separate legal personality in, 64–66, 67
Small Business, Enterprise and Employment Act 2015, 201
tax avoidance in, 58
Thalidomide in, 129
Third Parties (Rights against Insurers) Act 2010, 97
tort law in, 415
transparency rules in, 205, 208–9
undervalue transactions, avoiding in, 191–94, 196–97
unfair preferences, avoiding in, 191–92, 194–96
unlawful means conspiracy in, 351–52, 384, 386, 387, 389–90, 393–94
Vaccine Damage Payment, 14
veil-piercing in (*See* Veil-piercing)
vicarious liability in, 396, 397, 398, 399–400
Workers Compensation Act 1925, 106
wrongful trading in, 197–203
United Kingdom Shareholders' Association, 294
United States
antitrust law in, 53–54
asbestos industry in, 103, 118–21

United States (cont.)
Bankruptcy Code, 87–88, 118–21, 134–35, 225, 228
CERCLA, 254–60 (*See also* Comprehensive Environmental Response, Compensation and Liability Act of 1980 (US))
Coast Guard, 260, 265
conspiracy in, 388–89
contribution orders in, 222
Employee Retirement Income Security Act of 1974, 222
enterprise liability in, 178, 185
Environmental Protection Agency, 255
equitable subordination in, 228–31
financial responsibility, 261
Food and Drug Administration, 52–53, 129, 130–31, 134–37
forum non conveniens in, 92–93
Government Accountability Office, 120
Hazardous Substances Superfund, 258–59
institutional shareholders in, 292
judgment-proofing in, 119–20, 134–35
Kefauver-Harris Act of 1962, 129
liability rules in, 15
Minnesota Environmental Response and Liability Act of 1983, 259
MNEs in, 60
National Pollution Funds Center, 260, 263
National Vaccine Injury Compensation Program, 14, 253–54
negligence in, 376–79
Ocean Energy Management Bureau, 260
Oil Pollution Act of 1990, 260–65 (*See also* Oil Pollution Act of 1990 (US))
Oil Spill Liability Trust Fund, 263–64, 265
pharmaceutical industry in, 134–37
pre-packaged administration in, 87–88, 119–20
product liability in, 244–54
recharacterisation of debt as equity in, 232
regulation of corporate groups in, 10
separate legal personality in, 66
substantive consolidation in, 225–28
Thalidomide in, 129
unlawful means conspiracy in, 388–89
veil-piercing in, 339–42
vicarious liability in, 404–5
wrongful trading in, 198
Unlawful means conspiracy
overview, 381–82, 395
advantages of, 381
agreement requirement, 382–83
in Australia, 351–52
in Canada, 351–52
damages, 387
disadvantages of, 381–82, 389
extended shareholder liability and, 386–87
fault requirement, 383–85
injury requirement, 386
personal injuries, applicability to, 389–90
recklessness and, 384–85, 390–91
in UK, 351–52, 384, 386, 387, 389–90, 393–94
unlawful means requirement, 385–86
in US, 388–89

Veil-piercing
overview, 309, 415
agency as ground for, 336–38
alter ego test, 339–40, 341
in Australia, 325–27, 335–36, 338
in Canada, 325–26
CERCLA and, 256, 328
common law alternatives to, 343–45
concealment and, 316–17, 334
control and, 324–25, 339, 341
in corporate groups, 315–16, 318–23

deceit as ground for, 328–31
defined, 309–12
duty of care and, 363–64
elements of actions, 324–27
empirical evidence regarding, 323, 340–41
evasion as ground for, 316–17, 322–23, 331–34
evolution of, 314–18
failure of, 2
fraud as ground for, 328–31
general principles versus specific rules, 341
instrumentality doctrine, 339
insufficient policy guidance regarding, 341–42
limited liability and, 309–12, 323
minority shareholders and, 325
misuse and, 325
narrowness of doctrine, 317, 322–23
Oil Pollution Act of 1990 and, 328
power to pierce, 313–14
problems with, 341–43
as remedy of last resort, 330
separate legal personality and, 309–12, 323
sham or façade as ground for, 316, 322–23, 334–36
statutory grounds for, 328
as upward extension of liability to shareholders, 312, 316, 327
in US, 339–42
Vertical integration, 28–29, 30
Viagra, 124–25
Vicarious liability
overview, 396, 412, 416
contribution and, 398
control and, 417
of corporate groups, 398
dual vicarious liability, 398–99
general rules, 396–98
indemnity and, 398
judgment-proofing and, 401–3
limited liability and, 403–4
in New Zealand, 400–1
outside of employment context, 400
of parent, 399–404
problems with, 416–17
separate legal personality and, 403–4
in UK, 396, 397, 398, 399–400
in US, 404–5
Vindication, tort law and, 347–48
Vioxx, 130–31, 136
VTB Capital, 330

Weak board model, 58
Williamson, Oliver, 23, 27–28
Winfield, Percy, 394
Wrongful trading, 197–203